Guidelines for Determining Your Purpose

1. *What are the requirements of my writing project?*

If I am writing to fulfill an assignment, do I understand that assignment? If I am writing on my own, do I have definite expectations of what I will accomplish?

2. *As I proceed in this project, what do I need to know?*

Do I have a good understanding of my subject, or do I need more information? Have I considered the possible audiences who might read my writing?

3. *What hypothesis can I use as my working purpose?*

How many different hypotheses can I formulate about my subject? Which of them seems to direct and control my information in the most effective manner?

4. *What purpose have I discovered for this writing project?*

Has my purpose changed as I learned more about my subject and audience? If so, in what ways? Have I discovered, by working with a hypothesis or hypotheses, what I want to do in my writing?

5. *What is my thesis?*

How can I state my main idea about my subject in a thesis sentence? Does my thesis limit the scope of my writing to what I can demonstrate in the available space? Does it focus my writing on one specific assertion? Does it make an exact statement about what my writing intends to do?

Guidelines for Revising Your Style

1. *What is my general impression of my writing?*

Do I find my writing clear, unambiguous, and engaging? Have I carried out my purpose at every level; that is, am I satisfied that the *how* of my writing — its attitude, organization, and language — is equal to the *what*, to my ideas?

2. *What tone have I established in my writing?*

Is my tone informative, affective, or a blend of both? Is it appropriate for my subject and audience? How much distance have I maintained between myself and my readers? Is my tone maintained consistently?

3. *How can I characterize the overall style of my writing?*

Have I written this essay in a moderate style, opting for more or less colloquialism or formality as my purpose requires? Does my purpose in fact require me to be overtly colloquial or formal?

4. *Do my paragraphs work together to convey a sense of order and substance?*

Does my opening paragraph compel the reader's attention, because it either states its thesis impressively or offers an irresistible hook? Do the middle paragraphs of my essay reveal unity, completeness, order, and coherence? Are the transitions between paragraphs clear and effective? Does my closing paragraph conclude my essay convincingly?

5. *Are my sentences well constructed and easy on the ear?*

Have I written sentences of varying lengths and styles, so that the reader can follow them with interest? Have I avoided the choppiness that comes from too many basic or loosely coordinated sentences? Have I avoided the density that comes from too many complicated sentences with multiple subordinate clauses?

6. *Have I used words as effectively as possible?*

Do the connotations and denotations of my words support my purpose? Have I avoided unnecessary formalities and slang? Is my language specific and, when necessary, vivid? Have I inadvertently mixed metaphors? Have I used imagery to *heighten* effects, not merely to strive after them?

Writing With a Purpose

Writing With a Purpose

James M. McCrimmon

Eighth Edition

by Joseph F. Trimmer
Ball State University

Nancy I. Sommers
Rutgers
The State University of New Jersey

Houghton Mifflin Company

Boston   Dallas   Geneva, Illinois   Hopewell, New Jersey   Palo Alto

Text Credits

The authors of the writings quoted in the text are identified with the quotations. We would like to thank the following authors and publishers for permission to quote from their works:

The American Heritage Dictionary of the English Language. Boston: Houghton Mifflin Company, 1969, p. 289. Used by permission.   W. H. Auden from *The Dyer's Hand and Other Essays,* by W. H. Auden. Copyright © 1962 by W. H. Auden. Reprinted by permission of Random House, Inc., and Curtis Brown Ltd.   Russell Baker, © 1968 by The New York Times Company. Reprinted by permission. Also © 1983 by The New York Times Company. Reprinted by permission.   Louise Bogan: a selection from *Journey Around My Room: The Autobiography of Louise Bogan,* edited by Ruth Limmer. Copyright © 1980 by Ruth Limmer, Trustee, Estate of Louise Bogan. Reprinted by permission of Viking Penguin Inc.   Winston Churchill, from "Blood, Sweat and Tears" speech. © 1940 by The New York Times Company. Reprinted by permission of The New York Times and Cassell Limited.   "Dialect" (definition). By permission. From Webster's Third New International Dictionary. © 1981 by Merriam-Webster Inc., publisher of the Merriam-Webster © Dictionaries.   Joan Didion. Reprinted by permission of Farrar, Straus and Giroux, Inc. Excerpt from "On Keeping a Notebook" from *Slouching Towards Bethlehem* by Joan Didion. Copyright © 1966, 1968 by Joan Didion.   Ralph Ellison: "King of the Bingo Game" by Ralph Ellison. Reprinted by permission of William Morris Agency, Inc., on behalf of the author. Copyright © 1944 (renewed) by Ralph Ellison.   "Hunting Song" by Donald Finkel. Copyright 1959 by Donald Finkel. From *The Clothing's New Emperor (Poets of Today VI),* published by Charles Scribner's Sons, reprinted by permission of the author.   E. M. Forster, abridged from "My Wood" in *Abinger Harvest,* copyright © 1936, 1964 by Edward Morgan Forster. Reprinted by permission of Harcourt Brace Jovanovich, Inc. and Edward Arnold Publishers Ltd.   Ellen Goodman, copyright © 1981 by the Washington Post Company. Reprinted by permission of Summit Books, a division of Simon & Schuster, Inc.   S. I. Hayakawa, "Mr. Hayakawa Goes to Washington." Copyright © 1977 by *Harper's Magazine.* All rights reserved. Reprinted from the January 1978 issue by special permission.   Gerald Hawkins: excerpted from *Stonehenge Decoded* by Gerald S. Hawkins. Copyright © 1965 by Gerald S. Hawkins and John B. White. Reprinted by permission of Doubleday and Company, Inc.   Suzanne Britt Jordan, "That Lean and Hungry Look," © 1978 by Newsweek Inc. All rights reserved. Reprinted by permission.   Garrison Keillor: excerpted from "Drownings 1954." Copyright © 1976 by Garrison Keillor. Reprinted with the permission of Atheneum Publishers from *Happy To Be Here.* Copyright © 1982 by Garrison Keillor. "Drownings 1954" was first published in *The New Yorker.* Laurie Lee, from "Charm," in *I Can't Stay Long.* Copyright © 1976 by Laurie Lee. Reprinted with the Permission of Atheneum Publishers and Andre Deutsch.   Konrad Lorenz (pp. 166–167): specified material from pages 133 to 136 in *King Solomon's Ring* by Konrad Z. Lorenz, translated by Marjorie Kerr Wilson (T. Y. Crowell). Copyright 1952 by Harper & Row, Publishers, Inc. and Methuen & Co., Ltd.   George Orwell: from *The Road to Wigan Pier* by George Orwell. Reprinted by permission of Harcourt Brace Jovanovich, Inc., the estate of the late Sonia Brownell Orwell and Martin Secker & Warburg, Ltd.   Roger Rapoport: from "It's Enough to Make You Sick" by Roger Rapoport. Reprinted by permission of The Sterling Lord Agency, Inc. Copyright © 1972 by Roger Rapoport.   Adrienne Rich, "Bears" (p. 439), from *The Diamond Cutters and Other Poems,* Harper and Row, New York, 1955. Reprinted by permission of the author.   William H. Roberts, from *Psychology You Can Use.* New York: Harcourt, Brace, 1943.   William Saroyan: from *The Daring Young Man on the Flying Trapeze and Other Stories* by William Saroyan. Copyright 1954 by the Modern Library, Inc. Reprinted by permission of the author.   William Shakespeare, from *The Merchant of Venice.* From *The Complete Plays and Poems of William Shakespeare,* edited by William Allan Neilson and Charles Jarvis Hill. Copyright 1942 by William Allan Neilson and Charles Jarvis Hill, renewed

Illustrations

Contents

Foreword *by James M. McCrimmon*

The Eighth Edition of *Writing With a Purpose*, prepared by Joseph F. Trimmer and Nancy I. Sommers, is the most thorough-going revision the book has ever received. While the basic theme of purpose and the general organization of earlier editions have been retained, nine of the fourteen chapters of the Seventh Edition have been rewritten, expanded, or modified to conform to changing emphases in the teaching of freshman composition. The result, in my judgment, is a book that gives teachers and students everything of value that they had in previous editions and adds much that these editions did not provide.

The most significant changes are the expanded treatments of the writing process and of invention. Earlier editions tended to view the writing process as a linear progression — first prewriting, then writing, then rewriting — and in some editions each of these stages became a major unit of the book. However convenient this division may have been as a pedagogical device, it was certainly an oversimplification of how writers go about the process of writing. The Eighth Edition corrects this oversimplification by use of the concept of thinking-in-writing, a concept that fuses the linear stages into a cumulative progression in which writing and rewriting become means of invention: writers clarify their sense of purpose by reconsidering and revising what they have written. They do not think *and* write; they think *as* they write. Or — to be more accurate — they think before, during, and after the writing. This change of emphasis requires two organizational changes: first, *prewriting* becomes a misleading term and is dropped as a major unit; second, revision is emphasized as a necessary part of the process by devoting a whole chapter to it early in the book. The final result of these revisions is a description of the composing process that is both realistic and consistent with the belief that writing is a way of knowing.

The treatment of invention is both more comprehensive and more specific than in previous editions. It is at its best in Chapter 2, where Trimmer and Sommers present eight different means of acquiring information about a subject. These different means of invention merge into a continuing exploration, in which brainstorming, freewriting, journal keeping, scouting, mapping, speculating, interviewing, and reading provide investigative routes that lead to the same goal — a fuller understanding of the subject, an understanding that is made vivid by the effective use of the best student "case histories" I have seen in a freshman text.

Preface

Writing With a Purpose has always been distinguished by its emphasis on the role of purpose in the writing process, its comprehensive coverage of the materials and problems basic to introductory writing courses, and its effective use of examples and exercises to illustrate how writers make decisions that produce successful writing. Although the revisions embodied in the Eighth Edition retain and reinforce these traditional features of the text, they also introduce and incorporate the best of contemporary theory and practice in the teaching of writing. The result is a blend of familiar and new material invigorated by fresh approaches and examples and enlivened by student writing that moves through the various stages of the writing process.

Part 1, "The Writing Process," is completely new and covers all aspects of composing from planning through revising. Chapter 1, which provides an overview of this process, details the variety of approaches employed by individual writers to complete writing tasks and discusses those three activities common to every writing situation: selecting your subject, analyzing your audience, and determining your purpose. The third element, purpose, receives an expanded definition that is carefully reinforced throughout the text as the principal touchstone by which writers measure their progress through the writing process.

The remainder of Part 1 (Chapters 2, 3, and 4) takes up the three stages in the writing process — planning, drafting, and revising. Chapter 2 offers multiple planning strategies that illustrate how students can generate and evaluate their thinking-in-writing. Chapter 3 presents methods to arrange the material discovered during planning and provides instruction on how to formulate a preliminary hypothesis to guide the creation of a discovery draft. Chapter 4 defines the nature of the revising process, demonstrates methods for revising an essay, and then provides an extended case study of revising from discovery draft to final draft. Indeed, all the chapters in Part 1 are unified by recurring student writings-in-progress that encompass a full range of writing problems and lead to numerous exercises and writing assignments.

Part 2, "The Expression of Ideas," has been expanded and enriched by new examples and exercises. In particular, Chapter 5 has been completely rewritten to present all the methods of development from narration and description through the various forms of exposition. (Argument, because of its importance, continues to receive extended treatment in Chapter 10.) Each method is illustrated by carefully annotated selections from traditional writers such as George Orwell and W. H. Auden and more contemporary writers such as Ellen Goodman and Garrison Keillor. Chapters 6, 7, and 8 present familiar information on paragraphs, sentences, and words highlighted by new examples and exercises. Each of these chapters concludes with a special section on revision. Chapter 9, "Tone and Style," has been expanded to culminate in a summary analysis of revision for final style. Chapter 10, "Persuasion," discusses the thinking and writing strategies with which writers endeavor to change their readers' views.

Part 3, "Special Assignments," retains the valuable chapters on the essay examination and the critical essay (writing about literature) but presents completely new chapters on planning and writing the research paper (Chapters 13 and 14) and business writing (Chapter 15). These new chapters continue to focus on purpose as a crucial element in the writing process, but they also provide extensive analysis and illustration of the many steps embedded in the process of each special assignment.

For example, Chapter 13, "Planning the Research Paper," demonstrates how to select a subject for research; how to locate, assess, and analyze sources; and how to use current research tools, including the computer search, to help locate information. Chapter 14, "Writing the Research Paper," presents the methods by which information produced by other researchers can be incorporated into a student's own research paper. Special attention is given to the purpose and procedures of quoting, summarizing, and paraphrasing. The whole range of planning and writing activities required to produce a successful research paper is illustrated by one student's progress through the process. His paper, "Preparing for the Information Age: An Analysis of AT&T Advertising," which concludes the chapter, is fully annotated so that readers can assess the decisions made during the writing process and the methods used to embody those decisions in an appropriate format.

Although Chapter 15 provides information on the style and format of business writing, it also adapts the rhetorical principles of subject, audience, and purpose to such writing. Again, one student moves through the steps of planning, drafting, and revising as she writes various kinds of letters, memos, and reports.

New to this edition is *Practice For a Purpose,* by Muriel Harris of Purdue University. It offers a wealth of inventive activities in all phases of the writing process. The instructor's manual for the text, *Teaching With a Purpose,* by Doug Hunt of the University of Missouri at Columbia, features an introductory essay for new teachers, comments on all aspects of the Eighth Edition, and answers to the exercises.

It is a pleasure to acknowledge those who helped shape this edition of *Writing With a Purpose.*

For his counsel throughout the planning and writing of the Eighth Edition, thanks to James McCrimmon.

For their extensive comments on the plans for the Eighth Edition and for criticism of the evolution of those plans through several drafts of the manuscript, we thank the following persons: John L. Adams, Morristown College; Katherine Adams, University of Tennessee at Knoxville; Ruth Bauerle, Ohio Wesleyan University; Paul Batscha, Lincoln Land Community College; M. Elaine Bell, Harcum Junior College; Edwin J. Blesch, Jr., Nassau Community College; Mary Bly, University of California-Davis; Ed Booher, Lincoln Land Community College; Alice Heim Calderonello, Bowling Green State University; Glenna E. Campbell, Morehead State University; Fay Chandler, Pasadena City College; William Leon Coburn, University of Nevada at Las Vegas; V. J. Coleman, University of Arkansas; Robert J. Connors, Louisiana State University; Robert Cosgrove, Saddleback College; James Cruise, University of Pennsylvania; Julia Dietrich, University of Louisville; Bruce L. Edwards, Jr., Bowling Green State University; Sterling Eisiminger, Clemson University; David R. Ewbank, Kent State University; John P. Ferré, University of Illinois; David Fleming, Lincoln Land Community College; Douglas R. Friedlander, Hofstra University; E. J. Fulghum, Thomas Nelson Community College; Sara Garnes, The Ohio State University; Mary Ann Gatten, Lincoln Land Community College; Stephen H. Goldman, University of Kansas; Gwendolyn Gong, Texas A&M University; Robert R. Green, Community College of Allegheny County; Margaret Hagler, Lincoln Land Community College; Muriel Harris, Purdue University; Malcolm Hayward, Indiana University of Pennsylvania; Michael Hogan, University of New Mexico; Doug Hunt, University of Missouri; Kathryn Jenson, University of Oklahoma; Robert Keefe, University of Massachusetts; George R. Kennedy, Jr., St. Johns River Community College; E. Bruce Kirkham, Ball State University; Judy Koor, Office of Library Instruction, Bracken Library, Ball State University; Sharon L. Leahy, University of Notre Dame; Larry Longerbeam, Cleveland State Community College; Ambrose N. Manning, East Tennessee State University; Gretchen S. Marlotte, West Los Angeles College; Thomas Moore, University of Maryland; Calvin L. Myrbo, University of Wisconsin-Platteville; Edward C. Nolte, Norfolk State University; Virginia Oram, Southern Methodist University; Marcel Pacatte, Lincoln Land Community College; Peggy Pavlisin, Lincoln Land Community College; Mary Beth Pringle, Wright State University; Richard N. Ramsey, Indiana University-Purdue University at Fort Wayne; Bené Scanlon, Middle Tennessee State University; Mary Jane Schenck, University of Tampa; Marilyn L. Schiedat, Glendale Community College; R. Baird Shuman, University of Illinois; Hassell B. Sledd, Slippery Rock State College; Rita L. Sturm, Albuquerque; Karl Suess, Lincoln Land Community College; Frances G. Thomas, Hopkinsville Community College; Mary Turner, Lincoln Land Community College; Arthur E. Walzer, University of Minnesota; Barbara Weaver, Anderson College; Dick Williams, Lincoln Land Community College; and Leonora Woodman, Purdue University.

For their eager participation in a wide variety of writing experiments, the students in our writing classes deserve special acknowledgment. In particular, we are indebted to the inventive, humorous, and informative observations of the student authors whose writing gives this edition its unique voice. Their imaginative writing practice has helped us to understand both the theories of the writing process and the purpose of our own writing. Thanks to Wally Armstrong, Kurt Voss, Laurie Lindberg, Jody Gifford, Jenny Miller, Mary Brown, Larry Bush, Rod Myers, Ken Wickliff, and Maria Galvao.

Special thanks must be given to Mary Alexander, education specialist at the National Archives in Washington, D.C., for her energy in obtaining information about all sorts of subjects for this edition. Thanks also to Karen Taylor for typing numerous drafts of the manuscript.

J.F.T.   N.I.S.

Writing With a Purpose

Part 1

The Writing Process

Chapter 1

Toward Purposeful Writing

Some people seem to find writing easy. They sit down to write, they do not stop until they are finished, and their first draft is usually so good that it is their last draft. Everyone has heard stories about English majors who compose perfect term papers at their typewriters the night before the assignment is due. And many people remember the way in which Jack Kerouac wrote his novel *On the Road* — in fourteen days, typing on a continuous role of teletype paper so as to not waste time changing pages. But such ease of composition is rare. Most people experience at least a mild case of nervousness — and sometimes absolute alarm — when they begin a writing assignment. The blankness of the legal pad, typewriter paper, or word processor screen can be daunting. The right ideas and words can be elusive. The situation can seem interminable.

All writers — students writing papers for their college courses, business people communicating ideas in reports and memos, journalists composing news stories, even novelists writing yearly novels — know these basic frustrations. Writing is hard work. But writing is also opportunity: to convey something about yourself, to communicate ideas to people beyond your immediate vicinity, to learn something you didn't know. To make good use of those opportunities, you need to develop the confidence that will enable you to overcome whatever frustrations a writing assignment may present.

Fortunately, confidence is not a mysterious acquisition; you gain it by being willing to work at something and to learn from experience — your own and that of others. In fact, experienced writers — those individuals for whom writing is a primary occupation — have learned some lessons that you may find helpful. Consider, for example, what Ernest Hemingway (whose nickname, "Papa," suggests his legendary position among American writers) says about his early writing experiences in Paris in the 1920s.

> It was wonderful to walk down the long flights of stairs knowing that I'd had good luck working. I always worked until I had something done and I always stopped when I knew what was going to happen next. That way I could be sure of going on the next day. But sometimes when I was starting a new story and I could not get it going, I would sit in front of the fire and squeeze the peel of the little oranges into the edge of the flame and watch the sputter of blue that they made. I would stand and look out over the roofs of Paris and think, "Do not worry. You have always written before and you will write now. All you have to do is write one true sentence. Write the truest sentence that you know." So finally I would write one true sentence, and then go on from there. It was easy then because there was always one true sentence that I knew or had seen or had heard someone say. If I started to write elaborately, or like someone introducing or presenting something, I found that I could cut that scrollwork or ornament out and throw it away and start with the first true simple declarative sentence I had written. Up in that room I decided that I would write one story about each thing that I knew about. I was trying to do this all the time I was writing, and it was good and severe discipline. (Ernest Hemingway, *A Moveable Feast*)

Hemingway's words reveal some of the understandings that characterize the attitudes and work of experienced writers. They may be further explained as follows:

1. *Experienced writers have faith in their writing habits.* Because they have written successfully before, experienced writers believe they will write

successfully again. They risk this faith every time they write because each new writing task creates its own set of problems. And as they struggle to resolve these problems, they know that their faith in their abilities will probably fluctuate. But experienced writers do not lose faith. They believe that those writing habits that have worked before — a special environment, a disciplined schedule, and familiar tools — will work again to help them overcome the frustrations produced by any temporary difficulties.

2. *Experienced writers understand the stages in their writing process.* Because they have written so often, experienced writers are able to identify predictable stages in the evolution of their writing process. They know why each stage contains many smaller steps (some of which they can combine, some of which they can omit, but all of which they must consider); how each stage connects to the next stage; and when it is necessary to repeat one or all the stages several times to produce a successful piece of writing. As they move forward from stage to stage, or backward to repeat a stage, they are confident that they are making progress because they are identifying and solving problems.

3. *Experienced writers rely on the basic elements in any writing situation to guide them as they work.* Because they have had to write under many conditions and for many occasions, experienced writers have learned to focus on the factors that are constant in every writing situation. They may talk from time to time of "inspiration," or "the Muse," but experienced writers know that they cannot depend on magic to produce effective writing. They believe that effective writing emerges from effective decision making, and effective decisions are best made when writers understand their subject, their audience, and their purpose. To ensure their understanding of these primary elements of writing, experienced writers use practical guidelines to help them think and write more effectively.

One of the primary aims of this book is to offer you experience, and thereby confidence, in writing. Throughout the following chapters, you will learn the strategies with which writers approach their craft. You will watch both professional and student writers working their way through those strategies, and you will discuss and practice the strategies yourself. The best place to begin is with an overview of the writing process. The remainder of this chapter will discuss the writer's environment and working habits, the three-stage division of the writing process, and the central elements — subject, audience, and purpose — that every writer must understand in order to begin and to progress through the process.

The Writer's Environment and Habits

On your journey from kindergarten to college, you have probably had to produce dozens of stories, book reports, and themes on a wide variety of subjects. But if you are like many student writers, you may not feel as if you have learned much from this experience. The assignments were so divergent, the writing experiences so inconsistent, and the results so unpredictable that you may still feel like a beginner. Indeed, most beginning writers are so preoccupied with completing an assignment that they rarely think about how they did it, the process they used to produce it. If you were asked to describe the characteristic features of your writing process, you would probably begin by identifying your writing *habits* — those conditions and tools you believe you must have whenever you write.

Some of these writing habits are formed by chance. If you produced a paper you were proud of by secluding yourself in a quiet room, inscribing neatly shaped words in a spiral notebook with a soft-lead pencil, then you may be convinced that you need isolation, silence, and primitive tools to perform successfully. But chance could have ordained that you produced that same paper seated at the kitchen table, surrounded by family conversation, banging out your sentences on a portable typewriter. If so, you might believe that to write effectively you will always require a comfortable environment, reassuring noises, and efficient machinery. Indeed, after a time some writers look upon their writing habits as rituals, procedures to be followed faithfully and regularly each time they write. They wear the same flannel shirt, or choose the same background music, or sharpen an entire box of pencils before they begin.

Although many writing habits are formed by coincidental patterns of cause and effect and are sometimes perpetuated by ritual, most are chosen, almost unconsciously, to conform to a writer's other personal habits. If, like Felix (the finicky, exacting member of the comedy series

The Odd Couple), you must have a precisely arranged environment in order to accomplish any task from finding your socks to preparing dinner for guests, then you will no doubt accommodate your writing to the precision of your life. You will try to write regularly, at approximately the same time each day and for about the same amount of time, in a serene atmosphere uninvaded by other concerns. On the other hand, if, like Felix's opposite, Oscar, you thrive on disorder and cannot abide neat arrangements — of your life or anything else — then your writing habits are likely to reflect your preference for flexibility. Within reason (and within sight of your deadline), you will probably write when you find your attention most focused on the need to do so: at whatever hour of day or night and for varying stretches of time. As Felix and Oscar have proved to each other and to their viewers over and over, neither style of working is better than the other. What matters is that you find the conditions and tools that work best for you.

Exercise   Most people have developed special habits or idiosyncrasies when they write. Using the following questions as a guide, compile a list of your writing habits.

1. What particular experiences or people helped you form your writing habits?

2. Do your writing habits resemble your other work habits? Do you see any relationship between the way you write and the way you might make a piece of furniture, cook a large meal, or practice your favorite sport? Make a list of similarities and differences.

3. What kind of physical environment do you need in order to write effectively? Do you need the silence and solitude of your own isolated study or the sounds and activity of a more communal space such as the kitchen or the library? What happens to you when you are forced to write in a "hostile" environment?

4. What kind of tools do you prefer? Do you prefer composing with a special kind of pencil or pen, or do you prefer composing at a typewriter or word processor? What happens to you when you are forced to use an "alien" writing implement? What other special tools do you require — paper, pencil sharpener, eraser, correction fluid, scissors, tape, dictionaries, thesaurus?

5. When do you write best — early in the morning or late in the evening? How long can you write at one sitting? What kind of reasons do you give yourself

to stop working? What kind of rewards do you give yourself for finishing a piece of writing or a specific portion of it? How long does it take you to recover your train of thought once you have been away from a writing project for several hours or days? How do you re-establish contact with what you were thinking?

The Stages of the Writing Process

Whatever your writing habits, they are simply the enabling conditions that allow you to begin and pursue your writing process. These habits are the physical and psychological scenery for the central action — the intellectual procedure you perform as you move through a series of stages to produce a piece of writing. In this book, the writing process will be divided into three stages: *planning, drafting,* and *revising.* They will be discussed briefly in this chapter and at greater length, with examples, in Chapters 2, 3, and 4.

Planning

Planning is any orderly procedure used to bring about a desired result. As the first stage in the writing process, *planning is a series of strategies designed to find and produce information in writing.* When you begin any writing project, you need to discover what is possible. You need to locate and explore a variety of subjects. You need to invent alternative ways to think and write about each subject. And you need to consider all ideas, however mundane or unsettling, in order to select and create the substance out of which you will shape your subject. In Chapter 2 you will learn several planning strategies that will help you generate information you can transform into a first draft.

Drafting

Drafting is a procedure for drawing up a preliminary sketch. As the second stage in the writing process, *drafting is a series of strategies designed to organize and develop a sustained piece of writing.* Once planning has enabled you to identify several subjects and encouraged you to gather information on those subjects from different perspectives, you need to determine what you can best accomplish in writing. You need to select one subject and organize your information about it into meaningful clusters. Then you need to find connections among those clusters and discover the relationship that links the connections. In Chapter 3 you will learn how to use drafting techniques to produce a preliminary text that you can revise into a more effective piece of writing. Chapters 5 through 9 will give you additional techniques for drafting sections of the preliminary text.

Revising

Revising is a procedure for improving or correcting a work in progress. As the third and final stage in the writing process, *revising is a series of strategies designed to re-examine and re-evaluate the choices that have created a piece of writing.* After you have completed your preliminary draft, you need to stand back from your text and decide what actions would seem to be most productive. You may have to embark upon *global revision* — a complete re-creation of the world of your writing. Or you may be able to begin *local revision* — a concerted effort to perfect the smaller elements in a piece of writing you have already created. In Chapter 4 you will learn how to use global revision to rethink, re-envision, and rewrite your work. In Chapters 6 through 9 you will learn strategies for making those small rearrangements and subtle refinements that will bring your writing process to an appropriate conclusion.

Working Within the Process

One difficulty with this presentation of the writing process is that the three-stage division is deceptive. The words *planning, drafting,* and *revising* suggest a simple linear sequence in which you complete all the activities in one stage and then move on to the next stage. But such a sequence does not take into account the complexity of the intellectual activities you need to perform. You may have to repeat one stage several times before you are ready to move on to the next: that is, you may have to try any number of planning strategies until you feel that you have generated enough ideas and information to work with. And even when you arrive at the next stage, you may have to loop back to an earlier stage before you can go forward again. You may discover in drafting that the relationships you thought you saw in your material are in fact not there, or cannot be supported, so you have to return to planning. Or when you begin to revise a draft of your essay, you may find that it doesn't hang together, and thus you go back to drafting and/or planning. Indeed, although planning, drafting, and revising are in many ways distinct activities, they often appear to be the same activity. Or, to phrase the matter more precisely, at any point in the writing process you are likely to be performing all three activities simultaneously.

A second difficulty with the three-stage division is that experienced writers seem to work within the process in different ways. Some writers spend an enormous amount of time planning every detail in a writing project before they write. Others prefer to dispense with planning and discover their direction in the drafting or revising stage. For example, the American humorist James Thurber once acknowledged in an interview that he and one of his collaborators worked quite differently when writing a play:

> Thurber: Elliot Nugent ... is a careful constructor. When we were working on *The Male Animal* together, he was constantly concerned with plotting the play. He could plot the thing from back to front — what was going to happen here, what sort of situation would end the first-act curtain and so forth. I can't work that way. Nugent would say, "Well, Thurber, we've got our problem, we've got all these people in the living room. Now what are we going to do with them?" I'd say that I didn't know and couldn't tell him until I'd sat down at my typewriter and found out. I don't believe the writer should know too much where he's going. . . .
>
> Interviewer: Is the act of writing easy for you?
>
> Thurber: For me it's mostly a question of rewriting. It's part of a constant attempt on my part to make the finished version smooth, to make it effortless. . . . [My] wife took a look at the first version of something I was doing not long ago and said "Goddam it Thurber, that's high-school stuff." I have to tell her to wait until the seventh draft, it'll work out all right. (James Thurber interview, *Writers at Work: The Paris Review Interviews*)

A final difficulty with the three-part division of the writing process is that even for experienced writers, it may work differently on different projects. Virginia Woolf planned, drafted, and revised some of her novels with great speed, but she seemed bewildered by her inability to repeat the process with other novels:

> ... blundering on at *The Waves*. I write two pages of arrant nonsense, after straining; I write variations of every sentence; compromises; bad shots; possibilities; till my writing book is like a lunatic's dream. Then I trust to inspiration on re-reading; and pencil them into some sense. Still I am not satisfied.... I press to my centre. I don't care if it all is scratched out ... and then, if nothing comes of it — anyhow I have examined the possibilities. But I wish I enjoyed it more. I don't have it in my head all day like the *Lighthouse* and *Orlando*. (Virginia Woolf, "Boxing Day" 1929, *A Writer's Diary*)

These difficulties suggest that what appears to be a simple three-stage process is in reality a confused and even contradictory procedure. But experienced writers recognize that confusion and contradiction are temporary and even expected disturbances in the evolution of any piece of writing. Confusion occurs when you know too little about your subject; contradiction often occurs when you know too much. The secret to solving both problems is to consult the elements constant in every writing situation. These elements form a set of guidelines that you can use to begin the writing process and to measure your progress as you work your way through that process.

Making Decisions in the Writing Process

As you write, you will discover that you are constantly making decisions. Some of these decisions are complex because you are trying to shape ideas or define concepts; others are simple because you are arranging words and phrases. But each decision, large or small, affects every other decision so that you are continuously adjusting and readjusting your decisions to make sure that your writing is becoming increasingly consistent, coherent, and clear. The best way to test the effectiveness of your decisions is to measure them against the three elements in every writing situation: a writer is always trying to communicate a *subject* to an *audience* for a *purpose*.

Initially, you should think of these elements as *prompters,* as ways to consider what you want to write about and how you want to write about it. Later, as you move through planning, drafting, and revising your writing, you should think of these elements as *touchstones,* as ways to assess what you set out to accomplish. But mainly, you should think of these elements as *guidelines,* as ways to direct and control every decision you make during the writing process from formulating ideas to forming sentences.

Selecting Your Subject

Many writers complain that their biggest difficulty is finding a subject. Sometimes that difficulty appears less complicated because the subject is identified in a writing assignment. But writing assignments vary in how they are worded, what they assume, and what they expect. For example, you may be asked to discuss two characters in a play you have read. This open assignment does not identify a subject; it merely identifies an area in which a subject needs to be developed. Another version of that same assignment might ask you to compare and contrast the way the two characters make compromises. This closed assignment identifies a subject, but it assumes you know how to work with a specific form (the comparison and contrast essay) and it expects you to produce specific information (two ways of defining and dealing with compromise). In other words, although the second assignment restricts the subject, you must still select and arrange the subject matter of your essay.

When you have a free choice of subjects, your difficulties may appear more complicated. No one is helping you find your subject. On the other hand, no one is telling you what to do or how to do it. You are free to make all your own decisions. Rather than discuss two characters you have read about in a play, you may decide to compare and contrast two characters you know in your neighborhood. Or better still, you may decide to analyze how your favorite character (you) deals with the problem of making compromises.

"Write about dogs!"

Drawing by Booth; © 1976. The New Yorker, Inc.

Whether you are responding to an assignment or creating your own, you need to follow certain measures if you are to find an appropriate subject. First, you should write about a subject you know or can learn something about. The more you know about your subject, the more likely you are to shape it according to your unique perspective. In particular, if your subject is familiar to most of your readers, then your personal experience with or research on the subject will help you write about it in terms of *your* observations, *your* ideas, and *your* values. Second, you must determine if your subject is a general subject that you must limit to a specific subject. A *general subject* is a large category of information, such as situation comedies on television. A *specific subject* focuses on a particular topic within that category, such as the portrayal of women in sitcoms. Or a specific subject can reflect a particular attitude or judgment that expresses the writer's personal view of the general subject: "Sitcoms insult the intelligence of their viewers." The more you can limit or specify your subject, the more likely you are to concentrate your attention on concrete information rather than vague impressions. Third, to ensure that you are willing to spend time working on your subject, you need to ask yourself three questions about it. Is it significant? Is it interesting? Is it manageable?

The editors of a national magazine such as *Time* try to answer these three questions as they put together each week's issue. They followed the first two guidelines, of course, when they established the policies of the magazine. They have hired reporters who are either experts on particular subjects or who can become experts by using established research procedures. They have organized their magazine according to *general subjects* such as Science, Sport, and Show Business, but each week they must search for *specific subjects* to fit into those large categories. Their reporters have uncovered dozens of specific subjects that would be suitable for each section, but they select only one. At this point, the editors ask each other the key questions: which subject is more significant — photographs from the newest earth-observing satellite or the research breakthough of an important geneticist? Which subject is more interesting — the final standings in World Cup skiing or the probable pairings in the NCAA basketball tournament? Which subject can be developed most completely within the space allotted — a review of the splashy new musical from London now opening on Broadway or profiles of the Academy Award nominees?

As these examples suggest, the three questions do not have definitive answers. Each story must be considered on its own merits, in relation to the other stories, and in the context of the writing situation. The editors of *Time* must actually ask the three questions three times: (1) is a specific story inherently significant, interesting, and manageable? (2) is a specific story more or less significant, interesting, and manageable in comparison to the other stories available? (3) is a specific story significant, interesting, and manageable given the magazine's overall intentions?

As you select your subject, you will discover that significance, interest, and manageability are difficult criteria to define in any absolute sense. If you looked up these terms in a dictionary, you would find simply another set of abstract words.

significant: important, noteworthy

interesting: engrossing, intriguing

manageable: controllable, governable

Although these synonyms may add subtle shades of meaning to the primary terms, they do not really help you formulate three exact definitions. A significant subject does not need to be ponderous and weighty. It does need to be something that your readers are likely to have thought about or to find applicable to their lives and interests (for example, maintaining personal integrity, getting ahead, relations with one's family). Similarly, you should be genuinely interested in your subject and should be able to discuss it in a way that conveys your own distinct point of view, not merely the usual point of view associated with it. A manageable subject is not one so limited that you can reasonably hope to have written the final word about it; on the other hand, neither is it one so vast or complicated that lengthy articles and books, to say nothing of your own essay, only begin to discuss it adequately.

Ultimately, like the editors of *Time,* you must develop your own definitions as you examine the choices available and as you consider your audience and purpose. When you compare subjects in the context of the complete writing situation, you will naturally prefer some to others. To decide whether one of your preferences will produce a suitable subject, you can measure it against the criteria set forth in the following guidelines.

Guidelines for Selecting Your Subject

1. *What do I know about my subject?*

    Do I know about my subject in some depth, or do I need to learn more about it? What are the sources of my knowledge — direct experience, observation, reading? How does my knowledge give me a special or unusual perspective on my subject?

2. *What is the focus of my subject?*

Is my subject too general, too all-inclusive? How can I restrict it to a smaller, more specific subject that I can develop in greater detail?

3. *What is significant about my subject?*

What issues of general importance does it raise? What fresh insight can I contribute to my readers' thinking on this issue?

4. *What is interesting about my subject?*

Am I genuinely interested in this subject? What kinds of subjects do I usually consider interesting? Can I attract my readers' interest with this subject?

5. *Is my subject manageable?*

Can I write about my subject in a particular form, within a certain number of pages? Do I feel in control of my subject or confused by it? If my subject is too complicated or too simplistic, how can I make it more manageable?

Analyzing Your Audience

Most inexperienced writers assume that their audience is their writing teacher. But writing teachers, like writing assignments, often vary in what they teach, what they assume, and what they expect. Traditionally, such variation has prompted inexperienced writers to define their writing tasks as "trying to figure out what their teacher wants." This definition is both simple-minded and sophisticated. On the one hand, it suggests that the sole purpose of any writing assignment is to satisfy the whims of another individual. On the other hand, it suggests that once writers begin to analyze the knowledge, assumptions, and expectations of their readers they begin to develop a clearer perception of their subject and purpose. In order to make their analysis effective, however, writers must remember that they are writing for *three* audiences.

The most immediate (and in some ways the most important) audience for your writing is *you.* You write not only to convey your ideas to other readers but also to clarify and confirm them for yourself. But to think of yourself as an audience, you must change places: you must stop thinking like a writer and begin thinking like a reader. This change in perspective has advantages to offer, for of course you are the reader that you the writer knows best; accordingly, you can give your writing an unusually well-informed reading. You are also a fairly representative reader; that is, you do share broad concerns and interests with other people. If you feel that your writing is clear and lively and has something to say, your other readers will probably feel that way too. On the other hand, if you are not especially impressed with your writing, it is likely that your audience will be likewise unimpressed.

There is a drawback to considering yourself as an audience: at times you may deceive yourself. You want your every sentence and paragraph to be perfect, but you also know how much time and energy you invested in writing them, and you may allow that effort to blur your judgment if you aren't careful. That is, you may at times accept bad writing from yourself, even though you wouldn't accept it from someone else. For that reason, you need to consider a second audience for your writing. These readers — usually your teacher or editor — are simultaneously your most attentive and most artificial audience. They have helped you select your subject, guided you through the various stages of the writing process, and counseled you about how to improve many of your sentences and paragraphs. As you write, you must certainly anticipate the detailed advice you have learned to expect from these sympathetic readers. But you must remember that writing teachers and editors are essentially collaborators. They know what you have considered, cut out, and corrected. The more they have helped you shape your writing, the more eager they are to applaud it when it approaches acceptability.

The primary audience for your writing is a group of readers that does not care how much time and energy you invested in your writing or how many choices you considered and rejected. These readers are eager to read writing that tells them something interesting or important, and they are put off by writing that is tedious or trivial. It is this wider audience that you (and your collaborators) must consider as you work your way through the writing process.

At times this audience may seem indistinct, and you may wonder how you can direct your writing to it if you do not know any of its distinguishing features. In those cases, it may be helpful to imagine a reader to whom you are writing — an attentive, sensible, reasonably informed person who will give you an objective reading so long as you do not waste his or her time. This reader — whom various writers have termed "the general reader," "the universal reader," "the common reader" — is essentially a fiction, of course, but often a helpful fiction. If you can imagine this reader as an important person whom you respect and whose respect you want, then your writing can benefit from the objectivity and sincerity with which you address that reader.

Many times, however — especially as you learn more about your subject — you can discern a more specific audience for your writing. Sometimes, in fact, you may be able to discern a number of specific audiences, in which case you will ultimately have to choose among them. Consider the following example of how you might identify and analyze several audiences.

Perhaps your experience cooking or serving hamburgers last summer suggests that McDonald's might make an interesting subject. Although you know a great deal about this subject, you may find it difficult to focus your knowledge until you identify your audience. After some deliberation, you decide that you have at least three possible audiences: (1) those who love McDonald's — junk-food addicts who relish every item on the menu; (2) those who hate McDonald's — health-food addicts who despise every odor emanating from the Golden Arches; and (3) those who are indifferent to McDonald's — a group whose members have never tasted a Big Mac or have eaten one only on occasion.

Now that you have identified your audiences, you must analyze the distinctive features of each group. What do they know? What do they think they know? What do they need to know? The more you know about each group, the more you will be able to direct your writing to their needs and expectations. Your work experience will help you analyze the junk-food addicts. You saw them line up at the counter each day, eager to gulp down Quarter-Pounders and shakes. Some of the same people would line up for breakfast, lunch, dinner, and late evening snacks. McDonald's is very nearly a way of life with them.

Your school experience may help you analyze the health-food addicts. You have heard zealous dieticians lecture on the evils of junk food, and you have seen their disciples consume precise quantities of bean curd and sprouts. Some of these people spend most of their lives discussing dietary regulations and violations. They believe that a good life is a healthy life and that "you are what you eat."

At first you may have difficulty with the third group because they seem not to have a distinguishing point of view on the subject of McDonald's. They may have eaten there on occasion, but they do not share the junk-food addict's affection for burgers and fries. On the other hand, they do not adhere to the health-food addict's rigid culinary code. In some ways, this group is like "the general reader": you do not have firsthand knowledge of its members, and so you have to determine how to gain their interest. The more you think about it, the more you realize that this group shares some common knowledge with the other two and with you. Anyone who has been alive in the last twenty years knows that fast-food franchises such as McDonald's have had an enormous impact on American business, architecture, vocabulary, and eating habits. Whether people see the Golden Arches as marking a magic kingdom, a demonic power, or merely a burger joint, they cannot avoid seeing them — they are always "close by, right on the way."

As you think about each of these potential audiences, your knowledge of your subject may cluster itself into smaller, more specific subjects. For example, as you think about the junk-food addicts, you might recall the advertising rivalries between fast-food franchises, so you might restrict your subject to an evaluation of the McDonald's menu as compared to that of another fast-food franchise. As you think about the health-food addicts, you might recall the pep talks you received from your supervisor at McDonald's about the "all-natural" content of the food, so you might restrict your subject to the ingredients in McDonald's food. As you think about the neutral group, you might realize that although they are not interested in McDonald's itself, they are probably interested in the business conditions that support popular establishments like fast-food franchises. Thus you might restrict your subject to McDonald's growing profits. In other words, what you know about your audience or possible audiences affects how you look at your subject.

Finally, you have to decide which group would make the best audience for your essay. That decision, like the decision about subject, has to be made in the context of the complete writing situation. Both decisions are, in turn, closely related to your discovery of your purpose — what you want to do in your essay. In the next several pages, you will learn how purpose guides your decisions in writing. But first, look at the following guidelines for analyzing your audience.

Guidelines for Analyzing Your Audience

1. *Who are the readers that form the primary audience for my writing?*

   What is their probable age, sex, education, economic status, and social position? What values, assumptions, and prejudices characterize their general attitudes toward life?

2. *What do my readers know or think they know about my subject?*

   What is the probable source of their knowledge — direct experience, observation, reading, rumor? Will my readers react positively or negatively toward my subject?

3. *Why will my readers read my writing?*

   If they know a great deal about my subject, what will they expect to learn from reading my essay? If they know only a few things about my subject, what will they expect to be told about it? Will they expect to be entertained, informed, or persuaded?

4. *How can I interest my readers in my subject?*

   If they are hostile toward it, how can I convince them to give my writing a fair reading? If they are sympathetic, how can I fulfill and enhance their expectations? If they are neutral, how can I catch and hold their attention?

5. *How can I help my readers read my writing?*

   What kind of organizational pattern will help them see its purpose? What kind of guideposts and transitional markers will they need to follow this pattern? What (and how many) examples will they need to understand my general statements?

Determining Your Purpose

The central idea of this book is that writers write most effectively when they are "writing with a purpose." Inexperienced writers occasionally have difficulty writing with *a* purpose, because they see so many purposes. Most of them might be defined more accurately as *motives:* to complete the assignment, to earn a good grade, to publish their writing. These "purposes" are outside the writing situation, but they certainly influence the way you think about your purpose. For example, if your motive is to complete the assignment with a good grade, then you will define your purpose in terms of the requirements of your teacher's writing assignment. If your motive is to publish your writing, then you will have to define your purpose in terms of the editor's assumptions about the publication's subject, audience, and purpose.

When *purpose* is considered as an element inside the writing situation, the term has a specific meaning: *purpose is the overall design that governs what writers do in their writing.* When writers have determined their purpose, they know what kind of information they need, how they want to organize and develop that information, and why they think it is important. In effect, purpose directs and controls all the decisions writers make throughout the writing process. It is both the *what* of that process and the *how:* that is, the specific subject the writer communicates and the strategies — from establishing organization and point of view to perfecting tone and word choice — that the writer uses to communicate the subject most effectively. The difficulty with this definition is that finding a purpose to guide you through the writing process *is* the purpose of the writing process. Writing is both a procedure for demonstrating what you know *and* a procedure for discovering what you know. For that reason, you must maintain a kind of double vision of your purpose. First, you must think of it as a preliminary objective that helps illuminate the decisions you have to make. You must actually discover your purpose. Second, you must think of it as a final assertion that helps implement what you intend to do in your writing. You have discovered your purpose, and from that point you use it to guide all aspects of your writing.

Forming a Working Purpose: The Hypothesis

As you begin the writing process, you start to acquire a general sense of your purpose. You make tentative decisions about the nature of your subject and audience, and you begin to formulate ideas about what you want to accomplish in your writing, the impression you want to make. For example, suppose again that you choose to write about McDonald's. There are any number of ways you might approach the subject, but you have to begin somewhere, so you decide to focus on the food that is served at McDonald's. This tentative decision about purpose will help you gather and sort information, but as you step back to assess that

Drawing by Levin; © 1982 The New Yorker Magazine, Inc.

information, you may see that you do not yet have a real sense of what you want to do with it. You do not yet have a purpose, only some information and a general idea about purpose.

As you look at the information you have gathered, you realize that it can be organized into a number of patterns that suggest a number of perspectives on your subject. Any one of these perspectives might prove an interesting angle from which to approach your subject. That is, you can use any one of them to form a *hypothesis,* a tentative version of your purpose in writing about this subject — a working purpose.

Forming a hypothesis is a major step in determining your purpose. Sometimes you come to your writing already aware of your hypothesis: you know from the outset what you want to prove and what you need to do to prove it, or you are given an assignment that essentially specifies your purpose for you. More often, however, you need to consider the various possibilities that a writing situation offers you. After all, if you are going to convey something meaningful in your writing, something that bears your own mark, you need to keep an open mind and to explore your options as carefully as you can. Eventually, however, from various possibilities you must choose the one that you think most accurately establishes what you want to say about your subject and implies how you want to say it. You must establish a hypothesis, a preliminary or working purpose.

How do you know which of the possibilities to choose? There is no easy answer to this question. The answer ultimately emerges from your temperament, experiences, and interests, and also from the requirements of your writing situation — whether you are writing for yourself or on assignment and how much time you have for writing. Sometimes you can make the choice intuitively as you proceed; in thinking about your subject and audience, you see at once the perspective you want to adopt and how it will direct what you do in your writing. Other times you may find it helpful to write out the various hypotheses you see and then consider their relative effectiveness and interest to you. Which will be the most interesting to write about? Which best expresses your way of looking at things? With which are you most comfortable? With which can you make the strongest case or most intriguing assertions? You must decide, and then use your chosen hypothesis as a preliminary purpose statement that expresses what you want to prove about your subject.

For example, as you look at the information you have gathered about McDonald's and its menu, you might see a variety of hypotheses:

McDonald's menu has diversified considerably in recent years.

McDonald's food has little nutritional value; it is caloric and greasy.

People usually love or hate McDonald's food.

McDonald's food still is an extraordinary bargain.

Any one of these or other hypotheses might guide you through the next phases of writing about your subject. You must decide which one suits you best — a decision that, incidentally, should take into account the possible audiences you might have for an essay about the McDonald's menu.

Testing Your Hypothesis

After you have chosen your hypothesis, you need to determine whether this preliminary purpose statement really provides the direction and control you need to produce an effective piece of writing — that is, whether it really is a statement of what you intend to do. You can test your hypothesis by writing a first, or *discovery,* draft. Sometimes your discovery draft demonstrates that your hypothesis works. That is, the purpose you set out with, in a general way, is the purpose you arrive with, in a specific way. More often, however, as you continue in the writing process, you will uncover new information or arrive at realizations that cause you to modify your original hypothesis. In other cases, you will discover that you simply cannot prove what your hypothesis suggested you might be able to prove.

Whatever you discover about your hypothesis, you must proceed in writing. If your hypothesis does represent what you want to prove and needs only some modification, you must modify it. This may involve changing your perspective somewhat or finding additional information. If, on the other hand, you find that your hypothesis simply lacks conviction, or that you do not have, and suspect you cannot get, the information with which to prove it, or that in writing your discovery draft you have learned that you are not really very interested in your hypothesis, then you need to reconsider your working purpose. You need to choose another hypothesis that more accurately reflects your intentions, and you need to demonstrate to yourself that it can in fact become your purpose in writing your essay.

For example, if you choose a hypothesis about the lack of nutritional value of McDonald's food and start your discovery draft, you may realize that you have only a few sentences or a paragraph of actual information — probably not enough evidence on which to base an essay — and, further, that you don't consider that information to be especially convincing as you look at it in your first draft. You see holes in your reasoning, holes in your essay. In fact, as you consider the situation, you may recall certain newspaper and magazine articles about famous chefs who rated the food at McDonald's very highly. You have in effect uncovered evidence that might well disprove your hypothesis. You need either to modify that hypothesis or, more likely, to find another.

Purpose and Thesis

Whether you proceed with your original hypothesis, modify it, or choose another, you must eventually arrive at a final decision about your purpose. You make that decision when you know not only what you want to do in your writing but also that you *can* do it. You then use your established purpose to help you make or refine other decisions — about the organization, style, and tone of your writing. One way to express your purpose is to state your *thesis*. A thesis is a sentence that establishes your writing commitment by stating the main idea you are going to develop. The thesis sentence usually appears in the first paragraph of your essay. Although the thesis is often called a purpose statement, thesis and purpose are not precisely the same thing. Your purpose is both contained in and larger than your thesis; it is all the discoveries and decisions you have used to create that thesis, and all the strategies you will use to demonstrate it in a sustained and successful piece of writing.

As the preceding paragraph indicates, your thesis is usually an overt, written-out statement. It makes a restricted, unified, and precise assertion about your subject — that is, an assertion that can be handled in the amount of space you have, that treats only one idea, and that is open to only one interpretation. Deriving a thesis from the information you have about your subject and stating it well are key steps in the writing process; for that reason they will be discussed in more detail in Chapter 3. For now, however, you should remember that you state your thesis after you have determined your purpose, and your thesis expresses your main idea about your subject. For example, if you finally determine that you do not want to write about the nutrition of McDonald's food but rather about people's reaction to that food, your thesis might be stated in this way: "McDonald's food inspires extreme responses of loyalty or loathing from those who eat or think about eating it." In certain writing situations you do not need to write out your thesis. This does not mean that your writing in those situations lacks purpose or a main idea, only that you do not need to make an assertion about your subject in the form of a purpose statement. Writing that narrates a story or that straightforwardly describes an object, for example, does not necessarily need an explicitly written-out thesis; the thesis is rather suggested, or *implied*.

In many ways, the difference between a hypothesis — a working purpose — and a thesis — an assertion about an established purpose — explains why writing with a purpose *prepares* you to write with a purpose. That is, you may be able to speculate about your purpose before you write, but you can designate your purpose only after you have written. This evolutionary connection between your writing process and your writing purpose requires you to pause frequently to consult the criteria set forth in the following guidelines.

Guidelines for Determining Your Purpose

1. *What are the requirements of my writing project?*

   If I am writing to fulfill an assignment, do I understand that assignment? If I am writing on my own, do I have definite expectations of what I will accomplish?

2. *As I proceed in this project, what do I need to know?*

   Do I have a good understanding of my subject, or do I need more information? Have I considered the possible audiences who might read my writing?

3. *What hypothesis can I use as my working purpose?*

   How many different hypotheses can I formulate about my subject? Which of them seems to direct and control my information in the most effective manner?

4. *What purpose have I discovered for this writing project?*

   Has my purpose changed as I learned more about my subject and audience? If so, in what ways? Have I discovered, by working with a hypothesis or hypotheses, what I want to do in my writing?

5. *What is my thesis?*

   How can I state my main idea about my subject in a thesis sentence? Does my thesis limit the scope of my writing to what I can demonstrate in the available space? Does it focus my writing on one specific assertion? Does it make an exact statement about what my writing intends to do?

As you can see from this chapter, the writing process, although it centers on the constants of subject, audience, and purpose, is a fluid process. As you write, you must balance what you know, or think you know, against what you discover in order to create writing that is consistent, clear, and effective. You need to strike the right balance between finding your purpose and then demonstrating that purpose. The strategies you should learn in order to strike that balance are the subjects of Chapters 2, 3, and 4. Now it is time to move from an overview of the writing process into the process itself.

**Review
Exercise**

To review what you have learned in this chapter, read the following essay in which Wally, a student writer, describes his experiences painting for commission. Then discuss the questions that follow.

Brandon's Clown

Few of those words of wisdom that are passed from father to son are [1] followed. Most are simply acknowledged and forgotten. My father's advice about my adolescent love for painting was simple and direct: "Son, you have a special talent. Be smart. Use it to make money." With his words guiding me, I took my love to the marketplace. I began accepting commissions, painting fantasies for those who didn't have the skill or desire to paint their own.

Creating artwork for a client, I soon discovered, demands much [2] more than talent and a lust for money. A friend of mine in Art History 110 was offered $175 to paint a mural in the lobby of her home-town bank. Her only direction from the bank manager was to paint "something rural looking." Obviously, rural looking can be anything from cows lapping at a sunlit pond to combines ripping the heads from a field of golden wheat. Somewhere in that wide spectrum was the painting the manager wanted. Such flexibility forces the artist to play mind reader or simply follow his own desires and hope the client likes the result. A less common, perhaps even less desirable commission is the verbal blueprint. The client knows exactly what he wants. "I want a portrait," he says, "that makes me look like General Patton. I want two American flags in the background and a Doberman at my side." Although there is some security in knowing what the client expects, most artists aren't desperate enough to follow such instructions.

Once the actual work begins, the question that most frequently [3] plagues the artist is "Why am I doing this?" — especially when the commission calls for an uncharacteristic shift in creative expression. I am known on campus as "the guy who paints screaming faces," a tag I am quite happy with. I am proud of the dark maelstroms of anxiety I can create on my canvas. For hours after leaving the easel, I will walk about with my shoulders stooped and head down, frowning, lost in reflections on man's inability to overcome despair.

Naturally, my first commission was for a nursery painting. A young mother expecting her first child wanted an oil painting to hang in a newly remodeled nursery. Mutual friends had informed her that I was willing, able, and cheap. My father's advice prompted me to take the job and I soon found myself discussing infant tastes with the mother-to-be, a pleasant young woman whose only exposure to art was probably the Sunday funnies. 4

"You know, something happy and cheery," she said between snatches of dialogue on *General Hospital*. "The usual stuff for a kid's room." 5

"Is there any kind of theme to your nursery?" I asked hesitantly. 6

"Well, it's blue," she said. "If it's a boy, we're going to call him Brandon. Something like that would be nice." 7

I followed her finger to a baby stroller, decorated with circus animals. "Oh," I said, as the room began to darken and spin. "I see." 8

For the next several weeks, I had nightmares of pink giraffes and smiling zebras parading across my empty canvas. I spent hours hunched over my sketchbook, filling page after page with oddly shaped animal skeletons. Before long, the book looked like a Disneyland mortuary. The entire project seemed so pointless that I was exhausted with frustration. How would I satisfy my cheerful client and remain true to my creative vision? 9

Resolved to compromise my pride for a buck, I began gathering my paints, brushes and canvas with all the enthusiasm of the only girl in the eighth grade not chosen for the pompom squad. I reviewed my sketches hoping to find a subject and suddenly spotted a quick drawing I had made of a clown. Eureka! The answer seemed obvious: a clown. Of course. Clowns had screaming faces, even though they concealed their real pain behind their painted masks. I would mask my true intentions by painting a clown with a slightly sorrowful expression lurking behind his grease paint. He would hold the strings of two balloons, suggesting comparisons to a man behind prison bars. 10

So I began to paint. Every morning before class, I ran to my studio to reappraise the work I had done the night before. The glistening, bright arts were so inviting. Algebra could wait. I picked out my 11 favorite brush and dove back into the painting, detailing areas I had sketched before bedtime, making the highlights lighter and the shadows darker. Gradually, the clown's face began to emerge from the swirl of color. "Brandon's Clown" was my best work to date!

Feeling every bit like the proud parent myself, I carried the finished canvas home from my college studio to unveil it for my mother. As I held it up for her reaction, I was certain she would gush with glee and call the neighbors. But after a few moments of silence, she said "It's black." 12

My defenses flew to Red Alert. "It's supposed to be black. How can you emphasize light and shadow without using black?" 13

Leaving Mom to her *Reader's Digest,* I drove to my client's house in hopes of a better reception. Occasionally I glanced at the painting lying next to me on the seat. Perhaps it *was* a bit dark — for a nursery painting, that is. The expression on the clown's face suddenly seemed harsh and scolding. How could defenseless little Brandon lie in his crib and stare at this all day long? 14

"How do you like your painting, Mrs. Hobbs?" I asked meekly. For some reason, the canvas which had seemed so perfect that morning in my studio now looked totally out of place in Brandon's nursery. A beautiful, tiny wooden rocking horse swayed peacefully on the dresser top. An 8 × 10 hospital glossy of little Brandon, looking fresh and innocent, hung on the wall. And in the corner, nearly lost in a bundle of blankets, was Brandon himself, fast asleep and completely unaware of this ugly black thing that was about to disturb the harmony of his world. 15

"It's fine. Will you take a check?" his mother asked as she hung the painting right above Brandon's head. 16

As I left holding my first commission, I did not think about my father's advice or my artistic reputation. I thought only of poor Brandon. I will not be surprised if, twenty years from now, a deranged young man stops me on the street and smashes a clown painting over my head. I probably deserve worse. 17

Questions for Discussion

1. What kind of work habits does Wally follow when he paints? Where does he paint? What kind of tools does he use? What is the difference between his evening painting and his morning painting?

2. In what ways does the process of painting *Brandon's Clown* resemble the three-stage process of writing? How does Wally *plan* the painting? How does he *draft* the painting? In what sense does he *revise* it?

3. How does Wally select his subject? How do the two examples mentioned in paragraph 2 illustrate the difficulties in painting for a commission? What kind of painting assignment does Mrs. Hobbs give him? In what ways does his choice of a subject fulfill the "Guidelines for Selecting Your Subject" (pages 17–18)?

4. How does Wally analyze his audience? Who are the various audiences for *Brandon's Clown?* How does Wally assess the knowledge, assumptions, and expectations of each one? Which audience is he most concerned about pleasing? In what ways does he follow the "Guidelines for Analyzing Your Audience" (page 22)?

5. What is Wally's purpose? How many different purposes does he see for his work? What conflicts does he see among these various purposes? What hypothesis does he formulate as he begins work on the painting? What prompts him to reassess his original purpose once he has completed the painting? In what other ways does he follow the "Guidelines for Determining Your Purpose" (page 28)?

6. What is the subject of the essay "Brandon's Clown"? What general subjects are introduced in paragraphs 1 and 2? What specific subject is illustrated by the rest of the essay?

7. Who is the audience for this essay? What does Wally assume about the knowledge and expectations of his readers? How do his opening paragraphs help catch and hold his readers' attention?

8. What is the purpose of this essay? Does Wally imply his thesis or announce it in a direct statement? If it is implied, formulate his thesis. If it is stated, identify his thesis sentence.

Writing Exercises

1. Using the questions about writing habits on pages 9 and 10, interview a classmate about his or her writing habits. Try to select someone you suspect will answer these questions differently than you did. After you have compiled your information, write a brief description of this person as a writer.

2. Make a list of some of the writing assignments you had to complete in high school or in a business or professional situation. Pick the one that gave you the most difficulty or the most satisfaction and then explain the writing process you used to accomplish it.

3. Try to remember some words of wisdom that your parents or a trusted friend passed on to you as guidelines for giving your life a sense of purpose. Then describe what happened to you as you tried to follow those guidelines.

Chapter 2

Planning

Getting Started

All writers have trouble getting started. In Chapter 1, Ernest Hemingway was quoted as saying that when he was trying to get started he would stare into space, squeeze orange peels into the fire, or worry about whether he would ever write again. Not all these activities are a waste of time, and some of them may even be necessary if writers are to think their way into a writing project. Random thinking may seem pointless, but it often helps writers break away from outside distractions, thus allowing them to begin to focus on their writing. Random thinking becomes a waste of time, however, if it encourages writers to wait for the perfect moment to begin working. Those who wait for the perfect moment usually do a lot of waiting and very little working. Eventually, all writers must do what Hemingway recalls he did: give themselves a strong pep talk. "Stop worrying! Start writing!"

The best way to start writing is to begin planning. Inexperienced writers tend to think that planning is essentially a thinking activity. First, they plan inside their heads what they want to say, and then they transfer their thoughts onto a piece of paper. Unfortunately, inexperienced writers discover that such planning usually produces two kinds of failure: (1) they cannot think through everything they want to say before they begin to write, and (2) they cannot simply transfer their thinking into writing. In fact, planning is primarily a writing activity, as most experienced writers can testify. Although they admit that they do some planning before they write, they insist that they do their most productive planning after they have begun writing. For them, planning is not so much thinking *and* writing as it is *thinking-in-writing*. Notice what the poet William Stafford has to say about the relationship between thinking and writing in the following passage.

> When I write, I like to have an interval before me when I am not likely to be interrupted. For me, this means usually the early morning, before others are awake. I get pen and paper, take a glance out the window (often it is dark out there), and wait. It is like fishing. But I do not wait very long, for there is always a nibble — and this is where receptivity comes in. To get started I will accept anything that occurs to me. Something always occurs, of course, to any of us. We can't keep from thinking. Maybe I have to settle for an immediate impression: it's cold, or hot, or dark, or bright, or in between! Or — well, the possibilities are endless. If I put down something, that thing will help the next thing come, and I'm off. If I let the process go on, things will occur to me that were not at all in my mind when I started. These things, odd or trivial as they may be, are somehow connected. And if I let them string out, surprising things will happen. (William Stafford, "A Way of Writing," *Writing the Australian Crawl*)

Sources and Strategies

As the first stage in the writing process, planning helps you uncover, explore, and evaluate a topic. Whether you are assigned a topic by your teacher or are free, like Stafford, to accept any topic that occurs to you, planning helps you locate and produce information in writing. Hemingway, you will recall, located his "one true sentence" in one of *three* sources: (1) something he knew (memory), (2) something he had seen (observation), or (3) something he had heard someone say (research). These three sources contain an abundance of information — the raw material for your writing. To tap these sources, you will need to employ a series of practical thinking-in-writing strategies. These strategies not only identify familiar (or forgotten) information but also create, as Stafford suggests, new information. These strategies are also sufficiently flexible that they can be applied to all three sources of information. You may discover, for example, that a strategy designed to tap your memory — such as freewriting — works equally well as a method for observing or conducting research. As you use each strategy, you will need to answer two questions: (1) how much information can I produce about this topic in writing? and (2) how can I use this information to create an interesting piece of writing? You can only answer the first question after you have tried out various strategies. You can answer the second question by testing your information against those guidelines provided in Chapter 1 for selecting a subject, analyzing an audience, and determining a purpose.

Using Memory in Writing

Your own past is one of your best sources of information. Since infancy, you have been accumulating memories about people, places, and things; about growing up, falling down, leaving home, staying put — the list is endless. These memories will often pop into your head when you least expect them. A face in the crowd reminds you of your first date. The taste of cocoa takes you back to a snowball fight. A whiff of suntan lotion finds you playing volleyball at the beach. When you begin to write, however, you cannot remember on impulse. You must remember on purpose, searching your past for impressions, events, and ideas you may want to use.

Code Words

One of the best ways to remember is to use a *code word* to unlock your memory. Code words are similar to general subjects in that they identify a broad area in which you can search for information to shape into a more specific subject. Any code word will get you started thinking about some experience. And as you remember each experience, you will make associations and connections with other experiences you had forgotten or failed to find significant when they happened. Indeed, as you remember each experience you may find that you are replacing your first code word with a series of other words that provoke sharper memories. Some code words may be embedded in your writing assignments (for example, "How has *technology* changed the ways in which reporters gather news?"), but usually you will have to find your own. An easy way to find one is simply to make a list of words. One word will suggest another until you have compiled a fairly interesting group. The following list shows one group of code words that one writer compiled:

Family

Home

School

Work

Machines

Gadgets

Games

Ceremonies

First times

Successes

Disappointments

Secrets

Notice that the writer begins the list with what appear to be neutral words such as *family* and *school* and, through a string of associations, ends with what appear to be more provocative words such as *disappointments* and *secrets*. But only the writer can decide which of these words evokes the most interesting information and how best to use that information. When you compile your own list of code words, select the one (or two) that you think will evoke the most memories or responses from you. Next, use your word to practice one of the *thinking-in-writing* strategies designed to stimulate your memory, reproduce your memories in writing, and interpret what you have remembered. Three such strategies are *brainstorming, freewriting,* and *keeping a journal.*

Brainstorming

Brainstorming, as its name suggests, is supposed to produce a lot of intellectual thunder and lightning. Your code word functions like that first crack of lightning in a storm, illuminating the landscape and starting the downpour. Thinking as quickly and as broadly as possible, you try to remember everything that is provoked by your code word. In effect, you are practicing free association, letting your mind jump from thought to thought without censoring those thoughts. Nothing is "silly" in brainstorming, so don't make judgments while you are jotting down words and phrases. More important, write down everything that comes into your mind in whatever form seems most efficient. You can make another list of words, compose notes and diagrams, or even write out full sentences if they strike you as interesting. But you don't have to arrange anything in any particular order or worry about correcting your sentences as you write them. The point is to keep producing thunder and lightning regardless of how chaotic it looks on the page. If you have trouble generating more chaos, start writing your code word over and over again until you remember a new direction or a set of connections. After the storm is over, you will have time to look around and see what you have created.

One of your richest memory sources is probably your family. Using the code word "Mother," Kurt produced the following information in ten minutes of brainstorming.

Mother

glasses, wire rims

blue eyes

blonde hair in bun — hairpins

always remember her dressed in dull colors — gray, brown

against ERA types — troublemakers

likes to prepare food, talk about food, apologizes for food

born in Germany — saw too much destroyed under Hitler

still has German accent — can't say "enthusiasm" or "cucumber"

still loves Germany — in her blood, she says

family goes back to 16th century

no traces anymore, all wiped out

her family name known throughout Bavaria — Dad's too

must be hard to come to a new country — no one knows your name — sees you as a stranger — new language — new customs

always "Mother," never "Mom"

never understood Mother's moods — somber, serious

wanted her to be like other American mothers — den mother, car-pool organizer, family cheerleader

Mother had her own ways — listened to opera on radio on Saturday afternoon, always sang along with the singers, went to church on Sundays (sang there too), ate fruit at 11:00 a.m. and 3:00 p.m.

wants us to be successful, serious

made sacrifices, worked hard — ironing shirts in the basement, cleaning tile in shower with horrid-smelling cleanser, rubber gloves

did she ever want another life?

never saw her as a person — never let us — always as a parent. *Mother.*

After you have completed your brainstorming session, you should take time to examine your information carefully. What images and ideas seem to cluster together? What title would you give to each cluster? What connections do you see among these clusters? What images and ideas do you want to develop in greater detail? What subject seems to dominate your information? How many other subjects can you identify? What information is familiar? What information is surprising? You may decide that you can use most of the information you produced, or you may discover that only a few fragments or sentences are worth preserving. But one of those sentences may be what Hemingway called "a true sentence," a sentence that points the way to your subject, audience, and purpose.

In the brainstorming entitled "Mother," Kurt discovered that he could cluster his images and ideas around several general subjects:

The Immigrant Experience

The Children of Immigrants

Old Ways and New Ways

German Mothers and American Mothers

Mothers and Children

Although some of these subjects overlapped, each of them formed a body of information worth exploring. A couple of the subjects — "Old Ways and New Ways," "The Immigrant Experience" — seemed too large and remote. Another subject — "German Mothers and American Mothers" — seemed rather more restricted but still required additional research. The subject that seemed to connect most of the items on his list was "Mothers and Children." And he was particularly surprised by his last few phrases: "never saw her as a person — never let us — always as a parent. Mother."

Kurt had never thought of his mother as a person, as a separate individual with an identity apart from her life as his parent. That idea seemed to be a specific subject that was significant, interesting, and manageable. It also suggested at least two general groups of readers (mothers and children) for whom the subject might have some interest. But, most important, the idea hinted at a hypothesis about the relationship between mothers and children (or more specifically, his mother and her children) that Kurt wanted to explore in greater detail. With this new focus, he could repeat the brainstorming exercise or try out one of the other planning strategies described in this chapter. When he has collected enough information, he will begin to sharpen his sketchy hypothesis by composing a sustained piece of writing during the drafting stage.

Freewriting

Freewriting is similar to brainstorming in that both strategies are designed to help you write down what you can remember as quickly as possible. Freewriting differs from brainstorming in that it encourages you to remember blocks of information and to write them out in phrases and sentences. Freewriting is *free*, however, because you don't have to worry about writing perfect sentences. Your primary objective is to write for a sustained period of time (usually ten to fifteen minutes) without stopping. Under these conditions, you don't have time to think about where you are going, where you have been, or how anything looks. You don't even have time to correct misspelled words, cross out awkward phrases, or read what you are writing. Once you are finished, you will have time to read and evaluate what you have written.

Freewriting can be completely free, or it can be focused on a code word. When you are writing without a focus, you are really fishing for something you may want to write about. The result of this first exercise may be that you remember a word, idea, or incident that you would like to write about in another, more focused freewriting exercise.

Laurie, for example, began to freewrite in the hope that filling the page with words would coax something — a provocative word, an interesting recollection — from her mind.

> *Let's see, what can I possibly think of to fill all this blankness. I guess I'm blanking out already. Why not, I can't think of anything to write. Write write write write, right? No, wrong. Right and wrong — dilemmas — choices. That's a dead end. Freewriting is free, supposedly — free as a bird, free as — what? Where's my memory? Memory is free, isn't it? Maybe it costs something too. Not money of course, but cost is often worse when it's emotional. Everyone has regrets, things that never happened no matter how hard you wished. Like my father — never talked much, but I bet he dreamed of being a big league baseball player. Certainly not a warehouse worker. He liked a Yogi Somebody — Yogi Berra, that's it. Yogi is a funny name: Yogi Bear. Actually it's not all that funny, not for him, not for me either. What is "funny," anyway? Cartoon characters, the ones kids watch on Saturday mornings. But they're not really funny, they're violent, always beating up on each other. Boy, is this ever getting ponderous — a real soapbox. Violence on TV. There was that nutty character on TV who thought it was "violins on TV" wasn't there? Enough of this.*

In looking back over this freewriting, Laurie saw a number of ideas or topics that she might write about, but the sentence about her father and baseball struck her with special force. Those two words represented a subject she hadn't thought about for a while, whereas "violence on TV," she realized, seemed a topic that everyone was talking and writing about. She decided to write about her father and baseball, even though doing so risked her emotions, in a focused freewriting.

Father and Baseball

> *When I remember my father, I think about how he hated his work at the warehouse — belonged to my uncle. He loved sports, especially baseball.*

Worked at the warehouse for something like thirty years. Hated it for about the same length of time. Hated that place. Hated a lot of things. Came home from work to watch baseball on television — or basketball or football. Anything on TV was better than work. When he wasn't watching the Cubs or the White Sox, he would walk across the field to the park where the amateur teams played every summer. Watched those games. I could tell when I was still young that my father valued baseball more highly than most things. Suppose that was one reason, biggest reason, I became interested in baseball. I'd tag along to those games at the park and ask questions. He would answer. What he wouldn't do was teach me how to play. I still remember how he would ask my brother to practice batting, catching. Girls are never invited. I went anyway. Really wanted to know how to steal bases and hit home runs. Wanted to please him. He wasn't interested. Oh, he'd explain how to hold a bat or when to steal but it was my brother he wanted to teach. My brother wasn't interested. Who knows. Maybe he was at first. Father was a perfectionist. Impatient. Yelled at Rick for making mistakes. Rick would drop the bat and run home. Me and Dad on the field. "How about it, Dad? Now you can show me. I can do it." Shrugged his shoulders. Disgusted with Rick. Picked up the bat and ball and headed for home. Still makes me angry. When I was older, I fell madly in love with the catcher on our high school baseball team. Guess I thought I loved baseball. Beyond that now. No longer enjoy the game. I guess I liked it only to please him. Don't try anymore. When I am home, he is still watching sports on the portable. I guess that's why I hate baseball.

Laurie used her first freewriting to tap what William Stafford identifies as "receptivity": she accepted whatever occurred to her, even though it seemed quite trivial at first, and one thing led to another until, at the end of the freewriting, she had touched upon several potential topics. Her strong feeling about the topic she chose — "father and baseball" — is apparent in her second freewriting, which not only focuses closely on those two words but also begins to develop a story that her memories prompt her to tell.

Questions for Discussion

If Laurie wants to write a longer and more finished essay about her memories of her father and baseball, she will need to make a number of decisions about her subject, audience, and purpose. Reread both of her freewritings and then discuss your answers to the following questions.

1. **What do you think Laurie identifies as the most interesting and significant aspect of her subject? What do *you* think is interesting and significant about her subject? Do you think some of the information she remembers points to other subjects that are potentially more interesting and significant? What are they?**

2. **What aspects of her subject has Laurie managed to present in sufficient detail? What aspects will she need to develop? What aspects should she eliminate? Do the other subjects you see in this writing seem more or less manageable? Explain your answer.**

3. **How might Laurie consider the question of her audience (a) if she writes to sympathetic readers; (b) if she writes to readers who might be hostile or indifferent? What changes would you advise her to make to ensure a fair and sympathetic reading?**

4. **What do you think Laurie's hypothesis is? What is her attitude toward her subject? What is she attempting to prove by writing about it? Is she attempting to prove more than one thing? Make a list of hypotheses she could use to discuss this information.**

Keeping a Journal

Keeping a journal is a way of keeping track of what you are thinking-in-writing. Your first step is to purchase a notebook that appeals to you. It can be loose-leaf, if you like the idea of adding or rearranging pages; spiral, if you like the multiplicity of available sizes and shapes; or bound, if you like the permanence and stability implicit in binding. Whatever it looks like, the important thing is that you begin to write in it on a regular basis — preferably every day.

Although you are free to write whatever you want in your journal, you should not turn it into a diary that simply recounts each day's physical activities. A journal records the activities of your mind. It is a source book, a place where you can collect and preserve images, ideas, and commentaries on what you see, hear, and read that you may wish to use for some future writing assignment. Because you are keeping your journal for yourself, you don't need to be particular about how you record this information. You can compile lists of writing topics, brainstorm on code words, freewrite on any number of subjects, or even compose preliminary drafts — any activity that forces you to think-in-writing.

Throughout this book you will be asked to use your journal for a wide range of thinking-in-writing activities.

Keeping a journal has two advantages: it encourages you to *take risks* and to *take stock*. A journal provides a no-fault environment where you can try out all sorts of writing experiments. You can play memory games like describing your first day in elementary school, the emotions you felt during your first great success, or the reasons you never told anyone your deepest secret. Some of these experiences may seem hazy as you try to reconstruct them in your mind, but as you write down specific words and phrases, you will be surprised how much you will be able to remember. The rewards of such remembering are worth the risk.

A journal is also the perfect place to take stock of your progress as a writer. As you make lists or compose paragraphs, write to yourself about what you are trying to accomplish. If you are having trouble finding a focus for your subject, interview yourself on paper about your problem. What is the *key issue* in your subject? What do you really want to say about it? What is preventing you from saying it? Does everybody see this issue the way you do? As you try to answer your questions, comment on the choices you are making in the writing process. These comments will help you condense your information into a manageable subject, anticipate the objections of your readers, and underline the significance of your purpose.

In a previous brainstorming session, Jody had written a few sentences about her two grandmothers. In her journal, where she has more time for reflection and meditation, she tries to remember something special about these two women.

10/23 Dad called last night to say that they were finally going to have to put Grandma Rockwell in a nursing home. I know everyone is upset, especially Grandma Gifford. She's next. It wasn't always this way, trying to figure out what to do with old people. They are adults. We talk about them — treat them — like children.

I'd like to write something about the way we treat old people, but it is such a complicated subject. Besides, the only two old people I know are Grandma Gifford and Grandma Rockwell. When I was a kid I used to live at their houses in the summertime. But each one — house, that is — was different, smelled different, looked different, had a different personality. Maybe I can write something about those two houses.

Grandma Gifford's house was always warm — a very comfortable, almost drowsy warm. The thermostat was always set just below the borderline of perspiration. The house was so full of light. The sun shone through the many square-paned windows, through the African violets and made warm patches on the floor. No matter what the season, the house always smelled like Sunday dinner: just-baked bread, pot roast, and apple pie. Also, for some odd reason, I remember talcum powder and tobacco. Those smells don't fit somehow. Grandpa Gifford died before I was born. Maybe it was the old pipes in the pipe rack. Anyway, back to the house. The sounds of the house were drowned out at night by trucks droning by. I don't remember what the house sounded like without that noise. Strange. All I can remember is lying in bed counting the trucks as they rumbled past the house, down the hill into town.

Grandma Rockwell's house was almost warm in winter and nearly cool in summer. It was very dark but never scary. Sort of made it elegant and quiet, like some southern lady sitting in the shade of a stately tree. The house was full of dark woods, beautifully carved wooden doors and polished wooden floors. It was that wood that gave the house its clean smell — partly varnish, partly wax, partly plaster. The floors cracked and creaked when you walked on them. At night, the house groaned, settling into sleep.

That's why I'm so upset about Grandma Rockwell. That beautiful house, empty. I guess they'll sell it. I haven't got the two houses down yet. Maybe when I go home this weekend, I'll visit them both. But I'd rather write about them as I remember them. Now it is difficult for me to visit each house because I keep thinking how I am acting like an adult and my grandmothers are acting like children. But I know that's stupid and egotistical. That's the worst part. I don't feel anything anymore when I go into those houses. I just look around and touch things and wonder what they are going to do with all that stuff. Maybe I should write about that — how it used to feel and how it feels now. I liked remembering all those positive things about those two great houses. Maybe a comparison would spoil it. I'll think about it later.

Jody is making good use of her journal. She starts with a piece of news — as she might in a diary — but shifts quickly to consider what this news reveals about the changing relationships within her family. As she considers the fate of Grandma Rockwell (and the eventual fate of Grandma Gifford), she is compelled to write about them. She talks to herself about how she might write something about the general problem, old people in our culture, but she admits that she *knows* only two old people — her two grandmothers. And what she knows best about them is her childhood experiences in their houses.

This string of associations leads Jody to write about their houses. As she remembers specific sights, smells, and sounds, she uncovers some information that is useful, some information that is puzzling, and a strong sense that she has not recollected enough information to make her portraits complete. She thinks that a visit to the two houses might solve her problem, but she senses that her subject is not simply the two houses. It is how she felt about the two houses when she was a small girl. Visiting the houses now would only emphasize her loss. She speculates that maybe she should change her subject to comparing the way she felt then with the way she feels now. But she decides, for the moment, not to decide.

At this point in her writing process, Jody has not thought too much about her *audience* and has only thought a little about her *purpose*. Because growing old is a universal experience, she can assume that all her readers have faced or will face the kind of event that prompted her to write. But the focus of her writing is not so much the problems of growing old as the personalities of two houses. If her purpose is to make her readers see the uniqueness of each house, then she has to decide how much and what kind of descriptive detail she needs to present. But she also seems on the verge of proposing another purpose — making her readers see what she saw and feel what she lost. Although she uses her journal to take stock of the issues of subject and purpose, she decides to suspend her decision-making process. Perhaps her trip home will give her new insights into this material that she will want to explore in her next journal entry.

Exercises

1. **Pick a code word from the list below (or choose one of your own) and brainstorm about it for ten to fifteen minutes. When you have finished, examine your information and identify all the potential topics you see in it. Which do you find most interesting or surprising?**

computers	detective stories	skyscrapers	Hollywood
shyness	islands	obligations	travel
plastic	celebrity	zoos	cooking

2. **Choose a topic for a focused freewriting exercise and write about it for fifteen minutes. You might choose one of the topics you identified after your**

brainstorming in question 1 (for example, zoos and cruelty to animals; the unprivate lives of celebrities), or you might first brainstorm about one of the other code words in question 1 and then freewrite about a topic you have identified.

3. Try to maintain in your journal a regular commentary on any or all of the following:

interesting reading you do for other courses

the major news of the day, as reported by a newspaper or television commentator

letters from your friends or family

situations that cause you particular happiness or stress

striking images you see — in the media or on your daily rounds

individuals — present-day, historical, or fictive — who interest you

Using Observation in Writing

Although your memory is a rich source of information, you may discover that you have forgotten or never knew some of the information you need in order to write. Such a discovery should hardly surprise you. Why should you remember something you never noticed? Like most people, you spend much of your life as a casual observer, acknowledging but rarely examining the blur of activities you experience each day. You have learned to *look for* the things you have to see — the assignment on the syllabus, the stop sign at the intersection. And occasionally you will *look at* something new or unusual in your environment — a new student in the front row, a new store in the old building around the corner. But for the most part, you *look through* the world the way you look through a magazine, flipping pages and pictures without any particular purpose. When you begin to write, however, you must become a systematic rather than a casual observer. You must train yourself to look for interesting subjects, significant features, and telling details that will help you compose a vivid verbal picture.

Lookout Spots

Just as a code word can help you unlock your memory, so a *lookout spot* can help you focus your observation. Lookout spots function like a photographer's view finder, helping you scan, frame, center, and catalogue the scene you want to observe. In any scene, there are dozens of possible lookout spots, any one of which will enable you to see something from a slightly different perspective. If you decide to look at a stationary object (for example, a monument in your town square), you could observe it from any one of the following lookout spots:

1. Tourist's view
   a. front
   b. back
   c. side
   d. any other point on an imaginary circle that surrounds it
2. Bird's view
   a. top of a tree nearby
   b. top of a building faraway
3. Worm's view
   a. the base of the statue
   b. the flower bed several yards away
4. Commuter's view
   a. walking toward
   b. biking around
   c. driving by
5. Groundskeeper's view
   a. morning
   b. evening
   c. different seasons

Although establishing your lookout spot is essential for effective observation, you have to select what you want to observe, examine what you are seeing, and interpret what you have seen. Three strategies designed to help you think through these problems in writing are *scouting, mapping,* and *speculating.*

Scouting

Scouting is a method for selecting subjects suitable for sustained observation. It is similar to brainstorming in that it encourages you to record your impressions in writing as quickly as possible. It differs from brainstorming in that it requires you to venture out of your room, travel to several locations, and write down what you are seeing on the spot. In other words, scouting is a game of enforced concentration rather than free association. You write down what you discover about the world *outside* rather than what you recover from the world *inside* your self. You can scout by *free-lancing* or by *following a game plan.* In free-lance scouting, you simply wander around until you happen onto a possible location and wait for something to happen. In game-plan scouting, you compile a list of probable locations, often using a code word as you did in brainstorming or freewriting, to identify the kind of people, places, or objects you want to observe. Then you travel to each site and look for your subject.

Free-lance scouting may seem too unstructured because you simply roam from spot to spot without any particular purpose. But if you are prepared to observe all that you encounter, you can use free-lance scouting to make some surprising discoveries. By contrast, game-plan scouting may seem too systematic because you determine what you will observe before you observe it. But if you are ready to expect the unexpected, you are likely to see something you did not plan to see.

Whatever method you use to arrive at a location, you scout each one according to a three-step process.

1. With notebook in hand, you explore the location for possible lookout spots. If you are observing a large scene such as the foliage of a forest or the skyline of a city, you will need to find a spot that gives you a panoramic view of your subject. If you are observing a small scene such as the fish in a stream or a portrait in an art gallery, you will need to find a spot that gives you a more microscopic view of your subject. As you try out each spot, record it in your notebook along with a brief note about its advantages and disadvantages.

2. Select one lookout spot and write down everything you *see, hear, taste,* and *smell* for fifteen minutes. As with brainstorming, you don't need to compose this information in perfect sentences or in any particular order. Your primary task, rather, will be to capture your dominant

impression of the location. For that reason, you will be most conscious of what you are seeing. After all, you are *writing to observe*. But try to write down at least one comment on the other four senses so that you develop a more deeply textured sense of the place.

3. At the end of the session, read over your notes, observe the scene one more time, and then write a brief evaluation (no more than a few sentences) commenting on the subject's suitability for sustained observation.

In her journal, Jenny decided she wanted to observe a major intersection on the campus or in the nearby community. According to her game plan, such an intersection would provide her with an abundant supply of people and activities to write about. She compiled a list of intersections and began to scout them.

Crosswalks and Intersections

1. The quad

Lookout spots

a. in the center — no sense of shape or pattern, but a lot of people activity

b. from the edge — good sense of scene, no sense of people

c. second-story window — good overview of space and people, but detached, like TV without sound

From the center at 9:45 a.m.

center of campus — crossroad — everybody walks here.

scene changes every hour.

bells ringing inside buildings.

saw only two people when class was still in session — groundskeeper, man in a suit (prof?).

without people, you notice trees, squirrels, birds, dogs.

smell of grass, dirt.

bell rings, rush of people.

some follow the paths roped off by chains.

others cut across grass — short cuts.

students walk in groups — jocks, musicians carrying instrument cases.

talking, laughing — "Are you going to the game?"

professors walk alone — briefcase, papers.

how many people have walked across quad? history of this place!

changes in winter — people slipping on ice — in summer — guys throwing frisbee, dogs chasing them.

Evaluation

Interesting place to observe. Possible subject is how scene changes every hour — has changed every hour since school was built, almost a hundred years ago, I guess. Too many people. Too much activity.

2. *Laundry room in dorm*

Lookout spots

a. in the room — center of activity — doing laundry
b. from the door — outside observer

In the room at 4:00 p.m.

everybody comes here sooner or later.

nobody here now — quiet, good place to read except chairs are uncomfortable — red plastic mold.

soap smell, moisture.

three girls come into room, laundry bags.

coin changer, soap machine.

machines whirl, heat, noise.

washers in the middle, dryers on the side, one folding table.

two girls talk, can't hear because of machines, they leave.

other girl in red chair, reads a blue book, Introduction to Accounting.

waiting for machine to finish.

noise of machine changing cycles — wash, spin.

pull damp clothes out of washer, put in dryer, see clothes dancing through window of dryer.

dull — do your chores, your duty, get done.

waste of time — except you need clean clothes.

nobody can talk with machines running — shout.

Evaluation

Another interesting place to observe. More focused than quad — scene changes, too. But subject is dull. No real interaction. Nobody can talk.

3. *The block in the village*

Lookout spots

a. end of block — see length of street, store signs.
b. inside store looking out — watch shoppers pass by, some came in.

c. *bus stop — good place to watch activity. Not just college students. Real intersection of college and town.*

Bus stop at 12:00 noon

> *across the street is barbershop, coffee shop, pub.*
> *behind me is the bank — nothing to see there.*
> *people coming and going everywhere — groups of two's and three's.*
> *lot of traffic — horns, cars, bikes.*
> *bus stops — exhaust smell.*
> *two bus drivers change shifts — talk about ball game.*
> *one goes into pub — eat lunch?*
> *new driver climbs behind seat — nobody gets on.*
> *noise of doors closing, gears shifting, drives off.*
> *lots of people seem to be coming and going at barbershop, community crossroad.*
> *people talk to me at bus stop. "What are you doing?" "Assignment." "Oh."*
> *woman missed bus, knows schedule, sits down to wait for next bus.*
> *nothing much happens at stop between buses.*
> *places across the street seem more interesting — especially the barbershop. I've been in coffee shop and pub.*
> *never been in a barbershop — male place — don't belong.*
> *the barbers and their customers.*
> *what was barber's name on Andy Griffith Show?*
> *barbers could give shop personality.*
> *maybe it's like beauty parlor, you hear a lot of gossip.*

Evaluation

> *Could describe bus stop. The way people wait for buses, talk to other people, the drivers. That's sort of aimless, though, and there's not much to say. Barbershop looks like great place — atmosphere, people, personalities, process of cutting hair. I need to go inside.*

Jenny has used her scouting to select possible subjects for a sustained observation. At each location she considers several lookout spots, but the one she chooses is usually at the center of the activity because she wants to observe the interaction of people. As she reads over the information she has written down at each site, she makes some preliminary decisions about potential subjects: the quad is busy, the laundry room too dull, the bus stop too restricted, but the barbershop — she is surprised to discover — might be an interesting subject. Although she has not been inside the shop, Jenny is already thinking about how she might shape it into a subject ("barbershop, community crossroad"). She is also beginning to anticipate questions of audience ("male place — don't belong") and purpose ("barbers could give shop personality"). Although she thinks she has identified a subject to observe, Jenny will have to scout the interior of the shop before she makes her final decision. A good way to intensify her observation of this subject is to map it.

Mapping

Mapping is a method for examining a subject during an extended period of observation — usually thirty to sixty minutes. Its purpose is to force you to observe with a pencil in your hand in order to reproduce in lines and figures the general outline and the telling details you see in your subject. Once you have mapped your subject, you not only know it in greater detail but you also begin to see how you can convert your images into words.

Purchase a large sketch pad (the paper size should be at least eleven by fourteen inches or larger) and a box of sharpened pencils with good erasers. Then, with pad and pencils in hand, travel to the place you have selected. If someone owns or has responsibility for the place, you should explain what you want to do and ask for permission to complete your assignment. Once you have obtained approval, find a comfortable position at your lookout spot, and begin to map everything you see.

As you look at the scene in front of you and then at the large expanse of white paper resting in your lap, you will probably experience mapper's block, a fear of putting down the first line. If you have not sketched anything in a long time or are convinced that everything you sketch looks like something you drew in kindergarten, then you will be even more hesitant to begin. But remember you are making this map for yourself, not for the pages of *National Geographic*. Mapping is simply another strategy for thinking on paper. Its purpose is to provide you with a visual outline to frame, focus, and catalogue all the information you are observing — objects, activities, conversation, people.

Once you remind yourself of the purpose of your map, you must decide what kind of map you want to make. There are three basic formats:

1. *A spatial map* is the easiest to make because it resembles a traditional map or blueprint. The mapmaker looks down on the subject and outlines the spatial relationship among its various parts.

2. *An activity chart* uses the basic outline provided by the spatial map to document the kind and amount of action that occurs in the scene. Usually, the mapmaker will use a variety of dotted lines to illustrate where action originates or concentrates.

3. *A figure drawing* focuses on your subject in two- or three-dimensional detail. Drawing this kind of "map" requires the most time and talent, but it usually teaches you more about your subject than any other method.

Which format you choose depends in part on the nature of your subject and your purpose in mapping it. If you want to define the relationships among objects in a static space, use the spatial map. If you want to discover what people are doing in a particular space, use the activity chart. And if you want to examine the unique features of a particular object or person in the scene, use the figure drawing. You may decide to map your subject with all three methods.

Regardless of the format you choose, you should follow the same mapping procedure. First, you must determine how much of the material you see you want to include within the borders of your map. Hold your hands upright in front of your eyes to form the edges of an imaginary picture frame. Then move them out and back to see how much of your subject you want inside the frame. Second, identify the major landmarks on your map. In a spatial map, these landmarks are the most significant physical features you observe. On an activity chart, they are the energy centers you are able to discover — the places where things are happening. And in your figure drawing, they are the major focal points in the scene — the objects or features that attract and capture your attention. Third, catalogue all the telling details you can observe in the scene. Study your subject in the way a stage designer examines a theatrical set. Then locate and list everything you would need to reconstruct this set somewhere else — backdrops, characters, costumes, furniture, props.

Each line on your map discovers and defines information that you may want to use once you begin writing about your subject. But lines, shapes, and figures may not enable you to identify all the information you observe. For that reason, annotate your map, suggesting with a word or phrase the significance of some object you saw but somehow could not sketch in sufficient detail. Such annotations will help you comment on the distortions of space, activity, and shape you are likely to draw on your map. Inevitably, all mapmakers admit that they have failed to get the proportions right — the landmarks are too big, the energy centers too inconsistent, and the focal points too diffuse. Use your annotations to remind yourself of what you are learning about your subject as you try to map it.

Armed with her sketch pad and pencils, Jenny ventured into the Varsity Barbershop. When she asked the barbers for permission to complete her assignment, they agreed, but immediately began joking with one another about how famous they would all be once Jenny had mapped their wonderful world. As she started to work, one of the barbers or an occasional customer would look over her shoulder to inspect or comment on her map. But for the most part, she was absorbed into the atmosphere of the shop and began to concentrate on her subject. She spent almost an hour making the maps on pages 57 and 58.

Mapping is actually a two-stage procedure: (1) you make your map, and (2) you interpret what you have made. During the first stage, you focus on the *process* of creation. Your eyes move constantly back and forth between the objects you are observing and the shapes you are sketching with your pencil. As you frame, center, and catalogue all the details you see, you will be gathering more information about your subject than you will need in order to write about it. At this point, however, you are still discovering your subject. You don't know what details you will need. Everything seems interesting and significant because you want to make an accurate map. Although you may not need every detail on your map, you are acquiring an intimate sense of your subject's significant features and telling details. That knowledge will help you arrange and develop your information when you begin composing your first draft.

During the second stage of mapping, you focus on the *product* of your creation. Your eyes move across your map (side to side, top to bottom,

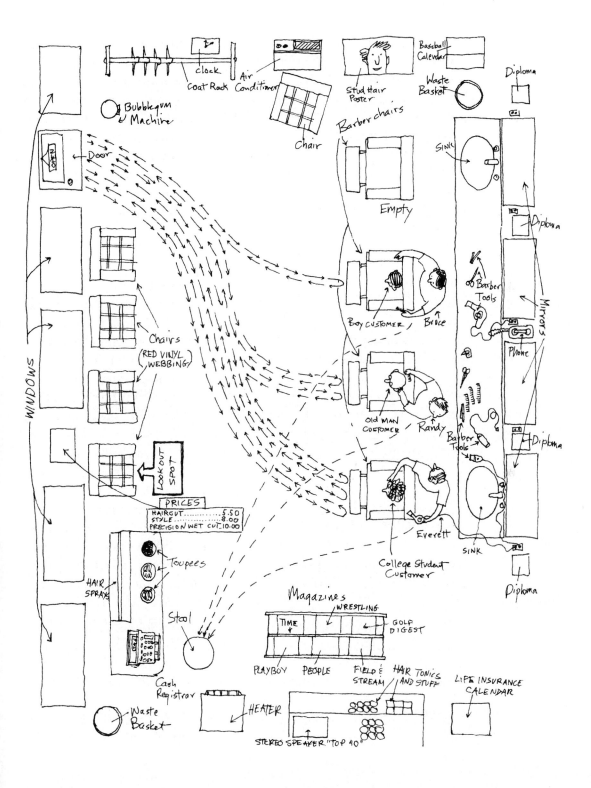

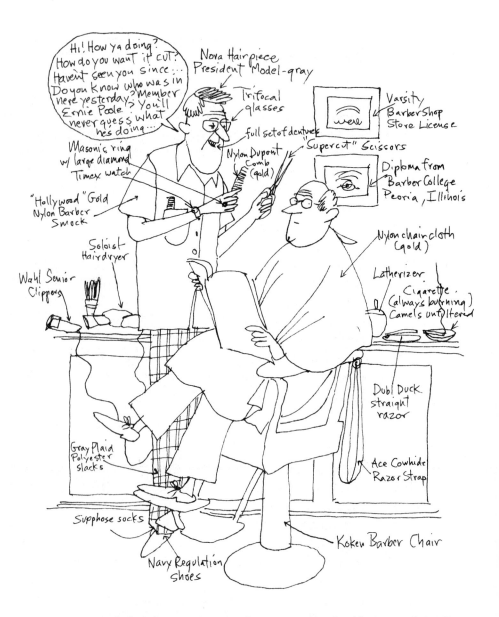

center to periphery) as you try to interpret the significance of the lines, figures, and shapes you have made. First, you form a general impression of these images. Next, you find the major landmarks, activity centers, or focal points in your drawing. Then, you examine the specific details in each portion of your picture, trying to establish their relationship to one another and to the major figures. And, finally, you define a *subject* that you can communicate to an *audience* for a *purpose*.

Jenny began by constructing a spatial map of the Varsity Barbershop. She established her lookout spot in the chair beneath a price sign and began to sketch. She blocked out the major areas in the shop (barber chairs, waiting chairs, cash register) and identified the individual details that created its atmosphere (barber tools, hair supplies, magazines). But she soon became more interested in the action in the shop than in its props and scenery. Her activity chart reveals the extent to which she saw one barber (Everett) as the central character in the shop's daily drama. Her character drawing suggests that she finds this man an appealing potential *subject.* Although her maps do not identify a specific *audience,* she has noted that men of all ages are customers of the barbershop. Her audience could be men (who are familiar with the rituals of a barbershop) or women (who either are interested in those rituals or suspect there may be similarities between the activities in barbershops and those in beauty salons). As she focuses on Everett, however, she thinks less about cutting hair and more about gossip. Everett is the energy center, the individual who dominates and orchestrates the conversations in the shop. She is close to formulating a *hypothesis* to try out in a draft: a single personality (Everett) gives a place (the Varsity Barbershop) its atmosphere and character.

Speculating

Speculating is a method for producing different interpretations of what you have observed. The word *speculate* suggests an imaginative, hypothetical kind of seeing: you examine what you observe, mull over its possible meanings, and make several conjectures about its significance. A secondary meaning of *speculate* is to take risks — such as when you speculate in the stock market in the hope of making a profit. Speculating as a thinking-in-writing strategy encourages you to take a few intellectual risks by considering your subject from three different perspectives.[1]

1. *Speculate about your subject as an object.*
   This perspective suggests that you see your subject at rest, as a static object or scene that at a given moment possesses a fixed identity.

---

1. Based on the tagmemic theory of invention in Richard E. Young, Alton L. Becker, and Kenneth L. Pike, *Rhetoric: Discovering and Change* (New York: Harcourt Brace Jovanovich, 1970).

2. *Speculate about your subject as an action.*

   This perspective allows you to see your subject in motion, as a dynamic, living process that changes its appearance as it progresses through various activities.

3. *Speculate about your subject as a network.*

   This perspective enables you to see your subject as a series of connections, as a complex system of relationships that extend and enhance its importance.

As you think about your subject from each of these perspectives, write down your speculations in your journal. If one perspective does not produce profitable information, move on to the next perspective. Remember, you are speculating, so don't be afraid to take risks. Write down what you see and make guesses about what you don't see. Don't try to write perfect sentences; you are still *planning*. You are trying to see something interesting and significant in your subject to present to an audience for a purpose.

Speculating is an effective procedure because it can be used both as a general strategy for generating information (provided, of course, that you have at least some notion of your subject) and as a specific strategy for focusing and interpreting information you have already observed. For example, after Jenny finished her mapping exercises, she decided to speculate in her journal about what she had seen at the barbershop.

Varsity Barbershop as an Object

The Varsity Barbershop has been a fixture in the university village for almost forty years. Probably never changed in all that time. A permanent set. If it had a checkerboard and an overhead fan it could be Floyd's Barbershop on the old Andy Griffith television series. There are four brown leather and chrome barber chairs facing the windows that look out to the street, and four red, webbed vinyl and aluminum waiting chairs facing the barber chairs. Behind three of the barber chairs stand the three barbers, waiting for somebody to come in. They watch the people who walk down the street outside. Sometimes they sit in their own chairs. They don't talk much when there are no customers. Manikins in a store window. Behind the chairs are large mirrors and a series of counters and sinks where they keep their tools. On the walls between the mirrors are their diplomas from barber school. At one end of the shop, near the door, is a coat rack, an air conditioner, and a large poster of this terrific-

looking stud with wonderful hair. At the other end, the cash register and the hair supplies, including a few sample toupees. Near the cash register is a magazine rack — Time, Field and Stream, Golf Digest, and Playboy — typical male reading. You can hardly see the price sign. When you sit in the waiting chair it's above your head. Too high to be reflected in the mirror. When you are in the barber's chair you can see it. As a fixed object, there's not much to see here. Drab. Dull. The shop comes to life when a customer walks in.

Varsity Barbershop as Action

There are so many things to see when the shop is busy. Above everything else there's the murmur of conversation. Listen carefully and you can pick out individual sounds — scissors snipping, razors trimming, and the vacuum whirring. But first you have to come in. "Hi, how are you?" Everybody gets a hello from every barber, but the biggest hello comes from Everett. Then you have to find a chair, pick out a magazine and wait your turn. Sometimes you talk to the barber while you wait, especially Everett, but mostly you wait. You can talk to the barbers once you get in their chair. Which barber you get depends on rotation — "Next?" Some people say "Go ahead" to somebody else. "I'm waiting for Everett." Once you get in the chair, you talk about how you want it cut. After a few jokes. Everett, who wears one of the "rugs" he sells, starts cutting your hair — combs, scissors, electric trimmers. He may turn you around a couple of times so you can see what he's doing in the mirror, but usually he waits to show you the result when he's done. All the time he talks. To you, to the other customers, to the other barbers. Randy is his straight man. Feeds him lines so he can get Everett to tell a joke. Bruce isn't as busy as Randy and Everett — he's only been at the shop a year. He picks up the broom and sweeps the hair clippings from under the chairs and pushes them down the floor to the wastebasket. When you're done, you pay at the cash register and say "Goodbye" to everybody. Customers come at different times. Sometimes there is a long waiting time. Sometimes you're next. A few people just come in to talk or say "Hi" to Everett. Always crowded at 5:00 p.m. on Fridays. When it's not busy, Randy likes to play the stereo. Works as a drummer on weekends. "Where you playing this weekend, Randy?" "Moose."

Varsity Barbershop as Network

Varsity Barbershop is definitely a network. Everett connects everybody with everybody. The shop is in the middle of the village, across from the bus stop and the bank. Everett owns some property nearby so he knows all about real estate.

Also knows all the other shopkeepers in the village. Probably knows their parents. When he goes out for coffee in the morning and the afternoon, he talks to everybody. Gets the lowdown, the latest. Comes back to the shop loaded with news about who's planning a sale, who's hiring, and who's selling out. Everybody who comes into the shop has news. The mayor, bankers, policemen, bus drivers, students, professors, kids — everybody has something to tell Everett. And Everett passes it on. Insurance man named Jerry comes into the shop. He's not getting a haircut — just wants to sell Everett some new life insurance. Everett says he cashed in his old policy and invested it in money market. "Oh, that Everett. He's a smart one," says Randy. Jerry takes bait. Soon they are shouting. "Insurance is something everybody's got to have," says Jerry. "Not really," says Everett. "You're crazy," shouts Jerry. "Why? I got money. I'm taken care of." "I'm talking about the average person," says Jerry. "Oh well then," Randy interrupts, "you're not talking about Everett." Everybody laughs. Bruce says that when the Brinks truck can't get through to the bank, "they just drive over here and ask Everett for a pile of hundreds." Everybody laughs again. Old gossip about Everett and his millions. Everett must know everybody in town. And when you think about how many students have gotten haircuts here in forty years, he probably knows half the state. During alumni week, the old grads come back to talk to Everett. He gets more news. Next week he'll pass it on. The Varsity Barbershop is an information switchboard and Everett is the chief operator.

Exercise

Jenny's planning activities have yielded a wealth of information about the Varsity Barbershop. Before she moves on to draft a full-length essay, she needs to consider all her information in terms of her potential subject, audience, and purpose. Re-examine her scouting, mapping, and speculating exercises, then write out your answers to the following questions. Your instructor may want you to discuss your answers in class.

1. How many subjects, general and specific, can you identify in the three speculations?

2. Which of Jenny's three speculations seems to produce the most interesting perspective on the barbershop? Why? How does that perspective define a significant and manageable subject?

3. Has Jenny discovered enough about her subject, or will she have to engage

in more planning activities before she is ready to write? **Explain your answer.**

4. **What kind of readers could Jenny assume to be the potential audience for her writing about the Varsity Barbershop? How might she assume a slightly different audience for each of her three speculations?**

5. **What possible hypotheses do you find in Jenny's scouting, mapping, and speculating exercises?**

6. **What purpose might Jenny choose for writing an essay about a small community barbershop? What thesis sentence could she write to control the purpose of her essay? How could she use information — description, dialogue, commentary — to demonstrate her purpose? Cite several examples.**

Using Research in Writing

Once you have explored your memories and examined your observations, you may decide that you still need more information about your subject if you are going to compose an effective piece of writing. Memory and observations, after all, define your subject in *your* terms — the way you remember or see it. To broaden and deepen your understanding, often you must move beyond the limits of your personal experience to determine how others have perceived your subject. Almost any subject you choose (worst flavors of ice cream, best hiking sites in your state, or most unusual gadgets sold on television) has been researched by other writers. Sometimes their conclusions, although different in focus and method, will enrich your perspective by confirming your preliminary hypothesis. Other times their conclusions, although apparently similar in pattern and detail, will expand your perspective by challenging your fundamental assumptions. As often as possible, you should ensure the accuracy and authority of your information by consulting the research others have done on your subject.

Search Questions

Before beginning your research, you need to determine generally what you hope to accomplish by it. A *search question* combines the primary features of the *code word* and the *lookout spot* by naming a subject and establishing a perspective from which to examine it. For example, the search question "How do historic preservation societies determine which buildings to designate as historic landmarks?" proposes to explore a subject (historic preservation societies) from a specific perspective (how they choose buildings for landmark status).

Some search questions are prompted by vague curiosity: "I wonder whether my grandparents had as much trouble understanding their parents as I seem to have understanding mine?" Others are provoked by a specific issue: "How has inflation affected the earning power of small businesses like barbershops or beauty salons?" Still others present an immediate problem: "If I purchase this wood-burning stove, will I actually save money?"

Although search questions guide you to a specific subject from a particular point of view, they often encourage you to ask additional questions — some direct, some diverting. Indeed, once you begin to pursue a search question in writing, you learn the true meaning of *research*. Experienced writers recognize that formulating new search questions is a predictable part of the research process. A new question simply means that your first question was (1) too general, (2) too restricted, or (3) not your real question. In any case, your discovery of new search questions will bring you closer and closer to producing informed answers. You should be able to convert one of these answers into a hypothesis — a preliminary statement that explains what you hope to prove by writing about your research. In Chapters 13 and 14 you will learn how to follow a search question through all the formal procedures of planning and writing the research paper, a more extended piece of writing than the expository writing discussed here. In this chapter, you will use your search question to practice two informal planning strategies designed to produce information in writing: *interviewing* and *reading*.

Interviewing

Interviewing someone is the easiest and most direct way to answer your search question, but the process is never as simple or as spontaneous as it appears on television. To be effective, you must learn (1) how to prepare for an interview, (2) how to manage and record the conversation during an interview, and (3) how to evaluate what you have learned once an interview is completed.

How to prepare for an interview   Begin by compiling a list of people who may be able to answer your search question. This list could include *experts* (people who have studied your subject), *participants* (people who have *lived* your subject), and *information brokers* (people who may know nothing about your subject but who know how to put you in touch with the people who do). It could just as easily include your roommate, your parents, or your family doctor. Contact the people on your list and ask for an interview. Tell them, in general terms, what you are trying to find out and why you think they may be able to help you. Ask if you can talk to them for a specific amount of time — no longer than an hour — and don't overstay your welcome. After you have set up your interviews, try to anticipate the attitudes that those you will interview will have toward you and your questions. Are they likely to be friendly, hostile, preoccupied, or merely puzzled when you arrive? Sometimes you can anticipate their attitudes because you have known them for a long time or because you have heard them express their opinions on your subject. Other times you can anticipate their attitudes by imagining yourself in their position. How would you feel about being interviewed on this subject? What topics would you want to be asked about? What topics would you want to avoid? What questions would you have about the interviewer's motives and methods?

After you have analyzed the people you are going to talk to, ask yourself what you really want to learn from them. Your search question helps you identify a general direction, but a successful interview requires you to ask more than one question. If you are interviewing someone you don't know, you want to appear prepared. If you are interviewing an old friend, you don't want to get sidetracked by other — more familiar — subjects. A useful strategy is to write out a list of questions about your subject according to the journalist's formula: Who, What, Where, When, Why, and How? This list of questions will help you organize what you want to learn. Most interviews are dynamic and therefore are often disorganized affairs. For that reason, you must remind yourself that you are likely to get surprising answers that will inspire you to ask new questions. The best interviewers prepare to uncover things they need to learn, and plan to discover things they had not expected to learn.

How to manage and record an interview   Interviews can be formal occasions — the interviewer acting like an attorney grilling witnesses; the witnesses acting like suspects, apprehensive about what they are saying and suspicious about why they are being asked. Or interviews can be informal occasions — a pleasant and productive conversation among friends. Sometimes you cannot control the mood of an interview because the person you are talking to is suspicious of you and your question before you arrive. But most of the time, you can put yourself and your subject at ease by following a few basic tips:

1. Don't *feel* that you have to apologize for your interview. You may want to *say* something about how much you appreciate your subject's willingness to talk to you. Such remarks are part of the expected etiquette of interviewing. But if someone has given you an interview, he or she is probably flattered that you are there and has already made time for you on the day's schedule.

2. Resist the temptation to use a tape recorder. Purchase a small notebook, keep it out of sight as much as possible, and write in it as little as possible. When you do write, copy down code words and phrases rather than complete sentences. Keep your eyes on the person you are talking to, not fixed on your notebook.

3. Begin your interview by talking about topics you know are comfortable, interesting, and safe. If you have arranged to conduct the interview on the subject's own turf (home, office), ask about some object or photograph you have noticed in the room. Even if you don't ask about these "props," try to list them in your notebook because they may help you interpret what your subject thinks is important in his or her life.

4. Don't tell your subjects everything *you* want to know before they tell you what *they* know. You are trying to learn what other people think, not prove what you think. The best strategy is to encourage your subjects to act like experts: ask them to help you understand and answer your own questions.

5. Use your prepared questions only when the conversation drifts far away from your major search question. For the most part, allow the conversation to develop naturally. Review your prepared questions as a final check before you begin to wrap up the interview.

6. Save two questions for the end of the interview: (1) what should I have asked that I didn't ask, and (2) who else do I need to interview (or read) to answer my questions?

How to evaluate an interview   Once you have completed your interview, you should return to your room and immediately reconstruct the conversation in writing. Try to describe the atmosphere of the room, the appearance of your subject, and the varying attitudes (eager, evasive, expansive) he or she expressed during the discussion. Transform all your code words and phrases into complete sentences. If your notes seem incomplete or if you want to be sure that you are quoting your subject accurately, call the person to double-check your information. Such follow-up calls are not invitations to censor. Subjects often want to revise what they said during an interview, but only you can decide whether their second thoughts should be yours. Your follow-up call is simply an effort to make the first version complete and accurate.

After you have reproduced the interview in writing, determine what you have learned. Did your subject provide useful answers to your prepared questions? What answers confirmed your assessment of his or her biases? What answers surprised you? What new questions did you discover as a result of the interview? If you were to write an essay trying to answer your search question, could you use the information gained from this interview to formulate a hypothesis?

This last assessment suggests the degree to which even the most informal interview can get you started on further planning activities. Once you try to write up what other people have told you, you will discover that you are making lists of questions you should have asked, people you want to talk to next, and material you think you better read. Such was the innocent beginning for Mary when she and her husband Bill first talked about the possibility of purchasing a wood-burning stove to reduce their winter utility bill. Because he had already conducted his own research, Bill was convinced that it would be a wise purchase. But Mary wanted to conduct her own independent research to determine whether Bill's hypothesis was really valid. In her journal, she decides to take on this family issue as a writing project for her composition class.

9/25   Bill doesn't usually jump into big investments without doing a lot of checking, but I feel he is taken with the pioneersy glamour of owning a wood-burning stove. I want to do some research on my own. Who should I talk to? I could talk to a couple of salesmen about stoves, but, of course, they will want to install a unit in the family room faster than Bill does. I know they'll give me a glowing portrait. I should ask them if they own one. I could talk to the energy consultant at the home show, but the article about him in last night's paper made him sound too theoretical and technical. I need to talk to a real person — someone who owns a stove, someone I can understand. George and Susie are perfect. But our conversations always ramble — kids, school, relatives, vacation, movies. I need a list of questions to help us stay on the subject.

1. *Who convinced you to buy a wood-burning stove?*

2. *What kind of stove did you buy? Why did you choose it? Are you satisfied with it?*

3. *Where did you buy it? Why?*

4. *When is the best time to buy and install a stove? Are they cheaper during a certain time of year?*

5. *Why did you buy your stove? Do you really think it would be a good investment for us?*

6. *How do you take care of a wood-burning stove? <u>Exactly</u> what is involved? Does it really <u>save</u> you money?*

7. *How much time is involved with this thing? Where do you get the wood? How about all the hidden extras — tools, paraphernalia? Is it really worth the hassle?*

9/28 Just returned from my interview with George and Susie. Now I am really confused. They were both eager to talk to me. And, of course, I got a grand tour of the big, black stove. Looks like one of those safes bank robbers used to blow up in the old western movies. We sat down in front of it and talked about it like it was a person. I got standard replies from George and Susie on my first few questions. But the closer I got to the <u>real</u> questions, the more they seemed to disagree with one another.

<u>Does it really save you money?</u> George hurried to his desk to pull out gas bills from before and after installation. He pointed to this month's bill: "The furnace hardly ever kicks on. It's incredible how much you can save." Susie went to the kitchen, rummaged in the junk drawer, and then came back reading from her list: "$50 for a fiber glass hearth rug; $35 for a wood crib; $35 for a chimney cleaning brush; $10 for stove polish; $12 for chimney fire extinguisher, etc., etc., etc." George admitted that there were <u>some</u> extras, but it was not that much, really.

<u>How much time is involved with this thing?</u> George said that the stove did take some of his free time, but he got a lot of great exercise chopping wood: "The

main thing is how it makes you feel. Self-sufficient. You don't have to depend on anybody. You really feel like you are accomplishing something." Susie started mumbling about ruined weekends ("spends all his Saturdays chopping") slipped discs ("he's gonna do it, sure"), and black soot ("you won't believe the mess").

I think I learned more about George and Susie than I did about stoves. Some of what George said made sense, but I sympathized with Susie. Maybe I am too close to them. George always sees the bright side. Susie loves to be the cynic. The question I should have asked them — "what has this thing really <u>cost</u> you?" — seemed like a powder-keg question, one that would probably start a family argument. So I didn't ask. I need other, less emotional, information. George gave me some consumer literature and a few sales brochures to read. I suppose I should talk to a few salesmen or that energy expert. At least, I have a better sense of the real questions I need to ask now that I have talked to George and Susie.

Mary began with what appeared to be a simple search question: "Will purchasing a wood-burning stove save us any money?" Her decision to interview friends rather than salespeople or experts also appeared to be a simple way to answer her question. What she discovered was that her search question and even her list of prepared questions contained many smaller, more complicated questions, such as how you calculate *cost* (lower utility bills versus ruined weekends). As she interviews other people and reads more about stoves, Mary knows that her *subject* is both larger and smaller than she first imagined. It is larger because it contains many controversial issues. It is smaller because all the controversy seems to focus on one question — how you measure *cost*. As she thinks about how Bill, George, and Susie have answered this question, Mary is beginning to formulate her own *hypothesis* about how people define the cost of a thing. She is also beginning to anticipate the kind of *audience* she will be writing for — people like Bill, George, Susie, and herself. Before she begins to test her hypothesis in a sustained piece of writing, she wants to search for more information.

Reading

Reading what other people have written about your subject is probably the most common strategy for gathering information for your writing.

For experienced writers, reading is always an active (never a passive) procedure. They select, analyze, and evaluate what they read for one purpose: to help them write. Chapters 13 and 14 will present several kinds of reading and writing activities that you engage in when you plan and write a formal research paper: checking bibliographies, assessing sources, taking notes, writing summaries, quoting evidence, and documenting sources. In this chapter, however, you will learn to use reading as a planning strategy, as an informal way to explore your search question in writing.

The easiest way to keep track of what you are reading is to write about it in your journal. You should think of reading as another form of interviewing — a way of talking to people who have answers to your search question. So, just as you did in interviewing, start by making a list of the kind of material you want to read. To find this material you can use your own instincts; ask an expert; consult popular magazines such as *Time, National Geographic,* or *Fortune;* or talk to a reference librarian at your library. You will discover once you start reading that each selection will refer you to other selections. Then your problem will be deciding when you have read enough. There is no easy way to make that decision — you can *always* read more — but usually you know that you have read enough when the same names, ideas, issues, and questions begin to repeat themselves in each article or book you read.

On most subjects, reading material falls into three categories: expert studies, eyewitness testimonials, and advocates' propaganda. Sometimes it is difficult to decide how to classify a specific selection because it may combine features of all three categories. For that reason, you need a set of questions to help you interpret what you are reading. These reading questions are similar to the guidelines you follow as you write, but in this case, you are deciding how another writer *selects a subject, analyzes an audience,* and *determines a purpose.*

1. Who is the author? What makes the author an authority on this subject? What reasons might the author have for being biased?

2. Where and when did the article or book appear? Sometimes you may know very little about the author, but you know something about the point of view of a particular magazine *(Cosmopolitan, New England Journal of Medicine)* and whether the date of the publication is likely to make the information current and reliable.

3. What is the author's subject? Within the general subject, how has the author restricted his or her subject? Does the author's particular perspective on the subject help you answer your search question, or does it lead you into areas that are only vaguely related to your question? What new questions does the author raise that you may have to account for as you define your subject?

4. To whom is the article or book addressed? What kind of knowledge does the author assume his or her readers already possess? What kind of information does the author presume his or her readers want to know?

5. Does the author make a specific purpose statement in the essay or do you have to figure it out on your own? If the author has written a thesis sentence, how does it guide you through the essay? How does it arrange and explain the information you read?

Armed with these questions, you can begin working your way through the readings on your list. Keep your journal with you so that you can write in it in three different stages:

Preview: Before you read certain selections, you can probably anticipate the kinds of information and the point of view you will find in them. Write a brief annotation beside each entry on your list, indicating why you selected it and what you expect to find when you read it.

Read: As you read each selection, write a few brief notes in your journal. Comment on the major points in the article, copy down a memorable sentence or some important data, and write out short answers to your reading questions. You will also want to write down any new questions the author raises that you have not considered.

Review: As you skim back through the articles, "talk" to yourself about your impressions. Evaluate what was said, what wasn't said, and what proved useful to you as you think ahead toward your own writing project.

In each of these three stages, keep your attention focused on the planning process. Do your thinking-in-writing. What are you learning about *your* subject by consulting another person's perspective? How does this perspective help you analyze your audience or determine your purpose?

After her interview with George and Susie, Mary continued to search for an answer to her question about wood-burning stoves by reading. First, she compiled a short reading list and annotated each entry by indicating her initial impression of it.

Reading List on Wood-burning Stoves

Preview

1. *Sierra Wood Stoves*   slick sales brochure picturing different models and special features. Sentences on cover: "When your home demands the finest in craftsmanship." Snowjob.

2. *Wood for Home Heating*   monograph from state agency on Forestry and Natural Resources. Probably written for energy experts. Filled with charts, graphs, and statistics. No doubt dry as dust and rigidly neutral.

3. *Mother Earth News*   article on "Wood Stove Safety." Magazine is filled with articles on conservation — "Growing Your Own Grapes," "Dental Medicine in the Kitchen," "Ten Commandments for Raising Healthy Rabbits." Article looks "consumer" oriented. Short; two simple graphs. Probably very "can-do" and pioneersy; no doubt romanticizes owning a stove.

Next Mary read and reviewed each selection and noted her assessments and reactions in her journal.

1. *Sierra Wood Stoves*   Each model is pictured as the centerpiece in a beautiful family room. Fire does look reassuring through glass doors. People in pictures are relaxing, dozing, reading — obviously warm. The Sierra ® Promise: "Under normal usage your Sierra Stove should last indefinitely." Words like heavy duty, fully approved, maximum efficiency throughout each paragraph. No prices listed. Tells you length of logs each stove uses. Do I have to measure my logs? Names for each model: Classic, Cricket, Regal, Contemporary, Cottage. What's Cricket doing in there — does it chirp? Extremely fine print: "*Heating capacities assume that your home is insulated and you encourage warm air circulation."

Review

Brochure shows the range of stoves available. But each one looks like the house was built around the stove. We're going to install one. Will it fit? Where are we going to get logs cut to the right size? Is our house properly insulated? How do you encourage warm air circulation? What's normal usage? Why don't *they list the prices? Like most catalogues, the brochure is a "wish-book." I just wish they would tell me more about how much all this is going to cost.*

2. *Wood for Home Heating   Monograph discusses potentials for using wood for heating and "the enjoyment of purchasing, cutting, and storing fire-wood." I never thought of that stuff as enjoyable, but George said he liked it. Table on kinds of woods — heavy (20), intermediate (6), soft (10). I never knew there were so many kinds of wood. Wood is wood. Finally found out what a BTU is — "British Thermal Unit is the amount of heat required to raise the temperature of one pound of water 1 degree F." Apparently different woods have different BTUs per cord. Fireplaces (as opposed to wood-burning stoves) very inefficient — only 10% of heat is actually used. You can purchase firewood in most communities. "It is important to understand what and how much the seller will deliver. Ricks are often sold as cords. Beware!" How will I know if I am getting "ricked"? Some people prefer to cut their own wood — chain saws. More money? Safety? How do you get permission to cut down trees? Do you have to pay? Storing. "Allow at least one full summer for proper drying." "Beware of termites." "Poisonous woods."*

Review

This article made perfect sense to me as I was reading it. I even understood the graphs and charts. But if someone were to ask me what it was all about I would probably say "wood is very complicated." My search question has blossomed (pardon the pun) into a whole new question: how do you get the wood for the stove? I could follow that question into the forest (sorry) and never find my way out.

3. *Mother Earth News   Article starts with a quote from Thoreau about pulling stumps: "They warmed me twice, once while I was splitting them and again when they were on fire." The article is dedicated to helping folks prevent an inadvertent third warming. Wood-burning stoves can burn down your house! Safe installation and operation. Picking a stove — too small, overheats and burns walls; too large, forms creosote (new term) and burns chimney. How will I know whether we need a Cricket or a Classic? Installation — specifications from NFPA (National Fire Protection Agency.) Extremely detailed and complicated. Also makes you wonder about guys who install stove. Will they follow regulations? The chimney — apparently a big deal. Never thought of chimney before — Santa Claus,*

chimney sweep. Another new term — stoking. Insurance company statistics on cause of wood stove fires — improper installation and maintenance.

Review

This article scared me to death. I can see our house in flames. The insurance man is standing there scratching his head talking about UL (Underwriters Laboratories) and NFPA violations. I think I know more about woodburning stoves than I want to know. Thoreau's quote reminds me of another one of his little gems of wisdom: "The cost of a thing is the amount of what I will call life which is required to be exchanged for it, immediately or in the long run." George and Susie?

Mary has certainly come a long way since her first talk with Bill about the possibilities of installing a wood-burning stove. Her subject has grown so large that she is about to retreat from it in despair. And when she tries to analyze the needs and expectations of her readers she is astonished at how much they have to know in order to understand the deceptively simple relationship between wood and stoves. Although her interview with George and Susie and her reading have raised a whole set of new search questions, her original search question seems, at first glance, to remain the same: "Will the purchase of a wood-burning stove save us money?" But the more she thinks about the information she has gathered during her research, the more she seems to be asking the question in a different way: "How much does a wood-burning stove cost?" The quote she remembers from Thoreau about "the cost of a thing" may provide her with an answer that can be converted into a hypothesis.

> If you calculate the cost of a thing in terms of how much time, energy, and money it requires, then a wood-burning stove costs too much.

Mary decides to test her hypothesis in two ways: (1) she agrees to allow Bill to install a stove if he agrees to allow her to collect more data on the *true* cost of this money-saving system, and (2) she decides to use all the information she gathers during her research to compose an essay that will prove her hypothesis. Mary's additional data appears as the first Drafting Exercise in Chapter 3. Her essay appears as the last Revising Exercise in Chapter 4.

Exercises

1. Think of a decision you need to make that will require you to gather some information before you can make it. For example, you may need to decide where to go on your next long vacation; which stereo components you ought to buy when you upgrade your system; whether to join an organization such as the photography club; whether to audition for a part in a play. You will gather your information by interviewing someone who knows a great deal about the subject of your decision: a travel agent, stereo equipment salesperson; club sponsor or member; drama coach; or other expert. Prepare for your interview by following the measures given on page 65, then conduct it. When you return from the interview, write out an evaluation in your journal, again following the advice on page 67.

2. Choose a subject about which you want or need to do some research. It might be the subject of your decision in question 1 above, or a subject such as high-interest bank accounts, chemical waste disposal, models of personal computers, or laboratory experiments involving animals. In your journal, compile and preview a short reading list about your subject. Be sure to look for variety in your reading material; that is, if your subject is bank accounts, do not confine your reading to bank brochures alone. When you have completed your reading, assess each source in your journal.

Mixing Sources and Strategies

Although the thinking-in-writing strategies presented in this chapter are organized according to three sources (memory, observation, and research), there is no reason why you cannot mix strategies and sources. You can brainstorm, freewrite, or make journal entries on anything you remember, observe, or research. You can also scout, map, or speculate about those same sources. For example, you may wish to visit your old home town to scout childhood hide-outs, map short cuts, and speculate about objects, people, and processes you have not observed in a long time. And certainly research strategies can be applied to any source. You could interview your grandmother about her attitudes on aging or read how another writer describes a local business. The Writing Exercises at the end of this chapter encourage effective planning by asking you to mix and match sources and strategies.

A Final Word About Planning

The most important thing to learn about planning is learning when to stop. You probably know people who spend their lives "making plans." If they have to study for a test, they will brainstorm about all the things they have to do, map out a schedule for when they are going to do each thing, and then talk to everyone else who is taking the test about how they plan to study for it. Somewhere in the midst of all this planning, they lose the project — the test. Planning as a part of the writing process has a specific and limited purpose: to think-in-writing. Once you have completed this thinking, you must come to some conclusion about what you have written. You must make choices about your *subject, audience,* and *purpose.* And you must be willing to try out those choices in a fuller, more sustained piece of writing. You must begin drafting.

Planning Exercises

1. **The two pictures that appear on pages 77 and 78 were engraved by William Hogarth, an eighteenth-century artist whose work satirized and criticized his world. Like Jenny, Hogarth has selected scenes that appear to be major intersections, places where there is an abundant supply of people and activities to observe. He has already selected his *lookout spots* and *framed* his subjects. But to understand what Hogarth observed, you must follow a procedure similar to the one described on pages 56 and 58 for analyzing your own map.**

   a. **Describe your general impression of the picture.**

   b. **Identify the major landmarks, activity centers, and focal points.**

   c. **Observe all the specific details in each section of the picture.**

   d. **Formulate a hypothesis about this picture that will allow you to communicate a subject to an audience.**

   Read through the following observation analysis of the first picture. When you have finished reading, you will find instructions on page 80 asking you to analyze the picture on page 78. The first Writing Exercise in this chapter (page 82), will ask you to compare your observations of these two pictures.

   Observation Analysis of First Picture

   A. *General impression:* **With some exceptions, the general impression of this scene is one of poverty, ruin, violence, and death.**

   B. *Major landmarks, activity centers, focal points:* **The major focal point in**

National Gallery of Art, Washington, Rosenwald Collection

National Gallery of Art, Washington, Rosenwald Collection

this picture is the woman on the staircase. Your attention is immediately attracted to her face and to the child falling over the railing. Other activity centers include the people at the pawnshop on the left and the crowd surrounding the wheelbarrow on the right.

C. *Specific details:*

1. In the foreground, we see a child falling from the lap of a woman who is taking something from a can (snuff?). Her clothes are tattered, her leg is scratched or bruised, her breasts are bare (has she been nursing the child?), and there is a vacant grin on her face.

2. Beneath her and to the right is a man who seems to be either dead or unconscious. Except for a coat, he is almost naked. In his left hand, he holds a bottle in a basket that contains a paper on which the most conspicuous word is *Gin*. In his right hand, he holds a glass, at which a dog seems to be gazing.

3. Below and to the left of the woman, a vessel of some kind (a pitcher?) is suspended over a door and shows the words *Gin Royal*. In this reproduction, you cannot read the inscription over the door, but if the picture were enlarged you would see:

   Drunk for a penny.
   Dead drunk for twopence.
   Clean straw for nothing.

4. Above the *Gin Royal* pitcher, an old man and a dog are gnawing at a bone; next to them, a woman is either asleep or staring vacantly upward.

5. Above this group are three people at the door of a pawnshop. One of them (the pawnbroker?) is well dressed and is examining a saw, which the man on his left is evidently trying to pawn. Next to them, a woman in tattered clothes is offering her cooking utensils.

6. To the right of this trio is a little mob scene in which the following details can be identified:

   a. Someone is being wheeled in a barrow while a woman is pouring a drink from a glass into the person's mouth.

   b. At the extreme right, a woman is giving her child a drink from the same kind of glass.

   c. Beyond her, two women are drinking from similar glasses.

      d. To the left of them, a group of men seem to be fighting: one of them has a bandaged head and is brandishing a stool; another is striking with a crutch; some others are carrying sticks.

   7. To the right of this group is a distillery displaying the same kind of pitcher noted before and containing stored barrels of something (gin?).

   8. Beyond the distillery is a building with a wall so broken that it reveals a man hanging (a suicide?).

   9. The next building has a coffin displayed on a pole (an undertaker's establishment?). This building seems to be in good shape.

  10. The next building is falling down.

  11. In mid-center, an almost naked corpse is being lifted into a coffin, beside which a man carrying a cross is standing (a priest or monk?). Beside the coffin is a child.

  12. To the right, a man carrying a pointed staff on which a child is impaled seems to be hurrying toward the fighting group.

  13. In the distance, at the end of the street, is a mass of buildings, one falling over and another being supported by posts.

D. *Formulate a Hypothesis:* The subject of the picture seems to be the drinking of gin. As you consider several interpretations of this picture, you might formulate a hypothesis about the connection between the drinking of gin and the condition of the people and the buildings. You might also formulate a hypothesis about the contrast between those who profit from the sale of gin and those who suffer from drinking it. Whatever hypothesis you selected, it would surely involve some assertion about the evils of drinking gin. If you were to give a title to the picture, you would want to feature the word *gin*. Hogarth called the picture *Gin Lane*.

Assignment

Now use the same method to interpret the picture on page 78. If your instructor prefers, the exercise may be done by class discussion. But because you are primarily concerned about transforming your observation into writing, you might want to write down in your journal what you (and your classmates) observe. As much as possible, document the specific details in the picture before you formulate a hypothesis. What title would you give this picture?

2. The following observations about keeping a journal were made by three

important writers: Henry David Thoreau, nineteenth-century American philosopher and essayist; Virginia Woolf, twentieth-century British novelist and essayist; and Joan Didion, twentieth-century American novelist and essayist. Read each passage carefully, then discuss all three in terms of the following questions:

a. How would you characterize the attitude of each writer toward keeping a journal?
b. Do you see any similarities among the three attitudes? Differences?
c. Which writer's remarks best approximate how you feel about keeping a journal? Explain your answer.

To set down such choice experiences that my own writings may inspire me and at last I may make wholes of parts. Certainly it is a distinct profession to rescue from oblivion and to fix the sentiments and thoughts which visit all men more or less generally, that the contemplation of the unfinished picture may suggest its harmonious completion. Associate reverently and as much as you can with your loftiest thoughts. Each thought that is welcomed and recorded is a nest egg, by the side of which more will be laid. Thoughts accidentally thrown together become a frame in which more may be developed and exhibited. Perhaps this is the main value of a habit of writing, of keeping a journal — that so we remember our best hours and stimulate ourselves. My thoughts are my company. They have a certain individuality and separate existence, aye, personality. Having by chance recorded a few disconnected thoughts and then brought them into juxtaposition, they suggest a whole new field in which it was possible to labor and to think. Thought begat thought. (Henry David Thoreau, *Journal*, 1852)

... I have just re-read my year's diary and am much struck by the rapid haphazard gallop at which it swings along, sometimes indeed jerking almost intolerably over the cobbles. Still if it were not written rather faster than the fastest type-writing, if I stopped and took thought, it would never be written at all; and the advantage of the method is that it sweeps up accidentally several stray matters which I should exclude if I hesitated, but which are the diamonds of the dustheap.... (Virginia Woolf, January 20, 1919, *A Writer's Diary*)

So the point of my keeping a notebook has never been, nor is it now, to have an accurate factual record of what I have been doing or thinking. That would be a different impulse entirely, an instinct for reality which I sometimes envy but do not possess. At no point have I ever been able successfully to keep a diary; my approach to daily life ranges from the grossly negligent to the merely absent, and on those few occasions when I have tried dutifully to record a day's events, boredom has so overcome me that the results are mysterious at best. What is this business about "shopping, typing piece, dinner with E, depressed"? Shopping for what? Typing what piece? Who is E? Was this "E" depressed, or was I depressed? Who cares? . . .

How it felt to me: that is getting closer to the truth about a notebook. I sometimes delude myself about why I keep a notebook, imagine that some thrifty virtue derives from preserving everything observed. See enough and write it down, I tell myself, and then some morning when the world seems drained of wonder, some day when I am only going through the motions of doing what I am supposed to do, which is write — on that bankrupt morning I will simply open my notebook and there it will all be, a forgotten account with accumulated interest, paid passage back to the world out there: . . . I imagine, in other words, that the notebook is about other people. But of course it is not. . . . (Joan Didion, "On Keeping a Notebook," *Slouching Towards Bethlehem*)

Writing Exercises

1. Reread the two observation analyses of the Hogarth engravings — the one on pages 76–80 and the one you did for Planning Exercise 1 on page 80. Then compose a freewriting exercise in which you compare and contrast the two scenes.

2. Conduct some research in your files, your home, or your family's home to locate old photograph albums or, better yet, old essays that you wrote in elementary or high school. Observe the photos or read the essays carefully, and then brainstorm in your journal, trying to remember "how it felt to be me" at that age.

3. Interview one of your grandparents, one of your family's oldest friends, or someone you know in the town you live in. Pick somebody unlike yourself, somebody who grew up in a different time and place. Instead of following the exact interview procedures outlined on pages 64–69, ask your subject to map his or her childhood neighborhood. As your subject sketches this world, ask questions about the relationship between its major landmarks

and specific details. Then speculate in your journal about the world your subject just created. Try to imagine it as an object, as a process, and as a network.

4. Pick a site that you do not often visit — or have never visited — in your town or city. It might be the lobby of a busy high-rise office building or hotel; a neighborhood delicatessen; a gallery in a museum; or a region like the waterfront, the financial district, the shopping district. Take a sketch pad and pencils, make sure that you will not be in anyone's way, and settle down to map the site. If you prefer, you can make character sketches of some of the people you observe there. Whichever method of mapping you follow, be sure to collect a variety of interesting details. When you have returned home, interpret your map to determine what possible topics it suggests for your writing (for example, a map of a hotel lobby might suggest the topic of tourism in your city; a map of a museum gallery might suggest the topic of artists' perspectives — how different artists have treated similar themes or objects). Choose one of the topics and use a variety of planning activities, including research strategies, to collect more information about it. Record in your journal all the information you uncover; you will be able to use it in a Drafting Exercise at the end of Chapter 3.

Chapter 3

Drafting

Drafting is a procedure for determining whether the information you discovered during planning can be shaped into a successful piece of writing. In Chapter 2, you learned to apply thinking-in-writing strategies to common sources of information so that you could explore a number of likely writing topics. You also learned to assess the potential of each topic by evaluating it according to the guidelines for selecting a subject, analyzing an audience, and determining a purpose. Now it is time for you to draft the most promising of these topics and try to transform it into the sentences and paragraphs of a complete composition.

Although drafting such a composition will require you to make specific choices about your subject, audience, and purpose, you should resist the temptation to think of these choices as final. Inexperienced writers often assume that writing the first draft is virtually the last stage in the writing process. They believe that, with a little quick repair work, they can convert their first drafts into final drafts. Experienced writers, on the other hand, presume that writing the first draft is merely the first major attempt to produce a sustained piece of writing. Planning allows them to examine a list of possible topics; drafting enables them to experiment with possible arrangements of one topic. They expect this experimentation to lead to new discoveries, some of which can be incorporated into the first draft relatively easily, but most of which will need to be embodied in a completely new draft. Indeed, experienced writers perceive drafting as the opportunity to produce several drafts. And they expect that as they complete each one, they will come closer and closer to discovering and refining what they want to say and how they want to say it.

In the following passage, writer May Sarton compares the art of arranging flowers to the art of writing. Her comparison provides an interesting though indirect commentary on how experienced writers view the process of drafting.

> After breakfast I spend an hour or more arranging and rearranging seven or eight bunches of flowers for the house. There are flowers indoors here all the year around — in winter, bowls of narcissus, geraniums brought in from the windowboxes in the autumn, cut flowers from a local florist when all else fails. But from late May on I have a variety to play with, and the joy becomes arduous and complex. Arranging flowers is like writing in that it is an art of choice. Not everything can be used of the rich material that rushes forward demanding utterance. And just as one tries one word after another, puts a phrase together only to tear it apart, so one arranges flowers. It is engrossing work, and needs a fresh eye and a steady hand. When you think the thing is finished, it may suddenly topple over, or look too crowded after all, or a little meager. It needs one more note of bright pink, or it needs white. White in a bunch of flowers does a little of what black does in a painting, I have found. It acts as a catalyst for all the colors. After that first hour I have used up my "seeing energy" for a while, just as, after three hours at my desk, the edge begins to go, the critical edge. (May Sarton, *Plant Dreaming Days*)

Although you may relax once you realize that drafting gives you more opportunities to discover your subject, audience, and purpose, you cannot relapse into inactivity. You must continue to exercise "the art of choice," examining your information, arranging and rearranging it so that you can shape it into a coherent first draft. The following pages discuss the four major steps you can follow in creating a first draft: (1) make a scratch outline, (2) draft a hypothesis, (3) compose a discovery draft, and (4) construct a descriptive outline.

The Scratch Outline

A *scratch outline* attempts to find some kind of order in the abundant but often chaotic-looking material you uncovered during planning. The scratch outline does not attempt to classify and name every major division and minor subdivision of your subject; it is a preliminary sorting tool designed to sketch a possible pattern for your writing. As such, it need not adhere to any prescribed format; you arrange your material in whatever fashion seems helpful. The point is to establish initial organization and relationships in your material. As you complete your first draft, you will find yourself learning more about your subject, audience, and purpose. Your new information and perspectives will enable you to create a more detailed organization for your writing and to establish more precisely the relationships among your ideas. But as you contemplate writing your first draft, a scratch outline should provide you with enough direction to get started.

To make a scratch outline, assemble all the writing you produced during planning — brainstorming, freewriting, journal notes, maps, speculations, annotated reading lists, research notes, whatever you have. Then, with a pencil in hand, read through your writing several times, looking for ways to cluster information, for recurrent patterns, for ideas or phrases that stand out. Use any marking system that seems comfortable — words, numbers, circles, charts — to code the common denominators you discover. Once you have clustered your information into groups, try to establish connections among the groups that will enable you to arrange them in a meaningful pattern. Then write out that pattern on another sheet of paper, but don't discard your planning materials, for you will need them as you proceed.

In all likelihood, you will use the pattern you create in your scratch outline to form the middle portion (or body) of your essay — the content and organization of your subject. Later you will use your preliminary hypothesis about this pattern to compose an introduction for your essay that will make a statement about your subject and give some indication of why you are writing about it. Of course, the *what* and *why* of your essay are so intricately related that when you identify one you usually define the other. But at the point at which you create a scratch outline, you may not be ready to make any final decisions about these matters. You are still trying to determine what kinds of patterns you can locate in the information you produced during planning, and you are still discovering what you want to do with them.

Sometimes you will discover that in compiling your information you have already organized it into a simple pattern, as in the case of Jody's memory of the houses of her two grandmothers or Jenny's observation of the routine at the Varsity Barbershop. More often, your information either sits there waiting to be arranged in some complex but as yet undiscovered scheme, or suggests several contradictory or inconsistent patterns of arrangement.

Such confusion usually occurs when you don't have enough information to work with (in which case you will have to do some more planning) or when you have too much information to work with (in which case you will have to make some tough choices). Because you cherish every single item you found during planning, all of it rushes forward "demanding utterance." But you cannot give equal attention to every piece of information. Some information may be significant enough to form a major division in your outline. Other information may be less significant but useful as a minor subdivision or illustrative example. Still other information — wonderful, colorful, delightful information — may have to be eliminated because it does not fit into your scheme. As you arrange and rearrange various sections of your scratch outline, certain information may even change status — information once identified as significant may be eliminated, whereas other information, once eliminated, may resurface to shape your material into a significant pattern. All the choices you make about how to use your information ultimately depend upon your decisions about the principal elements in the writing situation: "What arrangement best enables me to communicate my *subject* to an *audience* for a *purpose?*"

While planning, Larry explored several different subjects (his favorite movies, professional basketball teams, the kinds of people he saw at the mall), but every time he tried out a thinking-in-writing strategy he found himself making lists. During the next few days he began to find lists everywhere — going through the pockets of an old jacket, looking for something to watch in *TV Guide,* searching for a bicycle repair shop in the Yellow Pages. Lists, he decided, was an original subject that might lead to an interesting piece of writing. Using "lists" as his code word, he produced the following brainstorming exercise.

Lists

shopping list

Christmas list

old lists — forgot them, never used them?

check things off list

lists of checks — monthly statement

never can figure out how to check checkbook — never balances

business lists — Dow Jones, list of leading economic indicators

classified ads — help wanted, things to sell

scorecard — lists players by numbers. "Can't tell players without a scorecard."

Oscar nominees

Dick Clark — Top 40 "I'll give it an 80. It's gotta good beat to dance to."

Moving up on the charts

Lists of Famous People

The Book of Lists

Guinness Book of Records

Blacklists — Joe McCarthy

Ten Commandments — Moses

What is a list — things to do, to remember, to learn

syllabus — what's due tomorrow

Keep my lists in the back of my notebook — errands, phone numbers, birthdays

Why can't I find my list?

Why does everybody need a list? Does everybody make a list?

Are there different kinds of list makers — good, bad ones; beginners, experts?

Make a list

Now that Larry is ready to begin drafting, he needs to find a pattern in his information. As he reads through his brainstorming exercise, he begins to circle and number certain topics. Occasionally, he draws arrows to suggest how something from one part of his list belongs in another part. He also uses question marks and asterisks to indicate problems he needs to solve or explore in greater detail.

Lists

1. Kinds
   of
   lists

1. shopping list
   Christmas list
1. old lists — forgot them, never used them? 4.
3. check things off list
1. lists of checks — monthly statement
3. never can figure out how to check checkbook — 4. never
   4. balances
   business lists — Dow Jones, list of leading economic
   1. indicators
   classified ads — help wanted, things to sell

2. Famous
   lists and
   listmakers
   (same as
   # 1?)

2. scorecard — lists players by numbers. 3. "Can't tell players
   without a scorecard."
   Oscar nominees
   Dick Clark — Top 40 3. "I'll give it an 80. It's gotta good
   beat to dance to."

3. Ways to use
   list

?

3. Moving up on the charts
2. Lists of Famous People
   The Book of Lists
   Guinness Book of Records
   Blacklists — Joe McCarthy
   Ten Commandments — Moses

* 4. What is a list — 3. things to do, to remember, to learn
   1. syllabus — what's due tomorrow

4. Questions
   about
   lists

3. Keep my lists in the back of my notebook — 1. errands, phone
   numbers, birthdays
4. Why can't I find my list?
   Why does everybody need a list? Does everybody make a
   list?
   Are there different kinds of list makers — 2. good, bad ones;
   beginners, experts?

* 1. Make a list.

By clustering and numbering, Larry is able to identify and label several information groups. Some groups follow the pattern of associations he made during brainstorming (kinds of lists); other groups form incomplete but useful categories (ways to use a list); still others may overlap or require additional planning to make them more precise (famous lists and list makers). Many of the items on Larry's list could serve as code words for an additional brainstorming exercise (Christmas lists, scorecards, Top 40) that would generate a whole new list of information. But Larry decides that the information he discovered toward the end of his brainstorming (kinds of list makers) forms the most interesting cluster. He can also see how this cluster might make use of much of the information in the other clusters. His questions about what kinds of people make lists points to a new list. Indeed, he gives himself his own assignment — "make a list" of the different kinds of list makers. He hints at the organization for this new list when he speculates that there must be good and bad list makers. These final thoughts suggest a way for him to organize the thinking he has done in writing into a scratch outline.

Different Kinds of List Makers

1. Beginner, novice list maker

Christmas lists, shopping lists

Loses lists, doesn't check other people's lists,
*   doesn't follow his own list*

can live without list

2. Average, usual listmaker

daily list, weekly list

keeps list nearby (pocket calendar) — checks off assignments
*   read, phone calls made, checks that balance*

likes to read lists; buys scorecard at ballgame — keeps score for a
*   couple of innings*

likes to read famous lists — remembers some winners of famous awards —
*   MVPs, Oscars*

occasionally talks about lists of sports, movie, music trivia

3. Expert, compulsive — listomaniac

must have list for everything — annual report, five-year plan

every list is cross-referenced — fastidious about lists

> *writes things down on a list that he has done just so he can*
>   *check them off*
> *keeps lists in special notebooks, desk calendars, daily logs*
> *uses all sorts of schemes to organize list — most significant, most urgent,*
>   *most overlooked (carry-over list)*
> *loves to read lists — learns by making lists*
> *remembers all sorts of lists — best dressed, top ten, longest*
>   *losing streaks, biggest money makers*
> *The Book of Lists — the first book on his list of favorite books*

Making this scratch outline has prompted Larry to discover some information that wasn't on his original list (where people keep lists, how people organize their lists) and to eliminate some information on his original list that might have proved interesting (business lists, black-lists). His outline has helped him restrict his subject to three types of list makers. Although the three categories are still somewhat hazy, they look potentially significant, interesting, and manageable. Moreover, the notion of three kinds of list makers has helped Larry identify three specific readers for his essay — the novice, the usual, and the compulsive list maker. His readers will either identify themselves as one of these types, or see themselves as possessing some of the traits of each type. And he suspects that those readers who claim to be unaffected by lists and list making (if there is such a group) will nonetheless have some interest in the subject that he has sketched in his outline. Before he actually begins to convert his outline into a sustained piece of writing, however, Larry must draft a preliminary hypothesis about his material.

Drafting a Hypothesis

As you recall from Chapter 1 and from your assessments of the student writing in Chapter 2, a *hypothesis* attempts to make a statement about the possible purpose for your writing. Unlike the more formal thesis, which presents an assertion that your essay will demonstrate, the hypothesis expresses a purpose for your essay that is still tentative. You should *try* to make this first purpose statement as restricted, unified, and precise as you can, but you may discover that writing your first draft will usually modify rather than demonstrate your purpose. Indeed, once you have completed your first draft, you may decide to revise your purpose completely. The first draft functions like an experiment in a laboratory: it gives you an opportunity to test one possible explanation (hypothesis) for the pattern you have found in the material you produced during planning.

To draft a hypothesis, read through your scratch outline and consider answers for the following questions. If possible, write out your answers, for they will help you compose your introduction:

1. What are my expectations for this writing project? What, generally, do I want to accomplish?

2. What is my attitude toward the material I have gathered? What hypotheses could I prove by writing about it?

3. How can I state each of these hypotheses in a single purpose statement? Which of these statements seems the most restricted, unified, and precise?

Your answers to the first two questions can be lengthy and provisional. These questions are designed to clarify your aims and attitudes, so your answers will probably not appear as actual sentences in your introductory paragraph. But they will help you establish a point of view toward your material that will suggest appropriate introductory sentences. Your answers to the last question should be as simple and direct as you can make them. This question is designed to produce several conditional theses, one of which you can place in your introductory paragraph. This thesis sentence serves as a guide for you and your readers, enabling you to tell them what main idea you will develop in your essay.

When Larry started to draft his hypothesis, he was uncertain about what he wanted to prove by writing about list makers. His answers to the first two questions exhibit his uncertainty, but he answers the third question by proposing several provisional purpose statements.

> *1. What do I want to do with this material? When I was brainstorming, I thought it was funny. The whole notion of lists and list makers seemed so zany that I was convinced that the only reason to write about it was to be funny. What other reason could you have for talking about Moses and Dick Clark in the same essay? The more I think about lists though, the more*

interesting the subject becomes. There is a whole thought process behind list making that intrigues me. Teachers always say things like "You need to remember three things about this subject." And so down it goes in your notebook — 1, 2, 3. All those books in the drugstore — <u>Seven Steps to Total Happiness</u>, <u>Nineteen Ways to Thinner Thighs</u>. I like my outline with the three kinds of list makers. I'm not really sure about the names for my categories, but three seems like the right number. Maybe I want to tell my readers about these types — how they behave, what they look like, what their lists do for them. Maybe I want to persuade my readers that there are three types. That number three makes me seem so certain, authoritative — the expert in the white lab coat proving to those who may still have questions that "yes, indeed, research proves that there are three and only three kinds of list makers." Funny stuff. Maybe I can persuade my readers by being funny and informative. Where does it say that you have to prove something by being dull?

2. *I think my attitude toward this subject has definitely changed since I started writing about it. Now I am a believer. Lists and list makers rule the world. Everybody makes lists, uses lists, remembers lists. There are three — count them, 1, 2, 3 — ways to make lists. If I had to draft a <u>hypothesis</u> (man in the white lab coat) about list makers, it might have something to do with how everybody is a list maker and I can prove it. That's not really what I want to prove. I think I want to prove that there are three ways to make a list.*

3. *Possible hypothesis*
   a. *Everybody likes lists.*
   b. *There are different kinds of list makers in the world and they make lists according to different patterns.*
   c. *Everybody makes lists according to one of three basic patterns.*

As Larry tries to draft his hypothesis, he has created an interesting point of view toward his material that clarifies his subject, anticipates the reactions of his readers, and defines several different but related purposes. He knows that no matter what he does with his material, he cannot help but make it entertaining. But he also knows that he has discovered material that is informative and that he has organized it according to a pattern that seems persuasive. As he tinkers with various ways to word his hypothesis, he feels confident enough about his material to write a first draft.

The Discovery Draft

Novelist Dorothy Canfield Fisher once compared writing the first draft to "skiing down a steep slope she wasn't sure she was clever enough to manage." [1] Although you have compiled a large body of information during planning, organized that information into a scratch outline, and drafted several hypotheses about its meaning and significance, you cannot stand at the top of the hill forever. You must push off and see if your preparation has made you clever enough to manage the long white slope of blank paper in front of you.

This first draft is called a *discovery draft* because you should expect that in spite of all your advance preparation you will discover something new about the subject, audience, and purpose of your essay as you write each sentence. Some of what you discover will be disappointing. The groups of information you felt confident were complete may reveal themselves as sketchy and incomplete. The connections you saw between those groups may not be there or at least may not be there in the way you had anticipated. And the information you clustered into each group may not be as useful as you thought: you may discover that you cannot develop some items in any detail, that you cannot include interesting items because they merely duplicate other items, or that you must eliminate certain items because they do not contribute to your working purpose.

Most of the discoveries you make — even the negative ones — will help you learn more about what you want to say and how you want to say it. As you try to convert notes into sentences, connect sentences to sentences, and cluster sentences into paragraphs, your information will seem to talk to you — telling you things you didn't know, things you forgot to remember, and things you need to find out. Your scratch outline will expand, contract, and change before your eyes. Your hypothesis may reshape itself suddenly and subtly into a more precise statement. Your discovery draft gives you something to work with — a text. This text is a core of valuable material that you can refine and polish in your next draft.

Larry's discovery draft illustrates some of the points in the preceding paragraph.

1. Malcolm Cowley, "Introduction," in *Writers at Work: The Paris Interviews,* 1st Series (New York: Viking Press, 1958), p. 10.

LIST MAKERS

Everybody makes lists. It appears that everyone likes lists. Everybody likes the neat, point by point enumeration of "things done" or "things to do." Everybody makes lists according to one of three basic patterns.

First, there is the beginning list maker. He is the ordinary person who occasionally finds the need to write down something pertaining to the day's events. In listing circles, he is a novice. He deals with concrete things like Christmas gifts and household chores. His attitude is casual. If he forgets to write something down, or forgets to read it once it is written, he doesn't panic. The Beginning Lister doesn't count on a list to control his life.

The next type is the average list maker. He is a journeyman at the trade. His lists order his life. He makes lists regularly, sometimes by the week, often by the day, occasionally by the month. He deals with both the concrete and the abstract -- grocery lists and future plans. A careful lister, he controls the entries on his list in the hope that he can control his life. He's organized or at least wishes he were.

Third, is the compulsive list maker -- the listomaniac. He is fastidious about detail and frantic without a notepad. Every room in his house has a scrap paper and pencils. It's a ritual with him. Often he writes things down that he's already done just so he can check them off his list. Mostly his lists are written by the day, but often they include hours and portions of hours. The smaller time frame lists are balanced with his annual reports and twenty-year projections.

There are lists for the office, for his wife, and for his children.

The compulsive list maker has a cross-referencing system, a fail-safe back-up, and a check-off plan. A typical check-off plan would list items according to:

1. things that <u>need</u> to be done first
2. things that naturally come first
3. things left over from other lists

The compulsive list maker had his first mystical experience when he discovered Wallace's <u>Book</u> <u>of</u> <u>Lists</u> in the Public Library. (He found it listed in the card catalogue). He now owns a copy, hides it from his children, and regularly posts copies of lists on his bulletin board. Last week's list was 15 Famous Events that Happened in the Bathtub. The week before was 8 Known Cases of Spontaneous Combustion. Forthcoming is 3 People Who Died During Sex.

Upon rereading his discovery draft, Larry finds that he is vaguely disappointed by what he accomplished. Although he is pleased that his hypothesis helped him introduce the pattern of his essay, he is uneasy about its wording. He is certainly encouraged by his ability to describe three kinds of list makers, but he is uncertain about the way he has characterized each type. As he looks back at the information he produced during planning and even at the material he clustered in groups for his scratch outline, he can't help but conclude that by comparison to his aspirations for this writing project, his first draft looks "a little meager."

At this point, he is not quite sure why he is dissatisfied. Is his hypothesis too vague? Are his three types somehow inconsistent? Does he need to develop his description of each type in more detail? Is there some insight about lists and list makers that he has not yet discovered that would make his essay more interesting and significant? Before Larry begins another draft, he needs to describe what he has done so far and what he needs to do next. He can annotate his discovery draft, writing notes to himself in the margins and circling weak or unconvincing passages. A more thorough and potentially more useful means of proceeding, however, is to construct a descriptive outline.[2]

The Descriptive Outline

A *descriptive outline* is a method to help you assess what you have accomplished during drafting. In a sense, the descriptive outline forms a link between the preliminary scratch outline and the more conclusive formal outline. In the scratch outline, you describe an arrangement for a writing experiment. In the formal outline, you prescribe an arrangement for a writing demonstration. In the descriptive outline, you report what you have done with the scratch outline and speculate about what you might do if you decide to make a formal outline to guide the composition of your second draft.

To construct a descriptive outline, place your discovery draft on one side of your desk and some blank paper on the other side. Keep your scratch outline out of sight. Whether you adhered rigidly to that outline as you wrote, altered it dramatically as you discovered new information, or abandoned it completely once you realized that it would not work is of little real importance to you at the moment. Your objective is to make a new outline that actually describes the draft you have written. Counting the introductory paragraph as one, number in sequence each paragraph in your draft. Then list those same numbers on your blank piece of paper. Under each number, write down as briefly as possible (a) what each paragraph *says* and (b) what each paragraph *does*.

There is a subtle but significant difference between what a paragraph *says* and what a paragraph *does*. When you identify what a paragraph *says*, you are concerned with subject matter, with the major topic discussed in the paragraph. When you identify what a paragraph *does*, you are concerned with writing strategies, with the development of each paragraph and its function within the larger design of the essay. There

2. A technique developed by Kenneth A. Bruffee in *A Short Course in Writing* (Cambridge, Mass.: Winthrop, 1972), pp. 49–50.

are many things that a paragraph can *do:* it can tell a story, describe a scene, list examples, or compare evidence. You will learn more about what paragraphs can do both collectively and individually in Chapters 5 and 6. For the moment, simply try to describe in your own words what each paragraph in your discovery draft *says* and *does.*

After you complete the descriptive outline, read through your discovery draft one more time. Then read through your planning and drafting material. Now return to your descriptive outline. What kind of draft does it describe, and what is your response to that draft? How have you used the information you have gathered? Are you engaged or uninspired by the description of your discovery draft? Does it indicate an interesting progression and development of ideas, even though they are compressed in note form, or do you find routine statements and insufficient development?

All this rereading should prompt you to draw some important conclusions about what you have achieved so far in your writing and what more you need to do. Your first step is to list those conclusions, being as honest as you can.

Larry completed his descriptive outline, reread all his materials, and realized that he could do a number of things to improve his essay. His descriptive outline and conclusions are shown below. After you have read the outline, reread the draft on pages 96–97, then proceed to Larry's conclusions.

Descriptive Outline

1.
  A. Everybody makes lists.
  B. Introduces hypothesis that there are three ways to make lists.

2.
  A. The beginning list maker is casual, forgetful, and doesn't count on lists.
  B. Identifies the casual list maker by listing some of his listing activities and attitudes toward lists.

3.
  A. The average list maker is careful, attentive and uses lists to organize his life.
  B. Identifies the careful list maker by listing some of his listing activities and attitudes toward lists.

4.

    A. *The compulsive list maker thinks the world ought to live and learn by lists.*

    B. *Identifies compulsive list maker by listing some of his listing activities and attitudes toward lists.*

5.

    A. *The compulsive list maker has several cross-reference lists.*

    B. *Illustrates with examples (and lists) <u>how</u> the compulsive list maker uses his list.*

6.

    A. *The compulsive list maker's experience with the <u>Book of Lists</u>.*

    B. *Tells story about how compulsive list maker found and uses <u>Book of Lists</u>. Serves as a conclusion for essay.*

Conclusions

1. *I need to use more of the information I discovered in planning, maybe even do some more planning. There's not enough interesting detail in this draft.*

2. *Get more examples in the introductory paragraph to demonstrate that everybody makes and likes lists. The paragraph is weak.*

3. *Must rewrite my hypothesis to turn it into a decent thesis. My hypothesis talks about patterns of <u>list making</u>, but my essay talks about kinds of <u>list makers</u>. It's the behaviors of list makers that's interesting. Also, I don't say <u>why</u> I think my information is significant.*

4. *I need to rename my three basic types: got to have a catchy angle. Three <u>C</u> words make things neat: casual, careful, compulsive.*

5. *I should make some comparisons between each type to distinguish them from one another.*

6. *I need to include more examples of <u>how</u> each list maker uses lists — as I did with the compulsive list maker. And I need more humor.*

7. *Maybe I could conclude each section by discussing the list maker's knowledge of the <u>Book of Lists</u>. That would make my conclusion have more impact.*

8. *Mainly, I need to open up. Give my readers more information about list makers and how lists run their lives.*

Larry's descriptive outline has helped him identify what he has done right, what he has done wrong, and what he needs to do next. His conclusions establish an agenda for the next stage in the writing process — revising. Many writers can use their first drafts and descriptive outlines to spot major problems and propose specific solutions. Other writers have to compose more than one draft before they can discover a purpose and a design for their writing. Revising each draft, as you will see in Chapter 4, is a complex, though enormously satisfying, process. But before Larry revises his discovery draft, he must transform his hypothesis into a more precise controlling statement and he must consider how to organize all the material he wants to use in his next draft. He needs, in other words, to compose an effective thesis and to contemplate arranging his material in a formal outline.

Composing an Effective Thesis

A thesis makes an assertion about the main idea that you will develop in your writing. In a sense, it summarizes your conclusion about your subject and suggests your point of view toward it. You cannot make such an assertion until you have an understanding of your purpose in writing. That is, you cannot first compose a thesis and then write to its specifications. You must rather, as you have seen, consider and test various hypotheses about your subject, ultimately selecting the one that seems best to control your material. You can then transform that hypothesis into a thesis statement that reminds both you and your reader of the commitment you must fulfill in writing your essay.

An effective thesis, then, is derived from the material you work with and makes a compelling statement about that material. In this and earlier chapters you have seen how writers contemplate various arrangements of their information and consider possible hypotheses about their subjects, so you know how a thesis is derived from — and not imposed upon — material. But a well-supported thesis is nonetheless only as effective as its wording — that is, only as effective as the reader perceives it to be — so you need also to consider how to phrase your thesis statement.

Making Your Thesis Restricted, Unified, and Precise

You may recall the discussion in Chapter 1 of the meanings of *restricted, unified,* and *precise* when applied to theses. Those meanings are so important that they are worth amplifying here, for the more fully your thesis reflects those qualities, the better it controls your writing in your remaining drafts and your reader's reading of your final essay.

To be *restricted* a thesis must limit the scope of an essay to what can be discussed in detail in the space available. A thesis such as "The United States has serious pollution problems" might be suitable for a long magazine article, but you could not treat it in adequate detail in a three-page essay. You would be forced to make statements so broad that they would seem hackneyed to your readers, a mere summary of what everyone already knows. A better thesis about pollution might be phrased in one of the following ways:

The government has not been sufficiently aggressive in enforcing the regulations that control chemical waste disposal.

In many American cities, industrial expansion has resulted in severe damage to air and water purity.

Widespread use of pesticides in agriculture is threatening the survival of certain species of wildlife.

A carefully worded thesis indicates the specific subject you are writing about, not merely your general subject. Neither writer nor reader gets a clear focus from the thesis "Manufacturers often deceive their customers." That thesis could lead off in all sorts of directions and might result in no more than a list of miscellaneous deceptions. But if the thesis were restricted to "Some automobile manufacturers and dealers have withheld information about structural defects that a customer has a right to know," the real subject of the essay would be much clearer. Restriction of the thesis is so essential to effective communication that it is worth all the effort it requires.

A good thesis is *unified* as well as restricted. It must express only one idea. The following thesis contains not one idea but three: "The use of drugs has increased significantly in the last fifteen years. Hard drugs are admittedly dangerous, but there is considerable disagreement about marijuana." This thesis commits a writer to deal with three topics: (1)

the increase in the use of drugs, (2) the dangerous effects of hard drugs, and (3) the disagreement about marijuana. Each of these topics could easily be made the thesis of a separate essay. To try to deal with all three in a short essay would invite the kind of superficial treatment that is common with unrestricted theses and would almost surely result in an essay consisting of three unrelated parts and lacking focus.

Even such a thesis as "Compared with other languages, English has a relatively simple grammar, but its spelling is confusing" could lead to separate treatments of grammar and spelling. If these two topics are to be related in some way, that relationship has to be implied in the thesis, perhaps by such a statement as "In learning English, foreigners usually have less trouble with grammar than with spelling." In this form the thesis commits you to contrasting the ease of learning grammar with the difficulty of learning spelling and thus tends to prevent separate development of the two topics. If your chief interest is spelling, it would be still safer to ignore grammar and confine the thesis to spelling: "Foreigners have a hard time with English spelling."

As the previous examples show, lack of unity is most likely to occur in a thesis that contains two or more coordinate parts, each of which could be developed separately. For example, the thesis "The amateur ideal of the Olympic Games is being threatened; professionalism is on the increase" might trap you into treating each part separately and producing an essay that develops two ideas, not one. This possible fault can be avoided by embedding one part in the other: "Increasing professionalism is creating a serious threat to the amateur ideal of the Olympic Games."

In the following contrasted theses the possible lack of unity at the left is minimized by the rewording at the right:

Not unified	**Unified**
Many of the silent letters in English were once pronounced. The pronunciation changed, but the old spelling was standardized.	Many of the silent letters in English words are a result of standardizing the spelling while the pronunciation was still changing.
The nuclear bomb has immense destructive power, and there is no adequate defense against it.	There is no adequate defense against the immense destructive power of the nuclear bomb.

Baseball players have achieved a new independence, and there is nothing the owners can do about the situation.	There is nothing the owners can do about the new independence of baseball players.

Finally, a thesis should be *precise.* It should be so stated that it can have only one interpretation. For example, if your written-out thesis is "My home town is one of the most interesting in the state," that thesis does not indicate the content of your essay, because *interesting* is vague and can mean many things. Readers will want to know in what way the town is interesting. If they have to read the whole essay to find out, the thesis does not help them. Moreover, because of its vagueness, it does not help you see what you need to do to develop your essay.

Words such as *interesting, colorful, exciting, inspiring,* and *unusual* are too vague for a thesis. So are metaphors. The thesis "Where instructors are concerned, all that glitters is not gold" may seem clever, but what does it mean? That the best scholars are not always the best teachers? That instructors who put on a good show in the classroom do not always help students to master the subject? Or something else? The precise meaning of a thesis should be immediately clear. Metaphors may be effective in the text of an essay, but they can be troublesome in a thesis.

Larry's progress from hypothesis to thesis illustrates another aspect of ensuring precision in a thesis statement. Larry used his hypothesis — "Everyone makes lists according to one of three basic patterns" — to control his discovery draft, but upon studying the draft he spotted a discrepancy. His hypothesis promised an essay that discussed list makers in terms of three basic patterns, but his draft actually discussed three distinct groups of people, three types of list maker. If Larry had intended to discuss the three patterns, he might have been worried, for there is little in his planning materials or scratch outline to support such an intention. But, as he saw after composing a descriptive outline and listing his conclusions, his discovery draft did reflect accurately his purpose in writing about his subject. His next draft would need some more material, but his approach to lists and list makers was essentially on target. His hypothesis was not insupportable or wrong; it was merely misphrased. He had not paid enough attention to its wording but had rather assumed that what he wrote out on paper was what he was thinking. Aided by the insights his descriptive outline gave him, Larry can turn his hypothesis into a more precise thesis: "Three types of list makers make lists."

After stating his thesis, Larry must determine whether he can begin writing his next draft immediately, incorporating changes and new materials as he writes. He decides to give himself one more opportunity to organize all his material — from planning notes to descriptive outline to conclusions and new ideas — into a formal design from which he can write a more coherent, logical, and fully developed essay. He will write one more list about lists — a formal outline.

Discussion Problem

Some of the following statements would make acceptable theses; others, because they lack restriction, unity, or precision, would not. Reject those that are unacceptable and explain why you do so.

1. The Royal Family is very important to the British.

2. Almost every person has something secret he likes to eat.

3. The United Nations Organization has many weaknesses and cannot prevent a war between major powers.

4. It is easy to see the beginnings of things, and harder to see the ends.

5. The *Star Wars* trilogy films enjoyed enormous box-office success, and they proved that the science-fiction film must be taken seriously by the critics.

6. Social historians agree that the American Dream is no more than the snows of yesteryear.

7. The increasing cost of a college education is reducing enrollment in private colleges and universities.

8. The major cause of violence today is the influence of television and the fact that the courts are too lenient.

9. Although the average person usually thinks of gorillas as ferocious, chest-beating monsters, they are actually gentle creatures who live at peace with other animals.

10. The twentieth century is an exciting time in which to live.

Constructing a Formal Outline

A formal outline is an exact plan of organization that breaks your topic into major units (marked by Roman numerals) and subdivides these major units into minor units (marked by capital letters). These minor units may be further subdivided and the subdivisions marked by Arabic numerals. The Arabic-numeral subdivisions may be further broken into smaller units and marked by small letters. One warning about this format: if you make any division in your outline, you must have at least *two* subdivisions. You cannot divide something into one.

The best way to construct the formal outline is to lay out the major divisions before worrying about the various subdivisions. Establish all Roman-numeral headings first; then break each Roman-numeral heading into capital-letter entries, and so on, following the principle of completing one level of division before starting on the next lower level. Such a procedure keeps you in control of your outline: you will not be likely to distort the organization by developing some headings too much and others too little. As you work your way through each division, you may discover new patterns of organization that will require you to revise all the headings in your outline. You should welcome such discoveries because they will help you draft a more consistent outline. After all, your principal objective is to construct an outline in which all the parts function according to a coherent pattern.

As Larry looks at his two previous outlines, he decides that he wants his formal outline to follow pretty much the same order. The three kinds of list makers should form the three major divisions. When he starts to work his way down through the subdivisions, however, he finds that he is (1) reclaiming information from his brainstorming exercise that he had previously eliminated from his first outline and draft and (2) creating new information to fill in the slots that he has established in the subdivisions of his formal outline. Larry's experience thus illustrates why the formal outline is such a powerful tool. It is not always necessary to construct a formal outline to produce a new draft. Your discovery draft, descriptive outline, and reformulated thesis may give you all the direction you need. But a formal outline can serve as an additional planning strategy, helping you develop more information in greater detail, or it can provide you the security of knowing that you have already laid out your organization and emphasis before you begin a draft.

Formal Outline

Thesis: Three types of list makers make lists.

I. *The casual list maker*

    A. *The casual list maker makes lists only on rare occasions.*

        1. *He makes a Christmas list at the last minute.*

        2. *He makes a shopping list only when he has to purchase more than twelve items.*

    B. *The casual list maker does not know how to use a list.*

        1. *He often forgets to look at his list.*

        2. *He never checks things off his list.*

        3. *He often loses his list.*

        4. *He cannot read or remember other people's lists.*

    C. *The casual list maker does not need a list.*

        1. *He does not need a list to run his life.*

        2. *He is proud of his independence from daily list making.*

        3. *He views those who are always making lists as slaves to a silly system.*

    D. *The casual list maker has never heard of Irving Wallace's* Book of Lists.

II. *The careful list maker*

    A. *The careful list maker makes lists for most occasions.*

        1. *He always makes detailed Christmas and shopping lists.*

        2. *He usually makes a daily or at least weekly list of things to do.*

    B. *The careful list maker knows how to use a list.*

        1. *He uses his list to organize his daily and future plans.*

        2. *He consults his list to see if he has forgotten something he planned to do.*

        3. *He often has to make a new list of the things he failed to do on his old list.*

        4. *He likes to read lists of certain kinds of trivia.*

    C. *The careful list maker needs a list.*

        1. *He thinks that if he can control his list he can control his life.*

        2. *He thinks (or hopes) he lives an organized life because he makes lists.*

        3. *He views those who are not organized as somehow deficient or irresponsible.*

    D. *The careful list maker has skimmed Wallace's* Book of Lists *in the bookstore, but did not buy it because it wasn't on his shopping list.*

III. The compulsive list maker

    A. The compulsive list maker makes lists for absolutely every occasion.

        1. He makes lists by the day, by the hour, and by the portion of the hour.

        2. He makes lists for himself, his friends, his wife, his children.

    B. The compulsive list maker is always inventing new ways to use a list.

        1. He uses lists to organize the world — he thinks and learns in lists.

        2. He often writes things down on his list just so he can check them off.

        3. He invents elaborate cross-referencing systems to keep lists of his lists.

        4. He loves to read, analyze, and remember lists of all kinds.

    C. The compulsive list maker cannot live without a list.

        1. He believes that lists (and those who make them) rule the world.

        2. He is a list junkie, a list zealot, a listomaniac.

        3. He views those who live without lists as hopelessly and eternally lost.

    D. The compulsive list maker had his first religious experience when he discovered the <u>*Book of Lists*</u> *in the card catalogue at the Public Library.*

        1. He owns his own private copy but hides it from the members of his family as if it were some sacred relic.

        2. He occasionally posts tantalizing samples from the book on the refrigerator or the office bulletin board.

Testing the Outline: Evaluation and Discussion Problem

To test the effectiveness of Larry's formal outline, you need to evaluate it as a stage in a process and as a completed product. You can make the first evaluation by comparing Larry's previous writing on the subject of lists with this new "list."

1. How much of the old scratch outline appears in this new outline?

2. How much new information has Larry had to invent to complete this new arrangement of his material?

3. How many of the conclusions that Larry made at the end of his descriptive outline has he been able to build into this new document?

4. How does this new outline match Larry's perception of his *subject, audience,* and *purpose*?

You can make the second evaluation by testing Larry's outline according to the following criteria:

1. *Is the thesis satisfactory?* Because the thesis controls the whole outline, a faulty thesis invites trouble all along the way. A rigorous checking of the thesis is therefore the first and most important step in testing an outline.

   "Three kinds of list makers make lists" is certainly more restricted, unified, and precise than Larry's earlier hypotheses. It seems to control the whole outline, but does it say everything Larry wants to say about his purpose? How might he open up his thesis to assert more about the information he is trying to present? Why does he think this information is significant?

2. *Is the relationship among the parts clear and consistent?* In a good outline you should be able to see how each main unit brings out an important aspect of the thesis and how each subdivision helps develop its main heading. If there is any doubt about the relation of any heading to the thesis, that heading is either poorly stated or is a potential trouble spot in the outline.

   Larry's decision to rename his categories has helped him establish better connections among the three types. His subdivisions also seem to follow a clear and more consistent pattern. Do you see any potential trouble spots in the outline? Identify them and explain why you think they may produce difficulties.

3. *Does the order of the parts provide a logical progression?* Just as the sentences within each paragraph must follow a logical order, so must the parts of an outline. If any of the parts are out of order, the disorder will be magnified in the essay.

   Larry's major divisions — casual, careful, and compulsive — certainly form a logical progression. What about the logical order of the material he has grouped under his capital letters and Arabic numerals? How would you plot the progression in each group? Are there parts out of order?

4. *Is the outline complete?* This is not one question but two: (a) are all the major units of the subject represented, and (b) is each major unit subdivided far enough to guide the development of the essay? The first question is especially important for essays that classify something or explain how something is done: all classes or steps must be in-

cluded. The second question depends on the scope and length of the paper. For short papers, the outline may not need to go beyond the main headings. For longer papers, the outline needs to be developed in greater detail so that you can balance and control the amount of material you cluster under each heading.

Larry's three types *seem* to represent every class of list maker. Can you list any other type? What about the major units on Larry's outline? Do they need to be subdivided further to guide the development of the essay? Explain your answers.

5. *Can each entry be developed in detail?* Each entry in the outline should be fully developed when the essay is written. There is no rigid rule about how much development each entry should receive. Sometimes a single entry will require two or three paragraphs in your essay; occasionally several minor entries may be dealt with in a single paragraph. A useful rule of thumb, however, is that each entry should be developed into at least one paragraph.

In his discovery draft, Larry devoted one paragraph to the casual list maker, one paragraph to the careful list maker, and three paragraphs to the compulsive list maker. Does his formal outline suggest the same kind of arrangement? The four secondary divisions in Larry's outline (those marked with capital letters) appeared simply as sentences in Larry's discovery draft. Should these four items still be combined into one paragraph or should they be developed into four separate paragraphs? Do the entries Larry marks with Arabic numbers contain enough information to develop into separate paragraphs? Explain your answer.

A Final Word About Drafting

The most important thing to learn about drafting is not to be frustrated when your first or second drafts do not fulfill your expectations. You certainly know people who give up on a project when their first effort fails to measure up. They resist additional efforts, thinking of them as punishment for failing to succeed on the first try. But writing, like any other valuable work, requires additional effort. For that reason, drafting should be seen as an opportunity rather than an ordeal. Remember Sarton's comparison of arranging flowers and drafting a piece of writing. Both processes are arduous and complex, but they are also a joy. They require a fresh eye and a steady hand and, after awhile, they use up your seeing energy. Once you have completed a couple of drafts, you may feel as though your seeing energy is used up. In Chapter 4, you will study strategies for restoring that energy. Revising strategies help you *see* your material *again,* help you discover the catalyst that will enable you to continue the process of composing a successful piece of writing.

Drafting Exercises

1. **As you learned in Chapter 2, Mary decided that she would test the cost effectiveness of a wood-burning stove. She kept a list of what Bill had to do and how much it cost — in terms of time, energy, and money. Read through her list and try to cluster it into significant units of information. Give a title to each unit, and then see if you can establish connections among them. Next, make a scratch outline that organizes this information into a logical pattern. Finally, formulate several hypotheses about what this pattern means. Mary's essay — demonstrating her own thesis about this material — appears as the last Revising Exercise in Chapter 4.**

10/1	Purchase of one Sierra "on-the-hearth insert" Regal Stove	+ $1,000.00
	Projected savings on monthly utility bill during winter months $150 each month or $400 each year	− 400.00
10/4	Installation of stove	
	Projected cost if installed by workmen	+ 100.00
	Predicted cost if installed by Bill (and George)	− 0
	How will two 180 pound men install a stove that weighs ½ ton? (Hernia panic)	
	Will these two amateurs know enough about fire regulations, insulation, and air circulation to perform the job correctly?	
	Purchase of reflecting shield to protect mantel	+ 75.00
	Purchase of fireproof rug	+ 50.00
	2 full days labor for 2 men @ $5.00 per hour (24 hrs. × $10), not counting study time	

	for learning how to complete installation ($5.00? Why do do-it-yourselfers always calculate their work at minimum wage?)	+	240.00
	Purchase of stove polish	+	6.00
	Purchase of chimney cup	+	40.00
10/6	Stove finally installed and working with some wood George loaned us. Found Bill sleeping in front of the stove — "just in case," he said. Watchman's duty — 3 nights × 8 hours @ $5.00 per hour	+	120.00
10/10	Bill and George just drove up in their new purchase, a 1970 pickup they have nicknamed Big Red. Each is half-owner; our half is:	+	250.00
	I didn't ask about the cost of the license or insurance, but I did ask about whether we really needed Big Red. "How do you expect us to haul the wood?"		
	I thought they could buy it, but they insisted that cutting and hauling your own wood would save you money — in the long run. Well, it is a long run. George has this agreement with a farmer 50 miles away that if he and Bill give him half of what they cut, he will let them cut all the timber they want for free. One tank of gasoline for Big Red each weekend $20.00. Cutting and hauling season is like sharecropping season — April to November. Sometimes year-round if weather is bad. Stay conservative. April to November: 8 months × 4 weekends per month = 32 weekends. Gasoline cost per weekend = $20.00 × 32	+	640.00
	I'll forget about oil, oil filters, spark plugs, and tune-ups for Big Red.		
10/14	New — absolutely essential — purchases		
	Chain saw	+	200.00

Wood splitter	+	1,000.00
Wheelbarrow	+	50.00
Wood crib	+	35.00

Projected labor cost of sharecropping on 32
    weekends:

20 hours per weekend @ $5.00 per hour	+	3,200.00

10/20   New procedures to prevent furnace from turning on during night — 3:00 a.m. stoking. Bill's wrist alarm wakes him in the middle of the night — every night — so that he can stoke. Projected stoking costs: 4 peak winter months × 30 nights = 120 nights — 1 hour overtime @ $1.00 per hour   + 120.00

Two K-Mart window fans placed strategically in house to <u>encourage</u> air circulation = $5.00 per fan   + 10.00

10/22–10/25 Another new procedure — Chimney Cleaning

Projected cost of Chimney Sweep Service	+	60.00
Projected cost of Doing it Yourself	−	0

Actual cost
Chimney cleaner	+	150.00
Chimney cleaning brush	+	35.00
Chimney fire extinguisher	+	8.00
Scraping brush	+	5.00
Face mask	+	5.00

Unanticipated costs from ashes, soot, and creosote
Clean carpet in family room	+	35.00
Replace drapes in family room	+	400.00

10/26–11/15 Never leave house without thinking about or driving back to check stove — possible fire.

Party talk — comparing utility bills, wood supplies, chain saw repairman (our first repair bill was $25.00).

Over-the-fence talk (or observation) — calculating supply, stacking logs, moisture and insects in neighbor's wood crib.

2. Read the following essay by Suzanne Britt Jordan. State her thesis and then construct a formal outline for her essay. What is her purpose in this essay? (Remember, purpose and thesis are not identical.)

That Lean and Hungry Look

Caesar was right. Thin people need watching. I've been watching them for most of my adult life, and I don't like what I see. When these narrow fellows spring at me, I quiver to my toes. Thin people come in all personalities, most of them menacing. You've got your "together" thin person, your mechanical thin person, your condescending thin person, your tsk-tsk thin person, your efficiency-expert thin person. All of them are dangerous. 1

In the first place, thin people aren't fun. They don't know how to goof off, at least in the best, fat sense of the word. They've always got to be adoing. Give them a coffee break, and they'll jog around the block. Supply them with a quiet evening at home, and they'll fix the screen door and lick S&H green stamps. They say things like "there aren't enough hours in the day." Fat people never say that. Fat people think the day is too damn long already. 2

Thin people make me tired. They've got speedy little metabolisms that cause them to bustle briskly. They're forever rubbing their bony hands together and eying new problems to "tackle." I like to surround myself with sluggish, inert, easygoing fat people, the kind who believe that if you clean it up today, it'll just get dirty again tomorrow. 3

Some people say the business about the jolly fat person is a myth, that all of us chubbies are neurotic, sick, sad people. I disagree. Fat people may not be chortling all day long, but they're a hell of a lot *nicer* than the wizened and shriveled. Thin people turn surly, mean and hard at a young age because they never learn the value of a hot-fudge sundae for easing tension. Thin people don't like gooey soft things because they themselves are neither gooey nor soft. They are crunchy and dull, like carrots. They go straight to the heart of the matter while fat people let things stay all blurry and hazy and vague, the way things actually are. Thin people want to face the truth. Fat people know there is no truth. One of my thin friends is always staring at complex, unsolvable problems and saying, "The key thing is . . ." Fat people never say that. They know there isn't any such thing as the key thing about anything. 4

Thin people believe in logic. Fat people see all sides. The sides fat   5
people see are rounded blobs, usually gray, always nebulous and truly
not worth worrying about. But the thin person persists. "If you consume more calories than you burn," says one of my thin friends, "you
will gain weight. It's that simple." Fat people always grin when they
hear statements like that. They know better.

Fat people realize that life is illogical and unfair. They know very   6
well that God is not in his heaven and all is not right with the world. If
God was up there, fat people could have two doughnuts and a big
orange drink anytime they wanted it.

Thin people have a long list of logical things they are always spout-   7
ing off to me. They hold up one finger at a time as they reel off these
things, so I won't lose track. They speak slowly as if to a young child.
The list is long and full of holes. It contains tidbits like "get a grip on
yourself," "cigarettes kill," "cholesterol clogs," "fit as a fiddle," "ducks
in a row," "organize" and "sound fiscal management." Phrases like
that.

They think these 2,000-point plans lead to happiness. Fat people   8
know happiness is elusive at best and even if they could get the kind
thin people talk about, they wouldn't want it. Wisely, fat people see
that such programs are too dull, too hard, too off the mark. They are
never better than a whole cheesecake.

Fat people know all about the mystery of life. They are the ones   9
acquainted with the night, with luck, with fate, with playing it by ear.
One thin person I know once suggested that we arrange all the parts of
a jigsaw puzzle into groups according to size, shape and color. He
figured this would cut the time needed to complete the puzzle by at
least 50 per cent. I said I wouldn't do it. One, I like to muddle
through. Two, what good would it do to finish early? Three, the jigsaw
puzzle isn't the important thing. The important thing is the fun of four
people (one thin person included) sitting around a card table, working
a jigsaw puzzle. My thin friend had no use for my list. Instead of
joining us, he went outside and mulched the boxwoods. The three
remaining fat people finished the puzzle and made chocolate, double-
fudged brownies to celebrate.

The main problem with thin people is they oppress. Their good   10
intentions, bony torsos, tight ships, neat corners, cerebral machina-
tions and pat solutions loom like dark clouds over the loose, comfort-

able, spread-out, soft world of the fat. Long after fat people have removed their coats and shoes and put their feet up on the coffee table, thin people are still sitting on the edge of the sofa, looking neat as a pin, discussing rutabagas. Fat people are heavily into fits of laughter, slapping their thighs and whooping it up, while thin people are still politely waiting for the punch line.

Thin people are downers. They like math and morality and reasoned evaluation of the limitations of human beings. They have their skinny little acts together. They expound, prognose, probe and prick.   11

Fat people are convivial. They will like you even if you're irregular   12
and have acne. They will come up with a good reason why you never wrote the great American novel. They will cry in your beer with you. They will put your name in the pot. They will let you off the hook. Fat people will gab, giggle, guffaw, gallumph, gyrate and gossip. They are generous, giving and gallant. They are gluttonous and goodly and great. What you want when you're down is soft and jiggly, not muscled and stable. Fat people know this. Fat people have plenty of room. Fat people will take you in.

Writing Exercises

1. Select any item in Larry's brainstorming exercise that interests you, such as Christmas lists, top 40, or blacklists. Using the item as a code word, conduct your own brainstorming exercise. Then cluster your information into a scratch outline and formulate several hypotheses. Which do you find most interesting? Which can you best support?

2. Make a list of the people you know who can be characterized by their intense interest in one particular activity, such as buying record albums, eating chocolate, breaking rules, riding bicycles, taking chances, saving money. Use various planning strategies to produce enough information in writing so that you can compose an effective thesis about the casual, careful, and compulsive members of this group.

3. Pick one specialized kind of "writing assignment" such as completing a crossword puzzle, filling out a scorecard at a baseball game, or paying your monthly bills. Construct a formal outline of the procedures you follow to complete the assignment effectively. Reserve one division of your outline for special tips and warnings beginners might need to follow your procedure.

4. Reread in your journal the information you gathered for Writing Exercise 4 in Chapter 2 (page 83). You will also want to study the map you created in that exercise. Cluster that information in units, make a scratch outline, and decide which hypotheses you might be able to write about. Choose the one that most appeals to you and that you are most likely to be able to prove, word it carefully, and write a discovery draft. Then analyze your discovery draft, preferably by constructing a descriptive outline.

Chapter 4

Revising

Revising is the process of *seeing again,* of discovering a new vision for the writing you produced during planning and drafting. In a sense, you have been revising from the moment you began writing. As you experimented with thinking-in-writing strategies in planning, you revised your decisions about your subject, audience, and purpose. As you tried to embody those decisions in drafting, you revised again as you saw a better thesis or a more effective outline for your writing. Now that you are ready to begin the process of revising, you may wonder how you are going to see anything new in the writing you have already looked at several times. One thing is certain. You will not see much that is new if you think of revising as simply taking one last look.

Nothing distinguishes inexperienced writers from experienced writers more dramatically than the way they look at revision. For inexperienced writers, revision means *fixing* the first draft so that it can stand as the final draft. They suspect that somewhere in their text they have overlooked a few errors. Now they must search out and destroy these trouble spots by scratching out a sentence, rearranging a few phrases, or substituting one word for another. Once they have completed this correction process, inexperienced writers think they have revised their writing. For experienced writers, revision means *creating* the final draft. They know they have overlooked many errors and trouble spots, but before they embark on a search-and-destroy mission, they want to be sure they have written the final draft.

Revision is a two-stage process. During the first stage (the principal focus of this chapter), you employ various reading strategies to help you rethink, reorder, and often rewrite substantial portions of what you have already written. When you are satisfied with these "global revisions," you focus your attention on the second stage of the process — "local revision": fixing sentences, phrases, and words — polishing the essay. (Strategies for implementing local revision are presented in Chapters 6 through 9 of this text.) Yet even when you are at work on this second stage, you should be ready to return to the first stage if the relocation of a sentence or the tightening of a paragraph suggests a more effective way to revise a section of your essay or even the whole essay.

Novelist Eudora Welty once discussed with an interviewer her attitudes toward revising her work. Examine her comments carefully, paying special attention to what she implies about the importance of *seeing* in revision.

> My ideal way to write . . . is to write the whole first draft through in one sitting, then work as long as it takes on revisions, and then write the final version all in one, so that in the end the whole thing amounts to one long sustained effort. . . . [Using a typewriter] helps give me the feeling of making my work objective. I can correct better if I see it in typescript. After that, I revise with scissors and pins. Pasting is too slow, and you can't undo it, but with pins you can move things from anywhere to anywhere, and that's what I really love doing — putting things in their best and proper place, revealing things at the time when they matter most. Often I shift things from the very beginning to the very end. . . .
>
> [Writing] is so much an inward thing that reading the proofs later can be a real shock. When I received them for my first book . . . I thought, *I* didn't write this. It was a page of dialogue — I might as well have never seen it before. I wrote to my editor . . . and told him something had happened to that page in the typesetting. He was kind, not even surprised — maybe this happens to all writers. He called me up and read me from the manuscript — word for word what the proofs said. Proofs don't shock me any longer,

yet there's still a strange moment with every book when I move from the position of writer to the position of reader, and I suddenly see my words with the eyes of the cold public. It gives me a terrible sense of exposure, as if I'd gotten sunburned. (Eudora Welty, *Writers at Work: The Paris Interviews*)

Looking to Revise

Once you consider revising to be a creative rather than merely a cleaning-up activity, you will begin to look at yourself, your readers, and your text from a different perspective.

How You Look at It

Although you may never be quite able to see revision as a welcome opportunity — for it is admittedly hard work, and you have already been working hard on your writing — you should nevertheless overcome any sense of impending ordeal and allow yourself to look objectively at what you have done in writing. It is particularly important to keep an open mind at this stage, to be willing to rethink — and not merely glance over — every aspect of your writing, from your most abstract assumptions about your subject to your most concrete assertion of purpose. You should try not to be helplessly in love with your own words no matter how clever or ringing they seem; your real concern is not their eloquence but their effectiveness. Like Welty, you should anticipate that revision will bring coherence and clarity — moving "things from anywhere to anywhere . . . putting things in their best and proper place, revealing things at the time they matter most."

How Someone Else Looks at It

When you are ready to revise, you may welcome the perspective that someone else — a teacher, editor, or friend — can bring to your writing. Because these readers will see different things in your writing, you must learn to predict and take advantage of their reactions. Some readers will ask you about the larger elements in your writing (your selection of a subject, audience, or purpose). Other readers will point to the smaller elements of your writing (your choice of sentence structure, punctuation, or diction). Still others will talk to you about their general impression of your writing (whether it was interesting, funny, or dull). As you revise, you must consider all these reactions to your work — even if they seem threatening, trivial or trite. You must consider what your readers saw, why they liked or disliked what they saw, and whether you can use *their* observations to strengthen *your* vision of your writing. Because your various readers may, on occasion, give you confusing or contradictory advice, you must also remember that ultimately *you* are responsible for deciding how to use their advice — if you use it at all — to carry out the decisions entailed in revising. You cannot let someone else do it for you.

How It Looks

Once you start revising, your writing will often look different:

1. You may have written your first draft in pencil on patched pages of a yellow legal pad and then retyped your second draft on white bond. Your long messy manuscript now looks compact and complete. This new look can be seductive, suggesting that cosmetic surgery has somehow solved many of your writing problems. You must look beneath the surface of your beautifully typed manuscript to devise solutions for those problems that still require rethinking and rewriting.

2. Your writing will usually look different simply because of the passage of time. The writing you composed at the beginning of your project has been incubating in your unconscious while you have been doing other things — going to class, talking to friends, reading assignments, watching television. It has also been incubating as you have developed more material in writing. Now, after a few days — or even a few hours — as you re-establish contact with the overall design of your writing project, you may conclude that you have not restricted your subject, anticipated the needs of your audience, or used your purpose to control and carry out all the decisions you have made during the writing process. This new perspective compels you to look for those solutions that you now feel confident will make your writing sharper and more purposeful.

3. Your writing may look different because during your discovery draft you produced new information and new questions that in a subtle or

significant way have altered your perspective on your writing. You know that when you revise your discovery draft you must find ways to include this new information and answer these new questions. Once you incorporate these additions into your second draft, your writing will never look the same.

4. But mainly your writing will look different when you revise because you have changed positions. As the writer of your writing, your task was solving the problem of how to create and arrange your ideas. As the reader of your writing, your task is to evaluate the effectiveness of these solutions. Just as you used a set of guidelines to help you write your writing, so now you may need a set of guidelines to help you read and evaluate what you have written.

Reading to Revise

When you are reading to revise, you are still actively involved in the writing process. You are *not* proofreading. Proofreading presumes the existence of a completed manuscript. When you proofread, you are merely checking your writing one last time to prove that you have not mangled sentences, misplaced punctuation, or misspelled words. Reading to revise, on the other hand, assumes the existence of an evolving manuscript. When you read to revise, you are trying to identify the strengths and weaknesses of your subject. You are reading to sharpen your perception of what your audience knows (what *is* on the page) and to speculate about what your audience needs (what *is not* on the page). You are reading to determine whether your purpose establishes the direction of your whole essay and controls the connections among its various parts.

Each of these readings suggests a different reading strategy and a different kind of reader. Indeed, the following reading strategies encourage you to read your writing as though you were someone else — a fictitious person in a special situation who is reading for a particular reason. Anything you can do to sustain this momentary charade is worth doing because it will help you see your writing with a different set of eyes.

Reading for Subject

To prepare yourself for this first reading, imagine that you are seated in the waiting room of your dentist's office. As you flip through several magazines, you are looking for writing that will attract and sustain your attention for a brief period of time. You don't have a pen or pencil, and even if you did, you would not think of marking up the writing you are reading. You are simply trying to decide whether the subject of a particular piece of writing is worth your time. Now pick up your writing and read it through as quickly as possible. Once you have finished reading, put your writing aside, maintain your identity as an impatient patient in a waiting room, and, in a few brief sentences, write out your general reactions to the following questions:

1. Why was I attracted to this essay? Did the title or first few sentences — the lead — pull me into the essay and convince me that it is worth reading?

2. What is the subject of the essay? Does the essay focus on the subject immediately, or did I have to read a lot of preliminary material or prolonged digressions?

3. What is significant about the subject? Is it a subject I like reading about, one that I need to know about, or one that I ought to think about?

4. What is interesting about the subject? What makes it interesting: the attitude of the writer, the nature of the subject, or the way in which it is presented?

5. Does the essay seem the right length? Is it long enough to answer all my questions yet short enough to keep my mind from wandering?

Reading for Audience

On this second reading, imagine yourself seated in a large banquet hall about to listen to an after-dinner speech. You cannot avoid listening to the speech, so you decide to judge whether the speaker has correctly anticipated the needs and expectations of the audience. One way to simulate this situation is to read your writing aloud to a friend, spouse, or even the dog if it will listen. The important thing is that you *hear* yourself reading your writing to an audience. An excellent way to accomplish this objective is to read aloud into a tape recorder. Then, with your manuscript and pencil in hand, play back the "speech" for its audience. As you listen, use the following guidelines to judge the effectiveness of your writing; mark those passages that will need revision because they are not clear or because they fail to come across with as much authority as you imagined when you were composing them. Stop the recorder each time your annotations become too detailed for you to keep up with the tape. Once you have finished copying down your comments, punch the button and resume listening to your writing being read.

1. What kinds of people does this speaker expect to find in the audience? Does the speech acknowledge their values, assumptions, and prejudices?

2. In all likelihood, what do the members of the audience already know about the subject of this speech? How might their knowledge affect their reaction to the speaker's presentation?

3. Why do the members of the audience stay to listen to this person speak?

4. Does the speaker ask the same questions the audience will ask about this subject? Does the speaker answer those questions when they need to be answered? Does the speaker anticipate the hostile questions of the inevitable crank who is sitting somewhere in the audience?

5. Does the speaker help the audience focus on the subject and follow the development of the speech? Does the organization of the parts provide a logical transition from idea to idea? Where might the audience get bored, confused, or annoyed with the speech? Does the end echo and fulfill the promise of the beginning?

Reading for Purpose

On this third reading, imagine yourself seated in an attorney's office about to sign a contract that will have an enormous impact on your life. In this situation, you must read your writing slowly and deliberately. As you read, use your pen or pencil to underline your thesis statement and to trace its connection to each major topic of your essay. Your job is to determine, precisely, what the thesis of this contract promises and whether the various sections and subsections deliver on that promise. If there are sections that need to be rewritten, rearranged, or deleted, now is the time to insist on such revision. The following guidelines will remind you of the purpose of the "contract" and call your attention to how that purpose is connected by its various "clauses."

1. Does this essay rest on hidden and undocumented assumptions? Is there some way to introduce those assumptions into the wording of the essay?

2. What is the purpose of this essay? Is that purpose expressed openly or must it be inferred from the text?

3. What is the thesis of this essay? What specific promise does it make to its readers? Is that promise sufficiently restricted, unified, and precise so that it can be kept?

4. Does the body of the essay fulfill the promise of the thesis? Is there a direct, logical, and dramatic connection among the various parts of the essay?

5. Is each part of the essay sufficiently developed? Does the text provide an effective variety of evidence? Does each piece of evidence pertain to the thesis? Does new evidence need to be introduced to clarify and verify the thesis?

Revision Agenda

The purpose of reading to revise is to establish a *revision agenda*, a list of priorities for you to work through as you rethink, rearrange, and rewrite the next draft of your essay. You can prepare this agenda according to at least three different procedures:

1. You may decide that you cannot maintain the fiction of three separate readings. As you read for subject, you see something that pertains to purpose or overlaps with audience. For you, the easiest procedure is to keep the three imaginary readers in your head at the same time, so after one "combined" reading you can prepare a single revision agenda.

2. You may decide that you like the idea of separate readings because it gives you three different ways to re-envision your writing. You prefer to read through your text three times, answering the sets of questions that accompany each reading, but you would rather wait until you complete the three readings before you prepare one revision agenda.

3. You may determine that you will need to make three distinct revisions of your writing. According to this procedure, you read through your writing, attempting to answer the questions about subject. Your answers enable you to prepare a revision agenda that you can use to compose a new draft. After you write this new document, you repeat the whole process for audience and for purpose.

You will have to decide which of these procedures helps you produce the most effective revision agenda and the most polished revisions. Sometimes, the nature of the writing project will determine which procedure you should use. If you have to write under the pressure of time and if you have selected a fairly straightforward subject that contains relatively simple information, then you may be able to use one revision agenda to produce an effective revision. If, on the other hand, you have given yourself enough time to allow your writing project to evolve and if you have selected a complicated subject that contains a great deal of complex information, then you may need to generate several revision agendas to identify and solve all the problems in your writing.

Another factor you must consider in producing your revision agenda is the division between global and local revision. Often, as you are looking at the larger problems of focus and form, you will see smaller problems of sentence structure and diction that seem to demand immediate attention. Revision is an intuitive process. A sudden impulse inspires you to relocate a paragraph or realign the parts of a sentence. Revision is also a recursive process. You are constantly stepping back from your writing to see the big picture, moving forward to touch up some small detail, and stepping back again to see how the altered detail changes the composition of the whole.

But revision is also a logical process. In any piece of writing, you will discover a number of things that need revising. Your temptation is to fix the simple problems first and the more difficult problems later. But the logical way to proceed is to work on the difficult problems first, for in solving them you may eliminate the simple problems or at least discover an efficient method for dealing with them. As you prepare your revision agenda, sort out these priorities by asking yourself three questions.

1. What did I try to do in this draft?

2. What are its strengths and weaknesses?

3. What revisions do I want to make in my next draft?

Your recommendations should try to group the large problems (subject, audience, purpose) at the top of your agenda and the small problems (style, mechanics, usage) at the bottom.

Revising: A Case Study

At the beginning of his writing class, Rod decided that one of the subjects he wanted to write about was his high school trip to Washington, D.C. His junior class had spent almost a year preparing for the trip, had traveled miles across country in a crowded bus, and then had crammed several months of sightseeing into four days of frantic, nonstop touring. Rod learned so much during this year-long experience that he had difficulty sorting out all his information. What he remembered about the trip, what he saw in Washington, and what he read about Washington before he went and after he came home was all jumbled together in his mind. He decided to attack the problem slowly and systematically in several drafts — writing to discover what he remembered, reading to fill in the gaps of what he didn't know (or had forgotten), and then writing again to try out a revised perspective. Most writing assignments do not require you to revise as many times as Rod does as he shapes and reshapes his material into different drafts. But Rod, an architecture major, is obsessed with the problem of design. He wants to create something that captures the essence of his Washington experience. And since he has given himself enough time to work out his design in several drafts, his writing provides an interesting case study of how one writer rethinks, revises, and rewrites his work.

Rod began by planning. During a brainstorming exercise, he remembered the amount of time his teachers and parents had devoted to getting him ready for the "trip of his life." In a freewriting exercise, he remembered the people, the buildings, the monuments, and the heat of

Washington. As he sorted through this information, he decided to cluster it chronologically. The major headings on his scratch outline were I. Preparation; II. Trip; and III. D.C. Confident that he had gathered and arranged his information effectively, he wrote the following discovery draft.

OUR TRIP TO D.C.

(Discovery Draft)

In my junior year in high school, my class sold magazine subscriptions to make enough money to take a trip to Washington, D.C. Everything we did that year seemed to focus on Washington. In first period (Econ), we had market reports, pep talks, and strategy sessions. All of us had to make our quotas or there would be no trip. In second period (History) we learned about the history of Washington -- how it had been selected as the national capital and how it had been burned down by the British in the War of 1812. In third period (Art), we learned about the architect's design for the city, the famous museums, and all the monuments. I took really good notes in this class because I dreamed that I was going to be a world famous architect when I graduated from college. I still have that Art notebook and my notes actually make sense. Art class was the high point of my education for Washington.

By lunch time, everybody had had enough -- although I vaguely remember cutesy names on the cafeteria menu such as Lincoln Dogs, Congressional Burgers, and White House Shakes. In the afternoon, we learned about how the government worked -- the different branches and agencies -- in Civics, but I can't remember learning anything about D.C. in Math, Science, and Gym.

At home there was no relief. Mom and Dad were always
showing me articles and stuff about Washington, and my little
sister even pasted a picture of the Washington Monument on my
Art notebook. Even Uncle Fred -- the midwest's most fanatic
Bears' fan -- sent me a list of the Redskins' draft choices.

The trip was a real bummer. All the junior class, plus
our counselors, Mr. and Mrs. Franklin (my art teacher), and
our driver Dave crammed into this bus with lousy air
conditioning, and headed across Indiana, Ohio, West Virginia,
Pennsylvania, and Virginia to D.C. I don't remember too much
about the trip except that it was awful hot and kids were
always asking Dave to stop for a pit stop. When he did
somebody was always late getting their food or getting out of
the restroom, so that Mr. Franklin was always walking up and
down the aisle counting heads before Dave could pull out.

When we arrived in Washington, we had four days to see
the whole thing. We stayed in a motel in Virginia, but every
morning Dave would drive us into downtown D.C. On the first
day we saw our congressman, the Capitol, the Supreme Court,
the Library of Congress and then stood in line for a long time
for a brief tour of the White House. On the second and third
days, we visited the museums on the Mall. My favorite was
the Air and Space Museum, especially the film about flying.
Being in the museums was great because outside it was really
hot. After we were through at one museum, we would run to the
next one just so we could sit in an air-conditioned building.

Even though we drove by the monuments every day on our
way back to the motel, we didn't visit them until the last
day. The Jefferson and Lincoln were interesting and you could
see them quickly, but you had to stand in line -- a long, long

line — to see the Washington Monument. But I liked that
monument the best. Ever since we hit town, I kept seeing it
everywhere. I'd walk around a corner and there it was, or I'd
hear a jet plane going over and I'd look up and there it would
be again. It seemed big and yet so simple beside all those
other buildings. All the postcards I sent home, even the one
to Uncle Fred, had a picture of the Washington Monument on
it. Whenever I think of our trip, I think of that monument
standing in the middle of downtown Washington like a big
paperweight.

Revision Agenda

1. *What did I want to do in the draft?*

   I wanted to describe our junior class trip to Washington, D.C. It was such a big deal for our little high school that I've never forgotten it. I wanted to try to explain how much we had to learn to get ready, how awful the trip was, and how much I was impressed with everything I saw.

2. *What are its strengths and weaknesses?*

   When I read through the essay quickly I noticed that I had to get through all the stuff about school before I read anything about "Our Trip to D.C." In my scratch outline, I thought I would divide the paper into three parts — preparation, trip, and D.C. — but I spent so much time talking about school that I didn't say much about our trip or what we saw in D.C. We had only four days in Washington, so everything was jammed together — just like it is in my essay. I do like the last part about the Washington Monument, especially the sentence comparing it to a paperweight. I think the monument is interesting and its history is really significant. It took them over one hundred years to build it.

3. *What revisions do I want to make in my next draft?*

   a. *I know I have too many subjects, so I think I'll focus on our stay in Washington rather than try to talk about school or the trip.*

   b. *I think I'll restrict my subject to just our visit to the Washington Monument. It seems to represent the whole trip.*

   c. *I could include some of the people we met while we waited in line.*

> d. *I remember that the tour guides at the monument told some interesting stories. I had my Art notebook with me, so I wrote down what they said. Even asked a few questions.*
>
> e. *Mainly, I want to describe how wonderful the monument was and why I was so impressed with it.*
>
> f. *In my next draft, I will have to pay more attention to paragraphs. I don't really have an introduction or a thesis. My first paragraph just starts telling the story. It's also too long. Some of my other paragraphs are too short or deal with too many subjects.*
>
> g. *Also, I'll have to watch my sentences and vocabulary. When I write about high school, I sound like I am still in high school — I need to cut out "bummer," "lousy," and "stuff."*

Revising for Subject

Rod has too many subjects. Although his trip to Washington seemed like a specific subject, he now realizes that it contains many smaller subjects. Even his original division of his essay into three parts does not restrict his subject sufficiently so that he can develop each part in detail. He spends too much time on the first part, hardly any time on the second part, and then tries to cram too much information into the third part.

He decides to focus on his visit to the Washington Monument because it seems to represent for him everything he learned about Washington before he went and everything he saw while he was there. Now that he has a focus for his subject, he begins to think about what kind of information he can use to develop his subject in more detail and how he can introduce and interpret his subject for his readers. He tries to implement his revision agenda in a second draft.

VISITING THE WASHINGTON MONUMENT

(2nd Draft)

During my junior year in high school, my class sold
magazine subscriptions and made enough money to take a trip to
Washington, D.C. Our stay was brief, but we saw dozens of
historic sites and had our picture taken with our
congressman. I was certainly impressed with the large

government buildings and the elaborate architecture of the
monuments, especially the Jefferson and Lincoln Memorials with
their thick pillars and drafty halls. But for simple beauty
nothing I saw in Washington could compare with the Washington
Monument.

The afternoon was sunny and hot as our bus drove into the
parking lot near the Washington Monument. We jockeyed for
window positions where we could take photographs and let out
tremendous whoops to let everyone know that the folks from
Indiana had arrived. Our driver parked the bus, and we
squirmed in our seats for another five minutes while Mrs.
Franklin, our art teacher, told us to take notes on what the
guides said, and reminded us that young ladies and gentlemen
stood quietly in sweltering heat and refrained from squirting
others with water pistols. With that said, we stampeded off
the bus and raced through the maze of cars and buses toward
the monument.

The first of us there found a line over two hundred yards
long that snaked along the sidewalk like a Chinese dragon and
ended, oddly enough, with a middle-aged couple from Indiana.

"Are you kids from Indiana?" the lady asked. "We seen
your bus pull in just a minute ago."

"We sure are," I answered. "We sold magazine
subscriptions to get here." She seemed impressed and said
that they were from Indiana too. Then she treated us to a
detailed account of their vacation to date, naming every
battlefield, landmark, memorial, bridge, souvenir shop, rest
area and McDonald's they had visited. She placed special
emphasis on the Jack Daniels Distillery in Tennessee.

"I wish this line would get movin'. It's hotter than

blazes out here," grumbled her husband. He removed his Funk Hybrids cap and wiped the sweat off his forehead with a red handkerchief. "We got's plenty of buildin's to see before tonight." We all agreed that the line was slow and that it was "hotter than blazes." But before his wife could tell us about how quickly the line moved at Jack Daniels, we spotted a group of students in front of us. My friends and I spent the next quarter of an hour giving the eye to three young ladies, trying to figure out how we could meet them. But the girls played hard-to-get and ignored our leers, so we concentrated on spraying our own girls with our recently purchased "greenie-meanie" squirt guns.

Finally we stood at the base of the monument and craned our necks toward the top. It was bigger than I ever imagined, though I wouldn't admit it then. I thought about the guys who had to build the thing, particularly those guys who had to put the finishing touches on the peak.

When we finally moved inside, we were greeted by a tour guide (actually a park ranger) who told us that the Monument was 555 feet, 5 1/8 inches high, that it weighs 90,854 tons, and that it cost $1,187,710.31 to build. While I was writing these numbers down in my notebook, he explained that we could not walk up the 898 steps to the top, but would have to take a 13 second elevator ride. I was pleased in a way, because it was too hot to walk, but if it were cooler it would be fun to walk up to the top and count those steps.

Inside the elevator was another park ranger who told us historical facts about the monument. He only had a few seconds. He called it an obelisk, and told us that it took 105 years to build because they had trouble raising money and figuring out where to put it. The ground around the monument used to be a swamp or something.

When we got to the top another ranger walked us around the observation deck. There was a magnificent view out of each window. To the East, you could see the Mall rising up to Capitol Hill. To the West, we could see the Lincoln Memorial, if you stood on tiptoe. To the South, you could see the Pentagon straight ahead and, on tiptoe, the Jefferson. To the North you could see the National Cathedral up on the hill and the White House down below. Everybody was taking pictures, pointing to places we had been, and trying to see our bus in the parking lot and our motel across the river. I asked the ranger why there were bars on the windows. He said they installed them during the Depression after three people had committed suicide by jumping out one of the windows.

After awhile we came down and walked over to the souvenir shop where we loaded up on pamphlets, postcards, and little models of the monument. Our heads were groggy with information and our bodies were sticking with sweat, so we walked back to the bus, spraying an occasional victim with our "greenie-meanies." But strangely enough, I was in no mood for horsing around. I stopped and looked back at that stark, jutting obelisk. I was impressed. The Washington Monument, like the man it honors, is a rugged individual.

Revision Agenda

1. What did I try to do in this draft?

I wanted to describe our visit to the Washington Monument. Although we horsed around a lot while we were there, I was really impressed with the structure. Its design is so simple and rugged and it towers over much of the city. I wanted to explain why this monument is so interesting and significant.

2. *What are its strengths and weaknesses?*

   The best part of the essay is when I actually get inside the monument and tell what you can see from the top. Also, I like the end of the essay when I stop horsing around and think about what the monument means. When I read this draft aloud, I still sound like a high school kid. The only people who would like the beginning and the girl stuff is a bunch of high school kids. I guess that's part of the tourist atmosphere of the place, but I really learned more about the monument than how to squirt a "greenie-meanie." I keep thinking about that couple from Indiana and what I could have told them about the monument. I don't think they know the difference between a monument and a distillery.

3. *What revisions do I want to make in my next draft?*

   a. *I want to tell my readers something about this monument so they will understand its importance.*

   b. *As long as I talk about my high school trip, I'll sound like a high school kid.*

   c. *Also, I always get sidetracked when I start talking about my personal experiences.*

   d. *Everybody has seen pictures of the monument and a lot of people have been there, but I'll bet few of them know as much as I do about it. I've got all those notes from Art class, all the stuff the guides said that I wrote down, and those pamphlets I picked up at the souvenir shop.*

   e. *I'd like to try writing a history of the monument just to see how much I could tell people about it.*

   f. *My introduction and thesis was better in this second draft, but I'll have to change it — make it more objective — if I am going to write a history. But I also want to make it interesting — so that it's not dull history.*

   g. *I think if I imagine myself as a historian, or tour guide, then I won't have so much trouble with my vocabulary. I mean how can you take anybody seriously if they are running around squirting girls with a "greenie-meanie."*

Revising for Audience

Rod is beginning to recognize that he knows more about his subject than what he remembers about standing in line to observe it. He is also beginning to recognize the difference between *telling* what happened and *using* what happened to create a subject and develop a thesis. But his major reaction to his second draft is his discovery of audience. He wants to separate himself from the high school kids who don't care what they are seeing and the couple who don't understand what they are seeing. He wants to tell both groups that there is more to the monument than a place to find girls or yet another building to see. Its history is special and significant. Rod thinks that he has gathered enough information from his art teacher, the tour guides, and the souvenir shop to tell that history in some detail. This decision, made to enlighten his audience, also enlarges his subject and redefines his purpose.

THE STORY BEHIND THE WASHINGTON MONUMENT

(3rd Draft)

Since people first spoke, they have probably had a few good things to say about one another. Some people receive "high fives," some just congratulations. Others live in our books and a very few are important enough to have monuments built in their honor. When we look at those stone and steel structures, we often do not consider the time and work that went into their construction. The Washington Monument, for example, took 105 years to build and cost nearly 1.2 million dollars. Its construction was delayed repeatedly due to lack of funds and lack of interest. Once it was even stolen. The story behind the monument is in many ways as interesting as the story behind Washington himself.

The idea of building a monument to honor George Washington was discussed for several decades before it was finally examined seriously. In 1783, the Continental Congress voted to erect a bronze equestrian statue depicting the father of our country in Roman garb. This idea was not mentioned again until 1799, when Congress decided that a pyramid-type mausoleum might be more appropriate. Congress failed to provide the necessary funds, estimated at twenty-five cents per citizen. Only faint rumblings about the monument were heard during the next thirty years.

Senator Henry Clay of Kentucky revived the motion in 1832 and managed to allocate money for a twenty-ton statue of a toga-clad Washington, but this half-naked sculpture did not satisfy a group of local citizens who were more impressed with a 150-foot shaft erected in Washington's honor in Baltimore. The following year these people formed the Washington National Monument Society, and, during the next three years, collected $28,000 and sponsored a design competition. Robert Mills drew the winning plan, a 600-foot obelisk sticking out of a colonnade base, 250 feet in diameter, known as the National Pantheon. This temple was to contain statues of the signers of the Declaration of Independence, Revolutionary War heroes, and a colossal George Washington.

The laying of the cornerstone was scheduled for Washington's birthday in 1848, but Congress was slow in approving the site and the ceremony was rescheduled for July 4. Fifteen thousand people, including President Polk and Congressman Lincoln, watched Benjamin B. French lay the cornerstone with the same silver trowel that Washington had used to begin construction on the Capitol in 1793.

Although the cornerstone was laid, construction on the monument was delayed by a political group called the Know-Nothings. In 1855, they infiltrated the Monument Society, held a secret election, and took over the leadership of the Society, thereby "stealing" the monument. As a result, Congress promptly withdrew its pledge of $200,000 and the Society was discredited. Over the next three years, the

Know-Nothings collected $285.09 and added thirteen rows of inferior marble to the monument.

By 1858 the Society was back in reliable hands, but the Monument remained a 176-foot stump until 1876 when the U.S. Army Corps of Engineers began removing the work of the Know-Nothings. On July 5 Congress promised $200,000 and a completion date of October 19, 1881 was announced. Meanwhile, the U.S. Minister to Italy, George P. Marsh, suggested that the monument be simplified, leaving a stark, classical obelisk. The Society agreed and on August 7, 1880 President Hayes laid the second cornerstone. Four years later the final tip was set in place. On Washington's next birthday, the monument was officially dedicated; on October 9, 1888, it was opened to the public.

Despite lack of funds and lack of interest, the Washington Monument finally grew to be the tallest masonry structure in the world. And despite its simple appearance, it is one of the most visited memorials in the country. It is a tribute to both the father of our country and our country itself.

Revision Agenda

1. What did I try to do in this draft?

I tried to present a straight history of the monument — to inform people about how the idea got started, the different ways it was designed, and all the obstacles people had to overcome to build it.

2. What are its strengths and weaknesses?

I think I was pretty successful in using all the information I have collected on the monument to tell its story. There's a lot more I could have included — statistical information about its size, zany information about what people have done there. (The tour guide at the top of the monument told me some funny stories.) One of my problems is that I sound like a tour guide — a dull one. I read it aloud to one of my friends who said he thought it only got good when the Know-Nothings stole the monument. Of course, he's not a terrific audience — he likes cartoons and punk rock — but I know what he means. The style is kind of flat. The biggest weakness may be my thesis sentence. "The story behind the monument is in many ways as interesting as the story behind Washington himself." I guess I am promising to compare the story behind the monument with the story behind the man. I never talk about George during the whole essay.

3. *What revisions do I want to make in my next draft?*

   a. *I need to cut some of my historical information or at least present it in a more entertaining style. I think I can add some new stuff that focuses on some of the more unusual facts about the monument's history. The guide told me some good stories and the brochures I picked up at the souvenir shop tell a few fascinating stories about where some of the stones came from.*

   b. *I need to revise my thesis statement so that it focuses on the history of the monument — not a comparison between the monument and the man. I don't know enough about George Washington to write that comparison even if I wanted to — and I don't. I want to focus on the monument.*

   c. *I think my thesis should try to catch my readers' attention by simply telling them that this unique monument has a unique history.*

   d. *That's the way I'll begin. Everybody knows the facts, but here are some facts you don't know.*

   e. *Somehow I want to get my experience — or the experiences of tourists — back into the essay. Maybe that will confuse things again. But I want people to know more than just the facts — as crazy as they are. I want them to know what they are seeing and what it feels like to see it.*

   f. *My paragraphs seem more fully developed and clear this time, except for the fact that they don't relate to my thesis.*

   g. *My sentences and vocabulary are better too. Maybe it's because I'm writing about facts rather than my impression.*

Revising for Purpose

By trying to write a pure information essay, rather than a personal experience essay, Rod has created three problems. First, he has allowed his information to control his essay, thus making him sound — to himself, at least — as dull as a tour guide. Second, he has inadvertently allowed himself to write a thesis that promises a comparison between the monument and the man. Rod doesn't have the information to write the second half of this comparison — nor does he want to. His purpose is to discuss only the history of the monument. Third, somehow, he has eliminated himself from his essay. In trying to inform his readers about the significance of the monument, he has managed to prevent them from seeing why it impresses tourists (like himself) by its simple beauty. Some of the historical information is interesting, but Rod's attitude toward it (a mixture of admiration and amusement) does not really come through.

To tell the story behind the Washington Monument, he has to select and arrange his information differently so that it reflects his attitude, not the attitude of a tour guide. His decision to focus on the unusual history of the monument helps Rod formulate a more restricted, unified, and precise thesis. Certainly his decision to eliminate the comparison between the man and the monument makes his subject more manageable. Rod is finally confident that his new purpose will create an interesting subject that will appeal to his readers.

REVISING THE WASHINGTON MONUMENT

(4th Draft)

The raw facts are simple enough: The Washington Monument stands 555 feet 5 1/8 inches in the air. Its base is 55 feet 1 1/2 square inches. It is faced with 9,613 marble slabs, weighs 90,854 tons, can withstand a 145 m.p.h. gale, and cost $1,187,710.31. Many of the estimated two million tourists who visit the Monument each year can tell you those statistics. But there are some things they can't tell you. For example, in the two centuries since the idea was first mentioned, the Washington Monument has been revised, moved, stolen, ignored, held hostage, and almost blown up.

It all began in 1783 when the Continental Congress voted to erect a bronze equestrian statue of George dressed in Roman garb, wielding a spear. Sixteen years later, Congress

decided George might look better as a pyramid. Three decades
later somebody thought George looked best dressed in a toga.
This last idea was actually turned into a twenty-ton statue.
But George looked a little cold in his toga. Not satisfied
with a half-naked George, the good people of Washington formed
the Washington National Monument Society in 1833 to see if
they could create a fitting tribute for their hero.

In three years, the Society collected $28,000 and in 1836
they held a contest to select the best design. There were a
lot of crazy designs: One looked like a Gothic Cathedral,
another like an Egyptian Sphinx. But the committee selected
a drawing by Robert Mills that called for a 600-foot obelisk
rising out of a colonnade base, 250 feet in diameter, to be
known as the National Pantheon. This temple was to contain
statues of the signers of the Declaration of Independence,
Revolutionary War heroes, and a colossal statue of George. If
this description doesn't sound like the Washington Monument
you know, it's because it isn't. To cut costs, the monument
was stripped of all its ornamentation and shortened slightly
to conform to the classical proportions of an obelisk. For
years, however, artists included the National Pantheon in
their drawings.

George's Monument was not only modified, but it was also
moved. Pierre Charles L'Enfant, the architect who designed
the city, originally envisioned the monument resting on the
intersection of an axis running west from the Capitol and
south from the White House. This spot proved too marshy to
support much weight. If they had put George there, he would
have been a leaning or sinking tower. So they moved him one
hundred yards south.

Finally, in 1848, Benjamin B. French, Grand Master of the capital's Lodge of Free and Accepted Masons, laid the cornerstone with the same silver trowel George had used to begin construction on the Capitol. Fifteen thousand people attended the ceremony, including Martha's grandson, President Polk, and Congressman Abraham Lincoln. The odd thing is that nobody remembers which stone is the cornerstone.

The Society continued to raise money for George's monument. It also collected a number of carved stones from various states, Indian tribes, and foreign countries. Greece sent a block from the Parthenon, Egypt donated a stone from the Alexandrian Library, France sent a piece of Napoleon's tomb, and Italy sent a hunk of lava from Mt. Vesuvius. All these different stones (190 in all) decorate the monument -- with the exception of one. On March 6, 1854, a stone sent by Pope Pius IX from the Temple of Concord was stolen. A political group called the Know-Nothings was credited with the heist, but the stone was never found.

In 1848, these Know-Nothings added another page to the crazy history of the monument by infiltrating the Society, electing themselves as officers, and essentially "stealing" the monument. Congress promptly withdrew its $200,000 pledge. In their three year reign, the Know-Nothings collected $285.09 and added thirteen rows of inferior marble to the monument.

Twenty-five years later, when serious construction finally resumed, Col. Casey of the U.S. Army Corps of Engineers discovered that the rope used to lift supplies to the top of the monument had been pulled down. He solved this problem by killing a pigeon. He tied a long, thin wire to

the pigeon's leg which was attached to a rope. Then he let
the bird loose inside the monument and he fired a shotgun.
The pigeon flew out of the monument's top carrying the wire
and rope with it. But as soon as it cleared the monument it
was blown out of the sky by a sharpshooter. The wire was
retrieved, and the rope pulled through. A net was then
constructed around the base of the monument to prevent the
loss of another life during construction.

George's memorial was opened to the public in 1888 and
has been involved in some bizarre stunts ever since. In 1892
"Gabby" Street caught a baseball thrown out of one of the
windows at the top of the monument. In 1915, Dr. Alfredo
Warsaw, a New York baritone, sang two verses of a ballad while
friends dangled him from one of the windows. During the
Depression, three people committed suicide by jumping out the
windows. (Iron bars have since been installed.) In 1966, 76-
year-old Edna Rousseau made 307 round trip climbs on the 898
steps. In 1982, a man urging the cause of nuclear
disarmament, held the monument hostage and threatened to blow
it up if people didn't listen to him. He was shot by a
police sharpshooter and his bomb was discovered to be a fake.

There's obviously more to George's Monument than meets
the eye. Of course, you don't have to know the inside story
to like the monument. Most people who see a picture of the
monument on a calendar or a postcard like what they see. But
to truly understand and appreciate the monument, you do need
to know the inside story. When you visit George's monument on
some hot summer afternoon and have to stand in line for over
two hours for a thirteen second elevator ride to the top, you
need to know how long it took the planners and builders to

reach the top: all those false starts, crazy designs, and engineering obstacles that had to be overcome to produce this beautifully simple structure. When you see people in the line who don't know why they are there or who are just fooling around like they would at Disneyland, you need to know that the two hundred year history of the monument is filled with bewildered and misguided people. And when you have finished your visit, you need to take time to appreciate what you have seen. Turn and look at it one last time. There it stands — a solitary, rugged individual, indifferent to the confusion below. It is a peaceful and impressive sight.

Revision Agenda

1. What I tried to do in this draft.

I tried to tell the unusual history of the Washington Monument — to make the big paperweight seem more human and interesting for my readers.

2. What are the strengths and weaknesses of this draft?

I see mainly strengths in this draft. My thesis sentence actually names the topics of most of my paragraphs. And the other paragraphs — such as those about the stones and the pigeon — add to the spirit of the thesis. I managed to include a lot of statistical information at the beginning without boring my readers. I've selected a variety of historical information — some from my last draft and some new information that makes the essay easier to read and remember. I'm really happy with my conclusion. That was an inspiration. It pulls together everything I talked about in my second and third draft. I am still not sure about the way I talk about "old George." It may offend some of my readers or at least make them expect that I am going to talk about him somewhere in my essay.

3. What revisions do I want to make in my next draft?

a. Not many. Do I need another draft? No!

b. I think I am going to call this my last draft.

c. My purpose statement is clear.

d. My outline is solid.

e. My examples are funny and informative.

f. My conclusion is terrific.

g. I might need to fix up a few of my sentences and find some better words.

h. I still need to think about "the George problem."

i. Mainly, I think I am done. I wonder what the guy who laid the last stone in the monument said when he was done?

A Few Final Questions About Rod's Revising

1. How does Rod's *subject* change from his first (or discovery) draft to his fourth draft?

2. How does Rod's concern about *audience* affect his decision-making process? For example, how does his perception of his audience change in his second, third, and fourth drafts? How does his perception of himself change as he redefines his audience?

3. What is Rod's purpose for each draft? How does he try to combine several purposes in his fourth draft?

4. What is Rod's thesis in each draft? To what extent does each thesis control the decisions he makes in his writing?

5. How does Rod follow Welty's notion of revising? For example, how does he move things around in each draft — "putting things in their best and proper place, revealing things at the time when they matter most. . . . [shifting] things from the very beginning to the very end"? In each draft, what information does he drop, add, reduce, enlarge, or recycle?

6. Rod is obviously happiest with his last draft. Which draft do you like best? Explain your answer.

A Final Word About Revising

The final word about revising is that there is no final word. You can revise endlessly, always trying to rearrange information, rewrite paragraphs and sentences, and substitute new words. The more you look at your writing the more you will see that it needs revising. But at some point, revising becomes rationalizing, rethinking becomes idle tinkering.

The test of the revising process is whether a revision produces significant improvement.

Sometimes revision can actually destroy good writing, replacing spontaneous, original insights with self-conscious, overwrought commentary. Like Rod, you have to learn to know when to say "I am done" revising at the global level. Now you must presume that you have written your last draft. In Part 2 of this text, you will learn how to polish and perfect your last draft by examining such matters as common patterns to convey ideas, the shape and diversity of paragraphs and sentences, and the appropriateness of your words and style.

Revising Exercises

1. Each of the four designs shown on the following two pages was proposed to honor George Washington, the first president of our country. Compare and contrast the first three preliminary sketches for the structure with the photograph of the actual monument. In particular, examine the detail and annotations on each of the preliminary sketches. Then answer the following questions:

   a. What *subject* is suggested by each structure? What clues help you identify the subject? Which designs suggest more than one subject? What are they?

   b. What kind of *audience* does each designer imagine for his structure? What kind of values and tastes does the designer attribute to the audience who would be impressed with his design?

   c. What is the *purpose* of a national monument to George Washington? Which of these designs fulfills that purpose most effectively? Explain your answer.

2. In Chapter 2 you read about Mary's attempt to gather information about the cost effectiveness of wood-burning stoves by conducting some informal research — interviewing friends and reading a sales brochure, monograph, and magazine article. In Chapter 3 you examined Mary's research on the wood-burning stove that Bill installed in their house. You outlined her research and formulated several preliminary hypotheses she might use to demonstrate her findings. Reread her planning material on pages 67–69 and 72–74 and the Drafting Exercise on pages 111–113. Then read her essay below, and answer the following questions:

   a. What changes has she made in her subject?

   b. How has she revised her attitude toward her audience?

 Sketch #1   National Archives   **Sketch #2**   National Archives

c. How has she redefined her thesis?

d. In this final essay, what material does she keep, delete, reduce, enlarge, or rearrange from her earlier writing?

Burn Again

My life changed drastically awhile ago when my husband and I bought a wood-burning stove and he became a real Woodie. The Woodies are a loosely organized, but highly principled and dedicated cult whose members are not only stove owners, but also true believers. They are primarily male, but they do not discriminate on the basis of sex, race, age or marital status. Creed is the thing. Woodies believe in the spirit of independence, in the gospel of hard work, and in the wisdom of long range planning. Real Woodies are committed.

Sketch #3   National Archives

The Modern Monument
Robert Anderson/UNIPHOTO

    I had no idea what I was getting into when Bill broached the issue of buying the stove. The required initial $800 investment wasn't particularly appealing, but Bill convinced me that the house would be much warmer than the 60° we had our thermostat set on, and we could practically eliminate our monthly gas bill. So I agreed, and we purchased a Sierra on-the-hearth insert. What I did not realize at that time was that Bill was a newly converted Woodie for whom the doctrine of independence was already burning bright. He informed the dealer that he would install the stove <u>himself</u>.

    I wondered how it was possible for a 185 pound man to install a 385 pound stove himself, but he seemed confident and adamant, so I didn't ask. On the day of installation, visions of hernias danced in my head. But Woodies are a close-knit group, and even the Woodie code of

2

3

independence allows for in-group assistance. With the help of a friend in faith and a rented hoist, amidst much groaning (but never any complaining), Bill got the stove in its rightful place on the hearth. I cringed slightly when Bill told me that he had had to make a "few purchases": $60 for a heat reflecting shield to protect the mantel, $50 for a fiber glass rug to protect the carpeting in front of the stove, $6 for stove polish, and $8 for a chimney fire extinguisher to keep within reach. But, the true believer assured me, it would all pay for itself eventually. I was relieved. Now that the stove was in, we could relax, reap the economic benefits, and enjoy the warmth.

The implications, however, of Bill's new-found fervor started to become clear for me the next Saturday morning. He left early before I was awake and showed up in the driveway late in the morning in a rusty, 1970 pickup truck with the words "Big Red" stenciled in thick, square letters on its side. I recognized the gleam of new ownership in his eye, and my mouth must have dropped open when I saw him. He was quick to offer what he saw as the logical explanation. 4

"Well," he said impatiently. "How did you think we were going to get wood?" 5

"Get wood?" I came back ignorantly. "I assumed we'd buy it and have it delivered." 6

"Buy it? How can we save money if we have to buy wood?" 7

I wondered how much he'd "saved" on Big Red, but didn't have the nerve to ask. I tried to share his steadfast Woodie faith in "the long run." I wondered, though, where Bill planned on "getting wood." The trees on our half-acre suburban lot were barely kindling size, and we weren't blessed (to my knowledge) with any landed relatives or close friends. My skepticism, though, was based on an ignorance of Woodie determination and resourcefulness. The Word was that there were several area landowners (within 50 miles) who would trade access to their wood supply for every other load cut — a kind of modern day sharecropping for Woodies. The wood then is "Free," but for Bill Saturday has become a day of ritualistic pilgrimage to the woods, of cutting and stacking a load for himself and a load for his benefactor. Each tree is assessed in terms of its BTU potential, then felled, dissected and divied up. 8

This required ritual presupposes, of course, that a Woodie has 9 acquired not only a truck, but an ax, a chain saw, a wood splitter, and a wheelbarrow. It also presupposes that a Woodie will spend every autumn Saturday nowhere but in the woods and then in the back yard, hauling, stacking and restacking. The reward, of course, is in the growing stack along the back of the property and on the porch in the wood crib ($35). The reward is in estimating how long into the winter (and beyond) the accumulation will last, and in comparing the size of the stack to the size of the piles of other Woodies in the neighborhood.

But the size of the pile is not the only status symbol among the Woodies. The hierarchy within the group is based on an intricate balance between many variables. The obvious symbolic object — the stove itself — is not nearly so important as evidence of an adherence to Woodie principles. Whether one owns the expensive Norwegian Yotul, a cast-iron Buck, or a respectable, though economical Scottie is not nearly as important as how a Woodie makes his stove work for him. The real proof of the pudding is in the gas bill: the lower the bill, the higher the level of prestige. Woodie gatherings always involve the revelation and/or confession about last month's bill, and suggestions for how to improve stove efficiency. 10

A real Woodie goes to great lengths to ensure that his furnace won't inadvertently kick on. In our house, Bill has devised an elaborate network of fans which ensure that the warm, family room air will travel to the bedrooms and to the back hall where the thermostat is located. One night shortly after we began using our stove, I was jerked into wakefulness at 3 a.m. Through a cloud, something was buzzing, and Bill was thrashing wildly beside me trying in his own half-consciousness to discover the source of the disturbance. He reached violently for the phone, and, in the process of getting the receiver to his ear, realized instead that his watch alarm was making the noise on his wrist. 11

By this time I was rational. "You forgot to take off your watch," I said brilliantly. "I wonder why it went off." 12

He, too, was finally awake. "It went off because I set it for 3 o'clock," he answered as he began to climb out of bed. "I have to stoke the stove. Otherwise the furnace will come on." 13

Stoke the stove? In the middle of the night? I thought modern man had progressed beyond all that, but again I had underestimated the 14 depth of real Woodie dedication. Now the three o'clock offering is another of Bill's rituals, a sacrifice cheerfully made by him and by his fellow Woodies in their own homes.

The precepts of Woodie-ism remain sacred around our home, but lately I sometimes catch glimpses of doubt in Bill, and hear faint rumblings of a faltering commitment. I was somewhat surprised when he accepted a friend's invitation to attend a solar heat seminar (just to see), and I heard him mutter something that resembled a curse the last time the ashes needed to be hauled out. A few nights ago when at 3 a.m. his wrist alarm went off, I was either dreaming or I saw a sinful gleam from his eyes shine through the darkness and I heard him say, "What the heck. Gas company employees have to eat too." 15

Writing Exercises

1. Describe a personal experience you had creating or repairing something — an article of clothing, the engine of a car, the electrical hookup for your stereo, the menu for an important meal — in which you had to work through several possible solutions (or versions) before your revisions produced effective results.

2. Transform something that you have written exclusively from the point of view of your personal experience — an extended journal entry, a letter you haven't yet mailed to a friend or your family, an essay — into a more objective, informative piece of writing. Try to avoid the two problems that Rod discovered when he tried this assignment in his third draft: (a) his information took over his writing and (b) he lost his unique perspective on his information — his purpose for presenting it.

3. Find a magazine article that you know is directed to a very specific audience. Good sources for such articles are *Esquire, Cosmopolitan, Ms., New York* (or any "city" magazine), *Gourmet, Rolling Stone,* or any of various sports magazines such as *World Tennis.* Read the article carefully, then write a brief analysis of the audience for whom you think it was written. Now imagine another audience for the article — perhaps one that knows nothing about the subject or is indifferent to it, perhaps one whose lifestyle does not usually include the subject. Think of some ways in which the subject might be made appealing to these readers, then draw up a careful revision agenda indicating how you would revise the article for the new audience. You are revising primarily for audience, but you should not neglect to consider the article's purpose.

4. Return to the essay that you began planning in Writing Exercise 4 of Chapter 2 and drafted in Writing Exercise 4 of Chapter 3. Reread the list of conclusions you drew up when you analyzed it; then — looking to revise subject, audience, and purpose — reread the essay itself. Like Rod, you may want to read the essay three times, focusing each reading on one of the three elements; or you may feel comfortable and confident enough to read only once or twice, concentrating on all three elements simultaneously. Whichever method you choose, draw up a revision agenda, then revise your essay.

Part 2

The Expression of Ideas

Chapter 5

Common Methods of Development

In Part 1 of this text you learned how working your way through the stages of the writing process enables you to discover your subject, audience, and purpose. You also learned how making these discoveries helps you arrange your writing according to certain meaningful patterns. For example, once Laurie decided to write about her father and baseball, she began telling a story about her efforts to win her father's affection by learning the game he loved. And once Jody decided to write about her two grandmothers, she began describing their two houses where she had spent her summers. These patterns often emerge from your planning, drafting, and revising because they provide answers to some of the fundamental questions you ask about any body of information.

1. What happened? (narration)
2. What does it look like? (description)
3. How can you document it? (illustration)
4. How is it similar to or different from something else? (comparison)
5. What kind of subdivisions does it contain? (classification)
6. How do you do it? (process analysis)
7. Why did it happen? (causal analysis)
8. How would you characterize it? (definition)

As you move through the preliminary stages of the writing process you can use these questions to help you discover *your* purpose. For example, you can brainstorm about a code word by asking how many ways you can characterize it or what kind of subdivisions it has. If you select a subject from your brainstorming, you can explore it by framing a search question in terms of one of these fundamental questions. Say, for instance, that you have brainstormed about the word *artist* and, upon assessing your information, have decided to explore further the subject of women artists. You could form your search question this way: "Why are there comparatively few women among the ranks of the universally acknowledged great artists?" And you could further examine, organize, and assess much of the information you find on that subject in terms of other questions: "What happened in history to prevent women from freely becoming artists?" "How can I document the relative scarcity of women artists throughout history?" "How does the way women look at the world differ from the way men look at it, and does this difference have implications for their art?" And so on. As you can see, the point is that you can generate considerable information and establish significant perspectives on it by incorporating these questions into your planning strategies.

Once you have restricted and refined your writing project, you can convert one of more of these questions into specific writing strategies that help you *demonstrate* your purpose. On some occasions your information will suggest strategies for demonstrating your purpose: you will see that some of it traces stages or steps, suggesting that you explain how a process is accomplished or why something happened. Or some of it will elaborate upon the meaningful characteristics of someone or something, suggesting that you define your subject. On other occasions, your purpose will determine which strategy or strategies you need to impose on your information in order to sharpen and strengthen your writing. For example, if your purpose entails demonstrating that the United States Olympic gymnastics team is superior to the East German team, then your dominant strategy will be comparison.

Each of the strategies presented in this chapter can be used to develop a paragraph, a section of an essay, or a whole essay. When you select one strategy you do not necessarily exclude the others; in fact, you will very likely find it necessary to combine several of them to suit your needs. For example, Larry *classified* list makers, but he also needed to *define* his general category, *compare* his three subcategories, and *illustrate* how each type followed a certain *process* to compile and use lists. However you decide to employ the strategies, you need to understand the special techniques of each so that you can use them efficiently. The remainder of this chapter presents and analyzes examples of all the strategies except argumentation, which is sufficiently important to warrant an entire chapter of explanation and example (Chapter 10). In the following pages, the examples are annotated to show how writers use the strategies, singly or in combination, to advance their purposes in writing.

Narration

Narration is a story told to make a point. It can be used in an abbreviated form to introduce or illustrate a complicated subject — that is, writers often use narration to lead into the body of their writing — or in an extended form to provide a detailed, personal account of "what happened." An effective narration has a *plot;* it is arranged according to a meaningful and dramatic sequence of action, which may or may not follow the order in which events actually happened. Usually it focuses on some tension or conflict within the writer, or between the writer and others or the writer and the environment.

An effective narration also depends on pace and purpose. *Pace* is the speed with which events are narrated. Sometimes you will need to concentrate on one aspect of an event in great detail in order to *show* what happened. Other times you will need to summarize several related events in a few sentences. In both cases, you are making decisions about how you want to pace the development of your narrative so that you dramatize your purpose for your readers. When you write a narrative you need to choose a *point of view* to establish the person and position of the narrator. If you tell the story as "I" or "we," you are writing in the *first person;* if you recount what "he" or "she" or "they" did, you are writing in the *third person. Position* is the narrator's closeness to the action in both space and time: the narrator may be a participant or observer and may be telling the story as it happens, shortly thereafter, or much later.

In the following narrative excerpt, humorist Garrison Keillor recalls the terror and delight he experienced learning how to swim.

Introduces context for narration

When I was twelve, my cousin Roger drowned in Lake Independence, and my mother enrolled me in a swimming class at the Y.M.C.A. on La Salle Avenue in downtown Minneapolis. Twice a week for most of June and July, I got on the West River Road bus near our home in Brooklyn Park township, a truck-farming community north of Minneapolis, and rode into the stink and heat of the city, and when I rounded the corner of Ninth Street and La Salle and smelled the chlorine air that the building breathed out, I started to feel afraid. After a week, I couldn't bear to go to swimming class anymore.

Introduces point to be developed in the essay (fear of swimming class)

Focuses on one scene (one swimming class)

Never before had I stood naked among strangers (the rule in the class was no swimming trunks), and it was loathsome to undress and then walk quickly through the cold showers to the pool and sit shivering with my feet dangling in the water (Absolute Silence, No Splashing) and wait for the dread moment. The instructor — a man in his early twenties, who was tanned and had the smooth muscles of a swimmer (he wore trunks) — had us plunge into the pool one at a time, so that he could give us his personal attention. He strode up and down the side of the pool yelling at those of us who couldn't swim, while we thrashed hopelessly beneath him and tried to *look* like swimmers. "You're walking on the bottom!" he would shout. "Get your legs up! What's the matter, you afraid to get your face wet? What's *wrong* with you?" The truth was that my cousin's death had instilled in me a terrible fear, and when I tried to swim and started to

Identifies two conflicts
1. self and instructor
2. self and fear of drowning

1

2

sink it felt not so much as if I was sinking but as if something was pulling me down. I panicked, every time. It was just like the dreams of drowning that came to me right after Roger died, in which I was dragged deeper and deeper, with my body bursting and my arms and legs flailing against nothing, down and down, until I shot back to the surface and lay in my dark bedroom exhausted, trying to make myself stay awake.

Summarizes method for avoiding class (several scenes)

Identifies another conflict (self and moral code)

I tried to quit the swimming class, but my mother wouldn't hear of it, so I continued to board the bus every swimming morning, and then, ashamed of myself and knowing God would punish me for my cowardice and deceit, I hurried across La Salle and past the Y and walked along Hennepin Avenue, past the pinball parlors and bars and shoeshine stands to the old public library, where I viewed the Egyptian mummy and the fossils and a facsimile of the Declaration of Independence. I stayed there until eleven-thirty. . . .

Recalls how temporary order was disrupted by new complication (swimming at family picnic)

I still remember the sadness of wandering in downtown Minneapolis in 1954, wasting my life and losing my soul, and my great relief when the class term ended and I became a kid again around the big white house and garden, the green lawns and cool shady ravine of our lovely suburb. A weekend came when we went to a lake for a family picnic, and my mother, sitting on the beach, asked me to swim for her, but I was able to fool her, even at that little distance, by walking on the bottom and making arm strokes.

Explains temporary solution to new complication

Recounts how he resolved old conflicts through self-instruction

When I went to a lake with my friends that summer, or to the Mississippi River a block away, I tried to get the knack of swimming, and one afternoon the next summer I did get it — the crawl and the backstroke and the sidestroke, all in just a couple of weeks. I dived from a dock and opened my eyes underwater and everything. The sad part was that my mother and father couldn't appreciate this wonderful success; to them, I had been a swimmer all along. I felt restored — grateful that I would not be a bum all my life, grateful to God for letting me learn to swim. It was so quick and so simple that I can't remember it today. Probably I just stood in the water and took a little plunge; my feet left the bottom, and that was it. (Garrison Keillor, "Drownings 1954," *Happy to be Here*)

Concludes by emphasizing significance of the narrative

Like most narratives, "Drownings 1954" does not state an explicit thesis. But Keillor does use his introductory paragraph, and particularly the last sentence of that paragraph, to identify the major point of his story. In the second paragraph, Keillor slows down the pace of his narrative to show his readers what actually happened in swimming class. His exposure (no trunks) and immediate fears ("What's the matter, you afraid to get your face wet?") only added to the true anxiety he had felt ever since his cousin's death — his dream of drowning.

Keillor uses the middle of his narrative to summarize his method of avoiding his fears and to establish his sense of guilt about his escapes to the library. Toward the end of this middle section, however, he introduces a new complication — his mother's request that he "swim for her" — which is only temporarily resolved.

In the final section of his narrative, Keillor tells his readers that he finally resolved his conflicts by simply teaching himself how to swim one afternoon the next summer. Although his solution restored him, he acknowledges that his parents could never appreciate his success and that with the passage of time he can hardly remember how he did it.

Discussion Questions	1. **What is the subject of Keillor's narrative essay — learning how to swim, learning how to avoid your fears, learning how to solve your own problems? Explain your answer.**
	2. **What kind of readers does Keillor assume will be interested in his story? What kind of experiences does he assume they share?**
	3. **What is Keillor's purpose in telling this story? Although he does not provide a direct thesis sentence, he does give his readers enough guidance so that they can infer his thesis. Compose a thesis sentence for Keillor's narrative that is *restricted, unified,* and *precise*.**
Writing Exercise	Brainstorm in your journal about your most vivid childhood fears and the methods you used to avoid them. One item on your list should suggest a specific story that you can develop using the narrative strategies evident in Keillor's essay. As you write your essay, anticipate how your readers may relate to your experience and call their attention to your purpose for telling them about it.

Description

Description is a strategy for presenting a verbal portrait of a person, place, or thing. It can be used as a technique to enrich other forms of writing or as a dominant strategy for developing a picture of "what it looks like." A successful description does not depend on merely visual effects, however. It attempts to evoke all the senses by identifying a subject's significant features and by arranging those features in an appropriate pattern. When you describe something, you need to capture both detail and wholeness. You must select specific, vivid details so that you can make your readers see what you see. And you must present these details according to a pattern that helps your readers understand why you think your subject is interesting and significant. Like narration, description needs to make a point; it is not merely a catalogue of facts or a flourish of ornamentation. The following description is reprinted from Louise Bogan's autobiography, *Journey Around My Room.* In this particular passage, Bogan describes the signs that mark the beginning of a new season.

Presents dominant impression to be developed in the portrait

Although the houses stood securely fastened to the ground, as always, everything in the town went wild in autumn and blew about the streets. Smoke blew wildly from chimneys and torrents of leaves were pulled from the trees; they rushed across the sidewalks and blew against wagons and people and trains; they blew uphill and fell from great heights and small ones; they fell to the ground and into the river. Clouds rode high in the sky; the sun shone brilliantly everywhere. Or else half the town would lie in the shadow of a long cloud and half the town would stand shining bright, the weathervanes almost as still in a strong blast coming from one quarter as in no wind at all, the paint sparkling on the clapboards. Sometimes in the late afternoon the full sun came from two directions at once, from the west and reflected in a full blaze from the windows of houses looking westward.

Catalogues list of visual details — smoke, leaves, clouds, sun — that contribute to impression of a "wild" setting

Compares people to objects: children blown home like leaves

The children were blown home from school, shouting and running, along with the leaves. They were blown up paths to side doors, or through orchards, or into back yards, where perhaps their mothers stood, taking the last clothes in off the

1

2

Evokes smells of kitchen

Establishes major point of the description: "Everyone knew what he had to face."

Describes preparations for winter and their effect on the senses — touch (cold); smell (plaster), sight (piano, curtains, books, pictures); taste (tea); sound (low voices and dry leaves)

line, apron strings flying out from their waists. The children rushed into kitchens that smelled of baking or of ironed clothes. The doors swung behind them; some of the wind came in, and some of the leaves. . . .

The whole town, late in October, felt the cold coming on; in bleak afternoons the lights came out early in the frame houses; lights showed clearly across the river in the chill dusk in houses and in the mill. Everyone knew what he had to face. After the blaze of summer that had parched paint and shingle, winter was closing in to freeze wood and stone to the core. The whole house, in winter, turned as cold as a tomb. The upper rooms smelled of cold plaster and cold wood. The parlor was shut; the piano stood shut and freezing against the wall; the lace curtains fell in starched frigid folds down to the cold grain of the carpet. The little padded books on the table, the lace doilies under them, the painted china vases, and the big pictures hanging against the big pattern of the wallpaper all looked distant, desolate, and to no purpose when the door was opened into the room's icy air. The life of the house went on in the sitting room and in the kitchen, for in both these rooms there were stoves. If my mother happened to be on good terms with Mrs. Parsons or with Mrs. Gardner, who lived across the street, they would come to visit her in the early twilight, on those days when the lamps were lit at four o'clock. My mother made tea and the women sat talking in low secret voices beside the kitchen table. I sat in the sitting room, and heard their voices and the sound of dry leaves blowing along the walk at the side of the house. (Louise Bogan, "The Neighborhood," *Journey Around My Room: The Autobiography of Louise Bogan*)

3

Although Bogan does not attempt to prove a specific thesis, she does try to develop a dominant impression of what a change in seasons "looks like." Each detail she presents in her first paragraph — the smoke blowing wildly from the chimneys, the leaves being pulled off the trees and blown throughout the town, the clouds riding high in the sky, and the sun blazing into the windows — develops her opening statement that "everything in the town went wild in autumn."

In her second paragraph, she connects the natural world to the human world as she describes how children were blown home from school like leaves — up the paths, through the orchards, into the back yards, and finally into the warm, redolent sanctuary of the kitchen.

In her last paragraph, Bogan enriches the impression she has created in the first two paragraphs by describing how people prepared to face this change in seasons. Again, she arranges a series of specific sensory details that evoke the changes in the house, as some rooms are turned into cold tombs while others continue to be warmed by stoves, tea, and conversation.

Discussion Questions

1. There are two related subjects in Bogan's description — a change in seasons and the preparations people make to face the change. How are the two subjects connected? How does paragraph 2 help establish that connection?

2. What assumptions does Bogan make about the age and experience of her readers? Does central heating prevent contemporary readers from responding to the scene Bogan describes in the third paragraph? Explain your answer.

3. What is Bogan's purpose for describing this change in season? Does she want to portray simply what it looked and felt like, or does she want to convey some other impression? What impression does she evoke with her last sentence?

Writing Exercise

Freewrite in your journal about the events you notice as you move from any one of the four seasons to the next. Focus particularly on the rituals you and your family enact as you prepare for the new season. Then write a description in which you use specific sensory detail to create a dominant impression of the changes you have observed.

Illustration

Illustration is a method that explains or clarifies your purpose by presenting examples. In a sense, illustration is the most common method of development. Whether you are evoking specific sensory detail for a description or compiling pertinent evidence for an argument, you will need to provide examples to illustrate your purpose. As a distinct writing strategy, however, illustration focuses on either one extended example or a series of related examples. An extended example, if chosen carefully, is so rich in detail and meaning that it will illustrate everything you want to demonstrate about your purpose. A series of examples, if presented and arranged in a logically significant pattern, helps illustrate the extensive evidence available to document your purpose. In the following passage from *King Solomon's Ring,* naturalist Konrad Lorenz uses a series of illustrations to demonstrate his thesis about rearing birds in isolation.

Thesis stated and clarified

Birds reared in isolation from their kind do not generally know what species they belong to: that is to say, not only their social reactions but also their sexual desires are directed towards those beings with whom they have spent certain impressionable phases of their early youth. Consequently, birds raised singly by hand tend to regard human beings, and human beings only, as potential partners in all reproductive activities.

Example 1

A female barnyard goose which I now possess was the only survivor of a brood of six, of which the remainder all succumbed to avian tuberculosis. Consequently she grew up in the company of chickens and, in spite of the fact that we bought for her, in good time, a beautiful gander, she fell head over heels in love with our handsome Rhode Island cock, inundated him with proposals, jealously prevented him from making love to his hens, and remained absolutely insensible to the attentions of the gander.

Example 2

The hero of a similar tragi-comedy was a lovely white peacock of the Schönbrunn Zoo in Vienna. He too was the last survivor of an early-hatched brood which perished in a period of cold weather, and to save him, the keeper put him in the warmest room to be found in the whole Zoo, which at that time was in the reptile house with the giant tortoises. For the rest of his life this unfortunate bird saw only in those huge reptiles the object of his desire and remained unresponsive to the charms of the prettiest peahens. . . .

Example 3

Another tame adult male jackdaw fell in love with me and treated me exactly as a female of his kind. By the hour, this bird tried to make me creep into the nesting cavity of his choice, a few inches in width. He became most importunate in that he continually wanted to feed me with what he considered the choicest delicacies. Remarkably enough, he recognized the human mouth as the orifice of ingestion and he was overjoyed if I opened my lips to him, uttering at the same time an adequate begging note. This must be considered as an act of self-sacrifice on my part, since even I cannot pretend to like the taste of finely minced worms, generously mixed with jackdaw saliva. You will understand that I found it difficult to cooperate with the bird in this manner every few minutes! But if I did not,

I had to guard my ears against him; otherwise, before I knew what was happening, the passage of one of these organs would be filled right up to the drum with warm worm pulp, for jackdaws, when feeding their female or their young, push the food mass, with the aid of their tongue, deep down into the partner's pharynx. However, this bird only made use of my ears when I refused him my mouth, on which the first attempt was always made. (Konrad Z. Lorenz, *King Solomon's Ring*)

In the opening paragraph, Lorenz states his thesis and then clarifies it by a few additional sentences, so that his readers know, in general terms, the main idea he intends to develop. Next he presents three examples drawn from his personal experience to illustrate his thesis. The examples are arranged in a significant pattern that moves from the romance of a barnyard goose to the tragicomedy of a white peacock to the provocative seductive strategies of the jackdaw. The first example seems believable and mildly amusing; the second improbable and fairly absurd; but the third is both convincing and shocking because Lorenz presents it in such vivid personal detail. These three examples, taken collectively, provide dramatic evidence for Lorenz's thesis. Indeed, the examples give the essay its life by illustrating the significance and meaning of the assertions made in the first paragraph.

Discussion Questions

1. How has Lorenz restricted the subject of his essay? For example, what subjects does he mention in his introductory paragraph but exclude as he develops the remainder of his essay?

2. What assumptions does Lorenz make about the scientific knowledge of his readers? Does he think that he is illustrating familiar or new information? Explain your answer.

3. How do each of Lorenz's examples develop his thesis? Why does his last illustration provide the most convincing evidence for his thesis?

Writing Exercise

Compile a list of related examples drawn from your personal experience to illustrate an unusual or controversial thesis. Like Lorenz, you may want to demonstrate a theory you have about rearing animals. Or you may prefer to demonstrate a theory about repairing machines, restoring your body, or remembering information. Determine which of your examples is the most convincing and then arrange them so that they form a logical and dramatic sequence.

Comparison

A *comparison* is a systematic strategy for analyzing and evaluating the similarities of two or more things. (A *contrast* is simply a comparison that emphasizes differences rather than similarities.) An effective comparison attempts to demonstrate one of three general purposes: (1) two things thought to be different are actually similar, (2) two things thought to be similar are really quite different, and (3) two things, although comparable, are not equal — that is, one is better than the other. To demonstrate one of these purposes, you will need to develop your comparison according to one of two strategies: the divided (A + B) or alternating (A/B + A/B).

Before you decide which strategy you want to select, you will need to make some basic decisions about the two things you want to compare. You have to determine which item is the most interesting side of your subject, the most familiar to your readers, and the most important to your purpose. These decisions will help you select which item to place in the A position and which item to place in the B position.

The Divided Pattern of Comparison (A + B)

The most common strategy for developing a comparison is called the *divided pattern*. As its name suggests, this strategy divides the comparison into two separate sections, devoting the first half to a discussion of A and the second half to a discussion of B. The examples in A should be linked to those in B, to unify the contrast of the two parts. One way to achieve that linkage is to follow a similar pattern in both sections: if you make three basic points about A, you then make three basic points about B. You can also arrange your points in the same sequence and, where possible, devote the same amount of space to each point. But such exact pairings are not always necessary. It is more important that the overall effect of A — whatever its sequence or number of examples — establishes a direct contrast with B; thus the two are bound together in the working out of your purpose.

The two main parts of an A + B comparison must develop a cumulative comparison or contrast. A simple description of two unlike houses, for instance, is not necessarily a contrast. It becomes one only when it points up dissimilarities implied in a thesis. The chief exception to this statement is the situation in which one side of the contrast is so well known to readers that it need not be stated. Thus if you are contrasting English rugby with American football for an American audience, you might assume that your readers will be familiar with football but not with those details of rugby that show how different the two games are. In such a contrast, A is already in the mind of your audience, and you need only to explain the significant details of B and let the reader make the contrast.

In the following example, W. H. Auden uses the divided pattern to contrast American and European attitudes toward money:

Thesis identifies A and B and states the contrast.

A.

1. Europeans believe that money can be acquired only at the expense of others.

2. Europeans believe wealth available to only a few.

3. Europeans do not equate money with merit.

4. Europeans see wealth as the power to do what they want.

B.

1a. Americans acquired their money at the expense of national resources.

1b. Americans exploited people but did not make much money off of Indians and slaves.

The most striking difference between an American and a European is the difference in their attitudes towards money. Every European knows, as a matter of historical fact, that, in Europe, wealth could only be acquired at the expense of other human beings, either by conquering them or by exploiting their labor in factories. Further, even after the Industrial Revolution began, the number of persons who could rise from poverty to wealth was small; the vast majority took it for granted that they would not be much richer nor poorer than their fathers. In consequence, no European associates wealth with personal merit or poverty with personal failure. [1]

To a European, money means power, the freedom to do as he likes, which also means that, consciously or unconsciously, he says: "I want to have as much money as possible myself and others to have as little money as possible." [2]

In the United States, wealth was also acquired by stealing, but the real exploited victim was not a human being but poor Mother Earth and her creatures who were ruthlessly plundered. It is true that the Indians were expropriated or exterminated, but this was not, as it had always been in Europe, a matter of the conquerer seizing the wealth of the conquered, for the Indian had never realized the potential riches of his country. It is also true that, in the Southern states, men lived on the labor of slaves, but slave labor did not make them fortunes; what made slavery in the South all the more inexcusable was that, in addition to being morally wicked, it didn't even pay off handsomely. [3]

Thanks to the natural resources of the country, every American, until quite recently, could reasonably look for- [4]

2. Americans assume wealth is available to everyone.

3. Americans equate money with merit, with proof of oneself.

4. Americans see wealth as responsibility — to amass more and to give it away.

ward to making more money than his father, so that, if he made less, the fault must be his; he was either lazy or inefficient. What an American values, therefore, is not the possession of money as such, but his power to make it as a proof of his manhood; once he has proved himself by making it, it has served its function and can be lost or given away. In no society in history have rich men given away so large a part of their fortunes. A poor American feels guilty at being poor, but less guilty than an American rentier[1] who had inherited wealth but is doing nothing to increase it; what can the latter do but take to drink and psychoanalysis? (W. H. Auden, "The Almighty Dollar," *The Dyer's Hand and Other Essays*)

Auden identifies the contrast between Americans and Europeans in his thesis sentence and then quickly reverses their position in order to discuss Europeans first and Americans second. He devotes two paragraphs to each item and, with the exception of his discussion of Indians and slaves in paragraph 3, presents the same kind of information in the same sequence about Europeans and Americans. The directness of the contrast binds the two sections together as matching halves of one whole, thus developing the sense of balance imposed by Auden's purpose statement.

Discussion Questions

1. **Auden's thesis identifies his subject as American and European attitudes toward money. How does he expand and restrict that subject throughout the essay? For example, how does he link the concept of money to words such as *wealth, power, freedom,* and *self-worth?***

2. **Why do you think Auden reverses the A (American) and B (European) of his thesis statement? Whom does he consider his primary audience — Americans or Europeans? How do you know? How might his decision about the identity of his audience influence which subject he discusses first and which subject he discusses last?**

3. **Do all the items in Auden's essay contribute to the development of his thesis? How effective is his attempt to explain away the exploitation of**

---

1. French for "a person living on private means."

Indians and slaves? In what ways is the American *rentier* similar to his or her European counterpart?

Writing Exercise

Speculate in your journal on some of the similarities and differences you have observed between *your* world and another world *out there*. For example, you could compare your image of a particular place with the reality you discovered once you actually visited it. You could compare some of your family's routines inherited from its "foreign" background with the more familiar routines of American families. Or you could compare American attitudes toward a word such as *frontier* and another country's attitude toward that word (or similar words such as *border*). In any case, select a major point of comparison or contrast, line up the subpoints of your comparison, decide which items you want to present first and last, and then write an essay that demonstrates one of the three purposes for a comparison essay listed on page 168.

The Alternating Pattern of Comparison (A/B + A/B)

In the *alternating pattern* for developing your material, the details of A and B are not grouped separately but are presented in matched pairs, sometimes in the same paragraph, sometimes in the same sentence. The divided pattern is more common, perhaps, because it is an easier pattern to organize and control, particularly in short essays. But unless you have a clear, controlling thesis that establishes a connection between the two items, you may discover that you have written two separate essays. The alternating pattern requires you to organize your material more precisely, especially in a longer piece of writing. But the pattern is often easier and more interesting for your reader, because the point-by-point development reinforces the comparison with every pair of matched details, and often the balanced sentence structure emphasizes the comparison or contrast. Gerald Hawkins uses the alternating pattern in the following passage to compare the computer (A) and the brain (B):

Thesis

Presently it is a popular occupation among the computer fraternity to compare their mechanism to the human brain. The conclusions are not disheartening — marvelous as the machines are, the brain seems still a good deal more marvelous. Like the mills of the gods, it grinds slow compared to the machines, but it grinds exceeding fine — it is original, imaginative, resourceful, free in will and choice. The machine operates at a speed

A/B (speed)

A/B (path)

A/B (components)

B/A (size)

A/B (free will)

approaching that of light, 186,000 mi. per sec., whereas the brain operates at the speed at which impulses move along nerve fiber, perhaps a million times slower — but the machine operates linearly, that is, it sends an impulse of "thought" along one path, so that if that path proves to be a dead end the "thought" must back up to the last fork in the road and try again, and if the "thought" is derailed the whole process must be begun again; the brain operates in some mysterious multipath fashion whereby a thought apparently splits and moves along several different paths simultaneously so that no matter what happens to any one of its branches there are others groping along. And whereas even a transistorized computer has a fairly modest number of components, the brain, it seems, has literally billions of neurons, or memory-and-operation cells. To rival an average human brain a computer built by present techniques would have to be about as big as an ocean liner, or a skyscraper. And even then it would lack the capacity for originality and free will. To initiate free choice in a machine the operator would have to insert into its program random numbers, which would make the machine "free" but uncoordinated — an idiot. (Gerald S. Hawkins, *Stonehenge Decoded*)

This passage could have been written as a two-paragraph structure, with everything about the computer (A) in the first paragraph and everything about the brain (B) in the second. The structure of the two patterns is outlined below:

Alternating pattern	Divided pattern
A/B 1 Speed	A Computer
Computer	1 Speed
Brain	2 Path of thought
A/B 2 Path of thought	3 Number of components
Computer	4 Relative size
Brain	5 Free will
A/B 3 Number of components	B Brain
Computer	1 Speed
Brain	2 Path of thought
A/B 4 Relative size	3 Number of components
Brain	4 Relative size
Computer	5 Free will
A/B 5 Free will	
Computer	
Brain	

Discussion Questions

1. How does Hawkins's first sentence identify the source for the general subject of his essay? How does his second sentence restrict his subject to suit his own purpose?

2. In what ways does Hawkins's selection of the alternating pattern anticipate the needs of his audience? As a reader, what difficulties might you encounter if this essay were organized according to the divided pattern?

3. Consult the three general purposes for a comparison essay listed on page 168. How does presenting the computer first and the brain second emphasize Hawkins's thesis?

Writing Exercise

Read through several popular magazines or newspapers, looking for comparisons that are made in different areas: medicine (the heart is like a pump), politics (an election campaign is like a war), defense (a war is like a game), sports (professional sport is like professional entertainment), travel (country A is like a garden). Examine the points of comparison between the two items, and then write a comparison according to one of the two patterns. If the items you select allow you to argue that one is better than the other (school is better than jail), then arrange your essay so that you can present your information on the superior item in the second position.

Classification

Classification is a strategy for organizing information into groups and categories. An effective classification begins by defining a subject and then dividing it into major categories each of which shares some common trait. Next the categories are arranged in a sequence so that your reader can see that the division is *consistent* (the same principle is used to classify each category), *complete* (there are no major categories omitted), and *significant* (the categories and subcategories are arranged in order to demonstrate some purpose).

Like the process of comparison, classification builds on your readers' expectations of precision, balance, and order. First, call your readers' attention to the principle you have used to classify your subject by giving each category an identifying label. Next, be sure that you devote approximately the same amount of space to each category. And finally, arrange your categories and the subpoints within them so that your reader is able to follow the logic of your classification system. Larry's outline for his essay on list makers (pages 107–108) provides an effective illustration of classification. Classification is often used to advance a writer's humorous purpose, as shown in the following essay by Russell Baker, which classifies inanimate objects into three major categories.

States thesis that inanimate objects can be classified into three major categories; gives each category an identifying label	Inanimate objects are classified into three major categories — those that don't work, those that break down and those that get lost. 1
Explains principle of division, thereby expanding thesis to reveal a larger purpose	The goal of all inanimate objects is to resist man and ultimately to defeat him, and the three major classifications are based on the method each object uses to achieve its purpose. As a general rule, any object capable of breaking down at the moment when it is most needed will do so. The automobile is typical of the category. 2
Introduces category 1 (automobile as major example)	With the cunning typical of its breed, the automobile never breaks down while entering a filling station with a large staff of idle mechanics. It waits until it reaches a downtown intersection in the middle of the rush hour, or until it is fully loaded with family and luggage on the Ohio Turnpike. 3
	Thus it creates maximum misery, inconvenience, frustration and irritability among its human cargo, thereby reducing its owner's life span. 4
Cites other examples	Washing machines, garbage disposals, lawn mowers, light bulbs, automatic laundry dryers, water pipes, furnaces, electrical fuses, television tubes, hose nozzles, tape recorders, slide projectors — all are in league with the automobile to take their turn at breaking down whenever life threatens to flow smoothly for their human enemies. 5
Introduces category 2 (several examples)	Many inanimate objects, of course, find it extremely difficult to break down. Pliers, for example, and gloves and keys are almost totally incapable of breaking down. Therefore, they have had to evolve a different technique for resisting man. 6
	They get lost. Science has still not solved the mystery of how they do it, and no man has ever caught one of them in the act of getting lost. The most plausible theory is that they have developed a secret method of locomotion which they are able to conceal the instant a human eye falls upon them. 7

It is not uncommon for a pair of pliers to climb all the 8
way from the cellar to the attic in its single-minded determination to raise its owner's blood pressure. Keys have been known to burrow three feet under mattresses. Women's purses, despite their great weight, frequently travel through six or seven rooms to find hiding space under a couch.

Compares categories 1 and 2 (cites examples)

Scientists have been struck by the fact that things that 9
break down virtually never get lost, while things that get lost hardly ever break down.

A furnace, for example, will invariably break down at the 10
depth of the first winter cold wave, but it will never get lost. A woman's purse, which after all does have some inherent capacity for breaking down, hardly ever does; it almost invariably chooses to get lost.

Some persons believe this constitutes evidence that inanimate objects are not entirely hostile to man, and that a 11
negotiated peace is possible. After all, they point out, a furnace could infuriate a man even more thoroughly by getting lost than by breaking down, just as a glove could upset him far more by breaking down than by getting lost.

Not everyone agrees, however, that this indicates a conciliatory attitude among inanimate objects. Many say it 12
merely proves that furnaces, gloves and pliers are incredibly stupid.

Introduces category 3 (cites examples)

The third class of objects — those that don't work — is the 13
most curious of all. These include such objects as barometers, car clocks, cigarette lighters, flashlights and toy-train locomotives. It is inaccurate, of course, to say that they never work. They work once, usually for the first few hours after being brought home, and then quit. Thereafter, they never work again.

In fact, it is widely assumed that they are built for the 14
purpose of not working. Some people have reached advanced ages without ever seeing some of these objects — barometers, for example — in working order.

Explains importance of category 3 in system

Science is utterly baffled by the entire category. There are 15
many theories about it. The most interesting holds that the things that don't work have attained the highest state possible for an inanimate object, the state to which things that break down and things that get lost can still only aspire.

They have truly defeated man by conditioning him never 16

to expect anything of them, and in return they have given man the only peace he receives from inanimate society. He does not expect his barometer to work, his electric locomotive to run, his cigarette lighter to light or his flashlight to illuminate, and when they don't, it does not raise his blood pressure.

Analyzes relationship of system to human emotions

He cannot attain that peace with furnaces and keys and cars and women's purses as long as he demands that they work for their keep. (Russell Baker, "The Plot Against People")   17

Like Auden, Baker introduces certain expectations in his readers' minds in his thesis sentence, but then quickly scraps those expectations by scrambling his categories. His thesis argues for a sequence of (1) things that don't work, (2) things that break down, and (3) things that get lost. But his essay presents a different sequence: (1) things that break down, (2) things that get lost, and (3) things that don't work. For each category he presents at least one major example — automobile, keys, and barometer — and usually several other examples to suggest that he has exhausted each category. He also compares two of the categories to make sure that his readers understand the logical distinctions he is trying to establish. And finally, he underlines at several points the reason he is classifying inanimate objects — to prove that their goal is to resist, baffle, and defeat human beings.

Discussion Questions

1. How does the title of Baker's essay, "The Plot Against People," prepare you for the real subject of this classification of things? How "scientific" is his evidence for this plot?

2. What assumptions does Baker make about the reactions of his audience to this essay? What common experiences does he assume they share?

3. Why does Baker scramble the sequence of categories he presents in his thesis sentence? What logical pattern does he use to develop the sequence he presents in his essay? In what way is the last category the most important for demonstrating his purpose?

Writing Exercise

Interview your friends or members of your family about their experience with inanimate objects such as tools or machines. Instead of focusing on the objects, as Baker does, focus on their users. Try to classify at least three kinds of people according to how they relate to their tools or machines. Your categories may even allow you to reverse Baker's thesis. That is, you may be able to prove that machines do not destroy human beings, but rather, given the right kind of human being, provide creative extensions of the human imagination.

Process Analysis

A *process* is a sequence of operations or actions by which something is done or made. The development of the human embryo from conception to birth is one process; the procedure by which the citizens of the United States elect a president is another. To analyze a process effectively, you must know it thoroughly or learn as much as you can about it. Next, you must divide the process into steps or stages. You must make this division carefully because you may have to combine several small steps into one large step, advise that certain steps be suspended while others are completed, or warn that specific steps should not be overlooked or reversed. After you have divided the process into steps, you must explain each one, acknowledging as you go how each step connects to the next and what special knowledge or tools will be needed to complete it.

You must also make a careful assessment of your audience to determine whether you want to give them instructions on "how-to-do-something" or provide them with information on "how-something-works" or "how-something-is-done." In the first case, your readers will want to know enough about the process so that they can actually perform it; this kind of process often concerns assembling or making something (a volleyball set; an herb garden) or following directions (in a recipe; during travel). In the second case, they may be interested in the stages of a particular operation and how that operation is completed, even though they have no direct involvement in that process. In the following process analysis, writer George Orwell analyzes how the process of mining coal works:

Introduces process to be analyzed (acknowledges his own limits as an expert)

When you have been down two or three pits you begin to get some grasp of the processes that are going on underground. (I ought to say, by the way, that I know nothing whatever about the technical side of mining: I am merely

1

Compares unfamiliar process to familiar one

Explains earlier procedure

Analyzes step 1: describes special tool; details smaller steps within step 1

Acknowledges negative effects

Analyzes step 2: describes special tool; details smaller steps within step 2

Advises about possible dangers

Analyzes step 3: describes special tool; details smaller steps within step 3

describing what I have seen.) Coal lies in thin seams between enormous layers of rock, so that essentially the process of getting it out is like scooping the central layer from a Neapolitan ice. In the old days the miners used to cut straight into the coal with pick and crowbar — a very slow job because coal, when lying in its virgin state, is almost as hard as rock. Nowadays the preliminary work is done by an electrically-driven coal-cutter, which in principle is an immensely tough and powerful band-saw, running horizontally instead of vertically, with teeth a couple of inches long and half an inch or an inch thick. It can move backwards or forwards on its own power, and the men operating it can rotate it this way and that. Incidentally it makes one of the most awful noises I have ever heard, and sends forth clouds of coal dust which make it impossible to see more than two or three feet and almost impossible to breathe. The machine travels along the coal face cutting into the base of the coal and undermining it to the depth of five feet or five feet and a half; after this it is comparatively easy to extract the coal to the depth to which it has been undermined. Where it is "difficult getting," however, it has also to be loosened with explosives. A man with an electric drill, like a rather smaller version of the drills used in street-mending, bores holes at intervals in the coal, inserts blasting powder, plugs it with clay, goes round the corner if there is one handy (he is supposed to retire to twenty-five yards distance) and touches off the charge with an electric current. This is not intended to bring the coal out, only to loosen it. Occasionally, of course, the charge is too powerful, and then it not only brings the coal out but brings the roof down as well.

After the blasting has been done the "fillers" can tumble the coal out, break it up and shovel it on to the conveyor belt. It comes out at first in monstrous boulders which may weigh anything up to twenty tons. The conveyor belt shoots it on to tubs, and the tubs are shoved into the main road and hitched on to an endlessly revolving steel cable which drags them to the cage. Then they are hoisted, and at the surface the coal is sorted by being run over screens, and if necessary is washed as well. As far as possible the "dirt" — the shale, that is — is used for making the roads below. All that cannot be used is sent to the surface and dumped; hence the

Acknowledges negative effects of process

Explains how process is repeated

Summarizes the timing of the three-step sequence

monstrous "dirt-heaps," like hideous grey mountains, which are the characteristic scenery of the coal areas. When the coal has been extracted to the depth to which the machine has cut, the coal face has advanced by five feet. Fresh props are put in to hold up the newly exposed roof, and during the next shift the conveyor belt is taken to pieces, moved five feet forward and re-assembled. As far as possible the three operations of cutting, blasting and extraction are done in three separate shifts, the cutting in the afternoon, the blasting at night (there is a law, not always kept, that forbids its being done when there are other men working near by), and the "filling" in the morning shift, which lasts from six in the morning until half past one. (George Orwell, from *The Road to Wigan Pier*)

Orwell is not an expert on the technical side of mining, but he is a careful observer of this complicated and dangerous process. He divides the mining of coal into three major stages — cutting, blasting, and extraction. As he analyzes the many small steps he has observed within each of the large stages, he focuses his attention on the special tools required to complete each job — the coal cutter, the electric drill, and the conveyor belt. Operating these tools requires the skills of an expert, but even the most expert workers produce negative side effects with their work, such as the constant noise and dust, the possibility of mismanaged explosion, and the growing "dirt-heaps" outside the mine. Although Orwell's analysis is not detailed enough to tell his readers "how-to-do-it," it does provide them with enough information to understand "how-it-is-done."

Discussion Questions

1. **How does Orwell make this dingy subject interesting and significant? What specific sentences in his analysis enable you to understand why the process fascinates him?**

2. **What does Orwell assume about the knowledge of his readers? How does his second sentence help him to anticipate and control their expectations?**

3. **In addition to providing information on mining coal, what other purpose is Orwell trying to demonstrate? For example, does his analysis make this process seem easier or more difficult than you supposed?**

**Writing
Exercise**

Observe the steps in a process unknown to you (recall Jenny's observation of the processes in the Varsity Barbershop). Next divide the process into its major stages and the smaller steps within each stage. Then interview an expert who knows all the little tricks and hidden steps that must be performed accurately if the process is to produce successful results. Use this information to write a process analysis that allows your readers to "see" how it is done.

Causal Analysis

A *causal analysis* attempts to explain why something happened or happens. Like a process analysis, a causal analysis focuses on a sequence of steps that produce a result. It differs from a process analysis, however, in that it is primarily concerned with *causes* and *effects.* One strategy for developing such an analysis is to describe an action or event and then demonstrate what effects it produces. Another strategy is to describe the action or event and then determine what caused it to happen. A third strategy is to examine two related actions or events and try to prove that there is a cause-and-effect connection between them.

In each case, you must be careful not to oversimplify or exaggerate the cause-and-effect relationship. Sometimes you can mistake a simple coincidence for a cause-and-effect relationship. Other times you may be tempted to identify one cause as *the* direct cause when in fact any number of complex causes (working independently or in combination) could produce the same effect. In the following essay, journalist Ellen Goodman analyzes the causes and effects of secretary stress.

*Introduces subject of secretary stress
and its eventual effect — heart disease*

They used to say it with flowers or celebrate it with a somewhat liquid lunch. National Secretaries Week was always good for at least a token of appreciation. But the way the figures add up now, the best thing a boss can do for a secretary this week is cough up for her cardiogram.   1

*Suggests cause-and-effect relationship
between health of secretary and health
of boss*

"Stress and the Secretary" has become the hottest new syndrome on the heart circuit.   2

It seems that it isn't those Daring Young Women in their Dress-for-Success Suits who are following men down the cardiovascular trail to ruin. Nor is it the female profes-   3 sionals who are winning their equal place in intensive care units.

It is powerlessness and not power that corrupts women's hearts. And clerical workers are the number one victims.   4

Examines study that proves effect — heart disease — is higher among secretaries than other women

In the prestigious Framingham study, Dr. Suzanne Haynes, an epidemiologist with the National Heart, Lung and Blood Institute, found that working women as a whole have no higher rate of heart disease than housewives. But women employed in clerical and sales occupations do. Their coronary disease rates are twice that of other women.   5

"This is not something to ignore," says Dr. Haynes, "since such a high percent of women work at clerical jobs." In fact, 35 percent of all working women, or 18 million of us, hold these jobs.   6

Cites one cause of secretary stress — family situation

When Dr. Haynes looked into their private lives, she found the women at greatest risk — with a one in five chance of heart disease — were clerical workers with blue-collar husbands, and three or more children. When she then looked at their work lives, she discovered that the ones who actually developed heart disease were those with nonsupportive bosses who hadn't changed jobs very often and who had trouble letting their anger out.   7

In short, being frustrated, dead-ended, without a feeling of control over your life is bad for your health.   8

The irony in all the various and sundry heart statistics is that we now have a weird portrait of the Cardiovascular Fun Couple of the Office: The Type A boss and his secretary. The male heart disease stereotype is, after all, the Type A aggressive man who always needs to be in control, who lives with a great sense of time urgency . . . and is likely to be a white-collar boss.   9

Cites second cause — inability to express anger

Cites third cause — lack of job satisfaction

Cites fourth cause — Type A boss

"The Type A man is trying to be in control. But given the way most businesses are organized there are, in fact, few ways for them to be in control of their jobs," says Dr. Haynes. The only thing the Type A boss can be in control of is his secretary who in turn feels . . . well you get the picture. He's not only getting heart disease, he's giving it.   10

Cites fifth cause — the computer

As if all this weren't enough to send you out for the annual three martini lunch, clerical workers are increasingly working for a new Type A boss: the computer.   11

These days fewer women are sitting in front of bosses with notepads and more are sitting in front of Visual Display Terminals. Word processors, data processors, microprocessors . . . these are the demanding, time-conscious, new automatons of automations. 12

There is nothing intrinsically evil about computers. I am writing this on a VDT and if you try to take it away from me, I will break your arm. But as Working Women, the national association of office workers, puts it in their release this week, automation is increasingly producing clerical jobs that are de-skilled, down-graded, dead-ended and dissatisfying. 13

Describes effect of computer on work place

As Karen Nussbaum of the Cleveland office described it, the office of the future may well be the factory of the past. Work on computers is often reduced to simple, repetitive, monotonous tasks. Workers are often expected to produce more for no more pay, and there are also reports of a disturbing trend to processing speed-ups and piece-rate pay, and a feeling among clerical workers that their jobs are computer controlled. 14

"It's not the machine, but the way it's used by employers," says Working Women's research director, Judith Gregory. Too often, automation's most important product is stress. 15

Groups, like Working Women, are trying to get clerical workers to organize in what they call "a race against time" so that computers will become their tools instead of their supervisors. 16

Summarizes complex causes of stress and suggests solution (jogging) to minimize possibility of effect (heart disease)

But in the meantime, if you are (1) a female clerical worker, (2) with a blue-collar husband, (3) with three or more children, (4) in a dead-end job, (5) without any way to express anger, (6) with a Type A boss, (7) or a Type A computer controlling your work day . . . *You better start jogging.* (Ellen Goodman, "Being a Secretary Can Be Hazardous to Your Health," *At Large*) 17

Goodman examines one of the most discussed and least understood causes of heart disease — stress. Although her analysis is short, she is able to demonstrate that one particular group of people — secretaries — experience a great deal of stress. As she assesses each of the causes that produce this stress, she is also arguing that stress is the cause of something else. Indeed, each one of these causes, considered individually or collectively, can create the kind of stress that cardiologists identify as a contributing cause of heart attacks. Goodman uses a research study and personal testimony to concentrate on two causes in some detail. She suggests that there is a cause-and-effect relationship between the behavior of Type A bosses — likely candidates for a heart attack — and their secretaries. She also suggests that for all the good effects produced by the computer, its most important effect may be negative — it produces stress. In her final sentence, Goodman suggests another cause-and-effect relationship: jogging causes you to relax. In other words, its effect is to reduce stress.

Discussion Questions

1. Although Goodman's primary subject is the causes of secretary stress, she seems equally interested in the effects of stress. How does her title help you to identify both aspects of her subject?

2. Who does Goodman imagine as the primary audience for her essay — cardiologists, bosses, secretaries? How do you know? Which group does she address directly in her last paragraph?

3. What is Goodman's purpose in this essay? Is she merely interested in establishing the causes of secretary stress or does she have some larger, though unstated, purpose in mind? How would you state that purpose?

Writing Exercise

Stress is a normal emotion that you experience whether you are anticipating a weekend vacation or worrying about a week of final examinations. In other words, there is good and bad stress. Unfortunately, your body reacts the same way to each kind of stress. Select a job or activity that produces stress for you or for someone you know well. Examine it carefully, and then write an essay in which you analyze the causes that produce the stress.

Definition

The function of *definition* is to provide a necessary explanation of a word or concept. The explanation may be simply the substitution of a familiar word for the one being defined, as when you substitute *cancer* for

By permission of Johnny Hart and Field Enterprises, Inc.

carcinoma. It may be the addition of a phrase, as when you define *vintage* as "the yield of wine or grapes from a particular vineyard or district in one season." It may be a single sentence: "In the theater, a *prompter* is an individual who provides cues for the actors or singers on stage." Or the definition may consist of one or more paragraphs, or even a whole essay, in which you explain a subject in depth.

The length and complexity of a definition depend on your purpose.

That is, they depend on what you want to say about the subject and how you want to say it for the kind of reader being addressed. No definition of *thrombosis* would be necessary for a physician, but one might be advisable for most readers. In some situations, all that would be necessary would be to insert "a blood clot in an artery or vein" in parentheses after the word *thrombosis;* in others, you might feel it necessary to explain the process by which thrombosis develops and the effects it produces. How much definition is required is relative to the situation in which the definition is being made.

Definitions may be classified as three types: short, stipulative, or extended. A *short* definition, like the definitions of *carcinoma, vintage,* and *prompter* above, explains a word by a brief identification of its meaning. This is the kind of definition that dictionaries provide.

Stipulative definitions identify the particular meaning you intend to use in your writing. Because words may have several meanings, it is sometimes important to specify which meaning is being used in a particular passage. For example, in some parts of the United States the word *liberal* often has unfavorable connotations when applied to a politician. So a candidate for political office, on being called a liberal, is likely to reply, "I am not a liberal," or maybe, "Yes, I am a liberal, but only in the true sense of that word. I believe in the freedom of individuals to think, speak, and act according to their consciences. That is what the word *liberal* originally meant — freedom — and what it still means in reputable dictionaries." Here the candidate is making a stipulative definition by emphasizing one meaning to the exclusion of others. Provided that stipulative definitions are used to clarify an issue, not to obscure it, they are legitimate and useful means of defining. When the Supreme Court rules on how "due process of law" is to be interpreted, it is making a stipulative definition. It is saying in effect, "This is what *due process* must mean in a court of law." The definition of *purpose* on page 23 is another example of stipulative definition.

Extended definitions may include both short and stipulative definitions, but they go far beyond both. They are essentially essays that seek to explain the writer's view of a subject, something that cannot be done effectively in a short definition. An extended definition may begin with a dictionary definition, but it goes on to add to, modify, and illustrate that definition. In so doing, it may use any of the patterns of development discussed earlier in this chapter: it may compare or contrast one meaning with another; it may classify the subject by showing to what class it belongs and what its subclasses are; it may provide illustrative examples; it may treat the subject as a process. It may even combine two or more of these strategies, as poet Laurie Lee does in his extended definition of charm.

Thesis: Defines by simple substitution: "Charm is . . ."

Charm is the ultimate weapon, the supreme seduction, against which there are few defences. If you've got it, you need almost nothing else, neither money, looks, nor pedigree. It's a gift, only given to give away, and the more used the more there is. It is also a climate of behaviour set for perpetual summer and thermostatically controlled by taste and tact. . . .

Defines the "process" by which it is acquired

You recognize charm by the feeling you get in its presence. You know who has it. But can you get it, too? Properly, you can't, because it's a quickness of spirit, an originality of touch you have to be born with. Or it's something that grows naturally out of another quality, like the simple desire to make people happy. Certainly, charm is not

Defines negatively: "Charm is not . . ."

a question of learning palpable tricks, like wrinkling your nose, or having a laugh in your voice, or gaily tossing your hair out of your dancing eyes and twisting your mouth into succulent love-knots. Such signs, to the nervous, are ominous warnings which may well send him streaking for cover. On the other hand, there is an antenna, a built-in awareness of others, which most people have, and which care can nourish.

Defines by classifying qualities of charm

But in a study of charm, what else does one look for? Apart from the ability to listen — rarest of all human virtues and most difficult to sustain without vagueness — apart from warmth, sensitivity, and the power to please, what else is there visible? A generosity, I suppose, which makes no demands, a transaction which strikes no bargains, which doesn't hold itself back till you've filled up a test-card making it clear that you're worth the trouble. Charm can't withhold, but spends itself willingly on young and old alike, on the poor, the ugly, the dim, the boring, on the last fat

Defines by describing its effect on the person who possesses it

man in the corner. It reveals itself also in a sense of ease, in casual but perfect manners, and often in a physical grace which springs less from an accident of youth than from a

1

2

3

confident serenity of mind. Any person with this is more than just a popular fellow, he is also a social healer.

Charm, in the abstract, has something of the quality of music: radiance, balance, and harmony. One encounters it unexpectedly in odd corners of life with a shock of brief, inexplicable ravishment: in a massed flight of birds, a string of running horses, an arrangement of clouds on the sea; wooded islands, Tanagra figures, old balconies in Spain, the line of a sports car holding a corner, in the writings of Proust and Jane Austen, the paintings of Renoir and Fragonard, the poetry of Herrick, the sound of lute and guitar.... Thickets of leaves can have it, bare arms interlocking, suds of rain racing under a bridge, and such simplicities as waking after a sleep of nightmares to see sunlight bouncing off the ceiling. The effect of these, like many others, is to restore one's place in the world; to reassure, as it were, one's relationship with things, and to bring order to the wilderness. **4**

But charm, in the end, is flesh and blood, a most potent act of behaviour, the laying down of a carpet by one person for another to give his existence a moment of honour. Much is deployed in the weaponry of human dealings: stealth, aggression, blackmail, lust, the urge to possess, devour, and destroy. Charm is the rarest, least used, and most invincible of powers, which can capture with a single glance. It is close to love in that it moves without force, bearing gifts like the growth of daylight. It snares completely, but is never punitive, it disarms by being itself disarmed, strikes without wounds, wins wars without casualties — though not, of course, without victims. He who would fall in the battle, let him fall to charm, and he will never be humbled, or know the taste of defeat. **5**

In the armoury of man, charm is the enchanted dart, light and subtle as a hummingbird. But it is deceptive in one thing — like a sense of humour, if you think you've got it, you probably haven't. (Laurie Lee, "Charm," *I Can't Stay Long*) **6**

Defines by a series of illustrations

Defines by contrast with other qualities (aggression) and by comparison to similar qualities (love)

Defines by analyzing its effect on others

Lee uses most of the strategies of development to define what is both an immediately recognizable and yet somehow an ultimately unattainable quality — charm. He begins his definition by stating his thesis that "charm is the ultimate weapon" and then adds a few more aphorisms that suggest simple substitutions: charm is . . . the supreme seduction, a gift, a climate of behavior. In paragraph 2, he moves on to the process of "how-you-get-it." He argues that you can't acquire it or fake it with a few tricks but that it grows naturally out of a desire to make people happy. In paragraph 3, he tries to classify the various subqualities of charm — the ability to listen, warmth, generosity — before he describes its effect on the person who possesses it. In paragraphs 4 and 5, he illustrates charm through a series of examples and compares and contrasts it to other human qualities. He concludes by asserting that charm is a selfless, unconscious quality — "if you think you've got it, you probably haven't."

<table>
<tr><td>

Discussion Questions

</td><td>

1. How does Lee make his subject interesting and significant? For example, how does he use his opening sentence to make an apparently pleasant word seem controversial?

2. What kind of audience does Lee assume will read his essay? Are they people who, by his definition, possess charm? How does he "seduce" his readers into helping him define the word?

3. What is Lee's purpose in trying to define charm? Does he mean to prove that it is recognizable but undefinable, definable but unattainable, attainable but often deceptive? In what ways does Lee's last sentence about charm confirm or contradict his opening assertion about the word?

</td></tr>
<tr><td>

Writing Exercise

</td><td>

Select a word that you have encountered in some direct way such as *stress, trash,* or *glitter.* Try to avoid difficult, abstract words like *truth* or *happiness.* Begin by writing down a few simple statements about your word: "glitter is . . ." Then look the word up in a dictionary to determine its precise meaning and in a thesaurus to discover words that have similar meanings. Next write out a series of negative definitions ("glitter is *not* . . .") and subtle comparisons ("glitter may seem similar to flashiness, but . . ."). Finally, identify one extended example (or several related examples) from your personal experience that help you understand the word. Arrange this information into appropriate clusters, and then write an extended definition in which you demonstrate a particular thesis about your word.

</td></tr>
</table>

Review Exercise

The following essay by British novelist and essayist E. M. Forster reflects several strategies of development. Identify those strategies by annotating the essay in the manner in which the examples throughout this chapter are annotated. Do you think that any one of the strategies predominates — that is, can the essay be said to be an example of a particular strategy? What is Forster's thesis in this essay? His purpose?

A few years ago I wrote a book which dealt in part with the difficulties of the English in India. Feeling that they would have had no difficulties in India themselves, the Americans read the book freely. The more they read it the better it made them feel, and a cheque to the author was the result. I bought a wood with the cheque. It is not a large wood — it contains scarcely any trees, and it is intersected, blast it, by a public footpath. Still, it is the first property that I have owned, so it is right that other people should participate in my shame, and should ask themselves, in accents that will vary in horror, this very important question: What is the effect of property upon the character? Don't let's touch economics; the effect of private ownership upon the community as a whole is another question — a more important question, perhaps, but another one. Let's keep to psychology. If you own things, what's their effect on you? What's the effect on me of my wood?

In the first place, it makes me feel heavy. Property does have this effect. Property produces men of weight, and it was a man of weight who failed to get into the Kingdom of Heaven. He was not wicked, that unfortunate millionaire in the parable, he was only stout; he stuck out in front, not to mention behind, and as he wedged himself this way and that in the crystalline entrance and bruised his well-fed flanks, he saw beneath him a comparatively slim camel passing through the eye of a needle and being woven into the robe of God. The Gospels all through couple stoutness and slowness. They point out what is perfectly obvious, yet seldom realized: that if you have a lot of things you cannot move about a lot, that furniture requires dusting, dusters require servants, servants require insurance stamps, and the whole tangle of them makes you think twice before you accept an invitation to dinner or go for a bathe in the Jordan. Sometimes the Gospels proceed further and say with Tolstoy that property is sinful; they approach the

1

2

difficult ground of asceticism here, where I cannot follow them. But as to the immediate effects of property on people, they just show straightforward logic. It produces men of weight. Men of weight cannot, by definition, move like the lightning from the East unto the West, and the ascent of a fourteen-stone bishop into a pulpit is thus the exact antithesis of the coming of the Son of Man. My wood makes me feel heavy.

In the second place, it makes me feel it ought to be larger. 3

The other day I heard a twig snap in it. I was annoyed at first, for I 4 thought that someone was blackberrying, and depreciating the value of the undergrowth. On coming nearer, I saw it was not a man who had trodden on the twig and snapped it, but a bird, and I felt pleased. My bird. The bird was not equally pleased. Ignoring the relation between us, it took fright as soon as it saw the shape of my face, and flew straight over the boundary hedge into a field, the property of Mrs. Henessy, where it sat down with a loud squawk. It had become Mrs. Henessy's bird. Something seemed grossly amiss here, something that would not have occurred had the wood been larger. I could not afford to buy Mrs. Henessy out, I dared not murder her, and limitations of this sort beset me on every side. . . .

In the third place, property makes its owner feel that he ought to do 5 something to it. Yet he isn't sure what. A restlessness comes over him, a vague sense that he has a personality to express — the same sense which, without any vagueness, leads the artist to an act of creation. Sometimes I think I will cut down such trees as remain in the wood, at other times I want to fill up the gaps between them with new trees. Both impulses are pretentious and empty. They are not honest movements towards moneymaking or beauty. They spring from a foolish desire to express myself and from an inability to enjoy what I have got. Creation, property, enjoyment form a sinister trinity in the human mind. Creation and enjoyment are both very, very good, yet they are often unattainable without a material basis, and at such moments property pushes itself in as a substitute, saying, "Accept me instead — I'm good enough for all three." It is not enough. It is, as Shakespeare said of lust, "The expense of spirit in a waste of shame": it is "Before, a joy proposed; behind, a dream." Yet we don't know how to shun it. It is forced on us by our economic system as the alternative to starvation. It is also forced on us by an internal defect in the soul, by the feeling that in property may lie the germs of self-development and of exquisite or heroic deeds. Our life on earth is, and ought to be, material and carnal. But we have not yet learned to manage our materialism and carnality properly; they are still entangled with the desire for owner-ship, where (in the words of Dante) "Possession is one with loss."

And this brings us to our fourth and final point: the blackberries. 6

Blackberries are not plentiful in this meagre grove, but they are 7 easily seen from the public footpath which traverses it, and all too easily gathered. Foxgloves, too — people will pull up the foxgloves, and ladies of an educational tendency even grub for toadstools to show them on the Monday in class. Other ladies, less educated, roll down the bracken in the arms of their gentlemen friends. There is paper, there are tins. Pray, does my wood belong to me or doesn't it? And, if it does, should I not own it best by allowing no one else to walk there? There is a wood near Lyme Regis, also cursed by a public footpath, where the owner has not hesitated on this point. He had built high stone walls each side of the path, and has spanned it by bridges, so that the public circulate like termites while he gorges on the blackberries unseen. He really does own his wood, this able chap. And perhaps I shall come to this in time. I shall wall in and fence out until I really taste the sweets of property. Enormously stout, endlessly avaricious, pseudo-creative, intensely selfish, I shall weave upon my forehead the quadruple crown of possession until those nasty Bolshies come and take it off again and thrust me aside into the outer darkness. (E. M. Forster, "My Wood")

Chapter 6

Paragraphs: Units of Development

This chapter is the first of three that discuss the smaller units of expression — paragraphs, sentences, and words — with which writers work to create whole texts. You have seen in Chapter 5 the various strategies you can use in developing portions of an essay or even an entire essay. Now you will turn your attention to two kinds of paragraphs: *topical paragraphs,* those that actually develop a topic or idea; and *special paragraphs,* those that introduce or conclude a piece of writing or that provide a transition between major parts.

A paragraph is a set of related sentences that work together to express or develop an idea. Although it may stand on its own — and in some writing situations a writer needs but a single paragraph to fulfill his or her purpose — a paragraph is usually a unit in a complete piece of writing. It functions as a unit of development in that it organizes and advances the writer's ideas — that is, it helps develop the writer's thesis, or, in the case of narrative or descriptive writing, carries forward a story or provides significant details.

Paragraphing is useful for both writer and reader. A writer uses paragraphs to organize and present ideas — whether they are simple, elaborate, complex, or controversial — in manageable segments of prose. By grouping similar ideas together the writer ensures that they are fully and clearly explained before moving on to other ideas. Paragraphing also allows the writer to control emphasis (how much importance to lend to an idea) and rhythm (how to create and vary a pattern for presenting ideas). Readers need paragraphs in order to follow a writer's reasoning, more readily grasp key points, and avoid boredom or inattention. A long, solid block of undifferentiated prose is daunting to most readers, who can discern little or no emphasis or rhythm in it and thus little or no reason for struggling through it.

Paragraphing and Purpose

Most of the writing you do in college is expository writing — writing that tries to explain something. Paragraphs in expository writing are generally topical and work together to carry out your purpose in a given piece of writing. If you have planned your writing project carefully and accomplished some initial drafting, you will have an emerging sense of the intent and organization of your writing: your chosen hypothesis gives you a working purpose to try to demonstrate, and your scratch outline suggests the relationships in the information you have assembled. The paragraphs that you compose in a first draft must then be written in light of what your purpose requires you to do in your essay.

Of course, it is probably unlikely that you will know, in a first draft, precisely how many paragraphs you need or what each one must do. You are discovering whether you can demonstrate your purpose, after all; refinements come later. But you do know, from looking at your scratch outline and your planning material, that you need at least one paragraph apiece for each of the topics listed there, and you can see that your purpose requires you to define, compare, illustrate, or classify, or to combine these or other strategies. As you work through your draft you gain a sense of the emphasis you wish to give certain points, and you begin to see how you can compose an effective opening and ending for your essay. Then, when you step back to assess your draft and look closely at its paragraphs — in terms of how effective each single paragraph is and how effectively they all work together — you will learn either that you need to undertake global revision or that you can proceed with local revision — refining your paragraphs, sentences, and word choices. Although you will probably not be able to resist the temptation to perform some local revision — strengthening a transition here, changing the order of a paragraph there — during global revision, remember that local revision is most efficient and effective when it is accomplished on a text whose major issues (subject, audience, purpose, essential organization) have been resolved.

Before you can revise topical and special paragraphs, however, you need to know how they work and what their essential qualities are. The following pages discuss the four primary characteristics of topical paragraphs, offering illustrations of each, as well as varieties of special paragraphs. The chapter concludes with a discussion of revising paragraphs.

The Requirements of Topical Paragraphs

An effective topical paragraph must meet four requirements. First, it must discuss one topic only; that is, it must have unity of subject matter. Second, it must say all that your reader needs to know about the topic; that is, it must be complete enough to do what it is intended to do. Third, the sentences within the paragraph must follow some reasonable order that your reader can recognize and follow. Fourth, the sentences within a paragraph must have coherence; that is, they must be so tied together that your reader can read the paragraph as a unit, not as a collection of separate sentences.

Unity

Unity in a paragraph requires consistent development of the idea that your paragraph intends to explain. The paragraph as a whole should focus on that idea. If it is to achieve such a focus, each succeeding sentence must show a clear connection to the topic idea, such as is shown in the following paragraph:

(1) The fall of Rome was not a sudden event, but a slow process of disintegration which came from many causes, some so gradual that they were scarcely noticeable at the time. (2) Because of high taxes and harsh laws forbidding workmen to change their trades, the population of the city slowly melted away to find work at great country houses and estates. (3) This decline in population and taxes so reduced the imperial treasury that it became harder to man and pay the legions, and the resulting military weakness offered an inducement to provincial generals who found a march on the capital too great a temptation to resist. (4) Thus, slowly the machinery of government ceased to function. (5) And when the barbarians came there was no organized power to resist.

The first sentence states the slow process of disintegration that the paragraph is intended to develop. Each succeeding sentence contributes to the explanation of that process, so that all the sentences together focus on the disintegration that led to the fall of Rome. It is this close relationship among individual sentences that gives the paragraph its unity.

Any sentence that has no clear relation to the intent of the paragraph will blur the focus and obscure the point the writer is trying to make. Consider, for example, the following paragraph:

(1) Excavations in the past fifteen years have really formed the complete city of Pompeii. (2) As it stands now, most of Pompeii has been uncovered. (3) The ancient city of Pompeii covered one hundred and sixty-three acres, and at this time there are about fifty yards to go. (4) Scientists believe that Vesuvius is about to erupt again, and that would cover the city. (5) Archaeologists have not had to contend with Vesuvius at all in the past fifteen years, and progress has been faster. (6) Pompeii itself is now a museum, and people can walk on guided tours through all that the archaeologists have uncovered. (7) The techniques used in the past fifteen years have been more scientific and were more towards the preservation of this unknown city.

The first three sentences all deal with *the extent of the excavation of Pompeii.* Presumably, then, the paragraph is going to focus on that topic. A reader will have some difficulty with these sentences, because the first sentence suggests that the excavation is complete, whereas the second sentence says that *most* of the city has been uncovered. The third sentence gives the area of the original city but not the area of the uncovered part; instead, it gives only its length. But at least the sentences do deal with the extent of excavation.

Then in sentences 4 and 5 the focus shifts to Vesuvius, and neither sentence is clearly related to the extent of excavation. Sentence 6 shifts the focus again to Pompeii as a museum, a topic that does have some relation to the uncovered part of the city, though readers will have to discover the connection by themselves. The last sentence shifts again, this time to a contrast between old and modern techniques of archaeological investigation. All this is hard going for readers, who expect to be able to see the main idea and to follow its development through the paragraph. As they proceed they become less sure what the main idea is, or even whether there is one, and they begin to suspect that the lack of unity in the paragraph is a result of the lack of unity in the writer's perception of the subject.

When this paragraph is contrasted with the one on the fall of the Roman Empire you can see the difference between an integrated paragraph, in which each sentence contributes to the idea the writer intends to develop, and a paragraph that is merely a collection of inadequately related sentences that do not focus on any one idea. The author of the Pompeii paragraph moved from one sentence to another without proceeding in any consistent direction. If she had stuck to the intention of showing the extent of excavation, she might have begun with such a sentence as "During the last fifteen years so much of Pompeii has been uncovered that visitors can now take conducted tours through the ancient city." Such a beginning would have focused attention on the extent of excavation and would probably have suggested details about both the excavation and the tours that the paragraph obviously lacks. These details would have made the paragraph more informative than it now is.

Unless you have a clear idea of what you want to do in a paragraph, you can drift away from your opening sentences and end in a digression or, even worse, a contradiction. For example, the following paragraph ends up saying just the opposite of what its readers have been led to expect:

(1) In college writing the main emphasis is on content. (2) It is what you have to say that counts, and you are expected to think out the content of a paper before you begin to write. (3) Mechanical correctness — grammar,

punctuation, spelling, and the like — is still important, but you are supposed to have learned about those things in high school. (4) Such faults as period faults, comma splices, dangling modifiers, and faulty pronoun references can fail a paper. (5) So be sure you can recognize these errors and correct them. (6) I have found that it pays to go over my first drafts carefully to catch such mistakes, and I often wish we had spent more time on proofreading in high school. (7) Believe me, it is discouraging to plan carefully what you want to do in a paper and then have it returned with the comment, "The content of this essay is pretty good, but the grammar and spelling are atrocious."

The first two sentences clearly imply to a reader that the focus of the paragraph will be on content. The third sentence will be consistent with that focus if the writer immediately returns to content. But the introduction of "mechanical correctness" makes him forget his purpose and leads him astray. The result is that the second half of the paragraph digresses to a focus on correctness, which is the opposite of what the opening sentences require. The paragraph therefore becomes a conspicuous example of lack of unity.

Discussion Problem

Test the following paragraph for unity by checking whether each sentence clearly refers to the topic of the itinerant preacher announced in the first sentence. If you find any shift in focus within the paragraph, where does that shift occur? If you think the paragraph needs revision, can you suggest how it might be revised?

(1) The itinerant street preacher was a common sight in small Southern towns a generation ago. (2) He would come into town on Saturday afternoons in the summertime, after he had finished his week's work in his regular job, sometimes accompanied by a guitar player and one or two singers. (3) Once he had set up his microphone and loud speakers and had checked them by saying "Testing, testing, testing," he might begin the service with "Brothers and sisters, we have come here this blessed afternoon to bring the saving message of our Lord Jesus Christ to poor, lost, dying sinners! Amen!" (4) His audience would be located at various places in the block — some clustered around him, some scowling from the pool hall windows, some loafing on the taxi stand porch, and almost certainly a number sitting on the bank steps. (5) Almost certainly, I say, because the bank was a favorite

gathering place in those days. (6) Farmers came there to get their loans against crops that had not yet made. (7) Mill workers only a generation removed from the farm came to make small payments against money borrowed during the last strike or the last illness in the family. (8) And these people stayed to relax and talk with friends on the bank steps through Southern Saturday afternoons.

The Topic Sentence

The best way to keep your paragraphs unified is to be sure of what you intend them to do. One way to make your intention clear to yourself and your readers is to begin with a topic sentence. A *topic sentence* is a statement that summarizes the idea being developed in a paragraph. It is often a single sentence, though sometimes you will need two sentences to state the topic.

By beginning a paragraph with a topic sentence you immediately signal to your reader the main idea that you will develop in that paragraph. The reader can then follow the movement of the paragraph easily, for he or she will expect that all the remaining sentences help to explain and expand that idea. The following paragraph illustrates how an opening topic sentence controls a paragraph:

> Pictures are not easy to look at. They generate private fantasies, they furnish material for jokes, they recall scraps of historical knowledge, they show landscapes where one would like to wander and human beings whom one would like to resemble or adore, but looking at them is another matter, yet they must have been painted to be looked at. They were intended to appeal to the eye, but almost as if it were gazing at the sun itself the eye often reacts by closing as soon as it catches sight of them. The mind takes charge instead and goes off on some alien vision. The mind has such a congenial time that it forgets what set it going. Van Gogh and Corot and Michelangelo are three different painters, but if the mind is undisciplined and uncontrolled by the eye, they may all three induce the same mood; we may take just the same course through dreamland or funland from them, each time, and never experience anything new. (E. M. Forster, "Not Looking at Pictures," *Two Cheers for Democracy*)

Forster begins his paragraph with a simple, declarative sentence: "Pictures are not easy to look at." His purpose is to explain why they are not;

the remaining sentences in the paragraph advance that purpose by showing how the mind can embark on fantasies and take over from the eye when one is looking at pictures, thus obscuring a true *seeing* of the actual painting.

Not all topical paragraphs begin with topic sentences, however. At times a writer will place a topic sentence in mid-paragraph, where it often serves as a succinct commentary on (or provides specific meaning for) the sentences that come before and after it in the paragraph. The first sentence of the following paragraph by Paul Theroux seems to suggest a topic: the bilingualism of the Welsh. But Theroux defers his actual statement of topic until the next sentence, which affirms and sharpens the idea he has invoked in the preceding sentence.

> I wondered whether the Welsh could be explained in terms of being bilingual, which is so often a form of schizophrenia, allowing a person to hold two contradictory opinions in his head at once, because the opinions remain untranslated. The Welsh had that mildly stunned and slaphappy personality that I associated with people for whom speaking two languages was a serious handicap. It made them profligate with language, it made them inexact, it had turned them into singers — well, that was no bad thing, they said. I did not think it was a question of good or bad, but only of a kind of confusion. (Paul Theroux, *The Kingdom by the Sea*)

Sometimes a writer wants to build toward an idea or judgment and so defers the topic sentence until the end of the paragraph. The following paragraph by Lillian Hellman is a skillful example of such suspension:

> Old paint on canvas, as it ages, sometimes becomes transparent. When that happens it is possible, in some pictures, to see the original lines: a tree will show through a woman's dress, a child makes way for a dog, a large boat is no longer on an open sea. That is called *pentimento* because the painter "repented," changed his mind. Perhaps it would be as well to say that the old conception, replaced by a later choice, is a way of seeing and then seeing again. (Lillian Hellman, *Pentimento: A Book of Portraits*)

You will not always need to write a topic sentence for every paragraph. Sometimes what you want to say can be inferred from the way you say it, so that you do not need to compose a precise statement — indeed, such a statement would be gratuitous, out of place. The following paragraph, written by a master stylist, E. B. White, establishes how Americans feel about the beauty and timelessness of a summer's day, but White does not have to state that topic overtly:

> Summertime, oh, summertime, pattern of life indelible, the fade-proof lake, the woods unshatterable, the pasture with the sweetfern and the juniper forever and ever, summer without end; this was the background, and the life along the shore was the design, the cottages with their innocent and tranquil design, their tiny docks with the flagpole and the American flag floating against the white clouds in the blue sky, the little paths over the roots of the trees leading from camp to camp and the paths leading back to the outhouses and the can of lime for sprinkling, and at the souvenir counters at the store the miniature birch-bark canoes and the postcards that showed things looking a little better than they looked. This was the American family at play, escaping the city heat, wondering whether the newcomers in the camp at the head of the cove were "common" or "nice," wondering whether it was true that the people who drove up for Sunday dinner at the farmhouse were turned away because there wasn't enough chicken. (E. B. White, "Once More to the Lake," *Essays of E. B. White*)

As a rule, you should be sparing in your use of paragraphs without topic sentences. When used for effect they can be powerful and memorable — so long as the reader *can* infer your main idea, that is — but you risk misleading your reader and yourself if you routinely decline to write topic sentences. In most of your writing it is good practice regularly to begin paragraphs with topic sentences. Even though you can inadvertently depart from your main idea as you compose a paragraph, the topic sentence stands as a reminder of what you intend to do, and you can return to fulfill that intention in revision. As you gain experience and ease in writing, you will know intuitively when and why to divert occasionally from the topic-sentence-first pattern.

Completeness

Completeness, the second major requirement of an effective paragraph, is relative. How much explanation an idea requires depends on how much your reader needs. This is a decision you must make out of your knowledge of your subject and reader. It is an error to give too much information or not to give enough, though for the inexperienced writer lack of adequate detail is more common than too much detail.

Consider the following example:

> Under the 1968 Gun Control Act, any resident of a state can purchase a gun anywhere in his state provided he meets the established requirements. However, the law provides no foolproof way for gun dealers to check the background of the purchaser.

If that is all the writer is going to say about the Gun Control Act, this paragraph will be incomplete for most readers, since the two sentences do no more than state the topic. The only reader this paragraph will satisfy is one who already knows what "the established requirements" are and why the law provides "no foolproof way" to check a purchaser's identity. And such a reader would not need the paragraph in the first place. For one who does need it, the writer must provide a fuller explanation, perhaps something like this:

> Under the 1968 Gun Control Act, any resident of a state can purchase a gun anywhere in his state provided he meets specified minimum age requirements (twenty-one for hand guns and eighteen for long guns) and is not under indictment or has not been convicted of a crime punishable by more than a year's imprisonment. Nor can he be a fugitive from justice, a narcotics addict or unlawful user of drugs, an adjudged or committed mental incompetent, or anyone else otherwise disqualified from gun ownership by state or local laws. However, the federal law provides no foolproof way for gun dealers to check the background of a would-be purchaser or, for that matter, even to determine whether the person they are selling to is just who he says he is. A driver's license is usually considered sufficient identification to establish a person's name, address, and age. And so any proscribed person can easily get a gun, as well as ammunition for it, by presenting false credentials or by simply lying. (Carl Bakal, "The Failure of Federal Gun Control," *Saturday Review*)

The detailed information added in the expansion is necessary to make the meaning of the incomplete paragraph clear. Of course, you can begin with a short paragraph if all you intend to do is to state the idea you are going to develop and then explain it in a subsequent paragraph. In that case, the second paragraph completes the first.

The following example further illustrates incompleteness:

> Champagne is without doubt the most evocative word in the vocabulary of wine. It is made in a district in France. Both the district and the wine, which is white and sparkling, are called Champagne.

If the writer stops here, the reader is left with only an emphatic statement of opinion and two statements of fact, neither of which does much to illuminate the opinion. The reader needs to know what the word *Champagne* evokes, both literally and figuratively. With recasting and expansion, the paragraph will supply the answer:

> Champagne is without question the most evocative word in the entire vocabulary of wine. Strictly speaking, it refers to the district in France named Champagne and to the unique process invented there for producing sparkling white wine, as well as to the wine itself. But the word means so much more. It stands for gaiety, celebration and festivity, for wealth and splendor, for love. It means New Year's Eve, the launching of ships, toasts to Kings and Presidents. Its reputation has spread farther than that of any other wine. In fact, so unique is Champagne that many people do not even refer to it as wine, but rather as some sort of magical potion with an identity all its own. How often have you heard someone say, "I prefer Champagne to wine"? (Terry Robards, *The New York Times Book of Wine*)

The additions to the paragraph clarify the literal meaning of Champagne: it is a district, a method, and a wine. More than that, however, it is a mood, a symbol, a celebration — and, in the minds of some people, "a magical potion with an identity all its own."

The lesson to be learned from these examples is that you must spell out the implications of your topic sentences with facts, illustrations, explanations, definitions, or whatever is needed. Unless you give your readers the information they need, they will have difficulty understanding you. Incomplete paragraphing is an easy fault to fall into; yet it is likewise easy to correct if you realize that any generalization must be developed with supporting details.

Exercise   The following paragraphs are incomplete as they now stand. Complete them by adding a sustained illustration from any experience you have had or any activity you know well.

> You cannot and should not try to eliminate all anger from your life. If you react mildly to everything, you will often be suppressing your real feelings. But you must learn to recognize those situations when expressing anger is counterproductive.

> To excel in any skill, it is not enough just to be talented. Every kind of skilled activity has its special techniques that have to be learned by practice. You need a combination of talent and technical proficiency.

Order

So far in this chapter you have considered the need for unity and completeness in paragraphs. Now you need to study the third major requirement, *order,* the sequence of sentences within a paragraph. In a well-constructed paragraph the sentences follow a consistent order. As you saw in the paragraph on Pompeii (page 196), sentences that go in various directions are likely to bother readers by making it difficult for them to see the relationship among the sentences.

Order in a paragraph is like organization in an essay. But because paragraphs are smaller in scope, it may be simpler to consider order as *direction of movement.* In expository paragraphs the most usual directions are from *general to particular,* from *particular to general,* from the *whole to its parts,* and from *question to answer* or *effect to cause.* In the following pages you will see examples of each of these orders.

General to Particular

A common order in expository paragraphs is one that moves from a general statement, often a topic sentence, to specific explanation or illustration of that statement. The function of the paragraph is to make clear to a reader the meaning of the general statement. That meaning becomes increasingly clear as the paragraph progresses. You saw this kind of clarification in the paragraphs on gun control and Champagne.

In both these paragraphs the direction of movement was from a general statement to a particular explanation of that statement. The simplest prescription for a general-to-particular paragraph is to

1. begin with a general statement of the topic idea to be developed.

2. follow it with enough specific information to explain or illustrate the meaning of the opening statement.

Here is an additional example:

> There is another paradox in man's relationship with other creatures: namely, that those very qualities he calls animalian — "brutal," "bestial," "inhuman" — are peculiarly his own. No other animal is so deliberately cruel as man. No other creature intentionally imprisons its own kind, or invents special instruments of torture such as racks and thumbscrews for the sole purpose of punishment. No other animal keeps its own brethren in slavery; so far as we know, the lower animals do not commit anything like the acts of pure sadism that figure rather largely in our newspapers. There is no torment, spite, or cruelty for its own sake among beasts, as there is among men. A cat plays with its prey, but does not conquer and torture smaller cats. But man, who knows good and evil, is cruel for cruelty's sake; he who has a moral law is more brutal than the brutes, who have none; he alone inflicts suffering on his fellows with malice aforethought. (Suzanne K. Langer, "The Lord of Creation")

Particular to General

A particular-to-general order reverses the preceding pattern. A paragraph written in this order begins with specific information and leads to a general conclusion, as in the following example:

> When Michelangelo started work on the Sistine Chapel ceiling, five friends who were painters came to assist him and advise him in the techniques of fresco, in which they were practiced and he was not. Finding their work not what he desired, he resolved to accomplish the whole task by himself, locked the doors of the chapel until his friends gave up and went home, and through four painful years on a scaffold carried the work to completion, as Vasari tells us, "with the utmost solicitude, labor and study." That is what makes for quality — and its cost — and what helped to make Michelangelo one of the greatest artists, if not, as some think, the

greatest, of all time. Creating quality is self-nourishing. Michelangelo, Vasari goes on to say, "became more and more kindled every day by his fervor in the work and encouraged by his growing proficiency and improvement." Genius and effort go together, or if they do not, the genius will be wasted. (Barbara Tuchman, "The Decline of Quality")

Had Tuchman chosen, she could have followed a general-to-particular order, beginning with her final sentence about the relation of genius and effort and then illustrating her main idea with the example of Michelangelo and the Sistine Chapel. But she preferred instead to build to her conclusion about genius, thereby lending her chosen example an extra dimension of meaning.

Whole to Parts

Sometimes the function of a paragraph is not to explain an idea but to show the parts or divisions of a topic, as the following paragraph illustrates:

> The American vigilante phenomenon has gone through three distinct phases, though with considerable overlapping. The first was classic vigilantism, which erupted initially in South Carolina's back country on the eve of the Revolution and concerned itself with punishing ordinary badmen — horse and cattle thieves, counterfeiters, and assorted gangs of desperadoes. Classic vigilantism had as its main target the killers and spoilers who infested the early frontier. The second, or neovigilante, phase started with the great San Francisco committee of 1856 and had as its target ethnic and religious minorities and political opponents, usually clustered in urban areas. Neovigilantism was essentially urban and had little or nothing to do with cactus, horses, and gunslingers. The current phase, pseudo vigilantism, a less deadly but potentially volatile mixture of the first two, can be said to have started in response to the soaring crime and the racial upheavals of the 1960s. Both criminals and blacks have been the objects of pseudovigilante activities, and in a number of instances blacks themselves have organized vigilantelike groups to fight drug addiction among their own people. (William E. Burrows, *Vigilante!*)

Such an order is often called *partitive* or *enumerative*. The opening sentence announces the number of parts of the topic, and the rest of the paragraph identifies and defines each of the parts in turn. The partitive

or enumerative paragraph is often used in argument, either as an introduction to identify the issues that will be considered or as a conclusion to
sum up what has been done. It is also often used as an introductory
paragraph to present the categories under which a topic will be discussed
in an essay. In that case, it is usually less detailed than Burrows's paragraph on vigilantism, for the succeeding paragraphs supply details about
the categories.

Question to Answer, Effect to Cause

A paragraph may begin with a question and give the answer, or with an
effect and explain the cause. Such a paragraph may have no specific
topic sentence beyond the opening question or effect. The answer or
cause is given by the rest of the paragraph.

The following paragraph moves from question to answer — actually,
answers:

> What has the telephone done to us, or for us, in the hundred years of its
> existence? A few effects suggest themselves at once. It has saved lives by
> getting rapid word of illness, injury, or famine from remote places. By
> joining with the elevator to make possible the multistory residence or office
> building, it has made possible — for better or worse — the modern city. By
> bringing about a quantum leap in the speed and ease with which informa-
> tion moves from place to place, it has greatly accelerated the rate of
> scientific and technological change and growth in industry. Beyond doubt
> it has crippled if not killed the ancient art of letter writing. It has made
> living alone possible for persons with normal social impulses; by so doing, it
> has played a role in one of the greatest social changes of this century, the
> breakup of the multigenerational household. It has made the waging of
> war chillingly more efficient than formerly. Perhaps (though not provably)
> it has prevented wars that might have arisen out of international misunder-
> standing caused by written communication. Or perhaps — again not prov-
> ably — by magnifying and extending irrational personal conflicts based on
> voice contact, it has caused wars. Certainly it has extended the scope of
> human conflicts, since it impartially disseminates the useful knowledge of
> scientists and the babble of bores, the affection of the affectionate and the
> malice of the malicious. (John Brooks, *Telephone: The First Hundred Years*)

In the next paragraph the first sentence states an effect, the "immunity
gap." The rest of the paragraph shows what causes that effect. You have

seen this order earlier in this chapter, particularly in the paragraph showing the process of disintegration that led to the fall of the Roman Empire (page 196).

> The hard fact is that a wide "immunity gap" exists in our population between younger people and those fifty and over. The gap comes about in this way: the influenza virus, like other viruses, carries as part of its protein coating certain antigens that stimulate our immune systems to produce specific antibodies against it; because the swine type of influenza virus has not been in circulation for more than fifty years, people under fifty — and some above fifty as well — lack these protective antibodies and thus would be susceptible if such a virus were to be become active again. (Jonas Salk, "The Ultimate Flu Vaccine," *Saturday Review*)

The summary table that follows provides a quick review of the four common orders discussed in this chapter.

Summary of Main Orders of Paragraph Movement

General to particular *Opening general statement or topic sentence followed by illustration or details of explanation or proof. The paragraph may conclude with a restatement of the topic sentence.*

Topic sentence followed by supporting details.
Concluding statement optional.

Particular to general *From a series of detailed statements to a conclusion drawn from them. If there is a topic sentence, it occurs at or near the end of the paragraph.*

Explanatory details or illustrations leading to conclusion or topic sentence.

Whole to parts *Paragraph begins with an introductory statement about the number of parts and then explains each part; often a first, second, third order.*

Opening statement
1. _____
2. _____
3. _____

Question to answer, or **effect to cause** *Paragraph begins with question or effect, then answers the question or shows the cause.*

Question or effect followed by answer or cause.

Coherence

The fourth requirement of an effective paragraph is *coherence.* Literally, the word means "sticking together." A paragraph is coherent when the sentences are woven together in such a way that your reader can move easily from one sentence to the next and read the paragraph as an integrated whole, rather than as a series of separate sentences.

If you have a clear general plan when you begin writing, then you are not likely to have serious trouble with coherence. Most incoherent paragraphs come from thinking out the implications of the topic one sentence at a time, without considering the relationships among the sentences. If you work this way you will write one sentence, stop, think a minute, write a second sentence, stop, and continue in a series of spurts and pauses. Paragraphs written this way are likely to lack coherence, for you are starting afresh at every sentence. The sense of continuity between sentences is lost, and as a result the writing becomes jerky.

A paragraph that lacks orderly movement will not be coherent, because your reader will not see how two sentences are related and therefore cannot go easily from one to another. But though inconsistent order is a major cause of lack of coherence, it is not the only one. Anything that keeps your reader from making clear and quick connections between the sentences in a paragraph or between successive paragraphs interferes with your ability to communicate your subject to your audience.

Here is an example of incoherent writing that does not come from faulty order. The writer is composing a paper to show that Thomas Jefferson's writing is characterized by careful research and independent thinking. At one point in his paper he wants to illustrate that thesis by citing Jefferson's book *The Life and Morals of Jesus of Nazareth.* The writer has the material he needs in his notes, from which he writes the following paragraph:

> Jefferson could read Greek, Latin, French, and English, so he pasted texts of the New Testament in these languages side by side. He thought that the Bible should be read critically, like any other book, so he accepted those stories about Jesus which agreed with natural laws, and rejected those that did not. He kept the teachings of Jesus but rejected the miracles. He also rejected anything that had to be explained by revelation. "I think," he wrote in a letter to Adams, "that every Christian sect gives a great handle to

atheism by their general dogma that, without revelation, there would not be sufficient proof of the being of God." Jefferson considered Christianity the purest system of morality known.

Although this paragraph does develop the material in the notes into an orderly sequence of sentences, it has several weaknesses that could be removed in revision. Consider the following points:

1. What is the purpose of the paragraph? You know from the description of the assignment that the writer wants to illustrate Jefferson's habits of careful research and independent thinking. The information does illustrate these habits, but its significance would be clearer if the individual sentences were clearly related to a topic sentence that would bind them together. Without such a topic sentence a reader may wonder why Jefferson examined the New Testament in four languages and may have difficulty in seeing any connection between the first sentence and the second.

2. What is the relationship between this paragraph and the one that preceded it? You have been told that both are illustrations of the thesis of the paper, but this paragraph does not make that relationship clear. It needs some kind of introductory statement to show that it is another illustration.

3. Although the repetition of *he* provides some natural coherence within the paragraph and so ties the sentences together by giving them a common subject, the monotonous structure tends to emphasize the separateness of each sentence. The passage seems more like a collection of sentences than the development of a single idea.

4. The last sentence seems to have no relation to what has gone before. If it is not a digression, its function should be indicated.

Now consider the following revision:

Jefferson's book on Jesus of Nazareth provides another illustration of his careful collection and comparison of the evidence, and of his acceptance or rejection of it on the basis of reason rather than authority. To compare the evidence, Jefferson pasted texts from the New Testament in Greek, Latin, French, and English in columns side by side. As he was proficient in all four languages he felt he could come closer to the true meanings of the words by reading them in this way. To ensure that reason rather than the authority of tradition would guide him, he followed his own advice that the Bible should be read critically, like any other book. Accordingly, he accepted those parts which revealed the teachings of Jesus and rejected stories of miracles. He also rejected those passages which had to be supported by revelation. "I think," he wrote to Adams, "that every Christian sect gives a great handle to atheism by their general dogma that, without revelation, there would not be sufficient proof of the being of God." The result was a work which emphasized what Jefferson considered the purest system of morality known and toned down or omitted incidents which required a supernatural explanation.

Notice:

1. the topic sentence, which states the purpose of the paragraph (and so gives point to all that follows) and also relates this paragraph to the thesis of the paper.

2. the explanation of why Jefferson pasted the four different texts side by side. This explanation is necessary to illustrate the thoroughness of his working habits.

3. the clearer explanation of his selection and rejection of material ("To ensure that reason rather than the authority . . ."). This explanation helps to bind together four sentences that in the unsatisfactory version were connected only by a common subject.

4. the concluding sentence, which not only shows the pertinence of what previously looked like a digression but also, by showing Jefferson's emphasis, sums up the content of the whole paragraph.

5. the more pleasing effect obtained by slight but significant variations in the basic sentence pattern.

This contrast of the original and revised paragraphs shows how an unsatisfactory piece of writing can be improved by providing the connecting links that bring out the relationships among the sentences. In the revised paragraph these links were pieces of information that bridged the gaps in the original version and thus made the whole paragraph a fuller and clearer expression of the main idea, now stated as a topic sentence. Another way of linking sentences together into a coherent paragraph is to use such connective devices as pronouns, repetitive structure, contrast, and transitional markers, all of which are discussed in the following pages.

Coherence Through Pronoun Reference

Because it refers to an antecedent, a pronoun points back (or forward) and gives a simple and natural connection. Notice in the following example how the pronoun *it* ties the first half of the paragraph back to the antecedent *view*. Then, at mid-paragraph, *it* refers forward to *colour*. The overall effect of the pronoun repetition links all the details in the paragraph to the view that van der Post is describing.

> I wish I could describe the effect that view had on me, but I will say little more than that it seemed to me miraculous. It was so unlike anything else. It was deep in the heart of Africa and filled with the animals of Africa, and yet it was covered with the grasses, the flowers, and colours of Europe. Yet it was unlike any other colour I have ever seen: I expect, basically, it was a tawny gold, the gold of the leopard's rather than the lion's skin, but this gold was shot through with undertones of a deep blood red and a shadowy purple. (Laurens van der Post, *Venture to the Interior*)

Discussion Problem

One of these paragraphs is a revision of the other. Which is the revision, and what weaknesses is it trying to remove?

(1) Opera is a lavish kind of theater, to be sure, but it is not the silly art form that some people think that it is. (2) It is assumed by them that all singers are prima donnas who throw tantrums whenever a rival singer appears on the scene or whenever they don't get their way. (3) Those who think opera is silly can hardly have recognized that a new breed of singer now exists. (4) That singer is a capable actor, too. (5) Rivalries among singers are le-

(1) Although opera will always be grand, it has changed enough over recent years to give people who once avoided it reason to see what it is like. (2) One of the major changes has occurred in opera singers themselves. (3) Traditionally they have been considered prima donnas in the worst sense of the word: hefty, spoiled, screechy individuals who throw tantrums over imagined slights, presumed rivalries, and failure to get their way. (4) But today

gion, and there are some very funny stories about them. (6) Voltaire, an eighteenth-century writer, made one of the most famous remarks about opera: "What is too silly to be said is sung."

a new type of singer has appeared — the singing actor, who can convey both the drama and the music in opera with equal seriousness. (5) Voltaire's dismissive quip about opera — "What is too silly to be said is sung" — assuredly belongs, with him, back in the eighteenth century.

Coherence Through Repetitive Structure

Although unintended repetition should be avoided, deliberate repetition of key words, phrases, or sentence patterns can connect sentences into a coherent paragraph. In the following paragraph every sentence after the first has the same kind of structure and the same opening words, "There is nothing." This kind of repetitive structure, which will be discussed as *parallelism* in the next chapter, ties the sentences together as a consistent development of the topic sentence.

> America, the richest and most powerful nation in the world, can well lead the way in this revolution of values. There is nothing to prevent us from paying adequate wages to schoolteachers, social workers and other servants of the public to insure that we have the best available personnel in these positions which are charged with the responsibility of guiding our future generations. There is nothing but a lack of social vision to prevent us from paying an adequate wage to every American citizen whether he be a hospital worker, laundry worker, maid or day laborer. There is nothing except shortsightedness to prevent us from guaranteeing an annual mini-mum — and *livable* — income for every American family. There is nothing, except a tragic death wish, to prevent us from reordering our priorities, so the pursuit of peace will take precedence over the pursuit of war. There is nothing to keep us from remolding a recalcitrant status quo with bruised hands until we have fashioned it into a brotherhood. (Martin Luther King, Jr., *Where Do We Go from Here: Chaos or Community?*)

In the following paragraph the repetition of the pronouns *its* and *whose* combines with parallel sentence structure to provide effective links be-tween the sentences.

Those of us who came to know baseball when there was little television and no big-time professional football or basketball talked its language, heard its lore, and were taken with its special sense before we had ever played an organized game or pondered its beautiful mystery. There were giants on the field, men of legend whose voices we had never heard, whose faces we knew only from newspaper photographs or from the murky images on our bubble-gum cards, and whose records — batting average, home runs, runs batted in — suggested meaning beyond anything we understood. "Facts" supported myth, and myth magnified the facts on which it was supposed to be based. (Peter Schrag, "The Age of Willie Mays," *Saturday Review*)

Coherence Through Contrasted Elements

When the topic sentence calls for comparison or contrast, the pairing of contrasted or compared elements gives some coherence. In the following example successive contrasts between past and present relations of husbands and wives connect individual sentences and relate them all to the topic sentence:

Topic sentence
Contrast 1
Contrast 2

Topic sentence restatement in more specific form

Contrast 3

Contrast 4

Many men also find it hard to adjust to the stark contrasts between the new ways and the old. Their mothers stayed home. Their fathers made all the important decisions. In an argument, the father's word was final. And the mother cooked, sewed and cleaned up in silence. It can therefore be very unsettling for men to suddenly find that their wives are discovering activities and ideas so different from their mothers'. "My husband and I got along just fine until I went back to work," said a woman from Atlanta. "Then, suddenly, he started wanting to have people for dinner, take long vacations and have his undershorts ironed — issues that never came up when my time belonged more to him. It's really been a hassle. He keeps talking about the way his mother was with his father. I tell him times have changed. He answers, 'But *I* haven't.' " (Linda Bird Francke, "Do Strong Women Frighten Men?" *Ladies' Home Journal*)

Coherence Through Transitional Markers   *Transitional markers* are words or phrases often placed at or near the beginning of a sentence or clause to signal the relationship between a new sentence and the one before it. The commonest markers are the conjunctions *and, or, nor, but,* and *for.*

Others — sometimes called *transitional connectives* — also indicate the direction the new sentence is about to take. The commonest transitional connectives are used as follows:

1. to introduce an illustration: *for example, for instance, to illustrate*

2. to add another phase of the same idea: *second, in the second place, then, furthermore, next, moreover, in addition, similarly, again, also, finally*

3. to point up a contrast or qualification: *on the other hand, nevertheless, despite this fact, on the contrary, still, however, conversely, instead*

4. to indicate a conclusion or result: *therefore, in conclusion, to sum up, consequently, as a result, accordingly, in other words*

Exercise   Use the revised Jefferson paragraph (pages 210–211) as a model to convert this collection of sentences into a coherent paragraph. The purpose of the paragraph is to answer the question whether it ever gets too cold to snow. First write a topic sentence that will state a general answer to that question and thus suggest a focus for the information provided in the numbered sentences. Then work that information into a coherent paragraph.

1. Snow particles form when the temperature falls below 32 Fahrenheit.

2. At this temperature the particles are wet.

3. Wet particles mat together to form flakes.

4. As the temperature falls still lower, the air dries out.

5. Dry snow does not flake but becomes powdery.

6. At temperatures below zero, snow changes to fine, glittering ice-dust.

7. At temperatures below zero, a heavy fall of snow is rare, but it can occur.

8. The air is usually too dry to produce snow at subzero temperatures.

Coherence Through Connections Between Paragraphs

Coherence is necessary, not only within a paragraph, but also between the several paragraphs of an essay, so that your reader can see how any paragraph is related to those that have come before.

The following selection illustrates this coherence among paragraphs. The thesis is stated in the first sentence. The key terms are *myth* and *mathematical mind,* and they are repeated throughout the three paragraphs, keeping Tobias's thesis ever in front of the reader.

A common myth about the nature of mathematical ability holds that one either has or does not have a mathematical mind. Mathematical imagination and an intuitive grasp of mathematical principles may well be needed to do advanced research, but why should people who can do college-level work in other subjects not be able to do college-level math as well? Rates of learning may vary. Competency under time pressure may differ. Certainly low self-esteem will get in the way. But where is the evidence that a student needs a "mathematical mind" in order to succeed at learning math?

Consider the effects of this mythology. Since only a few people are supposed to have this mathematical mind, part of what makes us so passive in the face of our difficulties in learning mathematics is that we suspect all the while we may not be one of "them," and we spend our time waiting to find out when our nonmathematical minds will be exposed. Since our limit will eventually be reached, we see no point in being methodical or in attending to detail. We are grateful when we survive fractions, word problems, or geometry. If that certain moment of failure hasn't struck yet, it is only temporarily postponed.

Parents, especially parents of girls, often expect their children to be nonmathematical. Parents are either poor at math . . . or, if math came easily for them, they do not know how it feels to be slow. In either case, they unwittingly foster the idea that a mathematical mind is something one either has or does not have. (Sheila Tobias, "Who's Afraid of Math, and Why?" *The Atlantic*)

Special Paragraphs

So far in this chapter you have been dealing with topical paragraphs, those that develop your topic or some part of it. These are the main paragraphs in an essay. But certain other paragraphs have special functions. They are used to *introduce* or *conclude* an essay or to *mark a transition* from one main unit to another.

Introductory Paragraphs

The function of an introductory paragraph is to lead your readers into your essay. Readers want to know what you are writing about, as well as whether they will find it interesting and significant. In effect your introduction gives them a preview of your essay; if it captures their attention, they will find it easier to adjust themselves to the demands that you, the writer, will make of them. Introductory paragraphs are usually one of two types, or sometimes a blend of the two: suggestions of what you intend to do in the essay, or attention-getting devices that engage your readers' interest.

The first of these types is often a relatively short paragraph that states the thesis of an essay, usually with a brief explanation. Such an introduction may be called a *thesis paragraph*. Here are some examples:

> The future is to be read in the nature of America. It is, however, more difficult to know America than any other Western country. The Americans' picture of themselves and of their ideals is always controversial and deceptive. They exalt exaggerated virtues, deplore partly imaginary sins, overpraise the nobility of the original hopes, cry over the present betrayal, denounce the imminent ruin of everything decent and honorable, and extol the perfect Utopia which is only a few inventions away — all this sometimes within the same political speech or essay. (Luigi Barzini, *On Knowing Americans*)

> In the life of J. Robert Oppenheimer — the American physicist and scientist-statesman who directed the building of the first atomic bombs at Los Alamos, New Mexico, during World War II; whose government, discerning "fundamental defects" in his character, denied him security clearance in 1954; who died of throat cancer in 1967 — some have professed to see embodied the moral ambiguities of twentieth-century science, science charging breakneck over human institutions, scientists waking sacerdotal from Faustian dreams. Oppenheimer was not much of this, for these are tabloid notions, but he lived at the center of the century's most disturbing contradictions, and struggled with them, and suffered for them, and if he is often taken as their protagonist, it is partly because he was a man of disturbing contradictions himself. (Richard Rhodes, "J. Robert Oppenheimer, Shatterer of Worlds," *Looking for America*)

> The ghost of a lost, smudged Europe and its culture, and the ghost of the undefiled American continent: these, to me, are the two spooks of our

immigrant heritage. The most troubling American relation to beauty rests in our perception of our geographical body. It is this: we are aware that our presence on the continent has made it less beautiful. Our history presents us with emphatic before and after images of our land. Before us, after us. Before is beautiful. (Patricia Hampl, "Beauty," *A Romantic Education*)

A question raised by our culture of the last two or three decades is whether quality in product and effort has become a vanishing element of current civilization. The word "quality" has, of course, two meanings: first, the nature or essential characteristic of something, as in "His voice has the quality of command"; second, a condition of excellence implying fine quality as distinct from poor quality. The second, obviously, is my subject. (Barbara Tuchman, "The Decline of Quality")

As these examples show, the introductory paragraph can suggest an author's intentions in several ways. It can present a thesis and then clarify it, as does the Barzini paragraph. It can build toward a thesis, as does the Rhodes paragraph. It can link a series of related, evocative sentences together — as in the Hampl paragraph — to suggest a thesis. Or it can identify an issue or issues and state outright that the essay will deal with one of them, as in the Tuchman paragraph. Of course, there are more ways than these to structure a thesis paragraph. The point is that a thesis paragraph should give your reader a good idea of your subject and, if possible, a suggestion of your attitude toward it.

The second type of introductory paragraph is intended to lure the reader into the essay. Journalists and scriptwriters call this kind of introduction to catch reader interest a "hook." Often it is a dramatic example pulled out of its normal place and set at the beginning as bait to entice the reader into going on. Sometimes it is an analogy that points up the real subject of an essay; sometimes it is a question that challenges the reader or piques his or her curiosity.

You saw in Chapter 4 how Rod experimented with several opening paragraphs, finally opting for an introductory hook that gave his readers a barrage of facts about the Washington Monument and hinted that the Monument's story is more dramatic than mere facts can tell:

The raw facts are simple enough: The Washington Monument stands 555 feet $5\frac{1}{8}$ inches in the air. Its base is 55 feet $1\frac{1}{2}$ square inches. It is faced with 9,613 marble slabs, weighs 90,854 tons, can withstand a 145

m. p. h. gale, and cost $1,187,710.31. Many of the estimated two million tourists who visit the Monument each year can tell you those statistics. But there are some things they can't tell you. For example, in the two centuries since the idea was first mentioned, the Washington Monument has been revised, moved, stolen, ignored, held hostage, and almost blown up.

Following are some other examples of the introductory hook.

1. A question directed to the reader

> How many of you have ever wondered where certain slang expressions come from? Like "She's the cat's pajamas," or to "take it on the lam." Neither have I. And yet for those who are interested in this sort of thing I have provided a brief guide to a few of the more interesting origins. (Woody Allen, "Slang Origins," *Without Feathers*)

This paragraph is a clever illustration of the comic use to which the introductory question may be put; Allen's "Neither have I" answer is masterful. The reader, amused, begins in fact to wonder about slang origins. Of course, the introductory question may also be posed seriously.

2. A personal anecdote

> A time comes when creatures whose destinies have crossed somewhere in the remote past are forced to appraise each other as though they were total strangers. I had been huddled beside the fire one winter night, with the wind prowling outside and shaking the windows. The big shepherd dog on the hearth before me occasionally glanced up affectionately, sighed, and slept. I was working, actually, amidst the debris of a far greater winter. On my desk lay the lance point of ice age hunters and the heavy leg bone of a fossil bison. No remnants of flesh attached to these relics. The deed lay more than ten thousand years remote. It was represented here by naked flint and by bone so mineralized it rang when struck. As I worked in my little circle of light, I absently laid the bone beside me on the floor. The hour had crept toward midnight. A grating noise, a heavy rasping of big teeth diverted me. I looked down. (Loren Eiseley, "The Angry Winter," *The Unexpected Universe*)

Notice how Eiseley, telling a story about himself, builds suspense as skillfully as any detective novelist, linking present and past ages and suggesting — both in the details of his narrative and in his reflective opening sentence — that something is going to happen.

3. A statement to arouse the reader's curiosity

> Napoleon started it all. If it weren't for him, I might not be sitting here now writing these words. I am not thinking of a belligerent golden hamster I once owned, who went by that name, but of the original Napoleon — Bonaparte himself — for it was one of his cannonballs, fired in the Peninsular War, that shot off the arm of my great-great-grandfather, James Morris, and altered the whole course of my family history. (Desmond Morris, *Animal Days*)

Morris knows that the reader cannot begin to link Napoleon Bonaparte, a hamster, Morris's great-great-grandfather, and the Morris family history into any coherent sensibility. But he also knows that the reader will be intrigued and enticed by such enigmatic juxtapositions — in other words, hooked.

4. A statement of emphatic opinion

> If you must have an earthquake, 1755 is the year to have it: when you rebuild, you will get a full-blown eighteenth-century city. That is what happened to Lisbon. Yet, by a freakish and unjust oversight in the development of taste, Lisbon is not very famous. (Brigid Brophy, "Lisbon," *Don't Never Forget*)

Brophy flirts with — and actually indulges in — overstatement in this paragraph, but she does so with such energy that her words take on authority. Moreover, she lures the reader by implications: an eighteenth-century city is an object of admiration (why?), yet something has prevented Lisbon, an eighteenth-century city, from being justly famous (again, why?).

Transitional Paragraphs

A transitional paragraph is a signal of a change in content. Through transitional paragraphs you announce that you have finished one main unit and are moving to the next, or that you are turning from a general explanation to examples or applications. In their simplest form such signals may be as brief as the following:

So much for the woodwinds. We come now to the brasses.

Let us see how this theory operates in practice.

And this brings us to our fourth and final point: the blackberries.
(E. M. Forster, "My Wood")

A few examples will make this explanation clear.

I know of course that all this sounds vague. But don't worry. From this point on we are getting down to brass tacks. (Rudolph Flesch, *The Art of Plain Talk*)

Sometimes a writer supplements the bare signal with a concise summary of what has been done or with a hint of what is to come, as the next two examples show:

This chapter is the first of three that discuss the smaller units of expression — paragraphs, sentences, words — with which writers work to create whole texts. You have seen in Chapter 5 the various strategies writers can use in developing portions of an essay or even a whole essay. Now you will turn your attention to two kinds of paragraph: *topical paragraphs,* those that actually develop a topic or idea; and *special paragraphs,* those that introduce or conclude a piece of writing or that provide a transition between major parts.

Each of these "faces" has been symbolic of the multifaceted nature of New York. Each, in its own way, has made or "remade" sections of the city. There is emerging now a new, fourth face — New York, the cultural city. (Daniel Bell, "The Forces Shaping the City: The Four Faces of New York")

Concluding Paragraphs

Contrary to popular belief, not every paper needs a concluding paragraph. If an essay has adequately developed its thesis, nothing more is necessary. For example, the Lorenz passage about birds that are sexually confused (pages 166–167) needs no concluding paragraph, because the conclusion is implied in the thesis. All that essay needs to do is to explain its thesis. There would be nothing wrong with adding a concluding paragraph to this essay *provided that it strengthened the message.* But a merely mechanical conclusion that took the form "Thus we see that . . ." would be just a wordy anticlimax.

Yet an effective concluding paragraph can make a positive contribution by bringing your whole essay to a climax, by summing up the discussion in a few sentences that leave readers with the feeling, "Yes, that is what it is all about." Such a concluding paragraph gives you one final chance to drive the message home. Following are four examples of effective concluding paragraphs.

1. A paragraph that emphasizes main points in a summary

> The last three chapters have granted that at times language can be confusing, illogical, and infuriating; that it can play tricks on both speaker and listener; that though all human beings belong to the same species, they do not categorize their experience in any mutually intelligible way; that a mere flicker of the eyelids can sometimes belie the most carefully structured and grammatical utterance. In view of all this, can we regard the language game as an honest one? Yes, we can — despite the flaws. The flaws and limitations in language are a reflection of the flaws and limitations in our species, and an understanding of these will allow us to function within the boundaries of language with greater freedom and understanding than heretofore. (Peter Farb, *Word Play*)

2. A paragraph that draws a conclusion from preceding paragraphs

> Therefore, if you want to gain weight, you must do either of two things: eat more calories (units of heat, therefore energy), or use less through inactivity. If you want to lose weight, you do the reverse: decrease your input of calories or increase the amount of energy you spend. There is no other way. Gaining or losing weight is always a relation between intake and output of potential energy.

3. A paragraph that evaluates what has been done

> The procession which marked the conclusion of the ten-month Constitutional Convention set a symbolic seal on the long process and thus had the effect which many public ceremonies have of making it all seem a real and believable event. In the words of Benjamin Rush, the Philadelphia physician and signer of the Declaration of Independence, " 'Tis done. We have become a nation."

4. A paragraph that echoes an opening paragraph to express a judgment or realization, thus bringing an essay full circle

> In our own country we are so often unbeautiful. We almost take it for granted, tearing down fine old buildings and then racing off to Europe to gaze at old fountains, old villas, old this, old that. It may be our worst hurt — one which we inflict on ourselves and on other nations. It is a source of

whatever actual devastation we have wrought and comes from our impoverished sense of beauty, our grudge against loveliness. (Patricia Hampl, "Beauty," *A Romantic Education*)

Each of these paragraphs leaves a reader with a sense of completeness, a conviction that the point has been made and that nothing more needs to be said. And each makes a contribution to the essay that could not be made by a "Thus I have shown . . ." conclusion.

Revising Paragraphs

As you learned in Chapter 4, revision occurs at two levels: global revision, in which you are still creating your final draft, and local revision, in which you perfect your final draft. When you undertake local revision of paragraphs, you are ensuring that each paragraph in your essay not only helps to advance the overall purpose of the essay but also works internally. This chapter's discussion of the qualities of topical paragraphs has shown you some ways of thinking through local revision, especially in the case of the paragraph about Thomas Jefferson. Before you can revise your own paragraphs, however, you have to see why they need revision. To do so you must see your paragraphs as your readers will see them, and you must see them anew even though you have been looking at them in global revision. In other words, after you are reasonably sure that global revision has enabled you to refine the subject, audience, and purpose of your essay, and after you have established a reasonably firm organization for it, you must turn to another level of reading to revise: a sentence-by-sentence close reading that allows you to concentrate on the relation of sentences to each other and to the topic sentence. This reading is almost always better accomplished at some distance — preferably a day or two, if possible — from global revision.

One technique that may prove helpful in such close reading is the use of a descriptive outline (see Chapter 3, pages 98–101). As you recall, a descriptive outline is a method for determining what each paragraph in an essay *says* and what it *does*. What a paragraph *says* is its main idea — its topic sentence or, if the topic sentence is implied, a summary statement of its theme. What a paragraph *does* is conveyed in the way all the other sentences support and clarify the topic sentence or theme and how they do that: by illustrating, explaining, defining, narrating, and so on.

You should be able to state succinctly the main idea of every topical paragraph you write. If in reading a paragraph you find that you cannot really determine what it says, you probably need to reconsider your topic sentence — or you may need to create one in the first place. If you find that you cannot determine what a paragraph does, the problem may be that it does not in fact do anything: it may fail to support the topic sentence or fail to add up to any particular meaning. You need then to consider the paragraph's internal qualities: unity, completeness, order, and coherence. If a paragraph does not reflect each of these qualities — even if you have no trouble stating its main idea and what it does — it will not function as fully as it must in advancing your overall purpose. It will leave questions unanswered, details unsupplied, transitions incomplete; and the reader will receive less from your writing than you intended. To ensure these qualities in your paragraphs you must be willing to read painstakingly and to consider the effect of each sentence in a paragraph and the composite effect of all the sentences. A couple of examples of such close reading will help to illustrate its effectiveness.

In the following paragraph, a woman is reporting the difficulties she encountered on her first job as an editorial assistant.

> (1) I was accepted and started work in a large company. (2) My experience had been derived chiefly from books. (3) I was not prepared for the difficult period of adjustment. (4) I soon became discouraged with myself and so dissatisfied with my job that I was on the point of quitting. (5) My employer must have sensed this. (6) He called me into his office and talked to me about the duties of my position and the opportunities for advancement. I realized that there was nothing wrong with me or the job and I decided to stay.

This paragraph says that the writer began a new job as an editorial assistant in a large publishing company. It does the following: (1) explains the writer's difficulty in adjusting and her discouragement with the job; (2) narrates her employer's response to her reaction; and (3) states the resolution of her problem. The paragraph is fairly complete, although the writer omits interesting and vivid details for the most part, preferring instead to write in generalities. It is unified; all sentences relate to the main idea of the writer's difficulty in adjusting. Its order is acceptable: the writer follows the chronology of the situation, although, of course, she compresses it. Yet the paragraph is unsatisfactory. Why?

Primarily, this paragraph lacks coherence; the writer's ideas do not flow from one sentence to the next but rather come out in a series of jolts and jerks because the connecting links between them are not expressed. Also not expressed are the kinds of details that bring the situation to life for the reader, so that it does not seem simply a generic discussion of dissatisfaction on the job — any job. The writer's task in revising is to improve the coherence of the paragraph by providing transitions. As you will see, she did so by two means: sometimes by filling in a small gap in the thought, sometimes by connecting words and phrases. Her task is also to provide some significant details, concrete support for the general situations she is presenting. Study her revisions carefully.

I was accepted almost immediately after graduation, and I started work in the second week of June. Until that time, my experience had been derived chiefly from books, and those books always portrayed publishing as a glamorous world of fine ideas and famous writers. Unfortunately, they did not prepare me for the realities of being an inexperienced and overly idealistic editorial assistant in a very large and very busy publishing company. Consequently, I soon became so discouraged with myself for not knowing what I was supposed to know — and with my job for not being as glamorous as I had dreamed — that I actually thought about quitting. I think the sponsoring editor must have sensed this, for he called me into his office to discuss the nature of publishing and the opportunities my position could offer, including the possibility of advancement. That talk helped me considerably. From that time on I realized that glamour and famous writers are not everything — that pride in a job well done and making contributions to interesting books are more important to me. Needless to say, I didn't quit.

In the next example the writer reports his impression of the French Quarter of New Orleans.

(1) On Bourbon Street in the French Quarter of New Orleans there are a fifty-cent peep show and a theater that shows pornographic movies. (2) Pictures painted by talented artists are for sale in a shop down the street.

(3) Canned music blares through doors held partly open by hustlers of strip-joints. (4) There is a concert hall with no doors and no admission fee, where the crowd is entertained by jazz musicians. (5) In some places there are "dancing girls" who just walk across the stage and do "bumps" in what is supposed to be a dance routine. (6) Sometimes there is a young woman who dances gracefully. (7) She has mastered the techniques that the better burlesques made popular in earlier years.

This paragraph does not lack for detail; in fact, it is all detail and no framework. That fact is so immediately apparent that you need not bother trying to discern what the paragraph says or does. In its present state it is a list of details presented in no recognizable order and lacking a unifying idea. What can be done?

First you must identify or supply a controlling idea. On closer examination you can see that some of the details in the paragraph create an unfavorable impression of Bourbon Street and some a favorable impression: sentences 1, 3, and 5 are unfavorable; sentences 2, 4, 6, and 7 favorable. Once you have classified the details in this way, you realize that the paragraph probably intends to provide a contrast between the favorable and unfavorable aspects of the street. You can state this controlling idea in a topic sentence: "Bourbon Street in the French Quarter of New Orleans is a contrast of vulgarity and art." With that topic sentence as a controlling clue to the development of the paragraph, you can revise the structure of the paragraph in one of two ways: (1) an A + B contrast in which all details suggesting vulgarity (A) are placed in the first half and all those suggesting art (B) are placed in the second half, with a transitional marker *(But* or *On the other hand)* to mark the change; (2) an A/B + A/B contrast in which matched details of vulgarity and art alternate within each sentence. For this particular paragraph the second arrangement is probably better because of its repetitive balanced contrast. Here is the revised paragraph:

Bourbon Street in the French Quarter of New Orleans is a contrast of vulgarity and art. Just a few doors down the street from a fifty-cent peep show and a theater that presents pornographic movies is a shop displaying for sale paintings by talented artists. At strip-joints canned music blares out from doors kept ajar by hustlers seeking to entice passers-by; yet not far away is a concert hall with no admission fee, where musicians play first-rate jazz. Even the "dancing girls" offer a sharp contrast: most limit themselves to a slow walk across the stage, interrupted by exaggerated "bumps"; but a few gracefully demonstrate the techniques that once made burlesque at its best an art form.

Revising Special Paragraphs

Because they are used for special purposes and effects, introductory and concluding paragraphs require a somewhat different approach in revision. Of course, you need to ascertain that they do what they are meant to do, but that judgment must be made less in terms of their method than in terms of their effect. That is, you need to be sure that your introductory paragraph clearly presents the thesis that you intend to develop and that the thesis is advantageously positioned within the paragraph. Or, if you have opted for an opening hook, you need to look at it very carefully when you turn to local revision. If you were not the author of the essay, would you be enticed by its opening paragraph? Or would you find it merely enigmatic? Often writers commit themselves to opening paragraphs too early, before they have achieved a final draft of their writing. In those cases, the opening paragraph may no longer "fit" with the essay it opens, or it may provide only a weak or uncompelling prelude to what follows. A good practice to adopt is always to scrutinize your opening paragraph after you are satisfied with your final draft — and to maintain an open mind about redoing it altogether if that seems necessary.

When revising concluding paragraphs you need first to ascertain that a formal conclusion is in fact necessary. You do not want to belabor the obvious; so if you find that you have written an uninspired and unoriginal closing that merely repeats in capsule form all you have already said, you should not hesitate to delete it in revision. If, on the other hand, you reassure yourself that your essay does require a conclusion, then you need to decide what impression or effect you intended to leave in closing. Does your last paragraph achieve that impression? As in the case of introductory paragraphs, you will sometimes find that your original concluding paragraph is no longer appropriate for the essay you have written. There are numerous ways to close an essay — many more than are suggested in this chapter. Once you have carefully revised the other parts of your essay, you are in a good position to know what you must do to round off your work effectively, perhaps even memorably.

Exercise   Identify the problems in the following paragraphs and suggest a plan for revising each paragraph. Then revise each paragraph.

When CBS did a documentary recently on the late Edward R. Murrow, I was fascinated to see the respect my parents had for this radio and television commentator. Tears were almost in Mom's eyes when she spoke of the day it was announced that Murrow was dead of cancer. They spoke about his coverage of the bombing of London during World War II, about his service as head of the Voice of America in Europe after the war. Then there was his famous confrontation with Senator Joseph McCarthy that helped to put an end to the political witch-hunts of the 1950s. I can never understand how people who have good judgment in other matters can literally smoke themselves to death, as he did.

There is much talk today about "the new morality." People who use that term mean the new *immorality*. But what's new about immorality? In my opinion, young people today are no worse than their grandparents, and probably no better either. As in every generation, it takes all kinds to make a world. From what I've read about the Victorians there was plenty of immorality going on then and by some of the most respected people, even though it was all hushed up. Today young people are less hypocritical, at least most of them, but then again maybe they aren't. Maybe they just like to shock the older generation. It's hard to judge the morality of a whole generation, especially when you want to think the worst of young people anyway. My guess is that young people today are pretty moral, but not always.

In 1976 the United States government imposed a 55 m.p.h. speed limit. Many drivers do not think the speed limit is meant for them. It seems as though the 16–25 year old driving group doesn't believe in driving the speed limit even if it's going 30 m.p.h. in a 25 m.p.h. zone. They learn all the rules in drivers' education, but it suddenly leaves them once the drivers' test is passed. Young drivers should want to drive 55 m.p.h. to reduce wear on their car, the number of accidents, and the amount of gas needed for a trip. Also important is the need to make the United States independent from foreign oil.

It is natural for parents to want the best for their children. They want to protect them from as many of the hardships and difficulties of life. Some parents envision a perfect world for their children and do whatever is necessary to create that kind of atmosphere for them. The children are treated like delicate figurines, sheltered from the realities of life. The children are pampered and spoiled; everything is handed to them. The child believes that life is easy. All decisions are made by the parents. If any problems should arise in the child's life, they are quickly dealt with by the parent before it is allowed to affect the child. This type of treatment is detrimental to his life as an adult. The child develops into a frustrated adult who can not cope with adult problems because he or she was not allowed to deal with childhood difficulties.

Oklahoma stands tall among the other forty-nine states of the union as she is the last and lone dry state. Ever since 1920, liquor, and then later liquor-by-the-drink, have been outlawed in this last refuge of prohibition. Oklahoma earned the right to be called the last dry state in 1977, when South Carolina used the county option trick to bring liquor into their state. Oklahoma is now the only dry state, but that dryness is awful damp. The law states that anyone over 21 can buy a bottle of liquor if he takes the bottle to a private club where he can be served by a bartender from behind a bar. The law also states that everyone who is to drink from that bottle must have his name on the bottle; only one name can appear on a bottle. This law is abused excessively. Many bottles have several names on them and several bottles have no names on them at all.

Chapter 7

Sentences: Patterns of Expression

As you have seen in the last chapter, the sentences in a paragraph are not isolated statements. They are related to what has gone before and to what follows. Although it is traditional to call sentences units of composition, they are units chiefly in the grammatical sense that each sentence has its own subject and predicate and is not part of another sentence. Beyond these basic attributes, however, sentences vary widely in their styles — and therefore in their meanings — depending upon what a writer wants to accomplish. That is, writers have many options in constructing sentences: by making different arrangements of words, phrases, and clauses they can establish or relocate emphasis, shade meaning, and create various kinds of movement in their writing. The function of this chapter is to take a close look at sentences to see how writers work out the implications of their purpose by expanding, combining, and revising their sentences.

Expanding and Combining Sentences

A basic sentence is one that consists of a subject and a predicate expressed in their simplest forms. The predicate may be a complete verb or a verb that needs something to complete it. For example, the sentence *The dog barked* consists of the subject *dog* and the complete verb *barked.* But in the following two sentences the verb requires completion:

> The dog + *bit* + the letter carrier. (subject, verb, and object)

> The dog + *was* + vicious. (subject, verb, and complement)

A *basic sentence,* then, is a minimal main clause consisting of subject, verb, and any object or complement required to complete the verb.

Any element in a basic sentence may be modified by adjectives, adverbs, phrases, or clauses that describe or limit the words being modified. Or a modifier may modify the whole main clause rather than one of its elements. For example, in the sentence *If you can't do it, I'll ask Helena,* the introductory *if* clause modifies all of the main clause *(I'll ask Helena)* and is called a *sentence modifier.*

In the following examples the basic sentence is italicized; the modifiers are in parentheses and are connected by arrows to the words they modify.

> (Stray) *dogs are becoming a* (serious) *nuisance* (in our neighborhood).

> *The man* (who did that) *should be punished.*

> *I wrote* (for an hour), (steadily), (with unaccustomed concentration).

> (About two o'clock in the morning) *we were awakened* (by a quarrel) (in the next motel room).

> *Let me know your decision* (as soon as you make it).

As these examples show, modifiers may be single words, phrases *(about two o'clock in the morning, in the next motel room)*, or subordinate clauses *(who did that, as soon as you make it)*. The modifiers may come before, after, or within the main clause. In the last sentence the subordinate clause modifies the whole main clause and is therefore a sentence modifier.

Exercise   **To distinguish between basic sentences and their modifiers, first underline the basic sentences and then place parentheses around the modifiers.**

1. I did the assignment as well as I could.

2. The kitten was meowing plaintively under the porch.

3. Whatever it costs, I want it.

4. In the attic we found an album full of old family portraits.

5. On the walls of the stuccoed, crumbling villas, the paint peels, unnoticed by human eyes.

6. But as I approached the bridge, the euphoria dissolved. (David Yeadon)

7. With a crash of gears and a lurch we were off, bounding down a half-completed road, then swooping and looping the hairpins up the lower slopes of Mont San Angelo. (David Yeadon)

8. In May 1975, during the spring music festival that opens every year with a performance of Smetana's "Ma Vlast" ("My Homeland"), I went to Prague for the first time. (Patricia Hampl)

Expanding Sentences by Modification

As you have seen in earlier chapters, effective writing employs telling details to communicate specific information and gain the reader's interest. You can enhance and enrich any sentence by modifying any part or all of its main clause or clauses. Notice how much detail is added to the following sentences by the italicized modifiers:

Somehow my strongest memories of San Francisco are of me in a rented sedan *roaring up hills or down hills, sliding on and off the cable tracks.* (Tom Wolfe)

I debated whether I should join a sorority *so early in the term before I knew what college would be like for a small-town girl who was relatively unsophisticated.*

The drug companies, *usually operating through private physicians with access to the prisons,* can obtain healthy human subjects *living in conditions that are difficult, if not impossible, to duplicate elsewhere.* (Jessica Mitford)

Few travelers will find a better-appointed airport than Amsterdam's Schiphol — *clean, white, modern, uncrowded, and equipped with one of the best-appointed, free-port shopping areas in the world.* (Horace Sutton)

Until they are red all over, persimmons are not fit to eat, *as even the squirrels know.*

In sentences like these, the effect comes not from the main clause, which is too general to provide specific information, but from the information provided by the modifiers. This can easily be seen by isolating the main clauses from the italicized details in the fully developed sentences above.

My strongest memories of San Francisco are of me in a rented sedan.

I debated whether I should join a sorority.

The drug companies can obtain healthy human subjects.

Few travelers will find a better-appointed airport than Amsterdam's Schiphol.

Persimmons are not fit to eat.

Two observations should be made about the modifiers in these examples. First, they are not tacked on as afterthoughts during the writing but are rather an essential part of what the writers intended to say. A significant part of Tom Wolfe's memory of San Francisco was the way his car slid on and off the cable-car tracks; the student's debate about joining a sorority was occasioned by the doubt whether it was wise for a girl like her to join so early in the term; Horace Sutton's satisfaction with the airport at Amsterdam was based on the details he listed. In each case the modifying details are necessary to express the writer's complete thought.

Second, the modifications are grounded on previous observation. Wolfe knew from experience what it felt like to slide on and off the cable-car tracks. Sutton is writing from a clear memory of a visit to the airport. Mitford had researched her subject and knew about the doctors' cooperation and the conditions that made prisoners ideal subjects for the drug companies to work with. The writer of the last sentence had observed that not even squirrels will bite a persimmon until it is fully ripe, and he knows why. In each example, the content of the sentence comes directly from the writer's previous observations; modification is the grammatical means of getting these observations into the sentence. The relationship between modification and observation can be illustrated by contrasting two situations, in only one of which the observed details are provided. The four basic sentences below refer to Hogarth's picture of *Gin Lane* on page 77. Expanding these sentences simply requires you to look at that picture, select pertinent details, and use them to modify the basic sentences. For any basic sentence you need not try to get all the pertinent details into a single sentence; you need to use only those that provide an expanded content for each sentence. Look at the picture as you contrast the basic and expanded sentences.

Basic sentence	At the foot of the steps lies a man.
Expanded sentence	At the foot of the steps lies a man who has passed out and is still clutching a gin bottle and an empty glass.
Basic sentence	A woman is taking snuff from a can.
Expanded sentence	At the top of the steps a bare-breasted woman in tattered clothes grins drunkenly as she takes snuff from a can, oblivious that her child is falling over the railing.
Basic sentence	Two people are trying to pawn household utensils.
Expanded sentence	A pawnbroker critically examines a saw that a man has offered him, while a woman waits her turn to pawn a kettle and a cooking pot.
Basic sentence	A corpse is being placed in a coffin.
Expanded sentence	A priest watches two people lower a half-naked corpse into a coffin, beside which a child lies crying.

Now, suppose you were asked to expand the three following sentences by modification:

That attitude is indefensible.

Memories make me homesick.

Beauty contests exploit sex.

In order to expand these sentences, you must know what the writer had in mind when they were written, and you simply do not know. These basic sentences have almost no content. Therefore, asking you to expand them is asking you to provide *your* content for someone else's sentences. You can only do that by drawing on your own experience to decide which attitude is indefensible and why, which memories make you homesick, and why you think, or do not think, beauty contests exploit sex. For example, you might expand the first sentence as follows:

His attitude towards women's rights is indefensible, because he refuses to reexamine his old-fashioned stereotypes about men and women and their relationships in a modern society.

Drawing on your own experience, expand the other two basic sentences to make them fuller expressions of the ideas they suggest to you.

Exercise   **Study the photograph on the opposite page, select a cluster of related details, and for that cluster write a reasonably complete sentence. Repeat this procedure until you have communicated your major observation of the photograph. (Before beginning, you may want to reread the observation analysis of *Gin Lane* on pages 76–80.)**

Combining Sentences by Coordination

Coordination is the combining or joining of similar elements into pairs or series. Instead of writing

Wire-tapping is one kind of invasion of privacy. Breaking-and-entering is another.

you could combine the two sentences into one by compounding the subjects and giving them a common predicate.

Wire-tapping and breaking-and-entering are both invasions of privacy.

Instead of writing

At the tag sale a table could be bought for seventy-five dollars. A chest cost seventy-five dollars too. Seventy-five dollars bought a hand-braided rug.

Robert Doisneau/Rapho

you could combine the subjects in a series and give them all the same predicate.

> At the tag sale a table, a chest, and a hand-braided rug could be bought for seventy-five dollars each.

Exercise   Reduce each of the following groups of sentences to a single sentence by combining parts through coordination.

1. Many young people cannot afford college tuition.
   The expense of living away from home also keeps them from going to college.

2. Energy consumption is a major problem in this country.
   Inflation also causes us much trouble.

3. Journalism is an overcrowded field just now.
   Currently there are more licensed secondary school teachers than there are positions.
   The legal profession is overcrowded.

4. The camp director warned us against trying to shoot the rapids.
   Our class sponsor reminded us of the danger involved.
   A native of the area told us the same thing.

5. The prisoner lost 65 pounds by fasting.
   Then he escaped from his cell through a small skylight.
   After that he fled the state.

Using Parallel Structures

When two or more coordinate elements have the same form, they are said to have *parallel structure*. Parallel structures may occur unnoticed in any sentence but when the parallelism is conspicuous the whole sentence may be called a *parallel sentence*. Thus, "He was without a job, without money, without opportunity, and without hope" is a parallel sentence in which the four phrases have the same form (they all start with *without*) and the same grammatical function (they all complete the verb *was*).

This sort of repetition of parallel elements can be effective in either a sentence or a paragraph. Consider these contrasted sentences:

I am in favor of equal economic rights for women. Women should be able to compete with men for jobs for which they are both qualified. The pay should be the same for the same jobs. There should be the same opportunities for promotion.

I am in favor of equal economic rights for women: the right to compete with men for jobs for which they are both qualified, the right to get the same pay for the same job, and the right to equal opportunities for promotion.

Both versions assert the same three rights. The version at the left advances these assertions through four sentences, each of which has a different subject. The version at the right states all three rights in one sentence and focuses the reader's attention on rights by the repetition of the phrase "the right to" throughout the sentence. The parallel structure of the second version gives it a unity, a coherence, and an emphasis that the first version lacks.

Parallel elements always have the same form and grammatical function. They may be single words, phrases, or clauses; they may act as subjects, objects, verbs, or adverbial or adjectival modifiers. But in a pair or series of coordinate elements all members must be of the same kind. You cannot coordinate nouns with adjectives, verbs with infinitives, or phrases with clauses. Any such attempt would break the parallelism that coordinate structures require and would thus disappoint the reader's expectation and result in awkwardness.

For example, in each of the following sentences the italicized element breaks the parallelism of the sentence by switching from one grammatical form to another:

The children were laughing, squealing, and *danced.*

The sentence requires an *-ing* form, *dancing.* The switch from *laughing* and *squealing* to *danced* breaks the parallelism of the sentence.

My two ambitions are to own my own business and *having* enough money to give my children a good education.

Parallelism requires *to have* to go with *to own.*

My parents taught me such things as honesty, faith, *to be fair,* and *having patience.*

The first two elements in the series are nouns, the third is an infinitive, the fourth is a participle. Parallelism with the first two elements would be maintained by the nouns *fairness* and *patience*.

The diagrams in the following sentences set off the parallel structures to show their similarity in form and function:

1. **parallel predicates**

She
- wandered away from the group,
- climbed a grassy knoll,
- sat down on the grass, and
- leaned against a tree.

2. **a series of nouns followed by another series of adjectives**

Major food companies today are capable of producing foods with any
- flavor,
- texture, or
- color

to suit any
- dietary,
- aesthetic, or
- psychological

need or desire.

3. **a series of prepositional phrases**

We became involved
- in the fortunes of the football team,
- in the issues and personalities of student elections,
- in the letters written to the college paper, and
- in the ideas presented in class.

4. **a series of compound prepositional phrases**

Small children are notoriously deviationist. They totter
- from admiring a daisy to kissing a dog,
- from crawling under the sofa to crawling out again,
- from putting a couple of nails in their mouths to falling into the pond. (Virginia Graham)

5. **a series of objects of the preposition** *of*

But not even those wonderful clergymen who pray in behalf of——
- Congress,
- expressway ribbon-cuttings,
- urban renewal projects and
- testimonial dinners for ethnic aldermen

would pray for a demolition derby. (Tom Wolfe)

6. **parallel subordinate clauses as objects of the infinitive** *to realize*

The public needs to realize——
- that freedom for me is not enough,
- that in fact it is nothing at all. (Charles Rembar)

7. **a series of participial phrases**

I just walked,——
- stopping at coffeehouses,
- smoking unfiltered cigarettes and
- looking out from the blue wreath around me to other deep-drawing smokers. (Patricia Hampl)

Exercises

The following exercises will give you practice in recognizing and using parallel sentences.

1. To identify and point up the parallelism in the following sentences, diagram the parallel elements as shown in the examples above.

   a. We hold these truths to be self-evident: that all men are created equal, that they are endowed by their Creator with certain unalienable Rights. . . .

   b. The book is full of stories of sinking ships and burning towns, of killing cold and windlashed waves, and of reckless men engaged in dangerous pursuits.

2. Organize the following notes into parallel sentences by coordinating the notes in series. (The notes for *a* continue on the next page.)

   a. *Big cars*   but   *Small cars*
      More powerful   Repairs cost less
      Comfortable   Easy parking

Prestigious   Purchase price relatively low

Safer in a crash   Better gas mileage

b. *Watching football on TV*

Close-up of details of action

Expert commentators

Explanations of what happened

Replays

Comfort

3. **Using the notes in 2b as a model, list the advantages of watching football in the stadium; then using 2a as a model, write a parallel sentence that contrasts the relative advantages of watching a football game on television and in the stadium.**

4. **To get additional practice in writing parallel sentences, write three or four such sentences on subjects of your own choosing.**

When parallelism is extended through a paragraph, each sentence becomes an element in a series. You have seen an example of such a series of parallel sentences in the paragraph on page 213 in which Dr. Martin Luther King carried through the paragraph a series of sentences, each beginning with "There is nothing. . . ." As you will remember, this kind of deliberate repetition provides the coherence that ties the individual sentences into a repetitive whole. Here is another example. Do you recognize conspicuous parallelism in it?

H. G. Wells continues to be a biographer's dream and a book reviewer's waltz. His life stretches very nearly from Appomattox to Hiroshima. He was one of the world's great storytellers, the father of modern science fiction, an autobiographic novelist of scandalous proportions, a proselytizer for world peace through brain power, an unsurpassed popular historian, a journalist and inexhaustible pamphleteer, the friend and worthy adversary of great men and the lover of numerous beautiful and intelligent women. (R. Z. Sheppard, *Time*)

Combining Sentences by Subordination

Subordination is a way of reducing one sentence to a clause or a phrase so that it can be included as part of another sentence. For example, the second of the following two basic sentences

We left early. We had work to do.

may be included in the first as a subordinate clause:

We left early *because we had work to do.*

Or a basic sentence may be reduced to a phrase, as happens when you change

The man was evidently in great pain. He was taken to a hospital.

to

The man, *evidently in great pain,* was taken to a hospital.

As these examples show, subordination combines the information of two sentences into one by embedding one sentence in the other. Clearly the revised sentence contains more information than either of the original sentences alone. It is "denser" because it contains more information.

Within limits, the ability to convey more information within a sentence comes with maturity. A correlation exists between the length of sentences and the age of the writer: younger writers compose relatively short sentences, older writers compose longer sentences. This comparison does not mean that all short sentences are necessarily immature, for adult writers, including professionals, often use them for emphasis and variety. But the consistent use of basic sentences in a sustained piece of writing is more common among children than among adults.

The following example illustrates the conversion of four immature sentences into one mature sentence through subordination.

Last summer I camped for a week in Canada.

Three friends were with me.

We camped on the shore of a small lake.

The lake was fifty miles from the nearest settlement.

Last summer three friends and I camped for a week on the shore of a small Canadian lake fifty miles from the nearest settlement.

The original four sentences took 32 words; the revised sentence expresses exactly the same information in 24 words, thus saving one-quarter of the space and getting rid of the monotony of the immature sentences. These results were achieved by subordinating sentences 2, 3, and 4, by making them phrases and embedding them in the first sentence.

Exercise   To get practice in building denser sentences through subordination, reduce each of the following sets of sentences to a single sentence without omitting any of the information.

1. We bought a sturdy old farmhouse.
   I had always wanted the rustic country life.
   The house was a mile out of town.

2. State University won the Valley Tournament.
   State University's Karl Winster scored 35 points.
   He is all-conference.
   The game went into overtime.
   The score was 98–94.
   The game was played last night.

3. A railroad signal was faulty.
   An express plowed into the rear of a freight train.
   The accident happened last night.
   Five people were killed and fifty were injured.

4. The bull is mean and snarly.
   He looks like the devil.
   He is in the outskirts of the arena.
   He is waiting patiently for the ripe moment to attack his prey.

5. The exterior of the restaurant is rough and rugged.
   It resembles an old New England fishing shack.
   It looks like the restaurant should be on the coast of Maine.
   It is in Kansas.
   It looks like it is waiting for some old mariner to come back to port.

The Relation of Combination to Purpose

In combining basic sentences into denser patterns through coordination and subordination, you have a wide choice of combinations and should choose those that best suit your purpose. Suppose, for example, that you are writing a paper for an economics course and you need to trace the history of the competition between American and foreign car manufacturers. In your notes you find the following pieces of information:

1. Small foreign cars could be produced at less cost than the larger cars made in the United States.

2. Foreign-made cars captured a significant share of the American market.

3. American manufacturers began to produce compacts to compete with the foreign cars.

4. In 1972 the U.S. dollar was devalued on the international exchange.

5. The price of a foreign car to an American buyer rose proportionately.

6. Compacts made in the United States could then be sold for less than small foreign cars.

Strung together in a paper in this order, these sentences would have little meaning: they trace a sequence, to be sure, but what is important about that sequence and its implications? The answer, of course, depends upon your sense of your purpose. If you know what you want to do with this material, you can combine it by means of coordination or subordination into more focused sentences that establish relationships among facts and carry out your purpose.

For example, if you want to show the process by which the automobile industry responded to foreign competition, you can reduce 1 to a subordinate clause and embed it in 2, thus getting the sentence:

> Because small foreign cars could be produced at less cost than the larger cars made in the United States, they captured a significant share of the American market.

You can now add to what you have, with a slight change in word order.

> To compete with foreign cars, American manufacturers began to produce compacts.

You can repeat a similar procedure with 4, 5, and 6 to get the sentence:

> When in 1972 the U.S. dollar was devalued on the international exchange, the price of a foreign car to an American buyer rose proportionately, and the American compacts could then be sold for less than the foreign ones.

But if your purpose is to show how devaluing the dollar affected the American domestic market, you can combine the original sentences as follows:

The 1972 devaluation of the U.S. dollar on the international exchange caused foreign-made products to cost more in the United States and thus gave American manufacturers an advantage over their foreign competitors. For example, the small foreign economy cars, the low price of which previously had forced American car-makers to produce the compact, then had to be sold in the United States at prices higher than those of compact cars made in America.

In this version the material of the original is rearranged to form a two-sentence paragraph, of which the first sentence is the topic sentence and the second an illustration. The emphasis is no longer on the steps of a process but on the effect of devaluation. The means of achieving that emphasis are still subordination and coordination.

The three devices you have been studying — modification, coordination, and subordination — can be thought of as techniques for processing material into mature sentences. Organizing ideas into efficient form is just as important in a sentence as in an outline or a paragraph. In immature sentences each idea is stated separately; you put down one idea after another but do nothing to combine them into a denser, more coherent pattern. The ideas may all be there, but the relationships among them are not as clear as they should be. Moreover, immature sentences do not provide purposeful emphasis, for they do not distinguish between more and less important information: everything is treated as if it were equally important. By subordinating the less important to the more important, or by showing the equality of ideas through coordination, mature sentences give appropriate emphasis. They not only reduce monotony by providing more variety in the sentence structure, but they often provide better coherence.

Exercise   Read each of the following clusters of material and the purposes listed after each. Then combine as much of the material as you need (you may not be able to use it all) in sentences that fulfill the two purposes given for each cluster. You may need to write several sentences for each purpose. Your instructor may want your class to discuss the reasons for which you created your different sentences.

Cluster A

1. **Clothes reveal an individual's personality and attitudes.**

2. Clothes like blue jeans and tee shirts make a statement.

3. The color and style of clothing also make a statement.

4. Certain occasions, situations, or jobs require appropriate attire.

5. "Appropriate" attire is often formal: a dress, suit, tie.

6. People should be free to dress as they please.

7. In many professional situations, people judge others by their appearance.

Purpose 1: You want to assert why people should be free to dress as they please.

Purpose 2: You want to argue that people should dress appropriately in professional situations.

Cluster B

1. Frozen food has long been part of the American way of life.

2. Frozen dinners once consisted of such dull items as lima beans, gooey potatoes, and mystery meat.

3. Currently available frozen dinner entrees include beef bourguignon with glazed carrots, asparagus crepes with mornay sauce, and vegetarian lasagna.

4. Some frozen food companies have even developed gourmet dietetic dinners.

5. Americans have fast-paced, busy lifestyles these days.

6. They are also more concerned than before about eating healthful, interesting, and balanced meals.

Purpose 1: You want to propose a cause-and-effect relationship between the change in American lifestyles and eating habits and the change in frozen food offerings.

Purpose 2: You want to demonstrate that those who are particular about the nutrition and taste of their food now have reason to try frozen food.

Cluster C

1. Linda Ronstadt began her divergent career singing country-tinged ballads.

2. Gradually her music moved from country-rock to rock.

3. She has recorded acclaimed versions of songs by such diverse writers as James Taylor, the McGarrigles, and Elvis Costello.

4. Her range has been called "operatic" by a number of classical and rock music critics.

5. One recent album reflects a new repertoire for her — standards by such writers as Irving Berlin and Ira and George Gershwin.

6. She sang on Broadway in the soprano role of Mabel in Gilbert and Sullivan's operetta *The Pirates of Penzance*.

7. She is singing in Puccini's opera *La Bohème* in New York this season.

Purpose 1: You want to assert and illustrate Ronstadt's versatility as a singer.

Purpose 2: You want to speculate about a possible shift in focus in Ronstadt's singing career.

Types of Sentences and Their Effects

At the beginning of this chapter you saw the shape of a basic sentence and how that shape can be changed by modification or combination. Now you will consider two important sentence styles that you can use to good effect in your writing — the balanced sentence and the periodic sentence.

The Balanced Sentence

A *balanced sentence* is one in which two parallel structures are set off against each other like the weights on a balance scale. In each of the following sentences the italicized parts illustrate the balance:

Many are called but *few are chosen.* (Matthew 22:14)

Beauty without grace is *the hook without the bait.* (Ralph Waldo Emerson)

We undertook this project *to promote intercollegiate debate*, not *to kill it.*

The test of our progress is not whether we add more to the abundance of those who have much; it is whether we provide enough for those who have too little. (Franklin D. Roosevelt)

In reading these sentences aloud, you tend to pause between the balanced parts. That pause is marked often by a coordinating conjunction *(and, but, or, nor, yet)*, sometimes by *not* (as in the third sentence), and sometimes by punctuation alone (as in the fourth sentence). Whatever the marker, it serves as the fulcrum, the point at which the two parts balance against each other, as the following diagram shows:

but

| When a man dies on shore, his body remains with his friends, and the "mourners go about the streets," | when a man falls overboard at sea and is lost, there is a suddenness in the event . . . which gives it an air of awful mystery. (Richard Henry Dana) |

Here the similarity of thought and sentence structure on both sides of the conjunction sets up an equilibrium between the parts.

Although the balanced sentence is not limited to establishing a contrast, that is its most frequent use. It is an effective structure to use when, as in an alternating comparison, two subjects are being contrasted within the same sentence. It was used this way in the diagrammed example above, where the balanced structure points up the contrast.

Exercise
Generate a statement about each item in the following list of paired terms. Then combine the two statements into a balanced sentence.

dark chocolate	milk chocolate
compact car	full-sized car
jogging	swimming
rock singer	country music singer
celebrity	hero
education	unemployment

The Periodic Sentence

A *periodic sentence* is one that builds up, often through two or more parallel constructions, to a climactic statement in the final main clause. The italicized sentence below will introduce the structure:

Just before I went away to college, my father took me aside, as I had expected, and said, as I had not expected, *"Now, Son, if a strange woman comes up to you on a street corner and offers to take your watch around the corner and have it engraved, don't do it."* (Eric Lax)

The father's remarks lead up to the advice of the final main clause — "don't do it" — which provides a climax, like the punch line of a joke. All the rest of the sentence has been preparation for that statement.

Here is another, more serious, example, in which the main clause is preceded by a long participial phrase ("Having reached . . .") that includes a subordinate clause.

Having reached the murky grass flats of Tampa Bay, that place where under the hot sun and in rain squalls my father had so patiently taught me the unity of pain and beauty, I climbed over the side of the boat and scattered his ashes over the water.

One more example:

Unless we maintain the pure traditional meaning of the word [*freedom*], unless we can understand in common and as a nation that the only opinion established in this country by the Constitution is the opinion that a man is free to hold *any* opinion, unless we can agree among ourselves that by freedom we mean *precisely* freedom, we may end by finding ourselves "free" in the sense in which the Russians now find themselves "democratic." (Archibald MacLeish)

The structure of this sentence consists of three parallel subordinate clauses followed by the main clause, which contains a subordinate clause. The full revelation of the meaning is withheld until the final comparison. The sentence says, in effect, "Unless this and this and this happen, this will happen."

A basic sentence usually begins with a main clause; a periodic sentence ends with one. In this sense the periodic sentence reverses the standard order. But the difference between them is more than a change in order. There are also differences in procedure and effect. In a basic sentence you may work out the sentence while writing it, starting with the main clause and clarifying it by adding necessary modifications. But in a periodic sentence you must know from the beginning how it will end. For example, the writer of the following sentence is moving toward his main clause through a series of *if* clauses that successively deal with life, liberty, and the pursuit of happiness, and what he has to say about each of these subjects must be chosen for its contribution to the idea of the main clause.

> But if life hardly seems worth living, if liberty is used for subhuman purposes, if the pursuers of happiness know nothing about the nature of their quarry or the elementary techniques of hunting, these constitutional rights will not be very meaningful. (Aldous Huxley)

As these examples show, a periodic sentence allows you to put unusual emphasis on the main clause by holding it off until the end.

In the following sentence the main idea Norman Mailer wants to communicate is that Marilyn Monroe was a complex individual whose apparent inconsistencies were a reflection of her complexity. That purpose requires him to construct a brief argument in which selected inconsistencies are resolved as effects of an underlying cause — her complex but integrated personality.

> The boldness with which she could parade herself and yet never be gross, her sexual flamboyance and bravado which yet breathed an air of mystery and even reticence, her voice which carried such ripe overtones of erotic excitement and yet was the voice of a shy child — these complications were integral to her gift. (Norman Mailer)

Mailer could have written this sentence in standard order, starting with the main clause and following it with the series of apparent inconsistencies. But had he done so, the force of the main clause would have been weakened. A reader would have left the sentence, not with a statement about integrated complexity, but with a series of contrasting details about Marilyn Monroe's sexuality and innocence. By using a periodic rather than a basic structure, Mailer could put his conclusion where it would have the greatest force, at the end of the sentence. If you doubt this statement, try writing the sentence in standard order; or observe the difference in effect when the following sentence is written in standard order:

> From breakfast to lunch, from lunch to dinner, from dinner to midnight snack, he is thinking of only one thing, the next meal.

Exercise   **Write a periodic sentence describing the most frustrating, fulfilling, or comic day you have had in recent months. Use the opening clause in your sentence to**

cite details that will build up suspense for the reader. Reveal your major assertion about the day in the final main clause of your sentence.

Revising Sentences

So far in this chapter you have examined the structure of different types of sentences and the techniques for increasing the density of sentences through modification, coordination, and subordination. In this section you will learn how to work out another problem of local revision — revising sentences to make them more effective expressions of the ideas they are intended to convey. Much of the time, of course, you revise your sentences while writing them. The process of shaping ideas into sentences is a learning process, and you make changes in sentence structure and wording as you grope toward a satisfactory statement of your ideas. But here you will be trying to improve sentences that have already been written. This kind of revision will stress *clarity, emphasis, economy,* and *variety.*

In this section you will edit sentences by first detecting their weaknesses and then removing them. The experience you gain from this practice should make it easier for you to edit your own sentences.

Revision for Clarity

Lack of clarity can be a result of faulty grammar or punctuation, misleading pronoun reference, vague or ambiguous wording, or confusing sentence structure. Since you are revising sentence structure here, you should be aware of the lack of clarity that sometimes occurs when a writer tries to pack too much information into one sentence. The following example will introduce this problem:

> Last month while I was visiting the federal buildings in Washington on a guided tour, we went to the National Art Gallery, where we had been for an hour when the rest of the group was ready to move on to the Treasury Building and I told a friend with the group that I wanted to stay in the Art Gallery a while longer and I would rejoin the group about half an hour later, but I never did, even though I moved more quickly than I wanted to

from room to room, not having seen after about four hours all that there was to see.

As written, this sentence of 106 words consists of three main clauses and eight subordinate clauses. This involved structure is hard going for both writer and reader. The revision should seek to simplify the structure by reducing the number of clauses per sentence. This can be done by either or both of two methods: by distributing the clauses into two or more sentences, or by omitting material not necessary to the statement. The second method depends on the writer's view of what is necessary.

There are several ways of revising the sentence. Here are two.

> While I was visiting the National Art Gallery with a tour group last month, I decided to stay longer when the group left after an hour, and so I told a friend that I would rejoin the group at the Treasury Building in about half an hour. I moved from room to room much more quickly than I wanted to, but after four hours I still had not seen all there was to see. I never did rejoin the tour group that day.

This revision distributes all the original material into three sentences and makes the passage easier to read. In addition, the revision saves twenty-three words, a reduction of 20 percent.

The following revision cuts the original drastically by leaving out material not considered significant:

> While visiting the National Art Gallery with a tour group last month, I stayed for four hours after the group left. Even then I did not see all I wanted to.

This version reduces the original eleven clauses to four and condenses the 106-word sentence to 31 words in two sentences.

Both revisions are clearer than the original. The first revision may be considered minor, since it makes little change in content. The second revision is major, since it selects and reorganizes the content. Between these minor and major revisions, others are possible. Try a few variations to see which you prefer.

Notice that the revisions above reduce the amount of information in the original sentence. This statement may seem to contradict what was said earlier about combining sentences to increase their density. But in fact there is no contradiction. Some sentences should be combined to achieve greater density; others should be simplified by rewriting one sen-

"...And so it was, and so it was to be what it was to have been, and had what it was to have had, had it had what it was to be what it had to have been..."

Drawing by Maslin; © 1982. The New Yorker Magazine, Inc.

tence as two or three. The decision to combine or to separate, to enrich or to simplify, depends on the material and your best judgment of how to present it to your reader.

Exercise

Simplify the structure of the following sentences to make them easier to read:

1. His sister, who had been living in Springfield, where she had been directing a child-service program that screened reports of child abuse and made referrals to case workers, having been appointed to a position in the Department of Health and Human Services because she had performed so ably at the local level, has recently moved to Washington.

2. For several years controversy has centered upon a commonly used herbicide called 2-4-5-T, with producers insisting that it is not harmful to humans but with independent researchers saying there is evidence that it can contribute to miscarriages and development of cancer, among other problems, in people exposed to it, and the controversy has been highly publicized recently because the herbicide is similar in its chemical make-up to the defoliant

used by the American military in Vietnam that is now suspected of causing cancer and other serious diseases in people who were exposed to it there.

3. My father has a friend who insists that he is dirt poor and I suppose that in a sense he is because he invests almost all of his extra income in land, since he says he can't afford to put it in the bank because inflation decreases the value of his money more than interest increases it and he doesn't want to be bothered with the problems that go along with rental property and he isn't interested in stocks and bonds, all of which causes him to buy land on the theory that no more land is being made and that the only way its value can go is to keep rising.

Revision for Emphasis

Emphasis is a reflection of your purpose and helps you make that purpose clear to your readers. There are usually several ways of expressing any idea, and if one way gives greater emphasis than others to what you want to stress, that is the best way. Three ways of obtaining purposeful emphasis are *emphatic word order* (including *climactic order*), *emphatic repetition,* and *emphatic voice.*

Emphatic word order   The way word order is used for emphasis in a sentence depends on two considerations: What do you wish to emphasize? And what positions within a sentence provide the most emphasis? In an English sentence, both the beginning and the end are emphatic positions. The most important material is put in these positions, and less important material is placed in the middle. If unimportant details pile up at the end of a sentence, they may get more emphasis than they deserve, and your readers may feel that the sentence is "running down" because they expect important information at the end and do not get it.

Notice the difference between the following statements:

Unemphatic order	Emphatic order
On July 31, 1973, a plane crash which killed 88 people and which was the first fatal crash for Delta Airlines in 95 billion passenger miles occurred at Boston's Logan International Airport.	Eighty-eight people were killed in a plane crash at Boston's Logan International Airport on July 31, 1973, the first fatal crash for Delta Airlines in 95 billion passenger miles.

The version at the left puts the date and place in the most emphatic positions in the sentence (the beginning and the end) and the number killed and Delta's impressive safety record in the least emphatic position. The version at the right puts the most significant information where it will get the greatest emphasis and fills in the middle with the place and date.

Here is another example:

Unemphatic order	Emphatic order
Much debate focused on the effect that the Interior Department's decision about offshore drilling would have on the fishing industry in years to come.	The Interior Department's decision about offshore drilling caused much debate about the future of the fishing industry.

The two parts of the sentence that deserve most emphasis are "Interior Department's decision" and "future of the fishing industry." Unlike the version at the left, the version at the right places these two phrases in the most emphatic positions in the sentence, the beginning and the end.

Exercise

Revise the following sentences by changing the order to emphasize the parts you think important:

1. He said that the UN had failed in its chief function, to preserve peace, although it had done much of which it could be proud and was still performing valuable services in many areas.

2. It is entirely possible that morality consists chiefly in the courage of making a choice, I sometimes think.

3. A decision that has caused much concern about foreign policy is the one about legislative veto that the Supreme Court made.

4. A problem that is important to our environment, noise pollution, is one that we have only recently given much attention to.

5. He was accused of cheating and was expelled from college by the Disciplinary Committee yesterday afternoon at a meeting.

6. The governor said that he had considered the arguments for and against a

stay of execution and was in favor of mercy when everything was taken into account.

7. The doctor told me I could eat anything I pleased except animal fats while I was on this diet.

8. Thomas Marshall, Vice President under Woodrow Wilson, expressed our traditional neglect of the men in that office when he said, "If you're not coming in, throw me a peanut," to visitors looking curiously through his doorway.

9. In 1978 Proposition 13, which served as a stimulus for a nationwide concern about reducing taxes, was approved by the voters of California.

10. We can be sure that a reduction in taxes is what most political candidates will promise.

11. Though he hit the ball to the right-field wall, Pete Rose was called "Out!" after he rounded first and second and dived into third base in a head-first slide.

12. The situation faced by hundreds of American travelers stranded at the London airport was, because of a sudden airlines strike, a quite serious one.

Climactic order   Climactic word order is a form of emphatic order that arranges the material of a sentence so as to build up to a major idea. You have seen that the force of the periodic sentence comes from this order, but climax may also be used in standard sentences. The following examples contrast anticlimactic and climactic order. Study both versions of each sentence and explain what changes were made in the revisions.

Anticlimactic order	Climactic order
Near the end of *A Separate Peace,* Dr. Stanpole says to Gene that he must tell him that his best friend Finny is dead, the sort of news that the doctor fears the boys of Gene's generation will hear much of.	Near the end of *A Separate Peace,* Dr. Stanpole tells Gene that he must give him the sort of news he fears the boys of Gene's generation will hear much of, that Gene's best friend Finny is dead.
In a magnificent stretch run the favorite overtook six horses and	In a magnificent stretch run that thrilled the crowd, the favorite

won by a nose, thrilling the crowd.	overtook six horses and won by a nose.
The prosecution asked in its summing up that the jury bring in a verdict of guilty, which was the only possible verdict considering the violence of the crime and the lack of the provocation.	In summing up, the prosecution asked the jury to consider the violence of the crime and the lack of provocation and then bring in the only possible verdict — guilty.

Emphatic repetition   More often than not, unintentional repetition weakens a sentence, as the following examples show:

> Psychotic patients suffering from psychoses are sometimes hospitalized in hospitals operated especially for them.

> The writer who wrote the novel that won the prize for the best novel of the year did not attend the awards ceremony.

> The disappointing results were all the more disappointing because we were sure that the experiment would be a success, and so were disappointed in the results.

Intentional repetition, by contrast, can produce a desired emphasis. You have seen how repeated key words can help knit a paragraph together (page 216) and how the repetition of sentence structure through parallel and balanced elements creates desirable emphasis (pages 238–241; 248–49). Deliberate repetition, therefore, can be effective. Consider the following:

> If at first you don't succeed, *try, try* again.

> And this hell was, simply, that he had never in his life owned anything — *not* his wife, *not* his house, *not* his child — which could not, at any instant, be taken from him by the power of white people. (James Baldwin)

> It is easy to find scapegoats for the pollution problem: to *blame* the industrialist, to *blame* the scientist, to *blame* advertising or capitalism, or in one comprehensive condemnation, to *blame* society; but everyone who drives a car or burns electricity or flushes a toilet has a share of the *blame;* it is not *blaming* that is needed, but a conscientious and consistent attempt to make *blame* unnecessary.

Emphatic voice   It is a commonplace that writers should use verbs in the active rather than the passive voice. This advice is generally sound, because the active voice is usually more natural and the so-called weak passive sometimes leads to wordiness and awkward shifts in structure.

Weak passive	More emphatic active
Fashion design majors modeled the outfits that had been made by them during the term.	Fashion design majors modeled the outfits they had made during the term.
The length of the lake was swum by the six candidates for life-saving certificates.	The six candidates for life-saving certificates swam the length of the lake.
Thirty miles of rough road had been traveled before we realized that the tent had been forgotten.	We had traveled thirty miles of rough road before we realized that we had forgotten the tent.

Exercise   Revise the following sentences by changing passive verbs to the active voice:

1. Once the danger was gone, the safety precautions that had been so carefully observed by us were abandoned.

2. An almost perfect set was played by John McEnroe.

3. It was estimated by the garage mechanic that $200 would be needed for the repairs.

4. A local women's club was spoken to by Helen Caldicott about the nuclear freeze movement.

5. The path to the bottom of the canyon was descended by everyone in our group.

6. Gun control laws have been persistently opposed by the National Rifle Association.

7. A touchdown was scored by each of our running backs during the game.

8. He was not prepared for the test and so only half of the questions were answered.

9. The instructor said the papers would be graded and returned by him within three days.

10. It must surely be recognized by the American Hospital Association that such costs cannot be afforded by many families.

But there are situations in which the passive voice is more emphatic than the active. The beginning of a sentence is, as you have seen, a position of stress, and putting an unimportant word or phrase there tends to emphasize it — sometimes unwisely. For example:

The letter carrier delivers mail twice a day.

A person cannot smoke in this section of the plane.

People should expect some delay in these circumstances.

Someone stole her car from the parking lot.

The doctor performed the emergency surgery under battery-operated lights.

In these sentences the stress should not fall on the grammatical subjects, which are of almost no interest. Passive constructions, ignoring these subjects entirely, give more accurate emphasis:

Mail is delivered twice a day.

Smoking is prohibited in this section of the plane.

In these circumstances some delay is to be expected.

Her car was stolen from the parking lot.

The emergency surgery was performed under battery-operated lights.

The choice between active and passive is like any other choice you have to make. It is to be judged by the results: which form will provide the emphasis you want? But because misuse of the passive voice often results in an awkward or ungrammatical sentence, you should generally choose the active voice unless there is a clear gain from using the passive.

Revision for Economy

Economy is a relation between the number of words used and the amount of meaning they convey. A sentence is not economical because it is short, or wordy because it is long. The test is not the number of words but the amount of information they convey. Consider these two statements:

I should like to make it entirely   I want to make it clear to every-
clear to one and all that neither I   one that neither I nor any of my

nor any of my associates or fellow workers had anything at all to do in any way, shape or form with this illicit and legally unjustifiable act that has been committed.

associates had anything to do with this illegal act.

The version at the left takes forty-six words to say what is more clearly said at the right in twenty-four. The extra words do not add significant information; they merely make reading more difficult and annoy the reader by useless repetition of the same idea in different words.

Now contrast the following statements:

His defense is not believable.

His defense is not believable: at points it is contradicted by the unanimous testimony of other witnesses, and it offers no proof that that testimony is false; it ignores significant facts about which there can be no dispute, or evades them by saying that he does not recollect them; it contains inconsistencies that he is unable to resolve, even when specifically asked to do so.

The version at the right contains over ten times as many words as the one at the left, but its greater length is justified by the greater information it provides. Both versions share a common judgment, but the second goes on to show the reasons for that judgment. If these reasons are necessary, it would be foolish to omit them simply to get a shorter sentence. Decisions about economy must always be made in relation to meaning.

Wordiness — the opposite of economy — is a common problem in writing. When a whole essay is wordy, the trouble may lie in scanty planning or in a monotonous style that could be tightened up by better use of coordination and subordination. Some of these weaknesses require global revision. Here, however, you are considering local revision — omitting wordiness *within* a sentence. The two most common methods are cutting out useless words and substituting more economical expressions for wordy ones. Both methods are illustrated below.

Cutting out a useless introductory phrase

(H) ~~By way of response,~~ he said he would think about it.

~~With reference to your question,~~ I think we should accept the invitation.

~~It goes without saying that~~ (T) they certainly need help.

~~It seems unnecessary to point out that~~ I was in Chicago at that time.

Cutting out useless words within the body of a sentence

As we walked ~~in the direction of~~ home, I felt ~~as if~~ I had never been happier.

The task of English teachers is to help students ~~develop the ability to understand and~~ communicate in their native language.

She looked ~~as though she was~~ angry.

The truth ~~of the matter is, to call a spade a spade,~~ that he is afraid of her.

Richard Wright ~~was a person who~~ became disillusioned with the Communist Party ~~that was operating~~ in America because ~~of the fact that~~ he felt that it was not sufficiently sensitive to the problems of ~~most of the~~ black Americans.

Substituting an economical statement for a wordy one

We find the present situation ~~that exists at the moment~~ intolerable.

It is time to leave.
~~I think the time has come for us to be leaving.~~

The modern trend
~~The idea of communication has led the vanguard of the "New English."~~

is to emphasize
~~The emphasis now placed on~~ the teaching of linguistics ~~ties into the impor-~~
as an aid to effective communication.
~~tance implied in teaching children to communicate effectively.~~

Preceding the withdrawal of
The years ~~which preceded the time when~~ American troops ~~were withdrawn~~
of
from Vietnam were a time ~~when there was~~ much social and political unrest

~~among the people~~ in this country.

Exercise

Revise the following sentences to reduce wordiness:

1. Often the words that he uses do not convey the meaning that he intends.

2. She looked as though she was feeling indisposed.

3. As far as the average citizen is concerned, it is probable that most people are not greatly concerned about the scandals of politicians.

4. When we studied defense mechanisms, which we did in psychology class, I discovered that I use most of the mechanisms that are discussed in the textbook.

5. Just before the time when World War I broke out, Alsatians who were of French descent were outraged by the act of a German soldier's slapping a cobbler who was lame across the face with a sword.

6. Concerning the question of whether men are stronger than women, it seems to me that the answer is variable, depending on how one interprets the word *stronger.*

7. When, after much careful and painstaking study of the many and various problems involved, experts in charge of the different phases of our space flight programs made the decision to send a rescue ship to bring back the astronauts who were in space in Skylab II, about a thousand people set to work at Cape Kennedy, each with his or her own duties to perform, to get the rescue ship ready to fly into space and bring back the astronauts.

Revision for Variety

A discussion of variety in sentence structure in some ways belongs in a chapter on the paragraph, because variety is a characteristic not of single sentences but of a succession of sentences. But you need to understand how to achieve variety through modification, coordination, subordination, and word order, the issues discussed in this chapter. The following examples and exercises combine the techniques of local revision at both the paragraph and sentence level.

Consider the following series of sentences:

1. Maxwell Perkins was born in 1884 and died in 1947.

2. He worked for Charles Scribner's Sons for thirty-seven years.

3. He was head editor for Scribner's for the last twenty of these thirty-seven years.

4. He was almost certainly the most important American editor in the first half of the twentieth century.

5. He worked closely with Thomas Wolfe, Scott Fitzgerald, and Ernest Hemingway.

6. He also worked closely with a number of other well-known writers.

These sentences are all of similar length (10, 9, 14, 17, 11, and 11 words respectively), and they are all standard sentences of the same basic structure (subject + predicate). Their lack of variety becomes monotonous.

Now contrast the same passage revised for variety:

Maxwell Perkins (1884–1947), head editor of Charles Scribner's Sons for the last twenty of his thirty-seven years with that company, was almost certainly the most important American editor in the first half of the twentieth century. Among the many well-known writers with whom he worked closely were Thomas Wolfe, Scott Fitzgerald, and Ernest Hemingway.

The revision combines the original material into two sentences of thirty-seven and eighteen words respectively and results in greater economy (fifty-five words instead of seventy-two), greater density, and less monotony. These results were obtained by the following operations:

1. Sentences 1, 2, 3, and 4 of the original were combined in the first revised sentence by

    a. making Maxwell Perkins the subject of the new sentence.
    b. placing his dates in parentheses.
    c. reducing sentences 2 and 3 to a phrase in apposition with the subject of the new sentence.
    d. making sentence 4 the complement of the new sentence.

2. Sentences 5 and 6 of the original were combined by

    a. having them share a common verb, *were*.
    b. making sentence 6 the subject of that verb, and sentence 5 the complement.

Other revisions are possible. For example:

Maxwell Perkins (1884–1947), who as head editor for Charles Scribner's Sons for twenty years worked closely with such well-known writers as Thomas Wolfe, Scott Fitzgerald, and Ernest Hemingway, was almost certainly the most important American editor in the first half of the twentieth century.

This version reduces the original to a single sentence by making the statement about Perkins's importance the main clause and embedding the rest in a subordinate clause between the subject and predicate of the main clause. Still other revisions are possible. The point is not that one revision is better than another, but that subordination and coordination can get rid of the obvious weakness of the original — its lack of variety.

Exercise

As an exercise in using the procedure above, first consider the possible revisions that follow the paragraph about Henry V. Then decide which of these possibilities you want to use in rewriting the paragraph. It is not necessary to use all the possibilities. Use those that give you the best paragraph.

For ease of reference the sentences are numbered.

(1) Shakespeare's chronicle history of *Henry the Fifth* is a drama of kinghood and war. (2) It is essentially a play about a young king's coming of age. (3) Henry V had been an irresponsible young prince before his accession to the throne. (4) He had to prove his worthiness as king by leading his army in war. (5) He invaded France and captured Harfleur, and then tried to withdraw his troops to Calais. (6) He and his men were confronted by a numerically superior French army at Agincourt. (7) In a famous passage in Shakespeare's play, Henry urges his soldiers on to an incredible victory. (8) The superior mobility and firepower of the English proved too much for the heavily armored French.

Consider the possible revisions:

1. Combine 1 and 2 by omitting *is* in 1 and, with necessary punctuation, omitting *It* at the beginning of 2, thus making "a drama of kinghood and war" a phrase within the combined sentence. Write the sentence so formed.

2. Combine 3 and 4 by inserting a comma + *who* after *Henry V,* substituting a comma for the period at the end of 3, and omitting the *He* in 4. Write the sentence so formed.

3. Reduce the first half of 5 to a phrase, "After invading France and capturing Harfleur," and substitute *he* for *and then.*

4. Join 6 with 5 by *but* and change the *He* of 6 to *he.* Write the sentence thus revised.

5. Combine 8 and 7 by inserting *in which* after *victory* and making the necessary change in capitalization. Write the revised sentence.

6. Now, using any of these revised sentences, or any revisions of your own, rewrite the complete paragraph.

Here are three pieces of advice on sentence variety. First, *don't overdo it.* It is neither necessary nor wise to construct every sentence differently or to pack too much material into individual sentences. On the one hand, sentences that are too dense are hard to read. On the other hand, those not dense enough are monotonous and may seem immature. The main thing is to be sure you have *some* variety in sentence structure within your paragraphs. Most of your sentences will probably be basic sentences averaging about twenty words. But within a paragraph, individual sentences may range from ten words or fewer to thirty or more, and may include balanced or periodic structures. As the writer, you control the choice of length and structure. Knowing how to vary sentences helps you make intelligent choices.

Second, *postpone revision for variety until you have written your first draft.* You may find yourself reworking sentences as you write them, but your revisions will be more effective if you read the entire draft aloud and hear whether the sentence structure is monotonous. You can even *see* unvaried sentences by noticing that they all take about the same number of lines.

Third, *be aware of the effect that sentence length has on readers.* In general, long sentences slow down the reading, and short ones speed it up. Short sentences are often effective as topic sentences because they state a general idea simply, but longer sentences will often be needed to develop that idea through the paragraph. Short sentences are excellent for communicating a series of actions, emotions, or impressions; longer sentences are more likely to be appropriate for analysis or explanation. Short sentences are closer to the rhythms of speech and are therefore suitable when the style is conversational and you are adopting an intimate tone. The more formal the style, the more likely you are to use long and involved sentences. But all these statements are relative to the particular kind of material being presented to a particular kind of reader: as in all writing, the choice comes back to your purpose.

Review Exercises

1. **As a final demonstration of your ability to revise a collection of sentences into an effective, coherent paragraph, use all the information given below to write a paragraph on lobbyists.**

a. The most successful lobbyists working in state capitals are experts in legislative strategy.

b. They are highly paid.

c. They know more about the legislative process than do most state legislators.

d. They are skillful, professional workers.

e. They are available to almost any group with sufficient funds to pay for their services.

f. Lobbyists today are not likely to apply the old-fashioned direct pressure to politicians.

g. They are likely to try to persuade legislators' constituents to apply the pressure.

h. A pressure group wants something, and the public wants something.

i. Lobbyists hope to convince legislators that these are the same.

2. Edit the following paragraph into a more effective statement. First read the paragraph as a whole. Then go over it sentence by sentence, making whatever changes you think desirable. Finally rewrite the paragraph in its revised form.

One of the conceptions not founded in fact that many people have about the nature of language is that it is one of those things that will "hold still" and refuse to change. And many of those who know that this English language of ours has changed through the years, and continues to the present time to change, have the suspicion that there is something that is not good about this change from the status quo. You may have heard someone express his or her regret about the fact that our language is in this day and age no longer the "grand old language of Shakespeare." The person who would express that regret would be surprised to become cognizant of the fact that Shakespeare was one of those people who were denounced for corrupting and polluting the English language. But change in the language that we speak and write is not to be deplored: it is simply a fact that is with us in our lives.

Chapter 8

Diction: The Choice of Words

As you think your way through a sentence, you are inevitably concerned with finding the words that best convey your thought. Sometimes, especially when you are quite clear about what you want to say, the words come so easily that you are hardly aware of choosing them. At other times you find yourself scratching out one choice after another as you search for the word that will best convey the meaning you want. Such revisions are not necessarily a sign of indecision. Often it is the best writers who worry most about diction; and perhaps they are the best writers partly because they take pains to choose the right word.

But words are not right or wrong in themselves. What makes a particular word right for you is the effect it has in your sentence or paragraph. Readers do not read isolated words; they read words in a context provided by other words, and that context affects their response to any particular word. For example, they will respond quite differently to the word *disorderly* when it is used to describe a mob than they will when it is used to describe a house. Your choice of words must therefore take into account the context in which the selected word is to appear. Whatever words you use must be appropriate to the context. One way to determine whether a word is appropriate is to distinguish between two kinds of meaning.

Denotation and Connotation

The most familiar use of words is to name things — trees, cars, games, people, stars, oceans. When words are used this way, the things they refer to are called their *denotations*. The word *chair* most commonly denotes a piece of furniture for sitting on. The denotation of *Minneapolis* is the city of that name.

But words acquire *connotations* as well as denotations. Connotations are attitudes that are associated with particular words. When you call an action "courageous" or "foolhardy," you are not only describing it, you are expressing, and inviting a reader to share, an attitude toward it. Connotations are sometimes called *implicit* meanings, as contrasted with the *explicit* meanings of denotations, because they imply or suggest attitudes that they do not state outright.

In each of the following sentences, the writer is implying different attitudes toward similar events:

Our troops *routed* the enemy from the hill. The next day they made a *strategic withdrawal* from the same position.

Some of the stockholders charged that the corporation was *operating in the red,* but the chairman of the board explained that it was actually *achieving a programmed deficit.*

The difference between a *boyish prank* and an *act of vandalism* depends on whose child does the mischief.

When the principal announced that the teachers were *implementing a child-centered curriculum,* one disgruntled parent said they were *mollycoddling the kids.*

When our men started on *reconnaissance patrol,* they came across an enemy squad *sneaking behind our lines.*

Within each contrast in these sentences, the choice is not between denotations and connotations but between favorable and unfavorable connotations. "Boyish prank" is just as connotative as "act of vandalism" but implies a different attitude toward the event. "Operating in the red" and "achieving a programmed deficit" refer to the same financial situation; but whereas the first phrase will create unfavorable associations, the second may win approval from the stockholders.

Whatever words you choose should support your purpose. If you wish to report objectively what you saw or heard, you should choose words that imply no attitude. Thus you should prefer "reconnaissance patrol" to "sneaking behind the lines." If you wish to convey a tolerant or approving attitude, you should use words that invite such a response — "a boyish prank," "a strategic withdrawal," "a child-centered curriculum." But if you wish to suggest disapproval, you should select words with unfavorable connotations — "an act of vandalism," "mollycoddling the kids."

Three Qualities of Good Diction

Good diction is the choice of words that best allows you to communicate your meaning to your readers. That choice is always made with reference to a particular sentence. For this reason no dictionary will give you *the* right word. All a dictionary can do is to tell you what meanings a word generally has. It is up to you to decide which, if any, of these meanings meets your needs. But, as background for that decision, it will be useful to consider three qualities that should be taken into account: *appropriateness, specificity,* and *imagery.*

Appropriateness

Words are appropriate when they are suited to your purpose, which includes your analysis of the situation and of the audience for which you are writing. Imagine a doctor explaining to a patient the damage done by a heart attack, and the same doctor reporting on the same subject at a medical convention. The subject is the same, but the situation and the audience are so different that they will affect the content, the manner, and the language of the speaker. Differences in audience and situation affect the whole treatment of a subject and include choices that go beyond diction. These differences will be discussed in the next chapter, "Tone and Style." In this chapter you will concentrate on how to choose the right words to produce the right effect.

One of the major choices you have to make is how formal to be in a given situation. You know that in social situations the clothes you choose to wear depend on the occasion: a formal gown would be conspicuously inappropriate to the classroom; jeans and a shirt would not do for a formal dance. The same thing is true of diction. Some words are appropriate to some situations but not to others. The best way to understand this distinction is to consider four types of words: *learned, popular, colloquial,* and *slang.*

Popular and Learned Words   In English, as in other languages, a great part of the total vocabulary consists of words that are common to the speech of educated and uneducated speakers alike. These words are the basic elements of your language. They are indispensable for everyday communication, and by means of them people of widely different backgrounds are able to speak a common language. These are called *popular words;* they belong to the whole populace.

Contrasted with these are words that you read more often than you hear, and write more often than you speak — words more widely used by educated than by uneducated people, and more likely to be used on formal than on informal occasions. Such words are *learned words.*

The distinction between learned and popular words is illustrated in the following list, which contrasts the members of some pairs of words that have roughly the same meaning:

Popular	Learned	Popular	Learned
agree	concur	end	terminate
beggar	mendicant	fat	corpulent
behead	decapitate	hairdo	coiffure
break	fracture	lying	mendacious
clear	lucid	make easy	facilitate

near (in time)	imminent	surrender	capitulate
prove	verify	truth	veracity
secret	cryptic, esoteric	wordy	verbose

Colloquialisms The term *colloquial* is defined by *The American Heritage Dictionary* as "characteristic of or appropriate to the spoken language or to writing that seeks its effect; informal in diction or style of expression." Colloquialisms are not "incorrect" or "bad" English. They are the kinds of words that people, educated and uneducated alike, use when they are speaking together quite informally. In writing they are used to give the impression of talking directly and intimately with the reader. To achieve this effect you might use contractions — *don't, wasn't, hasn't* — and *clipped words,* like *taxi, phone,* which are shortened forms of longer words. The list below illustrates typical colloquialisms:

awfully (for *very*)	fix (for *predicament*)	over with (for *completed*)
back of (for *behind*)	it's me	party (for *person*)
cute	kind of; sort of (for *somewhat*)	peeve (for *annoy*)
exam		plenty (as an adverb)
expect (for *suppose*)	a lot of; lots of	movie (for *film*)
fellow	mad (for *angry*)	sure (for *certainly*)

Slang The *Oxford English Dictionary* defines *slang* as "language of a highly colloquial type." Notice that the adjective is *colloquial,* not *vulgar* or *incorrect.* Slang is used by people in all walks of life, though those with well-stocked vocabularies tend to use it less than those whose vocabulary range is limited. As with other types of words, the appropriateness of slang depends on the occasion. A college president, for example, would usually avoid conspicuous slang in a public address but might well use it in many informal situations.

Slang satisfies a desire for novelty of expression. Much of it is borrowed from the special vocabularies of particular occupations or activities: *zero in* (gunnery), *on the beam* (aerial navigation), *behind the eight ball* (pool), *raise the ante* (poker), *pad* (rocketry), *offbeat* (music), *tuned in* and *turned off* (radio). Some of it comes from the private languages of the underworld or the underground: *snow, grass, joint, mainliner, stoned.* Many slang expressions are words borrowed from the standard vocabulary and given new meanings: *flipped, split, cool, cat, soul, rap, high, trip, spaced out, wheels, bread, vibes.* Some slang proves so useful that it passes into the popular vocabulary, but most is a thing of the moment and soon dies.

These four types of diction can be arranged on a scale showing decreasing formality.

	Learned	Popular	Colloquial	Slang	
Most formal					*Least formal*

In most of your writing the degree of formality you use will be closer to the middle of this range than to either extreme. In general, therefore, your best choices will be popular words. Unfortunately, some inexperienced writers have the mistaken idea that formality is a virtue and that big, fancy words are preferred to short, common ones. This error is compounded when these writers cannot maintain the formality. Then their style becomes obviously inconsistent.

The following passage provides a humorous illustration of this kind of inconsistency. It is taken from George Bernard Shaw's play *Pygmalion*, perhaps better known by its musical and film versions as *My Fair Lady*. In this scene Liza Doolittle, a Cockney flower girl who is being taught by Professor Higgins to talk like a lady, meets her first test at a small party at the home of Mrs. Higgins, the professor's mother. Notice the contrast between Liza's first speech and her last.

Mrs. Higgins:	Will it rain, do you think?
Liza:	The shallow depression in the west of these islands is likely to move slowly in an easterly direction. There are no indications of any great change in the barometrical situation.
Freddy:	Ha! Ha! How awfully funny!
Liza:	What is wrong with that, young man? I bet I got it right.
Freddy:	Killing!
Mrs. Eynsford Hill:	I'm sure I hope it won't turn cold. There's so much influenza about. It runs right through our whole family regularly every spring.

> Liza: My aunt died of influenza: so they said.... But it's my belief they done the old woman in.... Why should *she* die of influenza? She come through diphtheria right enough the year before. I saw her with my own eyes. Fairly blue with it, she was. They all thought she was dead; but my father he kept ladling gin down her throat 'til she came to so sudden that she bit the bowl off the spoon.... What call would a woman with that strength in her have to die of influenza? What become of her new straw hat that should have come to me? Somebody pinched it; and what I say is, them as pinched it done her in.

Here the obvious switch from a formal to a highly colloquial style is justified by Shaw's purpose, which is to show Liza in a transitional stage at which she cannot yet maintain the pose of being a well-educated young woman. She does not see that her learned comment on the weather is inappropriate in this situation and therefore has no idea what Freddy is laughing at. Then when the subject changes to influenza, she forgets she is supposed to be a lady and reverts to her natural speech — which incidentally is much more expressive and colorful than her phony formality. Her inconsistency is amusing, as Shaw meant it to be.

But most inconsistencies in the compositions of inexperienced writers are not introduced for humorous effect. They slip in when writers are not in control of *how* they want to say *what* they want to say. They may start off like Liza, hoping to make a good impression, but their natural voice asserts itself and the final result is something that is neither formal nor informal, but an embarrassing mixture of both. The inconsistencies may, of course, be caught in revision. But it is better to avoid them in the first place by choosing words consistently appropriate to the situation.

Discussion Problems

1. **The following passage was spoken by a man on trial for murder and taken down by a member of the jury. As written here it is a harmonious statement because every word adds up to a consistent picture of the speaker. What happens if you try to refine it by "correcting" the language — for example, changing *goan* to *are going to* and substituting more formal diction such as *perceived* for *seen,* *ensnared* for *trapped,* and *prevaricating* for *tellin' lies?***

One time I seen a fly that was trapped in a spider's web and watched it suffer. These people that been tellin' lies to frame me goan suffer like that fly did. They goan lay awake at night worryin' 'bout it and it goan be with them in the mo'nin'. They goan live with their lies every day wonderin' when they goan be framed, or their chilren, or their friens and neighbors. On the Last Day they goan have to face Him with it, and I'm goan have a clean heart, 'cause I ain't done nuthin' wrong.

2. In the following paragraph the diction is inconsistent because some of the words are too informal for the context. Identify them and provide acceptable substitutes.

One serious rap that has been made against pressure groups is that they wield power without corresponding responsibility. Because they do not have to stand the test of power by winning elections, they are able to make beefed-up claims about the clout the people they represent give them. If these claims are made confidently, timid members of Congress are likely to be impressed. Some people think that this susceptibility of politicians to being hoodwinked is increased by the failure of the great political parties to support their members against the pressure groups. Others feel that Congress itself is too wishy-washy about propagandists. Whatever the cause, the irresponsibility of pressure groups has fostered rip-offs that distort their legitimate function to tip off legislators concerning public policy.

Another kind of inconsistency is the choice of a word that does not fit your intention. Usually in revision an obviously wrong word, like *urban* for *rural* or *figment* for *fragment,* is easy to detect and change. Implied meanings are more troublesome. While you would probably not write *skinny wench* in a context that called for *slender girl,* you could easily miss subtle distinctions and choose a word that does not exactly convey the right connotation. For example, *admonish, rebuke,* and *scold* all have the same general meaning, but in context they can have different effects. An employee would rather be admonished than rebuked by a supervisor, and rebuked rather than scolded. The supervisor would rather be considered a constructive critic than a faultfinder.

The choice of implied meanings should consistently support your purpose. Ideally you know what effects you want your words to produce

and will make the right choices. But under the pressure of writing you may overlook shades of meaning not suitable to your purpose, and thus introduce inconsistencies. The best time to catch these is in revision, when you are free to concentrate on particular words and to ask, "Is this exactly what I mean?" In the following sentences the blank may be filled with any of the words in parentheses, but each choice will change the meaning. The right choice is the one that best fits what you intend the sentence to mean.

1. She was a _____ reader. (compulsive, critical, perceptive)

2. The children were _____. (sleepy, exhausted, weary)

3. The candidate gave a(n) _____ answer. (judicious, ambiguous, evasive)

4. It was an _____ insult. (intentional, unmistakable, implied)

5. He was in a(n) _____ mood. (faultfinding, quarrelsome, irritable)

The only basis for choosing one of these parenthetical alternatives is its appropriateness in the context of the writing. Each right choice supports those that have gone before and strengthens the reader's interpretation. Each wrong choice introduces undesirable associations and creates at least momentary uncertainty in the reader. If there are enough wrong choices, the work will be so inconsistent that the reader will not know what to make of it.

Specificity

Specific and *general* are opposite terms. Words are said to be specific when they refer to individual persons, objects, or events: *Brooklyn Bridge, the Boston Massacre, Joe's mother, the next intersection, the man sitting nearest to the door.* Words are general when they refer not to individual things but to groups or classes — *bridge, massacre, mother, intersection, man.* As these examples show, a general term may be made specific by a modifier that restricts the reference to a particular member of the group.

Specific and *general* are also relative terms, since a word may be specific compared with one other word, and general compared with a second, as the accompanying diagram shows.

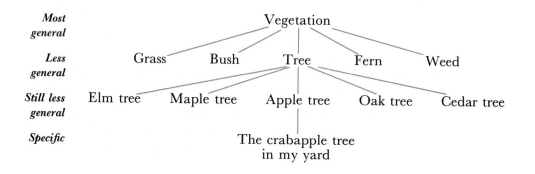

Exercise

For each set of terms below, show the gradation from general to specific by putting the most general term at the left and the most specific at the right, thus:

matter, food, fruit, citrus fruit, orange

1. football player, quarterback, Joe Montana, athlete

2. Labrador retriever, quadruped, bird dog, animal, dog

3. member of the CBS news staff, TV newsman, anchor man, Dan Rather

4. senator, legislator, politician, Senator Edward Kennedy

5. vacation spot, St. John Island, West Indies, U.S. Virgin Islands

6. bush, rosebush, plant, decorative bush, Tropicana rosebush

7. the man who stole my wallet, criminal, pickpocket, thief

Neither specific nor general words are good or bad in themselves. There are purposes that require generalities. A president's inaugural address cannot deal with specifics; it can be only a general statement of policy or intention. But generally the best policy is to be as specific as the situation permits. Notice how the specific language at the right communicates meaning not conveyed by the general diction at the left:

The child has a contagious disease.	The child has measles.
She was born in Europe.	She was born in France.
His grades last term were poor.	Last term he received two F's and a D.
After the strenuous activities of the day, I did not feel like dancing.	After playing twenty-seven holes of golf, I did not feel like dancing.

The term *concrete* is often used for some kinds of specific diction. *Concrete* is the opposite of *abstract*. Words are said to be concrete when they refer to particular things that can be perceived by your senses: details of appearance, sound, smell, touch, and taste. They are said to be abstract when they refer to qualities that many things seem to share: newness, width, size, shape, value, joy, and anger, for example. These qualities are not objects that you perceive directly by observation; they are concepts that you infer from what you see.

In the following paragraph the author provides concrete illustrations of the abstract opening sentence. The sensory details are so clear that, if you were an artist, you could paint the marshes turning pink, lilac, and golden green at sunset, the beach at low tide, a girl sliding down the sandhills on her bloomers, the lone sneaker beneath the sofa, and the shoes and towels in the closet. But you could not paint the "physical," the "appetite," or the "summertime" of the topic sentence.

> The memories of Beach Haven run all to smells and sounds and sights; they are physical, of the blood and appetite, as is natural to summertime. At the west end of Coral Street the marshes began, turning soft with color at sunset, pink and lilac and golden green. The ocean beach at low tide lay hard underfoot, wet sand dark below the waterline. On the dunes — we called them sandhills — we played King of the Castle or slid down on our bloomer seats, yelling with triumph and pure joy. The floors of Curlew Cottage, the chairs, even the beds were sandy. Always a lone sneaker sat

beneath the hall sofa; by August our city shoes were mildewed in the closets, and towels were forever damp. (Catherine Drinker Bowen, *Family Portrait*)

As the preceding paragraph illustrates, some words refer to sensory experiences: to what you see, hear, touch, taste, and smell. Because these words call up sensory images, they are particularly effective in writing such as Louise Bogan's description of the change of seasons (see pages 163–164). Some of the words in the following list could fit into more than one sensory category:

Touch chill, clammy, cold, corrugated, grainy, gritty, harsh, jarring, knobby, moist, nubby, numb, plushy, rough, satiny, slimy, slithering, smooth, sting, tingle, tickly, velvety

Taste bland, biting, bitter, brackish, briny, metallic, minty, nutty, peppery, salty, sour, spicy, sweet, tainted, vinegary, yeasty

Smell acrid, fetid, greasy, moldy, musky, musty, pungent, putrid, rancid, rank, reek, stench, sulphurous, woodsy

Sound bellow, blare, buzz, chatter, chime, clang, clatter, clink, crackle, crash, creak, gurgle, hiss, hum, murmur, pop, purr, rattle, rustle, screech, snap, splash, squeak, swish, tinkle, whine, whisper

Sight blaze, bleary, bloody, burnished, chalky, dappled, ebony, flame, flash, flicker, florid, foggy, gaudy, glare, glitter, glossy, glow, golden, grimy, haze, inky, leaden, lurid, muddy, roiled, sallow, shadow, smudged, spark, streak, tawny, turbid

Exercises

1. **As a demonstration of your ability to recognize concrete and specific diction, read the following passage and pick out the words or phrases that seem most concrete. Do you see any relation between the words being used and the writer's observation of the scene? Which came first, the observations or the words?**

The scullery was a mine of all the minerals of living. Here I discovered water — a very different element from the green crawling scum that stank in the garden tub. You could pump it in pure blue gulps out of the ground; you could swing on the pump handle and it came out sparkling like liquid sky. And it broke and ran and shone on the tiled floor, or quivered in a jug, or weighted your clothes with cold. You could drink it, smell it, draw with it, froth it with soap, swim beetles across it, or fly it in bubbles in the air. You could put your head in it, and open your eyes, and see the sides of the bucket buckle, and hear your caught breath roar, and work your mouth like a fish. (Laurie Lee, *The Edge of Day*)

2. The following pairs of contrasted statements deal with the same subject. From each pair choose the one that you think is more concrete and justify your choice.

   In the past, girls in rural communities had no facilities for bathing except those offered by some neighboring stream. In such circumstances a bathing suit was not always a necessity, but if one was worn it was likely to consist of nothing more than some discarded article of clothing tailored to fit the occasion.

   Forty years ago, if the farmer's daughter went swimming she swam in the crick below the pasture, and if she wore a bathing suit, which was not as customary as you may think, it was likely to be a pair of her brother's outgrown overalls trimmed with scissors as her discretion might suggest.

   Suddenly I felt something on the biceps of my right arm — a queer light touch, clinging for an instant, and then the smooth glide of its body. I could feel the muscles of the snake's body slowly contract and relax. At last I saw a flat, V-shaped head, with two glistening, black, protruding buttons. A thin, pointed, sickening yellow tongue slipped out, then in, accompanied by a sound like that of escaping steam.

   Suddenly I felt the snake moving over my arm. I felt the contraction of its muscles as it moved. Then I saw its ugly head and its evil-looking eyes. All the time its tongue kept moving in and out, making a kind of hissing noise.

3. For practice in using specific and concrete diction, recall some scene that impressed you vividly, or remember how you felt on some occasion; then describe your experience so that a reader can share it with you. Do not choose a large subject but think instead of something that can be treated fully in a substantial paragraph. Do not be in a hurry to start writing.

Meditate on the subject until you have the details clearly in mind. Then begin thinking in writing.

Imagery

As applied to diction, *imagery* has two general meanings: the images or pictures that concrete words sometimes suggest, and figures of speech such as similes and metaphors. The first meaning includes the pictorial quality we saw in the last section in such phrases as "green crawling scum," "pure blue gulps," "quivered in a jug." In this section you will learn about the second meaning — the figurative use of language.

The chief element in all figures of speech is an imaginative comparison in which two dissimilar things are described as being alike in some significant way. Here is an example:

The moon was a ghostly galleon tossed upon cloudy seas. (Alfred Noyes)

The basic comparison in this line of poetry is of the moon and a sailing ship. Now in most ways the moon is quite unlike a ship. But as the poet watches it alternately emerging from behind the clouds and disappearing into them again, it reminds him of the way a ship disappears from view as it goes down into the trough between two waves and then comes into view again as it rises on the next crest. In his imagination the moon is being *tossed* by the clouds the way a ship is tossed by the waves, and in this respect the moon and the ship resemble each other. The resemblance can be set up as a proportion.

$$\frac{\text{moon}}{\text{clouds}} = \frac{\text{ship}}{\text{waves}}, \text{ in respect to the tossing motion}$$

The figures of speech most commonly used are *simile, metaphor, analogy, personification,* and *allusion.* Each of these makes some kind of comparison, but each has its own characteristic form and use.

Simile A simile compares two things — A and B — by asserting that one is *like* the other. A simile usually contains the word *like, as,* or *so,* and is used to transfer to A the qualities or feelings we associate with B. Thus in

. . . there was a secret meanness that clung to him almost like a smell (Carson McCullers)

the abstract word *meanness* (A) is made concrete by likening it to a smell (B) that "clings" to the man the way tobacco smoke might permeate his clothing.

Here are other similes:

She crouched like a fawning dog. (John Steinbeck)

Records fell like ripe apples on a windy day. (E. B. White)

His face was as blank as a pan of uncooked dough. (William Faulkner)

Laverne wasn't too bad a dancer, but the other one, old Marty, . . . was like dragging the Statue of Liberty around the floor. (J. D. Salinger)

The Hovercraft looked like a single-decker bus fixed to the top half of a whale. (Anthony Bailey)

What the ad fails to mention is that smoking Carltons is like sucking air through a straw.

As the crowd left the scene of the accident, all that remained was a sprinkling of broken glass that shone like tears in the moonlight.

Metaphor A metaphor compares two things by identifying one with the other. It does not say that A is *like* B, but instead states that A *is* B. Thus when the Greek playwright Sophocles wrote,

Sons are the anchors of a mother's life

he was suggesting that a son gave stability to a woman's life the way an anchor held a ship in place, that in the culture of ancient Greece a woman without a son had nothing to hold her secure within the family.

Here are other metaphors:

California is the flashy blonde you like to take out once or twice. Minnesota is the girl you want to marry. *(Time)*

The President is asking Congress to join him in a crash landing, and the reason this presents difficulty is that they were not brought in on the take-off. (Eric Sevareid)

Europe was a heap of swords piled as delicately as jackstraws; one could not be pulled out without moving the others. (Barbara Tuchman)

Elliot Erwitt/Magnum Photos

I've climbed that damned ladder of politics, and every step has been rough. I've slipped many times and almost fallen back. . . . That top rung is never going to be mine. My fingernails are scraping it, but I don't have a grip. (Hubert Humphrey)

Good families are fortresses with many windows and doors to the outer world. (Jane Howard)

The script was more than four hundred pages long — overrich, repetitious, loaded with irrelevant, fascinating detail and private jokes, of which we loved every one. We spent two more weeks going through the pages with machetes — hacking away, trimming, simplifying, clarifying its main dramatic lines and yelling at each other all the time. (John Houseman)

Many words and phrases no longer thought of as figures of speech were originally metaphors or similes. Thus "foil" and "parry" derived from the sport of fencing; "checkmate" was a metaphor from chess; "rosy red" and "sapphire blue" were similes, as were "dirt cheap" and "silver hair." "At bay" once described a hunted animal when it finally turned to face the baying hounds; a "crestfallen" cock was one that had been humbled in a fight. Many other expressions retain their metaphorical appearance although you may no longer think of them as figures of speech — expressions such as the "mouth" of a river, the "face" of a clock, the "front" (originally "forehead") of a house, the "brow" of a hill. These are often called, metaphorically, *dead* or *frozen metaphors*. They are so common in the language that it would be hard to write a paragraph without one.

Analogy   An analogy is a metaphor or simile extended through one or more paragraphs to explain a difficult idea or to persuade a reader that because two things are alike, a conclusion drawn from one suggests a similar conclusion from the other. In the following analogy, the injury done to the soul of a black person is compared to a callus on the foot:

> . . . The Negro has a callus growing on his soul and it's getting harder and harder to hurt him there. That's a simple law of nature. Like a callus on the foot in a shoe that's too tight. The foot is nature's and that shoe was put on by man. The tight shoe will pinch your foot and make you holler and scream. But sooner or later, if you don't take the shoe off, a callus will form on the foot and begin to wear out the shoe.
> It's the same with the Negro in America. That shoe — the white man's

system — has pinched and rubbed and squeezed his soul until it almost destroyed him. But it didn't. And now a callus has formed on his soul, and unless that system is adjusted to fit him, too, that callus is going to wear out that system. (Dick Gregory)

As this analogy illustrates, a figure of speech is an effective way to make the abstract concrete. Abstractly stated, the argument is that blacks have become inured to white injustice, which has bruised their soul but also strengthened it, so that in time it will force a change in the system. The analogy with the callus pictorializes the argument by likening the process to something all readers will both understand and feel. There is therefore an emotional impact in the analogy that is lacking in the abstract argument.

Personification   Personification is a figure of speech by which abstractions and nonanimals are given human or animal characteristics. Thus winds are said to "roar" or "bite"; flames "eat hungrily" at a house on fire and may even "devour" it; a tree may "bow meekly" before a gale or in fair weather "lift its leafy arms to pray"; truth or virtue emerges "triumphant"; and justice is "blind." In all these examples, the writer imagines a resemblance between the actions being described and those of an animal or a person.

Such implied comparisons are often effective, but they should be used with restraint. If they seem exaggerated or far-fetched (as in "The waves roared their threat to the listening clouds while the palm trees nodded their approval"), your reader is likely to reject them as far-fetched or as a mistaken attempt to be "literary."

Allusion   An allusion is a reference to some historical or literary event or person seen to resemble in some way the subject under discussion. When the Prudential Insurance Company urges people to "own a piece of the rock," it is inviting the comparison that it is as solid and permanent as the Rock of Gilbraltar, which it uses as its symbol. Or when a political scandal is called another Teapot Dome or Watergate, it is being likened to the most notorious political scandals in our history.

A successful allusion provides a flash of wit or insight and gives your readers the pleasure of recognition. But if your readers do not recognize an allusion, it means nothing to them. Therefore you must be reasonably sure that the allusion is suited to your audience. Likening an uncomfortable cot to the bed of Procrustes will be received as a humorous exaggeration only by readers who know that Procrustes used to stretch or shorten his guests to fit the bed. If the allusion is not likely to be understood, what is the point of using it?

Exercises

As a review of what has been said about specific words and imagery, follow the directions for 1 and 2.

1. In each of the three selections that follow, underline whatever examples of specificity and imagery seem to you especially effective.

When wild ducks or wild geese migrate in their season, a strange tide rises in the territories over which they sweep. As if magnetized by the great triangular flight, the barnyard fowl leap a foot or two into the air and try to fly, . . . and a vestige of savagery quickens their blood. All the ducks on the farm are transformed for an instant into migrant birds, and into those hard little heads, till now filled with humble images of pools and worms and barnyards, there swims a sense of continental expanse, of the breadth of seas and the salt taste of the ocean wind. The duck totters to the right and left in its wire enclosure, gripped by a sudden passion to perform the impossible and a sudden love whose object is a mystery. (Antoine de Saint Exupéry, *Wind, Sand and Stars*)

The word is terracide. As in homicide, or genocide. Except it's terra. Land.

It is not committed with guns and knives, but with great, relentless bulldozers and thundering dump trucks, with giant shovels like mythological creatures, their girdered necks lifting massive steel mouths high above the tallest trees. And with dynamite. They cut and blast and rip apart mountains to reach the minerals inside, and when they have finished there is nothing left but naked hills, ugly monuments to waste, stripped of everything that once held them in place, cut off from the top and sides and dug out from the inside and then left, restless, to slide down on houses and wash off into rivers and streams, rendering the land unlivable and the water for miles downstream undrinkable.

Terracide. Or, if you prefer, strip-mining. (Skip Rozin, "People of the Ruined Hills," *Audubon*)

Smoke was rising here and there among the creepers that festooned the dead or dying trees. As they watched, a flash of fire appeared at the root of one wisp, and then the smoke thickened. Small flames stirred at the trunk of a tree and crawled away through leaves and brushwood, dividing and increasing. One patch touched a tree trunk and scrambled up like a bright squirrel. The smoke increased, sifted, rolled outwards. The squirrel leapt on the wings of the wind and clung to another standing tree, eating downwards. Beneath the dark canopy of leaves and smoke the fire laid hold on the forest and began to gnaw. Acres of black and yellow smoke rolled steadily toward the sea. At the sight of the flames and the irresistible course of the fire, the boys broke into shrill, excited cheering. The flames, as though they were a kind of wild life, crept as a jaguar creeps on its belly toward a line of birch-like saplings that fledged an outcrop of the pink rock. They flapped at the first of the trees, and the branches grew a brief foliage of fire. The heart of flame leapt nimbly across the gap between the trees and then went swinging and flaring along the whole row of them. Beneath the capering boys a quarter of a mile square of forest was savage with smoke and flame. The separate noises of the fire merged into a drum-roll that seemed to shake the mountain. (William Golding, *Lord of the Flies*)

2. Which of the following versions of the same scene do you prefer, and why?

He entered the tavern and took a seat comfortably back from the potbellied wood stove around which the regular customers sat drinking beer and exchanging the local gossip. The room was un-evenly lit by two suspended bulbs that swayed in the draft each time the door was opened, causing the shadows to swing eerily around the walls.

He entered the tavern and sat near the stove around which people were drinking and talking. The room was lit by two electric bulbs. Outside the wind was blowing, and every time the door opened it caused shadows to move around the walls.

Revising Diction

In a sense you have been reading about how to revise your choice of words through most of this chapter. In considering the qualities of good diction, you compared effective and ineffective ways of expressing ideas, and that comparison included a good deal of revision. But in this third stage of local revision you are changing your emphasis from good to bad qualities: you are trying to identify ineffective words that can be improved to emphasize your purpose. The four major weaknesses in diction are *vagueness, jargon, triteness,* and *ineffective imagery.*

Eliminating Vagueness

Words are vague when, in context, they do not convey one specific meaning to your readers. Consider this sentence:

I could tell by the funny look on her face that she was mad.

Words like *funny* and *mad* can have quite specific meanings, but not in this context. What does *mad* mean here? Certainly not "insane," which it might mean in another sentence. "Angry," then, or "annoyed," "irritated," "offended"? A reader cannot be sure. But the writer can remove any doubt by using more specific diction:

I could tell *by the way her face stiffened* that she was *offended.*

Words like *funny* and *mad* belong to a group called *utility words.* These, as their name implies, are useful. In ordinary speech, which does not usually permit deliberate choice and gives little chance of revision, they are common and often pass unnoticed. In writing they may be adequate if the context limits them to one clear interpretation. But because they are often left vague in student writing, they deserve a special caution here. The following list shows some of the most common utility words:

affair	condition	fierce	glamorous
aspect	cool	fine	goods
awful	cute	freak	gorgeous
business	factor	funny	great
circumstance	fantastic	gadget	line

lovely	nice	proposition	stuff
marvelous	organization	regular	terrible
matter	outfit	silly	terrific
nature	peculiar	situation	weird
neat	pretty	smooth	wonderful

In revising your papers, be sure that the meaning of a utility word is clearly implied by its context. Consider this:

In Bill's *situation* I would quit school.

If this sentence occurs in a context that clearly shows that Bill's problem is caused by low grades, lack of money, or family troubles, the sentence will present no difficulty. But if the context does not clarify the meaning of *situation*, the sentence should be rewritten to specify the intended meaning, as in

If I had Bill's grades, I would quit school.

Usually the simplest way to clarify a vague utility word or phrase is to substitute a specific word or phrase, as in the following examples:

It was a ~~peculiar~~ _{puzzling} statement.

Such scandals ~~are bad business for~~ _{weaken confidence in} politicians.

He is ~~in bad shape~~ _{seriously ill.}.

The news tonight is ~~terrible~~ _{alarming.}.

Other substitutions could have been made. The problem is to choose the one that specifies the intended meaning.

Exercise

Assuming that the italicized words are not made clear by the context, substitute more specific diction for the utility words to give a precise meaning.

1. He is a doctor, but I don't know what his *line* is.

2. Our *organization* is opposed to Brenda Ames for student president.

3. It was a *neat* party — *nice* people, *lovely* food, and *marvelous* conversation.

4. What a *terrific* surprise to meet so many *cool* people at the same *affair.*

5. The actors gave a *swell* performance.

6. The judge said the *matter* was *peculiar* but she would take it under advisement.

7. Mother is *fussing* about Jean's moving into her own apartment; she really is *fierce* about it.

8. One *aspect* of the *proposition* is its effect on prices.

9. I thought that the new TV series was *sort of cute,* but it got *awful* ratings.

10. The price they are charging for steak is *something else.*

Vagueness is not limited to unclear utility words. Any word or phrase that is more general than the intended meaning should be revised. The substitutions in the following sentences make the information more specific:

Antigone.

The class was discussing ~~a Greek play.~~

terminal cancer.

Her father has ~~an incurable disease.~~

getting along with other students.

Jim has difficulty ~~adjusting to his peers.~~

Exercise   In the paragraph below, choose the more specific expression in each parenthetical set.

The whole surface of the ice was (*a chaos* — *full*) of movement. It looked like an enormous (*mass* — *jigsaw puzzle*) stretching away to infinity and being (*pushed* — *crunched*) together by some invisible but irresistible force. The impression of its (*titanic* — *great*) power was heightened by the unhurried deliberateness of the motion. Whenever two thick (*pieces* — *floes*) came together, their edges (*met* — *butted*) and (*moved* — *ground*) against one another for a time. Then, when neither of them showed signs of yielding, they rose (*uncertainly* — *quiveringly*), driven by the (*implacable* — *tremendous*) power behind them. Sometimes they would stop (*altogether* — *abruptly*) as the unseen forces affecting the ice appeared mysteriously to lose interest. More frequently, though, the two floes — often ten feet thick or more — would continue to rise, *(rearing up — tenting up)* until one or both of them toppled over, creating a pressure ridge.

Eliminating Jargon

Jargon originally meant meaningless chatter. It later came to mean the specialized language of a group or profession, as in "habeas corpus" (law), "top up the dampers" (British for "fill the shock absorbers"), and "stand by to come about" (sailing). A third meaning is suggested by the following definition from *Webster's Third New International Dictionary,* which says jargon is "language vague in meaning and full of circumlocutions and long high-sounding words."

This section will focus on the third meaning of the word. There is no valid objection to the use of learned and technical terms for audiences and situations to which they are appropriate, but using them unnecessarily when addressing a popular audience is a violation of the basic rule that the style should fit your purpose and audience. Jargon in informal writing makes you seem pretentious and your audience feel frustrated. The following contrast will illustrate this charge. The version at the left comes from the King James translation of the Bible; that at the right is George Orwell's translation of it into modern jargon.

I returned and saw under the sun, that the race is not to the swift, nor the battle to the strong, neither yet bread to the wise, nor yet riches to men of understanding, nor yet favor to men of skill; but time and chance happeneth to them all.

Objective considerations of contemporary phenomena compel the conclusion that success or failure in competitive activities exhibits no tendency to be commensurate with innate capacity, but that a considerable element of the unpredictable must invariably be taken into account.

Although the Biblical version is more than three hundred and fifty years old, it makes more sense and is easier to read than the "translation," which destroys the simplicity and clarity of the original by smothering the meaning under a blanket of vague, polysyllabic words. As Orwell points out:

The first contains forty-nine words but only sixty syllables, and all of its words are those of everyday life. The second contains thirty-eight words of ninety syllables; eighteen of its words are from Latin roots, and one from Greek. The first sentence contains six vivid images, and only one phrase ("time and chance") that could be called vague. The second contains not a single fresh, arresting phrase, and in spite of its ninety syllables it gives only a shortened version of the meaning contained in the first. ("Politics and the English Language," *Shooting an Elephant and Other Essays*)

The three chief characteristics of jargon are:

1. Highly abstract diction, often technical, showing a fondness for "learned" rather than "popular" words: "have the capability to" for "can," "facilitate" for "make easy," "implementation of theoretical decisions" for "putting a theory to use," "maximize productivity" for "increase production," and "utilization of mechanical equipment" for "use of machinery."

2. Excessive use of the passive voice. If machines break down, they "are found to be functionally impaired." If a plan does not work, "its objectives were not realized." If management failed to consider the effects of certain changes on the workers, the error is reported as: "With respect to employee reactions to these changes, management seems to have been inadequately advised." If more than half the students in a class did not make a scratch outline before writing an essay, "It was discovered that, on the part of a majority of the class population, the writing of the essay was not preceded by the construction of a scratch outline."

3. Conspicuous wordiness, as illustrated in the examples given above.

These three characteristics combine inappropriateness, vagueness, and wordiness into one consistently unintelligible style. Most inexperienced writers have enough sense to avoid this kind of writing. Those who fall into jargon do so because they believe that ordinary language is not good enough. Like Liza Doolittle, they are trying to make a good impression. The best way to make a good impression in any writing situation is to have something to say and to say it clearly.

The only way to revise jargon is to get rid of it. Leaving it in only forces your readers to do the rewriting that you should have done, and your readers may not be sure what it means. As an exercise in revising jargon, take an example and see what you can do with it. Read the following paragraph to get a general impression of the difficulty it presents to a reader:

> (1) The innermost instincts of the infantryman, that unsung hero of the soldiery entrusted to wage our country's altercations, provide him with some of his fundamental feelings relevant to his fortune in war. (2) He lends more credibility to his instincts than he does to the reasoning faculties of his intellect. (3) The forefront of the field of battle is not a place where one intellectualizes rationally with maximum ease. (4) Indeed, a foot soldier is not desirous of contemplating the vicissitudes of his condition logically, for there are too many infelicities that the hazards of war may foist upon his person. (5) But though a human being can decline to reason intellectually, he cannot be inattentive to his instincts. (6) He was not instrumental in the formulation of these feelings of his inner self, and it is not within his capacity to deactualize them. (7) They are particles of his very essence, and he must coexist with them.

Now, take the paragraph sentence by sentence and see what the writer was trying to say.

Sentence 1.   There are two ideas in this sentence: that an infantryman's instincts provide him with his feelings about war, and that he gets little credit for his service. In the context of the whole paragraph the second idea does not seem to be important and might better be left out. But, assuming the writer thought it important, you could rewrite the sentence as follows: *The instincts of the indispensable but unappreciated infantryman determine his feelings about his conduct in battle.*

Sentence 2.   This sentence means that *he trusts his instincts more than his reasoning.*

Sentence 3.   *The front line is no place for reasoning.*

Sentence 4.   *A foot soldier does not want to think logically about his condition because there are too many unknowns that may affect him.*

Sentence 5.   *But though he can refuse to reason, he cannot ignore his instincts.*

Sentence 6.   *He did not create his instincts and he cannot stop them.*

Sentence 7.   *His instincts are an inseparable part of him.*

If you simply string these italicized revisions together, you get a version that says all that the original was trying to say, and says it more clearly and in fewer words — 84 instead of 152. But you might get a still better revision by combining some sentences and making some slight subtractions and additions.

> In battle an infantryman uses instinct rather than logic. There are too many unknowns in a battle to make logical reasoning either possible or trustworthy. So he acts on his instincts. He does what he feels he must do under the conditions that exist for him at the moment.

In this version, you have said nothing that was not said in the italicized revision above. But you have sharpened the focus of the paragraph by giving it a clear topic sentence and then explaining that sentence. In the process you have eliminated all the pomposities of the original version and have communicated its meaning in one-third the space.

Exercise

Following the procedure above, rewrite this paragraph:

> **(1) While on duty one evening, a colleague, who was interested in weightlifting, allowed me to peruse a book on the subject entitled *Big Arms,* by Bob Hoffman. (2) Not yet having realized my latent interest in athletic endeavors, I was surprised at the manner in which the book held my interest. (3) This I only realized after a while. (4) It was that book which stimulated me to make a purchase of a weightlifting set and, despite the inhibiting influences of long work hours, little sleep, and irregular meals, to exercise in my free moments.**

Eliminating Triteness

The terms *trite, hackneyed, threadbare,* and *cliché* are used to describe expressions, once colorful and apt, that have been used so much they have lost their freshness and force. Like outdated slang, trite expressions once called up original images and conveyed a sense of excitement and discovery. But the very qualities that make a phrase striking when it is new work against it when it has been used too much. Here are a few examples of triteness:

apple of her eye

birds of a feather

black sheep

blind as a bat

budding genius	mountains out of molehills
cool as a cucumber	raining cats and dogs
diamond in the rough	sober as a judge
fly in the ointment	teeth like pearls
hook, line, and sinker	thick as thieves
lock, stock, and barrel	water over the dam

Trite diction blocks thought. Writers who use ready-made phrases instead of fashioning their own soon have no thought beyond the stereotyped comment that the trite diction conveys. Consequently, their ideas and observations follow set patterns: any change in personnel becomes a "shakeup"; all hopes become "fond," "foolish," or "forlorn"; standard procedure for making a suggestion is to "drop a hint"; defeats are "crushing"; changes in the existing system are "noble experiments" or "dangerous departures"; unexpected occurrences are "bolts from the blue"; and people who "sow wild oats" always have to "pay the piper" even though they are "as poor as church mice." As these examples suggest, the use of trite phrases is habit-forming.

Whenever it can be recognized, triteness should be removed in revision. Unfortunately, what is recognized as trite by an experienced writer may seem original to some inexperienced writers. They may have had just enough experience with a cliché to think it sounds impressive, and not enough to realize that, like "water over the dam," it has been repeated so often by so many people that it is thoroughly stale. How, then, do you learn to detect and avoid triteness in your writing?

The only way to learn is by experience. One way to get that experience is to recognize triteness in the speech and writing of others. Note the italicized clichés in the following paragraph:

Money doesn't grow on trees and how well I've learned that. What a *rude awakening* when I finally realized that all the odd change I used to ask for at home wasn't available at school. I had thought my allowance was enormous and, *before I knew it*, it was gone. College has taught me that "*A penny saved is a penny earned.*" I have learned to live within my allowance and even to *save something for a rainy day*. What I have learned in college is *not all in the books*. I have also learned to *shoulder responsibility*.

How many of these phrases do you recognize as ready-made expressions that the writer did not invent but simply borrowed from the common stock of trite expressions? Many of them are like prefabricated units that can be fitted into any kind of structure. By using them, this writer did not have to shape her own ideas; she found them ready at hand. If you can see that triteness reduces a writer's comment to a parroting of stock remarks, you are more likely to avoid it in your own writing.

Discussion Problem

Read the following paragraph and discuss in class the question, "Does the writer provide any new insight into the value of football, or is he just repeating clichés that other people have used over and over again?" Support your judgments by reference to the text.

> Wherever the gridiron game is played in the United States — on a sandlot, a high school field, or in a college or professonal stadium — the players learn through the school of hard knocks the invaluable lesson that only by the men's blending together like birds of a feather can the team win. It is a lesson they do not forget on the gridiron. Off the field, they duly remember it. In society, the former player does not look upon himself as a lone wolf on the prowl who has the right to do his own thing — that is, to observe only his individual social laws. He knows he is a part of the big picture and must conduct himself as such. He realizes that only by playing as a team man can he do his share in making society what it should be — the protector and benefactor of all. The man who has been willing to make the sacrifice to play football knows that teamwork is essential in this modern day and age and that every citizen must pull his weight in the boat if the nation is to prosper. So he has little difficulty in adjusting to his roles in family life and in the world of business and to his duties as a citizen in the total scheme of things. In short, his football training helps make him a better citizen and person, better able to play the big game of life.

Exercise

Do *one* of the following:

1. As a result of the class discussion, rewrite the paragraph about football to get rid of the major objections to it made in class.

2. **Choose as your general subject the values of any college activity that interests you. Restrict that general subject to the one value that you think is most important to students, and write a substantial paragraph supporting your judgment. Then proofread it to catch any trite language you may have used.**

Eliminating Ineffective Imagery

You have seen that an effective figure of speech can lend concreteness to writing. But a figure that is trite, far-fetched, or confused is worse than useless, since it calls unfavorable attention to itself and distracts the reader. *Mixed metaphors* — metaphors that try to combine two or more images in a single figure — are especially ineffective.

Consider the following example:

> The mayor decided to test the political temperature by throwing his hat into the ring as a trial balloon.

This sentence mixes three different images, all of them so overused that no imagination is required to write them. "Testing the temperature" has a literal meaning in cooking and bathing, and a figurative use when extended to politics. "Throwing one's hat into the ring" comes from the old days of bare-knuckle prize fights, when this was a conventional way of issuing a challenge. "Trial balloons" were originally sent up to determine the direction and velocity of the wind. Each of these images can be adapted to a political situation, but fitting all three of them into one consistent figure of speech is impossible. The writer of the sentence should abandon the metaphor entirely and simply say, "The mayor decided to get a better sense of his chances of being re-elected by announcing his candidacy."

The lesson to be learned from the mixed metaphor given above is that a poor figure of speech is worse than none at all. The pictorial quality is ruined if no consistent picture is possible, and a device that is intended to strengthen communication actually weakens it. For this reason, it is wise to test every figure of speech by "seeing" the picture it presents. If you will visualize what your words are saying, you will have a chance to catch any ineffective images and revise them before they reach your reader.

Exercise   The following sentences try unsuccessfully to combine inconsistent images in the same figure of speech. Visualize the images they suggest and then revise each sentence either by providing an acceptable figure or by stating the idea in literal language.

1. A host of students flocked into the corridor like an avalanche.

2. You people have been selected for this program so that we can retread the cream of the crop.

3. The defense attorney expressed confidence that the real facts of the case would come out in the wash.

4. The president's ill-advised action has thrown the ship of state into low gear and unless the members of Congress wipe out party lines and carry the ball as a team, it may take months to get the country back on the track.

5. Some of the things those people say just make my hair crawl.

Chapter 9

Tone and Style

The last two chapters have examined sentence structure and diction separately. Now you need to consider their joint effect on the *tone* and *style* of a piece of writing. You are generally familiar with these terms, of course. You know what is meant when someone says, "Don't speak to me in that tone," or "The style of this book is unnecessarily difficult." But in this chapter *tone* and *style* are technical terms that require explanation.

Tone

Tone may be defined as the sum of those characteristics that reveal writers' attitudes toward their subjects and their readers. These attitudes are usually determined in planning and drafting an essay. For example, when (after all her intricate planning) Mary finally sat down to draft her essay about the cost of a wood-burning stove, she might have decided to take any number of approaches to her copious material. She might have written a sober essay about the potential dangers in owning such a stove, or an informative essay about the complex procedures entailed in maintaining it. But Mary wanted to put herself in this essay — after all, she had lived with its subject for some time — and she did: she styled herself as the skeptical, wryly witty, and ultimately vindicated narrator of a drama: her husband Bill's adventures (and misadventures) in living the precepts of Woodie-ism through installing and maintaining the stove. In making that decision Mary established an attitude toward her subject, one that suggested a similar attitude toward her readers. She and they will endure what is essentially a crash course in Woodie-ism, suspending (though not entirely successfully) their disbelief that *any*thing could cost so much in terms of time, energy, and not a little money, too. As you saw for yourself in Chapter 4, these attitudes combined to set the tone of Mary's essay, "Burn Again."

Informativeness and Affectiveness

One of the decisions about tone that will come out of your purpose is the degree to which your writing will be informative or affective — that is, the extent to which it will try to explain something to your readers (inform them) or to influence them in some way (affect them). The best way to understand these two emphases is to look at an extreme example of each.

Siemens, the big German electrical equipment maker, has become the latest bidder for the business of cleaning up automobile emissions. Siemens researchers in Erlangen, Bavaria, have developed a cigar-box-sized device that replaces the carburetor and, they claim, allows today's piston engine to run essentially pollution-free without use of complex and bulky devices to clean up the exhaust after it leaves the engine.

The device, called a "crack carburetor," uses a catalytic process to break down, or crack, gasoline into gaseous components, primarily methane, hydrogen, and carbon monoxide. These gases are mixed with air and burned in the engine. Automotive engineers have long known that gaseous fuels, such as liquid petroleum gas or natural gas, give very clean exhausts, but their adoption has been blocked by problems of distribution and on-board storage. Siemens gets around that by allowing the car to carry gasoline as its fuel and produce its own combustion gases. *(Business Week)*

You can observe the following things in this sample:

1. The writer is principally concerned with giving readers information about the subject. In writing for *Business Week,* a magazine sold chiefly to people who want to keep up with what is going on in the business world, the writer assumes that the readers will be interested in an invention that may reduce pollution, but that they do not know what a "crack carburetor" is. The writer's chief concern, therefore, is to explain to these readers the process by which Siemens hopes to get rid of harmful waste products. This is the real subject, and it establishes the writer's view of both the subject and the readers of *Business Week.*

2. The writing is completely *objective* — that is, the writer's own judgments and feelings and personality are not allowed to show in the writing. The readers are not assured that the invention will be successful, since that would require a judgment on the part of the writer. The article reports that the company *claims* the device will reduce pollution, but says nothing that would either support or cast doubt on that claim. As far as it is possible to do so, the writer stays out of the writing.

3. As a result of this procedure the tone of the writing is informative, factual, and impersonal.

Now contrast this sample with the one that follows.

You can also forget about *Guess Who's Coming to Dinner.* It's a comedy about a nice liberal family whose daughter decides to marry a black man (Sidney Poitier) who is so noble and wonderful that the issue of interracial marriage is completely blunted.

I feel a sadness bordering on anger that Mom and Dad were played by Katharine Hepburn and Spencer Tracy. It is infuriating that these two graceful people and glorious actors should have to make their last appearance together in such a heavy-handed, message-burdened vehicle. It's a travesty of the pictures they had previously — perhaps immortally — done. I think it's close to a moral act to avoid this dreadful work. It is an affront not only to movie art but to the difficult issue it pretends to examine. (Richard Schickel, "A Critic's Guide to Movies on TV," *Redbook*)

Your observations of this sample are quite different:

1. This piece is short on information. It tells us that Katharine Hepburn played Mom, Spencer Tracy played Dad, and Sidney Poitier played the black man who is going to marry their daughter. It does not tell who played the white girl or the black parents, although these three had important roles in the movie. Nor does it say anything about the conflicts among these people that made up the whole plot and theme of the story.

2. Instead, it is almost entirely concerned with the reviewer's personal reaction to the film. The review is an unfavorable judgment, presented without evidence in highly emotional language. The writer's attitude toward the subject is hostile; his attitude toward his readers is authoritative — don't waste your time on this movie: it's dreadful.

3. The writing is almost completely *subjective* — that is, it deals chiefly with how the writer *feels* about the movie. Not only does he say, "I think," "I feel," but the diction reflects his annoyance: "infuriating," "heavy-handed, message-burdened," "travesty," "dreadful work," "affront . . . to movie art" — these are all emotionally loaded terms that reveal his attitude to the subject. Another reviewer might be equally emotional in praise of the film: "It's a great movie, dealing in a sensitive way with an important social problem, and superbly acted. You leave it feeling some hope that the level-headedness of the younger generation will finally triumph over the stupidity of their parents." That is just as subjective a judgment as the first. The purpose of such reviews is not to inform readers about the movie but to affect their attitudes toward it.

We can place the two quoted passages on a scale going from informative to affective.

Informative ———————————————————— *Affective*

(Siemens article)   (Movie review)

Between the extremes you could place other samples showing varying degrees of informativeness and affectiveness, with those in the middle about equally balanced between the two.

In your writing you will have to decide how informative or affective you want to be. Certain assignments, such as reports of experiments, summaries of books or events, and essay examinations, usually require an informative treatment. Persuasive essays, which are intended to get a reader to believe or to do something, are usually affective. But most expository essays combine informative and affective elements. For such essays your choice will depend on the situation and your purpose. Rod's final essay on the Washington Monument, in Chapter 4, is informative because it gives his readers the facts of the Monument's history. But it is also affective because Rod wants his readers to understand that the Monument is special, not merely a building about which some facts can be given.

Inexperienced writers sometimes believe that the way to be objective is to avoid using the pronoun *I*. That rule of thumb may be true in some situations, but, as a general rule, it is misleading in two respects. First, when you are writing about your own experiences, ideas, and feelings, there is no reasonable objection to the use of *I*. Second, avoiding *I* will not in itself guarantee an objective treatment of the subject. The statement "I saw the car run through a red light" is more objective than "The crazy fool drove through a red light," even though the first contains *I* and the second does not.

You can determine whether the tone of an essay is informative or affective by examining *all* the evidence in the writing. If the writing emphasizes an objective description of the subject, you will decide that the tone is informative. If the writing seems designed to influence the reader's response by emphasizing the writer's feelings and opinions, you will decide that the tone is affective. If the writing seems to preserve an even balance between fact and opinion, the tone falls midway in the scale between informative and affective.

Discussion Problem

To what extent do you judge the following passages to be informative or affective? Where would you place each passage on the informative-affective scale? On what evidence do you base your judgment? (It is likely that you and your classmates will differ on these questions. Do not merely label passages, but examine each closely so that you can support your judgment by specific reference to details.)

Passage 1

Our church was built on brick pillars and stood about thirty inches from the ground. No lattice work fenced off the area under the church and, consequently, hogs chose that spot for their family bedroom, especially in winter. Sometimes there would be an argument among members of the hog family during the sermon. One of the hogs, possibly, would want to turn over and sleep on the other side for a while — this to the inconvenience of the others. Then we could hear a considerable oinking and squealing above the minister's voice. Sometimes the backs of the larger hogs would strike against the floor joists with such force that we could feel vibrations inside the church.

Hogs bred fleas in their under-the-floor beds, and the fleas came through cracks between the floor planks and into the church, seemingly seeking tender flesh. A prim young lady sitting in the choir in full view of everybody in the church could not reach handily under many layers of long skirts to get at the flea. She had to be dignified. So fleas bit at will. I heard women members of the choir complain of this. (Virgil Conner, *Life in the Nineties,* an unpublished dissertation)

Passage 2

It is a miracle that New York works at all. The whole thing is implausible. Every time the residents brush their teeth, millions of gallons of water must be drawn from the Catskills and the hills of Westchester. When a young man in Manhattan writes a letter to his girl in Brooklyn, the love message gets blown to her through a pneumatic tube — *pfft* — just like that. The subterranean system of telephone cables, power lines, steam pipes, gas mains and sewer pipes is reason enough to abandon the island to the gods and the weevils. Every time an incision is made in the pavement, the noisy surgeons expose ganglia that are tangled beyond belief. By rights New York should have destroyed itself long ago, from panic or fire or rioting or failure of some vital supply line in its circulatory system or from some deep labyrinthine short circuit. Long ago the city should have experienced an insoluble traffic snarl at some impossible bottleneck. It should have perished of hunger when food lines failed for a few days. It should have been wiped out by a plague starting in its slums or carried in by ships' rats. It should have been overwhelmed by the sea that licks at it on every side. The workers in its myriad cells should have succumbed to nerves, from the fearful pall of smoke-fog that drifts over every few days from Jersey, blotting out all light at noon and leaving the high offices suspended, men groping and depressed, and the sense of world's end. (E. B. White, *Here Is New York*)

Passage 3

I have lost friends and relatives through cancer, lynching and war. I have been personally the victim of physical attack which was the offspring of racial and political hysteria. I have worked with the handicapped and seen the ravages of congenital diseases that we have not yet conquered because we spend our time and ingenuity in far less purposeful wars. I see daily on the streets of New York, street gangs and prostitutes and beggars; I know people afflicted with drug addiction and alcoholism and mental illness; I have, like all of you, on a thousand occasions seen indescribable displays of man's very real inhumanity to man; and I have come to maturity, as we all must, knowing that greed and malice, indifference to human misery and, perhaps above all else, ignorance — the prime ancient and persistent enemy of man — abound in this world.

I say all of this to say that one cannot live with sighted eyes and feeling heart and not know and react to the miseries which afflict this world. (Lorraine Hansberry, *To Be Young, Gifted, and Black*)

Distance

Another element of tone is *distance*. In a discussion of tone the word is used to measure the impression of distance between writer and reader.

Consider a professor lecturing to a large audience. She is separated from her listeners by her position on the platform. She cannot speak to each member of the audience individually, though she may try to create the illusion of doing so. The situation requires her to speak more slowly, more loudly, more formally than if she were conferring with a student in her office. In the lecture room she is forced to be both physically and stylistically farther away from her audience than she would be in her office. Or contrast the distance in a statement in a printed syllabus that "Students are expected to hand in assignments on the date stipulated" and an instructor's after-class remark, "Joe, you've got to get your papers in on time." In the first statement the writer is impersonal and remote; in the second the speaker is personal and close.

The following selections further illustrate the difference between writing that tries to get close to the reader and writing that addresses the reader from a distance:

Example 1

It's Friday afternoon, and you have almost survived another week of classes. You are just looking forward dreamily to the weekend when the English instructor says: "For Monday you will turn in a five-hundred word composition on college football."

Well, that puts a good big hole in the weekend. You don't have any strong views on college football one way or the other. You get rather excited during the season and go to all the home games and find it rather more fun than not. On the other hand, the class has been reading Robert Hutchins in the anthology and perhaps Shaw's "Eighty-Yard Run," and from the class discussion you have got the idea that the instructor thinks college football is for the birds. You are no fool, you. You can figure out what side to take. (Paul Roberts, *Understanding English*)

The distance between writer and reader here is very slight. The writer gives the impression of speaking personally to an individual reader, whom he addresses as "you." The conversational tone, the diction, and the kinds of comments made about the subject suggest a close identification of writer and reader.

Example 2

White lies, first of all, are as common to political and diplomatic affairs as they are to the private lives of most people. Feigning enjoyment of an embassy gathering or a political rally, toasting the longevity of a dubious regime or an unimpressive candidate for office — these are forms of politeness that mislead few. It is difficult to regard them as threats to either individuals or communities. As with all white lies, however, the problem is that they spread so easily, and that lines are very hard to draw. Is it still a white lie for a secretary of state to announce that he is going to one country when in reality he travels to another? Or for a president to issue a "cover story" to the effect that a cold is forcing him to return to the White House, when in reality an international crisis made him cancel the rest of his campaign trip? Is it a white lie to issue a letter of praise for a public servant one has just fired? Given the vulnerability of public trust, it is never more important than in public life to keep the deceptive element of white lies to an absolute minimum, and to hold down the danger of their turning into more widespread deceitful practices. (Sissela Bok, *Lying: Moral Choice in Public and Private Life*)

This paragraph is addressed not to any particular reader, but to all readers. The writer makes no attempt to address her readers as "you" or to appeal to their special interests. She is more interested in what she has to say than to whom she is saying it. Therefore she makes no attempt to get close to her readers. The whole tone suggests much greater distance between writer and reader than was implied in the preceding passage.

This impression of distance comes chiefly from sentence structure and diction; these are the linguistic bases of tone and will be discussed below, under "Style." What you should remember from the discussion and examples in the preceding pages is that your tone depends partly on the decision you make about what distance, or degree of separation, to maintain between yourself and your readers. This is not an arbitrary decision. It is related to your decision about your attitude toward your subject, and it is consistent with your total purpose.

Style

The word *style* has many meanings, ranging from one's "lifestyle" to the latest fashion in clothes. Even when limited to writing, it can refer to anything from a writer's philosophy to his or her choice of words or sentence structure. It is a useful word, but it can be used with precision only when the context clearly implies its meaning. The rest of this chapter defines style as it applies to writing, discusses its chief components, and gives some practical advice about how you can improve the style of your essays.

Style Defined

The American Heritage Dictionary defines style as "the way in which something is said or done, as distinguished from its substance." In writing, *substance* means "what is said" — the message or content. The definition assumes that what is said can be examined apart from how it is said. But this assumption is not always true. In many subtle ways, a change in the style of a statement may change its meaning. For example, if you change "Please go!" to "Get lost!" the change in tone causes a change in the message. Only with this reservation can you accept the dictionary definition as a starting point and say, "Style is the way it is written."

But how do you describe the way something is written? Consider the following passage from *The Adventures of Huckleberry Finn*. Huck is staying with the Grangerfords after his raft has been wrecked. He has been reading a "poem" written by the youngest daughter, now dead. The poem is so maudlin and so badly written that it is funny. But it is supposed to be a sad poem about a young man who fell into a well and drowned. Huck thinks it is very good. After reading it, he says:

> If Emmeline Grangerford could make poetry like that before she was fourteen, there ain't no telling what she could a done by-and-by. Buck [her younger brother] said she could rattle off poetry like nothing. She didn't ever have to stop and think. He said she would slap down a line, and if she couldn't find anything to rhyme with it she would just scratch it out and slap down another one, and go ahead. She warn't particular; she could write about anything you choose to give her to write about just so it was sadful. Every time a man died, or a woman died, or a child died, she would be on hand with her "tribute" before he was cold. She called them tributes. The neighbors said it was the doctor first, then Emmeline, then the undertaker — the undertaker never got in ahead of Emmeline but once, and then she hung fire on a rhyme for the dead person's name, which was Whistler. She warn't ever the same, after that; she never complained, but she kinder pined away and did not live long.

You can notice the following things about this passage:

1. Mark Twain is having fun with the subject. He knows the poem is sentimental to the point of being ridiculous, and he expects the reader to see that, too.

2. Huck himself is serious. Twain is getting the humorous effect by letting Huck talk about the poetry. Huck is the narrator in the scene, who says what a boy like him, but not a man like Twain, would say. In other words, even though Twain is the writer, the *voice* you hear is that of Huck Finn. Twain creates an ironical situation in which everything Huck says about Emmeline's poetry will evoke a quite different judgment from readers.

3. The diction is appropriate to the speaker. The effect would be lost if Huck were made to speak like a sophisticated adult. He must speak in his own voice.

4. All these elements are so interrelated that a change in any one of them would spoil the total effect. They all add up to a consistent piece of irony that is making fun of extreme sentimentality.

Even so small a sample suggests that the decision about "how it is written" includes such considerations as (1) the writer's attitude toward the subject, (2) the writer's relationship with the readers, and (3) the language the writer uses to express his or her ideas. The first two of these considerations can be included in the general term *tone*. So the definition of *style* can be expanded as follows:

The *style* of a piece of writing is the pattern of choices the writer makes in developing his or her purpose. If the choices are consistent, they create a harmony of tone and language that constitutes the style of the work. A description of the style of any piece of writing is therefore an explanation of the means by which the writer achieved his or her purpose.

This definition relates purpose and style as cause and effect. As you have seen throughout this text, a clear sense of purpose guides you through all the choices you must make from planning your paper to revising it. If these choices are consistent with your purpose, your writing will show a harmonious pattern. This pattern is the style of your work. Style in the essays you write is not a vague literary quality, then; it is a common pattern evolving from all the particular choices you have made.

Language and Range of Styles

Style, of course, finally rests on language. So now you should look closely at the sentence structure and diction of selected passages to see what generalizations you can draw from them.

Example 1

You're going to paint that picturesque old barn. All right. One vertical line (better use charcoal) will place the corner of the barn, another line the base. A couple of lines for the trunk of the tree, and maybe a branch or two. Then a line to indicate the horizon — whatever divides the sky from whatever meets it (tree, barn, hill). That's all! No leaves, doorknobs, cats, mice, or daffodils. It's the painting that's fun, and any time wasted in getting into a mess of details is to be deplored. As we start to paint, anything resembling a real drawing on our canvas is purely accidental. . . .

Now squeeze out little blobs of color on your palette, and a big blob of white. And take a look at that sky. It is, let's say, cloudless. And it really is blue. Still not as blue as Uncle Ed's shirt. Take a half of a butter ball of white on your palette knife and plaster it on the front of your palette. Careful now! Just a pinch of blue and mix with the white until there are no streaks. Not blue enough? All right, just a tiny bit more—but easy! Satisfied? Dip your brush in the turpentine, then in the paint and slap it on! Boldly — never mind if you slop over the barn a bit. (Joseph Alger, "Get in There and Paint," *Recreation*)

Analysis of example 1: Sentence structure

The twenty-two sentences of this passage average only ten words in length, and over half of them are fragments. Most of the complete sentences consist of a main clause or two compound main clauses. There are no inverted constructions or periodic sentences, and few parallel structures. The sentences usually follow a straight subject-verb-object order, and most of them are commands.

Diction

In the whole passage there are fewer than a dozen words — about 5 percent — more than two syllables long. *Picturesque, accidental,* and *turpentine* are the most notable. Except possibly for *palette,* there are no "learned" words. Contractions are numerous — *you're, that's, it's, let's.*

Tone

The writer's attitude toward the subject is enthusiastic and subjective. His attitude toward the reader is both informative and affective, for he is trying to influence the reader's conduct by giving information and telling the reader how to use it. The distance between writer and reader is exceptionally slight: the writer creates the impression of standing beside the reader and giving advice on every move. The voice you hear is that of a teacher eager to share his knowledge, a little bossy in a friendly way, but encouraging and helpful.

Summary

All these components blend into a consistent style that aims at ease and clarity through simple sentences and diction. The writer gives the impression of talking in print. The diction and the rhythms of the sentences are those of informal conversation. In the last chapter you saw the word *colloquial* used to describe diction of this sort. Now that term can be expanded to cover the whole style. Such an obviously colloquial style is not common in college writing, but it is by no means an uneducated style, and it can be used — as it is here — when it suits your purpose.

Now contrast the following example with the one you have just studied. Read the paragraph aloud, slowly, to hear how it sounds.

Example 2

From those high storied shelves of dense rich bindings the great voices of eternity, the tongues of mighty poets dead and gone, now seemed to speak to him out of the living and animate silence of the room. But in that living silence, in the vast and quiet spirit of sleep which filled the great house, amid the grand and overwhelming stillness of that proud power of wealth and the impregnable security of its position, even the voices of those mighty poets dead and gone now seemed somehow lonely, small, lost and pitiful. Each in his little niche of shelf securely stored — all of the genius, richness, and whole compacted treasure of a poet's life within a foot of space, within the limits of six small dense richly-garnished volumes — all of the great poets of the earth were there, unread, unopened, and forgotten, and were somehow, terribly, the mute small symbols of a rich man's power, of the power of wealth to own everything, to take everything, to triumph over everything — even over the power and genius of the mightiest poet — to keep him there upon his little foot of shelf, unopened and forgotten, but possessed. (Thomas Wolfe, *Of Time and the River*)

Analysis of example 2: Sentence structure

This paragraph has only three sentences. There are no fragments, and the sentences are long — 38, 55, and 104 words respectively, or an average of 66 against 10 in the preceding example. All the sentences are involved; none of them is simple; none starts with the subject. Subjects and verbs are often separated — sometimes widely — by intervening modifiers. The last sentence, as the punctuation shows, is extremely involved. Throughout the paragraph parallel and periodic structures are used for rhythmic and other effects.

Diction

About 10 percent of the words are more than two syllables long, and there is a smaller proportion of monosyllables than in example 1. The diction is less concrete, and there are more learned words — *animate, impregnable, niche, compacted, garnished, mute.* Several phrases have a lofty, poetic ring — "high storied shelves," "great voices of eternity," "living and animate silence," "proud power of wealth," "the mute small symbols of a rich man's power," "unopened and forgotten, but possessed."

Tone

The writer's attitude toward the subject is clearly affective: Wolfe is expressing his indignation about people who reduce great books to mere symbols of their wealth. The distance between writer and reader is great; the emphasis is on the subject, not on the reader. The tone is impersonal, dignified, and eloquent.

Summary

As in the first example, all these components blend into a consistent style. But what a different style! This one aims at eloquence, not ease or familiarity. It is not the kind of style that you would use to give directions, explain a process, answer an examination, or report a story in a newspaper. It could be called a *grand* style, but the usual name for it is *formal.*

Example 3

Conant was the first Harvard president to recognize that meatballs [identified by the author as "commuting Irish, Jewish, and Italian youngsters from Greater Boston"] were Harvard men, too, and so he set apart a ground floor room at Dudley Hall where we could bring our lunches in brown paper bags and eat at a table, or lounge in easy chairs between classes. . . .

Dudley Hall was plowed regularly by Harvard's intellectual upper-class Communists, who felt that we were of the oppressed. Occasionally such well-bred, rich or elite Communist youngsters from the resident houses would bring a neat brown-paper-bag lunch and join us at the round tables to persuade us, as companions, of the inevitable proletarian revolution. . . . Most of us, largely Boston Latin School graduates, knew more about poverty than anyone from Beacon Hill or the fashionable East Side of New York. We hated poverty; and meant to have no share in it. We had come to Harvard not to help the working classes but to get out of the working classes. We were on the make. And in my own case, the approach to Harvard and its riches was that of a looter. Harvard had the keys to the gates; what lay behind the gates I could not guess, but all that lay there was to be looted. Not only were there required courses to be attended, but there were courses given by famous men, lectures open to all, where no one guarded the entry. I could listen. There were museums to be seen, libraries and poetry rooms of all kinds to tarry in — and stacks and stacks and stacks of books. It was a place to grab at ideas and facts, and I grabbed at history. (Theodore H. White, *In Search of History*)

Analysis of example 3: Sentence structure

All the sentences in this passage follow the standard pattern: subject-verb-object, each with its modifiers, and with subordinate clauses following their main clauses. There are no conspicuous parallel or periodic sentences and no sentence fragments. Sentences vary in length from 3 words to 48 and average 21, as contrasted with 10 in example 1 and 66 in example 2.

Diction

In this example there is only one learned word *(proletarian).* Slang words occur twice *(meatballs* and *on the make).* All the rest, including *grab,* are popular words. About 7 percent of the words contain more than two syllables.

Tone   The attitude toward the subject is serious and subjective. The author is describing his Harvard experience as he knew it, and what he has to say is influenced by his personal point of view. His attitude toward his readers, most of whom are probably college graduates, is mainly informative. The distance between writer and reader is greater than in example 1 but less than in example 2.

Summary   The style does not call attention to itself as do the styles of the other examples. The sentence structure is neither so simple as that of example 1 nor so involved as that of example 2. It contains none of the fragments that were so frequent in the first example and none of the conspicuous parallelism of the second. The average sentence length is between that of example 1 and example 2. This is an in-between style, a *moderate* style.

If these three styles are represented on a scale that extends from most to least formal, their respective positions can be shown as follows:

Formal	Moderate	Colloquial
∧	∧	∧
Example 2		*Example 1*
	Example 3	

This diagram is intended to suggest three things.

1. The scale measures degree of formality, from most to least; it does not measure degree of excellence, from good to bad. There is certainly no suggestion that a formal style is necessarily better than a moderate one, or that moderate is necessarily better than colloquial. All three are standard English styles, and each is appropriate in some situations. The most appropriate style for most of the writing that you do in college — and thereafter — is the moderate style.

2. Each stylistic classification is itself a range. Within the formal range a particular sample may be more or less formal than others. For example, in many ways a legal contract is more formal than the Wolfe paragraph.

3. There is no rigid dividing line between these styles. The overlapping shown in the diagram is intended to suggest that the moderate style has such a broad range that it can include some formal and some colloquial elements. These inclusions, however, must be consistent with the purpose and context of the writing. Theodore White was

justified in using *meatballs* in example 3, because that was what brown-bagging Harvard men were called when he was in college.

The table on the next page will give you a more complete summary of these three styles than it is possible to derive from a single example of each.

Exercise   Working individually, rate the styles of the following lettered paragraphs by placing the letter under the appropriate number on the scale. Then discuss your ratings in class.

Most formal ———————|———————|———————|———————— Most colloquial
1　　　2　　　3

A. What I have been talking about is knowledge. Knowledge, per-haps, is not a good word for this. Perhaps one would rather say my *Image* of the world. Knowledge has an implication of validity, of truth. What I am talking about is what I believe to be true: my subjective knowledge. It is this image that largely governs my behav-ior. In about an hour I shall . . . leave my office, go to a car, drive down to my home, play with the children, have supper, perhaps read a book, go to bed. I can predict this behavior with a fair degree of accuracy because of the knowledge which I have: the knowledge that I have a home not far away, to which I am accustomed to go. The prediction, of course, may not be fulfilled. There may be an earthquake, I may have an accident with the car on the way home, I may get home to find that my family has been suddenly called away. A hundred and one things may happen. As each event occurs, however, it alters my knowledge structure or image. And as it alters my image, I behave accordingly. *The first proposition of this work, therefore, is that behavior depends on the image.* (Kenneth Boulding, *The Image*)

B. This isn't the kind of thing you hear about during your orienta-tion period, partly because of the national aversion to history, partly because there are many more pressing matters. The prospect for a winning football season. What the kids are wearing. What the low-down is on the local Greeks, or activists, or literati, or jocks, whatever's

Summary of the Formal, Moderate, and Colloquial Styles

	Formal	Moderate	Colloquial
Sentences	Relatively long and involved; likely to make considerable use of parallel, balanced, and periodic structures; no fragments.	Of medium length, averaging between fifteen and twenty-five words; mostly standard structure but with some parallelism and occasionally balanced and periodic sentences; fragments rare.	Short, simple structures; mainly subject-verb-object order; almost no use of balanced or periodic sentences; fragments common.
Diction	Extensive vocabulary, some use of learned and abstract words; no slang; almost no contractions or clipped words.	Ranges from learned to colloquial but mostly popular words; both abstract and concrete diction; occasional contractions and clipped words; may contain some inconspicuous slang.	Diction limited to popular and colloquial words, frequent contractions and clipped words; frequent use of utility words; more slang than in moderate style.
Tone	Always a serious attitude toward an important subject; may be either subjective or objective and informative or affective; no attempt to establish closeness with reader, who is almost never addressed as "you"; personality of the writer not conspicuous; whole tone usually dignified and impersonal.	Attitude toward subject may be serious or light, objective or subjective, informative or affective; relationship with reader close but seldom intimate; writer often refers to himself or herself as "I" and to reader as "you"; but the range of moderate style is so broad that it can vary from semiformal to semicolloquial.	Attitude toward subject may be serious or light but is usually subjective; close, usually intimate, relation with reader, who is nearly always addressed as "you"; whole tone is that of informal conversation.
Uses	A restricted style used chiefly for scholarly or technical writing for experts, or for essays and speeches that aim at eloquence or inspiration; a distinguished style, but not one for everyday use or practical affairs.	The broadest and most usable style for expository and argumentative writing and for all but the most formal of public speeches; the prevailing style in nontechnical books and magazines, in newspaper reports and editorials, in college lectures and discussions, in all student writing except some fiction.	Light, chatty writing as in letters to close friends of the same age; on the whole, a restricted style that is inappropriate to most college writing except fiction.

your crowd. The food in the cafeteria. How to get into the dorm after hours. Where the john is in the library. With all this to assimilate, who has time or patience to consider the nature of the institution to which you've entrusted the next four years of your life? (Leonard A. Greenbaum and Rudolph B. Schmerl, *Course X: A Left Field Guide to Freshman English*)

I have, myself, full confidence that if all do their duty, if nothing is neglected, and if the best arrangements are made, as they are being made, we shall prove ourselves once again able to defend our island home, to ride out the storm of war, and to outlive the menace of tyranny, if necessary for years, if necessary alone. At any rate, that is what we are going to try to do. That is the resolve of His Majesty's Government — every man of them. That is the will of Parliament and the nation. The British Empire and the French Republic, linked together in their cause and in their need, will defend to the death their native soil, aiding each other like good comrades to the utmost of their strength. Even though large tracts of Europe and many old and famous States have fallen or may fall into the grip of the Gestapo and all the odious apparatus of Nazi rule, we shall not flag or fail. We shall go on to the end. We shall fight in France, we shall fight on the seas and oceans, we shall fight with growing confidence and growing strength in the air, we shall defend our island, whatever the cost may be. We shall fight on the beaches, we shall fight on the landing grounds, we shall fight in the fields and in the streets, we shall fight in the hills; we shall never surrender, and even if, which I do not for a moment believe, this island or a large part of it were subjugated and starving, then our Empire beyond the seas, armed and guarded by the British Fleet, would carry on the struggle, until, in God's good time, the new world, with all its power and might, steps forth to the rescue and the liberation of the old. (Winston Churchill, *Speech to the House of Commons, 1940*)

Some Practical Advice About Style

So far in this chapter you have examined other writers' styles, because by analyzing sample passages you can acquire a background that will help you see what kinds of considerations are involved in style. Now you should apply what you have learned to your own writing. The following advice about style, culminating in a brief checklist for revision, is a summary, so it will not introduce new ideas. But it will give you, in compact form, the chief stylistic considerations to keep in mind in all your writing.

1. *Let your purpose be your guide.* A clear sense of purpose acts as a control over all the choices you make at every stage in writing. Style is the result of that control. It is not some kind of literary covering that can be put on writing the way a coat of paint is added to a house. It must grow out of and reflect your purpose. Indeed, style is so dependent on purpose that it makes little sense to talk about it apart from purpose.

2. *Generally, choose a moderate style.* There is nothing wrong with either a formal or a colloquial style when it is appropriate, and there are times when each is right for a particular purpose. But these times are rare in college writing or in most of the writing you will do after you graduate. The trouble with unnecessary formality in writing is that it often leads to pretentiousness and wordiness; the writer tries too hard to be impressive and literary when it would be enough just to be clear. The trouble with a colloquial style is that, if used for serious treatment of a subject, it can easily degenerate into slovenliness and work against a serious purpose. The best general policy is to aim at something near the middle of the range between formal and colloquial. You can then be objective or subjective, informative or affective, and your writing is likely to seem more natural than at either extreme. The broad range of the moderate style gives you all the leeway you need.

3. *Keep your style consistent.* Probably the worst defect in style is inconsistency. A piece of writing that is completely inconsistent will have no discoverable purpose and therefore no discoverable style. But inconsistency usually occurs in particular paragraphs, sentences, or words and can be removed in revision.

    a. Inconsistency in tone. Conspicuous inconsistency in tone is likely to jar a reader. The inconsistency will be most obvious when colloquial elements appear in a formal style, or formal elements in a colloquial one. Because a moderate style can range from semiformal to semicolloquial, it can tolerate usages that would be more conspicuous in the extreme styles.

b. Inconsistency in diction. As early as the first paragraphs of an essay, you commit yourself to a recognizable approach to your subject and to your reader. Your thesis announces what idea you are going to develop, and the opening sentences establish the tone. A reader senses these commitments and expects you to honor them.

If your choices of words are harmonious, they will build to a consistent style; but unconsidered choices may make it difficult for a reader to see any pattern in your writing. Your choice of words should suit the style you have already established. Words that clearly suggest an undesired meaning are relatively easy to detect in revision. You are most likely to go wrong by choosing words that are close, but not close enough, to your intended meaning. Do you want *insensitive, naive, thoughtless,* or *undiscriminating* in a particular sentence? The answer, of course, depends on the context. It is not a question of which is the "best" word, but of which is the best word for your purpose at this point in your paper.

4. *Try to see your writing as your reader will see it.* Of all the advice given here, this is the hardest to follow. Everyone tends to assume that what is clear to them will be equally clear to others. Common experience demonstrates that this assumption does not always work. Even in ordinary conversation you often ask and are asked, "What do you mean by that?" Usually you can explain, but the point is that explanation is necessary. Clarity is even more necessary in writing, for the reader usually cannot ask for an explanation. As far as possible, try to anticipate your reader's difficulties.

Despite your best efforts to be clear, you may still get papers back with "Meaning?" in the margin. This is evidence that at least one reader had trouble understanding. A stock response is, "Oh, you know what I mean!" But this response is an evasion. The marginal question identifies a trouble spot at which the reader is asking for clarification. It is your responsibility as writer to provide it. If you cannot see what is causing the trouble, you can ask for advice.

5. *Be as specific as you can.* Language is often a difficult medium. What makes it so is its abstractness. The word *apple* is more abstract than any

"*The face of the pear-shaped man reminded me of the mashed turnips that Aunt Mildred used to serve alongside the Thanksgiving turkey. As he got out of the strawberry-hued car, his immense fists looked like two slabs of slightly gnawed ham. He waddled over to the counter and snarled at me under his lasagna-laden breath, 'Something, my little bonbon, is fishy in Denmark.' Slowly, I lowered my grilled cheese sandwich . . .*"

Drawing by Ziegler; © 1983. The New Yorker, Inc.

apple you ever ate or saw, because it leaves out most of our actual experience with apples — their shape, size, color, texture, and taste. The farther you get from the names of common objects, the more abstract language becomes. When you are talking about truth and beauty and justice, you are referring not to things but to highly abstract concepts.

The common problem of all writers is to make the abstractions of language concrete enough so that readers will get some clear image or idea from written statements. There are two common ways of doing this: one is to illustrate the meaning of a general statement by examples or details; the other is to choose words that are reasonably specific.

Try always to pin down your general statements by examples or details. If you do not have the details in mind, you are not ready to make the general statement, for generalizations are inferences drawn from details of observation and can be explained or supported only by reference to these details. The realization that you are not ready to be specific may force you to study your subject in greater depth, and this will contribute to your understanding of it.

The second way of avoiding abstractness in language is to use words that specify the meaning you want. Don't write "an *unsuccessful* attempt" if *abortive, blundering, botched, fruitless,* or *half-hearted* comes closer to your meaning. Don't write "walked," if *limped, lurched, sauntered,* or *strode* describes more accurately the kind of walking you have in mind. If you must use a utility word such as *mess,* restrict its general meaning by a specifying adjective, such as *cluttered, gooey,* or *untidy,* whichever describes the particular kind of mess you are writing about. But use sparingly adjectives that are themselves too general to be helpful — words like *awful, beautiful, grand, lovely, nice, terrible.*

6. *Revise for style.* Of course, in considerable measure you are revising for style from the moment you undertake global revision. As this chapter has emphasized, your style is wholly dependent on your purpose, and as you revise for purpose you make decisions that assuredly affect your style. Likewise, when you revise for subject you make choices that help you determine an appropriate style (some subjects are best conveyed by a style that is relatively colloquial; others demand an almost formal style; but sometimes you can gain an important effect by treating a subject in an unexpected style). And revision for audience can certainly cause you to reassess your tone, distance, and word choice. For example, when Rod decided that he wanted a wider audience for his Washington Monument essay than his peers, or people like the ones he had described in his initial drafts, he then needed to modify his style: to use fewer colloquial terms and less breezy references — in a word, to adopt a more moderate (even a more mature) style.

Local revision takes you to the nuts-and-bolts level of style, and in fact it is in local revision that you will probably make most of the changes that improve your style. But it helps to give your writing a final reading for style alone. This reading is best accomplished after you have completed local revision but before you have implemented the changes in a clean draft — unless, of course, your revisions are so extensive or messy that you cannot *see* your writing for all the clutter. In this reading for style (which should be done aloud if possible) you should concentrate on the overall effect your writing has on you. You can almost imagine yourself listening to a band or a singer performing a piece of music. As you listen you contemplate the style of the piece, and your ear is attuned to any faltering or inconsistency in that style.

The following checklist provides some basic questions to ask yourself when you are reading to put the final touches on your style.

Guidelines for Revising Your Style

1. *What is my general impression of my writing?*

   Do I find my writing clear, unambiguous, and engaging? Have I carried out my purpose at every level; that is, am I satisfied that the *how* of my writing — its attitude, organization, and language — is equal to the *what,* to my ideas?

2. *What tone have I established in my writing?*

   Is my tone informative, affective, or a blend of both? Is it appropriate for my subject and audience? How much distance have I maintained between myself and my readers? Is my tone maintained consistently?

3. *How can I characterize the overall style of my writing?*

   Have I written this essay in a moderate style, opting for more or less colloquialism or formality as my purpose requires? Does my purpose in fact require me to be overtly colloquial or formal?

4. *Do my paragraphs work together to convey a sense of order and substance?*

   Does my opening paragraph compel the reader's attention, because it either states its thesis impressively or offers an irresistible hook? Do the middle paragraphs of my essay reveal unity, completeness, order, and coherence? Are the transitions between paragraphs clear and effective? Does my closing paragraph conclude my essay convincingly?

5. *Are my sentences well constructed and easy on the ear?*

   Have I written sentences of varying lengths and styles, so that the reader can follow them with interest? Have I avoided the choppiness that comes from too many basic or loosely coordinated sentences? Have I avoided the density that comes from too many complicated sentences with multiple subordinate clauses?

6. *Have I used words as effectively as possible?*

   Do the connotations and denotations of my words support my purpose? Have I avoided unnecessary formalities and slang? Is my language specific and, when necessary, vivid? Have I inadvertently mixed metaphors? Have I used imagery to *heighten* effects, not merely to strive after them?

Once you have completed all your revisions and have typed your final draft, you should proofread your writing very carefully. Proofreading is a close reading of the final version to catch any errors in grammar, spelling, and punctuation — as well as any typographical errors — that may have survived your revisions or been introduced into the final copy. Proofreading should be done slowly, preferably aloud. If possible you should allow some time to elapse between your final work (revising, typing) on your essay and your proofreading — in that way you are more likely to read with a fresh eye.

Review Exercise

This exercise comprises two parts, one an in-class discussion, the other a written commentary.

The following essay by Russell Baker is concerned with the appropriateness of style in a particular setting. Baker's specific subject is what he calls "a raging epidemic of quaintness" in Nantucket, an island off the coast of New England, but that quaintness is not confined to Nantucket alone. All over America, cities and towns have been experiencing a "restoration boom," rushing to preserve the visible reminders of America's history and — in many cases — to reintroduce them into settings that have long since evidenced a modern style. Almost everyone has seen examples of the latter phenomenon: shopping centers with "Ye Olde Drugge Store" and McDonald's restaurants constructed in the style of colonial architecture are two prevalent types.

1. Read Baker's essay carefully; then discuss with your instructor and classmates the pros and cons of the kind of architectural and cultural revision for style that the essay discusses and illustrates.

2. Read the essay in terms of the categories presented in the "Guidelines for Revising Your Style" on pages 323–324. Then write an evaluation of Baker's style in the essay, commenting on each of the six major categories in the guidelines. What kind of style has Baker employed in writing about style?

The Taint of Quaint

I was not surprised to discover that Nantucket had suffered a severe outbreak of cobblestones in my absence. The symptoms of an onset were obvious before I left in January when a telltale rash of electrified fake gas street lamps was beginning to spread along the sidewalks.

I cautioned my friend Crowley. "If you're not careful, you may be caught here in a raging epidemic of quaintness," I said. I had seen these plagues before. The onset of fake gas lamps was always a bad sign.

"What's the worst that can happen?" Crowley asked.

I hesistated to tell him, but felt obliged by the duty of friendship. "In the worst cases, inhabitants find themselves dressed in wigs, hoop skirts, knee britches and such, while standing in public places stirring boiling vats of candle wax for tourist snapshots."

Did I think there was danger of that?

Not for two or three years yet, I said. "Usually the onset of fake gas lamps is followed by an intermediate stage characterized by a severe outbreak of cobblestones. In this stage, the disease's tendency is to expand the summer tourist season into the winter. Saloonkeepers start referring to their merchandise as 'wassail cups' while hotel keepers refer to their fireplace wood as 'yule logs'."

"But that's already happened here," Crowley cried.

"Then the disease may be progressing backward," I said. "I wouldn't be surprised to see a severe outbreak of cobblestones by summer."

I should note that Nantucket is an island located south of Cape Cod, 80 minutes by air from Columbus Avenue. Heavily dependent on tourism, it is highly vulnerable to the epidemics rampant among the middle class of the great northeastern megalopolis, a group in which the fever for chic smolders constantly alongside the damp smoke of nostalgia.

Thus, cobblestones were always easily predictable, just as the gourmet delicatessen was easily predictable. The cobblestones were Nantucket's reaction to the city dweller's hunger for nostalgia, just as the gourmet food shops were an attempt to assuage the city dweller's uneasiness about being denied Columbus Avenue cuisine.

If my diagnosis is correct, Nantucket's ailment results from a misreading of the chic urban crowd it yearns to attract. Consider the cobblestones. Nantucket has always had one cobblestone street, over-arched with giant elms and lined with architecturally handsome houses.

It is a magnificent street to photograph but, because of the cobble-stones, a terrible street to walk or drive on, and an agonizing street on which to ride a bicycle. For this reason, most Nantucketers try to avoid it as much as possible and leave it to the tourists.   12

Last year, a great many of the giant elms died of the elm blight, which diminished the street's grandeur. New plantings will improve matters 40 years from now, but in the meantime ...? The fake gas lamps sprouted, then cobblestones broke out all over heavily trafficked side streets.   13

It is obvious that Nantucket has overestimated the city dwellers' thirst for quaintness. What well-heeled spenders want when they depart Boston, New York and Philadelphia for the seashore is to take the elegance of Boston, New York and Philadelphia with them.   14

This is why gourmet food shops blossom wherever they go and why singles' bars replace the carpenters' beer joints in seaside towns. When the $100,000-a-year people take to the seaside, they don't want to eat the fried seafood platter at Cy's Green Coffee Pot while a television set blares the Red Sox game from the bar. They want to dine in a restaurant so exclusive that nobody else on the beach can get a reservation.   15

While they want the elegant side of city life waiting wherever they go, they do not want its seamy side. This is why most of the people you see standing around the streets of the Hamptons, Martha's Vineyard and Nantucket in what looks like underwear have it embroidered with alligators to show that it isn't underwear.   16

They don't want to be reminded that back home people sprawl all over the streets in real underwear. Nor do they want a lot of potholes. And what is a batch of cobblestones but an out-of-date precursor to the modern city pothole?   17

One cobbled street is amusing. Two cobbled streets remind us that quaintness was something Americans worked hard to put behind them, for good reason.   18

Whether the fever for quaintness has become terminal for Nan-tucket, it is too soon to say, but the crisis is now. Once total quaintness   19 occurs, as it has in Williamsburg, all you have left is a two-day town. I pray for Nantucket's recovery, if only so Crowley doesn't end up in a wig and knee britches, stirring hot candle wax in front of the camera shop. *(New York Times Magazine)*

Chapter 10

Persuasion

The chapters in Part 2 of this text have emphasized those strategies that enable you to demonstrate your ideas effectively. This last chapter in the section concerns itself with ways of persuading others to accept your demonstration.

Persuasion is verbal communication that attempts to bring about a voluntary change in judgment so that readers or listeners will accept a belief they did not hold before. The purpose of persuasion is to cause a change in thinking. That change may be simply the substitution of one belief for another, or it may result in action, such as voting for A instead of B, giving up smoking, or buying a product. This change of opinion must be voluntary: the people being persuaded must be free to accept or reject the belief or proposal. If they accept it, they do so because, all things considered, they want to. No persuasion is needed to make people believe what they already believe.

Persuasion is closely allied with *argument,* which is the process of reaching conclusions. Indeed, one way to persuade others is to show them how you reached your conclusions. In the following pages you will learn how to appeal to your readers and how to use argument to convince them.

Changing the Reader's Image

On page 316 you read a paragraph in which Kenneth Boulding explained what he meant by *image*. As he was using it, *image* meant the view or set of beliefs you have learned to accept. That view, or image, controls your behavior. If your image of democracy is associated with the right of people to choose their political leaders by secret ballot, to speak openly for or against their policies while they are in power, and to vote them out of office when their conduct is unsatisfactory, you will respond favorably to any proposal that is consistent with that image and reject any that seems to oppose it. Thus you will generally assume that democracy, as we understand it, is "good" and that communism and fascism are "bad." Your image of democracy becomes the standard by which you judge competing systems of government.

If in defining persuasion you substitute *image* for *belief*, you can say that the purpose of persuasion is to change the reader's image of something. To do this requires two kinds of knowledge: you have to know (1) what your reader's image is and (2) how it may be changed. The first requires a realistic understanding of your readers; the second requires familiarity with the principal means of persuasion. Only insofar as you meet these requirements will you be persuasive. Failure to realize this often results in arguments that, however logically constructed, have no effect because they do not reach the image that controls your reader's behavior.

Images are shallow-rooted or deep-rooted. A shallow-rooted image can be removed or changed without any drastic effect on the person who holds it. Many beliefs based on reason are of this kind. People can be persuaded to do things they would prefer not to do, such as submit to an operation, when the evidence leads them to conclude that the action is necessary or beneficial. Provided the reasons given are convincing, they can change their accustomed conduct without much trouble.

But some images are so deeply embedded in the personality that one cannot give them up. To abandon them would be to deny something essential to one's self-respect, to one's sense of integrity as a person. A reader who believes that creation is an act of God and that a child is created at the moment of conception must view deliberate abortion as murder and cannot give up that image without denying a basic article of faith. This image will not be changed by any argument that a woman has a right to decide whether she wishes to bear a child, because acceptance of that belief would be an admission that a woman has a right to commit murder. The image is so deeply rooted that it cannot be removed without tearing out a cluster of beliefs essential to the reader's view of his or her own character.

A reader's images cannot be changed by any one essay. If you attack them directly, you will only intensify resistance. If you ridicule them, you will create antagonism and may alienate other readers who are not committed to these images but resent your insensitivity. Your best course is to follow three steps:[1]

1. To recognize that you are confronted by a deep-rooted image that can be changed only by the reader, and then only when the emotional commitment given to the original image can be transferred to the new image.

2. To show understanding of the reader's position by restating it in terms acceptable to the reader.

3. To explore possible compromises between the reader's position and your own.

Even if you do not succeed in this third step, this procedure will help in at least three ways. First, it will reduce antagonism: the reader will feel less threatened and more inclined to listen to what you have to say. Second, your concessions may encourage concessions by the reader: no longer forced to defend an image, the reader may be willing to consider some modification of it, and so move closer to your position. Third, even if no acceptable compromise is possible, your fairness will impress other readers and so be persuasive for them. This third advantage will be discussed under the heading "Trustworthiness."

Fitting the Persuasion to the Audience

In all the preceding chapters you have learned that the more you understand your audience, the better chance you have of discovering and demonstrating your purpose. Readers of course vary. But even though you may not know them all individually, you can know where they, as a group, are likely to stand on the question you are dealing with. You can

1. This discussion is indebted to Anatol Rapoport's "Ethical Debate" in his *Fights, Games, and Debates* (Ann Arbor: University of Michigan Press, 1960).

estimate what they already know about the subject, what opinions and attitudes about it they now have, what issues they are most concerned with, and what kind of evidence will be most influential with them. Out of this knowledge you decide what kinds of appeals will best help you to persuade them. Making this decision is a major part of your planning.

Although some of the following advice echoes the instructions given in Chapter 1 in "Guidelines for Analyzing Your Audience," it is worth repeating here to remind you that a careful assessment of your readers is essential to persuading them to understand and believe in your purpose.

1. *Have specific readers in mind.* Whom are you trying to persuade — your parents, your instructor, your classmates, the readers of your college newspaper, or others? An essay written for one of these will not necessarily be persuasive to the others. A paper addressed to the world in general is not aimed at anybody in particular. You will write more purposefully if you begin by defining the particular set of readers for whom you are writing.

2. *Identify with your readers.* Once you have identified your readers, you can begin to identify *with* them. In this sense, *identify* means putting yourself imaginatively in their place and seeing the problem from their point of view. If persuasion is necessary, your readers do not at present share your beliefs. Your purpose is to lead them toward these beliefs. In order to lead them, you must start where they are. Only by understanding their present attitudes can you hope to change them. This kind of initial identification with the reader is not a trick; you are not pretending to be something you are not. You are simply trying to establish an area of agreement that you intend to broaden.

3. *Be careful about the tone of your writing.* As you saw in Chapter 9, your tone reveals an attitude toward your readers. Your tone should help strengthen your identification with your readers; it should certainly avoid anything that will increase the distance between you and them. You can be angry or indignant about the situation you are trying to change or about those who allow that situation to exist. But you cannot be angry or indignant with your readers, not if you want their agreement. Nor can you talk down to them. You are trying to establish a partnership with them. Such a partnership requires mutual respect, and anything in your tone that lessens that respect will work against your purpose.

4. *Provide the evidence your readers need to accept your beliefs.* If you respect your readers, you will not ask them to accept your unsupported opinions, any more than a businessman would expect his partner to take his word for it that a proposed investment will be profitable. Normally both partners would go over the evidence in detail until both were satisfied. As a writer you have an obligation to spell out in detail why you think your readers should accept your conclusions. It is not enough that you believe the argument is sound. It is your reader who must also be persuaded.

5. *Make your paper easy to read.* When you are asking your readers to agree with you, make their job as easy as possible. Highly complex arguments, confused structure, technical terminology, abstract diction, complex statistics — all these make communication difficult. Because you want to lead your readers, you should do everything you can to make it easy for them to follow your writing.

Means of Persuasion

In general you have three means of being persuasive: winning the trust of your readers (ethical appeal), appealing to their emotions (emotional appeal), and convincing them through the logic of argument (logical appeal). These means are not separate; you may use them together in the same essay so that each supplements the others. But in this chapter you will examine them one at a time.

Trustworthiness

Trustworthiness is the kind of persuasion that comes from the character or personality of the persuader. When writers seem trustworthy, readers have confidence in them and are inclined to agree with their arguments. This confidence may be a result of the writer's reputation, or it may be a response to what a writer does in a particular essay. In either case, the reader's trust is based on the belief that the writer is *knowledgeable* and *fair.*

Knowledgeability   To be judged knowledgeable you must appear to be fully and accurately informed on the subject. The standard of knowledgeability is relative. In medicine, specialists are usually considered more knowledgeable about their specialties than general practitioners would be, but outside of their specialties they may be less well informed. The knowledgeability of a student writer is usually measured in relation to that of other students. A student who has carefully studied a subject and shows familiarity with the pertinent facts will be considered more knowledgeable than another who has only a superficial grasp of the subject and is often wrong on significant details. The best way to be considered knowledgeable on any subject is to study it thoroughly.

When a piece of writing relies on information from printed sources, your trustworthiness depends in part on the reliability of these sources. If they are questionable, your trustworthiness suffers, because the ability to distinguish between reliable and unreliable sources is part of the test of knowledgeability. It is often hard to assess the reliability of printed sources, but the following advice will help:

1. If certain information is important to an argument, your readers will want to know where you got it. If you cannot or do not identify your source, you may raise a doubt about your knowledgeability. If you can identify your source, do so, either in the text of your paper or in a footnote.

2. Distinguish between primary and secondary sources. A *primary source* is the original source of the information; a *secondary source* is a report based on the primary one. Thus a television speech by a public figure or the text from which it was read is a primary source. Some newspapers, such as the *New York Times,* usually print the complete text of important speeches, and in this sense newspapers, too, may be considered primary sources. A newspaper report that summarizes the speech is, by contrast, a secondary source. It may or may not be accurate. If you are going to quote the speaker, it would be better to quote directly from the primary source. If that source is not available, you may have to quote and identify the newspaper report.

3. When using a secondary source, see whether it specifically identifies the primary source. Many reliable publications do. Be cautious about such vague identifications as "It was learned from usually reliable sources," or "Sources close to the President say . . ." These are

deliberate devices to conceal the primary source, either to protect the informant or to give the report credibility it may not deserve. The 1973 investigations of the Watergate affair were frequently confused by testimony identified as coming from "the highest levels at the White House." Investigators could not determine who these "highest levels" were.

The main point to remember in this discussion of knowledgeability is that if you want a reader to trust you enough to accept your opinions, you must be sure of the facts on which these opinions are based. If you are not sure, check your information in some reliable source. Certainly do not trust your memory on historical information. A student who writes "John F. Kennedy, twenty-first president of the United States, was assassinated in Houston, Texas, on November 16, 1963," makes three misstatements of fact that could easily have been corrected by checking any of several reliable yearbooks or almanacs. Even a dictionary would identify John F. Kennedy as the *thirty-fifth* president. The effect of such carelessness on your reader is to raise doubts whether any factual statement you make can be trusted.

Fairness Any obvious unfairness will weaken your trustworthiness. The most common kind of unfairness appears when you are so committed to your own views that you cannot see the question objectively, and so read into opposing arguments motives and inferences that are products of your own bias. Common signs of unfairness are *distortions of opposing views, slanting, quoting out of context,* and *name-calling.*

Distortion is misrepresentation of an opposing view by inaccurate reporting. A common trick is to exaggerate the view and then attack it in its exaggerated form. Here is an example:

Mr. A: With all the things that have to be taught in English, there is not much point in devoting a great deal of class time to questions of disputed usage. The distinction between *shall* and *will,* the use of *like* as a conjunction, saying *data is* for *data are* — these are not choices between educated and uneducated speech, since both forms are used by educated people. A teacher may prefer one form to the other and may encourage students to follow that preference. But it is a waste of valuable class time to teach over

and over again a distinction which, whatever its historical justification, is no longer a fact of English usage. We have more important things to do.

Mr. B: The difference between Mr. A and me is that I respect the purity
of the English language, and he does not. If we permit *will* instead
of *shall* and *data is* for *data are,* where do we draw the line? Mr. A
says that the incorrect forms become correct because educated
people use them. I say that no one who says *data is* is an educated
person. What Mr. A is doing is advocating the philosophy of
"anything goes." Many of our troubles come from the adoption
of that philosophy in various walks of life — in business, in government, in personal morality. It is a philosophy which reduces the
conventions of educated speech to the level of gutter talk, and I
think anyone who has any regard for the purity of his native
tongue should stand up against the corruptive effects of this false
philosophy.

Mr. A did not say "anything goes," nor did he advocate that educated
speech should be reduced to the level of gutter talk. He did not even say
teachers should accept usages they disapprove of. All he said was that
there is not much point in devoting class time to usages that are common
in the language of educated people. Mr. B is entitled to oppose that
opinion. He is not entitled to distort it by misrepresenting it. In persuasion it is often necessary to attack a statement one thinks unwise or
even quite wrong, but the attack should be directed at the statement
actually made, not at an unfair exaggeration of it. To avoid the temptation or the suspicion of misrepresenting your opponent's statement, it
is good policy and good manners to quote the statement fully and accurately before attacking it.

Slanting is the practice of selecting facts favorable to one's opinion and
suppressing those against it. The result is a distorted and unfair view.
For example, a writer who says there can be no real poverty in a country
where the average annual income is more than $10,000 ignores two facts:
that this average includes incomes of a million dollars or more, and that
great numbers of people do not have anywhere near the average income.
The omitted facts are just as pertinent to the question of poverty as is the
average figure. The evidence is slanted to support a conclusion that
would seem less true if the omitted facts were given.

A third kind of distortion is *quoting a statement out of context* and so making it mean what it was not intended to mean. You probably know that by deleting certain parts of a taped speech and then recording the edited tape, one can greatly distort the original speech. This may be amusing when done as a joke. It would be thoroughly dishonest if offered as evidence of what someone actually said. Yet writers sometimes produce similar effects by deliberately or carelessly omitting significant parts of a context. In reviewing a play, a critic writes: "The plot of this play is fascinating in a strange way: you keep waiting for something to happen, but nothing does. The characters never come close to greatness, and the few witty lines seem out of place among the platitudes of the dialogue." An advertisement based on this review reads: "Fascinating plot . . . characters close to greatness . . . witty lines." Even though some omissions are indicated, the effect of the advertisement is to distort what the critic said.

Name-calling is an attempt to discredit an opponent through the use of labels or descriptive words with highly unfavorable connotations. Examples are *male chauvinist pig, redneck, radical, reactionary, charlatan*. Within limits it is reasonable in persuasion to use connotations that advance your purpose. But when emotional language is carried to the point of name-calling, it provokes an unfavorable response from intelligent readers, especially when name-calling is substituted for logical argument. You do not have to call opponents names. It is enough to show that they are mistaken, or that what they propose is not in the readers' best interests.

Distortion, slanting, quoting out of context, and name-calling do more harm to the users than to their opponents. These devices are clear signs of unfairness, and readers resent them. Writers who create such resentment hurt their chances of being persuasive.

Exercise   The following excerpt is from an article written by a famous journalist about William Jennings Bryan. Bryan had been three times the Democratic candidate for president, had served as secretary of state under Wilson, and had been one of the prosecution lawyers in the Scopes trial in Dayton, Tennessee. At that trial Scopes, a biology teacher, was found guilty of breaking a state law by teaching the theory of evolution.

Study the diction in this excerpt. Do you find it persuasive or objectionable? Support your judgment by reference to particular words or phrases. What conclusions do you draw about the writer's fairness?

This talk of sincerity, I confess, fatigues me. If the fellow was sincere, then so was P. T. Barnum. The word is disgraced and degraded by such use. He was, in fact, a charlatan, a mountebank, a zany without shame or dignity. His career brought him into contact with the first men of his time; he preferred the company of rustic ignoramuses. It was hard to believe, watching him at Dayton, that he had traveled, that he had been a high officer of state. He seemed only a poor clod like those around him, deluded by childish theology, full of an almost pathological hatred of all learning, all human dignity, all fine and noble things. He was a peasant come home to the barnyard. Imagine a gentleman, and you have imagined everything that he was not. What animated him from end to end of his grotesque career was simply ambition — the ambition of a common man to get his hands upon the collar of his superiors, or, failing that, to get his thumb into their eyes. He was born with a roaring voice, and it had the trick of inflaming half-wits. His whole career was devoted to raising those half-wits against their betters, that he himself might shine. (H. L. Mencken, *Prejudices: Fifth Series*)

Emotional Appeal

Some people think of emotional appeal as an unworthy kind of persuasion. The term suggests to them a writer stampeding readers into thoughtless action by causing their feelings to overrule their judgment. This does happen, but abuses of emotional appeal do not negate the need for it. Readers feel as well as think, and to be thoroughly persuaded they must be both intellectually and emotionally involved. The need for emotional appeal is greatest when you are trying to persuade readers that the present situation is bad and something must be done about it. Because any action takes effort, people are not likely to act until they feel a compelling need to do so. Emotional appeal creates that need. Once they are emotionally persuaded that something must be done, they will be willing to consider possible solutions and choose the one that seems best. Someone has said that emotional appeal is the starter and logical argument the steering wheel. You do not need to choose between them. Both are necessary.

The strongest emotional appeals usually dramatize a situation through examples. Agencies seeking money to provide food, shelter, clothing, and medical care for suffering children often choose one child as typical and appeal for sympathy with a picture of that child. In the advertisement shown on the next page, the real problem is not so much the plight of the child in the picture as the negligence of parents. The statistics in the advertisement may persuade people who take the trouble to think about them. But it is the picture of the crippled child that gets their attention and makes them start thinking about the high risk of polio, diphtheria, and other preventable diseases among young children. The example personalizes the problem. From any parent who has not had a child vaccinated, it is likely to provoke the response, "That could be *my* child!" Once parents have identified their own children with the child in the picture, they are more likely to take protective action.

In using emotional appeal in your own writing, you will have almost no opportunity of presenting pictures; you must provoke the desired response through words alone. Your best means will probably be narration or description or a combination of both. If you want to show that a serious evil exists, dramatize that evil by showing it happening to somebody. If you want to show that the present situation is shocking, describe it in specific detail. The following paragraph combines both example and description:

> As I sit in my jail cell in Santa Fe, capital of New Mexico, I pray that all poor people will unite to bring justice to New Mexico. My cell block has no daylight, no ventilation of any kind. After 9 P.M. we are left in a dungeon of total darkness. Visiting rules allow only fifteen minutes per week on Thursdays from 1 to 4 P.M. so that parents who work cannot visit their sons in jail. Yesterday a twenty-two-year-old boy cut his throat. Today, August 17, two young boys cut their wrists with razor blades and were taken unconscious to the hospital. My cell block is hot and suffocating. All my prison mates complain and show a daily state of anger. But these uncomfortable conditions do not bother me, for I have a divine dream to give me strength: the happiness of my people. (Reies Lopez Tijerina, "A Letter from Jail," *We Are Chicanos*)

Discussion Problem

The following essay first appeared in *Ms.*, a magazine addressed to women. It views the husband-wife relationship through the eyes of a woman and argues that a wife is such a useful companion that even a *wife* would want one. Its persuasiveness for an audience of both sexes partly depends on whether the

If you forget to have your children vaccinated, you could be reminded of it the rest of your life.

There's no gentle way of putting it. Parents who don't have their children immunized against polio are risking a senseless tragedy. We only raise the point here because that's exactly what many parents seem to be doing.

In 1963, for example, 84% of all preschoolers had three or more doses of polio vaccine. Ten years later the number had plummeted to 60% — which is simply another way of saying that 2 out of every 5 children have not been immunized against polio.

And polio isn't the only childhood disease people seem to be ignoring.

Immunization against diphtheria has been so neglected that not long ago there was an epidemic of it in Texas.

In 1974, reports show there were 57,407 cases of mumps, 22,085 of measles, 94 of tetanus, and 1,758 of whooping cough — all preventable.

What about your children? Are they protected against these diseases?

The best way to make sure is to see your family doctor. He can help you check on which immunizations your children may have missed, and then see that your children get them.

Of course, one of the best weapons in preventing any disease is knowledge. So to help you learn about immunization in greater detail, we've prepared a booklet. You can get it by writing: "Immunization," Metropolitan Life, One Madison Avenue, New York, N.Y. 10010.

Our interest in this is simple. At Metropolitan Life, literally everything we do is concerned with people's futures. And we'd like to make sure those futures are not only secure, but healthy and long.

✳ Metropolitan Life
Where the future is now

Carl Fischer for Metropolitan Life

"husband" and "wife" in the article are typical. What do you think? Discuss the article with special attention to trustworthiness and emotional appeal.

I Want a Wife

I belong to that classification of people known as wives. I am a Wife. And, not altogether incidentally, I am a mother.

Not too long ago a male friend of mine appeared on the scene fresh from a recent divorce. He had one child, who is, of course, with his ex-wife. He is obviously looking for another wife. As I thought about him while I was ironing one evening, it suddenly occurred to me that I, too, would like to have a wife. Why do I want a wife?

I would like to go back to school so that I can become economically independent, support myself, and, if need be, support those dependent on me. I want a wife who will work and send me to school. And while I am going to school I want a wife to take care of my children. I want a wife to keep track of the children's doctor and dentist appointments. And to keep track of mine, too. I want a wife to make sure that my children eat properly and are kept clean. I want a wife who will wash the children's clothes and keep them mended. I want a wife who is a good nurturant attendant to my children, who arranges for their schooling, makes sure they have an adequate social life with their peers, takes them to the park, the zoo, etc. I want a wife who takes care of the children when they are sick, a wife who arranges to be around when the children need special care, because, of course, I cannot miss classes at school. My wife must arrange to lose time at work and not lose the job. It may mean a small cut in my wife's income from time to time, but I guess I can tolerate that. Needless to say, my wife will arrange and pay for the care of the children while my wife is working.

I want a wife who will take care of *my* physical needs. I want a wife who will keep the house clean. A wife who will pick up after me. I want a wife who will keep my clothes clean, ironed, mended, replaced when need be, and who will see to it that my personal things are kept in their proper place so that I can find what I need the minute I need it. I want a wife who cooks the meals, a wife who is a *good* cook. I want a wife who will plan the menus, do the necessary shopping, prepare the meals, serve them pleasantly, and then do the cleaning up while I do my studying. I want a wife who will care for me when I am sick and sympathize with my pain and loss of time from school. I want a wife to go along when our family takes a vacation so that someone can continue to care for me and my children when I need a rest and change of scene.

I want a wife who will not bother me with rambling complaints about a wife's duties. But I want a wife who will listen to me when I feel the need to explain a rather difficult point I have come across in my course of studies. And I want a wife who will type my papers for me when I have written them.

I want a wife who will take care of the details of my social life. When my wife and I are invited out by my friends, I want a wife who will take care of the babysitting arrangements. When I meet people at school that I like and want to entertain, I want a wife who will have the house clean, prepare a special meal, serve it to me and my friends, and not interrupt when I talk about the things that interest me and my friends. I want a wife who will have arranged that the children are fed and ready for bed before my guests arrive so that the children do not bother us. I want a wife who takes care of the needs of my guests so that they feel comfortable, who makes sure that they have an ashtray, that they are passed the hors d'oeuvres, that they are offered a second helping of the food, that their wine glasses are replenished when necessary, that their coffee is served to them as they like it.

And I want a wife who knows that sometimes I need a night out by myself.

I want a wife who is sensitive to my sexual needs, a wife who makes love passionately and eagerly when I feel like it, a wife who makes sure that I am satisfied. And, of course, I want a wife who will not demand sexual attention when I am not in the mood for it. I want a wife who assumes the complete responsibility for birth control, because I do not want more children. I want a wife who will remain sexually faithful to me so that I do not have to clutter up my intellectual life with jealousies. And I want a wife who understands that *my* sexual needs may entail more than strict adherence to monogamy. I must, after all, be able to relate to people as fully as possible.

If, by chance, I find another person more suitable as a wife than the wife I already have, I want the liberty to replace my present wife with another one. Naturally, I will expect a fresh, new life; my wife will take the children and be solely responsible for them so that I am left free.

When I am through with school and have a job, I want my wife to quit working and remain at home so that my wife can more fully and completely take care of a wife's duties.

My God, who wouldn't want a wife? (Judy Syfers)

Exercise   Choose any situation either on or off campus that you think is bad and ought to be changed. Then in two or three pages write an emotional appeal designed to make your readers feel as you do about the problem. You need not propose any specific changes. Your purpose in this paper is simply to make your readers feel that the situation is intolerable and thus make them willing to consider whatever changes are later proposed.

Argument

In addition to trustworthiness and emotional appeal, a third means of persuasion is argument. Argument is first of all a way of thinking. You observe something and draw a conclusion from it; the relation between the observation and the conclusion is an argument. Once you have convinced yourself that the conclusion is sound, you can use the argument to persuade others.

The Structure of Argument   In its simplest form an argument consists of two statements, one of which is a conclusion from the other.

Mary's temperature is 104 degrees.

She ought to go to the infirmary.

Here the second statement is a *conclusion* from the first. The first statement is what tends to make the second believable. In this chapter it is called a *premise*. The two statements taken together constitute an argument.

An inference is a thought process that moves from an observation through some knowledge or belief to a conclusion. Because anyone who concludes that Mary should go to the infirmary must believe that a person with a temperature of 104 degrees needs medical attention, the argument is an inference. *All arguments are inferences in which the conclusion is inferred from the premise.* The statement that

Mary's temperature is 104 degrees.

Her mother must be a lawyer.

is not an argument, since there seems to be no logical connection between her temperature and her mother's profession. There is no *premise-conclusion relation* between the two sentences.

Now consider these two statements:

Mary's temperature is 104 degrees.

She must have appendicitis.

The only reader who will accept the second statement as a conclusion from the first is one who believes that appendicitis is the *sole* cause of such a temperature. Few readers, if any, hold such a belief; therefore you must say that there is no premise-conclusion relation between the sentences and that the statements do not constitute an argument.

The difference between statements that are related as premise and conclusion and those that are not may be further illustrated by the examples below. Each pair of sentences at the left consists of a premise and an italicized conclusion. In the pairs at the right there is no premise-conclusion relation, since no reader can reasonably infer one sentence as a logical conclusion from the other solely on the information given.

Premise-conclusion relationship	No premise-conclusion relationship
These men and women are doing the same job. *They should get the same pay.*	These men and women are doing the same job. Some of them are married.
Professor Jones is a tough grader. A check of his grades for the past five years shows that less than 5 percent of his students got A's, and 20 percent got F's.	Professor Jones is a tough grader. He has a Ph.D. degree.
Unless you arrive on campus before eight o'clock, it is impossible to find a parking space. *Something ought to be done about the campus parking situation.*	This morning I had to park half a mile from campus. Students cannot afford to park in a metered area.

The arguments at the left are not necessarily convincing. Some readers might want additional premises before accepting the conclusion. But whether convincing or not, the paired sentences at the left are related as those at the right are not. We can make that relationship more obvious by inserting *because* before the premise or *therefore* before the conclusion. But no sentence at the right can be inferred as a conclusion from the sentence paired with it. If you disagree, first add *because* before the premise or *therefore* before the conclusion, and explain what a reader would have to believe in order to accept the conclusion.

Exercise   **Which of the following pairs of statements are related as premise and conclusion and are therefore arguments? At this time do not worry about whether the argument is convincing. Simply try to recognize premise-conclusion relations.**

Final examinations cause unnecessary hardships for both students and instructors. Final examinations are traditional ways of evaluating student performance.

Final examinations cause unnecessary hardships for both students and instructors. Final examinations should be abolished.

John Jones is the most politically experienced candidate for the Senate. He has served in the House of Representatives and in his state legislature.

John Jones is the most politically experienced candidate for the Senate. He has five children, all of whom have college degrees.

No woman should be penalized because of her sex. Some people are kept in inferior jobs just because they are female.

No woman should be penalized because of her sex. In a democracy women are absolutely indispensable.

Students have the right to disagree with their instructors. It is only through disagreement that they learn how to evaluate opinions.

Students have the right to disagree with their instructors. Some students are more disagreeable than others.

So far you have been examining arguments of the simplest structure — a single premise and a single conclusion. Many arguments are more complex. The next paragraph has five premises in sentence 3.

(1) But busing hasn't worked. (2) After almost a decade, it seems clear that the principal mistake was to assume that we could create a more

socially responsible society by putting the problem on wheels and expecting it to arrive at a daily solution. (3) The evidence is substantial that busing is leading away from integration and not toward it; that it has not significantly improved the quality of education accessible to blacks; that it has lowered the standard of education available to whites; that it has resulted in the exodus of white students to private schools inside the city or to public schools in the comparatively affluent suburbs beyond the economic means of blacks; and, finally, that it has not contributed to racial harmony, but has produced deep fissures within American society. (Norman Cousins, *Saturday Review*)

The first sentence makes an assertion. The second sentence explains the context for the assertion. And the third sentence gives five illustrations (or premises) that provide the evidence for the assertions stated in the first two sentences.

In a still more complex argument, a conclusion from one or more premises may become a premise for another conclusion, as one unit of the argument is built on another. In the following outline of a student paper, the marginal and parenthetical notations show the premise-conclusion relations among the parts of the argument:

Conclusion

Thesis: Teen-age marriages are not advisable.
(Conclusion from I, II, III — the main premises — below)

Main premise

I. The divorce rate for teen-age marriages is high. *(First main premise for thesis, but also a conclusion from A and B below)*

Subpremise

    A. Dr. Laura Singer, president of the New York Division of the American Association of Marriage Counselors, says that two out of three teen-age marriages end in divorce. *(First subpremise for I)*

Subpremise

    B. Dr. Harold Christensen, the author of many articles on marital adjustment, says that the younger the age of marriage, the higher the percentage of divorces. *(Second subpremise for I)*

Main premise

II. Teen-age marriage is especially difficult for students. *(Second main premise for thesis, but also a conclusion from A and B below)*

Subpremise

    A. Unless they are subsidized by their parents, married teen-agers have to divide their time between school and part-time jobs and have both academic and financial difficulties. *(First subpremise for II)*

Subpremise   B. In a recent study of married college students, Dr. Ruth Hoeflin of Ohio State University found that often either the husband or the wife had to drop out of school and work in order to meet expenses, and that between work and school they had little time to spend with their spouses. *(Second subpremise for II)*

Main premise   III. Teen-age marriages restrict individual development. *(Third main premise for thesis, but also a conclusion from A and B below)*

Subpremise   A. Early marriage deprives both partners of the maturing influences of travel, wide social acquaintances, independent decision making, and development of a sense of selfhood. *(First subpremise for III)*

Subpremise   B. A person who goes directly from responsibility to parents to responsibility to a spouse never has the experience of being responsible only to himself or herself. *(Second subpremise for III)*

This outline shows the structure of an argument in which the thesis states the conclusion, and the premises provide support for that conclusion. The whole argument breaks into three smaller arguments, any one of which you could develop into a separate paper by making a main premise the thesis. In its present form, this argument will be persuasive to any reader who believes that the three main premises with their supporting subpremises establish the soundness of the conclusion. When this happens, the premises *prove* the conclusion.

But proof is seldom as precise in argument as it is in mathematics. In Euclidean geometry you can prove that, without exception, the square of the hypotenuse is equal to the sum of the squares on the other two sides. But you cannot prove conclusively that teen-age marriages are *never* advisable. All you can do is show that they are *generally* inadvisable. You can do this only when your readers accept your premises and the conclusion drawn from them. Usually, therefore, *proof* in an argument means the *acceptance of the reasoning procedure.*

"It was the only thing to do after the mule died."

Three years back, the Hinsleys of Dora, Missouri, had a tough decision to make.

To buy a new mule.

Or invest in a used bug.

They weighed the two possibilities.

First there was the problem of the bitter Ozark winters. Tough on a warm-blooded mule. Not so tough on an air-cooled VW.

Then, what about the eating habits of the two contenders? Hay vs. gasoline.

As Mr. Hinsley puts it: "I get over eighty miles out of a dollar's worth of gas and I get where I want to go a lot quicker."

Then there's the road leading to their cabin. Many a mule pulling a wagon and many a conventional automobile has spent many an hour stuck in the mud.

As for shelter, a mule needs a barn. A bug doesn't. "It just sets out there all day and the paint job looks near as good as the day we got it."

Finally, there was maintenance to think about. When a mule breaks down, there's only one thing to do: Shoot it.

But if and when their bug breaks down, the Hinsleys have a Volkswagen dealer only two gallons away.

Discussion Problem

The text of this advertisement contains five premises for a conclusion that is unstated but hinted at in the statement immediately under the picture. See if you can agree in converting the ad into a premise-conclusion outline in which the conclusion is followed by five premises.

Exercise

The following three-part exercise should be done individually; then, if your instructor wishes, the final results may be discussed in class.

1. The following statements may be outlined as two main premises for the conclusion "In practice we are not able to define *heredity* or *environment* with precision." One of the premises has two subpremises; the other has none. Outline the argument to show all premise-conclusion relations.

   a. Some inherited characteristics of fruit flies appear only when the environment encourages their appearance.

   b. We are not able to define *heredity* except in terms of characteristics that may have been influenced by environment.

   c. An acorn will never grow into anything but an oak tree, but whether it becomes an oak tree depends on environmental conditions.

   d. The environment of individuals in a society is so complex that we cannot define it precisely.

2. The following statements can be outlined as three main premises for the conclusion "We cannot experimentally study heredity and environment apart from each other." Each main premise has one subpremise. Outline the argument to show all premise-conclusion relations.

   a. We cannot do this with newborn babies.

   b. We cannot do it with ordinary (fraternal) twins.

   c. A boy twin has a different environment than a girl twin.

   d. Identical twins come from the same egg and thus have the same inheritance, but we cannot be sure that they have had the same environment while growing up.

   e. Newborn babies have had nine months of prenatal environment.

   f. We cannot do it with identical twins.

3. Combine 1 and 2 into a larger argument, first by outlining the whole argument as in the outline on teen-age marriages (pages 346–347), then by writing the conclusion or thesis that your outline proves.

Common Types of Arguments

As you have seen, arguments are reasoning processes in which a conclusion is inferred from premises. Here we will consider common types of arguments by identifying common kinds of premises and inferences.

Types of Premises

The most common types of premises are *statements of fact, judgments,* and *expert testimony.*

Statements of Fact   Statements of fact may be verified by checking them against the facts they report. If the statement corresponds to the facts, it is "true"; if it does not, it is "false." Statements of fact make the most reliable premises. Among intelligent people the authority of facts is likely to be decisive; hence the common saying, "The facts speak for themselves." This is something of an exaggeration, since different conclusions can sometimes be inferred from the same factual premise, but controversies tend to dissolve when they are reduced to questions of fact. For this reason, the best preparation for argument is a diligent search for the facts.

Judgments   Judgments are conclusions inferred from facts. You saw that in the student outline on teen-age marriages the main premises were conclusions (judgments) from the subpremises beneath them. These judgments then became premises for the conclusion shown in the thesis. This procedure is common in complex arguments. For example, a doctor trying to find out what is causing a patient's symptoms may early in the examination make a tentative diagnosis that the symptoms are caused either by tuberculosis or by a tumor. If laboratory tests eliminate tuberculosis, the patient has a tumor, in which case it may be malignant (cancerous) or benign. That question can be decided only by surgery, and the facts revealed by the operation will determine the final conclusion. An outline of the doctor's reasoning would show the following steps:

1. *The symptoms are caused by either tuberculosis or a tumor.* This hypothesis, or tentative conclusion, is a judgment based on knowledge of the two diseases.

2. *It is not tuberculosis.* This conclusion is based on the laboratory tests.

3. *The patient has a tumor,* a conclusion based on an inference from 1 and 2 above.

4. *The tumor is benign and therefore the patient does not have cancer.* This is a further conclusion based on the operation.

If the first three steps in the doctor's reasoning are put in this form —

1. It is either tuberculosis or a tumor.

2. It is not tuberculosis.

3. Therefore, it is a tumor.

— the two premises from which the final conclusion is reached are judgments, since each is a conclusion inferred from the facts. A three-step argument in this form is called a *syllogism*. The doctor deduces or discovers the conclusion by making a logical inference from the two premises. Whether this syllogism is a sound argument or not will depend on whether the premises are true. For example, if the symptoms could be caused by a third disease — say emphysema — the first premise will be false, and the conclusion that the patient has a tumor cannot be accepted.

Expert Testimony   Expert testimony is a statement by a person presumed to be an authority on the subject. The statement may be factual, as when a doctor describes the conditions revealed by an autopsy; or it may be a judgment, as when a psychiatrist testifies that in her opinion a defendant is insane. Since expert testimony is always a statement of fact or a judgment, it could be dealt with under those two categories. It is here considered separately (1) because factual statements by an expert are often extremely difficult for a nonexpert to verify (for example, ordinary citizens cannot usually check the facts to determine whether a swimmer's death was caused by heart failure or by drowning); and (2) because the qualifications of the expert require special consideration.

Expert testimony is often abused. It is too easy to assume that the testimony of any prominent person is reliable, though you recognize — if you stop to think about it — that a person may be distinguished in one field but not in another, or may be expert in one phase of a subject and still know little about another phase of it. To be trustworthy, expert testimony must meet two requirements: the expert must be an authority on the particular subject, and there must be no reasonable probability of bias.

Exercise

The following material consists of four arguments in favor of simplified spelling. For each argument, mark the conclusion *C* and the premise *P*. Then

identify the premise as a statement of fact, testimony, or judgment. Finally, decide for each argument whether the premises persuade you to accept the conclusion. If they do not, what would the writer have to do to get you to accept the conclusion?

1. There is a tremendous lack of agreement between pronunciation and spelling in English. The sound of *a* in *ale* may also be spelled *ae* in *maelstrom, ai* in *bait, ay* in *day, e* and *ee* in *melee, ea* in *break, eigh* in *weigh, et* in *beret.*

2. The same letter may be used for different sounds. The letter *a* has different pronunciations in *sane, chaotic, care, add, account, arm, ask,* and *sofa.*

3. English is full of silent letters. It is estimated that two-thirds of all the words in the Merriam-Webster unabridged dictionary have at least one silent letter.

4. The cost of typing, printing, and proofreading illogical English spellings is high. George Bernard Shaw, who in addition to being a great playwright was a powerful advocate of simplified spelling, repeatedly stated his opinion in the London *Times* that by adopting simplified spelling Britain could have saved enough money to pay the costs of World War II.[1]

Types of Inferences

In this section you will examine three major types of inferences and one minor one. The major types are *generalization, causal relation,* and a combination of these two called *causal generalization;* the minor type is *analogy.*

Generalization   A generalization is the type of reasoning that draws a conclusion about a whole class from a study of some of its members. The members used are called a *sample,* and the conclusion infers that what is true of the sample will be true of the whole class. Well-known examples are questionnaires that attempt to describe public opinion on an issue by polling a sample and extending the results to the whole population.

Obviously a generalization based on a small sample is riskier than one

1. Much of the material in this exercise is from Falk Johnson, "Should Spelling Be Streamlined?" in *The American Mercury* for September, 1948.

based on a large sample, but the typicality of the sample is more important than its size. A sample is believed to be typical when there are good reasons for assuming that what is true of the sample will also be true of the unexamined part. For example, the butterfat content of a twenty-gallon can of homogenized milk will be the same in all parts of the can; therefore one part is as good a sample as another. Since there is no probability that increasing the size of the sample would increase the accuracy of the test, a single cupful — perhaps a few spoonfuls — would be a typical sample. But if the milk is not homogenized, the cream will rise to the top, and a sample taken from the top of the can will exaggerate the butterfat content, while one taken from the middle or bottom of the can will be lower in butterfat. In this case, there is no typical sample.

It is important to understand this distinction, because *the hasty assumption that a sample is typical is the chief cause of unsound generalizations.* It is often very difficult — sometimes impossible — to be sure that a sample is typical, and much useful reasoning is based on samples that can only be presumed so. But for any serious generalization, all possible care should be taken to see that the samples are probably typical. Any sample that tends to be "loaded" — that is, more likely to be true of part of a class than of all of it — should be rejected. Both the following samples are loaded:

1. A study of all members of a fraternity to answer the question, "Do fraternities help incoming students adjust to college life?"

This sample consists of students who have already answered this question in the affirmative and excludes those who have already answered it negatively. The sample is too biased to be typical of all male undergraduates. Even if all fraternities on campus were polled, the sample would still not be typical.

2. A study of college hospital records to determine how many days a semester a student is likely to be sick

This sample will exaggerate the amount of sickness because it ignores the healthiest part of the college population — those who did not need hospitalization.

The commonest safeguard against loading is to choose samples at random. A random sample is one in which the examined members are chosen by chance, as in a lottery, or by some other procedure so arbitrary that it is almost the same as a chance selection. The assumption behind this kind of selection is that any inference made from the sample is likely to be typical, since there is no reason for believing that the sampling procedure is likely to be loaded.

You will generally be safer with a large sample than with a small one. A conclusion about the advisability of teen-age marriages based on the testimony of eight teen-age couples you know would be a *hasty generalization,* one based on too small a sample to warrant any conclusion. In contrast, Dr. Christensen's testimony cited in the student outline on page 346 was based on 15,000 teen-age marriages. His sample may or may not have been typical, but its size would help to make it persuasive.

One way to avoid hasty generalizations is to be suspicious of any statement about *all* of a group or class — all women drivers, all teen-agers, all college professors. Such statements imply that your samples are typical and that the judgment is true without exception. Your generalization may be true of *many* or of *some* members of the class. If so, say so. Do not use *all* unless you are ready to prove that there are no exceptions. If you overstate the generalization, you invite doubts about your own trustworthiness. Notice that even if a generalization does not include the word *all,* it may still mean *all.* To say that college professors are absent-minded implies *all* college professors.

Exercises

A. Rate the acceptability of the lettered generalizations below, marking them by the following key:

3. True in all cases
2. True in most cases
1. True in some cases

Discuss your answers.

a. Athletes are not interested in the arts.
b. People who play slot machines a great deal lose more money than they win.
c. Qualified lifeguards are better-than-average swimmers.
d. The English have better manners than Americans.
e. Stockbrokers are experts on the economy.
f. College graduates earn more money in their lifetime than do noncollege workers.

g. Artists have low moral standards.

h. Advertising insults the public's intelligence.

i. Clothing sold in high-priced department stores is of the best quality.

B. The following selection from an essay attempts to find an answer to the question posed in the first paragraph. Read it and discuss the questions following it.

Why is America, blessed with the finest medical schools, the most extensive research facilities, the largest drug laboratories, the best-equipped hospitals and the highest-paid doctors, a "second-rate" country in the distribution of health care? That verdict doesn't come from Ralph Nader. It's the view of the nation's ranking public-health official, Dr. Roger O. Egeberg, Special Assistant to the Secretary for Health Policy of the Department of Health, Education and Welfare. . . .

Why is this so? My search for answers began in a utilitarian one-bedroom apartment awash in dirty hospital uniforms and copies of the *New England Journal of Medicine.* Slumped in the middle of her Levitz sofa, just off night-shift duty at one of the nation's major community hospitals, was a nurse, coughing badly from a cold, compliments of her patients. She was talking about a millionaire surgeon on her hospital staff. This physician, who specialized in diseases of the rich, was adored by high-society patients. His friends blessed him for finding imaginary breast masses on their wives and then subjecting them to needless mastectomies. Hardly a week passed when he didn't take out a normal stomach or a healthy uterus.

The nurse, still wearing her hospital whites and hacking steadily, went on for several hours about the outrages she had seen performed at the hands of this surgeon. The physician had tried to cure a woman's diarrhea with three totally unrelated surgeries: hysterectomy, thyroidectomy, and hemorrhoidectomy. The diarrhea did not abate. Another woman plagued by vaginal bleeding from her I.U.D. ended up with a hysterectomy (when the doctor simply should have removed the I.U.D.). After performing an appendectomy on one man, he closed the patient up before the pus could drain; he was in a hurry to make a baseball game with his son. The patient went downhill and the surgeon returned to pronounce him beyond hope. Several of the nurse's colleagues were so distraught they appealed to the chief of staff, persuading him to bring in other doctors, who drained the pus and saved the man's life. . . .

I remember feeling haunted by her stories when I drove home that night. I had read about such outrages in magazines and newspapers but somehow always managed to associate them with poor people who couldn't afford good medical care. Her firsthand accounts of this surgeon's work at the expense of his high-society patients jolted me. Now, dozens of hospitals and clinics later, the surgeon seems like a footnote to what I saw and heard during my travels about America's medical empire. I found:

> Patients denied admission to hospitals who dropped dead on their way home.

> Hospitals that falsify medical-committee-meeting minutes to win accreditation. . . .

> A state contracting with medical groups to provide prepaid health-care services at hospitals specifically disapproved by inspectors from that same state's medical association.

> A surgeon walking out in the middle of a hysterectomy because the nurse said something he didn't like (the anesthetist completed the operation).

> A medical-board-certified cardiovascular surgeon with impeccable medical credentials and a lengthy bibliography who has butchered a number of patients straight into their graves.

> Chiropractors, optometrists, and dentists handling emergency-room patients.

> Nurses who can't discriminate between live and dead patients.

(Roger Rapoport, "It's Enough to Make You Sick," *Playboy*)

1. Before answering the following questions, record your general response to the selection. Did you find it persuasive?

2. Insofar as it is persuasive, is the emotional appeal of the examples a significant factor in your response?

3. How satisfied are you that the examples are typical?

4. Which of the following seems to you a reasonable conclusion from the selection? If none of these satisfies you, state your own conclusion.

   a. The medical profession is a disgrace.
   b. Most doctors are incompetent and greedy.
   c. Some doctors are guilty of malpractice.

Causal Relation   As you learned in Chapter 5, causal relation is a method of developing your writing. It is also a form of reasoning. You want to know whether cigarettes really do cause lung cancer; you want to know what causes malnutrition, the decay of cities, the decay of teeth. You are equally interested in effects: what is the effect of alcohol on the formation of unborn infants, of sulphur or lead in the atmosphere, of mercury in tuna fish, of oil spills and raw sewage in rivers and the sea, of staying up late on the night before an examination?

You saw in Ellen Goodman's essay on secretary stress that causal reasoning may go from cause to effect or from effect to cause. Either way, you reason from what you know to what you want to find out. Sometimes you reason from an effect to a cause and then on to another effect. Thus, if you reason that because the lights have gone out the refrigerator won't work, you first relate the effect (lights out) to the cause (power off) and then relate that cause to another effect (refrigerator not working). This kind of reasoning is called, for short, *effect to effect.* It is quite common to reason through an extensive chain of causal relations. When the lights go out, you might reason in the following causal chain: lights out — power off — refrigerator not working — temperature will rise — milk will sour. In other words, you diagnose a succession of effects from the power failure, each becoming the cause of the next.

Causes are classified as necessary, sufficient, or contributory. A *necessary* cause is one that must be present for the effect to occur, as combustion is necessary to drive a gasoline engine. A *sufficient* cause is one that can produce an effect unaided, though there may be more than one sufficient cause of a given effect: a dead battery is enough to keep a car from starting, but faulty spark plugs or an empty gas tank will have the same effect. A *contributory* cause is one that helps to produce an effect but cannot do so by itself, as running through a red light may help cause an accident, though other factors — pedestrians or other cars in the intersection — must also be present.

In establishing or refuting a causal relation, it is usually necessary to show the process by which the alleged cause produces the effect. Such an explanation is called a *causal* analysis. The following selection refutes an alleged cause and suggests a more plausible one by examining the process between cause and effect.

What we know of prenatal development makes such attempts [attempts made by a mother to mold the character of her unborn child by studying poetry, art, or mathematics during pregnancy] seem utterly impossible. How could such extremely complex influences pass from the mother to the child? There is no connection between their nervous systems. Even the blood vessels of mother and child do not join directly. They lie side by side and the chemicals are interchanged through the walls by a process that we call osmosis. An emotional shock to the mother will affect her child, because it changes the activity of her glands and so the chemistry of her blood. Any chemical change in the mother's blood will affect the child — for better or worse. But we cannot see how a liking for mathematics or poetic genius can be dissolved in blood and produce a similar liking or genius in the child.

In our discussion of instincts we saw that there was reason to believe that whatever we inherit must be of some very simple sort rather than any complicated or very definite kind of behavior. It is certain that no one inherits a knowledge of mathematics. It may be, however, that children inherit more or less of a rather general ability that we may call intelligence. If very intelligent children become deeply interested in mathematics, they will probably make a success of that study.

As for musical ability, it may be that what is inherited is an especially sensitive ear, a peculiar structure of the hands or of the vocal organs, connections between nerves and muscles that make it comparatively easy to learn the movements a musician must execute, and particularly vigorous emotions. If these factors are all organized around music, the child may become a musician. The same factors, in other circumstances, might be organized about some other center of interest. The rich emotional equipment might find expression in poetry. The capable fingers might develop skill in surgery. It is not the knowledge of music that is inherited, then, nor even the love of it, but a certain bodily structure that makes it comparatively easy to acquire musical knowledge and skill. Whether that ability shall be directed toward music or some other undertaking may be decided entirely by forces in the environment in which a child grows up. (William H. Roberts, *Psychology You Can Use*)

The most common errors in causal reasoning are:

1. *Assuming that A causes B because A always precedes B.* Although it is true that a cause always precedes its effect, a mere time order is not necessarily a causal order. Night always follows day, and it is just as true that day follows night. But neither one causes the other. Each is caused by the rotation of the earth toward or away from the sun. The time order between A and B may suggest a causal relation, but that relation must be supported by other evidence, preferably an explanation of the causal process by which the effect is produced.

2. *Mistaking an effect for a cause.* Since a cause may produce more than one effect, two effects may be obvious at the same time. Getting rid of one effect will not necessarily get rid of the other. For example, certain medicines may remove a cough without curing the cold that causes the cough and other symptoms. But because effects are more obvious than causes, it is easy to assume that one effect is the cause of the other.

3. *Mistaking a contributory cause for a sufficient cause.* A tailgating driver who explains a crash by saying that the car ahead stopped suddenly is confusing contributory cause with sufficient cause. It is perhaps true that had the car ahead not stopped suddenly the tailgater would not have run into it. But without the tailgating, the stopping of the car ahead would not have resulted in an accident.

4. *Failing to recognize that the cause may be not a single event but a complex of causes.* This kind of oversimplification is probably the most common error in causal reasoning. You tend to think that every effect has *a* cause, and so you look for *the* cause. But the more complex the question is, the more causes may be at work. War, inflation, depression, a decline in the value of the dollar, and similar effects usually have a number of related causes. Even such a relatively simple event as losing your temper may grow out of an accumulation of irritations. Failure to realize this often results in a superficial analysis of a prob-

lem. A wife who blows up when her husband asks, "Isn't dinner ready yet?" may be responding not to his question but to a whole series of frustrations that occurred earlier. His question is not the cause; it is just the last straw.

Causal Generalization   The kind of causal analysis we have been considering works best when we are dealing with events in which all possible causes can be isolated and tested independently of each other. Many problems do not permit such a procedure. You cannot, for instance, test the hypothesis that fluorides prevent tooth decay by eliminating all other possible factors affecting decay — heredity, prenatal environment, diet, and so forth. All you can do is to contrast the amount of tooth decay in people who use fluoridated toothpaste or drink fluoridated water with the amount in people who do neither, and draw a conclusion from the contrast. Basically, you are generalizing from contrasted samples and making a causal-relation inference from the generalization. You are thus combining generalization and causal relation in a *causal generalization.*

The following selection is a causal generalization. The writer is reporting the results of a study to determine the effect of alcohol on Orientals. The generalization is a conclusion from the effect of alcohol on two groups of people. The causal relation is an attempt to establish a connection between race and the drinking of alcoholic beverages.

Orientals and Alcohol

Upon being offered the traditional one for the road, a Japanese will more likely than not decline with a polite *"Kao akaku naru"* (My face will get red). If he does accept the drink, he may feel uncomfortable after downing it. In any event, he — like most Asians — will probably never become an alcoholic. That fact has long been a puzzle to hard-drinking Westerners. The difference is often explained away by Oriental cultural or social traditions, like the strong Chinese taboo against public drunkenness. But now a group at the University of North Carolina has given new weight to a more recent explanation: the East-West drinking disparity may be primarily caused by genetic differences.

To check earlier findings by Boston psychiatrist Peter H. Wolff that Orientals blush more easily in response to alcohol than Westerners, the North Carolina team selected 48 test subjects, 24 Americans of European extraction and 24 Orientals, mostly Japanese, Chinese, Taiwanese and

Koreans. All of them lived in central North Carolina, mostly around the college town of Chapel Hill, and were modest to moderate drinkers.

The North Carolina team, led by psychiatrist John Ewing, gave laboratory cocktails of ginger ale and ethyl alcohol, measuring the amount of alcohol so that each subject drank an amount proportionate to his body weight. The volunteers were then questioned and tested for two hours to gauge the effect of the cocktail. The tests revealed a striking difference. After drinking, the Westerners tended to feel relaxed, confident, alert and happy; the Orientals were more likely to experience muscle weakness, pounding in the head, dizziness and anxiety.

Other test results were equally conclusive. Seventeen of the 24 Orientals became deeply flushed, some within minutes of drinking; that was established visually and by a special device that records pulse pressure of the earlobe. Only three of the Westerners blushed, none as heavily. Blood pressure dropped more sharply and heartbeat quickened more in Orientals than in Westerners. In addition, the alcohol tended to produce a higher level of acetaldehyde, a chemical with anesthetic and antiseptic properties, in the blood of the Oriental subjects. Ewing suspects that the production of this chemical may be partly responsible for the disagreeable reaction that the Orientals experienced.

Ewing's conclusion: "The general level of discomfort in drinking small amounts of alcohol would seem to offer protection to many Orientals from overusing alcoholic beverages as a psychological escape mechanism." He suspects that genetic differences may also account for the drinking habits of other ethnic groups. To check his theory, the North Carolina team has begun carrying out similar tests on blacks, Jews and other groups that tend to use alcohol sparingly. *(Time)*

Analogy　　On pages 285–286, you examined analogy as illustration in the form of extended metaphor. It can also be considered as argument based on similarities. From the premise that two very different things are alike in some significant way, the argument concludes that an inference about one will also apply to the other. The following famous Shakespearean analogy illustrates this type of inference:

I am a Jew. Hath not a Jew eyes? Hath not a Jew hands, organs, dimensions, senses, affections, passions? — fed with the same food, hurt with the same weapons, subject to the same diseases, heal'd by the same means, warm'd and cool'd by the same winter and summer, as a Christian is? If you prick us, do we not bleed? If you tickle us, do we not laugh? If you poison us, do we not die? And if you wrong us, shall we not revenge? If we are like you in the rest, we will resemble you in that. (Shylock, in *The Merchant of Venice*)

We can see the structure of this analogy better if we set up the compared characteristics in parallel columns, matching each characteristic of a Christian with a similar characteristic of a Jew. The whole combines to form a series of premises leading up to the conclusion that, like the Christian, the Jew will seek revenge if wronged.

	Christian		**Jew**
P	1. Has hands, organs, dimensions, etc.	→ 1.	Has hands, organs, dimensions, etc.
	2. Is affected in specific ways by food, weapons, disease, etc.	→ 2.	Is affected in the same specific ways by food, weapons, disease, etc.
	3. If pricked, bleeds.	→ 3.	If pricked, bleeds.
	4. If tickled, laughs.	→ 4.	If tickled, laughs.
	5. If poisoned, dies.	→ 5.	If poisoned, dies.
C	6. If wronged, seeks revenge.	→ 6.	If wronged . . .

In argument, analogy can be both useful and misleading. It is helpful in suggesting hypotheses for further investigation. For example, if you have found that the best protection against one virus disease is to isolate the virus and prepare an immunizing serum from it, you can predict that the same method will work with another virus disease. If the prediction proves true, the analogy has helped to solve the problem. If the prediction proves false, the suggested solution will be quickly rejected and no great harm will have been done.

When analogy is used as the sole proof of a conclusion, it should be examined very closely. It may be more persuasive than it should be and lead you to a conclusion that is not valid, for a single difference can make a whole analogy false. The test of an analogy is the question, "Are the two things analogous for the purpose for which the analogy is being used?" They may have many differences that are unimportant to the inference based on the analogy. But they must not be different in any detail essential to that inference. Thus the analogy that a motherless baby ape could be reared by feeding it as if it were a human baby would be sound because, despite many differences, young apes and human babies have similar digestive systems. But to reason that because two varieties of mushrooms look alike both will be good to eat is a dangerous analogy, because the possibility that one is poisonous would be more important than all their similarities.

Exercise

Study the following analogies and judge their persuasiveness. First, consider whether the alleged similarities offer a reasonable comparison. Then consider whether there is any difference that would cause you to reject the analogy no matter how similar are the things being compared. Finally, write a short critique of each analogy to show specifically why you accept or reject it.

Passage 1

Impeaching a President is like major surgery. It is an act that should not be done hastily nor emotionally, and only when it is necessary to restore the well-being of the patient, in this case the government of the nation. The purpose of surgery is not to punish the diseased organ; neither is the purpose of impeachment to punish a President. In both situations the only legitimate purpose is to remove a source of serious trouble and re-establish a healthy condition.

A surgeon does not initiate the decision to operate. Before he has been called into the case, the patient has been examined by a physician who must satisfy himself by the evidence of laboratory tests and x-rays that an operation may be necessary. When the surgeon is consulted, he reviews the evidence and makes the final decision. A similar procedure is followed in impeachment. The House first studies the question, seeks all pertinent evidence, and then decides whether the matter should go to the Senate. The Senate reviews the evidence and makes the final decision. The whole process of deciding what to do in either surgery or impeachment may take many months.

Both surgery and impeachment are periods of stress for everybody involved. And just as the patient may suffer post-surgical shock, so may the political body suffer from the shock of impeachment. In view of the possible consequences, neither should be undertaken unless there is no satisfactory alternative. But when the patient's health depends on cutting out the source of infection, failure to act, in both surgery and impeachment, may have serious consequences.

Passage 2

I believe that we all accept the principle that an affluent society must do what it can to prevent hunger and misery, and also to provide equality of opportunity to those who have been denied it. But how far can a society go in the redistribution of wealth without changing the very nature of society? I think this is a problem that we've got to face. I do not think that a majority in Congress are trying to face it, or realize that it is a problem, because so many of them are still hard at work at this business of redistributing income.

All that reminds me of what happened in the universities during the 1960's and 1970's — events that I witnessed from a ringside seat. During this period we had a fashion of giving A's to every student — there were no failures. The effect on academic life was devastating. When illiterate or lazy students could get an A average, good students stopped studying. The result was a profound change in academic life: formerly dropouts were those who failed in their studies; in the 1960's and 1970's most of the dropouts were the most gifted and brilliant students, who found that college had become meaningless.

What happens in the schools is not unlike what happens in society at large when the penalties of improvidence, laziness, or ignorance are not just softened, but removed. When there is no such thing as failure, there is no such thing as success either. Motivation, the desire to excel, the urge to accomplishment — all these disappear. The dynamism of society is lost.

This, I'm afraid, is the direction in which our society has been going steadily for many years. The biggest losers are the brightest and most capable men and women. But the average person is a loser too. Faced with no challenge, assured of a comfortable living whether they work or not, such persons become willing dependents, content with a parasitical relationship to the rest of society.

What is significant in our time is that there is a whole class of people interested in encouraging this parasitism. Many welfare officials and social workers are threatened with a loss of their power if there is a marked reduction in the number of their clients, so they are motivated to increase rather than decrease welfare dependency.

Politicians, too, have flourished by getting increased federal grants for this or that disadvantaged group. They go back to their constituents and say, "Look what I've done for you," and get reelected. These are the officeholders who are far more interested in being reelected than in doing what is good for people, good for the economy, good for the nation.

If everybody is rewarded just for being alive, you get the same sort of effect as you do when you reward every student just for being enrolled. You destroy not only education, you destroy society by giving A's to everyone. **This is a philosophical consideration that bothers me very much as I sit in the United States Senate and see its great budget allocations going through. (S. I. Hayakawa, "Mr. Hayakawa Goes to Washington,"** *Harper's*)

Refuting Fallacies

A *fallacy* is any error in the reasoning process that makes an argument unreliable. The following discussion will identify the most common fallacies and suggest how to refute them if your purpose requires you to deal with them in a paper.

Ignoring the Burden of Proof

It is a general rule in argument that *he who asserts must prove.* An *assertion* is a statement offered as a conclusion without a supporting premise. Since argument has been defined as a logical relation between a premise and a conclusion, an assertion is not an argument. You, as writer, must assume responsibility for making your reasoning acceptable to the reader. The least you can do is to give the premises on which you base your conclusion. The standard response by a reader to an unsupported assertion is to ask, "What is the evidence for that assertion?" Assuming that your assertions are true unless the reader can disprove them is *shifting the burden of proof.* It is the writer's job, not the reader's, to prove the truth of an assertion.

Example

College students spend four years of their lives and thousands of dollars of their parents' money trying to get as little as possible out of their college education, provided only that they get their coveted diplomas.

Analysis

This assertion is a generalization, but what is the evidence on which it is based? The writer gives none. If the evidence were given, the reader could evaluate the generalization and would probably dismiss it as a hasty one.

The best refutation is to expose the argument as an assertion and ask for the evidence.

Begging the Question

A question is "begged" when part of what has to be proved is assumed to be true. The best defense against this fallacy is to show how the begging takes place.

Example

In taking the position that persons accused of a crime cannot be interrogated without their lawyers being present, the Supreme Court is showing more concern for the protection of the criminal than for the protection of society. The laws were made to protect law-abiding citizens, not those who defy the law. A criminal loses the rights of a citizen on committing a crime. It is the duty of the police to get at the truth, and they have a right to question an accused person as long as they don't use force.

Analysis

This argument begs the question by assuming that anyone being interrogated by the police has defied the law and is a criminal. But this is what has to be proved. An accused person is innocent until found guilty by a judge or jury. Until then the accused is a "law-abiding citizen" and is entitled to the protection of the law.

Sometimes question-begging takes the form of a *circular argument,* one that goes from conclusion to unproved assertion and back to conclusion again.

Example

Much of this talk about spending millions for slum clearance is based on the fallacy that if we provide fine homes for people who live in the slums, they will suddenly become responsible and productive citizens. This argument puts the cart before the horse. The basic trouble is with the people who live in the slums. These people are shiftless and ir-

Analysis

In this argument the conclusion that slum dwellers are responsible for slums is supported by the unproved assertion that anyone who lives in a slum must be shiftless and irresponsible. That assertion begs the question, and the argument goes around in the following circle: "Slums are caused by shiftless tenants; this is true because shiftless tenants cause slums." The way to refute this argument is to show the cir-

responsible. The conditions under which they live prove this. If they had any initiative or industry, they would not be living in slums.

cularity of the reasoning and the question-begging assumption about the nature of slum dwellers.

Argumentum ad Hominem

The Latin phrase *argumentum ad hominem* means "argument against the man" and names the fallacy of attacking the person instead of the argument. Such an attack is legitimate when someone presents no argument except his or her own unsupported testimony. The device is frequently used in courts to discredit witnesses who are testifying as experts. If it can be shown that they are not experts or that their testimony cannot be relied on because of their characters, their trustworthiness as witnesses is seriously challenged. But if an argument rests on evidence and reasoning, it should be judged accordingly.

Example

No, I haven't read the bill. I don't need to. It's being supported by Congressman Blank, and there isn't a worse scoundrel in the country. If Blank's in favor of this bill, I'm against it.

Analysis

The bill should be considered on its own merits. If Blank is a scoundrel, that would be a factor in considering his trustworthiness, but Blank is not the issue here. It is the bill that should be attacked or defended.

Extension

Extension is the device of distorting an argument by exaggerating it. A college professor states that some high school graduates enter college inadequately prepared in English and mathematics. An opponent then charges that the statement belittles high school teaching. This charge greatly extends and exaggerates the original remark. If the professor makes the mistake of accepting the extension and of trying to show that high school instruction *is* bad, she falls into the trap and must defend a much weaker position. Her best response is to go back to her original statement and point out that, first, her statement was about *some* students, not *all;* second, it was about *two* high school subjects, not *all;* third, it did not place the blame for the students' deficiencies on the teachers. If the extension is not deliberate, the charge will be withdrawn. If it is deliberate and is not withdrawn, it will damage the accuser more than the accused. This fallacy is sometimes called the *straw man fallacy,* because the extension creates a "straw man" that is easier to demolish than a real one.

Red Herring

In hunting, a strongly scented object drawn across a trail will distract hounds and cause them to follow the new scent. In rhetoric, a *red herring* is a false issue used to lead attention away from the real one. Usually the false issue arouses an emotional response that creates a digression. The best defense is to show that the false issue is not pertinent to the discussion and then to refuse to follow it.

Example

As long as we're talking about whether women should be paid at the same rate as men for similar work and have equal chances of promotion, we should also be asking whether women want to be equal with men and still retain preferred treatment on social occasions, such as having men pay the expenses of a date, open doors for women, light their cigarettes, and so on. It seems to me that what women want is to have equal and preferred treatment at the same time.

Analysis

The question of how women should be treated socially is a red herring. The real issue is one of economic equality. How men treat women on social occasions has nothing to do with this issue. The best way to deal with this question is to show that it is irrelevant. Whatever courtesies a man extends to a woman on a date are social, not legal, practices. The best defense is to show that the question is irrelevant to the issue.

Unjustifiable Emotional Appeal

Ideally, emotional appeal supplements logical argument. When it is used as a substitute for argument, the test of its acceptability is the question, "Does it contribute to the best interests of the audience?" An emotional appeal to someone to give up an injurious habit is justifiable. One used in the sole interest of the persuader is not.

For example, if a politician is accused in the media of accepting bribes from companies seeking government contracts, it is in the public interest that these charges be investigated fully and fairly. An emotional appeal by the politician that he is being victimized by the media may prevent such an investigation and thus put the interests of the politician above those of the public.

Hasty Generalization

Any generalization drawn from an obviously small sample or one not likely to be typical is a hasty generalization.

Example

Women just aren't any good at logic. Although there are twelve women to ten men in our logic section, the four highest scores on the final exams were made by men and the four lowest by women.

Analysis

In the first place, what would make us believe that what is true of twelve women in one class will be true of all women? In the second, are the top four and bottom four scores typical of the scores in the class? Even as a comparison for this class alone, the sample is faulty. It would be better to take the median score of the women and compare it with the median score of the men. If the comparison favored the men, it would justify the conclusion that women in this class did less well than men in this class on an examination in logic. That is a less impressive conclusion than the one offered in the original argument.

Stereotype

A *stereotype* is a standardized mental image that pays too much attention to characteristics supposedly common to a group and not enough to individual differences. You begin with a number of individuals who have one thing in common (women who have married children); group them in a class (mothers-in-law); develop an attitude toward that class (mothers-in-law are interfering) based on a hasty generalization; then apply that attitude to individual mothers-in-law without waiting to see whether they actually are interfering.

To help avoid this fallacy, some students of language advise using index numbers after the class names to indicate that each member of a group has personal characteristics — that German$_1$ is not German$_2$, that college professor$_A$ is not college professor$_B$, that freshman$_{1984}$ is not freshman$_{1964}$. Whether you write these index numbers or merely think them, they are useful reminders not to assume that individuals with a common class name will be alike in all respects.

Either-or Fallacy

The either-or fallacy is the fallacy of ignoring possible alternatives. When you say you must either do this or do that, you are assuming that there are no other alternatives. This assumption may be right, in which case there is no fallacy. But if you have ignored alternatives, your reasoning is faulty. The way to refute an either-or fallacy is to show the alternatives that have been ignored.

Example

John's grades are not satisfactory. Either he lacks the ability to do college work or he is loafing.

Analysis

There are other possibilities. John may have an outside job that is using up much of his time and energy; he may be so concerned about some problem at home that he cannot keep his mind on his studies; he may be ill. These possibilities should be checked before any conclusion is drawn.

Oversimplified Cause

The two most common oversimplifications of a causal relation are mistaking a contributory cause for a sufficient one, and recognizing only one of several causes of an effect.

Example

The reason why so many people cannot find employment is that they do not have a college education.

Analysis

The lack of a college education may be a sufficient cause for unemployment in those jobs that require a college degree. But it does not explain why people without a degree cannot get other jobs. The suggested cause may contribute to unemployment, but it offers only a partial explanation.

The reason for the rush of American tourists to Europe is that a European vacation is cheaper than an American one, now that the dollar is so strong against European currency.

Even if it were proved that a vacation in Europe is definitely cheaper than one in America, there are other factors that help explain why Americans travel abroad: the urge to visit other cultures; interest in seeing relatives, finding homesteads, or tracing ancestry; awareness of European attractions as a result of increased tourism promotion by European countries.

Unexamined Analogies

As was pointed out earlier, an analogy should be carefully examined to be sure the things being compared are alike in ways essential to the conclusion being drawn. The fact that they are alike in *some* ways is not enough. If there is one difference that would cause rejection of the conclusion, the analogy is fallacious.

Example

We can orbit people in space and communicate with them while they are there. Surely we can learn to communicate with one another here in our own country and so live together harmoniously.

Analysis

There is an essential difference in the type of communication between astronauts and the space administration on the one hand, and the discussion of economic, political, and social issues on the other. Astronauts in flight limit themselves to matters of fact that can be quickly checked. Living together harmoniously requires sensitivity to other people's images and needs, and tolerance of opposing points of view. It is probable that astronauts have as much difficulty communicating at this level as other people do!

Discussion Problem

The following arguments contain various kinds of fallacies. Evaluate each and explain clearly what is wrong with it. Do not be content with naming the fallacy. The skill you are trying to develop is not identification, but analysis. It is more important to explain the errors than to name them.

1. Of course he's guilty. If he were innocent, he would have disproved these charges long ago.

2. Dad, I think you will be making a mistake if you take out a big insurance policy now. The mortality tables show you have a life expectancy of sixty-nine and you are only forty-four. That means you have a reasonable expectation of living twenty-five years more. In four years both Madge and I will be through college and self-supporting. If you postpone the insurance until then, we won't have to skimp to pay the premiums.

3. Careful research shows that the most successful people have the largest vocabularies. This proves that one way to be successful is to develop a large vocabulary.

4. Teen-agers are not mature enough to get married. They have the highest divorce rate of any age group. If they were mature, they would make a go of their marriages.

5. We can recognize that athletes who participate in major sports must be given special consideration within our grading system, <u>or</u> we can let the university sink into athletic oblivion.

6. Bill, you're a superb mechanic; you seem to have a natural talent for detecting what the trouble is and remedying it. Surely, then, you can analyze the rough drafts of your papers and turn them into polished essays.

7. Students here are rude. Last night the fellows in the room next to mine played their radio at full blast until two in the morning, and as I was on my way to class this morning a bicyclist almost ran me down.

8. The <u>only</u> reason the human race has survived is that human flesh is less palatable than that of other animals. A beast of prey will dash right past a defenseless human being to kill a gazelle or an impala.

9. A: When Thomas Wolfe was at his best, he was very good, but too often he was painfully verbose.

   B: You have no appreciation of the sort of spontaneity and lyricism Wolfe was capable of. I suppose you also think that Faulkner was no good and that Flannery O'Connor and Carson McCullers were decadent writers. What have you got against the South?

10. I went to a feminist meeting last night. The speakers were about as homely a group of women as I've ever seen. No wonder they hate men. A man would have to be pretty desperate to want to have anything to do with them.

11. It comes down to this: <u>either</u> NATO should require the European countries to finance and man the European part of the program <u>or</u> the United States should pull out.

12. The reason for the epidemic of violent student demonstrations in the sixties was that these students had been brought up under Dr. Spock's permissive theories of child rearing.

13. I don't know what the colleges are teaching nowadays. I have just had a letter of application from a young man who graduated from the state university last June. It was a wretched letter — badly written, with elementary errors in spelling, punctuation, and grammar. If that is the kind of product the university is turning out, it does not deserve the tax support it is getting.

14. The argument that football is a dangerous sport is disproved very simply by showing that the death rate — not total deaths, but deaths per thousand — among high school, college, and professional players combined is much less than the death rate of the total population.

15. According to the newspapers, venereal disease is rising at an alarming rate among children in their early teens. If this is true, it raises a serious question about the wisdom of teaching sex education in junior high schools.

16. All right-thinking people will support the board of education's decision to destroy novels in the school libraries which are offensive to the moral

standards of the community. If there were an epidemic of typhoid, the health authorities would be expected to do everything in their power to wipe it out. Pornography is worse than typhoid, since it corrupts the minds and morals of the young, not just their bodies. The school board is to be applauded for its prompt action in wiping out this moral disease.

17. I dined in a London restaurant last summer, and the filet of sole was almost inedible. What's more, a friend of mine traveled on a British liner, and she said the menus were boring — too much roast beef and Yorkshire pudding. The English seem to have no talent for cooking.

18. The fundamental problem in a democratic society is education. In a democracy the citizens are continually faced with alternatives. Whether they choose wisely or not will depend on how well educated they are. It is for this reason that each state must support public education generously. The better the support, the better the educational system; and the better the educational system the wiser the citizens and thus the state.

Exercise

The following essay, written by a high-school teacher, addresses an important issue in contemporary secondary-school education: how much time students do or do not spend in the classroom. Read the essay carefully; then, drawing on your own high-school experience or that of a high-school student you know, write an essay in which you defend or contradict the writer's point of view. Because your essay will itself be an example of persuasion, take the time to make your reasons as complete, clear, and convincing as you can. In planning your essay you may want to brainstorm or freewrite about the comparative advantages offered by the two types of activity — classroom instruction and extracurricular activities — that the writer discusses. You may also want to consider your own definition of "learning."

Excuses, Excuses

By and large, the report of the National Commission on Educational Excellence has been received favorably by those of us in the teaching profession, even though the blame for a shoddy educational system falls so often on our shoulders. For example, recently we have been hearing a lot about teacher competency and the need for merit pay, as if this would solve our problems.

   Somewhere in the commission's report and lost to sight in the hue and cry is a recommendation that received little publicity. This is the suggestion that schools make more effective use of the existing school day.

As a teacher I understand this to mean that I had better make sure my students spend every minute they have with me studying and learning the subject I teach. Now, we teachers have some control over time on task. We have no one to blame but ourselves if we fill up half a period Monday entertaining our classes with stories about what we did over the weekend. However, even those of us with the best intentions find our classes interrupted, depleted or canceled by forces beyond our control day after day after day. For under the guise of "education," a plethora of social activities has sprouted in our schools which draw students from our rooms. This situation is particularly destructive at the high-school level where I am now teaching.

Sometime in the summer, our school district, like others across the country, will publish a school calendar for the coming year. In my state, students must attend school 180 days. This means that each of the students assigned to me will have 180 periods of classroom instruction in the subject I teach. However, I know that this will never happen. If I consider only the classes I lose to "necessities" such as fire drills, bomb scares, three days of state-mandated testing, three days of registration and one entire day for school photos, my students have already missed 10 periods out of the 180. Now, depending upon how many pep rallies are needed, how many assemblies we can afford and the degree to which my students participate in a host of activities offered during school time, I will lose all of them again, and most of them again and again.

It might be helpful to compare the situation in our high schools with that in our colleges, where an intellectual atmosphere still prevails. Think back a moment. Do you remember your college classes being canceled for pep rallies, assemblies or class meetings? Not once, but often during a semester? When you want to attend some social function or help prepare for a dance were you excused with the blessings of the administration, or did you cut? Do you remember lectures interrupted routinely by a hidden sound system? Did office aides make it a practice to appear with urgent memos which your professors had to read and respond to while you waited impatiently? Was it a common occurrence for football players to rise en masse in the middle of a discussion to go to practice or a game?

And yet this is precisely the kind of situation we high-school teachers put up with day after day. Is it any wonder that many students don't value much of what goes on in the classroom?

At the latest count my syllabus is at the mercy of 45 different activities sanctioned by our school system. I lost students this past year for the following reasons: club trips to Atlantic City, student-council elections, bloodmobile, appointments with guidance counselors and Army representatives, an art show, community show, tennis, track, baseball, swimming, football, cheerleading, club meetings, class meetings, drama and band workshops, yearbook, PSAT, chorus and orchestra rehearsals, science day, cattle judging, attendance at the movie "Gandhi" and graduation rehearsal.

This list is by no means complete.

The rationale which allows this charade to continue is that if students miss classes they can make up the work and no harm is done. Of course, this idea carried to its logical conclusion means that we need less school for students, not more as the president's commission recommended. It is true that many students can read assignments outside of class, copy notes and keep up with their work. Others may opt for lower grades. But much of what takes place during class cannot be made up. How do you make up a class discussion where you have a chance to test and clarify your ideas on a subject? A group discussion where you must come to a consensus? An oral reading?

When I cannot organize a group discussion in advance because I am never sure who will show up, when "Romeo" is off to a band rehearsal and "Juliet" has a swim meet on the day the class reads "Romeo and Juliet" aloud, how can I generate seriousness of purpose and respect for intellectual effort?

Obviously many of these activities are worthwhile. But there is no pressing reason why any of them have to take place during class hours. Days could be added to the school calendar for state-mandated testing and registration. And why not let communities sponsor dances, sports, college and Army representatives and clubs after school hours? At the very least we would then discover which students wanted to participate in activities and which simply wished to escape from class.

The culmination of this disrespect for intellectual effort occurs in my school when the seniors are allowed to end classes and prepare for graduation three weeks before the rest of the student body. The message which comes across is that the senior curriculum is so negligible it can be cut short, and that when you get older, you have it easier than anybody else, not harder.

I am not a kill-joy. I know that kids need fun just as much as adults do and that clubs are educational in their own way. But as a member of a profession which is accorded only the most grudging respect and which is continually suspected of not doing its job, I say start by giving us a chance. Guarantee me those 180 periods I'm supposed to have. I'll know the public and the people who run the schools are serious about improving them the year my classes have not been shortened, delayed, canceled, interrupted or depleted for any reason short of illness, an emergency or the Second Coming. (Helen C. Vo-Dinh, *Newsweek*)

Part 3

Special Assignments

Chapter 11

The Essay Examination

The essay examination is one of the most practical of all writing assignments. By asking you to compose in one or more paragraphs an answer to a specific question, it calls on most of the skills you have developed as a writer. It also tests your ability to read carefully and to write purposefully within a rigidly limited time.

Instructors often complain that students write their worst on essay examinations. Of course, the pressure of an examination hardly encourages stylistic polish. But the chief weakness of examination answers is not that they are unpolished or ungrammatical or awkward, but that they are not composed at all. Many students do not first plan what they want to say and then develop their intention into an adequate answer. Too often they begin to write without a clear purpose and assume that as long as they are writing they are somehow answering the question. The result is often an answer that is irrelevant, inadequate, unclear, and even self-contradictory.

This chapter attempts to improve the quality of essay answers through applying to them the principles of purposeful writing discussed in earlier chapters of this book. You cannot, of course, learn the subject matter of your examinations in this chapter. But many weaknesses in examination papers are caused not by ignorance of the subject matter, but by carelessness, haste, or panic. The recommendations in the sections that follow should help you avoid such weaknesses.

Read the Question Carefully

Before beginning to answer any part of an examination, read the question carefully to see what it asks you to do. If you misinterpret the question, your whole answer may be off the point, even if it shows detailed knowledge of the subject and is otherwise well written. So before you begin to write, ask yourself, "What does this question require me to do?" Notice especially whether it asks you to explain, summarize, discuss, evaluate, or compare. These are often key words in an essay question. If you are asked to *evaluate* a paragraph or a poem, a *summary* or an *explanation* of the paragraph or a *paraphrase* of the poem will not satisfy the requirement. If you are asked to *compare* two characters in a play, a *description* of each character may not develop a comparison. Presumably, the wording of the question has been carefully thought out, and you will be expected to follow the directions it implies. *Never begin to write until you have a clear idea of what kind of answer is asked for.*

To see how a writer can drift into a bad answer by not reading the instructions carefully and seeing clearly what they require, study the following question and the two answers to it.

Using Le Corbusier's Savoye House and Frank Lloyd Wright's Kaufmann House as typical examples, contrast the architectural styles of these two men as expressions of their beliefs of what a house should be.

Answer 1:
Thesis stating basic
contrasting views

The major differences in the architectural styles of Le Corbusier and Wright came from their different views of what a house should be. For Le Corbusier a house was "a machine for living" which should be efficient and attractive; for Wright a house should integrate the needs of its owners with its surroundings. The Savoye House and the Kaufmann House are good illustrations of the results of this fundamental difference.

Topic sentence of enumerative paragraph showing characteristics of Savoye House

Four characteristics of the Savoye House are typical of a Le Corbusier residential design. First, the emphasis is on the house itself; its environment is just the location on which it is built, and a similar house could be constructed in a different place. Second, it is built on three levels, each of which meets a different need of the family. The ground level is an open space which can serve as a garage; the middle level, which is raised from the ground on piers and cantilevered out from the ground level, is the living area; the top level, the flat roof, is a recreational area with a space for sunbathing and a small garden. Third, the different levels are painted in different colors to emphasize their different uses. Fourth, the whole structure is built of steel and cement in a harmonious arrangement of horizontal and vertical lines relieved only by the curved cement windbreak around the roof garden. The major emphasis throughout is on utility. The whole effect is one of efficient regularity in an attractive design.

Summary statement

Topic sentence stating Wright's view

Frank Lloyd Wright referred to such buildings as "structures on stilts." He saw the machine as a potential enemy of modern man and, through his houses, he rebelled against it. In designing a house he started with the family needs and the environment, and he sought to unite these two elements in the building. This makes it more difficult to identify any one Wright house as "typical," since each house is designed for a different set of conditions. The Kaufmann House, named *Falling Water,* is a good example of this uniqueness. Because the Kaufmanns were fond of their natural waterfall, Wright designed the house to be built partly over it. Indeed, he made the house a vertical extension of the waterfall by projecting two massive cement cantilevers which, in effect, added two stories to the falls. The house proper was designed to blend into the environment. Its basic materials were wood and a native stone that harmonized with the surrounding colors. To increase this color-blending, Wright sometimes mixed local dirt with cement. The house itself is built into a hillside and is on several levels which merge into the surrounding landscape through a series of porches and terraces. This identification of the house with its environment, achieved through structure and materials, is what Wright calls his "organic architecture."

Summary statement

This is an excellent response to the examiner's directions. It first establishes in the introductory paragraph the basic contrast between the two architects' views from which the specific differences follow. Then it examines each house to show how it illustrates the architect's objectives.

Les Heures Claires, Le Corbusier Villa Savoye, Poissy-sur-Seine, France, 1931.
Photograph courtesy The Museum of Modern Art, New York.

Falling Water, Kaufmann House, Frank Lloyd Wright, 1936–37.
Photograph by Ezra Stoller © ESTO.

386 / *Special Assignments*

Every detail of the second paragraph adds to the theme that a Le Corbusier house is "a machine for living." Every detail in the third paragraph supports the relation between house and environment in a Wright design. No digressive details are allowed in the answer. The writer knows what the directions demand. That determines her purpose, which in turn controls what she has to say.

Answer 2

    The Savoye House is a rectangular building. Its main part, the living area, is raised above the ground, and the space under it can be used for a combination garage and open basement. On top of the living quarters is a flat roof on which there is a small garden almost surrounded by a curving wall. The rest of the roof is vacant, except for some vents and a pipelike metal chimney.

    Around the middle level is an almost continuous band of windows, so the living quarters are well lighted. There are no windows on the lower level, since that is completely open, except for the supports on which the rest of the house stands. The exterior of the house is made of painted concrete with a different color for each level. This helps to break the monotony of the rectangular structure.

    The Kaufmann House is one of Frank Lloyd Wright's most famous creations. It has an unusual setting because it was built over a waterfall. The base of the house consists of three great cement slabs. Two of these project over the waterfall like huge diving boards. Rising above these slabs is a large chimney that looks like the funnel of a ship. As a matter of fact the whole building makes you think of a battleship.

    Frank Lloyd Wright calls this kind of architecture "organic." This means that he uses chiefly organic materials like wood and stone, where other architects would use steel and cement. There is quite a lot of cement in the Kaufmann House, but mostly in the slabs. The house itself is made chiefly of stone. It is a one-level house, but the big slabs give it the appearance of several stories.

Even though it shows good observation of details, answer 2 is unsatisfactory, chiefly because it does not respond directly to the question. The purpose imposed by the directions was *to show the differences between the architectural styles of Le Corbusier and Wright* by contrasting two representative examples of their work. Answer 2 does not achieve this purpose. It simply describes each house separately, paying almost no attention to what the descriptions were supposed to illustrate. Except for the definition of "organic architecture" (which is incomplete), it fails to relate the observed details to a contrast of architectural styles. From this answer a reader learns what each house looks like but is not told the major differences between the styles of Le Corbusier and Wright.

The composition of these answers is a practical application of the A + B contrast discussed in Chapter 5. The structure of answer 1 is similar to that of W. H. Auden's essay contrasting European and American attitudes toward money (pp. 169–170): an introductory paragraph identifying the two elements of contrast (A and B), followed by information illustrating A and then information illustrating B. You may recall the warning given in the discussion following the Auden essay: "A simple description of two unlike houses, for instance, is not necessarily a contrast. It becomes one only when it points up dissimilarities implied in a thesis." The thesis of answer 1 is clearly expressed in its introductory paragraph. But answer 2 has no thesis, and the reason it has no thesis is that the writer has not made up his mind what basic contrast his answer should establish. By ignoring the final part of the directions and plunging too soon into descriptive details, he fails to answer the question satisfactorily. Because the first answer would probably be graded at least two full grades higher than the second, the writer of answer 2 would pay a stiff price for his failure to apply a principle established in Chapter 5.

Think Out Your Answer Before Writing

Think out your general answer before you begin to develop it. Because there is almost no chance for extensive planning or revising in an essay examination, your answer must be correctly drafted the first time. If you have your thesis or topic sentence clearly in mind, you probably also have explanatory and illustrative details in mind, and you can supply them as you write. But if you have not decided what you want to say before you begin, you may veer away from the question or write a series of unrelated sentences that do not add up to a unified answer. For many, if not most, questions, it is wise to make a scratch outline, organizing the information you want to work into your answer and formulating a thesis statement or, in the case of short answers, topic sentence about it. This advice repeats what was said in the chapter about drafting, but the advice becomes even more important in an examination because there is so little chance to revise.

The answer given below shows a carefully planned response to the following question:

> Just before he dies, Laertes says to Hamlet, "Mine and my father's death come not on thee, nor thine on me." In view of the facts of the play, how do you interpret this statement?

The student thinks over the question and the facts of the play and frames a general answer thus:

> Laertes' statement fits some of the facts but not all of them and is best understood as a request to let bygones be bygones.

This is the topic sentence or thesis of his answer. It requires him to do three things: (1) to show that Laertes' statement fits some of the facts, (2) to show that it does not fit other facts, and (3) to explain what he means by interpreting the statement as a request to let bygones be bygones. Notice how he satisfies his own intention and the requirements of the question.

Answer 1
Laertes' statement fits some of the facts but not all of them and is best understood as a request to let bygones be bygones. True, Hamlet is not responsible for Laertes' death, because Hamlet thought he was engaging in a friendly bout with blunted swords. When he picked up Laertes' sword in the mix-up he did not know it was poisoned. Since Laertes deliberately put the poison there, he was responsible for both Hamlet's death and his own. Hamlet killed Polonius by mistake, thinking that the person behind the curtain was the king. To that extent it was an accidental killing, but a killing nevertheless. I think Laertes' statement is not intended as a literal description of the facts but as a reconciliation speech. I interpret the statement as meaning: "We have both been the victims of the king's treachery. Forgive me for your death, as I forgive you for mine and my father's."

This answer is an excellent example of purposeful writing in a paragraph: topic sentence, followed by supporting details, followed by a restatement of the topic idea in a concluding statement. The structure of the paragraph is implied in the topic sentence. Because the student planned his whole answer before beginning to write, he controls the content of the paragraph. He knows that he must document his topic sentence from the facts of the play.

Contrast that answer with one by a student who has not thought out his general answer and plunges into a summary of the facts without considering how they relate to the question he is supposed to be answering.

Answer 2

Laertes returns from France and learns that his father has been killed by Hamlet. He is almost mad with grief and rage and in a stormy scene with the king he demands revenge. He and the king conspire to arrange a duel between Laertes and Hamlet in which Laertes will use a poisoned sword. The duel takes place after Ophelia's funeral, and Laertes cuts Hamlet with the poisoned sword. Then, in a scuffle, their swords are knocked from their hands and Hamlet picks up Laertes' sword and wounds him. Meanwhile the king has put poison in a goblet of wine he intended for Hamlet, but the queen drinks it instead. When Hamlet sees she is dying he kills the king; then both Hamlet and Laertes die.

This paragraph does not answer the question asked, nor does it interpret Laertes' final speech. It simply summarizes the action of the play from the time of Laertes' return from France until his death in the duel. Since the question assumes that the facts of the play are known to everyone in the class, the answer contributes nothing.

Failure to read the question carefully enough to see what it asks and failure to plan your answer are related faults. If you know the subject, careful reading of the question suggests an answer, and planning the answer gives you a check against the wording of the question. A student who misses the first step will probably miss the second also. The sensible thing is to postpone the writing until you know what you are trying to say, and why.

Write a Complete Answer

Unless the directions specify a short answer, do not write a one- or two-sentence answer in an essay examination. This advice requires you to distinguish between a short-answer test and an essay examination. A short-answer test tests knowledge of the facts. Accordingly, the questions can be answered satisfactorily in one or two minutes. Usually there are from twenty to thirty such questions in a fifty-minute quiz. An essay examination, by contrast, requires a *discussion* of the question to show your ability to select and organize information to support a thesis. Because such an answer needs one or more paragraphs, the examiner assumes it will take from fifteen to thirty minutes. Sometimes the directions specify how much time to allow for an answer. But if they do not, the number of questions asked indicates the average time for each. Therefore, you should know from the situation how much time to allow for each question.

A complete answer is one that deals with the subject as fully as possible within the time limits. An answer that is complete for a short-answer test will be inadequate for an essay examination. For example, the second sentence of the first answer on the styles of Le Corbusier and Wright

> For Le Corbusier a house was "a machine for living" which should be efficient and attractive; for Wright a house should integrate the needs of its owners with its surroundings.

would be complete for a short-answer test, but it would be inadequate for an essay examination because it lacks the detailed contrast of the two houses that the directions required.

The following answers further illustrate the difference between a complete and an incomplete answer in an essay examination. Here is the question:

Explain the real issue behind Alexander Hamilton's bargaining with Pennsylvania, Maryland, and Virginia on the site of the projected national capital.

Answer 1
The real issue was whether Alexander Hamilton's desire to have a strong central government would prevail. To enlist support for this idea Hamilton proposed that the federal government should assume responsibility for the existing state debts. This won over the heavily indebted states but was opposed by those states that were relatively free of debt. Hamilton knew that the vote would be a close one and that the votes of the delegates from Pennsylvania, Maryland, and Virginia (who all wanted the capital to be in their state) might be decisive. After considerable negotiation with the delegates from these states he arranged a compromise that Philadelphia should be the temporary capital for ten years while Washington was being

built on the Potomac on land ceded by Maryland and Virginia. In return, the delegates from these three states would vote for federal assumption of state debts. This compromise worked. The advocates of assuming state indebtedness won, and the arrangement for the location of the capital was ratified by Congress.

Answer 2   Alexander Hamilton bargained with Pennsylvania, Maryland, and Virginia, and finally worked out a plan making Philadelphia the temporary capital for ten years while Washington was being built between Maryland and Virginia.

Answer 2 is incomplete for two reasons: it leaves out Hamilton's motivation and the issue of the federal government's assumption of the state debts; and by doing so it does not explain the real issue behind the bargaining but merely states some of the results. The answer is not appropriate to the situation for which it was written, though it would have been adequate as a short answer to the question, "What compromise did Alexander Hamilton arrange to get Pennsylvania, Maryland, and Virginia to agree to the location of the national capital?"

Completeness in an examination essay is no different from completeness in paragraphs, discussed in Chapter 6. The topic sentence of a paragraph or the thesis of an essay is necessarily a general statement. To make that statement clear and convincing to a reader, you must develop it in specific detail. This is especially true when the examination question calls for a judgment. That judgment is only a topic sentence until it is developed into a complete answer by the evidence needed to support or explain it. If the writer of answer 1 on Laertes' statement had stopped with the general answer, "Laertes' statement distorts the facts. It is not an accurate report of what happened. He is rationalizing his own guilt and that of Hamlet by blaming Claudius," he would have written an incomplete answer. His explanatory details make his answer complete.

Do Not Pad Your Answer

Padding an answer is more likely to hurt than help. A writer who pads an answer with wordiness, repetition, or irrelevant detail draws attention to the fact that he or she has little to say and is trying to conceal this lack of knowledge. It is naive to think that a grader will accept padding as a

The bargaining that led to the establishment of the U.S. capital in Washington, D.C., was an example of how important political decisions are made in a democracy. Whatever state the capital was located in would get prestige and political influence by having the capital located in that state. So many states were eager to get ~~this prestige and political influence by having~~ the capital in that state that there was bound to be jealousy no matter which state won. The only logical solution was to have the capital in no state but in a separate area called the District of Columbia which was governed by the federal government, not by a state government.

But what was the bargaining — who bargained with whom about what, and why?

The bargaining that led to this decision was an attempt to find a solution that would avoid state jealousies by treating every state the same. If no state had the national capital, there would be no need to be jealous of any one state. Therefore all states would be likely to support this proposal, because every state would feel that the next best thing to having the capital within their boundaries would be to let no state have the capital. This was done by setting up the District of Columbia as an independent area under the control of Congress. In that way the capital was in no state but belonged to the whole country.

This ¶ merely restates what was said in ¶ 1 and does not give further information about the nature of the bargaining.

Not only does the second paragraph repeat the content of the first, but neither paragraph gives any detailed explanation of the bargaining between Hamilton and the delegates of Pennsylvania, Maryland, and Virginia. The independence of the District of Columbia was not an issue in the bargaining, but assumption of state debts was.

contribution to the answer. There is a relationship between length and content, because presenting content takes space. For example, the good answers in the preceding pages could not have been reduced in length without losing significant content. But no experienced grader equates mere length with content. Graders are not easily persuaded that an answer is good just because it is long. They are more likely to be annoyed at having to spend time to separate a few kernels of wheat from a bushel of chaff. It is your responsibility to select and present what is relevant to the question.

The essay on page 392 is a padded response to the question on the bargaining by which the site of the national capital was decided. The grader's comments identify the two major weaknesses of the answer — failure to explain the reason for Hamilton's negotiations with the delegates from Pennsylvania, Maryland, and Virginia; and the useless repetition of the content of the first paragraph in the second. It is obvious that the writer was not prepared to answer the question and that she said in the first paragraph all she could say. But she seemed to feel that saying it over again in the second paragraph would somehow make her answer acceptable. Notice the irritation the grader expresses in both the crossed-out paragraph and the marginal comments. However harsh this criticism may seem, it is the kind of response that conspicuous padding may provoke. Even if a grader does not so openly express irritation, it will be a factor in deciding the grade given to the answer.

Discussion Problem

For each of the following paired answers choose what you think is the better one and discuss your reasons in class. The first pair is for a course in library science, the second for a course in psychology, and the third for a course in humanities. Even though you may not be familiar with the subjects being discussed, you should be able to decide which answer better satisfies the requirements of the directions.

Question 1

1. *Discuss the contribution of William Morris to book design, using as an example his edition of the works of Chaucer.*

Answer 1

William Morris's *Chaucer* was his masterpiece. It shows his interest in the Middle Ages. The type is based on medieval manuscript writing, and the decoration around the edges of the pages is like that used in medieval books. The large initial letters are typical of medieval design. Those letters were printed from woodcuts, which was the medieval way of printing. The illustrations were by Burne-Jones, one of the best artists in England at the time. Morris was able to get the most competent people to help him because he was so famous as a poet and a designer of furniture (the Morris chair) and wallpaper and other decorative items for the home. He designed the furnishings for his own home, which was widely admired among the sort of people he associated with. In this way he started the arts and crafts movement.

Answer 2   Morris's contribution to book design was to approach the problem as an artist or fine craftsman, rather than as a mere printer who reproduced texts. He wanted to raise the standards of printing, which had fallen to a low point, by showing that truly beautiful books could be produced. His *Chaucer* was designed as a unified work of art or high craft. Since Chaucer lived in the late Middle Ages, Morris decided to design a new type based on medieval English script and to imitate the format of a medieval manuscript. This involved elaborate letters and large initials at the beginnings of verses, as well as wide borders of intertwined vines with leaves, fruit, and flowers in strong colors. The effect was so unusual that the book caused great excitement and inspired other printers to design beautiful rather than purely utilitarian books.

Question 2

2. Explain the chief differences between neurosis and psychosis.

Answer 1   The chief differences between neurosis and psychosis are the extent to which a person is alienated from reality and his chances of making a workable adjustment to normal living. The boundary between the two cannot be precisely drawn; therefore the differences are best illustrated at their extremes.

A person suffering from neurosis may feel serious anxieties but still be able to handle the ordinary activities of daily living. For example, a woman may have a phobia about being left alone with a red-headed man because a male with red hair once assaulted her. But as long as she avoids that particular situation, she is able to conduct her domestic and business duties in a normal manner. Through psychiatric counseling she may learn to understand the cause of her phobia and either get rid of it or control it. Fears of heights and crowds are other examples of neuroses. They are not central to the way one organizes his life and can be alleviated either by counseling or by avoidance of situations in which the neurotic response is likely to occur.

But a psychotic person is so divorced from reality that in severe cases, like paranoid schizophrenia, he lives in a private world which has little relation to the real one. A man who thinks he is Moses and feels a divinely granted right to punish those who break any of the Ten Commandments has reorganized experience around a delusion that makes life bearable for him. His delusion is necessary to his continued existence. In a sense he has found a therapy that works for him. He will resist psychiatric help because he thinks he no longer has any problem: it is the sinners who have problems. Such a person may be helped to some degree by specialized, institutional care, but the chances of a complete recovery are slim.

Between these extremes are conditions which may be classified as either neurosis or psychosis. In such cases psychiatrists may disagree in their diagnoses.

Answer 2

Because there is some neurosis in all of us, we all utilize defense mechanisms against our frustrations. For that matter, a psychotic person may also use such defenses, but he is less likely to be aware of what he is doing. We may repress our frustrations — simply refuse to think about them. Or we may defend by consciously developing characteristics the opposite of those we disapprove of. For example, a person who is troubled by his tendency toward greediness may force himself to be generous in giving away possessions he wants to keep. We can also escape frustration and low self-esteem by projection of our faults, blaming them on other people. Or we can use rationalization by devising excuses to justify our behavior. Finally, we may save our pride by fantasizing. That is, a young man may imagine that the girl who has declined to date him is cheering wildly in a basketball gymnasium while he sets a new school scoring record and that she will be waiting for him with bated breath at the locker-room door.

Neurotic people may need the help that defense mechanisms can give them, but excessive use of such devices can make a problem worse. And if a neurotic condition becomes so serious that the person is out of touch with the real world and locked into his private world, he is psychotic. As I think back over my answer it seems to me that a

Madonna with Child, Filippo Lippi, 1406–1469.
Scala/Art Resource, Inc.

psychotic person would be more likely to use some of these mechanisms than he would others.

Question 3

3. *To illustrate the differences between early and late Renaissance painting, contrast Fra Filippo Lippi's* Madonna with Child *with Raphael's* Sistine Madonna.

Answer 1

Fra Filippo's picture is a good example of early Renaissance naturalism. The Madonna — his own wife — is wearing a stylish gown, which is painted in faithful detail. Her hair is dressed in the mode of the time. She is seated — as though in her own home — on an elaborately carved chair, with a framed painting of a landscape serving as the background. Her pose and expression are calm, perhaps devout, but neither exalted nor humble. She is an ordinary worldly mother with a chubby baby, who is being lifted to her rather ungracefully by a saucy angel. The entire scene is intimate, personal, and joyous, but hardly reverent. Filippo, pleased with the new-found technical mastery of his age, is content to paint what he sees.

Raphael was able to get above his technique and make it expressive of lofty emotion. The figures in the *Sistine Madonna* are monumental and stand out against a subdued background. The Madonna, her feet resting weightlessly on a cloud, wears an expression of sublime dignity. She holds with graceful ease the Child, whose sober eyes reveal the portent of His future. The figures wear classic robes, whose flowing lines give a wonderful, circling movement to the painting. A cloud of tiny cherubs' heads, peeping through the effulgence surrounding the Virgin, completes the heavenly setting. Where Filippo's work is mere copying, Raphael's is imaginative and spiritual. This loftiness of conception combined with grace of design and beauty of execution is the flower of the High Renaissance.

Answer 2

Filippo's picture is simply designed, and the figures are naturalistic. The Madonna is sweet, gracious, and human, dressed in the mode of the times. The Bambino is a natural, playful child. He is being lifted up by two older boys — undoubtedly Fra Filippo's family posed for the picture. The background is a stylized landscape of rocks and streams, bounded by a frame. The Madonna is seated in a chair with an elaborately carved arm which stands out in the foreground.

Raphael designed the Sistine Madonna in a pyramid with the Madonna herself at the apex. She carries the curly-haired Child, and although she is standing still, her garments swirl as in a strong wind. One's eye is first caught by the figure of Pope Sixtus at the lower left and, through the folds of his garment and his uplifted eyes, drawn toward the central figure of the Virgin. Her garments, billowing to the right, draw the eye downward again to the figure of St. Barbara, kneeling on a cloud. Her eyes are cast down, and the glance follows hers to discover two jaunty cherubs leaning on the lower frame. They look upward, thus deflecting the eyes of the beholder up again, completing the movement of the design.

Exercise

Take from your file any essay examination you have previously written, preferably an unsatisfactory one. Review the wording of the question to determine what assumptions the examiner made about *what* you knew and what instructions he or she gave you about *how* to present what you knew. Reread your answer. Does it suggest that you (1) read the question carefully, (2) thought out your answer before you wrote, (3) composed a complete answer, and (4) avoided padding your answer? One way to answer these questions is to outline your essay to determine whether it says what you think it says. Such an outline may help you understand your instructor's comments. Now that you have reassessed your answer, revise your essay so that it provides a more effective answer to the question.

Sistine Madonna, Raphael, 1483–1520.
Scala/Art Resource, Inc.

Chapter 12

The Critical Essay

Planning

A critical essay is one that attempts to analyze, interpret, and evaluate its subject. The word *critical* in this context does not mean "fault-finding." Its Greek root means "to separate, discern, or choose," and a critical essay is chiefly an exercise in analysis, interpretation, or evaluation. It may deal with any subject worthy of serious study — a book, a film or television program, a painting, a building, a political or social movement. But because a favorite subject for critical essays in a writing class is often literature, this chapter will focus on that subject.

The procedure for planning a critical essay is similar to that for other papers. You discover your purpose through planning and then select, organize, and develop your material to show your reader what the work means to you, or how you respond to it.

The chief difference is that, more than in any other kind of writing, the critical essay depends on reading. The first stage in planning a critical essay is a careful, sometimes a repeated, reading of the novel, short story, play, or poem you are writing about. Because everything depends on a sound knowledge of the work, your planning will be more efficient if you know what to look for in your reading. Accordingly, you should begin by examining the basic elements that you will be concerned with in reading literature. These are *situation, character, plot, dramatic conflict, theme, structure, symbol, irony, point of view,* and *voice.* In any particular work some of these elements will be more important than others. Which one or what combination of them you want to emphasize will be part of your decision about your real subject.

One of the best ways to understand these elements is to see how they work in a literary source. Accordingly, read Ralph Ellison's "King of the Bingo Game" and the commentary that follows.

King of the Bingo Game
by Ralph Ellison

The woman in front of him was eating roasted peanuts that smelled so good that he could barely contain his hunger. He could not even sleep and wished they'd hurry and begin the bingo game. There, on his right, two fellows were drinking wine out of a bottle wrapped in a paper bag, and he could hear soft gurgling in the dark. His stomach gave a low gnawing growl. "If this was down South," he thought, "all I'd have to do is lean over and say, 'Lady, gimme a few of those peanuts, please ma'm,' and she'd pass me the bag and never think nothing of it." Or he could ask the fellows for a drink in the same way. Folks down South stuck together that way; they didn't even have to know you. But up here it was different. Ask somebody for something, and they'd think you were crazy. Well, I ain't crazy. I'm just broke, 'cause I got no birth certificate to get a job, and Laura 'bout to die 'cause we got no money for a doctor. But I ain't crazy. And yet a pinpoint of doubt was focused in his mind as he glanced toward the screen and saw the hero stealthily entering a dark room and sending the beam of a flashlight along a wall of bookcases. This is where he finds the trapdoor, he remembered. The man would pass abruptly through the wall and find the girl tied to a bed, her legs and arms spread wide, and her clothing torn to rags. He laughed softly to himself. He had seen the picture three times, and this was one of the best scenes.

On his right the fellow whispered wide-eyed to his companion, "Man, look a-yonder!"

"Damn!"

"Wouldn't I like to have her tied up like that . . ."

"Hey! That fool's letting her loose!"

"Aw, man, he loves her."

"Love or no love!"

The man moved impatiently beside him, and he tried to involve himself in the scene. But Laura was on his mind. Tiring quickly of watching the picture he looked back to where the white beam filtered from the projection room above the balcony. It started small and grew large, specks of dust dancing in its whiteness as it reached the screen. It was strange how the beam always landed right on the screen and didn't mess up and fall somewhere else. But they had it all fixed. Everything was fixed. Now suppose when they showed that girl with her dress torn the girl started taking off the rest of her clothes, and when the guy came in he didn't untie her but kept her there and went to taking off his own clothes? *That* would be something to see. If a picture got out of hand like that those guys up there would go nuts. Yeah, and there'd be so many folks in here you couldn't find a seat for nine months! A strange sensation played over his skin. He shuddered. Yesterday he'd seen a bedbug on a woman's neck as they walked out into the bright street. But exploring his thigh through a hole in his pocket he found only goose pimples and old scars.

The bottle gurgled again. He closed his eyes. Now a dreamy music was accompanying the film and train whistles were sounding in the distance, and he was a boy again walking along a railroad trestle down South, and seeing the train coming, and running back as fast as he could go, and hearing the whistle blowing, and getting off the trestle to solid ground just in time, with the earth trembling beneath his feet, and feeling relieved as he ran down the cinder-strewn embankment onto the highway, and looking back and seeing with terror that the train had left the track and was following him right down the middle of the street, and all the white people laughing as he ran screaming . . .

"Wake up there, buddy! What the hell do you mean hollering like that! Can't you see we trying to enjoy this here picture?"

He stared at the man with gratitude.

"I'm sorry, old man," he said. "I musta been dreaming."

"Well, here, have a drink. And don't be making no noise like that, damn!"

His hands trembled as he tilted his head. It was not wine, but whiskey. Cold rye whiskey. He took a deep swoller, decided it was better not to take another, and handed the bottle back to its owner.

"Thanks, old man," he said.

Now he felt the cold whiskey breaking a warm path straight through the middle of him, growing hotter and sharper as it moved. He had not eaten all day, and it made him light-headed. The smell of the peanuts stabbed him like a knife, and he got up and found a seat in the middle aisle. But no sooner did he sit than he saw a row of intense-faced young girls, and got up again, thinking, "You chicks musta been Lindy-hopping somewhere." He found a seat several rows ahead as the lights came on, and he saw the screen disappear behind a heavy red and gold curtain; then the curtain rising, and the man with the microphone and a uniformed attendant coming on the stage.

He felt for his bingo cards, smiling. The guy at the door wouldn't like it if he knew about his having *five* cards. Well, not everyone played the bingo game; and even with five cards he didn't have much of a chance. For Laura, though, he had to have faith. He studied the cards, each with its different numerals, punching the free center hole in each and spreading them neatly across his lap; and when the lights faded he sat slouched in his seat so that he could look from his cards to the bingo wheel with but a quick shifting of his eyes.

Ahead, at the end of the darkness, the man with the microphone was pressing a button attached to a long cord and spinning the bingo wheel and calling out the number each time the wheel came to rest. And each time the voice rang out his finger raced over the cards for the number. With five cards he had to move fast. He became nervous; there were too many cards, and the man went too fast with his grating voice. Perhaps he should just select one and throw the others away. But he was afraid. He became warm. Wonder how much Laura's doctor would cost? Damn that, watch the cards! And with despair he heard the man call three in a row which he missed on all five cards. This way he'd never win . . .

When he saw the row of holes punched across the third card, he sat paralyzed and heard the man call three more numbers before he stumbled forward, screaming,

"Bingo! Bingo!"

"Let that fool up there," someone called.

"Get up there, man!"

He stumbled down the aisle and up the steps to the stage into a light so sharp and bright that for a moment it blinded him, and he felt that he had moved into the spell of some strange, mysterious power. Yet it was as familiar as the sun, and he knew it was the perfectly familiar bingo.

The man with the microphone was saying something to the audience as he held out his card. A cold light flashed from the man's finger as the card left his hand. His knees trembled. The man stepped closer, checking the card against the numbers chalked on the board. Suppose he had made a mistake? The pomade on the man's hair made him feel faint, and he backed away. But the man was checking the card over the microphone now, and he had to stay. He stood tense, listening.

"Under the O, forty-four," the man chanted. "Under the I, seven. Under the G, three. Under the B, ninety-six. Under the N, thirteen!"

His breath came easier as the man smiled at the audience.

"Yessir, ladies and gentlemen, he's one of the chosen people!"

The audience rippled with laughter and applause.

"Step right up to the front of the stage."

He moved slowly forward, wishing that the light was not so bright.

"To win tonight's jackpot of $36.90 the wheel must stop between the double zero, understand?"

He nodded, knowing the ritual from the many days and nights he had watched the winners march across the stage to press the button that controlled the spinning wheel and receive the prizes. And now he followed the instructions as though he'd crossed the slippery stage a million prize-winning times.

The man was making some kind of a joke, and he nodded vacantly. So tense had he become that he felt a sudden desire to cry and shook it away. He felt vaguely that his whole life was determined by the bingo wheel; not only that which would happen now that he was at last before it, but all that had gone before, since his birth, and his mother's birth and the birth of his father. It had always been there, even though he had not been aware of it, handing out the unlucky cards and numbers of his days. The feeling persisted, and he started quickly away. I better get down from here before I make a fool of myself he thought.

"Here boy," the man called. "You haven't started yet."

Someone laughed as he went hesitantly back.

"Are you all reet?"

He grinned at the man's jive talk, but no words would come, and he knew it was not a convincing grin. For suddenly he knew that he stood on the slippery brink of some terrible embarrassment.

"Where are you from, boy?" the man asked.

"Down South."

"He's from down South, ladies and gentlemen," the man said. "Where from? Speak right into the mike."

"Rocky Mont," he said. "Rock' Mont, North Car'lina."

"So you decided to come down off that mountain to the U.S.," the man laughed. He felt that the man was making a fool of him, but then something cold was placed in his hand, and the lights were no longer behind him.

Standing before the wheel he felt alone, but that was somehow right, and he remembered his plan. He would give the wheel a short quick twirl. Just a touch of the button. He had watched it many times, and always it came close to double zero when it was short and quick. He steeled himself; the fear had left, and he felt a profound sense of promise, as though he were about to be repaid for all the things he'd suffered all his life. Trembling, he pressed the button. There was a whirl of lights, and in a second he realized with finality that though he wanted to, he could not stop. It was as though he held a high-powered line in his naked hand. His nerves tightened. As the wheel increased its speed it seemed to draw him more and more into its power, as though it held his fate; and with it came a deep need to submit, to whirl, to lose himself in its swirl of color. He could not stop it now, he knew. So let it be.

The button rested snugly in his palm where the man had placed it. And now he became aware of the man beside him, advising him through the microphone, while behind the shadowy audience hummed with noisy voices. He shifted his feet. There was still that feeling of helplessness within him, making part of him desire to turn back, even now that the jackpot was right in his hand. He squeezed the button until his fist ached. Then, like the sudden shriek of a subway whistle, a doubt tore through his head. Suppose he did not spin the wheel long enough? What could he do, and how could he tell? And then he knew, even as he wondered, that as long as he pressed the button, he could control the jackpot. He and only he could determine whether or not it was to be his. Not even the man with the microphone could do anything about it now. He felt drunk. Then, as though he had come down from a high hill into a valley of people, he heard the audience yelling.

"Come down from there, you jerk!"

"Let somebody else have a chance . . ."

"Old Jack thinks he done found the end of the rainbow . . ."

The last voice was not unfriendly, and he turned and smiled dreamily into the yelling mouths. Then he turned his back squarely on them.

"Don't take too long, boy," a voice said.

He nodded. They were yelling behind him. Those folks did not understand what had happened to him. They had been playing the bingo game day in and night out for years, trying to win rent money or hamburger change. But not one of those wise guys had discovered this wonderful thing. He watched the wheel whirling past the numbers and experienced a burst of exaltation: This is God! This is the really truly God! He said it aloud, "This is God!"

He said it with such absolute conviction that he feared he would fall fainting into the footlights. But the crowd yelled so loud that they could not hear. Those fools, he thought. I'm here trying to tell them the most wonderful secret in the world, and they're yelling like they gone crazy. A hand fell upon his shoulder.

"You'll have to make a choice now, boy. You've taken too long."

He brushed the hand violently away.

"Leave me alone, man. I know what I'm doing!"

The man looked surprised and held on to the microphone for support. And because he did not wish to hurt the man's feelings he smiled, realizing with a sudden pang that there was no way of explaining to the man just why he had to stand there pressing the button forever.

"Come here," he called tiredly.

The man approached, rolling the heavy microphone across the stage.

"Anybody can play this bingo game, right?" he said.

"Sure, but . . ."

He smiled, feeling inclined to be patient with this slick looking white man with his blue sport shirt and his sharp gabardine suit.

"That's what I thought," he said. "Anybody can win the jackpot as long as they get the lucky number, right?"

"That's the rule, but after all . . ."

"That's what I thought," he said. "And the big prize goes to the man who knows how to win it?"

The man nodded speechlessly.

"Well then, go on over there and watch me win like I want to. I ain't going to hurt nobody," he said, "and I'll show you how to win. I mean to show the whole world how it's got to be done."

And because he understood, he smiled again to let the man know that he held nothing against him for being white and impatient. Then he refused to see the man any longer and stood pressing the button, the voices of the crowd reaching him like sounds in distant streets. Let them yell. All the Negroes down there were just ashamed because he was black like them. He smiled inwardly, knowing how it was. Most of the time he was ashamed of what Negroes did himself. Well, let them be ashamed for something this time. Like him. He was like a long thin black wire that was being stretched and wound upon the bingo wheel; wound until he wanted to scream; wound, but this time himself controlling the winding and the sadness and the shame, and because he did, Laura would be all right. Suddenly the lights flickered. He staggered backwards. Had something gone wrong? All this noise. Didn't they know that although he controlled the wheel, it also controlled him, and unless he pressed the button forever and forever and ever it would stop, leaving him high and dry, dry and high on this hard high slippery hill and Laura dead? There was only one chance; he had to do whatever the wheel demanded. And gripping the button in despair, he discovered with surprise that it imparted a nervous energy. His spine tingled. He felt a certain power.

Now he faced the raging crowd with defiance, its screams penetrating his eardrums like trumpets shrieking from a jukebox. The vague faces glowing in the bingo lights gave him a sense of himself that he had never known before. He was running the show, by God! They had to react to him, for he was their luck. This is *me,* he thought. Let the bastards yell. Then someone was laughing inside him, and he realized that somehow he had forgotten his own name. It was a sad, lost feeling to lose your name, and a crazy thing to do. That name had been given him by the white man who had owned his grandfather a long lost time ago down South. But maybe those wise guys knew his name.

"Who am I?" he screamed.

"Hurry up and bingo, you jerk!"

They didn't know either, he thought sadly. They didn't even know their own names, they were all poor nameless bastards. Well, he didn't need that old name; he was reborn. For as long as he pressed the button he was The-man-who-pressed-the-button-who-held-the-prize-who-was-the-King-of-Bingo. That was the way it was, and he'd have to press the button even if nobody understood, even though Laura did not understand.

"Live!" he shouted.

The audience quieted like the dying of a huge fan.

"Live, Laura, baby. I got holt of it now, sugar. Live!"

He screamed it, tears streaming down his face. "I got nobody but YOU!"

The screams tore from his very guts. He felt as though the rush of blood to his head would burst out in baseball seams of small red droplets, like a head beaten by police clubs. Bending over he saw a trickle of blood splashing the toe of his shoe. With his free hand he searched his head. It was his nose. God, suppose something has gone wrong? He felt that the whole audience had somehow entered him and was stamping its feet in his stomach, and he was unable to throw them out. They wanted the prize, that was it. They wanted the secret for themselves. But they'd never get it; he would keep the bingo wheel whirling forever, and Laura would be safe in the wheel. But would she? It had to be, because if she were not safe the wheel would cease to turn; it could not go on. He had to get away, *vomit* all, and his mind formed an image of himself running with Laura in his arms down the tracks of the subway just ahead of an A train, running desperately *vomit* with people screaming for him to come out but knowing no way of leaving the tracks because to stop would bring the train crushing down upon him and to attempt to leave across the other tracks would mean to run into a hot third rail as high as his waist which threw blue sparks that blinded his eyes until he could hardly see.

He heard singing and the audience was clapping its hands.

Shoot the liquor to him, Jim, boy!
Clap-clap-clap
Well a-calla the cop
He's blowing his top!
Shoot the liquor to him, Jim boy!

Bitter anger grew within him at the singing. They think I'm crazy. Well let 'em laugh. I'll do what I got to do.

He was standing in an attitude of intense listening when he saw that they were watching something on the stage behind him. He felt weak. But when he turned he saw no one. If only his thumb did not ache so. Now they were applauding. And for a moment he thought that the wheel had stopped. But that was impossible, his thumb still pressed the button. Then he saw them. Two men in uniform beckoned from the end of the stage. They were coming toward him, walking in step, slowly, like a tap-dance team returning for a third encore. But their shoulders shot forward, and he backed away, looking wildly about. There was nothing to fight them with. He had only the long black cord which led to a plug somewhere back stage, and he couldn't use that because it operated the bingo wheel. He backed slowly, fixing the men with his eyes as his lips stretched over his teeth in a tight, fixed grin; moved toward the end of the stage and realizing that he couldn't go much further, for suddenly the cord became taut and he couldn't afford to break the cord. But he had to do something. The audience was howling. Suddenly he stopped dead, seeing the men halt, their legs lifted as in an interrupted step of a slow-motion dance. There was nothing to do but run in the other direction and he dashed forward, slipping and sliding. The men fell back, surprised. He struck out violently going past.

"Grab him!"

He ran, but all too quickly the cord tightened, resistingly, and he turned and ran back again. This time he slipped them, and discovered by running in a circle before the wheel he could keep the cord from tightening. But this way he had to flail his arms to keep the men away. Why couldn't they leave a man alone? He ran, circling.

"Ring down the curtain," someone yelled. But they couldn't do that. If they did the wheel flashing from the projection room would be cut off. But they had him before he could tell them so, trying to pry open his fist, and he was wrestling and trying to bring his knees into the fight and holding on to the button, for it was his life. And now he was down, seeing a foot coming down, crushing his wrist cruelly, down, as he saw the wheel whirling serenely above.

"I can't give it up," he screamed. Then quietly, in a confidential tone, "Boys, I really can't give it up."

It landed hard against his head. And in the blank moment they had it away from him, completely now. He fought them trying to pull him up from the stage as he watched the wheel spin slowly to a stop. Without surprise he saw it rest at double zero.

"You see," he pointed bitterly.

"Sure, boy, sure, it's O.K.," one of the men said smiling.

And seeing the man bow his head to someone he could not see, he felt very, very happy; he would receive what all the winners received.

But as he warmed in the justice of the man's tight smile he did not see the man's slow wink, nor see the bow-legged man behind him step clear of the swiftly descending curtain and set himself for a blow. He only felt the dull pain exploding in his skull, and he knew even as it slipped out of him that his luck had run out on the stage.

Situation

The situation is the combination of circumstances, including the setting, out of which the action emerges. Much of what happens in "King of the Bingo Game" occurs because the main character is "up North," where he is a stranger, without a job and with little hope of getting one, and because his wife is " 'bout to die 'cause we got no money for a doctor." To obtain the money to save his wife's life has become his main compulsion. The only solution he can think of is to win the jackpot at the bingo game played in a local movie theater. To increase his chances of winning he has somehow acquired five bingo cards and has decided just how hard to spin the wheel to make it stop on the double zero.

This desperate need for money provides the immediate motive for his actions, but there is another element in the situation that is not made explicit. As a disadvantaged black, he has apparently been pushed around by whites and by events he could not control. He therefore has a psychological need to assert his dominance in the control of his own fate. Once he wins the bingo game and goes to the stage, this second motive becomes irresistible. What he is fighting for at the end of the story is not money but power. Much of what happens results directly from this dual-level situation.

In thinking about situation in whatever work you are dealing with, you may find the following questions helpful:

1. What is the situation here? Be sure you have a clear understanding of it before you move on to more complex problems in analysis and interpretation.

2. How is the situation revealed? Through description or explanation by the narrator? By dialogue? By historical information that the reader already possesses? In "King of the Bingo Game" it is chiefly revealed by an unnamed narrator who describes what the main character thinks of his plight.

3. How important is the situation in the total work? In Ellison's story it is so important that it supplies the motivation for the man's actions throughout the story. In other works, it may be less important.

Character

The word *character* is used in two senses in literature: first, to identify the people who appear in the story, play, or poem; second, to describe the personality of any of these people, especially those traits that affect the development of the work. The second meaning is the important one in this chapter.

In "King of the Bingo Game" the main character's reaction to his frustrating situation is all-important. All his life he has reacted to other people; now they must react to him. Though he has temporarily forgotten his name and is confronted with the age-old question of identity ("'Who am I?' he screamed"), he thinks that if he can just hold onto the power that accompanies the pressing of the button he can show his audience "how to win": "I mean to show the whole world how it's got to be done." He must instruct the "poor nameless bastards" who think he

*"All right, children, who wants to open our discussion of
the Papa Bear's sense of rage? Tommy?"*

Drawing by Ziegler; © 1982. The New Yorker Magazine, Inc.

is crazy and laugh and applaud. He is, temporarily at least, a man with
a mission: "I'll do what I got to do."

The minor characters may be essential to the main action of a story, or
they may be introduced for some special purpose — to provide comic
relief, to serve as narrator, to act as a mouthpiece for the author, or to
provide a foil through which some quality of the major character is
emphasized. The theater manager in "King of the Bingo Game" serves
as a foil: he asks the right questions, makes the right comments, and takes
the right action to portray the main character in this story.

In thinking about the characters in a literary work, consider the following questions:

1. Do you have a clear impression of the major characters? If so, how
   did you get it? Through what they do or say? Through what others
   say about them? Through the author's or narrator's comments?

2. Do the characters change as the story proceeds — that is, do their
   experiences make them stronger or weaker, nobler or more corrupt,

than they were at the beginning? If so, do you feel that the change is justified by what happens in the story?

3. Does the dialogue ring true? Do characters speak in a way consistent with their regional and social backgrounds?

Plot

The term *plot* is generally familiar. The plot is the sequence of actions that make up the core of the story. It is what the characters do or what is done to them as the story proceeds. Thus the plot of "King of the Bingo Game" is what happens to the main character in his attempt to win the money he needs.

Dramatic Conflict

Dramatic conflict occurs when opposing forces meet. The conflict may be physical, as in a fight; or it may be psychological, as in Huck Finn's difficulty in reconciling his friendship with Jim and his sense of guilt in aiding a runaway slave. The conflict is likely to be resolved by decisions the characters make and by the actions they take or refuse to take.

In "King of the Bingo Game" the main character experiences several kinds of conflict. The most interesting is that between him and the wheel. He says of it, "This is God!" and he feels he must control this life-sustaining force if he is to save Laura. He shouts, "Live, Laura, baby. I got holt of it now, sugar. Live!" He feels that the wheel controls him, too, and that if he stops pressing the button, the wheel will stop and Laura will die. When he is subdued, the wheel does stop, ironically at double zero. His only victory is in having tried.

There are other conflicts, between him and the manager who tries to interfere with his plan, and with the audience who call him a "jerk" and taunt him until he feels as if "the whole audience had somehow entered him and was stamping its feet in his stomach."

Theme

In addition to showing characters in action or in conflict, a work may express a general idea or theme that gives unity to the action. Often the theme is not stated explicitly. For example, in much of *The Adventures of Huckleberry Finn* there is a contrast between Huck's sense of values and the values that the adults in the story proclaim or reveal. Mark Twain's criticism of society, as it is represented in Miss Watson, the Grangerfords, the King, and others, so permeates the story that it can be said to be the theme of the book. If what these adults stand for is "sivlization," Huck wants none of it. As he says at the end, "But I reckon I got to light out for the territory ahead of the rest, because Aunt Sally she's going to adopt me and sivilize me, and I can't stand it. I been there before." In "King of the Bingo Game" the author does not actually say that the man's attempt to control the symbolic wheel and thus assert his own power and save Laura is futile, but you can infer that theme from the facts of the story.

Sometimes there is a statement within a work that does state the theme explicitly. For example, Lieutenant Frederick Henry, the narrator of Hemingway's *A Farewell to Arms,* reflects on his days with Catherine Barkley and says:

> If people bring so much courage to this world the world has to kill them to break them, so of course it kills them. The world breaks every one and afterward many are strong at the broken places. But those that will not break it kills. It kills the very good and the very gentle and the very brave impartially. If you are none of these you can be sure it will kill you too but there will be no special hurry. (Ernest Hemingway, *A Farewell to Arms*)

When at the end of the story Catherine dies giving birth to a stillborn child and Lieutenant Henry walks from the hospital out into the rain a broken man, you realize the statement you read seven chapters earlier does indeed express the unifying idea of the novel.

Structure

The structure of a literary work is the pattern into which the parts fit so as to form a unified whole. In some kinds of writing the pattern is so common that it is perceived as a conventional structure. For example, a five-act play is likely to proceed from (1) an explanation of the situation, to (2) the complication, to (3) the climactic action or decision, and then through a relatively brief (4) falling action to (5) the resolution, or final outcome. Most detective stories move through six stages: (1) the situation preceding the murder, (2) the murder, (3) identification of a number of suspects, (4) elimination of innocent suspects, often through *their* murders, (5) identification of the real murderer, (6) concluding explanations that resolve the mystery.

Each of these structures imposes certain limits on writers that influence what they can say and how they can say it. For example, in the conventional detective story the writer must conceal the identity of the murderer until the end and must build a plausible case against each of the suspects before he or she is absolved of the crime.

In addition to the requirements imposed by conventional structures, writers can structure their work to suit their own purposes. "King of the Bingo Game" is organized in two scenes, the first of which is introductory to the second. The first scene shows the man in the theater audience, watching a movie he has seen three times before. He is paying more attention to the people eating and drinking around him than to the movie, and finally he checks his bingo cards as the numbers are called. The second scene, the main one, shows the man on the stage trying to win the jackpot. As the action develops, the man gets carried away by the power he attributes to the wheel and cannot let go of the button that controls it until he is wrestled to the floor and finally hit over the head. This two-scene structure is the author's choice. He could have started the story with the man's going up on the stage, but evidently he felt the introductory scene was necessary as background for the main action.

Within this two-scene structure "King of the Bingo Game" has smaller structural elements that contribute to the meaning of the story. For example, at the beginning the main character watches his favorite scene in the movie for the fourth time, a scene in which a woman bound on a bed is rescued by her lover. The melodramatic quality of the rescue foreshadows his equally unrealistic scheme for rescuing Laura, who is also bound to a bed by her illness. Another structural device is the use of two train scenes, one near the beginning and the other near the end of the story. These scenes "frame in" the view of a man always on the run from threatening forces, and emphasize his need to seize control of his fate. Such structural details tie different parts of the story together and so help them underscore the common theme. They are thus important clues to our interpretation of the story.

Symbol

The simplest kind of symbol is one that stands for or represents something else, as two bars on an army officer's uniform are a symbol of the rank of captain. When the symbol can be interpreted in only one way, it is a *closed* symbol. The jerk of an umpire's thumb in a baseball game is a closed symbol; it means only one thing — the runner is officially out. A symbol is *open* when different people can interpret it in different ways. Thus the flag is a symbol of the United States, but it can mean much more than just the country; it can also suggest to different people different clusters of associations about the nation and its history.

In literature the most interesting symbols are open ones, because their ambiguity presents a challenge that makes interpretation more difficult but more satisfying. For most readers the realization that they can read into an open symbol a whole cluster of associations gives them a sense of discovery that more than compensates for the difficulty. Even though they may sometimes read into the text more than other readers would accept, the interpretation of an open symbol is a source of pleasure, because readers add something of themselves to the work and so make their reading of it a personal experience. When this happens, readers become involved in the work.

The most important symbol in "King of the Bingo Game" is the wheel of fortune, with its double zero and the attached cord and button. When the man first goes onto the stage, he considers the spinning of the wheel to be a ritual, and rituals are symbolic performances. As the story progresses, the wheel becomes much more than a device to decide whether the man will win the prize. It becomes a means of controlling fate, and confers the godlike power of deciding whether Laura will live or die. Anyone who controls the wheel controls the future. That is why the man cries excitedly, "This is God!" Clearly he associates the wheel with some supernatural or magical power.

There are other symbols in the story. The double zero is an ambiguous symbol within the symbol of the wheel. It can mean "jackpot" or it can mean "absolutely nothing." The two trains mentioned in the story are also symbols of the man's fantasy that he can escape from poverty, illness, and insignificance by some magical solution that gives him control over his destiny. Notice that the main character is never named. By standing for nobody, he can be a symbol of everybody. He can be a symbol of the frustration of blacks in a white-dominated world, or a symbol of the frustrations and delusions of all humankind.

Irony

Irony is a stylistic device by which a writer conveys to readers a different meaning than would result from a literal interpretation of the words. You have seen an example of irony in the excerpt from *Huckleberry Finn* (page 310) in which Huck praises Emmeline Grangerford's poetry.

The plot of a story may develop ironically when the action seems to lead one way but actually leads another. In "King of the Bingo Game" the man's original strategy was to give the wheel "a short quick twirl" to make it stop at double zero and so win enough money to take care of all his problems. The reader's attention is focused on that event; it seems to be the culmination of the story. Then the man is caught up in the symbolic power of the wheel and tries to keep it running forever. When he is forced to let go of the button, the wheel stops, ironically, at double zero. But again, ironically, the winner gets nothing; he is hit on the head and dragged off the stage. Even if he had won the jackpot, it would have been of little use, since it came to only $36.90. That situation, too, is part of the irony of the story. Even the word *King* in the title is ironical. A bingo game is a small realm for a king. This king's rule lasted but a few minutes, and his fall from power was complete. At the end he, like the members of the audience, is just another "poor, nameless bastard."

Point of View

Literally, a point of view is the position one occupies in viewing an object. Applied to literature, the phrase refers to the way an author views a subject or tells a story. Generally either an *omniscient* or a *limited* point of view can be used. With an omniscient view the author can know everything about the characters, and can tell not only what they do and say, but also what they are thinking. What happened in the past or will happen in the future can be reported, as well as what is happening at present. A limited point of view, by contrast, requires the author to tell the story as some one person knows it. That person may be one of the characters, or someone who witnessed the events but did not share in them, or even the author but without omniscience.

A third point of view combines the omniscient and the limited. This is the one Ellison uses in "King of the Bingo Game." The narrator is omniscient regarding the main character and so can say that the character thought of a terrifying train in a half-dream, that he felt the manager was making a fool of him, and that he knew "his luck had run out" when he "felt the dull pain exploding in his skull." But this narrator does not speak this way about other characters; he only reports what they say and do and *seem* to feel. His point of view is omniscient for the main character but limited for all the others.

Voice

The term *voice* identifies the person or personality speaking in a literary work. The question "Who is speaking here?" is often important to the interpretation of a work. A story written in the first person need not be about the author or even represent the author's thinking. Huckleberry Finn is not speaking for Mark Twain when he says that people who behave as he has done — that is, who have helped a slave escape — go to hell. This is Huck's voice expressing ideas that he believes but Twain does not.

Sometimes a narrator speaks with a dual voice, as Ellison's narrator does. At times he speaks in the author's relatively detached standard English ("Tiring quickly of watching the picture he looked back to where the white beam filtered . . ."); at other times he speaks in the dialect of the main character ("Well, I ain't crazy. I'm just broke, 'cause I got no birth certificate to get a job . . ."). This duality in voice enables Ellison's narrator to move into the mind of the character, revealing in the man's own language what he is thinking, while still retaining the right to comment as narrator.

Your familiarity with these ten elements of imaginative writing can be useful when you restrict your subject for any paper you write on a literary work. You may decide to concentrate on one of the elements or on two or three of them. And you certainly will find yourself drawing on your knowledge of these elements as you analyze, interpret, or evaluate an entire work.

Now read William Saroyan's story "Snake" and the comments that follow it. Because this story poses some interesting problems of interpretation, it provides a good example to illustrate the usefulness of careful planning.

Snake

by William Saroyan

Walking through the park in May, he saw a small brown snake slipping away from him through grass and leaves, and he went after it with a long twig, feeling as he did so the instinctive fear of man for reptiles.

Ah, he thought, our symbol of evil, and he touched the snake with the twig, making it squirm. The snake lifted its head and struck at the twig, then shot away through the grass, hurrying fearfully, and he went after it.

It was very beautiful, and it was amazingly clever, but he intended to stay with it for a while and find out something about it.

The little brown snake led him deep into the park, so that he was hidden from view and alone with it. He had a guilty feeling that in pursuing the snake he was violating some rule of the park, and he prepared a remark for anyone who might discover him. I am a student of contemporary morality, he thought he would say, or, I am a sculptor and I am studying the structure of reptiles. At any rate, he would make some sort of reasonable explanation.

He would not say that he intended to kill the snake.

He moved beside the frightened reptile, leaping now and then to keep up with it, until the snake became exhausted and could not go on. Then he squatted on his heels to have a closer view of it, holding the snake before him by touching it with the twig. He admitted to himself that he was afraid to touch it with his hands. To touch a snake was to touch something secret in the mind of man, something one ought never to bring out into the light. That sleek gliding, and that awful silence, *was* once man, and now that man had come to this last form, here were snakes still moving over the earth as if no change had ever taken place.

The first male and female, biblical; and evolution. Adam and Eve, and the human embryo.

It was a lovely snake, clean and graceful and precise. The snake's fear frightened him and he became panic stricken thinking that perhaps all the snakes in the park would come quietly to the rescue of the little brown snake, and surround him with their malicious silence and the unbearable horror of their evil forms. It was a large park and there must be thousands of snakes in it. If all the snakes were to find out that he was with this little snake, they would easily be able to paralyse him.

He stood up and looked around. All was quiet. The silence was almost the biblical silence of *in the beginning.* He could hear a bird hopping from twig to twig in a low earthbush near by, but he was alone with the snake. He forgot that he was in a public park, in a large city. An airplane passed overhead, but he did not see or hear it. The silence was too emphatic and his vision was too emphatically focused on the snake before him.

In the garden with the snake, unnaked, in the beginning, in the year 1931.

He squatted on his heels again and began to commune with the snake. It made him laugh, inwardly and outwardly, to have the form of the snake so substantially before him, apart from his own being, flat on the surface of the earth instead of subtly a part of his own identity. It was really a tremendous thing. At first he was afraid to speak aloud, but as time went on he became less timid, and began to speak in English to it. It was very pleasant to speak to the snake.

All right, he said, here I am, after all these years, a young man living on the same earth, under the same sun, having the same passions. And here you are before me, the same. The situation is the same. What do you intend to do? Escape? I will not let you escape. What have you in mind? How will you defend yourself? I intend to destroy you. As an obligation to man.

The snake twitched before him helplessly, unable to avoid the twig. It struck at the twig several times, and then became too tired to bother with it. He drew away the twig, and heard the snake say, Thank you.

He began to whistle to the snake, to see if the music would have any effect on its movements, if it would make the snake dance. You are my only love, he whistled; Schubert made into a New York musical comedy; *my only love, my only love;* but the snake would not dance. Something Italian perhaps, he thought, and began to sing *la donna è mobile,** intentionally mispronouncing the words in order to amuse himself. He tried a Brahms lullaby, but the music had no effect on the snake. It was tired. It was frightened. It wanted to get away.

He was amazed at himself suddenly; it had occurred to him to let the snake flee, to let it glide away and be lost in the lowly worlds of its kind. Why should he allow it to escape?

He lifted a heavy boulder from the ground and thought: Now I shall bash your head with this rock and see you die.

To destroy that evil grace, to mangle that sinful loveliness.

---

* "Woman is fickle." The libertine Duke of Mantua in Verdi's opera *Rigoletto* sings an aria entitled "La donna è mobile." One of the stanzas says, "Women are all the same — Never believe them! Love them and leave them — That's how to play the game!"

But it was very strange. He could not let the rock fall on the snake's head, and began suddenly to feel sorry for it. I am sorry, he said, dropping the boulder. I beg your pardon. I see now that I have only love for you.

And he wanted to touch the snake with his hands, to hold it and understand the truth of its touch. But it was difficult. The snake was frightened and each time he extended his hands to touch it, the snake turned on him and charged. I have only love for you, he said. Do not be afraid. I am not going to hurt you.

Then, swiftly, he lifted the snake from the earth, learned the true feel of it, and dropped it. There, he said. Now I know the truth. A snake is cold, but it is clean. It is not slimy, as I thought.

He smiled upon the little brown snake. You may go now, he said. The inquisition is over. You are yet alive. You have been in the presence of man, and you are yet alive. You may go now.

But the snake would not go away. It was exhausted with fear.

He felt deeply ashamed of what he had done, and angry with himself. Jesus, he thought, I have scared the little snake. It will never get over this. It will always remember me squatting over it.

For God's sake, he said to the snake, go away. Return to your kind. Tell them what you saw, you yourself, with your own eyes. Tell them what you felt. The sickly heat of the hand of man. Tell them of the presence you felt.

Suddenly the snake turned from him and spilled itself forward, away from him. Thank you, he said. And it made him laugh with joy to see the little snake throwing itself into the grass and leaves, thrusting itself away from man. Splendid, he said; hurry to them and say that you were in the presence of man and that you were not killed. Think of all the snakes that live and die without ever meeting man. Think of the distinction it will mean for you.

It seemed to him that the little snake's movements away from him were the essence of joyous laughter, and he felt greatly pleased. He found his way back to the path, and continued his walk.

In the evening, while she sat at the piano, playing softly, he said: A funny thing happened.

She went on playing. A funny thing? she asked.

Yes, he said. I was walking through the park and I saw a little brown snake.

She stopped playing and turned on the bench to look at him. A snake? she said. How ugly!

No, he said. It was beautiful.

What about it?

Oh, nothing, he said. I just caught it and wouldn't let it go for a while.

But why?

For no good reason at all, he said.

She walked across the room and sat beside him, looking at him strangely.

Tell me about the snake, she said.

It was lovely, he said. Not ugly at all. When I touched it, I felt its cleanliness.

I am so glad, she said. What else?

I wanted to kill the snake, he said. But I couldn't. It was too lovely.

I'm so glad, she said. But tell me everything.

That's all, he said.

But it isn't, she said. I know it isn't. Tell me everything.

It is very funny, he said. I was going to kill the snake, and not come here again.

Aren't you ashamed of yourself? she said.

Of course I am, he said.

What else? she said. What did you think, of me, when you had the snake before you?

You will be angry, he said.

Oh, nonsense. It is impossible for me to be angry with you. Tell me.

Well, he said, I thought you were lovely but evil.

Evil?

I told you you would be angry.

And then?

Then I touched the snake, he said. It wasn't easy, but I picked it up with my hands. What do you make of this? You've read a lot of books about such things. What does it mean, my picking up the snake?

She began to laugh softly, intelligently. Why, she laughed, it means, it simply means that you are an idiot. Why, it's splendid.

Is that according to Freud? he said.

Yes, she laughed. According to Freud.

Well, anyway, he said, it was very fine to let the snake go free.

Have you ever told me you loved me? she asked.

You ought to know, he said. I do not remember one or two things I have said to you.

No, she said. You have never told me.

She began to laugh again, feeling suddenly very happy about him. You have always talked of other things, she said. Irrelevant things. At the most amazing times. She laughed.

This snake, he said, was a little brown snake.

And that explains it, she said. You have never intruded.

What the hell are you talking about? he said.

I'm so glad you didn't kill the snake, she said.

She returned to the piano, and placed her hands softly upon the keys.

I whistled a few songs to the snake, he said. I whistled a fragment from Schubert's Unfinished Symphony. I would like to hear that. You know, the melody that was used in a musical comedy called *Blossom Time.* The part that goes, *you are my only love, my only love,* and so on.

She began to play softly, feeling his eyes on her hair, on her hands, her neck, her back, her arms, feeling him studying her as he had studied the snake.

Your first reaction to this story may be puzzlement. What is it about? You can begin to find out by asking questions about the chief elements. As ever, you should jot down brief answers to these questions — or even answer them more fully in your journal, if you wish.

1. What is the situation here? There seem to be two: the scene between a man and a snake in a park, and another between the same man and a woman in a house. Since this is one story, the two scenes must be related. Obviously they are related through the snake, which is the main subject of conversation between the man and the woman, and through the title, which suggests that the whole story is about a snake. But *what* about the snake? The answer to that question seems to be a major problem of interpretation.

2. As you consider the story of a snake in a park (*park* can be used to include a garden), you need to remember another snake and another garden, which are part of the context of Saroyan's story. You can read the Biblical account in the second and third chapters of Genesis.

3. Now look at the characters. Assuming that the snake is a character, you can say there are three, two in each scene. What does the man think about the snake? At the beginning he calls it "our symbol of evil." Later he says, "To touch a snake was to touch something secret in the mind of man, something one ought never to bring out into the light." Then he associates the snake with Adam and Eve and echoes that association with the statement, "In the garden with the snake, unnaked, in the beginning, in the year 1931." Adam and Eve were naked in the beginning; it was only after they met the snake that they were unnaked. It becomes increasingly clear that this is not just a little brown snake, but a symbol of some relationship between a man and a woman. What is the relationship? The Biblical snake is asso-

ciated with both knowledge and sin. Is the man sexually attracted to the woman, and if so does he feel guilty because he thinks that to know her sexually would be sinful? Sex, Sin, and the Snake. Do they all go together?

4. At first the man experiences "the instinctive fear of man for reptiles" and intends to kill the snake. That is his "obligation to man," though he sees that it is "a lovely snake, clean and graceful and precise." He starts to bash its head with a rock, "to destroy that evil grace, to mangle that sinful loveliness." But then he begins to feel sorry for the snake and says, "I see now that I have only love for you." He picks it up and finds it pleasant to the touch. He has been all wrong about the snake. Is his attitude toward the woman similar to his attitude toward the snake? Before you answer, reread the last part of the dialogue, beginning with "I'm so glad, she said. But tell me everything." What is the man likely to conclude about the woman on the basis of what he has learned about the snake?

5. Consider carefully the dialogue that begins with the woman's asking "Have you ever told me you loved me?" and concludes with "I'm so glad you didn't kill the snake." She says here, "And that explains it." What explains what? If you can answer this question, you will have gained considerable insight into their relationship. What is there near this statement that will help you answer the question?

6. Does the woman seem to be wiser than the man, or at least more perceptive about the nuances of his adventure with the snake? It is *he* who asks *her*, "What does it mean, my picking up the snake? . . . Is that according to Freud?" What does her answer reveal about her interpretation of the snake incident and about her relationship with the man? Is she happy or offended when, in the last paragraph, she begins to play the piano and feels him "studying her as he had studied the snake"?

7. Consider what you do not know about these people — what they look like, how long they have known each other, even their names. Since the story is written from an omniscient point of view, Saroyan could have told his readers these things. Why didn't he? Are the characters themselves symbolic, so that they represent not particular people, but Man and Woman? Are they a twentieth-century Adam and Eve resolving through the snake the doubts and confusions of falling in

love? Or are readers simply meeting a neurotic young man who can profess his love to a snake but not to a woman?

8. It is now clear that the snake is a symbol. Does the structure of the story bear this out? Consider how details in the second part echo details in the first: the man's wanting to kill the snake and leave the woman because he thinks they are both evil, his admission that he loves the snake, the woman's realization that he loves her, the song "You are my only love" referred to in both parts, and his studying the woman as he studied the snake. What at first seemed to be two situations not clearly connected are now blended into an integrated story.

After you have finished your reading, review your notes and consider what you might write about. If you have a fairly good idea of your subject, you have finished planning and may be ready to begin drafting. You have a preliminary notion of your purpose and probably have the information needed to develop it. If your notes seem sketchy, you might want to expand them now. It is often wise, before beginning to write, to outline your paper and check your notes to see if you have all the information you need to do what your outline requires. At this stage much of the hard work of the paper has been done.

Exercises   **As preparation for writing a paper on "Snake," first discuss in class in as much detail as you can the following questions:**

1. **Suppose Saroyan had made the man kill the snake in the first part. How would that change affect the structure of the story? Would there be a second part? If so, what would it do? Would the man have to kill the woman at the end of the story?**

2. **Suppose Saroyan had identified the man as Joe Doakes, a used-car salesman, and the woman as Jane Doe, a typist. How would this change affect the story?**

3. **Why does the woman call the man "an idiot" on page 422, and what is it that is "splendid"?**

4. **If you agree with the partial interpretation of the story suggested in this chapter, what additional information can you provide to support that interpretation?**

5. **If you disagree with that interpretation, can you provide textual evidence to support your disagreement?**

As a result of your discussions, choose any thesis you please about "Snake" and write a paper supporting that thesis.

Types of Emphasis

A critical essay is likely to discuss one or more of the following three types of concerns: *technical analysis,* or the methods used to achieve the effects revealed in the work; *interpretation,* or what the work means; *evaluation,* or the essayist's judgment of the effectiveness or significance of the work or of any part of it. These three kinds of criticism are not independent of each other. Interpretation, as you have seen in "Snake," sometimes depends on technical analysis, and evaluation sometimes includes both technical analysis and interpretation. But in any one paper a critic can emphasize the kind of criticism he or she is most concerned with. The pages that follow will explain these three kinds of emphasis in some detail.

Technical Analysis

Technical analysis is chiefly concerned with technique, with the means a writer uses to develop situation, characters, theme, structure, or any of the ten elements we considered earlier. The preceding discussion of the relation between the man, the snake, and the woman, and the parallelism betwen the two parts of the story is an example of technical analysis. In Chapter 9 *style* was defined as the way a work is written; technical analysis deals also with those stylistic features of a work that the analyst wishes to discuss.

The following extract from a student essay makes a technical analysis by showing how James Thurber handled contrasts and transition in his short story "The Secret Life of Walter Mitty." The subject of the story is a timid, incompetent man married to a domineering woman who constantly criticizes him for his shortcomings. To escape from his wife's henpecking, Mitty resorts to fantasies in which he can imagine himself a powerful, brave, resourceful, and confident hero who distinguishes himself in every imaginable situation.

What makes "The Secret Life of Walter Mitty" more than just another amusing short story is Thurber's unique and effective use of contrasts. Consider, for example, the first three paragraphs. Here the Walter Mitty of imagination is placed side by side with the Walter Mitty of reality. The contrast between the iron-hearted Naval Commander, bravely giving orders to his men, and the chicken-hearted Walter Mitty, timidly taking orders from his wife, is quite apparent. But the use of contrasts is by no means restricted to the beginning of the story. On the contrary, it is employed all the way through to the very last word. Compare the quick-thinking Doctor Mitty, famous surgeon, to the Walter Mitty who cannot park his car, remove his tire chains, nor readily remember to buy a box of puppy biscuits. Compare also the "greatest shot in the world" or the daring Captain Mitty, or the "erect and motionless, proud and disdainful Walter Mitty the Undefeated" with the Walter Mitty who seeks the quiet refuge of a big leather chair in a hotel lobby. Contrasts are effective tools for any writer, but the straightforward manner in which Thurber employs them enhances their effectiveness considerably.

After briefly skimming through the collection of contrasts that makes up "The Secret Life of Walter Mitty," one might feel that there is little connection between the paragraphs describing the imagined Walter Mitty and the Mitty of reality. However, closer observation reveals that Thurber does, by the use of suggestive words and phrases, cleverly establish links between the Mitty of fact and the Mitty of fancy. . . . Consider how Mrs. Mitty's mention of Doctor Renshaw and the event of driving by a hospital lead to a daydream in which Walter Mitty, a distinguished surgeon, assists Doctor Renshaw in a difficult operation. Take note also of how a newsboy's shout about the Waterbury trial initiates the trial of Walter Mitty in the following paragraph. Such skillful employment of transitions, by which an event in reality triggers an event in the imagination, is sound not only from the literary standpoint, but also from the psychological point of view.

This critic has not concerned himself with interpretation, for the meaning of Thurber's story — that a timid, insecure, and weak character can take refuge in heroic fantasies — is easily grasped by any perceptive reader. The critic has instead analyzed Thurber's method of conveying this meaning. First he treats the repeated use of contrasts in moving back and forth between the "real" world of Walter Mitty and the more satisfying life of his daydreams, and gives illustrations of this movement. Next he demonstrates that the opposing elements in any contrast have a subtle connection in thought or language.

The writer of the paper on pages 429–430 had the advantage of a group of study questions intended to help him analyze the poem "Hunting Song." Only after he had done the technical analysis as a planning exercise did he attempt to write his essay. Here are the poem, the analytical questions, and the essay:

The poem

Hunting Song
by Donald Finkel

The fox came lolloping, lolloping,
Lolloping. His tongue hung out
And his ears were high.
He was like death at the end of a string
When he came to the hollow
Log. Ran in one side
And out of the other. O
He was sly.

The hounds came tumbling, tumbling,
Tumbling. Their heads were low
And their eyes were red.
The sound of their breath was louder than death
When they came to the hollow
Log. They held at one end
But a bitch found the scent. O
They were mad.

The hunter came galloping, galloping,
Galloping. All damp was his mare
From her hooves to her mane.
His coat and his mouth were redder than death
When he came to the hollow
Log. He took in the rein
And over he went. O
He was fine.

The log, he just lay there, alone in
The clearing. No fox nor hound

Nor mounted man
Saw his black round eyes in their perfect disguise
(As the ends of a hollow
Log). He watched death go through him,
Around him and over him. O
He was wise.

The questions

1. In what ways do *Log* (line 6 in each stanza) and *O* (line 7 in each stanza) draw your attention to the log?

2. Read aloud the first sentence in each stanza. How does the poet rely on contrast in sound and rhythm to draw your attention to the log?

3. Contrast the use of *death* in stanzas 1, 2, and 3 with its use in stanza 4. Observe the irony of the dead log's construing the live characters to represent death.

4. Contrast the effect of the final word in stanzas 1, 2, and 3 with the effect of the final word in stanza 4.

5. By now you see (1) that much in the poem says "Pay attention to the log," (2) that contrast and irony contribute to meaning, (3) that death is prominent in the theme, and (4) that the log's relationship to the action of the poem is different from that of any other "character."

The student's essay

The Detached Interpreter

Donald Finkel's "Hunting Song" speaks of a fox chase and of a hollow log's reaction to the chase. By watching the log carefully throughout the poem, by observing contrasts between the log and the other characters, and by being alert to ironical implications about the characters' proximity to death, the reader can discover what the poem says about the living and the dead.

There is much evidence that the reader must pay attention to the log. The word *Log* appears as the first word in line 6 of each stanza, even though it is the last word in its sentence. The word's being out of its normal position, the capital letter it normally would not have, the period that follows it even though it is the first word in the poetic line — all these draw attention to *Log*. So does the *O*, surely a representation of the end of a hollow log, which is conspicuous as the end word in line 7 of each stanza.

Contrast operates to draw the reader's attention to the log — contrast in cadence, for example. The first sentences of the first three stanzas are action statements:

The fox came lolloping, lolloping,
Lolloping.

The hounds came tumbling, tumbling,
Tumbling.

The hunter came galloping, galloping,
Galloping.

But the cadence in the log's stanza is different:

The log, he just lay there, alone in
The clearing.

Clearly the log is different from the rest in that it is not caught up in the action of the chase.

Another difference between the stanza about the log and the first three develops from the ironical use of *death*. The animate characters are very much alive; yet the fox "was like death at the end of a string," the hounds' "breath was louder than death," and the hunter's "coat and his mouth were redder than death." By the fourth stanza these characters are no longer compared with death; they *are* death. The log "watched death go through him, / Around him and over him." It is the log, so long dead that it is hollow, that can serve as the interpreter of the scene. On the figurative level the literally dead log is alive (his eyes are only disguised to look like the ends of a hollow log); the literally alive characters are representative of death.

If matters proceed as they are likely to, the fox will die within a few minutes. Before long the hounds will be dead and then the mare. A few years more and the man will be gone. The log lived and died long ago — so long that he is detached from the sound and the fury of the hunt. He knows that this chase and others like it will soon end and that the participants will experience the detachment of the dead rather than the involvement of the living.

Finally, while the fox is sly, the hounds are mad, and the hunter is fine, the log — this log so long dead that he is free from involvement in temporal matters and so can watch the chase with sublime detachment — is wise.

The writer of this paper has interpreted, but not without first engaging in careful analysis. Notice that the study questions do not ask for comment on what the poem says until an analysis has been completed. Only after you know *how* a literary work says, should you feel confident that you know *what* it says.

Interpretation

An interpretation shows how the interpreter reads a work, what the work means to him or her. It is thus a personal response, and because it is personal, different readers may interpret a piece of literature in somewhat different ways. But to say that different interpretations may be possible is not to say that "anything goes" or that any one interpretation is as good as any other. To be acceptable to your readers, your interpretation must be consistent with all of the facts of the work. You may emphasize some facts more than others, but you cannot ignore significant facts just because they are not convenient to your interpretation. Thus no one can reasonably argue that "Snake" is a story about a man who falls in love with a snake and so abandons his fiancée. There is too much evidence in the story against that interpretation.

It is possible to jump to a hasty interpretation of a poem because you fail to pay attention to all its details. You may then draw a hasty conclusion from some details and ignore others. The result is a slanted interpretation similar to the slanted arguments discussed in Chapter 10. The best defense against hasty interpretation is, first, to observe all the details; second, to see how individual details fit into patterns; third, to generalize these patterns into a unified view of the whole work. If you follow this procedure, your interpretation will be grounded on the facts and will develop from them.

Interpretation is never mere summary. Telling the story of a play or novel, or paraphrasing a poem, is not what is expected in a critical essay. The critical-essay assignment requires you to discover a meaning in the work, but a summary does not interpret: it simply reports, or gives a statement of fact. A critical essay uses the facts to support a judgment about meaning, and is thus a statement of opinion based on facts.

Discussion Problem

The following student essay about "Hunting Song" (pages 428–429) was written as an exercise in analysis and interpretation. What details in the poem support the interpretation given in the paper? What details oppose it? What details does the interpretation ignore? What is commendable about the student's method of arriving at the interpretation? What is not commendable about the method? In view of your answers to these questions, how acceptable is the interpretation?

Symbolism in "Hunting Song"

The first reading of "Hunting Song" gave me a pleasant description of the fox hunt. This was evident particularly in the first three stanzas. The fourth stanza, with a definite change in tone, suggested a deeper meaning than a mere fox hunt. Donald Finkel very carefully chose a simple description to convey a significant and moving incident of religious belief.

If the poet's intent was to give a mere description of the fox hunt, the first three stanzas could be complete by themselves. But he doesn't stop here. He presents a fourth stanza which alters our image of the hunt. The words of this stanza give much deeper meaning to the poem. The rhythm becomes very slow and the tone calm; the hunt is over and all is quiet. "... he just lay there, alone in / The clearing." But what does it all mean?

To discover a meaning, I look to the title, "Hunting Song." Like "Song of Solomon," this conveys a religious feeling. To me it represents man's hunt, or search, for a reason to believe. The question becomes — Believe in what?

On reading the poem several more times I begin to see the symbols, not just the participants of a fox hunt. The fox becomes the redheaded Judas. "His tongue hung out / And his ears were high" as he lolled about awaiting the opportunity to betray. "He was like death at the end of a string" seems almost like a prediction of the fate, the hanging, which awaits Judas. The line "Ran in one side / And out of the other" indicates the sneaking movement of Judas to his master, the kiss of betrayal, and then his moving right along with the crowd.

Oh — he was sly.

In the second stanza we see the "hounds ... tumbling." This symbolizes the soldiers and masses of people jumping about in a complete state of disorder. Some in the crowd were ashamed of their actions and stood with "their heads ... low and their eyes ... red." But for the majority, "The sound of their breath was louder than death" as they shouted a demand for action. They were in disorder only until "a bitch found the scent" — until someone let out a yell, "Crucify Him!" — and thereby set the direction of action for the masses to follow.

Oh — they were mad.

The third stanza brings us to the hunter. He is not alone; he is mounted. The mount is symbolic of his royal position, that of emperor. The hunter also wears the red coat of royalty, but his mouth is "redder than death" when he realizes the task before him. Rather than make a decision by himself, Pilate washes his hands to symbolize the purging from head to foot. This action is evident in the line "All damp was his mare [his royal position] / From her hooves to her mane." Pilate would not be guilty of such a crime; the people could decide and take the blame.

Oh — he was fine.

The fourth stanza gives the tone which is in great contrast to the preceding action. This is the end of the poem, but it portrays an unending scene. This is the verse which makes you reread the poem for deeper meaning. The log now becomes a symbol of the Cross of Crucifixion. Though he has "watched death go through him, / Around him and over him" Christ, now on the Cross "alone in the clearing," was not recognized by Judas, the masses, or Pilate as the true Son of God in the perfect disguise of man.

Truly — he was wise.

Evaluation

In technical analysis you discuss the ways in which effects are achieved in a work of literature. In interpretation you show what the work means to you. In evaluation you judge the effectiveness or significance of the work.

The judgment you make in an evaluation may be favorable or unfavorable or may consider both merits and weaknesses. It may be a judgment about the whole work or about any important element of it, such as the characters, the plot, the theme, the structure, or any combination of these elements. The following evaluation by a professional critic is chiefly unfavorable and focuses on the main character:

In "A Perfect Day for Bananafish," the first of J. D. Salinger's remarkable short stories to attract widespread attention, a young veteran recovering from a nervous breakdown in Florida takes a little girl out swimming, in a charmingly described interlude, and then goes to his hotel room and shoots himself when he is confronted by his shallow wife. In "For Esmé — with Love and Squalor," one of the best and most moving of all his stories, an American soldier in Germany suffering from an extreme case of combat fatigue is brought back by a message from a little girl he had met in England. And in the climactic scene of his first novel, *The Catcher in the Rye*, the sixteen-year-old hero who has been wandering around New York alone for three days, ever since his expulsion from boarding school, in a state somewhere between reality and unreality, abandons his dream of running away to the West and goes home (and subsequently to a sanitarium) when his ten-year-old sister, whom he has met secretly, is clearly broken-hearted at the thought of his leaving.

In all three cases the children and the boy-men are exceedingly well done. In each case, despite the similarity of situation, they are quite different and distinct individuals. The final scene in *The Catcher in the Rye* is as good as anything that Salinger has written, which means very good indeed. So are a number of other episodes. But the book as a whole is disappointing, and not merely because it is a reworking of a theme that one begins to suspect must obsess the author. Holden Caulfield, the main character who tells his own story, is an extraordinary portrait, but there is too much of him. He describes himself early on and, with the sureness of a wire recording, he remains strictly in character throughout:

> I shook my head. I shake my head quite a lot. "Boy!" I said. I also say "Boy!" quite a lot. Partly because I have a lousy vocabulary and partly because I act quite young for my age sometimes. I was sixteen then, and I'm seventeen now, and sometimes I act like I'm about thirteen. It's really ironical because I'm six foot two, and I have gray hair. I really do. The one side of my head — the right side — is full of millions of gray hairs. I've had them ever since I was a kid. And yet I still act sometimes like I was only about twelve.

In the course of 277 pages the reader wearies of this kind of explicitness, repetition and adolescence, exactly as one would weary of Holden himself. And this reader at least suffered from an irritated feeling that Holden was not quite so sensitive and perceptive as he, and his creator, thought he was. In any case he is so completely self-centered that the other characters who wander through the book — with the notable exception of his sister Phoebe — have nothing like his authenticity. *The Catcher in the Rye* is a brilliant tour de force,* but in a writer of Salinger's undeniable talent one expects something more. (Anne L. Goodman, "Mad About Children," *New Republic*)

---

* *Tour de force:* literally, "a feat of skill or power"; in literature, a triumph of the author's artistry over the limitations of the subject.

The structure of this 500-word essay is worth a close look. It consists of three paragraphs. The first relates *The Catcher in the Rye* to two of Salinger's short stories. The second states the thesis of the essay ("the book as a whole is disappointing . . .") and presents the main evidence for the critic's judgment, the quotation from the book. The third offers a final explanation of the judgment contained in the thesis.

The position of the thesis — exactly in the middle of the essay — may seem a bit unusual, but the long introductory paragraph performs two important functions. First, by showing the critic's familiarity with some of Salinger's earlier stories and her appreciation of them, it establishes her credentials: she knows Salinger's work and likes it. That suggests to a reader that she is not predisposed to be hostile to *The Catcher in the Rye,* and helps to emphasize her "disappointment." Second, her comparison of the two stories and the novel lays the groundwork for her judgment that *Catcher* is "a reworking of a theme that one begins to suspect must obsess the author." This judgment is part of her reason for being disappointed in the book.

The second paragraph deals with her main point, that Holden's character is presented in such explicit detail that we get too much of him. Her readers need some evidence for this assertion, and Ms. Goodman gives it in the quotation. Whether or not you agree with her judgment, does the quotation show you why she finds Holden a bit tedious? That is what it is intended to do.

The final paragraph expands the criticism of Holden's character: not only is he wearisome, but the reader begins to doubt his sensitivity and perceptiveness. Yet, despite the irritation that Holden causes, Salinger succeeds in making him an authentic and unforgettable character. This is the tour de force that the critic speaks of, the triumph of Salinger's artistry in making such a character the hero of an immensely popular novel.

Writing the Paper

For two reasons, the actual writing of a critical essay needs only brief attention here. First, much of the work on this kind of paper is done in planning, because once you have decided what you are going to say

© 1966 United Feature Syndicate, Inc.

about the work you are discussing, the content of your paper has been established. Second, the writing of a critical essay is not significantly different from the writing of any other essay. The advice that follows merely applies the principles of purposeful writing to this kind of assignment.

1. *Make clear to your readers what your specific subject is.* The specific subject, as explained on page 16, identifies the particular view of the general subject you are going to deal with and thus provides the focus of your paper. Sometimes the specific subject will be implied in the title; usually it is stated in an introductory paragraph containing a thesis. Such an introduction prepares your readers for what you are going to do. It also commits you to doing that, and so helps control the choices you will make during the writing. If you are bothered about how to start, review the discussion of introductory paragraphs on pages 217–220.

2. *Select and evaluate your material.* Your material will be the judgments you make about the work and the details that support those judgments and so make your criticism acceptable to your readers. The best way to make your judgments persuasive is to base them on the facts of the text and, through quotations and descriptions, to show those facts, so that your readers will see why you say what you do. The basis for selecting your material is its pertinence to your subject. If you know what you want to do, you should have no trouble choosing pertinent evidence. But, especially during revision, it will be wise to ask yourself, "Does this evidence clearly prove what I want it to prove?" If you have any doubt, remove it by choosing stronger evidence, or by establishing a clearer connection between the evidence and the judgment you are making from it, or by revising the judgment.

Especially be cautious when dealing with symbolism. If you think something is being used as a symbol, take pains to establish that belief. Notice how much evidence was gathered in the investigation of "Snake" by asking a series of questions. The answers to these questions helped support the belief that the snake in Saroyan's story is a sexual symbol. Notice, also, how little evidence was used to support the assertions in "Symbolism in Hunting Song" that the hunter on his horse is a symbol of the emperor and that "all damp was his mare / From her hooves to her mane" is a symbol for Pontius Pilate's washing his hands. You have a right to see symbols wherever you want to; but if you expect other people to accept your interpretations, you must be prepared to defend them with more than unsupported assertions.

3. *Summarize the work when necessary.* One of the decisions you must make in writing a critical essay concerns summarizing. The best procedure is to summarize only when necessary and then only as much as necessary. But what is "necessary"? If your readers are not familiar with the work you are writing about, they will need some kind of background information to appreciate the pertinence and significance of your comments. It is therefore necessary to give them enough information about the content of the work so that they can readily follow you. If you are writing a criticism of a story or novel, do not let this necessity of providing enough information lead you into a retelling of the story, or of considerable parts of it. Select and summarize only

that information that your readers will need in order to appreciate your criticism. More than that is a waste of space. But if your essay is a criticism of a poem, it is usually necessary to give the full text of the poem so that your readers can refer to it.

4. *Use quotations when they help, but do not overuse them.* An apt quotation from the work can be helpful in two ways: it can illustrate the point you are making, and it can provide evidence to make your judgments acceptable. The essays included in this chapter use quotations skillfully to make their comments clear and convincing. But the overuse of quotations may result in padding; so, in general, keep quotations short and to the point. It is customary to indent and single-space prose quotations of five lines or more, or two or more lines of a poem.

5. *Use source references if necessary.* If you refer only to the work you are writing about, you may include page numbers (line numbers of a poem) in parentheses within the text of your paper, thus: "(page 12)" or "(lines 5–6)." Unless a reader needs such references, however, they can be omitted; notice that very few of the essays in this chapter use page or line references. But if you are writing a long paper that makes use of several sources, it is customary to cite these sources in a note either at the bottom of the page *(footnote)* or at the end of the paper *(endnote)*. That note should identify at least the author, the title of the work, and the page number or numbers. The conventional forms of such notes are discussed and illustrated in Chapter 14, "Writing the Research Paper."

6. *Always proofread your finished essay carefully, preferably more than once.* This is standard procedure for all essays.

Exercise   In this exercise you are asked to study two poems, on one of which you are to write a critical essay emphasizing interpretation. Do not try to interpret either of the poems as soon as you have read it. Instead, let your interpretation develop gradually as you write responses to the study questions. The questions are designed to enable you to employ the method for analyzing and interpreting that you have learned earlier — observing significant details and then fitting related details together into meaningful patterns.

Bring your planning notes on both poems to class to use in discussion. If necessary, revise your notes as a result of the discussion. Then decide which poem you will write about. Do your responses to the questions allow you to make a general interpretive statement about the poem? If so, you are ready to develop that statement in an essay. If not, you may want to write about the problems that prevent you from arriving at an interpretation in which you have confidence.

Bears
by Adrienne Cecile Rich

Wonderful bears that walked my room all night,
Where are you gone, your sleek and fairy fur,
Your eyes' veiled imperious light?

Brown bears as rich as mocha or as musk,
White opalescent bears whose fur stood out
Electric in the deepening dusk,

And great black bears who seemed more blue than black,
more violet than blue against the dark —
Where are you now? upon what track

Mutter your muffled paws, that used to tread
So softly, surely, up the creakless stair
While I lay listening in bed?

When did I lose you? whose have you become?
Why do I wait and wait and never hear
Your thick nocturnal pacing in my room?
My bears, who keeps you now, in pride and fear?

Questions

1. In the first two stanzas the narrator speaks of the bears' "sleek and fairy fur," the "veiled imperious light" of their eyes, their being "as rich as mocha or as musk," and the "opalescent" effect of their fur. Is the narrator a child who admires the bears or an adult who is reflecting on the admiration she felt for them as a child?

2. From what sources might a child's imagination have created the bears?

3. Attempt to answer the narrator's questions "Where are you gone ...?" (asked in stanza 1 and repeated in stanzas 3 and 5) and "When did I lose you?" (stanza 5).

4. The narrator seems to wish that she could once again hear the bears treading on the stair and pacing in her room. Why does she have this wish?

5. The narrator wonders who keeps her bears. Offer her an answer.

6. If someone is keeping the bears "in pride and fear," what is the source of the pride? of the fear? (*Fear* is conspicuous for being the final word in the poem. Give it close attention.)

The Going Away of Young People*
by Eleanor Ross Taylor

1

This was the day
The crumbs from last night's dinner
Lay all day on the table.

Your room filled only by sunlight
Is darkened by the late sleeper.

　　You forgot your love.
　　I'd mail it but
　　There's the chore of string
　　And paper and
The timbre of hi-fi turned off
Strings the psyche.
　　Anyway it's stuff I'm used
　　To stumbling over in various
　　Recesses of my house
　　Wondering why I haven't
　　Given it away, put it
　　To some use —
　　But keep on hoarding it, ashamed.

2

And our sailers-away hang yet full sail
In our autumn windows,
The windows across the street
Becalmed of young people.
Grass infiltrates their marigolds.
The garage cries out.

* Reprinted by permission; © 1976 The New Yorker Magazine, Inc.

3

I won't say goodbye.
But all leave-taking is a permanence.
We can't be sewed back up.
My mother's face at the window
Like a postage stamp
Hinges a faded September.

4

And over a drink my old friend fights tears,
Fights impatiently sympathy,
At her window cuts at the traffic
With her hand — "It was all woods!
Gone! And I've failed, too."

5

Windows between Septembers,
More and more windows,
Muffling, fogging over,
At last reflect only me
In car window, kitchen window,
Across-the-street windows,
This window I open over your bed
In case you should come back
For what you forgot.

Questions:
Stanza 1

1. Why have the crumbs not been cleared from the table on this particular day?

2. Literally, the room is filled with sunlight. Why, then, does it appear to be darkened? Does your answer explain the term "late sleeper"?

3. What does the speaker have in mind when she considers mailing the forgotten love?

4. What is "the chore of string / And paper" that the speaker refers to? What is the "stuff I'm used / To stumbling over"?

5. Why and how does the "timbre of hi-fi turned off" affect the speaker?

6. In the light of your answers to these questions, can you describe briefly the state of mind of the speaker?

Stanza 2

This stanza contains a metaphor in which one house is likened to a ship under sail, the other to a ship becalmed.

1. Who are the "sailers-away"?

2. What are the signs that the house across the street is becalmed?

3. Why is the first house not becalmed?

4. Does this stanza suggest to you that in time the first house, too, will become becalmed? (If you cannot answer this question now, skip it and come back to it after you have answered all the other questions.)

5. Who is the speaker in stanza 2 — the same person as in stanza 1, or somebody else?

6. Do you see any relation between the ideas expressed in stanza 2 and those expressed in stanza 1 and suggested by the title of the poem?

Stanza 3

1. Who is it who won't say goodbye: the same speaker as in stanza 1 or a different speaker?

2. To what situation does the first line refer: (a) the same situation as in stanza 1, (b) a situation that occurred much earlier, (c) both *a* and *b?* Explain your answer.

3. Why "faded September"?

Stanza 4

1. Assuming that the person speaking in the first three lines is offering sympathy to a friend, what is the occasion for the sympathy?

2. Why does the friend say, "I've failed, too"? Why "failed" and why "too"?

3. Do you see any relation between this conversation and what has been said in earlier stanzas?

Stanza 5

1. Why the emphasis on windows in this stanza? When windows have been mentioned earlier, what has been their function?

2. Why do these windows finally "reflect only me"?

3. Do the last three lines return the poem to the situation in stanza 1 and to something forgotten there?

Chapter 13

Planning the Research Paper

The research paper (also called the library paper or term paper) may be the most frequently assigned and therefore most important kind of paper you will be asked to write during your formal education. You will probably write a number of research papers about a number of subjects over the coming years; and those papers will not only figure prominently in determining the grades you receive in your courses but will also give you an opportunity to learn a number of valuable ways of thinking and writing.

In many ways, the research paper assignment is similar to other writing assignments in that you must discover information on a subject, arrange your information to satisfy the needs and expectations of an audience, and present your information to fulfill a specific purpose. It differs from other writing assignments, however, in that the source of your information is not your interpretation of memory, observation, or informal research (as in most informal essays), your textbook or lecture notes (as in the essay examination), or even one or more literary or artistic creations (as in the critical essay), but the books, articles, and documents housed in your university library. To locate the precise information you need in this vast collection of material and then to incorporate it into your own writing will require certain thinking, reading, and writing skills that you have not encountered in your other assignments.

A good way to begin learning these skills is to approach the writing of the research paper as a process that can be divided into stages, each of which contains a sequence of smaller steps. As in any process, alternatives and short cuts can be used to eliminate some of the more time-consuming steps in the process. Your ability to see alternatives or discover short cuts will grow as you learn more about the subject, audience, and purpose of your research paper, and as you learn how to perform efficiently each of the steps in the research process. Just as you form certain writing habits over time, so too you form certain research habits with practice. But in your first few research paper assignments you will probably feel more comfortable following certain precise steps. The purpose of this chapter is to introduce those stages you must work through in *planning* your research paper — for careful planning, as you have seen throughout this text, establishes an essential foundation for any writing project. Chapter 14 takes up the stages involved in *writing* the research paper. Throughout both chapters you will follow Ken, a student writer, as he moves through the various procedures in planning, drafting, and revising his research paper about the implications of the advertising campaigns conducted by the American Telephone and Telegraph Company over the past half century. Ken's final paper is presented at the end of Chapter 14; it is fully annotated so that you can see at first hand how he made important decisions about the content of his paper and how he worked those decisions into the format of the paper.

The planning stages that will be discussed in this chapter are listed below. Each is treated in detail in the following pages.

1. Understanding the assignment

2. Making a schedule

3. Selecting a subject

4. Finding sources

5. Evaluating sources

6. Taking notes

7. Filling gaps

Understanding the Assignment

As you begin your research paper, you will no doubt have many questions about the exact requirements of the assignment. Some of these questions (such as the preferred length of the paper or the style of documentation) can be answered immediately. In fact, your instructor will usually provide such information on the assignment sheet. Other questions (such as how to locate and evaluate particular sources) can only be answered once you have started planning and writing your paper. But before you begin working, you need to determine the kind of research paper you are expected to produce.

There are two basic kinds of research paper. In one you are expected to compile a *survey;* in the other you are expected to construct an *argument.*

The Survey

The survey is a factual report that reviews what other researchers have already written about a specific subject. When you select a subject for a survey, you need to focus on an issue or problem that has provoked extensive commentary (or controversy), such as the causes of acid rain, the effects of gun control, or the merits of educational reform. You must imagine your readers as curious about your subject but uncommitted, at least in theory, to any particular position. They expect you to review all sides of the subject objectively and to document your sources accurately so that they can read more information on your subject. Your general purpose in a survey is not to present your own argument about a subject but to select and summarize the major arguments that have already been written.

The Argument

The argument presents an original analysis of a subject that has already been researched by others. Your subject for such an argument cannot be completely original, of course, because you are creating the argument by interpreting the sources you have uncovered in your research. But your perspective on your subject and your method of organizing and analyzing your sources will be your own. You must imagine your readers as curious and uncommitted but ready to be convinced of the accuracy of your analysis. They will expect you to acknowledge opinions that do not support your own, but they also expect you to present your analysis forcefully and to cite the proper authorities to support your thesis. Your general purpose, then, is not to compile a neutral survey of what others have written about a particular subject but to make your own contribution to the growing body of research that your subject has generated.

In longer research projects, such as a thesis or dissertation, these two kinds of research paper are often combined. Writers will use their first chapter or so to "survey the literature" that has already been written about their subject, and then they use the remaining chapters to argue the case for their own conclusions. Such a format assures an audience that all previous interpretations of a subject have been considered carefully and fairly before a writer sets out to demonstrate his or her own interpretation.

In the research papers you write for most writing classes, however, you will not have the time or the space to compile a complete survey of the literature *and* to construct a convincing, original argument. Therefore, some writing teachers suggest that you study the controversy provoked by your subject by surveying what other writers have written about it. But most writing teachers prefer that you use the material you have read to become an informed writer — a writer who uses sources to argue your own thesis. For that reason, these two chapters will focus on the skills you will need to complete that assignment. But, as in every writing assignment, you should not make any assumptions. If your instructor does not tell you what kind of research paper is expected, ask for clarification by discussing the alternatives available.

Making a Schedule

As you plan and write your research paper you will learn to appreciate the importance of managing your time effectively. Your writing assignment will specify when your paper is due and may even provide a timetable that requires you to submit your work in stages so that both you and your instructor can keep track of your progress. If your instructor's assignment does not provide a timetable, your first task should be to make one of your own. Start with the deadline and then, working backward through the process, assign a specific amount of time to each stage. Be as cautious as possible by allowing yourself plenty of time to complete each stage. Be as conscientious as possible by working in the library for a certain number of hours each week. And be as pragmatic as possible by producing some kind of written material (journal entries, note cards, drafts) at the end of each stage. Post the schedule in a prominent place in your room or notebook and consult it often. A typical schedule for a research paper might look like this:

Time	Activity	Written product
Week 1	Study assignment. Make out schedule. Use journal to assess subject, audience, and purpose. Pick general subject. Read background material.	Schedule; journal entries; general subject; notes on background reading
Week 2	Select a specific subject. Formulate several hypotheses. Begin compiling bibliography of possible sources.	Specific subject; several hypotheses; source cards
Week 3	Locate and evaluate possible sources. Begin reading and taking notes.	Note cards
Week 4	Restrict subject. Analyze most valuable sources. Identify gaps in research.	Restricted subject note cards; new source cards
Week 5	Locate and read additional sources. Take notes.	New note cards
Week 6	Select hypothesis. Develop outline.	Hypothesis; outline
Week 7	Write first draft. Prepare revision agenda for next draft. New outline.	First draft; revision agenda; new outline

| Week 8 | Write final draft. Check quotations. Complete documentations. Compile bibliography. Type and proofread final manuscript. | Completed assignment |

Even if you start the day you receive your assignment and follow a schedule like the one above, you will soon discover that you will have to adjust your timetable. A good rule of thumb is to anticipate some difficulty with your project by adding two weeks to your schedule for work on some activity you cannot complete in the time allotted. You may need this extra time for situations like the following:

1. *Some things take more time than you planned.* Because the article you must read by Friday has to be ordered through interlibrary loan, you will have to wait for two weeks.

2. *Some procedures don't work exactly the way they are supposed to.* Because only a few of the items on your list of possible sources deal directly with your subject, you will have to look for new sources.

3. *Many of the deadlines on your schedule will have to be adjusted, making it more difficult to meet the next deadline.* Because you had difficulty completing the final draft of your manuscript, it can no longer be typed in time: the typist you hired two months ago has contracted for other work or has suddenly become ill.

The research paper is often called the term paper because it represents a significant investment of time. Writers who start early, map out a reasonable timetable, make allowances for setbacks, and practice efficient procedures can produce a successful research paper on time. But those who leave everything to the last minute will discover too late that they cannot throw together a satisfactory research paper in a few days. You need to live with your research project over a period of several weeks so that you can read and assimilate the most important sources and then use those sources effectively to plan, draft, and revise your paper. A good schedule provides you with a written reminder of your overall goal in writing the research paper and encourages you to work at a steady pace throughout the term, committing your work to writing as soon as you begin to discover your purpose.

Selecting a Subject

Selecting the appropriate subject for a research paper is like staking a prospector's claim. You may suspect that the claim will produce gold, but you will not know for sure until you begin digging. For that reason, some instructors prefer that you select your subject from a list they have prepared and pretested to meet certain requirements. If your instructor prefers that you select your own subject, you need some rules of thumb so that you can assess the potential of subjects that attract you. Some of the following rules of thumb are similar to the more general Guidelines for Selecting a Subject discussed in Chapter 1, but they have been reformulated here to focus on the special conditions of the research paper.

1. *Select a subject you can research.* This seems like an obvious requirement, but many of the subjects you may consider cannot be researched because

   a. *They are too autobiographical.* A research paper that draws primarily on your personal experience does not require you to search for information in other sources.

   b. *They are too subjective.* No amount of research will resolve a question of personal taste, such as "Which is the better poet — Yeats or Eliot?"

   c. *They are too restricted.* A mechanical process that can be explained by one source does not require any additional research.

   d. *They are too current.* Events or problems that produce today's headlines may not have been studied in sufficient detail to enable you to find enough information for your research.

   e. *They are too specialized.* Subjects that require an examination of certain documents cannot be researched if your library does not own (or have access to) that special collection.

2. *Select a subject you can restrict.* Before you begin researching your subject, you may be concerned that you will not be able to find enough information. Once you are involved in the research process, however, you are likely to discover that you have unearthed too much information. Every source you read seems to reveal a new feature of your subject, expanding it to the point that you feel overwhelmed. At this point, you must control your project and reduce it to manageable size. Two criteria should help you decide how to restrict your subject:

a. *Be reasonable about the amount of time you have for planning your research paper.* Whether you select a subject that you already know something about or one that is new to you, you must be realistic about how much you can learn during the weeks you have scheduled for planning. If you select a subject such as heart disease, for example, you will scarcely have enough time to compile a list of all the sources in the card catalog, let alone enough time to read, analyze, and understand them. You would do better to restrict your subject to *one* of the suspected causes of heart disease, such as high blood pressure or heavy smoking. Even these subjects could be restricted further to focus on the methods used to control high blood pressure or eliminate heavy smoking.

b. *Be realistic about the amount of space you have in which to develop your research paper.* If your writing assignment suggests a particular page length, then you must be realistic about how much you can say about any subject in that restricted space. If you selected a subject such as word processors, for example, you would barely be able to list all your sources in ten pages, let alone use any of that information to develop your own argument about the subject. You would do better to restrict your subject to how the word processor is changing the way American businesses correspond with their customers, or, perhaps better, how the word processor will change the way students complete their assignments.

3. *Select a subject you can live with.* Writing a research paper requires that you work on your subject for a considerable amount of time. If your subject does not fascinate you, if you finally do not care about the questions it poses or the answers you can provide, then you will soon become bored with the whole project. Boredom is a serious problem for a researcher because it leads to careless planning and uninspired writing. To avoid such difficulties, be sure your subject is varied enough to sustain your interest and significant enough to justify your time.

4. *Select a subject that will appeal to your readers.* Although the immediate audience for your research paper is the instructor who gave you the assignment, you must imagine at least two other audiences for your paper. One audience is that group of researchers you have come to know as you have investigated your subject. In a sense you are carrying on an extended conversation with these writers about a new direc-

tion you have discovered in a subject they have already studied. The other audience is a group of intelligent readers who are always interested in examining new information or new approaches to old information. You are asking this group of readers to pay attention to a new thesis you intend to prove. Formulating your subject to appeal to both these audiences will require you to strike a delicate balance. Your subject should be sufficiently substantial so that previous researchers will not consider it trendy, and sufficiently innovative so that intelligent readers will not consider it time-worn.

5. *Select a subject you can prove something about.* If the point of your research paper is to use your sources to argue a thesis, then you must select a subject that will allow you to accomplish that objective. Your research paper is, after all, the product of *your* research. It is not a scrapbook of the research conducted by other people. It is your paper not only because it carries your name on the title page but also because it presents your own argument, an argument you have discovered during your research and that you now wish to demonstrate to your readers. For that reason, you should select a topic that is focused enough so that you can arrange and control your information to support your argument, and complex enough so that you can develop and sustain your argument throughout your paper.

Discussion Problem

One effective way to begin thinking about your research paper is to use your journal to explore what you already know about certain general subjects and to examine how you might restrict them. Ken, an engineering major, follows this procedure as he thinks through his choice of subjects and hypotheses. Read his journal entry and then discuss how he has applied the requirements discussed above.

I got the research assignment today. Need to think about possible topics. Should do something on radio — that's a subject I know inside and out. Wrote a short paper on it last term. But I might get bored. Reading the same material, trying to find a new angle. I do want to write something about technology. Most people think technology is a dull subject, but it is really fascinating. Maybe the telephone. A simple little system that everybody uses. Used to work at the phone company in the summer, so I have some idea how complex that "simple little system" really is — all those wires, cables, and switching systems under the streets. That's the problem. The topic is so big. How can I possibly cover it in ten pages?

What interests *me* about the phone? Problem! If given a free hand, I would probably write about the telephone from the perspective of an engineer — electrical equipment, switching systems, maybe the microchip. But that's really getting too technical. My readers don't care how their calls get from point A to point B. What do they care about? Phone bills! Maybe I should focus on the phone *company* rather than phone *technology*. What could I do with that — "how to cut costs of phone bills"? Sounds too much like a magazine article. "How phone bills are figured"? Sounds too dull. Besides, I am not sure I could find any information on the subject.

What else is there except making calls and paying bills? How does the company touch people? "Reach out, reach out and touch someone." Advertising. Of course! AT&T touches more people, more frequently, more colorfully through advertising than any other method. You see ads on TV and in all the magazines. *Telephone advertising.* I like it. Still too big. Good place to begin.

Finding Sources

Once you have selected your subject and considered several hypotheses about it, you must begin the formal process of researching it in the library. You may feel at home in the comfortable surroundings of a library as you browse through newspapers or check the new books shelf. But when you have to conduct research in a library you are more likely to feel intimidated or overwhelmed, like a visitor to a large city. Most libraries, like most cities, try to help visitors by providing organized tours, publishing maps and directories, and hiring special guides (librarians) to work at specific locations throughout the building. Because no two libraries are organized exactly alike, even the most experienced researchers depend on this kind of assistance to help them learn how to work in a new facility. Experienced researchers, like seasoned travelers, know that the best way to find your way around a strange place is to ask advice from someone who lives there. Thus, as you try to find your sources, you will save yourself considerable trouble and frustration if you realize at the outset that your best allies are librarians. No matter how difficult or seemingly ridiculous your question, they have probably heard it (or one like it) before. And even if they cannot answer your question, they can show you where and how to look for your answer. Indeed, they can direct you to many more sources than the few representative samples noted in this chapter. Librarians will help you formulate a *search strategy* — a systematic, logical procedure for finding information on any subject.[1] The following diagram shows you the terrain and the routes entailed in a search strategy.

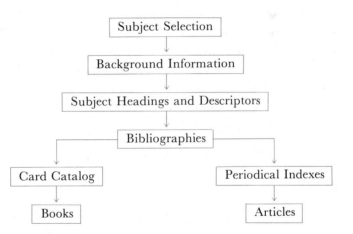

Search Strategy

You have already considered how to select a subject for research. Now you need to learn how to use each of the major sources of information to find resources for researching your subject.

Background Information

Your first step is to read several overviews of your subject so that you can learn something about its history, major ideas, and principal figures.

---

1. Some of the information on finding sources has been adapted from a series of excellent study guides prepared by the Office of Library Instruction, Bracken Library, Ball State University.

Such background information can be found in the general and specialized encyclopedias located in the reference collection of the library.

General Encyclopedias   These are written for a general audience and cover a wide variety of subjects. The entries are not technical or scholarly, but they often conclude with a brief list of sources that treat the subject in more depth. You can find the entry on your subject by pulling down the volume identified by the initial letter of your topic. Or you can consult the index, usually the last volume in the set, to help you locate all the pertinent references to your subject. This second method is, in many ways, more efficient because it enables you to see how your subject is subdivided and cross-referenced. By reading these additional entries you may gain a perspective that will help you restrict or revise your subject in a way that you had not considered. Several standard encyclopedias are

Collier's Encyclopedia

The New Columbia Encyclopedia

Encyclopedia Americana

The New Encyclopaedia Britannica

World Book

Specialized Encyclopedias   These, usually devoted to one or two disciplines or broad subject areas, provide a narrower, more detailed coverage of particular subjects within those disciplines. The information tends to be more technical than that in a general encyclopedia, and longer lists of sources are often included. Because specialized encyclopedias are available on a wide range of academic and popular subjects, you will need to locate them by looking in the card catalog under your subject heading and then finding the subheading "Dictionaries." For example, the *Encyclopedia of Philosophy* is listed under the subject heading "Philosophy — Dictionaries." The brief sampling of specialized encyclopedias listed below will give you some idea of the range of reference material available.

The International Encyclopedia of Higher Education

McGraw-Hill Encyclopedia of Science and Technology

The Physical Fitness Encyclopedia

Rock on: The Illustrated Encyclopedia of Rock 'n Roll

Biographical Sources These give brief accounts of notable figures, listing such information as family history, educational background, major accomplishments, and significant publications. Although the accounts are brief, they often include a short list of additional sources. If your background reading on a particular subject suggests that one or two people have played significant roles in its development, then you should look up these figures in several of the following kinds of biographical sources.

Biography Index. Directs you to biographical material on well-known people from our time or from earlier periods in history.

Dictionary of American Biography. Contains biographies of notable Americans who are deceased.

Dictionary of National Biography. Similar to DAB in that it contains biographies of notable people who lived in the British Isles (or various colonies) but who are now deceased.

Who's Who. Offers brief biographies of notable living people. The three major collections are *Who's Who in America*, *Who's Who* (primarily British), and *The International Who's Who*. The first two have companion volumes for the deceased: *Who Was Who* and *Who Was Who in America*. And the series also includes specialized *Who's Whos* that focus on people in particular professions, ethnic groups, or religious groups.

Discussion Problem

Ken uses his journal to take some preliminary notes on the background information he discovered in several general and specialized encyclopedias. As you read through his notes, discuss how his background reading is helping him shape his subject. What information seems to expand or enrich his original subject? What information seems to complicate and confuse his original subject? What information seems difficult to find? Can you identify any information in his notes that might lead to sources that might deal more directly with his subject?

Over twenty-five separate headings on "Telephone and telecommunications" in *Britannica*. About as many on "Advertising." No headings that deal with both, except selling over the phone. Two separate tracks. Need to find a way to make them connect. Surely somebody talks about advertising the telephone. Stay with telephone for now. Two major entries: (1) history of the company — Bell's invention, Edison's innovations, growth of system; (2) developments in the equipment — electromagnetic switching systems, satellite communications, video telephone. Entries in all general encyclopedias seem to start with Bell as a teacher of the deaf (*Who Was Who in America* says he was professor of vocal physiology at Boston University). Invented telephone (1876) as part of electrical experiments to help students. One of his students became his wife. First message transmitted over two-wire contraption was to his lab assistant — Watson (naturally). Call for help: "Mr. Watson, come here. I need you." All inventions seem to start with these little "once upon a time" Mr. Wizard stories: Franklin, Whitney, Ford, Wright Brothers. Bell invented all kinds of other things that nobody remembers him for. 18 patents.

Once phone is invented, trouble begins. Bell tries to obtain patent. Challenged by competitors. Most complex patent litigation in American history: over 600 challenges. Eventually Bell wins. Bell system becomes world's largest monopoly, AT&T. Now the courts are breaking that up. Could devote my whole paper to all these incredible stories of buying and selling competitors and stock options. But I'm not *Fortune* magazine, and my readers won't put up with that stuff. I'd rather focus on how company sells itself to others.

After the Mr. Wizard to Ma Bell story, most encyclopedias deal with all the equipment. The *McGraw-Hill Encyclopedia of Science and Technology* defines almost thirty different devices that make the system work from *dials* to *ringers*. Each device is a complete process, with its own history — telephone lines, telephone cables, microwave, satellites. Telephone becomes Telecommunications. Impact of all this technology on ordinary people? What was it like before the phone — quiet, unconnected, isolated? How did you get messages to people? How long did you have to wait for a reply? Telephone connects people, speeds up communication (business). McLuhan's "Global Village." Maybe he has some stuff on telephones — or advertising.

Subject Headings (or Descriptors)

Once you have done some background reading, you will discover that there are many ways to classify, subdivide, and cross-reference your topic. The cluster of categories you encounter should tell you three things: (1) you must restrict your general subject (in Ken's case, telephones) to the specific subject you want to write about (telephone advertising); (2) you may find that your specific subject listed under several headings (telephone advertising, AT&T advertising; television commercials); and (3) you may have to consult material that does not deal directly with your subject in order to discover a perspective that will help you organize your information (business history, social history, communications theory).

The best way to discover subject headings related to your subject is to consult the reference book entitled *Library of Congress Subject Headings.* This guide, usually located near the card catalog, will enable you to see how your subject is classified and cross-referenced in the card catalog. Sometimes you will have to use some ingenuity to determine how your subject might be listed. For example, if you try to look up *Equal Rights Amendment* under *E* you will not find anything. But if you look under "Women's Rights — United States or United States Constitution," you will find a wealth of material. Other times you will have to use your ingenuity to determine which of the many subheadings you locate provide the most promising leads. For example, when Ken looked up *telephone* he discovered two pages (three columns per page) of subject headings. Although there was no heading entitled "Telephone advertising," there were headings on "Social history" and "Communications theory" that looked promising. Similarly, although the word *advertising* did not produce a specific reference to "Telephone advertising," it did provide headings such as "Media" and "Market research" that might lead to sources that involved information on the telephone.

Throughout your research you will be revising your descriptors. You will eliminate some because they fail to turn up sources that focus on your subject. You will add others because they lead to sources that give you new ideas and insights about your subject. You may strike out in a completely new direction once you cannot find the information you want, discover that the information you find is more complicated or less interesting than you had anticipated, or read something that suggests another way to define or analyze your subject. For example, Ken's list of initial descriptors *(telephone* and *advertising)* is beginning to look like an accordion, expanding to include such subjects as social history and communication theory and contracting to eliminate such subjects as telephone selling and telephone soliciting. Although such revisions might suggest that his subject is getting out of control, Ken is actually developing several hypotheses about the historical impact of inventions that will enable him to organize his subject once he begins drafting.

Bibliographies

When you have compiled a preliminary list of descriptors, you are ready to begin building your bibliography. A bibliography is a list of books and articles on a particular subject. There are two kinds of bibliographies: *a working bibliography,* a list of books and articles you intend to consult as you research your subject; and *a final bibliography,* a typewritten list of the sources you used to write your paper, included at the end of your finished paper.

At this point you will need to build a working bibliography. A good way to begin is to consult a reference guide to reference books, such as The American Library Association's *Guide to Reference Books* (and supplement), compiled by Eugene P. Sheehan. (Ninth edition published 1976, supplement 1980.) Another way to get titles for your bibliography is to determine whether someone else has already published a specialized bibliography on your subject. Specialized bibliographies not only save you a great deal of time but also guarantee that you have consulted the most significant books and articles written about your subject. Another advantage is that some specialized bibliographies are *annotated,* which means that they contain a brief description (and perhaps an evaluation) of each book or article listed. One disadvantage of specialized bibliographies is that they may be dated. If a bibliography was published in 1950, for example, you will have to locate information that has been published since that time.

There are three ways to locate specialized bibliographies:

1. You can check the *Bibliographic Index,* a reference work that lists articles, parts of books, and pamphlets devoted in whole or in part to bibliographies.

2. You can check the card catalog by searching under your topic (and various descriptors) for the subheading " — Bibliography." For example:

   Advertising — BIBLIOGRAPHY

   Communication — BIBLIOGRAPHY

   Technology — BIBLIOGRAPHY

3. You can check the notations on the catalog cards under your subject heading for books that contain bibliographies. For example:

Bibliography note —————

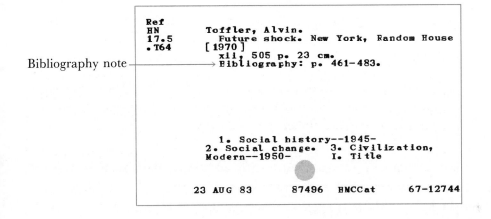

```
Ref
HN          Toffler, Alvin.
17.5           Future shock. New York, Random House
.T64        [ 1970 ]
               xii, 505 p. 23 cm.
            Bibliography: p. 461-483.




            1. Social history--1945-
            2. Social change.  3. Civilization,
            Modern--1950-      I. Title


    23 AUG 83        87496      HMCCat       67-12744
```

Card Catalog

After locating a specialized bibliography or determining that none is available, you are ready to begin constructing your own bibliography with the two major tools in the library — *the card catalog* and *the periodical indexes.* The card catalog lists books and other materials available in your library in three ways: (1) by author, (2) by title, and (3) by various subject headings.

If you know the author of a book about your subject, or suspect that a certain author might have written about the subject, locate in the card catalog the author (or main) card. This card will give you not only the title but also a good deal of other useful information. The information given on the author card is categorized below.

Author card

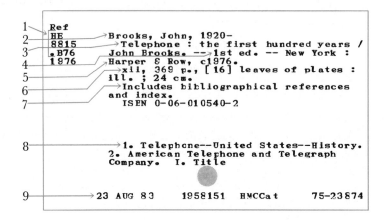

1. The *call number* (and location symbol if applicable). The total combination of letters and numbers in the order they appear on the card comprises the call number and indicates the book's precise location on the shelf.

2. *The author.* Last name first with additional data such as titles of nobility and birth and death dates.

3. The *title.* As it appears on the title page of the book.

4. *Edition statement.* Appears particularly if work is in at least a second edition.

5. *The imprint.* Included here are the place of publication, the publisher, and the date of publication.

6. *Number of pages, size of book,* and *maps, charts,* or *illustrations.* The first number (xii), in small Roman numerals, indicates the number of pages of front matter: preface, introduction, table of contents, etc.

7. *Special features.* Indicates if there are a bibliography, appendixes, and index.

8. *Tracings.* Lists subject headings under which the book is cataloged. Tracings are most useful for locating other subject areas that might have information related to your subject.

9. *Codes* pertaining to computer cataloging. They are *not* pertinent for locating the book.

If you know the title of the book but have forgotten the author, of if you suspect that one of your descriptors might be included in a book title, locate the title card.

Title card

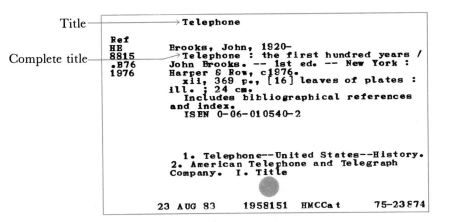

If you know only your subject or several related subject areas (as will often be the case, especially if you haven't found a specialized bibliography of your subject), locate the subject cards.

Subject card 1

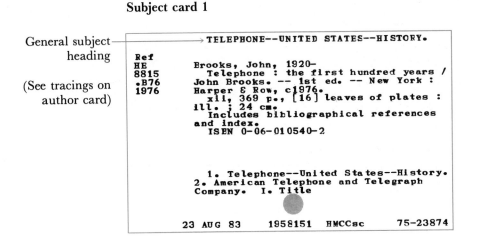

Subject card 2

More specific
subject heading

(See tracings on
author card)

```
                →AMERICAN TELEPHONE AND TELEGRAPH
                   COMPANY.
   Ref
   HE
   8815         Brooks, John, 1920-
   .B76           Telephone : the first hundred years /
   1976          John Brooks. -- 1st ed. -- New York :
                 Harper & Row, c1976.
                   xii, 369 p., [16] leaves of plates :
                 ill. ; 24 cm.
                   Includes bibliographical references
                 and index.
                   ISBN 0-06-010540-2



                   1. Telephone--United States--History.
                 2. American Telephone and Telegraph
                 Company. I. Title


       23 AUG 83      1958151    HMCCsc        75-23874
```

After you have located a book in the card catalog, your next job is to locate it on the shelf. Most libraries are now organized by the Library of Congress system, although some libraries still retain the Dewey Decimal system or are in the process of converting to the Library of Congress system and so have part of their collection classified by one system and part by the other.

Library of Congress   In the Library of Congress system, materials are arranged by the letters of the alphabet to represent various subject areas.

A	General Works	L	Education
B	Philosophy, Psychology, Religion	M	Music
		N	Fine Arts
C–D	History and Topography (except America)	P	Language and Literature
		Q	Science
E–F	America	R	Medicine
G	Geography, Anthropology, Sports and Games	S	Agriculture, Forestry
		T	Engineering and Technology
H	Social Sciences	U	Military Science
J	Political Science	V	Naval Science
K	Law	Z	Bibliography and Library Science

Dewey Decimal   In the Dewey Decimal system, materials are arranged by numbers representing subject areas.

000–009	General works	600–699	Technology (applied sciences)
100–199	Philosophy and related disciplines	700–799	The arts. Fine and decorative arts
200–299	Religion	800–899	Literature (belles-lettres)
300–399	Social sciences	900–999	General geography and history and their auxiliaries
400–499	Language		
500–599	Pure sciences		

The chief advantage of knowing the classification system in your library is that it helps you find a specific book. But because books are shelved by subject, you may discover other interesting books in the area where your book is located. Once you have found *the* book you are searching for, spend some time browsing on the shelves looking for intriguing titles that you didn't know about or failed to notice in the card catalog but that may relate to your subject. Ken, for example, began browsing on the specific shelf where he had located John Brooks's *Telephone: The First Hundred Years* and found a series of little volumes bound in gray cardboard. These little volumes turned out to be a nearly complete collection of AT&T's annual reports. Similarly, when he was browsing in the general area designated as Engineering and Technology (T), he found a book he had overlooked in the card catalog, *The Telephone: A Historical Anthology,* part of a series, "Historical Studies in Telecommunications," published in cooperation with the Smithsonian Institution.

Periodical Indexes

Periodicals (magazines and journals) exist on almost every conceivable subject. They are a valuable source for your research because they provide you with current information, often on a specific aspect of your subject, and reveal (through their back issues) the way your subject has been treated in different historical periods. There are two major types of periodical indexes, *general* and *subject.*

General Index   The general indexes list articles from hundreds of magazines, most of which are nontechnical and nonscholarly. Individual articles are classified by author and by subject, and most general subjects are further subdivided by other subject headings. The most useful general index is *Readers' Guide to Periodical Literature,* which is issued monthly and bound into cumulative volumes annually.

Selected Subject Indexes   Subject indexes list articles on specific subjects. The articles tend to be more detailed and more scholarly than the more popular articles listed in the *Readers' Guide.* For that reason, you should supplement your search for periodical literature by checking several subject indexes that include specialized investigations of your subject. Here is a brief sampling of the subject indexes available.

Art Index

Humanities Index

Social Sciences Index

Business Periodicals Index

Education Index

Music Index

Most periodical indexes are located in the reference area of your library. When you have selected the best indexes for your subject, use your descriptors to find major subject headings and then check any subheadings or cross-references for additional information.

The following excerpt is from the *Readers' Guide.* The actual list of articles on the telephone for this particular year (March 1978–February 1979) was over two pages long. Notice that the general subject heading ("Telephone") is expanded to include other subject headings — "Apparatus and supplies," "Installation," "Rates." Notice also that there are cross-references to other categories ("*See also* Telephone apparatus industry") and cross-references to other general categories ("*See* Wiretapping").

When you look at a specific entry you see that it contains (1) the title of the article; (2) the name of the author; (3) the abbreviated title of the periodical; (4) the volume number of the periodical; (5) page references for the article; and (6) date of publication of the article:

1
Faster than a speeding electron beam; picture-phone.

2   **3**   **4 5**   **6**
L. Mandel.   Car & Dr   23:20   F '78

Reader's Guide entry

1. General heading

2. Subject headings

3. Cross references

TELEPHONE
Automating office communications: the policy dilemmas. M. A. Sirbu, Jr. bibl il Tech R 81:50-7 O '78
Electronic telephone. P. P. Luff. il Sci Am 238: 58-64 bibl (p 154) Mr '78
Hold the line: even more startling telephonic tricks are on the way. M. Grosswirth. Sci Digest 85:47-8+ Ja '79
New phone age. N. Potter. il N Y 11:64-6 D 18 '78
Now there's a telephone to suit every taste. E. R. Mark. il Good H 188:174-5 Ja '79

Answering service
How to start an answering service. F. Weinstein. il Work Wom 3:20-1 F '78

Apparatus and supplies
Before you buy your own phone. Changing T 32:21-2 N '78
Fear of phones? Junk calls go automatic. Consumer Rep 43:66 F '78
Instant tracing system shows you who's calling. S. Walton. il Pop Mech 150:16 Ag '78
New all-in-one speaker-phone. H. R. Camenzind. il Radio-Electr 49:37-40 N '78
Pen registers: the appropriate technology approach to bugging. D. Shapley. Science 199: 749-51 F 17 '78
Plugging into Bell. L. Wessner. il Pop Sci 214: 72-5+ Ja '79
Pros and cons of owning a phone. S. Weiss. McCalls 105:47 Mr '78
Protect your home—build autodialer and cassette interface. J. H. Gilder. il Radio-Electr 49:41-3 My '78
Remote telephone ear—listen via long distance. J. H. Gilder. il Radio-Electr 49:67-8 D '78
Should you buy your own phones? B. Price. il Fam Handy 29:42-3+ Ja '79
Superphone: new ways to make your phone do more, better. D. Sagarin. il Pop Mech 149: 116-17+ Ap '78
Telephone answering machines: how to buy one and get your callers to talk to it. Glamour 76:53 Ap '78
Where the action is. D. Sutton. il Peter Phot Mag 7:24 Ag '78
See also
Telephone apparatus industry

Installation
Planning for new phone service. Bet Hom & Gard 56:205 Ap '78

Rates
Pros and cons of owning a phone. S. Weiss. McCalls 105:47 Mr '78
What this country needs is a free phone call. E. Garfield. Bull Atom Sci 34:56-9 F '78
Wisconsin students tackle Ma Bell's sales methods. Consumer Rep 43:372-3 Jl '78

Recorded announcements
Dial on, America! M. E. Marty. Chr Cent 95: 967 O 11 '78

Switching systems
See Telephone switching systems, Electronic

Television combination
Faster than a speeding electron beam; picturephone. L. Mandel. Car & Dr 23:20 F '78

Wiretapping
See Wiretapping

1

2
2

3
2
2

2

2
3
2

2
3

All the information in the entry shown at the bottom of page 466 is necessary for locating the periodical and will be used in your final bibliography. Copy the author, title of the article, periodical title, volume, pages, and the complete date onto your source card (see "Taking Notes," pages 474–481). You may also want to copy the title and volume of the index in case you need to recheck the information at some later time. The abbreviations used in the entries are spelled out in the *front* of most periodical indexes. Sometimes reading through this list of abbreviations can produce valuable information. For example, as Ken started to glance through the list of abbreviations in *Readers' Guide*, he noticed several journals devoted exclusively to the telephone: *Bell Journal of Economics, Bell Laboratories Record, Bell Telephone Magazine,* and *Bell Telephone Quarterly.*

Newspapers, Documents, Microforms, and Computer Search

In addition to the general and subject indexes, four other tools will be helpful to you in your search for information on your subject.

Newspapers Most major newspapers, such as *The New York Times, The Times* (London), and *The Washington Post,* publish their own indexes. Newspapers give day-to-day accounts of historical events and provide details often omitted in later, more general discussions. Consulting them will help you identify important factual information about your subject and enable you to trace its historical development. For example, Ken used the *Index to the Wall Street Journal* to locate information on the size of AT&T's advertising budgets in different historical periods.

Government Publications The United States Government publishes an enormous amount of information on a wide variety of subjects. These publications are housed in a separate area of the library and cataloged according to a separate classification system. There are indexes to this information — such as *American Statistics Index* and the *Monthly Catalog of United States Government Publications* — but to use the collection effectively you will need the help from the government documents librarian. (If your library does not have a documents librarian, one member of the reference staff is probably knowledgeable about the library's documents collection.) Although Ken did not consult any government materials in his research, he discovered that a number of the social historians he read depended on the statistics published by the Bureau of the Census to chart social change. For example, the 1920 census revealed that for the first time more Americans lived in urban than in rural areas, although "urban" was defined as a population center of 2,500 people. Such statistical information made Ken wonder whether AT&T had begun to direct its advertising to those who lived in cities during this period.

Microforms Most libraries have difficulty finding space for all the documents they wish to keep in their collection. For that reason, many periodicals and other materials are photographically reduced in size and stored on either *microfilm* (reels of film) or *microfiche* (sheets of film). With the aid of mechanical viewers, you can enlarge and read these documents quite easily. You can even make photocopies of the enlarged images. Librarians can advise you about which books and periodicals are stored in microform and can help you learn to operate the microreaders.

Computer Search An increasing number of libraries make use of the computer to store and access information. The Library of Congress in Washington, D.C., for example, is entering its entire card catalog into a computer. Instead of flipping through cards, users must now search for sources by learning how to operate one of the many computer terminals placed throughout the building.

Many fields of knowledge are storing their research in data bases that can be accessed through a computer. Medical information, government statistics, stock-market figures, law cases, and abstracts of educational articles, studies, and bibliographies are among the types of material that a computer can search quickly, thoroughly, and accurately. The results can be printed out while you wait, in some cases, or, if you need extensive material, can be supplied in a few days.

If your library offers such a computer search, you should inquire about the possibility of using it (you should also inquire how much it costs). Normally, you consult with a librarian about your subject and the descriptors you are using to conduct your research. If your subject proves suitable for a computer search, the librarian will use your descriptors (as well as a few others) to search data bases for books, articles, and other documents. Some computer searches cost as little as ten dollars; others cost a good deal more. Your librarian can advise you whether, given your subject, you should invest in the service.

Evaluating Sources

Once you have compiled a working bibliography of books and articles that might pertain to your subject, you must decide which items will prove most useful to your project. The best way to make that decision, of course, is to read each source carefully. But you will soon discover that you do not have time to read every source you uncover. If Ken attempts to read every source that he finds on *telephones* and *advertising,* he will never complete his reading in time to write his paper. And if he decides to read all the books and articles he can find on *technology, communication,* and *social history,* he will spend his lifetime trying to keep up with his growing reading list. What all researchers need is a set of guidelines and short cuts to help them make intelligent guesses about the potential value of the sources they uncover. Following such guidelines will help you eliminate some sources immediately, discard others after you have read enough to determine that they do not focus on your subject, and concentrate on those sources (or parts of sources) that will make the most significant contribution to your subject.

Guidelines for Evaluating Sources

1. *The source should be relevant.*

   This seems like an obvious requirement, but the relevance of a particular source is not always apparent. First, you may not have a clear perspective on your subject as you begin your research, therefore every source may seem potentially relevant. Second, the titles of some articles and books can be misleading or vague: some titles that seem to deal directly with your subject may actually deal with a completely unrelated subject, while other titles that seem to deal with general or theoretical ideas may deal in whole or in part with the precise focus of your subject. Third, your reading will occasionally change the status of some sources. What seemed irrelevant to yesterday's perspective of your subject may suddenly seem crucial to today's more informed definition of your purpose. The key to evaluation, of course, is restriction. The quicker you can limit your subject, the quicker you can decide whether a particular source is likely to be relevant.

2. *The source should be current.*

    Again, this requirement seems obvious, but it can be tricky. You want to be sure that the information in your sources is reliable and up to date. There is no point, for example, in reading an article published in 1945 on the latest cures for cancer. On the other hand, if you are analyzing the public's attitude toward cancer in different historical periods, then such an article might be extremely "current." Then, too, for many subjects there are acknowledged "classic" books or articles that have advanced major interpretations; you should read any classics that are truly relevant to your subject.

3. *The source should be comprehensive.*

    As you begin reading you will discover that some sources focus on an extremely narrow aspect of your subject and others attempt to examine its every feature plus those of several related subjects. Because your schedule demands that you set priorities about which sources you read first, you should always begin with the most comprehensive source, on the assumption that it will probably cover the information contained in the more specialized source in sufficient detail so that you may not have to read the second source.

4. *The source should direct you to other sources.*

    Checking the information on the catalog card will tell you whether a book contains a bibliography. Skimming an article will tell you whether it contains extensive notes. The most helpful notes include brief annotations about the importance of the sources cited. Books and articles that describe and evaluate other sources are valuable because they help you decide whether you want to read sources you have already found and they enable you to discover sources you have overlooked.

Additional Short Cuts for Evaluating Sources

Locate Annotated Bibliographies If you are lucky enough to find an annotated bibliography on your subject or if the notes in one of the articles you read contain extensive annotations, you can determine quickly whether the sources they describe are worth reading.

Read Book Reviews   If you want to determine whether a particular book is reliable, you can see how the book was reviewed when it was first published. Reference guides such as the *Book Review Digest* or the *New York Times Index* contain either summaries or references to book reviews that should help you evaluate both the book's content and critical reception.

Obtain the Advice of Experts   There are many people on your campus or in your community who are experts on certain subjects. A quick phone call or visit to these people can help you identify the "must-reads" or classic treatments of your subject. They can also direct you to annotated bibliographies and special indexes that will help your research. And, finally, they can refer you to sources that you would not find when following a normal search strategy. These sources, often written about other subjects, may provide you with ideas you can use to integrate your other sources or with methods of interpretation you can imitate to analyze your information.

Review the Table of Contents   To determine the way a book develops its major ideas, study the table of contents. The chapter titles and subheadings work like an outline, giving you a general sense of the author's understanding and organization of the subject.

Read the Introduction   To discover the particular focus of a source, read its introduction — the preface (and often the first chapter) of a book, the first few paragraphs of an article. In a few pages you can usually detect the author's thesis and decide whether the thesis is relevant to your subject and the source valuable to your research.

Browse Through the Index   The most useful part of a book is probably its index. An index works like a miniature card catalog, helping you see whether a source has any information on your subject, how it has classified and cross-referenced your subject, how much information it has devoted to each of the subject's various features, and precisely where that information is located.

Exercise

Following is a list of titles from Ken's working bibliography on telephone advertising. The best way to evaluate these sources, of course, is to locate them, check their indexes, skim their introductory material, and then assess their relevance to the subject. But, if you were Ken, what guesses would you make about the usefulness of the sources from the information provided below? Use the Guidelines for Evaluating a Source to rank these sources according to the order in which you would consult them. Be prepared to defend the reasons for your choices.

Field, Kate. *The History of Bell's Telephone.* London: Bradbury, Agnew, 1878.

Atwan, Robert, Donald McQuade, and John W. Wright. *Edsels, Luckies, and Frigidaires: Advertising the American Way.* New York: Dell Publishing Company, 1979.

MacKenzie, Catherine. *Alexander Graham Bell: The Man Who Contracted Space.* New York: Grosset and Dunlap, 1928.

Danielian, N. R. *A.T. & T.: The Story of Industrial Conquest.* New York: The Vanguard Press, 1939.

Mubon, Prescott C. *Mission Communication: The Story of Bell Laboratories.* Murry Hill, NJ: Bell Telephone Laboratories, 1975.

McLuhan, Marshall. *Understanding Media: The Extensions of Man.* New York: McGraw-Hill Company, 1964.

American Telephone and Telegraph Company. *The Yellow Pages as an Advertising Medium.* New York: American Telephone and Telegraph Company, 1963.

Federal Communications Commission. *Investigation of the Telephone Industry in the United States.* House Document No. 340, 76th Congress, 1st Session, 1939.

Clarke, Arthur C. "Communication in the Second Century of the Telephone." In *The Telephone's First Century — And Beyond.* Ed. Arthur C. Clarke, et al. New York: T. Y. Crowell, 1977.

Mumford, Lewis. *Technics and Civilization.* New York: Harcourt Brace and World, Inc., 1963.

Brooks, John. *The Telephone: The First Hundred Years.* New York: Harper and Row, 1976.

Weiner, Jerome. "Technology and the Telephone." In *The Telephone's First Century — And Beyond.* Ed. Arthur C. Clarke, et al. New York: T. Y. Crowell, 1977.

Taking Notes

After you have found your sources and selected those that you suspect will prove most useful, you must start taking notes.

Source Cards

The first step in the note-taking process is to fill out a 3″ × 5″ *source card* on every item you intend to read. This card will help you to keep track of each source from the beginning of your research (when you locate the source in the card catalog or periodical index) to the point at which you type up the results of your research (when you enter the source in your final bibliography).

Here are two sample source cards, the first for a book, the second for a periodical.

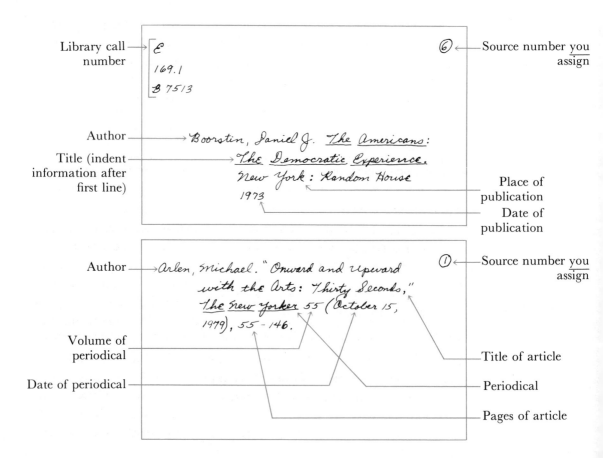

Two pieces of information on the source card help you during the research process. The call number at the left enables you to locate the book on the shelf; the source number on the right enables you to locate your source in your stack of source cards and to code the note cards you make as you read that source with the same number. The rest of the information on the source card not only helps you during the research process but also during the writing process. The information — author, title, place of publication, publisher, and date of publication — should be entered according to the format for books and articles required in the final bibliography. (See "Listing Sources" on pages 507–513.) Although you may not know at this point which of your sources will surface in your paper, you can save time later by filling out each source card properly as you begin your research. Then when you are ready to type your final bibliography, you can simply arrange the sources you have used in alphabetical order and type the information you have provided on the source card.

After you have filled out source cards on the material you plan to read, use the evaluation guidelines to establish some priorities: What sources seem most crucial to your subject? What sources will take the most time to read? What sources are likely to help you find other sources? Then sort through your cards and organize your reading to make the most efficient use of your time.

Note Cards

As you begin reading your sources you will need to start taking notes. Note taking is perhaps the most critical stage in the research process because it demands that you read, select, interpret, and evaluate the information that will form the substance of your paper. When you return the books and articles to the library, you will have to depend on your notes for information. If you have taken careless notes, you will be in trouble when you begin writing your paper. Many students inadvertently commit plagiarism (see "Quoting Sources," pages 494–500) because they work from inaccurate note cards. The wise procedure is to take your notes precisely from the beginning.

Most researchers prefer to use large cards (4" × 6" or 5" × 7") for note cards and small cards (3" × 5") for source cards. The two sizes make it easy to distinguish between the types of cards, and the large cards provide more space for writing down information. Just as your source cards may eventually become part of your final bibliography, so each of your note cards may eventually become one of the ideas you will document in the final text of your paper. For that reason, you need to make a separate note card for every piece of useful information you discover in each source. Identify the note card with the source card number, the author, and the page(s) where you found your information so that you have a complete record of the information on each card. By using separate cards for each note, you can shuffle your cards as you begin to look for ways to organize your paper. In fact, as you become familiar with your topic, you may wish to write specific subheadings on the top of each card to help you discover a preliminary pattern in your information.

To understand how to read, react, and write during the note-taking process, look at the following passage, reprinted from Marshall McLuhan, *Understanding Media: The Extensions of Man* (New York: McGraw-Hill Company, 1964), page 232, and then read the commentary that follows.

> Ads have proved to be a self-liquidating form of community entertainment. They came along just after the Victorian gospel of work, and they promised a Beulah land of perfectibility, where it would be possible to "iron shirts without hating your husband." And now they are deserting the individual consumer-product in favor of the all-inclusive and never-ending process that is the Image of any great corporate enterprise. The Container Corporation of America does not feature paper bags and paper cups in its ads, but the container *function*, by means of great art. The historians and archeologists will one day discover that the ads of our time are the richest and most faithful daily reflections that any society ever made of its entire range of activities.

Before you actually write down a note, you should read quickly through your source to determine if there is any information worth noting. If there is, then on a second, more careful reading you should employ one of the three methods for taking notes: quotation, summary, and paraphrase. No matter which method you use, you should leave room at the bottom of the card for your own comment. In this space consider how you might use the note or how it might connect to other note cards you have written.

Quotation Quoting an author's views word for word is the easiest way to record information from your source. But you should use this method selectively, choosing to quote only those passages that deal directly with your subject in particularly memorable language. When you write down a quotation on your note card, remind yourself that you are quoting by placing quotation marks at the beginning and end of the passage. If you decide to leave out part of the quote, use three ellipsis dots (. . .) to indicate that you have omitted words from the middle of a sentence or four ellipsis dots (. . . .) to indicate that you have omitted one or more sentences between the beginning and end of the passage. (See the discussion of ellipses on page 677 in the Handbook of Grammar and Usage.) Finally, be sure that you have quoted the passage accurately. Proofread your note against the original to confirm that every word and mark of punctuation is in its proper place.

Note card: Quotation

Subject heading	→ *Advertising as History* → ⑨
Source card number	*McLuhan* *p. 232*
Author	" *The historian and archeologists will one day discover that the ads of our time*
Page	*are the richest and most faithful*
Quotation marks	*daily reflections that any society has ever made of its entire range of activities.* "
Your comment	*Good introductory quote ?*

Summary Summarizing an author's views is an easy way to record the major direction and overall design of a text. You should use this method when the author's argument seems to state a thesis or analyze evidence in a way that anticipates or contradicts your emerging perception of your argument. You can summarize by outlining the principal points in an argument, by copying down key words, or by restating the essence of the argument in two or three phrases.

Note Card: Summary

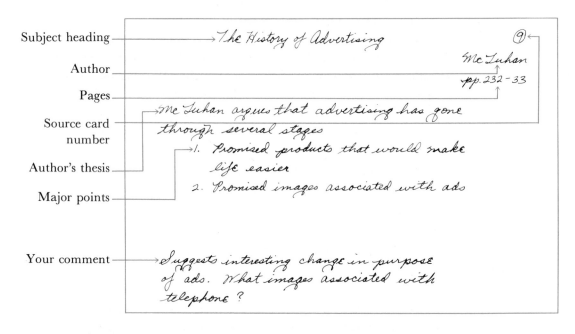

Subject heading → *The History of Advertising* ⑨

Author → *Mc Luhan*

Pages → *pp. 232 – 33*

Source card number

Author's thesis → *Mc Luhan argues that advertising has gone through several stages*

Major points →
1. Promised products that would make life easier
2. Promised images associated with ads

Your comment → *Suggests interesting change in purpose of ads. What images associated with telephone?*

Paraphrase Paraphrasing an author's views is the most useful and the most misused method of note taking. It is *not* simply a casual way of reproducing the author's views approximately word for word without using quotation marks. Rather, it is the process of thinking through what the author has said and then restating the information *in your own words*. To accomplish this objective you must understand what the author has said and then reformulate his or her opinion without adding or deleting significant information or without distorting the intent of the original passage. The paraphrase combines the advantages of quotation and summary because it allows you to reproduce the essence of the author's argument and adapt it to the flow of your own argument.

Note card: Paraphrase

Subject heading — → *Historical value of ads* → ⑨

Source card number → *Mc Luhan*

Author — → *p. 232*

Page —

Although McLuhan thinks that ads have changed their purpose over the years, he argues that future historians and archeologists will see them as a valuable record of our society.

Your comment — → *Good argument to justify the study of ads as a reflection of society. Compare Boorstin and Toffler*

Exercise

The following passage is from Alvin Toffler's *The Third Wave* (New York: William Morrow and Company, 1983), page 248. Read it carefully and then, following the procedures discussed above, make out *three* notecards: (1) select a few important sentences to quote; (2) summarize the major points of the passage; and (3) paraphrase Toffler's thesis. Remember to write a comment at the bottom of each card stating what you think of the note and how you might use it in a paper.

Today, as the Third Wave strikes, the corporate manager finds all his old assumptions challenged. The mass society itself, for which the corporation was designed, is beginning to de-massify. Not merely information, production, and family life, but the marketplace and the labor market as well are beginning to break into smaller, more varied pieces.

The mass market has split into ever-multiplying, ever-changing sets of mini-markets that demand a continually expanding range of options, models, types, sizes, colors, and customizations. Bell Telephone, which once hoped to put the same black telephone in every American home — and very nearly succeeded — now manufactures some one thousand combinations or permutations of telephone equipment from pink, green, or white phones to phones for the blind, phones for people who have lost the use of their larynx, and explosion-proof phones for construction sites. Department stores, originally designed to massify the market, now sprout "boutiques" under their roofs, and Phyllis Sewell, a vice president of Federated Department Stores, predicts that "we will be going into greater specialization ... with more different departments."

The fast-increasing variety of goods and services in the high-technology nations is often explained away as an attempt by the corporation to manipulate the consumer, to invent false needs, and to inflate profits by charging a lot for trivial options. No doubt, there is truth to these charges. Yet something deeper is at work. For the growing differentiation of goods or services also reflects the growing diversity of actual needs, values, and life-styles in a de-massified Third Wave society.

Photocopying

Along with microtexts and the computer, the most significant technological advance in the research process has been the introduction of photocopying machines throughout the library and in other accessible locations. Photocopying is especially pertinent to the discussion of note taking because it is simultaneously (1) a great time-saver and (2) a great time-waster.

If you discover a particularly valuable source, you may decide that the smartest thing to do is to photocopy all of it (if it is an article) or significant sections of it (if it is a book). You can then reread the pertinent information in the original when you begin writing your paper. You can even cut out appropriate passages and paste them on to individual note cards, thus ensuring that you have precise quotations.

If you decide that you are going to photocopy every source you uncover, you are wasting a lot of time and paper. The purpose of reading and note taking is to extract the essence of an article or book, to select the information most pertinent to your argument. If you photocopy all your sources, you have not tried to understand or evaluate them. You have simply compiled a large stack of paper that you will have to read, examine, and interpret at some future time.

The best advice about photocopying is to use it as an extension of, rather than a replacement for, the note-taking process. Always make out a source card, even if you plan to photocopy the source, so that you have an exact bibliographical record of your source. Always read the source carefully and begin taking notes before you decide to photocopy it. You may discover that it yields only one or two notes and is therefore not worth copying. Finally, if you find that you are taking more than six notes on an individual source, perhaps you should consider photocopying those sections that seem to be the most fruitful. A final caution. Be sure that you photocopy the whole page (and page number) so that later you can identify where you found particular quotations or information.

Filling Gaps

Planning the research paper is like planning any other paper because what you discover as you evaluate your information is that you need more, or at least different, kinds of information. As you follow the research process through its various stages, you are constantly refining and restricting your subject. By the time you finished taking notes on the sources you discovered at the beginning and the sources you have uncovered along the way, you know precisely where the holes in your research are, what gaps you have to fill if you are to present a thorough and coherent argument on your subject.

At this point the research process, like the writing process, becomes recursive. You must loop back to the beginning to check other subject headings (or descriptors) and specialized bibliographies to find the sources to fill the gaps in your information. You may even have to make another loop once you begin writing your paper to discover information to bridge missing connections. But because you have been through the process once and know what you are looking for, these additional journeys should be quick and to the point.

Chapter 14

Writing the Research Paper

In every writing project there comes a time when you must stop gathering information about your subject and begin drafting your paper. As you look at the large stack of note cards you have prepared, you realize that you have learned a great deal about your subject (and related subjects) as you have explored leads and examined sources. In fact, that stack of cards represents two accomplishments: (1) you have learned a systematic procedure for gathering information (a procedure you can apply to other subjects) and (2) you have acquired a detailed knowledge of the research that has already been published on your subject. Unfortunately, that stack of cards also presents two problems: (1) you have gathered more information than you can possibly use in any one paper, and (2) you have become so preoccupied with discovering what other researchers have written about your subject that you may no longer know what *you* want to write about it. For most writers, the easiest way to solve these problems is to settle down and write a first draft.

This chapter will discuss the basic steps entailed in writing that first draft. It will also show you some of Ken's initial difficulties and resulting revision agendas as he attempted to determine his purpose and get his first draft started. And, further, it will give you detailed advice on working the substance of your planning — your notes — into your research paper and documenting them accurately. Be sure to read Ken's paper and accompanying annotations once you have completed the chapter: they offer a preview of the reasoning and writing strategies you may want to bring to your own research paper.

The major topics to be discussed in this chapter, then, are as follows:

1. Organizing a preliminary outline

2. Developing a thesis

3. Writing the first draft

4. Quoting sources

5. Documenting sources

6. Listing sources

7. Typing the final draft

8. General format

9. Ken's research paper

Organizing a Preliminary Outline

As you will remember from Chapter 3, there are different kinds of outlines — a preliminary (or scratch) outline that helps you sort and arrange your information into meaningful clusters; a descriptive outline that may help you assess the strengths and weaknesses of your first draft; and a formal outline that enables you to define the sections and subsections of your paper. As you begin to organize your research paper, you need to try out several preliminary outlines to determine which one imposes the most effective pattern on your information. When you are ready to write the final draft of your research paper, you will need to produce a more formal outline to guide your composing process. You may also need to include this formal outline as a kind of "table of contents" in the final copy of the paper when you submit it to your instructor (see Ken's formal outline, pages 519–521).

To organize a preliminary outline, read through your note cards as if you were playing a game of solitaire, matching up cards that deal with certain subdivisions of your subject. If you have been conscientious about composing specific subheadings at the top of each card, your large stack of cards will quickly organize itself into a series of smaller stacks. Each of these stacks could become a major section or a minor subdivision on your outline. But you may discover that several stacks focus on similar aspects of your subject, contain too few cards to represent a significant subdivision, or deal with subheadings no longer appropriate to the emerging design of your paper. In such cases you will have to eliminate some of your note cards or relabel them so that you can make more precise and meaningful subheadings.

Once you have established your categories, arrange them into several possible patterns to determine which one seems most effective. You may wish to review Chapter 5, "Common Methods of Development," to remind yourself of some of the most familiar patterns. Some of your subject headings may suggest a simple pattern (a *narrative* account of Bell's invention of the telephone), while others may require a more complicated pattern. For example, Ken's research led him to study the history of AT&T's expanding technology, the manner in which AT&T advertised this technology, and the impact of this technology and advertising on the changing social history of the American people. Because he knew that there was probably some kind of complex cause and effect relationship among these various factors, he considered writing a *causal analysis*. But he was perplexed about how to arrange his information. Should he analyze causes first and then effects? Which factors were causes (technology, advertisements, social history) and which were effects (technology, advertisements, social history)? He decided that he didn't know enough about all these factors to analyze their relationship; and, even if he did, he would need more space and time than his assignment allowed to compose such an analysis. He decided instead to *illus-*

trate the changing nature of telephone advertising by organizing his information chronologically. Here is his preliminary outline.

Working Title: Changes in Telephone Advertising

I. *Advertising for telephone during World War II*
   A. *Importance and necessity of technology on battlefield*
   B. *Appeal to sense of patriotism for phone system in Civil Defense*

II. *Advertising for phone in mid-to-late fifties*
   A. *Concentrated on increasing technology available*
   B. *Explained process for getting equipment in place for total phone system*
   C. *Appeal to "Good Life" theme*

III. *Advertising in early-mid-late sixties*
   A. *Concentrated on improving technological capacity of AT&T*
   B. *Focus on phone as the business tool*
   C. *Began to focus on variety of domestic services — Direct Dial Long Distance*

IV. *Advertising in the late seventies*
   A. *More emphasis on service than equipment*
   B. *Fusion of phones with computers*

V. *Early eighties*
   A. *Show increasing level of human interaction with machines — information transmission and information processing became one process*
   B. *Explain rationale for break-up and new organization of AT&T*

Organizing a preliminary outline helps you determine what kind of paper your sources will allow you to write. You should be able to see at a glance whether you have staked out too much territory to cover in a single paper, settled for giving your readers a tour of your note cards, or proposed a paper that, given the limits of your time and resources, you will not be able to write. As Ken looks at the preliminary outline, he sees that he has fallen into the "survey" trap. Because he has read several histories of AT&T and traced AT&T advertising campaigns through the back issues of several national magazines, he has developed a historical perspective on his topic. But rather than allowing him to advance an argument about this paticular history, his material — as evidenced in his outline — simply surveys what happened. The outline's major headings, for example, designate fairly arbitrary and inconsistent historical periods. Its subheadings look more promising, but they suggest so many potential theories about AT&T advertising that it is difficult to see how they will help Ken (or his readers) find a coherent sense of purpose in his paper. Ken needs to revise his outline so that it will demonstrate a thesis.

Developing a Thesis

As you learned in Chapter 3, the relationship between an outline and a thesis is often complicated and unpredictable. For some writing projects you can develop a thesis almost immediately that will suggest a method for outlining your information. For other projects, you may devote most of your planning and drafting to hunting for the right thesis to shape and control an outline. And, as you know, you may have to write more than one draft of your paper before you discover what you want to demonstrate about the material you have found.

No matter what process you use, developing your thesis remains the most difficult task in composing the research paper. Your copious note cards, even when they are sorted and arranged into precise stacks, represent the voices of authority. It is easy to be intimidated by your own research, easy to let your sources speak for you. But you must remember that your aim in this writing project is to advance your own argument — to discuss and analyze a topic from your own point of view. As is true of all writing assignments, the research paper requires you to write with a purpose.

To find that purpose, read back through your note cards, paying particular attention to the space you reserved for your own comment at the bottom of the card. If you used this space consistently to comment on or pose questions about the ideas in your notes, then you have already established a degree of independence from your sources. As you reread these comments, look for some common denominators in your thinking. What fascinated you about your subject? What questions did your authorities leave unanswered? What connections did you see among the various sources you read? Now as you review your notes and comments, what new insights can you discover? What is your informed opinion of the subject, now that you have researched it?

Once you have established some common themes in your thinking, convert them into hypotheses and try to match them to your preliminary outline. Some may match up immediately, providing an assertion that explains all the divisions in your outline. Others may require you to revise the internal divisions of your outline or expand the range of information you will need to consider. Still others may suggest that you reorganize it completely. The particular hypothesis you try to advance in your first draft depends on a number of factors, among them your personal preference, your understanding of the information you have gathered, and your confidence in your ability to demonstrate what you propose to prove.

As Ken looked back through his comments, he discovered that two ideas advanced by other writers seemed to explain what he was trying to prove in his own research. Marshall McLuhan's observation that advertising would provide future historians with a faithful record of a changing society gave Ken a rationale for the subject of his paper — tracing the changes in society by tracing the changes in the ads of one corporation. But McLuhan's comment did not really assert anything about the nature of those changes or their impact on society. Alvin Toffler's theory in *The Third Wave* that civilization has moved through three waves or stages — agriculture, industry, and information — suggested a way for Ken to organize the historical periods he was trying to analyze, but he would have to reconsider the early history of the telephone, a period that he had excluded from his preliminary outline, which began with the Second World War.

The more he thought about Toffler's theory, however, the more Ken realized that it helped him see a pattern in AT&T advertising. The corporation began by introducing its product to a predominantly rural country (agriculture), soon began to manufacture its product on a mass scale (industry), and then started to emphasize its services rather than its product (information).

Ken began to examine specific AT&T ads in the light of Toffler's theory. Most of them seemed concerned about preparing the public for the most recent innovations in telephone technology. The messages seemed to be: (1) the new product works; (2) the product is useful; (3) the product is not intimidating; (4) the product will produce valuable social change; (5) the change is inevitable; (6) the change will be gradual. Like today's ads for computer hardware and software, the telephone ads tried to present the excitement of a new technology while at the same time reassuring potential customers that the technology was not cold and impersonal — it was, in the jargon of computer ads, "user-friendly." Once the ads had sold the hardware (the phone in all its various shapes and sizes), they began to sell the software (the variety of services the phone could provide). As Ken began to see these new connections in his information, he decided he was ready to formulate several hypotheses about AT&T advertising.

1. The advertisements for one product, the telephone, reveal how Americans have changed their attitudes toward technology.

2. The advertisements for the telephone illustrate how AT&T prepared Americans for the introduction of new technology.

3. The advertisements for the telephone document America's growth from an agricultural to an industrial to an information-based society.

4. AT&T's advertisements helped change Americans' perception of the telephone from a novelty to a convenience to an essential tool.

Exercise   **Discuss the way each of Ken's hypotheses matches up with his preliminary outline on page 486. In what ways will each hypothesis require Ken to change the major headings and subdivisions of the information listed on his outline? What information will he have to add, eliminate, or relabel?**

Writing the First Draft

Writing the first draft of your research paper is like writing the first draft of any other paper — it is a discovery exercise. You have to discover whether all your advance planning will enable you to communicate a subject to an audience for a purpose. Some of your discoveries will seem familiar because they are common to every writing structure: the blocks of information that seemed so complete in your notes prove sketchy; the connections that seemed so logical on your outline appear strained; and the overall purpose of your paper, so clear in your mind when you began, now strikes you as confused or inconsistent. Other discoveries may prove unsettling because they seem unique to the research paper: your first draft may follow your outline and support your thesis but it may seem stiff, mechanical, and dull.

For most inexperienced writers, first-draft dullness derives from difficulties they encounter in two undertakings: (1) composing a simple, straightforward introduction to their paper that asserts a thesis; and (2) weaving quoted material gracefully and naturally into the body of the paper. The remainder of this section will illustrate the first problem. The next section ("Quoting Sources") will discuss some methods for solving the second problem.

Creating the Right Introduction

You should not be surprised if you have to struggle with the introduction to your research paper. You have learned a great deal about your subject and you are eager to display that learning in the body of your paper. But in order to "get there" you have to write an introduction that establishes the focus of your subject, attracts the attention of your audience, and asserts the purpose of your paper. Some writers feel that they cannot write such an introduction until they have discovered precisely what they are going to say in the body of their paper. For that reason, they prefer to write their introduction after they have written the rest of their paper — when they know exactly what they want to introduce. Other writers feel that they cannot develop the body of their paper until they have defined its direction. For that reason, they prefer drafting several versions of the opening of their paper, hoping to learn what they want to introduce. Either method will require writers to make a series of readjustments — some large, some small — between the introduction and the body of their paper as they compose the final draft. Those readjustments are made by the procedures for global and local revision that you have been practicing throughout this text.

Ken's first two attempts at finding a purpose and direction for his research paper produced two different introductions. His revision agendas illustrate that he was not satisfied with either one because each failed to establish his subject or clarify his thesis. Both introductions and revisions agendas are shown below; examine them carefully, recalling what you have learned so far about research papers in general and Ken's project in particular.

FIRST DRAFT: INTRODUCTION

Watching history as it takes place is difficult because, as participants in society, we are blinded by our proximity to events. We see changes as a continual, ill-defined blur rather than as progressive steps toward an end. One of these changes we may have difficulty seeing is the movement from an industrial to an information-based society. Alvin Toffler writes in The Third Wave that this change began around 1955 and is spreading at various rates through all of society's institutions.[1]

One way to observe this change is to focus on corporate America, since innovations in the U.S. usually have their beginnings there. Because it is currently at the forefront of this information-revolution and has been in existence for over one hundred years, American Telephone and Telegraph is a natural corporation to choose for close observation.

Since AT&T is too large and complicated to study as a complete unit, it is necessary to choose one element of the corporation as an indication of its general activities. Its advertising is a good choice for three reasons. First, ads can be easily studied by examining back issues of national magazines. Second, since ads are paid for by the company, they can be expected to highlight changes and trends in a fairly dramatic fashion. Third, advertising is aimed at the general public, which means that the changes it illustrates can be expected to be of interest to the average person. As Marshall McLuhan has suggested, "the ads of our times are the richest and most faithful daily reflections that any society ever made of its entire range of activities. . . ."[2]

Revision Agenda

1. *What did I try to do in this draft?*

   I tried to illustrate the historical change from an industrial to a technological society. Argued that one way to illustrate change was to focus on the advertising of our corporation — AT&T.

2. *What are its strengths and weaknesses?*

   Toffler's theory helps give paper three part division — agriculture, industrial, information-based. Good rationale for selecting AT&T as the corporation and advertising as the specific subject. McLuhan's quote helps readers see the importance of advertising to historical research. But I take too long getting to the point. Spend too much time explaining the reasons for my choice. I think I sound defensive. Maybe I should simply present my argument. What is it? I don't have a specific thesis statement that pulls everything together.

3. *What revisions do I want to make in my next draft?*

   a. *Collapse my first three paragraphs into one — get to stuff on telephone quicker.*

   b. *Keep Toffler's three waves — say that technology caused each one.*

   c. *Keep reader involved by stressing confusion about technology — "what does it all mean to me?"*

   d. *Establish transition from technology to advertising to telephone so that I can end with a clear thesis.*

SECOND DRAFT: INTRODUCTION

In the last hundred years, technology has pushed us through two eras (agricultural and industrial) and propelled us into a third (the information age) with such dazzling speed that we often find it difficult to explain what has happened to us.[1] Marshall McLuhan, prophet of the information age, has suggested that future historians and archeologists may discover that one easy way to explain the impact of technology is to study advertising — "the richest and most faithful daily reflections that any society ever made of its entire range of activities."² If McLuhan is right, then perhaps we can learn something about the transformations in our time by sampling the advertisements for a common technological system -- the telephone.

Revision Agenda

1. <u>*What did I try to do in this draft?*</u>

   I tried to show the relationship of major ideas — technology, social change, advertising, and the telephone. Again, concluded by saying that studying one case (AT&T) could illustrate connections.

2. <u>*What are its strengths and weaknesses?*</u>

   Toffler's ideas help me establish causes of historical change. I include the reader by using "We" and "us" — all of us are confused by change. McLuhan's quote seems to provide transition between technology and telephone advertising, but maybe it gets in the way — too obvious. I still don't like last sentence. Not sharp enough. "Learn something" — what? "Sampling" — sounds too casual.

3. <u>*What revisions do I want to make in my next draft?*</u>

   a. *Dump McLuhan quote. The point is obvious.*

   b. *Focus on audience — "our" attitudes toward technological change.*

   c. *Use audience as way into thesis — how AT&T thinks about these attitudes when it designs its advertising.*

   d. *Focus and simplify thesis — AT&T uses ads to create and exploit our need for a personal relationship with impersonal technology.*

   e. *Use thesis to explain periods of technological change in history of telephone.*

   f. *Explain history (and thesis) by analyzing specific ads.*

   g. *Include ads in paper as illustrations.*

When he had completed his second revision agenda, Ken felt that he had put himself on the right track in his research paper. Having discovered his purpose in writing the paper, he knew that he could use the information he had researched to demonstrate that purpose. Like any writer, he made a number of false starts and encountered some tricky problems that required careful solutions as he began writing the body of the paper. A number of those problems concerned how best to use his sources to support his point of view. You will see how Ken worked through those problems when you read his paper and the annotation accompanying it.

Because he had worked carefully on the introduction to his paper, and because he then felt so confident about the direction of the paper, Ken did not need to undertake global revision after writing his full first draft. Not all writers of first-draft research papers are so lucky, however. It is always wise to subject your first draft to thorough scrutiny, even though you may think, after so many weeks of work, that your subject, audience, and purpose *must* be in order. Draw up a revision agenda, and, if global revision is indicated, settle down to accomplish it. If it is not required — or, in any case, once you are satisfied that you have handled the major issues of your paper successfully — you can move on to local revision, perfecting your paragraphs, sentences, and words, and ensuring that you have indeed woven your sources smoothly into your paper. The next section of this chapter gives some advice about how to accomplish that weaving.

Exercise

Compare Ken's first two introductions with the introduction that appears in his final paper. (See his research paper, page 523.) How do his revision agendas help him sharpen and focus his thesis? What specific decisions seem to produce the biggest changes in his final draft?

Quoting Sources

The most persistent challenge of the research paper is deciding *when* and *how* to use your sources to support your argument. For every division on your outline, you have a stack of note cards that contains the words and ideas of other writers. If you use this material, you will be expected to acknowledge the source of your information (see "Documenting Sources"). But many inexperienced writers do more than use their sources. They develop their papers by quoting extensively from their notes. Excessive quoting creates two problems: (1) it distorts the balance between your writing and the writing of others by suggesting that you have simply pasted together a scrapbook of other people's opinions; (2) it disrupts the natural flow of your own argument by introducing ideas and images that do not deal directly with your thesis.

To avoid these problems, you should be selective about when you quote. Because each quotation creates a special effect in your writing, you should ask yourself the following questions when deciding whether to quote a passage.

1. *Will the substance of the passage make a significant contribution to my subject?* Sometimes a passage may seem significant because it provides extensive evidence for its conclusions. But you may be able to make the same point more effectively and efficiently by paraphrasing rather than quoting the passage.

2. *Will the phrasing of the passage seem memorable to my readers?* You do not want to blur the effect of a quotation by quoting too much material. Nor do you want to waste a quotation by quoting uninspired or unintelligible writing. You should quote only those key sentences or phrases of a passage that convey the author's meaning in especially vivid language.

3. *Will the reputation of the author give credibility to my argument?* There is no point in quoting certain "experts" because the mere mention of their names produces controversy. You cannot evoke the authority of your sources if their authority is suspect.

When you determine that you want to use a particular quotation, you have to decide how to incorporate it into your own writing. There are several methods for quoting material; the one you choose depends on your reason for quoting the passage and how much of it you intend to quote.

Introduction to Quotation

All quotations must either be placed within quotation marks or be set off from your text, and they must be documented with a number referring your reader to a note that identifies the author and source. You can help your readers follow your reasoning and prepare them for the special effect of a quotation by introducing the quoted passage. Use a lead-in phrase or sentence to identify the person you are quoting and the reason he or she is being quoted. Because these introductions provide the transition from your words to another's words, their length and format depend on the writing context. Here are three ways to introduce the same passage.

> As noted social critic Alvin Toffler points out in <u>Future
> Shock</u>, "once a techno-society reaches a certain stage of
> industrial development, it begins to shift energies into the
> production of services as distinct from goods."³

This is the most common method of introducing a quote. The phrase identifies the person to be quoted (Alvin Toffler) and his expertise *(noted social critic)* and his book *(Future Shock),* but it does not explain why Toffler is being quoted. Presumably, this passage would appear in a paragraph in which you have already established a context or reason for the quotation. The transitional phrase, in this case, helps your reader see how your argument is advanced by another authority.

> "Once a techno-society reaches a certain stage of industrial
> development," Toffler argues, "it begins to shift energies
> into the production of services as distinct from goods."³

This method of identifying the source of your quotation (Toffler) assumes that you have already introduced his full name and credentials earlier in your paper. At this point, he can be referred to by his last name.

> Social critic Alvin Toffler explains the causes for this
> social change in <u>Future Shock</u>: "Once a techno-society reaches
> a certain stage of industrial development, it begins to shift
> energies into the production of services as distinct from
> goods."³

In this introduction the person being quoted (social critic, Alvin Toffler, author of *Future Shock*) and the reason he is being quoted (he explains the causes of this social change) are both identified in a full sentence that concludes with a colon. The quotation follows this complete introduction.

Length of Quotation

The length (and look) of your quotation will determine the effect it will produce. As a general rule, citing a brief, pointed quotation or working parts of a quotation into the syntax of your own sentence is the best way to advance your argument. But on rare occasions (perhaps no more than two or three times in a ten-page research paper) you may want to quote a long passage that embodies the major ideas you are trying to present.

Longer quotations (four or more lines of prose; three or more lines of poetry) are usually introduced by a colon or comma, set off from your text by triple spacing, and indented ten spaces from the left margin. Setting off the passage from your text tells your readers that they have encountered a quotation, so you do not need to enclose it in quotation marks. Here is an example:

In its 1982 Annual Report, AT&T acknowledged that the corporation had reached a turning point in its history:

As a general comment on the changing nature of this business, competitive inroads continue to be made in markets that in the past were, for all practical purposes, virtually ours alone to serve. Indeed, telecommunications is on its way to becoming one of the most competitive of U.S. industries.⁹

Shorter quotations (less than four lines of prose; less than three lines of poetry) are usually incorporated into your text, unless special emphasis is required. You can introduce the shorter quotation by one of the three methods illustrated above, or you can work parts of the passage into the syntax of your own sentence, as in this example:

Although AT&T announced that it was ready for the information age, it acknowledged that "competitive inroads continue to be

```
made in markets that in the past were, for all practical

purposes, virtually ours alone to serve."⁹
```

Manipulating Quotations

Sometimes to make a quoted passage fit smoothly into the flow of your sentence you will have to make use of *ellipsis marks* and *brackets*. Use ellipsis dots when you want to omit part of the quoted passage to make it conform to your sentence. Use *three* dots (. . .) to indicate omission of material within the sentence. Use *four* dots (. . . .) to indicate the omission of a whole sentence or more. (For more information, see the treatment of ellipsis marks in the Handbook of Grammar and Usage, pages 677–678. Use brackets when you need to add your own words to a quotation to make the passage complete or grammatically correct or, on occasion, to make an editorial comment. (See the treatment of brackets in the Handbook of Grammar and Usage, page 679.) Notice how ellipses and brackets are used to manipulate the following quotation:

```
    In 1982, AT&T announced that "the changing nature of

[its] business. . . . [had made] telecommunications . . . one of

the most competitive of U.S. industries."⁹
```

Paraphrase

Often the most efficient way to work your sources into your own writing is to paraphrase them. A paraphrase is not simply rearranging the words of the original source. Rather, it is a restatement of the ideas in the source *in your own words*. Because the words of the paraphrase are yours, they do not need to be enclosed within quotation marks. But because the ideas for the paraphrase come from someone else, you do need to cite the source in your text and document the passage with a note.

The following passage is quoted from an original source, Sonny Kleinfield's *The Biggest Company on Earth: A Profile of AT&T* (page 149):

One of the idiosyncrasies of the phone company is a policy — dating back to its earliest days — that advertising should be considered an instrument not solely of the system's attempts to sell its services, but also of its attempts to polish its image and deal politically with the public.

Here is the same passage in paraphrase:

Sonny Kleinfield, author of <u>The Biggest Company on Earth: A</u>
<u>Profile of AT&T</u>, argues that the phone company has always
considered advertising an instrument of public relations.[3]

Plagiarism

Plagiarism is the use of someone else's writing without giving proper credit — or perhaps without giving any credit at all — to the writer of the original. Whether plagiarism is intentional or unintentional, it represents a serious academic offense that can be easily avoided by adhering scrupulously to the following advice. You should document your sources whenever

1. you use a direct quotation
2. you copy a table, chart or other diagram
3. you construct a table from data provided by others
4. you paraphrase a passage in your own words
5. you present specific examples, figures, or factual information taken from a specific source and used to explain or support your judgments

The following examples illustrate the problem of plagiarism.

Original Version

Still, the telephone was only a convenience, permitting Americans to do more casually and with less effort what they had already been doing before. (Daniel J. Boorstin, *The Americans: The Democratic Experience,* page 391)

Version A

The telephone was a convenience, enabling Americans to do more
casually and with less effort what they had already been doing
before.

This is plagiarism in its worst form. Because the writer does not indicate in the text or in a note that the words and ideas belong to Boorstin, he asks his readers to believe the words are his. He has stolen the words and ideas and attempted to cover the theft by changing or omitting an occasional word.

Version B

```
Daniel J. Boorstin argues that the telephone was only a
convenience, permitting Americans to do more casually and with
less effort what they had already been doing before.[1]
```

This version is also plagiarism, even though the writer acknowledges her source in her text and documents the passage with a note. Obviously she has copied the original almost word for word, yet she has supplied no quotation marks to indicate the extent of her borrowing.

Version C

```
Daniel J. Boorstin has noted that most Americans
considered the telephone as simply "a convenience," an
instrument that allowed them "to do more casually and with
less effort what they had already been doing before."[1]
```

This version represents one, although not the only, satisfactory way of handling this source material. The author has identified her source at the beginning of her paragraph, thus enabling her readers to know who is being quoted, and she has provided a complete note directing them to the exact source of the statement. She has paraphrased some of Boorstin's words and quoted others, making it perfectly clear to the reader which words are hers and which belong to Boorstin.

Documenting Sources

When you have completed your revisions and are satisfied that you have a final draft, you need to document your sources. This means that all the information you derived from your research and used in your paper must be indicated by a citation that gives the exact source from which it was taken. The purpose of this convention is twofold: (1) to avoid the appearance of representing somebody else's work as your own, and (2) to let interested readers consult your sources if they want further information about the subject of your investigation or if they want to check your accuracy. Although there is general agreement about the purpose of documentation, different fields of knowledge, periodicals, and publishers prefer different styles of documentation.

The two most commonly used styles are those recommended by the Modern Language Association in its *MLA Handbook for Writers of Research Papers, Theses, and Dissertations* (1977) and by the American Psychological Association in its *Publication Manual of the American Psychological Association* Third Edition (1983). The principal difference between the two styles is:

MLA	APA
Sources are documented with footnotes cited at the bottom of the page or endnotes listed at the end of the paper.	Sources are documented by parenthical author-date-and-page-number citations within the text, or date-and-page number alone if the author's name is mentioned in the text.

Here are some examples of how one source is documented according to each style.

MLA   Arthur C. Clarke suggests that the telephone could be mass produced quickly because it was "near the absolute zero of technological complexity."[4]

_____

[4]Arthur C. Clarke, "Communication in the Second Century of the Telephone," The Telephone's First Century -- and Beyond (New York: Thomas Y. Crowell Company, 1977), p. 87.

APA   *Version 1 (name/year/page)*

One writer (Clarke, 1977, p. 87) suggests that the telephone could be mass produced quickly because it was "near the absolute zero of technological complexity."

APA   *Version 2 (year/page)*

Arthur C. Clarke (1977, p. 87) suggests that the telephone

```
could be mass produced quickly because it was "near the
absolute zero of technological complexity."
```

Notice that in MLA style the reader finds the full citation in the note.[1] In APA style the reader finds the full citation in the list of sources at the end of the paper.

Instructors in different departments of a college or university will tell you which style of documentation they require you to use in your research papers. If you are writing a research paper for a class in educational psychology, your instructor is likely to require APA style. If you are writing a research paper for a class in American literature, your instructor is likely to require MLA style. Because this chapter is designed to help you write a research paper in a composition class, its examples, including Ken's research paper, follow MLA style.

MLA style requires that documentation consist of two parts: a numbered marker, beginning with "one" and continuing consecutively throughout the paper, and a corresponding note that provides the exact source for each statement. When notes are placed at the bottom of the page, they are called *footnotes*. When they are listed at the end of the paper they are called *endnotes* or simply *notes*. (When footnotes or endnotes include information or commentary to support the argument in your text they are called *discursive notes*.) Most research papers, like the one Ken is writing for his composition class, use endnotes. Unless your instructor suggests some modification, you can use the following instructions to type your notes. These instructions are illustrated in Ken's paper at the end of this chapter:

1. *Spacing.* Begin your notes on a separate page following the text of

1. At the time this text went to press, the Modern Language Association had received a report from its Committee on Documentation Style that proposed a number of significant changes in MLA style. Perhaps the most important of the changes would bring MLA style closer to that of APA. Footnotes and endnotes would be eliminated in favor of in-text parenthetical citations of author, work, and page reference, or, where appropriate, simply page reference. A list of works cited would be appended to the research paper. Discursive notes would continue to be styled as footnotes or endnotes.

The MLA expects to publish these and other changes in the next edition of its *Handbook* (scheduled for Spring 1984) but also advises that current MLA style — as reflected in the 1977 edition of its *Handbook* and in this chapter — will remain in effect for a period of time after the new edition of the *Handbook* appears.

your paper. Begin each note with the number you used in the text: 1 for the first note, 2 for the second, and so on. Each number is indented five spaces and is placed slightly above and one space before the author's name. If the note takes more than one line, all lines after the first start flush with the left margin. Double-space between lines and between notes.

2. *Author's name.* Begin with the author's given name — "John Smith," not "Smith, John." If the work has more than two authors, use "and others" after the first one — "Leon Edel and others," instead of "Leon Edel, Thomas H. Johnson, Sherman Paul, and Claude Simpson." This shorter form is used only in endnotes, not in the bibliography. When a book has an editor instead of an author (as in an anthology or a book of readings), the editor's name goes in place of the author's and is followed by "ed." After the first reference to a work, the author's or editor's name is shortened to surname only — "Smith," not "John Smith." If there is no author's or editor's name, the note begins with the title.

3. *Title.* In the first reference to any source you need to provide the complete title, but in the second and subsequent references the author's surname and the page number are enough — for example, "Bonington, p. 11" — provided that only one author by that name is being cited, and only one book or article by that author. Unless both these conditions are met, it will be necessary to add a short title — "Richards, *Principles,* p. 24."

After the first reference to an *unsigned* newspaper article, the title of the newspaper is used without the title of the article. Obviously this short form can be used only if no ambiguity results; if other notes are going to refer to different issues of that newspaper, a fuller reference will be needed. The short form can be used only when the note refers to a newspaper article already cited. When it refers to another article in the same newspaper, it requires a full citation.

4. *Facts of publication.* The place of publication, the name of the publisher, and the date of publication are enclosed in parentheses in the first citation of a work, but are omitted in subsequent references. When used, the facts of publication follow the form used in a bibliography.

5. *Volume and page numbers.* In reference to a one-volume work, the abbre-

viation *p.* is used for "page" and *pp.* for "pages." When the reference is to a work of more than one volume, both the volume and the page number must be given. When both are given, the abbreviations *Vol.* and *p.* are dropped; instead the volume is indicated by a Roman numeral and the page by an Arabic numeral — "II, 28," not "Vol. II, p. 28." The page number must refer to the exact page of the source being cited; if the material comes from more than one page in the source, all necessary pages must be shown — "p. 5," or "pp. 5–6," or "pp. 5–8."

But when the reference is to a periodical rather than to a book, both the volume and the page numbers are in Arabic numerals, with the volume number first and the page number last and the date coming between these two numbers — "22 (1976), 45–46." Usually, however, no volume number is given for magazines published monthly, semi-monthly, or weekly. Then the citation is by date and page numbers — "Oct. 1978, p. 140," or "10 Sept. 1976, pp. 21–23." Many newspapers are numbered in sections, with the page numbers starting over again in each new section — "Sec. A, p. 12," or "Sec. B, p. 4," or "Sec. 2, pp. 4–6." For such newspapers the order is title, date, section, page, and sometimes column number.

6. *Punctuation.* Notes are punctuated like sentences, with a period at the end of the note and after abbreviations, and commas between the parts except where colons are needed.

Sample Notes

The following sample notes illustrate and supplement the preceding discussion. They may be used as models against which to check your own notes.

First reference to a book

[1] Roderick Nash, <u>The Nervous Generation: American Thought, 1917–1930</u> (Chicago: Rand McNally and Company, 1970), 78.

Subsequent reference

    2 Nash, p. 153.

Reference to a multivolume work

    3 Martin Blumensen, The Patton Papers (Boston: Houghton Mifflin, 1972, 1974), I, 134–35.

(Note: The two dates are necessary here because the first volume was published in 1972, and the second in 1974.)

Subsequent reference

    4 Blumensen, II, 27.

Reference to a second or later edition

    5 John Hope Franklin, From Slavery to Freedom: A History of Negro Americans, 3rd ed. (New York: Knopf, 1967), p. 506.

Subsequent reference

    6 Franklin, p. 302.

Reference to an essay in an edited collection

    7 Henry Beston, "The Golden Age of the Canoe," in The Great Lakes Reader, ed. Walter Havighurst (New York: Macmillan, 1966), pp. 31–32.

Subsequent reference

    8 Beston, p. 35.

Reference to a magazine article

⁹ William H. Isbell, "The Prehistoric Ground Drawings of Peru," Scientific American, Oct. 1978, p. 140.

Subsequent reference

10 Isbell, p. 142.

11 Mario Pei, "Prospects for a Global Language," Saturday Review, 2 May 1970, p. 23.

Subsequent reference

12 Pei, p. 25.

Reference to a newspaper article

13 Roger Kenneth Field, "Automated Medicine," New York Times, 31 Jan. 1971, Sec. 3, p. 8, col. 2.

Subsequent reference

14 Field, p. 8.

15 "Senate Unit Moves to Set Aside Alaska Lands," Washington Post, 30 Sept. 1978, p. A6, cols. 3-5.

Subsequent reference

16 Washington Post.

Reference to an article in an encyclopedia, signed or unsigned

17 Thomas Babington Macaulay, "Johnson, Samuel," Encyclopaedia Britannica, 11th ed., XV, 463.

Note that "1910 ed." could be used in place of "11th ed."

Subsequent reference

> 18 Macaulay, p. 465.
>
> 19 "Entelechy," Encyclopaedia Britannica: Macropaedia,
> 1974 ed., XXIII, 908.

Subsequent reference

> 20 Britannica, 1974, XXIII, 908.

Biblical reference by book, chapter, and verse (or verses)

> 21 Genesis 25:29-34.

(The title of the book is not underlined.)

Reference to a play by act, scene, and line

> 22 Hamlet III, i, 56.

Listing Sources

As you planned your research, you compiled a stack of source cards as a working bibliography. When you are ready to write your final draft, you must list these sources in a final bibliography on a separate page(s) that will be placed at the end of your research paper. Final bibliographies usually list only those sources that you have cited in your paper, although occasionally your instructor may ask you to expand this list to include those sources you consulted in preparing your paper. A bibliography of sources cited is included at the end of Ken's research paper (pages 565–567). In typing your final bibliography, follow these instructions:

1. List all entries in alphabetical order according to the surname of the author.

2. Double-space between successive lines of an entry and between entries. Also leave one extra space — that is, two spaces in all — between author and title, and title and facts of publication.

3. After the first line of an entry, indent successive lines five spaces.

4. If you are listing more than one book by the same author, do not repeat the author's name; instead of the name, type ten hyphens followed by a period, thus:

```
Lanham, Richard A.   The Motives of Eloquence: Literary

     Rhetoric in the Renaissance.   New Haven: Yale Univ.

     Press, 1976.

----------.   Style: An Anti-Textbook.   New Haven: Yale Univ.

     Press, 1974.
```

In this example the books are listed in alphabetical order, but they could also be listed in the order of their publication dates.

Sample Entries

The exact form of each entry on your bibliography will vary according to the kind of publication being cited. The major variations are illustrated in the sample bibliographical entries given below:

A book by a single author or agency

```
Brooks, John.   The Telephone: The First Hundred Years.   New

     York: Harper and Row, 1975.
```

a. The author's surname comes before the given name or initials for ease in alphabetizing. Use the name exactly as it appears on the title page.

b. If the book is the work of an agency, committee, organization, or department, instead of an individual, the name of the agency takes the place of the author's name.

c. If no author or agency is given, the citation begins with the title.

d. The title of the book is underlined.

e. The facts of publication are the place of publication, the publisher, and the date of publication, in that order.

f. If more than one place of publication is given on the title page, use only the first.

g. If no date of publication is given, use the latest copyright date, usually found on the reverse of the title page.

h. The punctuation and spacing in the sample show the preferred form.

A book by two or more authors

```
Ashby, Eric, and Mary Anderson.  The Rise of the Student

     Estate in Britain.  Cambridge, Mass.: Harvard Univ.

     Press, 1970.
```

a. The names of authors after the first are not inverted (Thomas, Joseph M., Frederick A. Manchester, and Franklin W. Scott). Otherwise the form of the entry is the same as that of example 1.

b. The order of the authors' names is the same as that on the title page; hence Ashby comes first, even though Anderson would be alphabetically earlier.

An edition other than the first

```
Bailey, Sydney D. British Parliamentary Democracy.  3rd ed.

     Boston: Houghton Mifflin, 1971.
```

a. If the work is a revised or later edition, the appropriate abbreviated designation (Rev. ed., 8th ed.) is placed immediately after the title and separated from it by a period.

b. Only the date of the edition being cited is given.

c. The edition number is not included in the title but follows it after a period and two spaces.

A work of more than one volume

```
Johnson, Edgar.  Charles Dickens: His Tragedy and Triumph.  2

     vols.  New York: Simon and Schuster, 1952.
```

The number of volumes follows the title, is separated from it by a period, and is always abbreviated as shown.

An edition of another author's work

> Smith, Grover, ed. <u>Letters of Aldous Huxley</u>. New York: Harper
>   and Row, 1969.

An edited collection or anthology

> Rothenberg, Jerome, ed. <u>Shaking the Pumpkin: Traditional</u>
>   <u>Poetry of the Indian North Americas</u>. Garden City, N.Y.:
>   Doubleday, 1972.

A translation

> Hesse, Hermann. <u>Beneath the Wheel</u>. Trans. Michael Roloff.
>   New York: Farrar, Straus and Giroux, 1968.

A pamphlet

Because there is considerable variation in the bibliographical information given in pamphlets, they are sometimes difficult to cite. Whenever possible, treat them like books, with or without an author. If the bibliographical information is so incomplete that you cannot confidently describe the pamphlet, get your instructor's advice. Following are four variant forms:

> Lichtman, Gail. <u>Alcohol: Facts for Decisions</u>. Syracuse, N.Y:
>   New Readers Press, 1974.
> Florida Dept. of Highway Safety and Motor Vehicles. <u>Florida</u>
>   <u>Driver's Handbook</u>. Tallahasee, Fla., 1976.
> U.S. Dept. of Interior, Teton Dam Failure Review Group.
>   <u>Failure of Teton Dam: A Report of Findings</u>. Washington,
>   D.C.: GPO, 1977. [GPO is a standard abbreviation for the
>   U.S. Government Printing Office.]

<u>Your Library: A Guide for Undergraduate Students.</u> University

of Illinois, n.d.

a. The last example shows a difficult pamphlet, since the only bibliographical information given is the title and publisher.
b. The symbol *n.d.*, meaning "no date," is used to show that no date of publication or copyright is given and that the omission is not your oversight.

An essay in an edited collection

Tyler, Anne. "Still Just Writing." In <u>The Writer on Her</u>

<u>Work</u>. Ed. Janet Sternburg. New York: Norton, 1980.

a. This entry requires two titles and both an author and an editor.
b. The title of the essay (or story or poem) is in quotation marks.
c. The title of the book is underlined and is preceded by *In*.

An article in an encyclopedia.

Green, Benny. "Jazz." <u>Encyclopaedia Britannica:</u>

<u>Macropaedia</u>. 1974 ed.

"Rome." <u>New Columbia Encyclopedia</u>. 1975.

a. Some encyclopedia articles are initialed, and the authors are identified in a special list. The article on jazz is signed "B. Gr." If the author is not identified, the entry begins with the title of the article, as in the *Columbia* example.
b. The British spelling *Encyclopaedia* is often bothersome to American students. Copy the title exactly as it is given on the title page.
c. The only fact of publication necessary is the edition or the year of publication. Pages may be omitted, since the topics are arranged alphabetically.

An article in a journal

Journals are periodical publications dealing with a particular area of study. Examples are *The Journal of Library History, The Book Collector,* and *PMLA* (Publications of the Modern Language Association). The following samples show respectively the forms for periodicals published annually, quarterly, and monthly.

```
Stewart, George R.  "A Classification of Place Names."  Names,
     2 (1954), 1-13.
Hoffman, Frank A.  "Place Names in Brown County."  Midwest
     Folklore, 11 (Spring 1961), 57-62.
Stitzel, Judith.  "Reading Doris Lessing."  College English,
     40 (Jan. 1979), 498-503.
```

a. For all three of these entries the information following the title is volume, date, and page numbers in that order, with the volume in Arabic numerals and the date in parentheses.

b. For a journal published only once a year, the year alone is a sufficient date. For one published quarterly, the season (Spring, Summer, Fall, Winter) is added to the year, and for monthly periodicals the date consists of month and year.

c. When using quarterly or monthly issues bound in an annual volume by the library, check to see whether the page numbers are continuous through the volume or whether they start again from page 1 for each issue. Some journals use continuous pagination through a volume; others do not. As long as the date of each issue is given, the page numbers are not likely to be confused.

A magazine article

```
George, Phyllis.  "Sports: A Joy to the Spirit."  Saturday
     Evening Post, Oct. 1978, pp. 34-36.
Kramer, Hilton.  "The New American Photography."  New York
     Times Magazine, 23 July 1978, pp. 8-13.
```

a. The first entry shows the standard form for an article in a monthly magazine. No place of publication or publisher is given, but the month, year, and page numbers are shown. Notice the abbreviations: *p.* for "page," *pp.* for "pages."

b. The second entry shows the form for magazines published oftener than once a month and magazines issued as newspaper supplements. The day as well as the month is given.

A newspaper article

```
Whited, Charles.  "The Priceless Treasure of the Marquesas."

     Miami Herald, 15 July 1973, p. 1.

"Fall Brings Road Hazards."  The [Champaign, Ill.]

     News-Gazette, 25 Sept. 1976, p. 8, col. 4.

"Culture Shock: Williamsburg and Disney World, Back to Back."

     New York Times, 28 Sept. 1975, Sec. 10, p. 1.
```

a. The first example shows the standard form for a signed article. The definite article before the name of the city is not used because it does not appear in the title of the newspaper.

b. The second example illustrates the form when the name of the city does not appear in the title, but the definite article does. In this example the column number is given because the story is not conspicuous on the page, and the column number makes identification easier.

Typing the Final Draft

As you type the final draft of your research paper, adhere to the following requirements.

1. Use white, twenty-pound, $8\frac{1}{2}'' \times 11''$ paper.

2. Use a pica typewriter, if possible; its type is easier to read.

3. Avoid fancy print typewriters or dot matrix word processors; their type is hard to read.

4. Double space the text throughout, including quotations and notes.

5. Observe well-balanced margins of one inch at top, bottom, and both sides of your paper.

6. Indent five spaces for paragraphs.

7. Leave two spaces after periods and other terminal punctuation.

8. Leave one space after commas and other marks of punctuation.

9. Number paper consecutively throughout the manuscript in the upper-right-hand corner.

10. Do not punctuate page numbers by adding periods, slashes, or hyphens.

11. Do not number the title page or the pages of the outline.

12. Do not number the first page of the text, the first page of the notes, or the first page of the bibliography, but count such pages in the total pagination of the work.

13. Proofread your paper carefully, including outline, notes, and bibliography.

14. Make a carbon or photocopy of your paper for your own files.

15. If your instructor requires you to turn in your note cards along with your paper, be sure they are arranged in the correct order and securely bound together or placed in an envelope.

General Format

A research paper consists of five parts:

1. *Title page.* The information on the title page is spaced so that it appears balanced on the page. The title is centered about a third of the way down, and is followed by the author's name, the course and section number, the instructor's name, and the date.

2. *Final outline.* The final outline serves as a table of contents for the final paper. It follows the format discussed in Chapter 3 and may be a topic or full sentence outline. The thesis is written at the top of the page, but neither the introduction nor the conclusion appears as a heading.

3. *Final text.* The title is repeated on the first page of the final text. The format of the paper adheres to the instructions in "Typing the Final Draft."

4. *Notes.* The notes for a paper can appear as footnotes at the bottom of the page or as endnotes at the end of the paper. Ken's paper uses endnotes. The notes begin on a new page titled "Notes" following the text and preceding the bibliography. The notes are numbered con-

secutively and conform to the pattern outlined in "Documenting Sources."

5. *Bibliography.* The bibliography begins on a new page following the notes and is titled "Bibliography." A bibliography usually lists only those sources cited in the notes. If the bibliography is expanded to include other sources consulted during research, the list is entitled "Works Consulted." In either case, entries are arranged alphabetically and conform to the pattern outlined in "Listing Sources."

1. **Title** Ken's final title is more appealing and more pointed than his earlier working title, "Changes in Telephone Advertising." The first part of the title suggests a general direction and point of view ("preparing for the information age"); the second part identifies his method for examining a specific subject ("an analysis of AT&T advertising").

1

Preparing for the Information Age:

An Analysis of AT&T Advertising

Ken Wickliff

English 104, Section 2

Mr. Johnson

May 12, 1983

2. **Thesis** Compare Ken's final thesis with his preliminary hypotheses on page 489 and with the two drafts of his introduction on pages 491–493. His new thesis, which grew out of the revision agenda for his second draft, advances a specific argument about the purpose of AT&T advertising. Notice the way this reformulated thesis directs and controls each of the headings in Ken's final outline.

3. **Outline** At first glance, Ken's final outline looks vaguely similar to his preliminary outline on page 486. It follows a chronological development, but it contains three significant revisions.

   a. Ken has included the early history of telephone advertising (Sections I and II) to make his argument more comprehensive and conclusive.
   b. He continues to use historical periods for his major headings but he characterizes each one in such a way that his readers see its relationship to his thesis and developing argument.
   c. The word *advertising* (or *ads*) is repeated in parallel phrasing and at parallel levels throughout the outline to establish the focus and coherence of his paper.

Preparing for the Information Age:

An Analysis of AT&T Advertising

2 <u>Thesis:</u> American Telephone and Telegraph uses advertising to create and exploit its customers' need for a personal relationship with an impersonal system.

  I. Early advertising is used to sell reliability of new technology.

    A. Alexander Graham Bell exhibits new technology.

    B. Ads assert that new technology is available to America's predominantly rural population.

    C. Telephone technology expands and enriches personal lives of rural Americans.

3   II. Advertising in the 20s and 30s reveals tension between old and new technology.

    A. Ads celebrate values of rural life.

    B. Ads introduce innovations that accelerate growth of urban life.

    C. Ad for direct dial telephone assures consumers that technological change is manageable.

 III. Advertising in the 40s and 50s explains and then exploits industrial expansion.

    A. Ads explain value of new technology for winning the war.

3. **Outline** (continued)

    d. The outline is placed between the title page and the text, and its pages are not numbered into those of the research paper itself. Ken numbered his outline with a lowercase Roman numeral, omitting the numeral on the first page of the outline. (Numbers are omitted on the opening pages of all major sections of the research paper — i.e., first page of text, first page of notes, first page of bibliography.) He could have chosen to leave a two-page outline unnumbered.

ii

B. Ads exploit post-war affluence by encouraging the purchase of more technology.

C. Ad for extension telephones appeal to consumer's desire for convenience and status.

IV. Advertising in 60s and 70s sells service rather than products.

A. AT&T establishes technology for global communication.

B. Ads encourage long distance calling.

C. "Reach out and Touch" campaign tries to personalize the use of new technology.

V. Advertising in the 80s prepares customers for the information age.

A. AT&T adjusts to competition and divestiture.

B. AT&T recognizes commercial implications of information age.

C. "Your Gateway to Tomorrow" ad conveys excitement and the efficiency of new technology.

D. "Let's Talk" device reassures customers that they can still have a personal relationship with an increasingly impersonal system.

4. **Introduction** Ken opens his essay by identifying a common experience that he and his readers share: the dazzling and confusing impact of technology on their lives. He uses Toffler's three-stage theory to characterize this shared history, but acknowledges Toffler in a note rather than allowing a third party to interfere with his direct appeal to his audience.

5. **Thesis** The transition to Ken's thesis now grows naturally out of his introductory comments about the need to explain "ambivalent attitudes toward technological progress." His actual thesis makes an assertion about how one corporation has used advertising to capitalize on that ambivalence.

6. **Common knowledge** Because Bell's invention of the telephone falls into the category of common knowledge (information educated people are expected to know), Ken does not need to document the first sentence of his second paragraph. He is not certain, however, that most people know Bell exhibited his telephone at the Philadelphia Centennial Exhibition. Ken didn't know about this event until he read Boorstin, so he acknowledges his source.

Preparing for the Information Age:

An Analysis of AT&T Advertising

In the last hundred years, technology has pushed us through two eras (agricultural and industrial) and propelled us into a third (the information age) with such dazzling speed that we often find it difficult to explain what has happened to us.[1] We see the advance of this technology as a mixed blessing -- as a cold, impersonal force that has taken control of our lives and as an exciting, liberating creation that has expanded and enriched our lives. Perhaps the most effective way to explain our ambivalent attitudes toward technological progress is to study the way one corporation, American Telephone and Telegraph, has used advertising to create and exploit our need for a personal relationship with an impersonal system.

On March 10, 1876, when Alexander Graham Bell first transmitted the human voice over a couple of wires, he faced the same problem that every inventor faces -- how to sell his product to the public. His first task was to demonstrate that his invention really worked, and he could find no better place to display his product than the large "sales conference" that was

7. **Advertisements** Ken's biggest technical problem throughout his paper is to establish a consistent policy for documenting advertisements. In some cases, he characterizes advertising campaigns by quoting corporate policy. In other cases, he analyzes specific ads by including them as illustrations in his text. In this case, he quotes the copy of Bell's first ad from a numbered illustration on an unnumbered page in John Brooks's book. See note 3.

8. **Analysis** This analysis of American life in the early years of the telephone grows out of Ken's historical reading and his speculation (in the comment portion of his note cards) about what rural life must have been like before the introduction of the telephone.

2

held in Philadelphia that same year, the Centennial
Exhibition.[2] Bell published his first ad for the
telephone the following year, encouraging people to
come to Old St. John's Church in New York to examine
the "Speaking and Singing Telephone, . . . giving the
tones of the voice so that the person speaking can be
recognized by the sound at the other end of the
line."[3] These early exhibitions seemed to carry two
messages: you can see a new invention work and you can
use it for your own pleasure -- to hear the voice of
someone you recognize at the other end of the line.

Once people realized that Bell's telephone worked,
they had to be convinced that it could become a
dependable product, superior to its new competitors and
to other forms of communication. In these early days
the challenge was to develop a reliable telephone
network for an essentially rural population that had
learned to trust the letters delivered by personable
mail carriers, or, in the case of an extreme emergency,
the messages relayed by friendly telegraph operators at
a nearby town or railroad crossing. From the
perspective of the isolated and self-reliant family
farm, advertisements for technological inventions such

9. **Discursive note** Because Ken wants to maintain his focus on advertising, he does not want to introduce too much information about the early innovations in telephone technology or the corporate battles that eventually led to the creation of AT&T. He alludes to these developments in his text, but he provides his readers with further information on both subjects in a discursive note. See note 4.

3

as the telephone were identified with life in the city
-- a life filled with newfangled contraptions and old
fashioned corruptions. But as technological advances
and organizational developments allowed Bell's
invention to evolve into the Bell system and eventually
into the American Telephone and Telegraph Company, the
corporation's advertisements soon were able to
proclaim that telephone service was available to
everyone.[4] An 1890s ad assures potential consumers
that "the mail is quick, the telegraph is quicker, but
long distance telephone is instantaneous. You don't
have to wait for an answer."[5]

By the turn of the century, more and more wires
were strung across rows of crops and down dirt roads
connecting country to city. In fact, "the increase in
the number of rural phones between 1902 and 1907 was
truly phenomenal -- from 260,000 to 1,465,000 or 49
percent."[6] This high demand suggested that farmers did
not perceive telephones as the intrusion of an
impersonal technology into their homes, but as the
extension of their personal relationships into a new
community. Because most rural phones were on the party
line, they created a new network of friends and a new

10. **Indirect source** Ken wants to use this quotation from a farm wife to drive home his point about the effect of the party line on the lives of rural Americans. But he does not have access to the original source (a 1905 issue of a magazine entitled *The World's Work*). Brooks quotes this source, but supplies no page number in his notes. Ken must therefore acknowledge Brooks as the indirect source of his quotation. See note 7.

11. **Paraphrase** Notice the way Ken uses the information paraphrased in his notes to develop his own paragraph:

---

8   *Early Advertising*   Brooks

                                               p. 117

Brooks argues that one side-effect of the installation of the telephone was creation of the "heroic, rural operator. In the natural course of things, she became an involuntary message center." Brooks uses magazine articles, popular literature, and popular songs to illustrate the importance of this woman named Central.

Interesting side-effect. Self-reliant farmer suddenly becomes dependent on operator. How do people feel about operators now? Annoying voice of phone company -- Lily Tomlin being Ernestine, nasal and snorting. No longer personal advisor.

---

12. **Selecting quotations** To establish the theme of the Norman Rockwell-type ads he has seen in the early issues of national magazines, Ken selects a few vivid phrases characterizing those ads from Sonny Kleinfield's book and then works those phrases into the syntax of his own sentences. See notes 9 and 10.

4

form of entertainment -- eavesdropping. When asked how she liked her new telephone service, a farm wife replied, "Well, we liked it a lot at first, and do yet, only spring work is coming on so heavy that we don't have time to listen now."[7]

Another factor that helped personalize this new technology was the operator. Since most rural customers made their calls through a switch board, they soon transformed the central operator into a community heroine.[8] Intelligent and vigilant, she could always be counted on to supply information, gossip, or emergency warnings. Along with the mailman, the country doctor, and the local store owner, she soon entered the folklore of rural America, representing not the rapid advances of AT&T but the reassuring presence of Ma Bell.

By the 1920s the phone had become a commonplace in most American homes. The advertisements created by Bell's ad agency (N.W. Ayer) for magazines such as Colliers described "the good intentions and social benefits" of the telephone in "friendly-folksy, all-is-well themes."[9] In Norman Rockwell-type pictures, AT&T's ads depicted "family groups with glowing

13. **Quoting factual information** Although Ken has not read the 1920 census, he has read several social historians who cite it as providing the first factual evidence that America was no longer a rural nation. To advance his own thesis, Ken uses the historian's interpretation of the census rather than the census itself. He could have selected any major historian, but he quotes Roderick Nash because Nash's interpretation of the 1920s often focuses on how new technology made Americans "nervous." See note 11.

14. **Introducing quotation** Because Brooks's study is one of Ken's most important sources, he wants to work the author's name and book into the text (he has already quoted silently from Brooks in notes 3, 5, 6, and 8). Notice that Ken uses an introductory phrase to characterize and name the source and its author before he presents the quotation. Notice also that even though this quotation provides a crucial transition in the paper — asserting that the phone helped create the psychology of urban America — Ken quotes only the key words of Brooks's assertion.

5

healthy, apple-cheeked youngsters and beaming, silver
topped grandmas and grandpas."[10] But all was not well
on the family farm. The industrial revolution, which
had begun in the late nineteenth century, had reached
its first boom period, luring more and more apple-
cheeked youngsters to the thriving factories in the
city. The 1920 census confirmed the effect of this
social change: for the first time in the nation's
history more Americans lived in urban areas than in
rural areas.[11]

In a sense, telephone advertising not only
accelerated this change by encouraging communication
between country and city, but also created the
psychological attitudes that helped shape industrial
America. In his comprehensive study, Telephone: The
First Hundred Years, John Brooks points out that the
telephone (and certainly the advertising that lauded
its innovations) created "a new habit of mind -- a
habit of tenseness and alertness, of demanding and
expecting immediate results."[12] The art work in many
of AT&T's ads still celebrated the leisurely,
predictable routines of rural life, but the copy
announced a new technology that could assist city

15. **Analysis** Again, Ken's independent thinking causes him to speculate on the effects of a new, impersonal technology on people familiar with a more personal, established technology. The source of such speculation can be seen in Ken's comments on the role of the rural operator and in his analysis of his first major illustration, the ad for the direct dial telephone.

16. **Documenting illustration** Because three major ads appear in the text with an accompanying credit line, Ken is uncertain how to document them, particularly given that he quotes extensively from each one. His decision is to document his first reference to each ad and then explain in his note that "subsequent references to the ad will be documented by quotations in the text." See notes 13, 16, and 29.

17. **Interpreting illustration** Ken's purpose in selecting these three ads is to provide his audience with vivid illustrations of his thesis — that AT&T advertising creates and exploits its consumers' need for a personal relationship with an impersonal system. Although he discusses other ads in his paper, he uses these three to highlight AT&T's policies during Toffler's three historical periods. The three-wave theory gives Ken concepts to work with, but his interpretation of the copy (words) and art work (pictures) of each ad emerge from his own analysis.

6

go—getters, big and small, to do business efficiently
and effectively.

This tension between the personal society
established by a familiar technology and the impersonal
world created by a new technology is certainly apparent
in AT&T's attempt to convert party lines to private
lines and the central switch board to the direct dial
system. Although both changes were appropriate for
urban living — encouraging privacy and independence in
a world that was becoming increasingly public and
interdependent — they were nevertheless changes in a
fixed system and therefore viewed with some
apprehension.

An advertisement from the early 1930s, "The Dial
Telephone . . . How it Works," symbolizes AT&T's desire
to prepare its anxious customers for one of these
technological innovations.[13] The copy at the top of
the ad begins with the known, making "a call from a
telephone served by operators," and then moves on to
describe the unknown, making a call "without the aid of
an operator." The instructions assure readers that the
system is essentially the same system and that they
know how to control it. Rather than talk to an

18. **Introducing quotations** Ken introduces this quotation by identifying who is being quoted, the source of his statement, and the reason he is being quoted. The quotation following the colon is compact and dramatic, providing Ken with an efficient example of the thinking that guided most of AT&T's advertising for a whole decade. His decision to name and quote AT&T's chairman of the board allows him to evoke the authority of the person responsible for the corporation's policies.

7

operator, they can use "the dial on your telephone to tell this apparatus the number of the line you wish." The art work to the right of the copy shows a young man calmly using the "finger wheel" to complete this process. Finally, after explaining the electrical mysteries that allow such calls to be completed, the copy concludes with the reassuring news that although the conversion to direct dial is inevitable it will be gradual.

AT&T was forced into a period of rapid change during the forties. Not surprisingly much of its technological energy went into the war effort. In the 1942 Annual Report, Chairman of the Board Walter Clifford, Jr. stressed a theme that was to highlight much of AT&T's advertising during this period: "The science underlying electrical communication is at the heart of modern war."[14] Not only did the telephone prove crucial to planning military campaigns abroad, but it also proved essential to the nation's civil defense. Patriotic ads assured Americans that AT&T was developing a highly advanced communications technology to preserve their personal freedom and livelihood.

When the war ended, AT&T, like most American

19. **Selecting supporting evidence** One of Ken's discoveries during his research was an almost complete series of AT&T's annual reports. Each report, written for an audience of stockholders, comments on corporate policy and provides ample statistical evidence to support that policy. In the *1953 Annual Report* Ken finds sales figures to document AT&T's eager response to post-war consumers.

20. **Interpreting illustration** Ken interprets AT&T's exploitation of the age of affluence by carefully examining the copy, artwork, and "hidden persuaders" in this ad for extension phones. He incorporates words and phrases from the ad into the syntax of his own sentence, summarizes significant points of the copy, and introduces the major argument of the ad in a full quotation. He also tries to interpret what the art work communicates *directly* (the convenience of extension phones in certain rooms of the house) and what it communicates *indirectly* (the status required to own such a home). Of course, Ken continues to underline his thesis by directing his readers' attention to AT&T's attempt to personalize technology: "custom planned (by you!) for comfortable living."

8

corporations, turned its mobilized industrial power on
the newly affluent American consumer. After years of
scrimping and sacrificing, Americans were ready to
invest their resources in a new generation of gadgets,
from air conditioners to television sets. The
telephone, which during the war had provided an
emergency connection for many families, was at the top
of the shopping list. In 1953, AT&T reported that it
had installed over 19 million phones since the war and
was currently trying to fill a million requests for
private lines.[15]

In this new age of affluence, AT&T decided to
change the thrust of its advertising from explaining
the benefits of one telephone to extolling the value of
extension telephones. The basic telephone, now
considered a domestic necessity, could be multiplied
throughout the household, fulfilling each family
member's need for personal access to communications
technology. In a 1960s ad, AT&T suggests that
extension telephones make it possible for homes to be
"custom planned (by you!) for comfortable living."[16]
The copy reminds readers that the telephone dominates
their lives — helping them plan social engagements,

21. **Longer quotations** Ken decides to include this long passage in his text because it makes a major point about the expanding market for telephones, and because it *looks* like the point it makes. In other words, the effect of reading this long quotation about the "ever-multiplying ... sets of mini-markets" is to *see* these markets expand into a wide "range of options, models, types, sizes, colors, and customizations." Ken identifies the author of the passage by his full name, evoking the authority of this writer whom most readers identify with intriguing forecasts about social change. He then sets off Toffler's comments from his own text by triple spacing above and below, double spacing the quote, and indenting the blocked quotation ten spaces from the left margin.

9

shop for goods and services, keep in touch with family
and friends. The argument seems unassailable: "Because
the telephone is so useful to everyone, extension
phones should be handy throughout your home, in
locations to fit your family needs" -- in the kitchen,
the bedroom, the game room, and the den.

Although this ad sells telephone technology as a
"Home-wide convenience," it appeals to the notion of
technology as status. The copy assures the reader that
additional phones don't "cost much to enjoy," but the
art work portrays the telephone, "available in your
choice of decorator colors," amidst the technological
trappings of luxurious suburban dwelling. In this new
environment, the telephone, once perceived as an
instrument for transmitting messages, is converted into
a badge for communicating achievement.

The more AT&T created and exploited consumer
desire for status, the more it had to personalize its
technology to satisfy individual tastes. As Alvin
Toffler points out,

> The mass market has split into ever-
> multiplying, ever-changing sets of mini-
> markets that demand a continually expanding

22. **Shorter quotations** Although Toffler's long quotation helps Ken catalogue the full industrialization of telephone hardware, Toffler's shorter quotation about the change from goods to services is more important to Ken's argument. Ken leads into the quotation with his own assertion that AT&T was "moving toward Toffler's prediction" and then completes the syntax of his own sentence with Toffler's prediction. Because Ken has already introduced Alvin Toffler to his readers, he can now refer to him by his last name.

23. **Summary** Ken cannot possibly explain the creation and impact of all the new technology that evolved into AT&T's total system and maintain his focus on advertising. He decides to mention some of the changes and then cite a page in Sonny Kleinfield's book that summarizes how these systems created the remarkable accessibility of direct long distance calls. See note 19.

10

range of options, models, types, sizes, colors and customizations. Bell telephone, which had once hoped to put the same black telephone in every American home -- and very nearly succeeded -- now manufactures some one thousand combinations or permutations of telephone equipment from pink, green, or white phones to phones for the blind, phones for people who have lost the use of their larynx, and explosive proof phones for construction sites.[17]

Although this catalogue suggests that AT&T was preoccupied with selling hardware, the corporation was actually moving toward Toffler's prediction that "once a techno-society reaches a certain stage of industrial development, it begins to shift energies into the production of services, as distinct from goods."[18] During the early seventies, inventions such as the micro-chip, computer switching systems, and orbiting satellites finally became part of the total AT&T system, making it possible for customers to make inexpensive direct dial long distance calls within the United States and to other countries throughout the

24. **Quoting special terms** Ken's primary source for AT&T's "Reach Out and Touch" campaign is Michael Arlen's article in *The New Yorker*. Much of that article is based on interviews with the advertising executives responsible for creating the ads. As the note card below indicates, Ken selects only two words from one of these interviews, but quotes the source because these words require special definition.

---

21   "Reach Out and Touch"   Arlen
                                                                p. 21

Phil Shyposh (great name for an ad-man) on the philosophy of the campaign: "To begin with, what you have to remember about residence long-distance calling is that it is a discretionary purchase. By that I mean there is nothing about a telephone that compels a person to make a long distance call; you could even say that it's a reorder every time. So, basically, we've been trying to focus on a user strategy that appeals to people who are comfortable making a long distance call..."

Wonderful ad-man talk. "Discretionary purchase," "user strategy." Never thought of long distance call as a reorder (goods vs. services). Use one long quotation full of ad-man talk to explain motives for advertising

11

world.[19] This global service prompted AT&T to launch
a vigorous advertising campaign (especially on
television) encouraging its customers to use this new
technology.

The "Reach Out and Touch" advertising campaign
epitomizes AT&T's effort to create and exploit its
customers' need for a personal relationship with an
impersonal system. Post-war Americans were not only
affluent, they were mobile, moving their households
every five years.[20] As members of the family scattered
across the country, they needed some method to maintain
personal contact with one another. But long distance
calling had always been reserved for special
occasions. The cost accountants at the corporation
referred to it as a "discretionary purchase."[21] No
customer has to make a long distance call. To
encourage such calling on a regular basis, AT&T had to
convince people that they were purchasing a service
that would enrich their lives. Jerry Pfiffner, account
executive for N.W. Ayer, explains the corporate motives
for this campaign.

> From the very beginning, A.T. and T. wanted
> us to overcome the negative emotions

24

25. **Using a source effectively** It is clear from the cluster of notes in this paragraph that Ken thinks AT&T's *1982 Annual Report* is a major source for the last part of his paper. First, Ken quotes a phrase that the report has given special meaning, "turning point." Second, he explains one reason for this change by working part of a quotation into his own sentence. Third, he explains another reason for this change by summarizing the results of a complicated court order. And, finally, he provides his own interpretation of the meaning of this material, an interpretation that simultaneously advances and gives an ironic twist to his thesis: "the corporation had to create a new personality to manage the technology it had created."

12

associated with long distance -- you know the
way people used to think about the high cost
of long distance, the bad-news phone call in
the middle of the night . . . A.T. and T.
wanted us to emphasize the casual, positive
aspect; long distance is fun, it's easy, it's
cheap.[22]

The real motive for the campaign was more likely AT&T's
recognition of a new technological era -- an era in
which services rather than products were going to have
to carry "more and more of the revenue burden in the
system."[23]

In 1982, AT&T announced that it had reached a
"turning point" in its history.[24] On the one side, the
corporation faced increasing competition "in markets
that in the past were, for all practical purposes,
virtually ours alone."[25] On the other side, it was
faced with a court order to divest itself of its local
companies and form a new AT&T.[26] For the first time,
the corporation had to create a new personality to
manage the technology it had created.

As it assessed the situation, AT&T realized that
the information age had come of age:

26. **Longer quotation** Ken uses this long quotation from the *1982 Annual Report* to define the information age ("about half the workers in the United States are engaged in generating, gathering or otherwise processing information") and to demonstrate AT&T's decision to fashion a new corporate policy to take advantage of this new era. He introduces the quotation with a full sentence that prepares his readers for the special significance of the passage.

27. **Analysis** Although this long quotation establishes AT&T's relationship to the information age, Ken does not let the quote stand alone. He comments on its importance by paraphrasing AT&T's account of its technological achievements and its assertion that it will continue to be a leader in information services. Ken also speculates that the social change documented in the quote will evoke the old ambivalence about new technology. Such speculation enables Ken to make a direct transition to his analysis of the third ad.

28. **Interpreting art work** The photograph accompanying the "Your Gateway to Tomorrow" ad provides a dramatic illustration of the information age. But Ken's own interpretation of the details of the photograph establish its full significance. He compares the telephone cradle/gate to a "Star Wars launching platform" and comments on the relative proportions of the compact telephone and the expansive horizon. In effect, he transforms the picture into a symbol to illustrate the goods versus services argument.

13

26

Today, about half the workers in the United States are engaged in generating, gathering or otherwise handling information. And they are doing it with increasingly modern technology – from hand-held or desk-top computers to advanced information systems that not only process business data but actually control business processes.[27]

27

AT&T felt confident that it could be a leader in this new era because it had created most of the technology that had brought it into being.[28] But as this complex of new systems began to bombard and penetrate the personal lives of every American, it evoked the traditional ambivalence about technology: were we eager citizens of the information age or anxious victims of information overload?

28

In 1983, AT&T tried to answer this question by announcing its newly fashioned corporate identity while at the same time reaffirming its old fashioned relationship with its customers. A typical ad suggests that the telephone is about to become "Your Gateway to Tomorrow."[29] The art work conveys all the mystery and excitement of a new age. The cradle of a touch-tone

29. **Interpreting copy** Because the complete copy for the advertisement is included in the illustration, Ken knows his readers can examine its language and arrive at their own conclusions. But he wants to direct them to those sections of the copy that advance his own thesis. The ad does catalogue a wide range of technological innovations that are about to change the way we live, but Ken recognizes that AT&T is introducing these innovations according to a recognizable pattern, with an appeal to new conveniences and the assurance of familiar tools. It is "your simple, basic, everyday telephone" that will provide these new services.

14

phone (presented in the image of a Star Wars launching platform) sits at the bottom of the page while a vast horizon stretches to the top of the page. The relative proportions of the two images suggest that the telephone (barely recognizable as a phone) will become less important than the incredible array of new services it will provide.

The copy in the ad continues to emphasize the "dramatic and exciting changes" that are about to take place, but it follows the theme of earlier AT&T advertising by reassuring its readers that these changes will be both practical and manageable. It is "your simple, basic, everyday telephone," after all, not some monstrous computer, that is about to become the gateway to the information age. As the copy describes the changes that will affect the way we work, live, and play it encourages us to use the simplicity and efficiency of this new technology. Every activity -- managing your household, arranging your entertainment, operating your business, escaping emergencies -- can be controlled by your familiar telephone.

The copy concludes by acknowledging that to bring

30. **Introducing quotation** Ken uses a simple phrase (identifying author and source) for his lead-in to Kleinfield's summary quotation about the future of AT&T. Because the passage is longer than four lines, Ken should probably set it off from his text. But he does not want to distract his readers. He wants to preserve the look of a regular paragraph as he prepares for his conclusion.

31. **Conclusion** Although the conclusion provides a final statement of your thesis, it is not a mere restatement of your introduction. It echoes and fulfills the promise of the earlier sections of your paper, but it also offers the final, clinching evidence for your argument. Ken tries to accomplish both objectives by focusing on the "Let's Talk" service announced in his last ad. He has actually called the number to determine whether he would be connected with a real person or a recorded message. His own experience seems to offer conclusive evidence of his thesis: Even as we prepare for the exciting and unsettling mysteries of the information age, Ma Bell still provides an intelligent and vigilant person to explain "what's going on" and "what it all means to you."

15

about these changes, the telephone company will have
to change. As Sonny Kleinfield, author of The Biggest
Company on Earth, predicted in 1981, "it is probable
-- in the long run -- that the telephone will no longer
be called the telephone. And so the name, the
American Telephone and Telegraph Company will become a
misnomer (the telegraph portion is already a misnomer)
and it, too, will undoubtedly be changed in time to
something like the American Communications Company.[30]

Although the exact character of the information
age may still be as vague as the horizon beyond the
phone cradle, AT&T wants to assure its customers that
this new technology will liberate rather than overwhelm
them. At the conclusion of the ad, AT&T invites
customers to call a toll-free number to "talk about
what's happening today to make a new tomorrow." The
"Let's Talk" number does not connect callers with an
impersonal recorded message, but a personable operator
reminiscent of that heroic operator from rural
folklore. Perhaps there is no better way to prepare
for the information age than to talk about this ominous
blessing with an intelligent and vigilant operator who
can help "you understand what's going on. What it all
means to you."

32. **Format of notes** The word *Notes* is centered two inches from the top of the page and is followed by four lines of space. The note pages are counted as part of the total pages of your paper, but the first page of the notes is not numbered. This page is actually page 16. The first line of each note is indented five spaces and preceded by a raised number. All notes are double spaced and follow the pattern discussed in "Documenting Sources" (pages 500–507).

33. **First reference to book by single author** Notes 1, 2, 3, 9, 11, and 18 illustrate citations from books by single author.

34. **Discursive note** Ken uses note 4 to provide additional information on the economic and technological evolution of AT&T. Although the information is interesting and important, including it in the text would detract from the development of his thesis about advertising.

35. **Subsequent reference** Notes 5, 6, 8, and 12 illustrate the use of subsequent references to a source once it has been established in the text.

Notes

[1] Alvin Toffler, The Third Wave (New York: William Morrow and Company, 1980), p. 26. Toffler argues that human history can be divided into three great stages or waves: agricultural, industrial, and information-based.

[2] Daniel Boorstin, The Americans: The Democratic Experience (New York: Random House, 1973), pp. 390-91.

[3] John Brooks, The Telephone: The First Hundred Years (New York: Harper and Row, 1975), plate 16.

[4] The complete story of the economic evolution of AT&T is recounted in N. R. Danielian, A.T. and T., The Story of Industrial Conquest (New York: The Vanguard Press, 1939). The speed of AT&T's technological success may be explained in part by Arthur C. Clarke's contention that the telephone could be mass produced quickly because it was "near absolute zero of technological complexity." Arthur C. Clarke, "Communication in the Second Century of the Telephone," The Telephone's First Century and Beyond (New York: Thomas Y. Crowell Company, 1977), p. 87.

[5] Brooks, plate 30.

[6] Brooks, p. 116.

36. **Indirect sources** Because Ken does not have access to the original source, he must cite Brooks as the indirect source of this quotation.

37. **Corporate author** AT&T's ads and annual reports are the work of the corporation instead of a single author. AT&T is thus listed as the author.

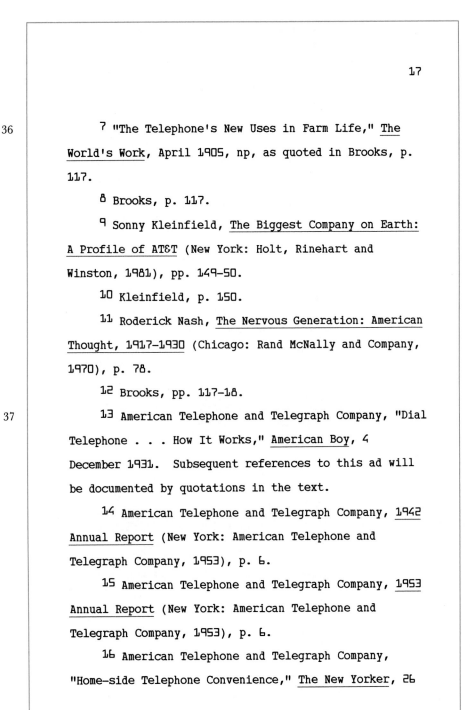

17

36

7 "The Telephone's New Uses in Farm Life," The World's Work, April 1905, np, as quoted in Brooks, p. 117.

8 Brooks, p. 117.

9 Sonny Kleinfield, The Biggest Company on Earth: A Profile of AT&T (New York: Holt, Rinehart and Winston, 1981), pp. 149-50.

10 Kleinfield, p. 150.

11 Roderick Nash, The Nervous Generation: American Thought, 1917-1930 (Chicago: Rand McNally and Company, 1970), p. 78.

12 Brooks, pp. 117-18.

37

13 American Telephone and Telegraph Company, "Dial Telephone . . . How It Works," American Boy, 4 December 1931. Subsequent references to this ad will be documented by quotations in the text.

14 American Telephone and Telegraph Company, 1942 Annual Report (New York: American Telephone and Telegraph Company, 1953), p. 6.

15 American Telephone and Telegraph Company, 1953 Annual Report (New York: American Telephone and Telegraph Company, 1953), p. 6.

16 American Telephone and Telegraph Company, "Home-side Telephone Convenience," The New Yorker, 26

38. **Subsequent references to author of more than one source** Because Toffler is cited as author for two books, *The Third Wave* and *Future Shock,* "Toffler, p. 70" is not a sufficient documentation. To distinguish between the two books, author and title must be included.

39. **First reference to an article by single author** Note 21 follows the format for documenting an article discussed in "Documenting Sources," pages 500–507.

40. **Subsequent reference to article** Like books, articles can be documented in subsequent references by citing the author's name and page number.

41. **Subsequent references to pamphlet** Once Ken has provided a complete citation for AT&T's *1982 Annual Report,* he refers to it in subsequent citations by simply listing title and page number.

42. **Discursive note** For readers interested in reading AT&T's explanation of the causes and effects of the court ordered divestiture, Ken refers them to appropriate pages in the *1982 Annual Report.* He quotes the same report to demonstrate AT&T's acknowledgment of the new competition in telecommunications.

18

March 1960. Subsequent references to this ad will be documented by quotations in the text.

[17] Toffler, p. 243.

[18] Alvin Toffler, Future Shock (New York: Random House, 1970), p. 221.

[19] Kleinfield, p. 301.

[20] Toffler, Future Shock, p. 78.

[21] Michael J. Arlen, "Onward and Upward with the Arts: Thirty Seconds," The New Yorker, 15 October, 1979, p. 99.

[22] Arlen, p. 59.

[23] Arlen, p. 100.

[24] American Telephone and Telegraph Company, 1982 Annual Report (New York: American Telephone and Telegraph Company, 1982), p. 3.

[25] 1982 Annual Report, p. 1.

[26] The causes and effects of divestiture are explained in the 1982 Annual Report, pp. 3–5. The Report also acknowledges that "telecommunications is on its way to becoming one of the most competitive of U.S. industries" (p. 1).

[27] 1982 Annual Report, p. 6.

[28] 1982 Annual Report, p. 6.

43. **Documenting illustrations** Even though all three illustrations carry a full credit line, Ken documents each one with a complete citation and an explanation that "subsequent references to this ad will be documented by quotations in the text." See notes 13, 16, and 29.

19

43

     29 American Telephone and Telegraph Company, "Your Gateway to Tomorrow," <u>Money</u>, March 1983. Subsequent references to this ad will be documented by quotations in the text.

     30 Kleinfield, p. 304.

44. **Format of bibliography** Like the first page of "Notes," the first page of the Bibliography is not numbered. The word "Bibliography" is centered two inches from the top of the page and followed by four lines of space. All entries are double-spaced. The first line of the entry begins at the left margin, but each subsequent line is indented five spaces — a simple reversal of the format for the notes. All entries are alphabetized by the last name of the author.

45. **Two or more works by the same author** Multiple works by the same author are indicated by giving the name(s) of the author in the first entry only. Thereafter, in place of the author(s) name, type the appropriate number of hyphens. In citing two or more works, sources can be arranged chronologically (as with the dates of the *Annual Reports*) or alphabetically (as with the first word of the ads).

46. **Entry for article by one author**

47. **Entry for book by one author**

48. **Entry for essay by one author in collection of essays**

Bibliography

American Telephone and Telegraph Company. <u>1942 Annual Report.</u> New York: American Telephone and Telegraph, 1942.

———— . <u>1953 Annual Report.</u> New York: American Telephone and Telegraph, 1953.

———— . <u>1982 Annual Report.</u> New York: American Telephone and Telegraph, 1982.

———— . "Dial Telephone . . . How it Works," <u>American Boy,</u> 4 December, 1931. (advertisement)

———— . "Home-wide Telephone Convenience," <u>The New Yorker,</u> 26 March 1960. (advertisement)

———— . "Your Gateway to Tomorrow," <u>Money,</u> March 1983. (advertisement)

Arlen, Michael J. "Onward and Upward with the Arts: Thirty Seconds," <u>The New Yorker,</u> 15 October 1979, pp. 55-146.

Boorstin, Daniel. <u>The Americans: The Democratic Experience.</u> New York: Random House, 1973.

Brooks, John. <u>The Telephone: The First Hundred Years.</u> New York: Harper and Row, 1975.

Clarke, Arthur C. "Communications in the Second Century of the Telephone," <u>The Telephone's First</u>

44

45

46

47

48

49. **Entry for unsigned source with no page numbers (np) as cited in another source**

50. **Entries for two or more works by the same author** The titles are arranged alphabetically.

21

Century -- and Beyond. New York: Thomas Y.
Crowell Company, 1977.

Danielian, N.R. A.T. and T.: The Story of Industrial
Conquest. New York: The Vanguard Press, 1939.

Kleinfield, Sonny. The Biggest Company on Earth: A
Profile of AT&T. New York: Holt, Rinehart and
Winston, 1981.

Nash, Roderick. The Nervous Generation: American
Thought, 1917-1930. Chicago: Rand McNally, 1970.

"The Telephone's New Uses in Farm Life," The World's
Work, April 1905, np, as quoted in Brooks, p.
117.

Toffler, Alvin. Future Shock. New York: Random House,
1970.

---------- . The Third Wave. New York: William Morrow
and Company, 1980.

Chapter 15

Business Writing

Business is paperwork. As Ken discovered in his research paper, "about half the workers in the United States are engaged in generating, gathering or otherwise handling information." Some of this information can be communicated orally, over the phone or over lunch, but most of it must be communicated for the record in writing. The purpose of this chapter is to acquaint you with some of the conventional forms of business correspondence and to enable you to apply the lessons you have learned in this book to practical writing situations.

Letter of Complaint

Your first correspondence with the world of business may be as a consumer who feels that a particular business (or person) has failed to provide proper goods or promised services. If you want to write a letter of complaint, you are probably angry, feeling that you have been cheated or misled. But venting your anger in a letter is not the best way to remedy the situation you want corrected. In some cases, the person who will read your letter may not be aware of or responsible for the situation that has made you mad. In other cases, the person may be responsible but may also feel that he or she has a logical explanation for the situation you find offensive. In any case, your reader will probably respond to your hostility by becoming defensive.

If you want your reader to recognize the possible legitimacy of your complaint, you must adjust the tone of your letter so that you sound like a reasonable citizen rather than a crank. The best procedure is to analyze the situation carefully, consider the point of view of your reader, and then determine your real purpose in writing the letter — what, specifically, you want to accomplish. Once you have made this assessment, draft a letter that states your complaint in an objective tone, support your case with pertinent facts, and request a specific solution.

Consider the case of Maria and her fellow tenants at the Devon Apartments. In May, Maria learned that she would be working at the university during the summer and would need a place to live. After examining several possibilities, she selected Devon Apartments because it had a large swimming pool. Other tenants, mostly college students, and the building's supervisor, Billy Ray Burford, had promoted the pool as the complex's social center during the summer. However, on the first day of June the tenants were informed by a notice on the bulletin board that the pool would be closed for the summer. The notice (signed simply "The Management") gave no explanation for the closing, and Billy Ray was away on vacation visiting relatives in Tennessee.

Weather predictions forecast the hottest summer in years, the temperature of the tenants reached the boiling point, and a meeting was scheduled in the Devon Apartments' recreation room. After some shouting and screaming, someone suggested that a formal letter of complaint be written to the owner of the facility. Maria, the English major, was elected to write the letter.

As she began to plan what she wanted to say in the letter, Maria made a list of all the comments she had heard at the tenants' meeting.

1. *Who closed the pool?*

2. *Where's Billy Ray? When is he supposed to get back?*

3. *This is supposed to be the hottest summer in years.*

4. Why are they closing it this summer?

5. Who's "The Management"?

6. Let's sue the owner.

7. I'm getting a lawyer and breaking my lease.

8. The pool is the reason I moved here. It's in all the ads.

9. That's false advertising.

10. What reasons could they have for closing it — money, insurance, repairs?

11. Let's offer to pay a few extra bucks a month to keep it open.

12. Let's all move out.

Maria decided that her first job was to obtain some facts. Her lease listed the owner of the Devon Apartments as a Mr. Oliver Pendragon of Mesquite, Texas. Did he order the pool closing, or did Billy Ray (or one of the "managers") make the decision without his knowledge? Because neither Maria nor any of the other tenants had ever met Mr. Pendragon, she was uncertain about how to address him. A careful examination of her lease also revealed that the pool was not mentioned anywhere in it. Did the tenants have a legal right to complain about its closing? Was false advertising a sufficient reason to complain?

As she reviewed her notes from the meeting and considered the questions she had raised by examining her lease, Maria realized that she needed to select the information that would support her case most effectively. Her letter should not plead (we'll pay extra) or threaten (we'll move out). It should be polite but firm. She should adopt the tone of a concerned tenant speaking on behalf of her fellow tenants. She might hint that others were charging false advertising or contemplating legal action, but she would simply request an explanation. She decided not to mention the lease because to do so might escalate the legal issue and close off all discussion. The purpose of her letter, Maria decided, was to inform her absentee landlord of the situation, request an explanation, and suggest that he reverse his decision before the next tenants' meeting. She wrote an effective letter, which appears on page 573. And she prevailed. The pool — closed for repairs that the management had not wanted to invest in just yet — was reopened on the Fourth of July weekend.

The Form of the Business Letter

The typical business letter conforms to a relatively standard format and consists of eight parts. Study each of the numbered descriptions below, then look at Maria's letter to see how each part of a business letter appears in type. The numbers in the margin of the letter are coded to the descriptions below.

1. *The return address*   This part is omitted, of course, if the writer uses stationery with a printed letterhead, because the letterhead itself is the return address. The lines are blocked, and no punctuation is used at the end of them, although conventional punctuation is followed within them.

2. *The date line*   The date line is placed directly below the return address heading, unless you are using letterhead, in which case the date line is centered five spaces below the last line of the letterhead. The order of the date may be month-day-year with a comma between day and year (June 7, 1983) or day-month-year without a comma (7 June 1983).

3. *The inside address*   The heading of three or more lines is placed flush with the left margin and presents information in the same sequence as the return address. Abbreviations such as *Co.* and *Inc.* are used only if these terms are abbreviated in the company's official letterhead.

4. *The salutation*   When an individual is being addressed, the salutation usually takes one of the following forms: "Dear *Mr.* (or *Mrs., Ms.,* or *Miss*) Woy," or "Dear *Sir* (or *Madam*), followed by a colon. The form "Dear Sirs" or "Gentlemen" is seldom used in modern business letters. If you do not know to whom to address your letter, address the position, such as "Dear Editor" or "Dear Manager." If you do not know the position, use "Dear Sir or Madam." Informal salutations such as "Dear Lynn" are acceptable only in writing to a friend.

5. *The body*   The body of the letter usually consists of one or more paragraphs of single-spaced text, with double-spacing between paragraphs. All paragraphs start at the left margin, with no indentation to mark the opening of the paragraph.

6. *The complimentary close*   The most common endings are "Yours truly," "Yours sincerely," or "Sincerely yours." Such closings as "Cordially" or "Cordially yours" are used when you are on familiar terms with the

Standard business letter format

1   3200 Devon Road, Apartment 18
    Muncie, IN 47304
2   June 7, 1983

3   Mr. Oliver Pendragon
    Owner, Devon Apartments
    72 North Skyway Drive
    Mesquite, TX 75150

4   Dear Mr. Pendragon:

5   The tenants of Devon Apartments recently received a notice from The
    Management informing us that the complex swimming pool would be
    closed this summer. Many of us chose Devon Apartments because it
    was the only apartment complex featuring a swimming pool. The
    pool is pictured in the apartment's brochures and in the
    advertising printed in the local newspapers. Also, your
    supervisor, Mr. Billy Ray Burford, emphasizes the advantages of the
    pool when he takes prospective tenants on a tour of the facility.

    At a recent tenants' meeting, we discussed the pool closing. All
    agreed that closing the pool during what promises to be a very hot
    summer is both disheartening and inconvenient. We also agreed
    that advertising the pool but closing it down is not a good
    business practice. In fact, one resident is considering consulting
    his attorney.

    Clearly, the residents of Devon Apartments, who had anticipated
    another enjoyable summer at the complex pool, would like to know
    why the pool is being closed. They have asked me to inform you of
    the situation, to request some explanation for the closing, and to
    urge you to reconsider this unpopular decision. I look forward to
    hearing from you soon so that I can make a progress report at our
    next tenants' meeting on June 21, 1983.

6   Sincerely yours,

                            Maria Galvao

7   Maria Galvao

8   cc: Tenants of Devon Apartments
         Billy Ray Burford, Superintendent

addressee. "Respectfully" is a formal close used chiefly in reports. The complimentary close is punctuated with a comma.

7. *The signature* The signature consists of two parts: the written signature and the writer's typed name. The written signature is the legal identification of the writer; the typed name below it is a safeguard against misreading. If a woman wants to be addressed as *Mrs.* or *Miss,* she may indicate the preferred form in parentheses before her typed name; otherwise, she will probably be addressed as *Ms.* in a reply to her letter. The complimentary close and typed signature are in alignment with one another and start in approximate alignment with the return address and date.

8. *The reference* Three types of reference information are often included at the bottom of a business letter. Each item is typed flush with the left margin, placed below the author's signature, and separated from one another by three spaces.

   a. *Initials of sender and typist:* When a letter is typed by someone other than the writer, the typist includes the writer's initials, a colon, and his or her own initials — JFT:kmt.

   b. *Enclosure:* When other material has been included along with the letter, the typist tells the person receiving the letter that there is an enclosure and what has been enclosed — Enclosure: color chart.

   c. *Recipient of copies:* When copies of the letter have been sent to other people, the typist provides the names of those people by typing *cc,* a colon, and the recipient's names — cc: Tenants of Devon Apartments.

Job Search

Perhaps the most important contact you have with the business world is the correspondence you write seeking employment. Many jobs do not require extensive written application. For example, if you are seeking part-time work selling shoes in a department store or pumping gas in a service station, you should apply in person at the personnel office or to whoever is doing the hiring for that job. But most job openings listed in formal advertisements call for special skills, are quite competitive, and therefore require a two-stage application procedure. First, you must present yourself to your prospective employer in writing. Second, if you are fortunate enough to pass this initial screening, you will probably be invited to interview for the position. There are two parts to the written application — the résumé and the letter of application. The purpose of both documents is to convince an employer that you are an excellent candidate for the position — certainly someone who should be interviewed. Once you reach the second stage, you can find out more about the job and present your qualifications in greater detail.

Résumé

A résumé is the basic tool in any job search because it lists in summary form what you know, what you have done, and what you have to offer a prospective employer. Because the preparation of a résumé is essentially a writing assignment, when you compose your résumé you should work your way through the three stages of the writing process.

1. *Planning* Before you create a formal résumé, you should analyze your abilities and achievements in writing. Make a list of your *educational achievements* (degrees, dates, institutions, major, minors, honors); *work experience* (business, position, responsibilities, dates of employment); and *personal characteristics* (special skills, social attitudes, work habits).

2. *Drafting* Once you have compiled this list, organize your information according to a logical format such as the one illustrated on page 579. Because the most effective résumés are brief (preferably not longer than one typed page), you will need to make some decisions about the information you uncovered in planning. Some of it is essential; some of it is inappropriate; and some of it could be important if it were presented in the right way.

3. *Revising* As you examine the preliminary draft of your résumé, you may need to consider two kinds of revision. First, you may want to rearrange your information to emphasize those skills and experiences that make you particularly suited for a specific job. Second, you may want to rearrange the design or spacing of your résumé to make it more attractive or easier to read.

The three elements that guide you through the writing process work equally well to guide you through the process of preparing a résumé. Your *subject*, after all, is you. Your résumé should present you as a significant and interesting applicant whose experience and skills match those required for the job. Your *audience* is your prospective employer. You need to think about the kind of information he or she wants and needs to make a decision about your qualifications. You also need to think about how to present this information in a way that will allow him or her to make an efficient and informed judgment. Your ultimate *purpose* is to get the job (if you discover you want it), but your immediate purpose is to get an interview so that you and your prospective employer can find out more about each other. Your résumé should therefore argue convincingly that you possess credentials worth discussing in some detail.

Maria's experience during her summer of working on campus provides some interesting examples. When Maria began in the spring to consider the possibility of summer employment, she conducted a personal inventory of her educational achievements, work experiences, and personal skills.

Education

1969-1975 — Grade School — Captain of Safety Patrol
Student Council President

1975-1977 — Middle School — Drama Club, Choir, Student
Council

1977-1981 — High School — Valedictorian, Drama Club,
Madrigal Singers

1981-   College — English and Speech Communications major
Royalty Scholarship, 1982
Madrigals

Experience

1976 —   Babysitting
1978-1979 —   Waitress for Emily's Catering Service (Summer)
1979 —   Elf at Santa Claus Land at Mall (Christmas)
1980 —   Copy kid for Muncie Evening Star (Summer)

1981 —	*Campaign volunteer for congressional candidate (Summer)*
1982 —	*Freelance arts writer and arts calendar editor, The Indianapolis Evening Globe (Summer)*
1982-present (school year)	*Student secretary and research assistant for Dr. Duffy*
	Tutor, Writing Center
	Editor, The Expositor

Personal Skills and Characteristics

Good writer, responsible, cheerful — get along with people. Good listener. Good interviewer. Variety of interests — music, theater, jogging, politics.

As she assessed her preliminary list, Maria realized that her major, most of her really important and interesting jobs, and certainly her most marketable skills suggested that she look for a job in communications. She read the classified ads in the newspaper, visited the university placement center, and asked friends and faculty members about possible job openings. Several possibilities presented themselves — a secretary's job in a public relations-firm, a free-lancing assignment for the local paper, and an internship at a university publication, *Campus Update.* Although she knew that competition for the last job would be intense (several of her friends had already applied), Maria thought that the ad argued for someone with her qualifications.

Campus Update, a publication of the Office of University Relations, is accepting applications from qualified students for a summer internship as the magazine's editorial assistant. The editorial assistant will research, write, edit, and proof material for the magazine; work with the university's Photo Service in assigning photographs to accompany articles in the magazine; and assist with design and paste-up. The applicant should be a full-time student, possess strong writing skills, and be able to meet deadlines. Application Deadline, April 15, 1983. Submit résumé to Rae Morrow, Editor, Campus Update, Ball State University, Muncie, IN 47306.

Exercise   Study Maria's original inventory and her completed résumé, shown on page 579. What information from her inventory does Maria include, omit, or relabel in her résumé? How does the information listed in the ad help her decide what details to include? **If you were the editor of *Campus Update,* what specific experiences listed on Maria's résumé would you say suggest her qualifications for the position of editorial assistant? Why?**

The Form of the Résumé

Because every individual possesses unique qualifications and each job situation is different, there is no standard format for a résumé. The example on the facing page illustrates common presentations featured in many résumés. It is typed according to the block style, major sections are single spaced, and spacing between sections is double-spaced.

1. *The heading.* Center the title, Résumé (in capital letters), at the top of the page and follow it with your name, address, and telephone number. The last piece of information may be the most important, particularly if your prospective employer wants to call you to arrange an interview.

2. *Position desired.* Because Maria is responding to an ad for a specific job, she lists that job on her résumé. *Job Objective* is sometimes included in this space to indicate your ultimate career objective.

3. *Education.* List the college(s) you are attending or attended in reverse order. Include the dates you attended each one, any degrees received, your major and minor fields of study, and any honors you were awarded. Because Maria is presently a college student, she decided to include her high school, its location, the dates she attended, and a special honor she received.

4. *Work experience.* List all your work experience, starting with the most recent and working backward. In particular list those jobs that illustrate your experience performing tasks similar to those listed in the ad. Give the details of your experience, such as the dates of employment, the job title, the name of your employer, and a brief description of your responsibilities. Use *action* verbs to emphasize the nature of your responsibilities, particularly when they correspond to the qualifications in the job description.

5. *References.* You can include the names of people who know you and your abilities as references in your résumé, particularly if listing their

RESUME

Maria Galvao
3200 Devon Road, Apartment 18
Muncie, IN 47304
317-555-5721

Position desired   Publications Intern (Editorial Assistant)

Education
    1981-present   Ball State University
                    Current standing: Sophomore
                    Major: English and Speech Communication
                    Honors: Royalty Scholarship, 1982

    1977-1981   East Central High School, Indianapolis
                    Valedictorian

Work Experience
    1982-present   Editor, The Expositor. Selected, edited,
                        proofread articles for college literary
                        magazine.
                    Tutor, The Writing Center. Tutored students
                        with writing problems.
                    Student secretary and research assistant, Dr.
                        Maureen Duffy. Typed manuscript.
                        Conducted library research.

    1982 (Summer)   Freelance arts writer, The Indianapolis
                        Evening Globe. Wrote theater reviews and
                        compiled weekly arts calendar.

    1981 (Summer)   Campaign volunteer for Congressional candidate
                        Phil Nightingale. Wrote press releases,
                        worked on phone banks, and helped organize
                        fund-raising events.

    1980 (Summer)   Copy kid, Muncie Evening Star. Delivered news
                        copy and mail.

References   Academic references and college transcripts
                  available from Placement Office, Ball State University,
                          Muncie, IN 47306

References

Dr. Maureen Duffy   Larry Horney, Editor
Professor of English   Indianapolis Evening Globe
Ball State University   Indianapolis, IN 46208
Muncie, IN 47306   317-936-5520
317-555-6055

Elizabeth Hockney
Director, The Writing Center
Ball State University
Muncie, IN 47306
317-555-5754

positions suggests your qualifications for a particular job. Always ask these people in advance before you use their name as a reference. Include their name, title, address, and telephone number. Your prospective employer may want to call your references for detailed information that would not appear in a letter of reference. You can also indicate that your references are on file (as Maria does) or can be furnished upon request.

Letter of Application

The letter of application (sometimes called the cover letter) is submitted with your résumé and is designed to accomplish five objectives:

1. To inform your prospective employer what job you are interested in and where you learned about it.

2. To persuade him or her that your qualifications match the requirements listed for that position.

3. To refer him or her to those features listed on your résumé that are particularly relevant to the position advertised.

4. To indicate that you are available for an interview.

5. To present yourself *in writing* as an intelligent, confident, and responsible applicant.

To accomplish these objectives, you need to consider the person reading your application. Faced with a large stack of applications, that person — being only human — will find an efficient method for reducing the large stack to a small stack. The easiest way to eliminate paper is to discard the letters of all those applicants who fail to mention or are uncertain about the position for which they are applying. The next task is to determine whether an applicant's qualifications actually match the requirements listed for the position. Your reader will be particularly quick to spot "Although-letters," as in "*Although* most of my experience has been in the area of selling, I feel confident that my experience in oral communication will enable me to master the skills of written communication."

Once the confused and unqualified are eliminated, your reader still

Letter of application

3200 Devon Road, Apartment 18
Muncie, IN 47304
April 3, 1983

Ms. Rae Morrow
Editor, Campus Update
Ball State University
Muncie, IN 47306

Dear Ms. Morrow:

I am applying for the summer internship as editorial assistant for Campus Update, Ball State University's magazine for faculty and staff. Dr. Maureen Duffy, Professor of English, called my attention to your advertisement in the Daily News and encouraged me to apply for the position.

I am a sophomore working toward a bachelor's degree in English and speech communication. My courses have given me extensive experience in public speaking, interviewing, writing, and conducting research. As the enclosed résumé illustrates, my work experiences include writing for an Indianapolis newspaper, editing a student literary magazine, and composing press releases for a congressional candidate. In addition, my two years working as secretary and research assistant for Dr. Duffy and as a tutor in The Writing Center have helped me learn a great deal about the diverse research activities and professional services of Ball State University's faculty and staff.

I feel that my education, writing experience, and understanding of the university will enable me to be an efficient and effective editorial assistant for Campus Update. This internship will provide me with valuable experience as I work toward my career goal as a writer or editor for a commercial magazine. I am available for an interview and will be happy to submit samples of my writing. My local telephone number is 555-5721.

Sincerely yours,

Maria Galvao

Maria Galvao

Enclosure: Résumé

may face a fairly large stack of applications. At this point, he or she will study the major section of each letter with some care. What specific training or experiences make this candidate qualified for this position? How does this candidate's letter and résumé suggest that he or she is familiar with and confident about the "hidden" responsibilities of the job? An ad cannot list all the responsibilities of a specific job. If you can anticipate some of those responsibilities in your letter (and résumé) and explain why you are particularly qualified to assume them, then your letter will distinguish itself from the rest of the stack.

As this last comment suggests, your reader must discover some way to choose from among equally qualified candidates. All sorts of criteria — some objective, many subjective — now enter the picture. Eventually, your prospective employer will want to verify his or her judgment of your credentials by asking you questions during the interview and by talking to those people you have listed as references. But at this stage in the process, he or she is still dealing with the impression that your written correspondence creates. Does your letter attract and hold his or her attention? Is it neat, to the point, and free of error? Is the tone of your letter appropriate — confident without being aggressive, professional without being stuffy, personable without being chatty? In sum, does the person who emerges from the writing in this letter seem like someone who is responsible, intelligent, and imaginative?

Because Maria was applying for a job as an editorial assistant, she knew that her written application would be submitted to a rigorous evaluation. Her résumé and letter of application had to follow the correct format. Her writing had to be accurate, graceful, and cogent. And her letter had to demonstrate not only that she was qualified for the job but also that her experience, achievements, and personal characteristics make her especially qualified to perform the job. How successfully do you think Maria presented herself and her credentials in writing? Her letter, shown on page 581, conforms to the traditional format for a business letter.

Writing on the Job

When you start to work at a particular job, you may be asked to draft *external* or *internal* business correspondence. External correspondence involves writing letters to people in the "outside" world — customers and competitors not employed at your place of business. Internal correspondence involves writing memos and reports to people in the office — your immediate supervisor or fellow employees. The following discussion and examples illustrate how each type of business writing is directed to different audiences for different purposes.

Letters of Inquiry and Response

Inquiry

Letters of inquiry are written to other people and businesses to request information or services. Such letters usually fall into two categories: (1) those that request information appealing to the self-interest of the other company, such as a request for its latest catalog, and (2) those that request special services (or favors) motivated by your self-interest, such as a request for the other business's mailing list. The best letter of inquiry, of course, is one written to persuade the reader that a prompt reply is in the mutual interest of all parties concerned.

Because your objective is to solicit a favorable reply, you should do some planning before you draft your letter. Conduct preliminary research so that you know you need to write the letter. Often the information you want may be readily available if you spend a little time looking on your own. Identify the specific person or office within a business that can provide you with the information you want. Because many letters are sent to the wrong place, they are often ignored or routed to another office (which may also be the wrong office). Or they elicit a terse form letter telling you that (a) the office does not have the information you seek (and doesn't know where you can find it), or (b) you will have to draft another inquiry to another office (which, again, may or may not be the right place to inquire). Finally, as you plan your letter, be clear in your own mind what you want to know. Many letters ask too many questions, ask questions that cannot be answered, or ask questions that are essentially rhetorical — that is, they ask questions that the writers do not really expect the reader to answer.

As you draft your letter, think about the common elements of the writing situation. Restrict the *subject* of your letter by keeping your

Letter of inquiry

P. O. Box 5732
Modoc, IN 47358
July 7, 1983

Ms. Rae Morrow
Editor, Campus Update
Ball State University
Muncie, IN 47306

Dear Ms. Morrow:

I recently came across a back issue of your fine magazine, Campus
Update, and was delighted to read about the many wonderful
research activities of the Ball State faculty. I am writing to
inquire whether you would be interested in doing a story on my
research on regional beers.

Although I am not a Ball State faculty member, I was, until my
recent retirement, Professor of Business at North Central Business
College for twenty-five years. During my tenure at NCBC, I began
to document the closing of local breweries in the Midwest. Some
were bought out. Some simply went bankrupt. I tried to explain
the reasons for these developments in an article I submitted to the
Midcentral Historical Quarterly in 1969. But that's ancient
history.

What I thought might be of interest to your readers is my extensive
beer can collection. I have converted my barn into a "beer-can
library." I think I have a can or bottle from every brewery that
ever made beer in the Midwest, plus many cans and bottles in my
national and international collections. Some of the individual
cans are really quite attractive and are certainly interesting
relics from another period in our nation's history.

I am here most of the time, so feel free to call me if you are
interested in my story. Is there any way I can subscribe to Campus
Update? It's a wonderful magazine.

Sincerely yours,

Donald Harvey

Donald Harvey, Ph.D.
317-515-4437

questions brief, clear, and to the point. Avoid long-winded accounts of how you became interested in the subject or tedious explanations of what you already know about the subject. Anticipate the needs of your *audience* by making it easy for your reader to answer your questions. Put yourself in your reader's place. Ask yourself, "If I received this request, what would I do with it?" State your *purpose* directly by indicating in a few words why you need the information and what you plan to do with it once you receive it.

Response

Letters of response may seem to be simple writing assignments ("Here is the information you requested"; "We do not have the information you requested"), but they often require a considerable amount of planning. When you write most business letters you are not speaking for yourself; you are speaking for your business. Indeed, for that moment you *are* the business. In addition to responding to the letter of inquiry, you are promoting the good will of your business. Accordingly, just as the writers of letters of inquiry should think about you by making it easy for you to answer their questions, so you should think about them as you plan your letter explaining what you can and cannot do for them.

The best strategy is to begin on a courteous note by acknowledging the writer's letter and interest in your business. Then, if you can respond positively to the letter, answer as many questions as you can, as completely and as efficiently as you can. If you cannot respond positively, cushion the bad news somewhere in the middle of your letter. You may need to explain your negative response by citing a company policy ("we do not release our mailing list"), but you should try to avoid the impersonal impact of policy statements by adopting a reasonable, polite tone that acknowledges the legitimacy of the writer's request and your understanding of his or her problem. Your letter can also promote the good will of your business by providing information not requested in the letter of inquiry. For example, you may want to include material that the letter writer did not know about but that may enhance his or her understanding of the subject. Or you may want to refer the writer to someone who can provide the information or supply the services requested.

Maria's first assignment as an editorial assistant at *Campus Update* was to draft a letter of response to Dr. Donald Harvey's letter of inquiry, shown on page 584. Her assignment was somewhat complicated because she was drafting the letter for someone else's signature — that of editor Rae Morrow. It is not uncommon in business for a letter to be written by one person and signed by another. Indeed, much important business correspondence is written and revised by several people before it actually reaches the desk of the person who reads it, approves it, and signs it. As Maria planned Ms. Morrow's response to Dr. Harvey's letter, she began by making a list of the things "she" could say to him:

1. *Campus Update is for Ball State faculty members.*

2. *You are not a Ball State faculty member.*

3. *Your research project does not conform to the policy of the magazine to report on BSU faculty research.*

4. *Your research is not really research.*

5. *Beer can collecting does sound like an interesting subject.*

6. *Disappearance of local breweries is a significant historical fact.*

7. *Sounds more like a feature story for a newspaper or commercial magazine.*

8. *Larry Horney at Globe.*

9. *I'd like to see beer can collection — might even want to do free-lance piece on it for the Globe.*

10. *Can't subscribe to Campus Update. It's given away. (Is last sentence polite close or subtle bribe?)*

Maria read through her list and decided that the issue was fairly simple. Dr. Harvey was not a faculty member so his request could be easily denied by stating magazine policy. But she was interested in the story and thought it should be written for some publication. As *Ms. Morrow,* however, she could not volunteer to visit the "beer-can library" or write the feature story for the *Globe.* She decided to write Dr. Harvey a friendly rejection letter, suggesting that he consider a wider audience for his story and providing him with the name of a newspaper editor who might be interested in it. Her letter, signed by Ms. Morrow, is shown on page 587.

Exercise

Reread Dr. Harvey's letter, Maria's notes, and Ms. Morrow's letter. How does Maria open her letter? How does she deliver the bad news? How does she promote the good will of Ball State University and *Campus Update*?

Letter of response

BALL STATE UNIVERSITY / MUNCIE, INDIANA 47306

July 13, 1983

Dr. Donald Harvey
P. O. Box 5732
Modoc, IN 47358

Dear Dr. Harvey:

Thank you for your letter expressing interest in the research
conducted at Ball State University and suggesting a story for
Campus Update.

As you may know, Campus Update is an internal magazine for Ball
State University faculty and staff. By distributing this magazine
free of charge we hope to inform university employees about the
research activities of their colleagues. Ball State University
employs 2,900 people, and reporting their achievements takes up a
lot of space. Unfortunately, we do not have room to write about
the many research activities of people outside the university even
though they may be doing valuable work. We feel that our first
obligation is to our own employees.

Perhaps you should consider a wider audience for your story on your
beer can collection. Larry Horney, editor at the Indianapolis
Evening Globe (317-936-5520), is interested in business history and
may want to consider doing a feature story on the demise of
regional breweries.

Thank you again for your interest in Campus Update. We wish you
the best of luck in your research.

Sincerely yours,

Rae Morrow

Rae Morrow, Editor
Campus Update

Memorandums

The standard form of communication among members of the same business organization is the memorandum (or memo). Because memos contain a permanent record of an organization's daily activities — information requested, decisions made — many businesses supply their employees with a standardized "memo form" to facilitate efficient reading and filing. Such forms provide specific spaces for the date, the names of the recipient and sender, and the subject of the correspondence. If such forms are not available, or if your memo is too long to fit on a standard form, you can easily duplicate the memo format. (See the examples of standardized form on page 589 and individualized form on page 590).

Although memos may be short (a brief note requesting sales figures) or long (an extended argument for a new sales policy), they require writers to give serious attention to subject, audience, and purpose.

1. *Subject.* The *subject line* restricts and controls the subject of the memo. Effective memos maintain the focus identified by the subject line; ineffective memos introduce extraneous information, circle the subject, or seem somehow to avoid the subject completely.

2. *Audience.* An accurate assessment of the audience for a memo is essential to effective business communication. If you are writing *up* the organizational ladder to your superior or to more than one person, you should adopt a relatively formal tone. If you are writing *down* the ladder or to people on the same rung, you can adopt a more informal tone. In all cases, you should consider the needs and expectations of your reader. You probably know much more about the subject of your memo than your reader does. In fact, you are probably supplying information at his or her request. The question is this: does your reader *need* to know everything you know? You may want to provide a brief introduction to inform (or remind) your reader of the reason for your memo, but your principal objective is to get to the point. Deliver the information briefly and effectively in a format that will enable your reader to find information and make a decision. Divide your subject into convenient subheadings and number them in a logical sequence.

3. *Purpose.* Memos usually have a quite focused purpose, such as to request information, to supply information, to urge the adoption of a

---

INTER-OFFICE CORRESPONDENCE

TO: Maria Galvao, Editorial Assistant   DATE: July 20, 1983

FROM: Rae Morrow, Editor

SUBJECT: Cover Story for Campus Update on Alcohol Abuse

A recent issue of The Chronicle of Higher Education carries the
headline "Higher Education's Drinking Problem." The article cites
a national survey showing that anywhere from 70-95 percent of
students on any one campus drink alcoholic beverages. No other
U.S. population segment has a higher proportion of drinkers.

Although this is hardly earth-shattering news, I think we need to
do a story on campus drinking. Are any of our faculty members
conducting research in the area of alcohol abuse? Try to find a
story that offers a positive solution to the problem rather than
negative evidence to support the old party-school stereotype.

---

new policy, or to argue for the removal of an old policy. A memo is
like an essay in that you need to announce your purpose at the beginning and then supply the information that will support your purpose
in the body of your correspondence. If your purpose is clear and well
developed, your reader will understand at once what you have written
and how he or she is supposed to respond.

After Maria had worked at *Campus Update* for about six weeks, she
received a memo (shown above) from her supervisor, requesting that she
research and recommend a cover story for the magazine on the subject of
alcohol abuse.

Maria determined that Ms. Morrow had actually defined the kind of
story she wanted: a story about a faculty member who was conducting
"positive" research on the problem of alcohol abuse. As she began her
research, Maria discovered a surprising number of stories on alcohol
abuse, but few that met her editor's requirements. For example, she
talked with a faculty member who was gathering data on student attitudes and practices regarding the use and misuse of alcohol. She also
talked to a visiting lecturer from the Johnson Institute, a treatment
center for chemically dependent persons located in Minneapolis, Minnesota. But the research of the faculty member and the visiting lecturer

To: Rae Morrow   July 27, 1983

From: Maria Galvao

Subject: Alcohol Abuse Cover Story

After considering several possibilities, I want to recommend that
we do a cover story on the new Chemical Dependency Project that is
being co-sponsored by Ball Memorial Hospital and the University's
Human Performance Laboratory. The purpose of the project is to
initiate a program of regular, monitored exercise for people who
are chemically dependent -- on drugs or alcohol. I think this
story would be effective for the following reasons:

1. The story is positive. Regular exercise helps restore the
   body's natural working order. Once they substitute exercise for
   alcohol, patients eat better, sleep better, experience less
   stress, and feel generally more in tune with their body. The
   social support of the exercise group is also crucial to the
   patient's increased self-confidence and improving self-concept.

2. The story is based on research of Ball State faculty members.
   Although the program is still in its initial phases, the
   researchers at the Human Performance Laboratory are confident
   that their program will be able to duplicate the results of
   similar programs which have reported an 85 percent recovery
   rate. Recovery is a clinical word. It does not mean cured.

3. The story would appeal to a large segment of the university
   population. Those who are social or heavy drinkers will be
   interested in the research team's findings about the effect of
   alcohol on the body. Those who are interested in physical
   fitness will be interested in how exercise can restore the
   body. And those who are in both categories -- occasional
   drinkers and joggers -- will be interested in the physical and
   psychological effects of both activities.

I can see only two major problems with this story:

1. The program is so new that the research findings are not
   complete. But I think the pattern has been established by
   comparable programs, and our faculty will be interested in the
   progress of this program. Some may want to sign up.

2. We may have difficulty with the patients' right to privacy.
   Some patients may not want to talk about the program, much less
   be named in or photographed for the story. I will have to
   consult with Ball Hospital and the Human Performance Laboratory
   to determine their policies on this matter. If you like the
   idea for this story, I can resolve this issue, one way or the
   other, in a few days.

seemed to focus on documenting the causes and explaining the effects of the problem. Neither seemed to meet Ms. Morrow's requirements for "a story that offers a positive solution." After several days of hunting, the only "positive solution" story Maria was able to uncover was the work of a neighborhood committee (composed of officers of fraternities and home owners who lived near fraternity row). The committee was trying to find a solution to the noise problem produced by excessive partying. Although such a story could be considered positive, it was not based on faculty research and it certainly did not help counter "the old party-school stereotype."

Finally, Maria learned about a new research program cosponsored by the local hospital and the university's Human Performance Laboratory. She talked with a doctor from the hospital on the phone and visited with several members of the research team at the laboratory. Because these conversations convinced Maria that she had uncovered a story that communicated the right subject to the right audience for the right purpose, she wrote a memo to her editor recommending the story for the cover of *Campus Update*. The memo appears on the opposite page.

Exercise

A. **Analyze the subject, audience, and purpose of Maria's memo.**

1. **Why does she omit from her memo the other stories she researched?**

2. **How does she present the case for the story she recommends?**

3. **What effect does Maria create in her memo by introducing potential problems with the story? Why does she propose to solve them?**

4. **If you were Ms. Morrow, how would you respond to this memo?**

B. **Review the sections in Chapter 1 of this book that discuss making decisions about your subject, audience, and purpose (pages 15–28). To what extent has Maria followed the Guidelines for Selecting Your Subject, Analyzing Your Audience, and Determining Your Purpose in recommending her cover story?**

Handbook of Grammar and Usage

A POINT OF VIEW TOWARD USAGE

The Evolution of English

The language that Americans speak and write is descended from the language spoken by the English, Scottish, and Irish immigrants who founded the British colonies in America. Their language, in turn, was descended from the languages of Germanic tribes who, during the fifth and sixth centuries, invaded Britain and settled there. One of these tribes, the Angles, later became known as the Englisc (English) and gave their name to a country and a language, both of which they shared with other peoples — the Saxons, the Jutes, and, later, the Danes and the Normans.

The language that has come down to us from that Anglo-Saxon beginning has undergone great changes. Modern college students find Chaucer's fourteenth-century English something of a puzzle. And before Chaucer — well, judge for yourself. Here is the opening of the Lord's Prayer as it was written in the ninth, fourteenth, and seventeenth centuries, respectively:

Old English	**Middle English**	**Modern English**
Fæder ūre þū þe eart on heofonum, sī þīn nama gehālgod. Tōbecume þīn rīce, Gewurþe ðīn willa on eorðan swā swā on heofonum.	Oure fadir that art in heuenes, halwid be thi name; thi kyng- dom cumme to; be thi wille don as in heuen and in erthe.	Our Father which art in heaven, Hallowed be thy name. Thy kingdom come. Thy will be done on earth as it is in heaven.

A contrast of these three versions offers a brief but revealing impression of the changes that occurred in the language during eight hundred years, and these differences would seem even greater if we could reproduce also the changes in sound that took place. For example, Old English *ū* and *ī* were pronounced like the *oo* in *boot* and the *e* in *me* respectively, so that *ūre* was pronounced "oo'ruh" and *sī*, "see."

In grammar the major change has been the simplification of grammatical forms. Old English (700–1100) was a highly *inflected* language, one that made grammatical distinctions by changes in the form of a word. For example, nouns were declined in five cases (nominative, genitive, dative, accusative, and instrumental) as well as in singular and plural numbers. Adjectives and the definite article were declined to agree with the nouns they modified. Here is the declension, in the singular only, of "the good man" with the approximate pronunciation enclosed in quotation marks at the right:

Case	Declension	Pronunciation
N. (*man* as subject)	sē gōda mann	"say goada man"
G. ("of the good man" or "the good man's")	ðaes gōdan mannes	"thas goadan mannes"
D. ("to the good man")	ðǣm gōdan menn	"tham goadan men"
A. (*man* as object)	ðone gōdan mann	"thonna goadan man"
I. ("by the good man")	ðȳ gōdan menn	"thee goadan men"

In Modern English the article and the adjective are not declined at all. The noun retains the genitive case and has singular and plural forms. We distinguish between subject and object by word order, and we have replaced the dative and instrumental endings by the prepositions *to* and *by*. As a result, the whole declensional system has been greatly simplified. Verbs still show considerable inflection, though much less than in Old English.

Along with this simplification of grammatical forms went a great increase in vocabulary as new words were introduced through association with foreign cultures. During the eighth and ninth centuries Scandinavian raiders settled along the coast and brought into the language some fourteen hundred place names and about one thousand common words. In 1066 the Normans conquered England, and for three hundred years their French language dominated the court and the affairs in which the nobility was most involved — government, army, law, church, art, architecture, fashions, and recreation. Between 1100 and 1500 over ten thousand French words were absorbed into the language. During the fourteenth, fifteenth, and sixteenth centuries English writers borrowed heavily from Latin. It is estimated that more than half of the present English vocabulary came from Latin, either directly or through one of the Romance languages, especially French. And as the English-speaking countries grew in political, economic, and cultural importance, their language borrowed from all over the world the words it needed to name the things and ideas that Anglo-Americans were acquiring. Today the vocabulary of the English language is international in origin, as the following list illustrates:

algebra (Arabic)	dollar (German)	polo (Tibetan)
amen (Hebrew)	flannel (Welsh)	silk (Chinese)
bantam (Javanese)	garage (French)	shampoo (Hindi)
boor (Dutch)	garbage (Italian)	ski (Norwegian)
caravan (Persian)	inertia (Latin)	tag (Swedish)
cashew (Portuguese)	kimono (Japanese)	toboggan (American Indian)
chorus (Greek)	leprechaun (Old Irish)	vodka (Russian)
coffee (Turkish)	polka (Polish)	whiskey (Gaelic)

Standards of Usage

A description of a language is a description of the speaking and writing habits of the people who use it. Since there are some 300,000,000 users of English, widely separated geographically, culturally, and socially, many differences distinguish the English of one group from that of the others. These variations within a common language are called *dialects*. For example, in some ways the English spoken in Britain differs from that spoken in the United States. The British say "lift" when we would say "elevator," "torch" when we would use "flashlight," "bonnet" when we would speak of "the hood of a car"; they pronounce *garage* with the accent on the first syllable and *controversy* with the accent on the second; and they pronounce *schedule* as though it were written "shedule." Yet, despite many such differences, American and British English are mutually understandable dialects of a common language. A visitor to either country may be often amused but seldom confused by national differences.

Within the United States there are noticeable differences between the speech of natives of Atlanta and that of people raised in Boston, the Bronx, or Chicago. Even in a single city there will be language variations that can be attributed to differences in education and cultural background. But seldom do these differences interfere with communication. A Harvard professor and a Detroit factory worker would be able to carry on a conversation about the World Series, enjoy "Cheers" or Johnny Carson on television, and read the news in the *Detroit Free Press*. Their individual dialects would be less important than the language they have in common.

The dialect that American schools have historically taught is called *Standard English*. This is a social rather than a regional dialect. *Webster's Third New International Dictionary* defines it as

> the English that with respect to spelling, grammar, pronunciation, and vocabulary is substantially uniform though not devoid of regional differences, that is well-established by usage in the formal and informal speech and writing of the educated, and that is widely recognized as acceptable wherever English is spoken and understood.

This definition can be simplified by saying that Standard English is the usage of educated speakers and writers of English. Schools generally stress this dialect, and it is the standard by which expository writing in schools and colleges is judged.

Even within Standard English, though, decisions about what is acceptable usage are sometimes troublesome for three reasons. First, in an evolving language, usage will change. The change will be greatest in the vocabulary, as new words are introduced, old words are given new meanings, and some words cease to be used. Spellings, pronunciations, styles of punctuation, and grammatical constructions that were not recognized by one generation may be accepted by another, and there is likely to be a "usage gap" between what people think standard usage is and what it has, in fact, become.

Second, educated speakers and writers vary their usage with the situation, so that there are differences between the way they speak with their friends and the way they write on serious matters for strangers. These differences are not between educated and uneducated usage but between different styles within the standard dialect. Whether formal or informal usage is preferable depends not on which is more "correct" but on which is more appropriate to the writing or speaking situation.

Finally, many people have strong opinions about usage and approve or condemn certain uses no matter what the facts are.

These three conditions sometimes make it difficult for people to agree on whether particular constructions are or are not standard usage. For example, even on such an apparently simple question as whether "alright" is an accepted spelling, reputable dictionaries disagree. *Webster's Third New International* says it is, *The American Heritage Dictionary* calls it "a common misspelling," and *Webster's New World Dictionary* labels it "a disputed spelling."

When judgments about particular usages are so divided, the division suggests that the usage is changing and that the two forms are in competition. This is a common situation in a living, hence changing, language. In the past *honour, labour,* and *valour* have lost out to *honor, labor,* and *valor* in American usage; *shirt* and *skirt,* which were originally English and Norse variants of the name for a garment worn by either men or women, have become different words with different meanings; foreign pronunciations have been naturalized (French *coupé* has lost its accent and changed its pronunciation from "coo-pay" to "coop"); foreign plurals have been forced into English patterns *(gymnasia* became *gymnasiums; data are* has retained the plural verb in formal and scientific writing, but become *data is* in informal writing). No doubt each of these changes was first condemned as a mistake, then called a disputed usage, and finally accepted as standard. The history of the language shows that when mistakes become common enough they cease to be mistakes.

Despite specific disagreements, there is still general agreement about the main conventions of Standard English. These conventions are generalizations about how the language is used, and as long as the generalizations actually report educated usage, they provide norms against which we can check our own practices. If we want to call these generalizations "rules," we can do so, as in "rules of spelling," "rules of punctuation," "rules of grammar"; but it would be misleading to include them all under the heading "rules of grammar," since spelling and punctuation are not parts of grammar. The blanket term to cover them all would be "rules of usage."

The handbook that follows is a reference section in which you can check your usage against the norms of Standard English. The material is organized under eight main headings, the first five of which are marked by an identifying letter: *sentence structure* **(S),** *diction* **(D),** *word order* **(WO),** *grammatical forms* **(GF),** *punctuation*

(P), *mechanics* (spelling, capitalization, italics, and so on), a *glossary* of grammatical and literary terms, and a *checklist* that identifies particular words and constructions that frequently give student writers trouble. Under each lettered heading, the numbered sections deal with specific parts of the subject. Thus sections **S2–S4** deal with the distinction between sentences and nonsentences; **S6–S9** deal with inconsistencies in sentence patterns. It is assumed that your instructor will decide from your writing which conventions you need to study and will refer you to the section or sections dealing with them.

S SENTENCE STRUCTURE

S1 Review of Sentence Elements

Know how to recognize the basic elements in any sentence.

The basic elements of a sentence are subject, verb, object, complement, modifier, and connective. These elements can be represented by the symbols S, V, O, C, M, and +; they are identified in the following examples:

      S   V

1. Nobody came.   (Simple subject followed by *intransitive* verb — a verb that does not require an object.)

      S   V   O

2. We have time.   (Subject followed by *transitive* verb and its necessary object.)

    M   S   V   C

3. Her father is a lawyer.   (Subject preceded by its modifier, then followed by *linking* verb and its noun complement.)

    S   V   +   V

4. They washed and polished the   (Compound verb connected by *and*.)

    O

car.

Each of these four sentences says something about its *subject*. What it says about that subject is called the *predicate*. The predicate may be just an intransitive verb (example 1), a transitive verb and its object (example 2), or a linking verb and its complement (example 3). The subject and one of these basic forms of the predicate make a basic, or kernel, sentence.

The most common **subjects** are nouns and pronouns, but a group of words (a *phrase*) may also serve as a subject, as in the following examples:

Most of the books were damaged.

The end of the story puzzled me.

When a group of words has a subject and verb of its own, it is called a *clause*. A clause, too, may serve as the subject of a sentence. In

What everyone wants is more time

the italicized words make up a clause that serves as the subject.

Verbs may be single words or phrases, but never clauses. When they require an object to complete the predicate, they are called *transitive* verbs, as in "He caught the ball," in which the transitive verb *caught* is completed by the direct object *ball.* When a verb does not require an object to make a complete predicate, it is called *intransitive,* as in "I refused"; "They arrived"; "The child cried." Many verbs may be transitive or intransitive according to the structure of a sentence: "She *sings* (transitive) the National Anthem at every game," or "She *sings* (intransitive) beautifully." A verb is called a *linking* verb when it completes the predicate by linking the subject to a following noun or adjective. For example, compare these two sentences:

She telephoned a doctor.

She became a doctor.

In both sentences *doctor* is necessary for a complete predicate. In the first sentence *doctor* is the **object** of the transitive verb *telephoned,* because the doctor received the action performed by the subject. But in the second sentence no action is performed on the doctor. The verb *became* merely links the subject to the doctor. In such sentences we may say that *doctor* is not the object but the **complement** of the verb. In the following sentences the italicized adjectives are complements of linking verbs:

Mary looks *tired.*

That offer seems *reasonable.*

Dad remained *unconvinced.*

The most common linking verb is some form of the verb *to be* (*is, are, was, were, have been,* and so on), but *become, get, feel, look, seem, smell, taste,* and some other verbs may serve as links between the subject and the complement.

Exercise   Identify each of the underlined elements as a subject, verb, object, or complement by writing the appropriate letter above it.

1. They tried it and it worked.

2. Nobody likes her; she is too sarcastic.

3. That dog looks vicious.

4. Those who trust you will not need an explanation.

5. I doubt that he will go, but I'll ask him.

6. Did <u>you</u> get <u>the tickets?</u>

7. <u>Part of the sentence</u> is <u>illegible.</u>

8. They <u>paid</u> <u>you</u> a <u>compliment.</u>

9. <u>The trouble with Bill</u> is <u>that he is too sensitive.</u>

10. We <u>discovered</u> <u>that it was our fault.</u>

In general, a **modifier** describes a subject, object, complement, or another modifier or tells where, when, why, how, or under what conditions the action of the verb takes place. The italicized modifiers in the following sentences illustrate these uses:

Old soldiers never die.	(Modifies the subject.)
We had a *second* chance.	(Modifies the object.)
Honesty is the *best* policy.	(Modifies the complement.)
They came *early.*	(Modifies the verb — tells when.)
What do you have *in your hand?*	(Modifies the verb — tells where.)
I will go, *if you pay my way.*	(Modifies the verb — tells under what conditions.)
She had a *disturbingly* hostile look.	(Modifies the modifier *hostile.*)

Connectives (or *conjunctions*) are sentence elements that join other elements in a sentence. They usually come between the elements they join. The two most common types are coordinating and subordinating connectives. A **coordinating connective** (*and, or, nor, but, either . . . or, neither . . . nor, yet*) joins two grammatically similar elements:

He fought cleverly *and* courageously.	(Connects two adverbs.)
I'll do it, *but* I won't like it.	(Connects two main clauses.)

A subordinating connective does two things: it joins two clauses and subordinates one to the other. Thus if we change "He is cross. He is tired" to "He is cross because he is tired," we have connected two main clauses and reduced the second one to a subordinate clause by the use of the subordinating connective *because.* In the following examples the subordinate clauses are in parentheses and the connectives are in italics:

I don't know (*why* he did it).

He did not say (*when* he would return).

You may go (*whenever* you please).

In these examples the subordinating connective comes between the clauses it joins. But a subordinate clause may precede the main clause, and then the connective will come at the beginning of the sentence:

(*If* you seriously object), I won't do it.

(*Because* I flatter him), he likes me.

(*Since* you are in a hurry), I won't bother you about it now.

Exercise

Using subordinating connectives as clues, enclose in parentheses all subordinate clauses in the following sentences, and state whether they act as subjects, objects, complements, or modifiers.

1. I will do whatever you say.

2. What he told me is none of your business.

3. The book that I bought cost eight dollars.

4. The man who is wearing the plaid shirt is his uncle.

5. If that is how you feel, why don't you leave?

6. The people who lived in that house moved to Minnesota.

7. He said that he was terribly embarrassed.

8. This is the book that I want.

9. I would like to know why they did it.

10. When you are ready, call me.

Verbs and Verbals

Much of the trouble with verbs comes from a failure to distinguish verbs from verbals. A **verbal** is derived from a verb but does not act as one in a sentence. In the sentences

Wrestling is a body-building sport.

To wait is sometimes not easy.

He spoke in *threatening* terms.

the italicized words may look like verbs, but they do not act as verbs. *Wrestling* and *to wait* are the subjects of their sentences; *threatening* modifies *terms*.

Verbals are of three types: infinitives, participles, and gerunds. **Infinitives** are verbals of the type *to do, to choose, to be seeking, to have said.* Usually, but not always, they begin with the infinitive marker *to.* They often serve as subjects, objects, or complements and may occasionally act as modifiers.

To do that takes nerve.	(Infinitive phrase is the subject.)
He asked *to be excused.*	(Infinitive phrase is object of *asked.*)
He seems *to be worried.*	(Infinitive phrase is complement of *seems.*)
I bought it *to read,* if I have time *to spare.*	(Infinitives are modifiers.)

A **participle** is a word or phrase that is derived from a verb but acts as a modifier. The present participle ends in *-ing (crying, smiling, sulking).* Most past participles end in *-ed (disgusted, abused, inspired),* but many are irregular *(chosen, grown, kept, slung).* The following sentences illustrate forms and uses of participles:

His *fighting* days are over.	(Present participle modifies subject.)
He is a *fighting* fool.	(Present participle modifies complement.)
Discouraged by the lack of public support, the mayor resigned.	(Past participle modifies *mayor.*)
Goldsmith wrote a poem about a *deserted* village.	(Past participle modifies *village,* the object of *about.*)
Having been deserted by her husband, she supported the family.	(Passive form of past participle modifies subject *she.*)

A **gerund,** or verbal noun, has the same form as the present participle but is used as a subject, object, or complement in a sentence.

Thinking is hard work.	(Gerund is subject of *is.*)
That will take some *doing.*	(Gerund is object of *will take.*)
What bothers them is his *swearing.*	(Gerund is complement of *is.*)

Exercise

Identify infinitives, participles, and gerunds in the following sentences and tell whether they act as subjects, objects, complements, or modifiers.

1. **Nobody wants to tell him.**

2. **This is a thrilling story.**

3. The course requires too much reading.

4. To play as well as she does takes more time than I can afford.

5. A drunken man is usually a bore.

6. Disappointed by the results, he gave up the experiment.

7. With screeching brakes, the car came to a jarring stop.

8. That will take some thinking.

9. Not to have invited her would have caused trouble.

10. Feeling sorry for yourself will not solve the problem.

S2   Period Fault and Sentence Fragment

Use complete sentences, not sentence fragments, in expository writing. Especially avoid separating a subordinate clause or phrase from its main clause by a period.

Sentence fragment	Explanation	Full sentence
We decided to stay home for the holidays. *Because the gasoline shortage made driving too uncertain.*	*The italicized element is a subordinate clause and therefore only part of a sentence. It must be included in the full sentence, as shown at the right.*	We decided to stay home for the holidays because the gasoline shortage made driving too uncertain.
Professor Carlson gave us a choice. Either *to write a 1000-word essay out of class or to take a midterm exam in class.*	*The infinitives* to write *and* to take *are verbals, not verbs; therefore, the words after the first period are not a sentence.*	Professor Carlson gave us a choice, either to write a 1000-word essay out of class or to take a midterm exam in class.
Several of my friends earn a major part of their college expenses. *Attending* classes during the day, *working* in the early evening, and then *studying* later at night.	*The italicized words are verbals, not verbs. They are changed to verbs at the right.*	Several of my friends earn a major part of their college expenses. They attend classes during the day, work in the early evening, and then study later at night.

In the examples to the left above, a period comes between a main clause and a subordinate clause or phrase. The words following that period are a **sentence fragment** — a part of a sentence punctuated as if it were a complete sentence.

The incorrect use of the period represented here is a **period fault.** As the revisions indicate, period faults may be corrected either by changing the period to a comma, thus incorporating the separated phrase or clause into the sentence to which it belongs, or by expanding the fragment into a main clause so it can stand as an independent sentence.

Exercise   In the following sentences correct the period faults:

1. He has only one ambition. To play professional football.

2. Having come this far. We must see the matter through.

3. In a persuasive speech you should try to appeal to the whole audience. Not just to those who believe as you do.

4. We made our way up the mountain trail with much difficulty. Slipping on rocks and snagging our clothes in the underbrush.

5. Anticipating that our team would be named to the top twenty. We forgot that our defense was only mediocre.

6. Whatever challenge the office presents. I believe our new member of Congress will meet it successfully.

7. When our mayor announced, "I will not compromise on any issue on which I have taken a stand." That's when I began to question his judgment.

S3   Fused Sentences

Do not fuse two sentences by omitting necessary terminal punctuation between them.

Fused sentences

There are several words similar in meaning to the word *happiness* three of them are *bliss, contentment,* and *felicity.*

Be sure to set your alarm by dawn we must be well on our way.

Fused sentences can be quite confusing to a reader when we know how to revise them we can easily avoid the confusion.

Why do you ask how does it concern you?

Separated sentences

There are several words similar in meaning to the word *happiness.* Three of them are *bliss, contentment,* and *felicity.*

Be sure to set your alarm. By dawn we must be well on our way.

Fused sentences can be quite confusing to a reader. When we know how to revise them, we can easily avoid the confusion.

Why do you ask? How does it concern you?

Exercise   Revise the fused sentences in these examples:

1. At the half it seemed that the Celtics would be in the playoffs when the game was over they were out of the running.

2. Let's make up our minds about this matter there is certain to be much disagreement, whatever we decide.

3. The food service in the student union must be investigated unless better food is served business will drop drastically.

4. We must know what we mean when we punctuate we use punctuation marks to make our meaning clear.

5. Every lesson we have learned so far in the campaign has proved to be helpful in the last half of the campaign, though, there will certainly be much more to learn.

6. I find it difficult to believe he would act in such a way that is not at all like him.

7. Why do you want to make such an offer if you know they will refuse it what do you hope to gain?

S4   Run-On Sentences

Do not string together a number of main clauses with *but, and, for, so,* or *and so.*

Sentences so formed are called **run-on sentences.** They can be improved if part of the material is made subordinate to the rest, as shown in the following revisions:

Run-on sentence	Revision
The committee was trying to coordinate the events for Homecoming weekend, but various campus organizations were secretly engaged in plans to outshine each other, for competition among these organizations goes far back into the school's history, and so persuading them to cooperate was no easy task.	While the committee was trying to coordinate the events for Homecoming weekend, various campus organizations were secretly engaged in plans to outshine each other. Because competition among these organizations goes far back into the school's history, persuading them to cooperate was no easy task.

Exercise   Remove the run-on effect in the following examples:

1. I was not sure which flight Jim would arrive on, so I met all the planes coming in from Atlanta, but he was on none of them and so I decided that I was wrong about which day he was coming.

2. You object to having been misled, and so do I, and so we should be able to find a common ground for agreement.

3. I examined all reasonable transportation possibilities and I concluded that indeed I was stranded, so I called the professor whose exam I was to take next day and told her that I would probably be absent, and then I started to hitchhike back to school.

4. I was interested in learning about Thomas Wolfe's method of writing autobiographical fiction, and so I read his first novel and then I read the section of the Nowell biography dealing with his early life, and the comparison was fascinating.

5. John Malcolm Brinnin wrote a book called *Dylan Thomas in America,* but Mrs. Thomas disapproved of it, so she insisted that a statement from her appear at the beginning of the book, for she wanted to record her disapproval.

6. Our freshman writing instructor told us about various theories for teaching writing, and then we asked him what scholarly research had to say about the matter, and so he explained the difficulty of conducting research on the subject, and then he said, "There's not much that is conclusive."

S5 Comma Splice

Do not join main clauses by only a comma unless they are in series.

The use of a comma instead of a period or a semicolon between main clauses not linked by a coordinating conjunction is a **comma splice.** A comma by itself is a purely internal mark of punctuation, and a reader may read through it and be confused:

Registration for the new term begins Monday, on Wednesday classes begin.

In the following example, the italicized element could attach to either clause:

The United Fund drive was a great success, *thanks to several citizens' groups,* the campaign was better organized than ever before.

Which clause is the writer qualifying? Readers are free to guess, but they will get no help from the sentence. It could mean either

The United Fund drive was a great success, thanks to several citizens' groups. The campaign was better organized than ever before.

or

The United Fund drive was a great success. Thanks to several citizens' groups, the campaign was better organized than ever before.

Comma splices can be corrected in any one of three ways.

1. The simplest way is to change the faulty comma to a period or a semicolon, whichever gives the more desirable degree of separation.

Comma splice	Revision
No conclusive evidence has been un-covered, the committee will meet again tomorrow.	No conclusive evidence has been un-covered. The committee will meet again tomorrow.
The team lost six games, at least three of these losses were due to fumbles.	The team lost six games; at least three of these losses were due to fumbles.

2. A second way is to provide a coordinating conjunction between the two main clauses, thus making the comma acceptable.

Comma splice	Revision
Much has been said, we believe that much more needs to be said.	Much has been said, but we believe that much more needs to be said.

3. The third way is to subordinate one main clause to the other.

Comma splice	Revision
Members of the Drama Guild have rehearsed carefully for tonight's show, the director feels certain it will be a success.	Members of the Drama Guild have rehearsed so carefully for tonight's show that the director feels certain it will be a success.

When two main clauses are joined by a transitional connective — *consequently, however, moreover, nevertheless, therefore* — the usual punctuation between them is a semicolon, though a period is not uncommon.

It's too late to get a plane reservation; however, you could go by bus.

When two short independent clauses are closely related, informal usage permits a comma by itself.

The war is over, the fighting is not.

Exercise   **Using whatever method seems best, correct the comma splices in the following sentences:**

1. Practice ran very late tonight, Coach said that we would not work out tomorrow morning.

2. The comma splice can confuse the reader, it is usually less troublesome, though, than the fused sentence.

3. You don't have to pay for it today, all you need is a five-dollar deposit.

4. Professor Thompson refused to miss our final class to attend a professional meeting, moreover, he definitely expected us to be in class to hear his summarizing lecture.

5. I made the best decision I could at the time, looking back, I see what I should have done differently.

6. Pay attention, before you go you must be familiar with the entire plan.

7. We never once questioned Luke's integrity, strange as it now seems, we would have trusted him with anything.

8. On the first day of our tour our guide took us to the Senate because it was so close, the House of Representatives was our next stop.

9. We were able to notify all the committee members of the emergency meeting, although there were others who should have attended, enough were present to make a quorum.

10. Although the election was over, the excitement among the campaign workers wasn't, enjoying their memories of ten months together, they stayed around campaign headquarters until daylight.

S6   Faulty Parallelism

Sentence elements that are parallel in function should be parallel in grammatical form.

For a detailed discussion of parallel and balanced sentences, see pages 232–242 and 248–249.

Faulty parallelism

The two matters that most concern the leading candidates for class president are *winning* the election and then *to persuade* opposing factions in student government to work together harmoniously.

Explanation

The first part of the compound complement of are *is a gerund phrase starting with* winning; *the second part is an infinitive phrase starting with* to persuade. *The two should be in parallel form. In the revision the infinitive has been changed to a gerund.*

Revision

The two matters that most concern the leading candidates for class president are winning the election and then persuading opposing factions in student government to work together harmoniously.

Faulty parallelism	Explanation	Revision
The report is chiefly about *inflationary trends* in the last decade and *that the consumer has lost confidence* in the quality of many products.	*The compound object of* about *consists of a phrase and a subordinate clause. Each part of the object should be a phrase.*	The report is chiefly about inflationary trends in the last decade and the consumer's loss of confidence in the quality of many products.

Sentence elements in a series should have the same form: a phrase should be followed by a phrase, a clause by a clause, a noun by a noun, and a verb by a verb. The following sentence contains a series that lists the powers of a commission:

The commission has the power *to investigate, to conciliate, to hold* hearings, *to subpoena* witnesses, *to issue* cease-and-desist commands, *to order* reinstatement of a discharged employee, and *to direct* the hiring of a qualified applicant.

Most of this sentence consists of a series of infinitive phrases, each identifying one of the powers of the commission and modifying the noun *power*. Since all elements in the series have the same function, they all have the same form. They could have been put in a form other than the infinitive: "The commission has the power *of investigating, of conciliating, of holding* hearings," and so on. But the forms should not shift, as they do in the following sentence — from noun, to infinitive, to gerund, to verb-verb-verb, and back to infinitive again:

The commission has the power *of investigation, to conciliate, holding* hearings, *subpoena* witnesses, *issue* cease-and-desist commands, *order* reinstatement of a discharged employee, and *to direct* the hiring of a qualified applicant.

Exercise

Rewrite the following sentences to correct faulty parallelism:

1. In high school we were asked to write legibly and that we should be concerned with accuracy.

2. The evangelist ended the service with a hymn and calling on sinners to repent.

3. Sentence elements performing parallel functions but that are not written in parallel grammatical form should be revised.

4. The article cites three main causes for the energy crisis: the greatly increased demand for oil in industrialized countries; the fact that the big oil companies had not built new refineries to meet this demand; and that the supply of oil depends to some extent on the political situation, which has become more unstable.

5. The narrator in *Invisible Man* was idealistic, intelligent, and tried to advance the cause of black people.

6. By examining newspaper files, magazine articles, and obtaining interviews with knowledgeable people, I was able to gather the information I needed.

7. The executives of a corporation must be concerned with keeping the price of their product competitive and that the stockholders make a reasonable profit.

8. In the president's first term in office, his main challenges were to persuade Israel and the Arab nations to reach a peace agreement and finding a way to control inflation in the United States.

9. Manipulative commercials encourage people to want things they do not need and in buying things that they cannot afford.

10. Because he has always been wealthy and with indulgent parents, he has never been forced to accept responsibility.

S7 Dangling Modifiers

Avoid dangling modifiers.

Any modifier that does not clearly relate to some word in the sentence can be said to dangle. The most troublesome dangling modifiers are verbal phrases at the beginning of a sentence. As the revisions below show, a writer can remove an opening dangling modifier by either (1) revising the main clause so that its subject can be modified by the introductory phrase, or (2) rewriting the opening phrase as a subordinate clause.

Dangling modifier	Explanation	Revised version
Expecting an important call, the telephone was always at my elbow.	*There is nothing in the sentence for* expecting *to modify. Making* I *the subject of the main clause (method 1 above) removes the dangling modifier.*	Expecting an important call, I stayed close to the telephone.
Discouraged by the score, the stadium began to empty.	*Without something in the main clause to modify,* discouraged *dangles. Making* fans *the subject of the main clause (method 1) corrects the error.*	Discouraged by the score, the fans began to leave the stadium.

Dangling modifier	Explanation	Revised version
Waiting for my date in the lobby, two men in tuxedos got into a violent argument.	*The introductory phrase does not modify anything in the main clause. Changing the phrase into a subordinate clause (method 2) corrects the error.*	While I was waiting for my date in the lobby, two men in tuxedos got into a violent argument.

Sometimes a dangling modifier is an elliptical clause — that is, a subordinate clause some elements of which are not expressed. The simplest way to revise a dangling elliptical clause is to supply the missing elements to complete the clause.

Dangling modifier	Revised version
When only five, my father began to teach me how to swing a golf club.	When I was only five, my father began to teach me how to swing a golf club.
While in training, Mother did not have to insist on my getting plenty of sleep.	While I was in training, Mother did not have to insist on my getting plenty of sleep.

A dangling modifier at the end of the sentence is more likely to be awkward or unemphatic than ambiguous:

Dangling modifier	Revised version
Every member of our research team worked conscientiously, thus producing one of the best projects Professor Ames has ever received.	Because every member of our research team worked conscientiously, we produced one of the best projects Professor Ames has ever received.

The cause-to-effect order is presented more emphatically if the sentence begins with a subordinate clause and ends with a main clause, as in the revised version.

Exercise   Correct the dangling modifiers in the following sentences:

1. **Although working steadily each day, time ran out before I could complete the job.**

2. **To qualify for the award, the committee requires that candidates have perfect attendance.**

3. **When a senior in high school, my English teacher had so many students that he was not able to give close attention to individual students' writing problems.**

4. Having heard the weather report, our trip was postponed.

5. By telling the story in the first person, the reader is more likely to grant the narrator's credibility.

6. In order to study the effects on their hearts, pigs are jogging up to five miles.

7. By quoting two authoritative sources, my reader should realize that my information is trustworthy.

8. Studying about life during the Middle Ages, Chaucer's work became more meaningful to us.

9. Secure in the knowledge that we had finally arrived safely, a good night's sleep was welcome.

10. Upon hearing a sharp click the suds subsided and the dial on the top of the washing machine read "drain."

S8   Shifts in Subjects and Verbs

1. Avoid any unnecessary shifts in the person and number of a pronoun subject.

Shifted pronouns	Explanation	Revised version
One hopes that an effective speaker is a good person, but *you* cannot prevent a bad person from learning and using all the means of persuasion.	*The subject shifts from the impersonal pronoun* one *to the second person pronoun* you. *The revisions remove this shift. (A shift from* one *to* he *or* she *would also be acceptable as a revision.)*	One hopes that ... , but one cannot. . . . *or:* You hope that ... , but you cannot. . . .
I cannot understand how a *person* can have so many different feelings about something *they* plan to do.	Person *is singular and should have a singular pronoun, as shown at the right.*	I cannot understand how a person can have so many different feelings about something he or she plans to do.

Exercise   Remove the shifts in person or number in these sentences:

1. When one gets through a three-hour examination, you are exhausted.

2. I tried to understand quadratic equations, but there is a limit to how much math a person can learn.

3. In a situation like that, so many things can happen that one cannot foresee them all. All we can do is decide on a plan and then make whatever changes you have to.

4. Loyalty means having complete confidence in someone, even if they are under suspicion.

5. The book says that the battle took place in 1847, but they are wrong.

2. Avoid unnecessary shifts in the subject within successive sentences of a paragraph.

Although it is not necessary for all sentences in a paragraph to have the same subject, keeping the same subject running through a paragraph whenever possible is one means of preserving unity.

Shifting subjects	Explanation	Revision
When *we* began our composition course, there was little *knowledge* about the importance of strategy in the writing of a paper. *Correctness* in spelling, punctuation, and grammatical usage was what had been drilled into us; but the *effects* of interrelationships among speaker, audience, and occasion were foreign to us.	*Both these sentences have the same logical subject, the students' unawareness of the role of rhetorical strategy in their writing; but the two sentences contain four grammatical subjects. This unnecessary shifting of subject weakens the unity of the passage. The revision reduces the subject to one form — we.*	When we began our composition course, we knew little about the importance of strategy in the writing of a paper. We knew the necessity for correctness in spelling, punctuation, and grammatical usage; but we were unaware of the effects of interrelationships among speaker, audience, and occasion.

Exercise

Rewrite the following passages to improve unity by keeping a common subject in all sentences of each passage:

1. The worries about entrance examinations leave the minds of the students before they depart for the campus. The last days are spent shopping for clothes during the day and partying with friends at night. Their families receive little attention, and entrance examinations are no longer thought of.

2. I often have difficulty writing the first draft of a paper. The chief problem is finding a main idea to write about. A blank page seems to produce a blank mind. When possible topics do occur, they don't work out. After a few sentences or a paragraph, there is nothing more to say and the wastepaper basket begins to fill up with discarded sheets. All this shows lack of concentration, which seems to be the main weakness in my writing.

3. Avoid unnecessary shifts in the forms of verbs. Keep voice and tense consistent.

Shifted verb forms	Explanation	Revised version
Members from the House and Senate *met* in conference committee for five consecutive days, but no agreement *was reached*.	*The shifting from active voice in the first clause to passive in the second clause is awkward. The revision keeps both verbs in the active voice.*	Members from the House and Senate met in conference committee for five consecutive days but reached no agreement.
The older girls *had* a party to get us acquainted, and it *was* deeply *appreciated* by me.	*The shift from active voice in the first clause to passive in the second is unnecessary and awkward. The revision subordinates one clause and keeps both verbs in the active voice.*	I appreciated the party that the older girls gave to get us acquainted.
As centuries *passed,* the dress patterns *become* more and more complicated.	*The tense changes from past to present. Since both actions happened in the past, both verbs should be in the past tense.*	As centuries passed, the dress patterns became more and more complicated.
He *said* he *will* call for me at eight.	*The writer is confusing the tenses for direct and indirect discourse. Either form at the right will do.*	He said he would call for me at eight. He said, "I will call for you at eight."

Exercise   Revise the following sentences to get rid of awkward shifts in voice and tense:

1. The more we learned about the proposal, the clearer the issues become.

2. We spent the whole class hour discussing that question, but no agreement was arrived at.

3. I wrote inviting her to the party, but no answer was received.

4. When the problem was discussed in class, it becomes quite simple.

5. As Douglas talked, I reminded myself that we will have to reserve judgment about him but that he will have to prove himself.

6. One behavioral scientist has said that he believed permissiveness in the schools leads to student contempt for the schools.

7. Professor Wallingford said that she will return our papers at the next class session.

8. The rescue party worked for hours to extricate the child from the wreckage, and finally the efforts were successful.

9. He said we would be late for class anyway, so let's finish our Cokes and not worry.

10. In choosing a mate for the rest of your life, certain qualities should be looked for.

S9   Incomplete Constructions

Do not omit words necessary to the structure of a sentence.

Leaving out a word or phrase that is necessary to the structure or meaning of a sentence may result in an awkward or ambiguous statement. The following sentences illustrate this error, which should be caught in proofreading:

Incomplete	Explanation	Complete
The playwright tried for months, but no play.	*Incomplete contrast. The conjunction* but *requires a verb to balance the sentence.* Could not finish *is necessary to complete the contrast.*	The playwright tried for months but could not finish the play.
I don't approve of the assumption which he began.	*Omitted preposition. With a choice of two forms for the subordinate clause —* "with which he began" *or* "which he began with" *— the writer has failed to supply* with *in either position.*	I don't approve of the assumption with which he began. *or:* I don't approve of the assumption which he began with.
Investigation showed that the foreman took the defect in the engine more seriously than his employers.	*Omitted verb causing a possible ambiguity. The comparison is not of en-gine and* employers, *but of* foreman *and em-ployers. The clause with* employers *as sub-ject needs a verb.*	Investigation showed that the foreman took the defect in the engine more seriously than his employers did.

Incomplete	Explanation	Complete
The problem was his cousin was too honest to cooperate in the scheme.	*Omission of the subordinating conjunction* that *allows the subject of the subordinate clause,* cousin, *to be misread for a moment as the complement of* was.	The problem was that his cousin was too honest to cooperate in the scheme.
This decision is as hard, if not harder, than any we have had to make.	*This construction mixes two expressions: "as hard as" and "harder than." Than will not serve as connective for both expressions. The sentence could be revised to read: "This decision is as hard as, if not harder than, any we have had to make"; but this construction is so awkward that many people prefer to avoid it and use instead one of the revisions at the right.*	This decision is one of the hardest we have had to make. *or:* This decision is at least as hard as any we have had to make. *or:* This decision may be the hardest we have had to make.

Exercise

Revise the following sentences to complete the incomplete constructions:

1. We studied the subject as carefully as our opposition.

2. I question the premise which the argument depends.

3. I scribbled and outlined until I had exhausted my imagination, but no satisfactory result.

4. Jason Compson, in *The Sound and the Fury,* is as despicable, if not more despicable, than any character in all of Faulkner's fiction.

5. Senator Benson has spoken more convincingly against the denial of civil rights than his opponent.

6. We have insisted, and continue throughout the campaign, on equal opportunity for every ethnic group.

7. I sometimes think our professor has a better understanding of *Macbeth* than Shakespeare.

8. The recommendation that is as valuable, or perhaps more valuable, than any the steering committee received came from a housewife whom the committee chairman inadvertently failed to mention.

9. Our expectation is the proposal will be rejected at the polls.

10. In the last quarter State launched a furious passing attack and its fifth straight victory.

D   DICTION

D1   Using a Dictionary

Become familiar with at least one good college-level desk dictionary.

Because a good dictionary may well contain more useful information on more subjects than any other one book you are likely to use, it is a good idea to own one. Useful dictionaries are of two sizes: the so-called unabridged, and the collegiate, or desk, size. The following desk dictionaries are those most commonly recommended for student use:

The American Heritage Dictionary of the English Language

Funk & Wagnalls Standard College Dictionary

The Random House Dictionary of the English Language, College Edition

Webster's New Collegiate Dictionary

Webster's New World Dictionary of the American Language, College Edition

All these dictionaries are equipped with useful study aids that are supplied by their publishers on request.

When you look up a word in a dictionary, try to find out as much as you can about it. A good desk dictionary records many kinds of information about a word, as the entry on page 620 shows.

Although dictionaries vary in detail, they all give the following kinds of information. Check your dictionary against this list and make notes on any variations.

1. *Spelling and syllabication.* The entry word is spelled and is divided into syllables, usually by dots: con•tract. When a given word has more than one acceptable spelling, all accepted spellings are listed: *ax, axe.* (For your own and your readers' peace of mind, it is a good idea to choose one of these accepted spellings and to stand by that spelling in all the writing you do.)

2. *Pronunciation.* Immediately after the entry word is the pronunciation, usually in parentheses. Each dictionary has its own pronunciation key, usually printed at the foot of the page. Words of more than one syllable also include one or more accent marks (´ ʹ) placed before or after syllables to indicate secondary or primary stress. Note that *contract* has alternative pronunciations depending on whether it is used as a noun or a verb.

Spelling and
syllabication

Pronunciations

Parts of speech

Grammatical features:
principal parts

Abbreviations

Meaning within
part-of-speech groupings

con·tract (kŏn′trăkt′) *n. Abbr.* **contr., cont.** **1.** An agreement between two or more parties, especially one that is written and enforceable by law. **2.** The writing or document containing such an agreement. **3.** The branch of law dealing with contracts. **4.** Marriage as a formal agreement; betrothal. **5.** In the game of bridge: **a.** The last and highest bid of one hand. **b.** The number of tricks thus bid. **c.** **Contract bridge** *(see).* —*v.* (kən-trăkt′, kŏn′trăkt′) **contracted, -tracting, -tracts.** —*tr.* **1.** To enter into by contract; establish or settle by formal agreement. **2.** To acquire or incur. **3.** To reduce in size by drawing together; shrink. **4.** To pull together; wrinkle. **5.** To shorten (a word or words) by omitting or combining some of the letters or sounds; for example, *I'm* for *I am.* —*intr.* **1.** To enter into or make a contract. **2.** To become reduced in size by or as if by being drawn together. [Middle English, from Old French, from Latin *contractus,* from the past participle of *contrahere,* to draw together, bring about, enter into an agreement : *com-,* together + *trahere,* to draw (see *tragh-* in Appendix*).] —**con·tract′i·bil′i·ty, con·tract′i·ble·ness** *n.* —**con·tract′i·ble** *adj.*

Etymology

Synonyms

Synonyms: *contract, condense, compress, constrict, shrink.* These verbs refer to decrease in size or content of a thing and sometimes to a resultant change in its form. *Contract* applies to internal drawing together that reduces the volume of a thing. *Condense* refers to an increase in compactness produced by the removal or reduction of parts or by a change in physical form of the thing involved, such as a change from gas to liquid or from liquid to solid. *Compress* applies to increased compactness brought about by external force; the term implies reduction of volume and change of form or shape. *Constrict* refers to decreasing the extent of a thing, usually by external pressure. *Shrink* refers to contraction that produces reduction in physical extent.

3. *Part of speech.* The abbreviation is given for the part of speech in which the word is used (*n., v., adj.,* and so on). If a word is used in several parts of speech, all meanings for each part of speech are grouped together: all noun meanings are grouped, all verb meanings, and so on.

4. *Abbreviations.* Most dictionaries list common abbreviations, though not always near the beginning of the entry.

5. *Grammatical features.* Irregular plurals are given for nouns *(mice, oxen),* principal parts for verbs, and comparative forms for adjectives and adverbs that do not take *more* and *most.*

6. *Meanings.* Within part-of-speech groupings, meanings are given in historical order, in order of frequency of use, or from primary or basic to secondary or extended. Check the front matter of your dictionary to see which order it uses.

7. *Etymology.* When it is known, the origin of the word is given. Thus *contract* is one of a large class of words that came into English from Latin via Old French. It is made up of the prefix *con-* (from Latin *com-,* "together") and the root *tract* (from Latin *trahere,* "to draw").

8. *Labels.* Labels are used to indicate usage *(Nonstandard, Slang, Informal),* dialect

(*Dial.*), region *(Brit., Southern)*, and specialization *(Law, Med.)*. A word not labeled (*contract,* for example) is in standard general use.

9. *Synonyms and antonyms.* Dictionaries vary in the positioning of these elements and in the space given to them. Check the front matter of your dictionary if in doubt.

Exercise

The following quiz will test your knowledge of your own dictionary. Check your answers by the introductory pages and by reference to particular entries.

1. Does your dictionary record variant spellings of the same word in one entry or in different entries? Is one spelling necessarily "more correct" than an alternate spelling?

2. How is pronunciation indicated in your dictionary? Is there a key to the symbols at the bottom of the page, or only in the introductory matter?

3. Where are the etymologies shown: after the inflectional forms, or at the end of the entry? In many dictionaries, *L* is the symbol for Latin. Other common origins are *Gr* (Greek), *F* (French), *N* (Norse), *O* (Old, as in *Old English, Old French*). If you are not sure how to interpret these symbols, where in your dictionary can you find out?

4. In what order are the definitions given? If you are not sure, where can you find out?

5. How are foreign words identified — that is, words that are still considered foreign rather than English, and so have to be underlined in manuscript or italicized in print? If you are not sure, how can you find out? (Hint: Check *gestalt, bon voyage, in absentia.*)

6. For which of the following entries are synonyms or antonyms given: *ambition, deface, fiendish, luster, restive, voracious?*

7. How are the following words pronounced: *acclimate, alias, banal, data, ennui, impious, impotent, joust, schism, Wagnerian?*

The things you most need to know about a new word are its pronunciation, etymology, and meanings. Knowing the pronunciation not only helps you pronounce a word correctly in reading aloud or in speaking, but also helps you fix the word in your memory. Because the way a word looks is often no safe clue to how it sounds, everyone has had the embarrassing experience of making a very obvious mispronunciation when called upon to read an unfamiliar word aloud. Even such fairly common words as *abyss, blatant, caprice, decade, echelon, façade, gauge,* and *ribald* can be troublesome for a person who has met them in reading and has never heard them spoken.

The etymology of a word gives you its family history and thus makes your knowledge of it more complete. When you learn that *crucial* comes from the Latin word for *cross,* you can see that in a crucial decision, you figuratively stand at a crossroads and decide which way to go; and you may discover an unsuspected relationship among *crucial, crucify, crusade,* and *crux.*

As for the meaning of a word, it should be clear that unless you know what a word means, you cannot use that word effectively in speech or in writing. Failure to use the right word or to use the word right is an error in diction.

The errors in diction identified in sections **D2** through **D6** have all been discussed earlier in the text, chiefly in Chapter 8. For help with avoiding any of these errors in your writing, consult the pages referred to.

D2   Wrong Meaning

The italicized word does not mean what the writer intended it to mean:

The state's attorney said that the man would be *persecuted.*

The word wanted here is *prosecuted.* The error may be a misspelling, or it may reveal a confusion of two words of similar appearance but different meanings, like *casual–causal, concave–convex, detracted–distracted, official–officious,* and *prescribe–proscribe.* For a fuller list of such pairs, see the Checklist of Troublesome Usages at the end of this book.

D3   Inconsistent Diction

Words may be inconsistent for two reasons: (1) because they are too formal or too colloquial for the context in which they are being used, or (2) because they are not appropriate to the writer's purpose.

1. Avoid diction that is too formal or too colloquial for the style of your paper.

See pages 271–275.

2. Avoid connotations that work against your purpose.

Example: *Notorious* and *famous* both have the general meaning of being well known, but the first has unfavorable connotations, the second favorable: "a notorious criminal," but "a famous writer."

D4   Vague Diction

See "Eliminating Vagueness," pages 289–292.

D5   Trite Diction

See "Eliminating Triteness," pages 295–298.

D6   Inappropriate Image

A figure of speech will be inappropriate if:

1. it attempts to combine one or more images in one *metaphor* (see pages 298–299).

2. it presents a *personification* that is so exaggerated that a reader will not accept it (see page 286).

3. it makes an *allusion* to some person or event that a reader is not likely to understand (see pages 286–287).

WO WORD ORDER

WO1 Normal Order and Accepted Inversions

Normal Order

The normal order of words in English sentences may be summarized as follows:

1. Except in questions and expletive-type sentences ("Why do you despair?" "There is a ray of hope"), the standard order of the main sentence elements is subject-verb-object or complement. An indirect object precedes the direct object: "He sent me flowers."

2. Single adjectives or series of adjectives precede, and adjective phrases follow, their headword — the word they modify: "a *trusted* man *of the people*."

3. Adverbs usually follow the verbs they modify, but may come elsewhere. Adverbs modifying adjectives or other adverbs precede the headword: "He is *very* old"; "They dance *remarkably* well."

4. Main clauses usually precede subordinate clauses, but the following exceptions are common:

   a. Adjective clauses immediately follow their headwords: "The man *who did it* should be punished."

   b. Adverbial clauses, especially conditional clauses, often precede the main clause: "*If you do that,* you'll be sorry."

   c. Noun clauses acting as subjects or objects occupy the subject or object position: "*That he will accept* is taken for granted." "He says *that you are afraid.*"

5. Closely related elements are kept as close together as possible. Thus a preposition precedes the object and its modifiers ("the top *of the highest mountain*"); modifiers remain close to their headwords; and subject-verb, verb-object, and pronoun-antecedent combinations are not separated more than the special needs of the sentence require. In short, the order of elements in a sentence should reveal relationships, not obscure them.

Accepted Inversions

Any inversion of normal word order tends to attract attention and to emphasize the inverted expression. If this emphasis is desirable and if the departure from normal order is not outlandish or unidiomatic, a writer may gain interesting variety in sentence structure by moderate use of inversion.

If it does not create misinterpretation or awkwardness, an element may be transposed from its normal order for emphasis.

Normal order	Emphatic inversion
They laid him down *slowly and sadly.*	*Slowly and sadly* they laid him down.
The Celtics don't stand a chance *without Larry Byrd.*	*Without Larry Byrd,* the Celtics don't stand a chance.
The doctor arrived *at last.*	*At last* the doctor arrived.
Will you help me *if I agree?*	*If I agree,* will you help me?
Don't take his word for it *under any circumstances.*	Don't *under any circumstances* take his word for it.
Oliver asked, "Please, sir, may I have some more?"	"Please, sir," Oliver asked, "may I have some more?"

In this last example the inversion is made not so much for emphasis as to provide variation in the order of the "he asked," "she said," "they answered" tags that accompany direct discourse. These tags may come at the beginning, the middle, or the end of the quotation.

WO2   Ambiguous Order

Be sure that the relationship between modifying words, phrases, or clauses and the elements they modify is clear.

If a modifier is so placed that it could modify either of two elements, its reference will be ambiguous and the intended meaning will be unclear. Even if the reader is able to make the correct interpretation, the writer's carelessness will be apparent.

Ambiguous order	Explanation	Revised order
I thought of writing *often* but never did.	*The adverb* often *can modify either* thought *or* writing. *If it is intended to modify* thought, *put it immediately before or after that verb.*	I often thought of writing but never did.

Ambiguous order	Explanation	Revised order
The Chinese vase was a wedding gift *that was stolen.*	*Since adjective clauses follow the nouns they modify, a reader may interpret* gift *as the antecedent of* that. *The revision removes this possibility.*	The Chinese vase that was stolen was a wedding gift.

Exercise   Remove possible ambiguities in the following sentences by changing the position of misleading modifiers:

1. My mother planted the rosebush in her garden that I gave her on Mother's Day.

2. The children watched while the magician drew out a rabbit with shining eyes.

3. No boy would treat his father like that unless he was spiteful.

4. The list of expenses tells the story of the man who wrote it quickly and clearly.

5. There is a panel discussion tonight about drug addiction in the student lounge.

6. Bill promised on his way home to pick me up.

7. I was so surprised that I forgot what I intended to say to her when I met her.

8. At one time his neighbors said he had been in jail.

9. Richard Burton played the part of the man who was corrupted by power superbly.

10. There was a noisy disturbance when the speaker said that at the back of the hall.

11. The car is in the garage that he wrecked.

12. They talked about going on a second honeymoon frequently but never did.

WO3   Awkward Separation of Elements

Avoid unnecessary separation of a subject and its verb, a verb and its object or complement, a modifier and its headword, or a preposition and its object.

Unnecessary separation of closely related elements can distort the sentence pattern and interfere with ease of reading.

Awkward separation	Explanation	Revised order
My *father,* after considering what the trip would cost and how long it would take, *refused* to go.	*Awkward separation of subject and verb. The unnecessary interruption of the main clause by a phrase and two subordinate clauses distorts the structure of the main clause.*	After considering what the trip would cost and how long it would take, my father refused to go.
Who *will believe,* considering his reputation and the lack of any confirming evidence, *what he says?*	*Awkward separation of italicized verb and object.*	Considering his reputation and the lack of any confirming evidence, who will believe what he says?
Her parents are neither in favor *of* nor opposed to the *marriage.*	*Awkward separation of preposition of and its object. The revision at the right is the best way of expressing the idea.*	Her parents neither favor nor oppose the marriage.

WO4   Unemphatic Order

Any word order that reduces a desired emphasis in a sentence should be avoided or revised. This principle was discussed in "Emphatic Word Order" and "Climactic Order" on pages 255–258. What follows is a supplement to that earlier treatment, not a substitute for it.

1. Do not place relatively unimportant material at the end of a sentence.

The end of a sentence is a point of major stress. Putting unimportant information there will give that information more emphasis than it deserves and produce an anticlimax. For example, in the sentence

Last night our car was stolen while we were in the theater.

the most important information — that the car was stolen — is in a position of less emphasis than the less important information that the owners were in the theater at the time. A more appropriate emphasis can be obtained by putting the theft at the end:

Last night, while we were in the theater, our car was stolen.

This kind of faulty emphasis is most conspicuous when an unimportant qualification ends the sentence. Compare:

Unemphatic ending	More emphatic ending
He has never been married, *as far as I know.*	*As far as I know,* he has never been married.
She is innocent, *in my opinion.*	*In my opinion,* she is innocent.

2. Do not weaken an important concluding statement by reducing it to a participial phrase.

Many a good sentence ends with a participial phrase, but to use such a phrase for an idea that is important enough to deserve a main clause often makes a lame ending. For example, in

He fell from the roof, *thus breaking his neck.*

the italicized phrase is at least as important as the main clause, yet it is grammatically subordinate and trails off weakly. The idea in the phrase is important enough to come at the end, but it deserves a stronger grammatical form:

He fell from the roof and broke his neck.

3. Do not put a conjunctive adverb at the end of a sentence.

Conjunctive adverbs, also called transitional connectives, are words like *accordingly, consequently, furthermore, however, nevertheless, therefore* that connect and make a transition between two sentences or two main clauses of a compound sentence:

He thinks she deceived him deliberately; *consequently,* he is in no mood for a reconciliation.

We have repeatedly tried to make friends with them and have been consistently repulsed. *Nevertheless,* we'll try again.

I am willing to advise you. I will not, *however,* accept responsibility for what you do.

Since a connective should come between the things it connects, the normal positions for a conjunctive adverb are at the beginning of the second sentence or clause, as in the first and second examples above, or *near* the beginning of the second clause, as in the third example. For maximum emphasis on the conjunctive adverb, place it at the very beginning of the second sentence.

Exercise   Revise the following sentences to improve awkward or unemphatic order:

1. The cause of death was heart failure rather than drowning in the coroner's judgment.

2. Her parents, even, do not know where she is.

3. The challenger knocked down the champion six times in two rounds, thus shocking the crowd.

4. The plane made a successful takeoff although its tires had been riddled by the FBI marksmen, who were there to prevent the hijacking.

5. The Supreme Court refused to consider the appeal, according to the late news last night.

6. I think Wayne's personality will irritate other members of the council. I'll have to vote for him, however.

7. The chairman said the minutes would be accepted, there being no objection.

8. The best argument for democracy is to consider its alternatives, I firmly believe.

9. The instructor promised that she would give the class some sample questions to study for the exam after much pleading from the students.

10. The evidence shows, if you examine it carefully and impartially, that the best baseball is played in the National League.

11. I am neither in support of nor opposed to the bill.

GF GRAMMATICAL FORMS

GF1 Principal Parts of Verbs

1. Use the accepted principal parts of verbs.

The great majority of English verbs form the present participle by adding *-ing* to the present-tense form *(walk, walking)*; they form the past tense and the past participle by adding *-ed* to the first principal part *(walked, walked)*. All exceptions are specifically listed in a good dictionary. The following list contains the principal parts of the irregular verbs that cause most trouble:

Present tense	Present participle	Past tense	Past participle
am, is, are	being	was, were	been
bear	bearing	bore	borne
beat	beating	beat	beaten
begin	beginning	began	begun
bite	biting	bit	bitten
blow	blowing	blew	blown
break	breaking	broke	broken
bring	bringing	brought	brought
burst	bursting	burst	burst
cast	casting	cast	cast
choose	choosing	chose	chosen
come	coming	came	come
deal	dealing	dealt	dealt
do	doing	did	done
draw	drawing	drew	drawn
drink	drinking	drank	drunk
eat	eating	ate	eaten
fall	falling	fell	fallen
fly	flying	flew	flown
forbid	forbidding	forbade	forbidden
forsake	forsaking	forsook	forsaken
freeze	freezing	froze	frozen
give	giving	gave	given
go	going	went	gone
grow	growing	grew	grown
hang*	hanging	hung	hung
have	having	had	had

* The verb *to hang*, used in the sense of "to execute," is regular: *hang, hanged, hanged.*

Present tense	Present participle	Past tense	Past participle
know	knowing	knew	known
lay	laying	laid	laid
lie	lying	lay	lain
ride	riding	rode	ridden
ring	ringing	rang	rung
rise	rising	rose	risen
run	running	ran	run
see	seeing	saw	seen
shake	shaking	shook	shaken
shoe	shoeing	shod	shod
shrink	shrinking	shrank (shrunk)	shrunk
sing	singing	sang (sung)	sung
sink	sinking	sank (sunk)	sunk
sit	sitting	sat	sat
slay	slaying	slew	slain
slink	slinking	slunk	slunk
speak	speaking	spoke	spoken
spin	spinning	spun	spun
spring	springing	sprang (sprung)	sprung
steal	stealing	stole	stolen
strive	striving	strove	striven
swear	swearing	swore	sworn
swim	swimming	swam	swum
take	taking	took	taken
teach	teaching	taught	taught
tear	tearing	tore	torn
throw	throwing	threw	thrown
wear	wearing	wore	worn
weave	weaving	wove	woven
win	winning	won	won
write	writing	wrote	written

2. Distinguish between the forms for the past tense and the past participle.

In verb phrases the past participle, not the past-tense form, should follow an auxiliary verb ("has *been*"). Except when a verb is acting as an auxiliary ("*had* gone," "*was* crying"), its past-tense form is not used in combination with another verb.

Nonstandard form	Standard form
It is *broke*.	It is *broken*.
These tires are *wore* out.	These tires are *worn* out.

Nonstandard form	Standard form
He has *began* all over again.	He has *begun* all over again.
I *seen* him do it.	I *saw* him do it.
The river is *froze* solid.	The river is *frozen* solid.
Everybody has *went* home.	Everybody has *gone* home.
Have you *wrote* to him?	Have you *written* to him?
They *come* back yesterday.	They *came* back yesterday.

3. Distinguish between the uses and forms of *lie* and *lay*, *rise* and *raise*, *sit* and *set*.

The principal parts of these verbs are as follows:

Present	Present participle	Past	Past participle
lie	lying	lay	lain
lay	laying	laid	laid
rise	rising	rose	risen
raise	raising	raised	raised
sit	sitting	sat	sat
set	setting	set	set

Each pair has principal parts that are similar, though not the same, in form and general meaning. The chief difference in each pair is that the first verb is *intransitive*, the second *transitive*. That is, the first does not need an object to complete the action of the verb; the second does need an object. Determining the accepted form, therefore, depends on the answers to two questions: (1) Does the sentence require a transitive or an intransitive verb? (2) What are the principal parts of the required verb?

In the examples that follow, the unacceptable forms at the left are revised at the right.

Unacceptable	Explanation	Acceptable
We *laid* breathless with suspense.	*The sentence contains no object; therefore, the intransitive verb is wanted. The past form of* lie *is* lay.	We lay breathless with suspense.
It was *setting* on the table.	*No object; therefore, the intransitive form* sitting *is required.*	It was sitting on the table.

Unacceptable	Explanation	Acceptable
They have *lain* the carpet.	Carpet *is the object; therefore, the transitive* laid *is required.*	They have laid the carpet.
He *raised* up and went to the bench.	*No object; intransitive* rose *is required.*	He rose and went to the bench.
It has been *laying* there all night.	*No object; intransitive* lying *is required.*	It has been lying there all night.

Exercise   **Write the acceptable form in the following sentences:**

1. We (lay, laid) on the pier and dozed.

2. I would like you to (rise, raise) my wages.

3. Go out and (rise, raise) the flag.

4. (Set, Sit) down and rest for a while.

5. Finally, the curtain (raised, rose).

6. They were (laying, lying) in wait for us.

7. We (laid, lay) down for a rest.

8. They were (setting, sitting) the chairs in a circle.

9. He (raised, rose) himself on his elbow.

10. Clothes were (laying, lying) all over the room.

GF2   Tense Forms

(For identification of the basic tenses, see pages 630–631.)

1. Avoid illogical sequence of tenses.

a. Keep the tenses of main clauses consistent. Do not shift needlessly from one tense to another.

Inconsistent	Explanation	Consistent
She laughed, and I asked her what she knew about him. She *laughs* again, this time much louder.	*In the first sentence all verbs are in the past tense; in the second,* laughs *is in the present tense. There is no reason for the shift to occur here.*	She laughed, and I asked her what she knew about him. She *laughed* again, this time much louder.

Inconsistent	Explanation	Consistent
For five rounds the young challenger danced and ducked and jabbed and piled up points. Then the champion found an opening — and Bam! The fight *is* over.	*All the verbs except the last one are in the past tense. The last shifts to historical present. Either that tense or the simple past should be used throughout.*	For five rounds the young challenger danced and ducked and jabbed and piled up points. Then the champion found an opening — and Bam! The fight *was* over.

b. Keep the tense of a subordinate clause in logical sequence with that of the main clause.

Illogical	Explanation	Logical
They *have made* so much money last year that they *bought* a second store.	*The present perfect (have made) suggests action more recent than the simple past (bought); it is illogical to use the present perfect for the earlier action.*	They *made* so much money last year that they *have bought* a second store.
Before I was introduced to her, I *heard* rumors about her reputation.	*Since the rumors came before the introduction, the past perfect tense should be used in the main clause.*	Before I was introduced to her, I *had heard* rumors about her reputation.

2. In converting direct discourse to indirect discourse, observe the normal change in tense.

Direct discourse repeats the actual words of the speaker, and verbs should be in the tense the speaker used. When direct discourse is converted to indirect, the tenses of the original are, when possible, pushed one stage farther into the past. Thus present becomes past, and past becomes past perfect. Since there is no tense more past than past perfect, a verb in that tense does not change.

Direct discourse	Explanation	Indirect discourse
He said, "I *want* to read that novel."	*Change simple present to simple past.*	He said that he *wanted* to read that novel.
He said, "I *wanted* to read that novel yesterday."	*Change simple past to past perfect.*	He said that he *had wanted* to read that novel yesterday.

Direct discourse	Explanation	Indirect discourse
He said, "I *had wanted* to read that novel until I *saw* the movie."	*Leave the verbs as they are. There is no way to make* had wanted *more past than it is, and to change* saw *to* had seen *would destroy the sequence of tenses.*	He said that he *had wanted* to read that novel until he *saw* the movie.

The following examples contrast faulty and correct conversion from direct to indirect discourse:

Direct discourse	Faulty conversion	Correct conversion
I said, "She *is* a good risk."	I said she is a good risk.	I said she *was* a good risk.
I asked, "*Have you talked* to your doctor?"	I asked if he talked to his doctor.	I asked if he *had talked* to his doctor.

3. Observe the relationships of tense between verbs and verbals.

The tense of a verbal is not determined by the tense of the verb in the main clause. Regardless of the tense of the verb, a present participle expresses an action occurring at the same time as that of the verb. A perfect participle expresses time before that of the verb. A present infinitive indicates either the same time as that of the verb or a later time. A perfect infinitive suggests time before that of the verb.

Rounding the last turn, he *was* ahead by two yards.	*The present participle* (rounding) *and the past-tense verb refer to actions occurring at the same time.*
Having unblocked the drain, she *washed* her hair.	*The perfect participle* (having unblocked) *refers to an action before that of the verb* (washed).
I *tried to telephone* you.	*The verb* (tried) *and the present infinitive* (to telephone) *refer to actions occurring at the same time.*
I *expect to hear* from him tomorrow.	*The expectation is now; the hearing has yet to occur. Therefore, the present infinitive refers to a time later than that of the verb.*
They *are reported to have reached* an agreement.	*The perfect infinitive* (to have reached) *points to a time before the reporting.*

Faulty sequence	Explanation	Correct sequence
Asking the blessing, we began to eat.	*Since the blessing was asked before the eating began, the perfect participle is required.*	*Having asked* the blessing, we began to eat.
Having faced the spectators, the referee signaled a holding penalty.	*Since both actions took place at the same time, the present participle is required.*	*Facing* the spectators, the referee signaled a holding penalty.
We meant to *have told* you earlier.	*The perfect infinitive suggests that the telling occurred before the intention. The present infinitive is the required form.*	We meant *to tell* you earlier.
I am sorry *to overlook* that fact.	*Since the overlooking occurred before the regret, the perfect infinitive should be used.*	I am sorry *to have overlooked* that fact.

Exercise   Revise the following sentences where necessary to correct illogical or faulty sequence of tenses:

1. Because the social committee has planned so carefully, everything went just fine.

2. Billy insisted that his antique Cadillac runs as smoothly as last year's model.

3. Practicing all week against a zone defense, our team was puzzled when Riply played man to man.

4. It was clear that just before I arrived they had a serious quarrel.

5. We were told to have packed our bags before breakfast.

6. The treasurer is lucky to find the error before the meeting on the budget.

7. Even before the jury pronounced her guilty, the accused woman sensed that they were not sympathetic toward her.

8. Finishing the planning of my essay, I was ready to begin my discovery draft.

9. We arranged to have submitted our papers before leaving campus.

10. I had planned to write the letter before I had gone to the party, but Karen asked me to come earlier than I intended.

GF3　Case

Case is a system of inflection that shows the relation of nouns and pronouns to other words in the sentence. English has three cases: **subjective** (or *nominative*), **possessive** (or *genitive*), and **objective** (or *accusative*). In general, a noun or pronoun is in the subjective case when it acts as a subject, in the objective case when it acts as an object, and in the possessive case when it modifies a noun as in "*his* bicycle," "the *boy's* dog," "the *girl's* future."

English nouns, pronouns, and adjectives were once fully inflected to show case, but in modern English, word order and idiomatic constructions have largely replaced case endings. Adjectives are no longer inflected for case; nouns are inflected only in the possessive case: "the *fireman's* hat." Only pronouns (and chiefly the personal pronouns) still make any considerable use of case forms. The study of case in modern English, therefore, is pretty much restricted to pronouns.

1. The case of a pronoun is determined by its function in its own clause.

If a pronoun is the subject of its clause, it takes the subjective case; if it is an object within its clause, it takes the objective case; if it is a modifier, it takes the possessive case. But notice that: (1) a pronoun subject of an infinitive takes the objective case ("I want *him to see* it"); and (2) the complement of the verb *to be* takes the subjective case in formal usage ("It was not *I* who said that").

Pronouns take the *subjective* case when

1. they are subjects of verbs: "*I* think that *he* missed."

2. they are in apposition with subjects: "Three men — Fred, Roy, and *I* — were elected delegates."

3. they are complements of the verb *to be:* "I am sure it was *he.*"

Pronouns take the *objective* case when

1. they are objects of verbs: "Mother likes *her.*"

2. they are objects of prepositions: "They pointed at *me.*"

3. they are in apposition with objects: "They gave *us* — Dave and *me* — the money."

4. they are subjects or objects of infinitives: "I want *her* to go"; "We didn't expect to see *him.*"

Pronouns take the *possessive* case when

1. they modify a noun or a pronoun: "Those are *my* six children, this is *his* one."

2. they precede and modify a gerund: "What's wrong with *her* swimming?" "*His* winning was a surprise."

Troublesome Constructions

In general, errors in case occur for two reasons: (1) because the function of a pronoun is obscured; and (2) because a case form inappropriate in writing is so often used in speech that the colloquial form seems more natural than the more formal one. Often these two reasons merge. That is, a particular construction requires more deliberate analysis than speakers have time to give it and so encourages a colloquial usage that competes with the formal one.

The following pages point out the constructions that create most of the irregularities in the use of case forms.

2. Most errors in case occur in a few constructions. Learn to recognize and deal effectively with the following:

a. Interrupting constructions with *who* or *whom*.

Any construction that interrupts the normal pattern of a clause is likely to obscure the function of a pronoun in the clause. In the following sentence it is quite clear that *who* is the subject of *won* and takes the subjective case:

That is the man who won the prize.

But if we introduce an interrupting clause — "they say" — into the sentence, the function of *who* becomes less clear:

That is the man who they say won the prize.

There is now a tendency to assume that *who* is the object of *say* and to put it in the objective case. But its function has not changed. "They say" has no grammatical relationship to any element in the sentence. The faulty analysis suggested by the interrupting construction often leads to the use of the wrong case.

Wrong case	Explanation	Correct case
The man *whom* they think did it has been arrested.	*Pronoun is subject of* did, *not object of* think.	The man *who* they think did it has been arrested.
She introduced me to a man *whom* she said was her boss.	*Pronoun is subject of* was, *not object of* said.	She introduced me to a man *who* she said was her boss.

Wrong case	Explanation	Correct case
The police identified the woman *who* they had arrested.	*Pronoun is object of* had arrested, *not a subject.*	The police identified the woman *whom* they had arrested.

b. *Whoever* and *whomever.*

These two relative pronouns follow the rule that the case of a pronoun is determined by its function in its own clause. But because they often follow a transitive verb or the preposition *to,* they are often mistaken as objects when actually they are not objects.

Faulty	Explanation	Correct
Invite *whomever* will come.	*Pronoun is subject of* will come; *object of* invite *is the clause* whoever will come.	Invite *whoever* will come.
Send it to *whomever* you think would like it.	*Relative pronoun is subject of* would like. *The preposition* to *and the qualifying clause* you think *do not affect its case.*	Send it to *whoever* you think would like it.

c. Complement of the verb *to be.*

In written usage a pronoun complement of the verb *to be* takes the subjective case: "It was *he.*" See page 725 in the Checklist of Troublesome Usages.

d. Comparative with *than* or *as.*

The case of a pronoun following *than* or *as* in a comparison often causes difficulty. In such comparisons as the following, *than* and *as* are connectives between a full clause and an elliptical (incompletely expressed) one:

He is at least as old as *she.*	(If the elliptical clause were completely expressed, the sentence would read: "He is at least as old as *she is.*")
I am about twenty pounds lighter than *he.*	("I am about twenty pounds lighter than *he is.*")
The judge liked us better than *them.*	("The judge liked us better than *he liked them.*")

In the expanded form it is clear that *than* and *as* are connectives joining two clauses. Pronouns in shortened comparisons take the same case they would take if the comparisons were fully expanded. That is, a pronoun takes the subjective case if it is the subject of an unexpressed verb and the objective case if it is the object of such a verb.

e. Possessive with a gerund.

A pronoun preceding and modifying a gerund takes the possessive case: "I am opposed to *his going*." In formal writing, a noun modifying a gerund also takes the possessive case: "Imagine *John's saying* that!" Both colloquial usage and informal usage usually ignore this latter convention and put the noun modifier in the objective case: "Imagine *John saying* that!"

   The following sentences further illustrate the use of the possessive case when a noun or a pronoun modifies a gerund:

There is really no excuse for *his failing* the course.

We are embarrassed by *their* continual *begging*.

They object to *my having signed* the petition.

Mary's interrupting annoys him.

Their believing that doesn't surprise me.

We could not sleep because of the *baby's crying*.

Exercise

In the following sentences some of the italicized case forms are acceptable and some are not. Where a wrong form has been used, write the acceptable form.

1. Reverend Clark is the person to *whom* we'll go for advice.

2. Barbara and she are the ones *who* I believe should receive the award.

3. *Us* union members are happy about the *company's* being so generous.

4. You, not *me*, must make the decision.

5. You suspect Jennifer's friends, but she is more likely to be guilty than *they*.

6. Our school officials did not like *us* heckling the visiting speaker.

7. I will be pleased to work with *whomever* you appoint to the job.

8. I will be pleased to work with *whoever* accepts the job.

9. Nielson is the candidate *who* the party leaders prefer.

10. The comments were directed at *we* two, you and *I*.

11. I'll support *whomever* has the best chance of defeating the incumbent.

12. In the dim light I thought *her* to be Mary.

GF4   Subject-Verb Agreement

In grammar the term **agreement** is used to describe the relationship between the inflectional forms of different elements within a sentence. When two related elements (subject and verb, pronoun and antecedent) show the same kind of inflection, they are said to agree. Thus a verb agrees with its subject if its form shows the same number and person as the subject. A pronoun agrees with its antecedent if both show the same gender, number, and person. The fundamental convention of agreement is that *the inflectional endings of two related elements should agree as far as possible.*

1. Verbs agree with their subjects in number and person.

A singular subject requires a singular verb, a plural subject a plural verb. If the subject is a personal pronoun, inflected for person, the verb agrees in person. If the subject is a noun, it is always considered to be in the third person and takes the third-person form of the verb.

I *am* late.	(subject first person singular; verb first person singular)
He is sorry.	(subject third person singular; verb third person singular)
The *man works* slowly.	(*works* third person singular to agree with *man*)

Troublesome Constructions

The following constructions cause most troubles in subject-verb agreement:

a. When two or more singular subjects are connected by *and,* a plural form of the verb is required.

He and his brother *are* identical twins.

Tom, Sarah, Griff, and I *make* a good foursome.

A fool and his money *are* soon parted.

There are three exceptions to this rule: First, when each of the singular subjects is considered individually, the verb is singular. This usage is most frequent after *each* or *every*.

Here, every man and woman *works* for the good of the organization.

Each boy and girl *makes* a separate report.

Second, when the two singular subjects refer to the same person or thing, the singular verb is used.

His pride and joy *is* his new car.

Grape juice and ginger ale *is* a good drink.

Third, mathematical computations may take either a singular or a plural verb.

Five and five *is* ten.
or:
Five and five *are* ten.

Two times three *is* six.
or:
Two times three *are* six.

b. When two or more singular subjects are connected by *or, nor,* or *but,* a singular form of the verb is required.

Quigley or Stein *is* to be elected.

Neither Lawrence nor Hugh *has* a chance.

Not Sue but Betty *was* invited.

Not only his wife but even his mother *finds* him selfish.

c. When one of two subjects connected by *or, nor,* or *but* is singular and the other is plural, the verb agrees in number with the nearer one.

Neither Lewis nor his lawyers *were* there.

Not only the boys but also their father *encourages* it.

d. When two subjects connected by *or* or *nor* differ in person, the verb agrees with the nearer.

Neither you nor Ted *works* this evening.

Jean or you *are* to go.

Either Red or I *have* won.

When following this rule creates an awkward sentence, restate the idea in a form that is both correct and natural. For example, rather than write

Neither Ben nor I am to blame.

You or he is the leading contender.

restate these sentences as follows:

Ben is not to blame, and neither am I.

You and he are the leading contenders.

e. A singular subject followed immediately by *as well as, in addition to, including, no less than, with, together with,* **or a similar prepositional construction, requires a singular verb.**

The husband as well as the wife *needs* advice.

The senator together with his assistants *was* praised.

The president no less than the secretary *is* responsible.

The store in addition to the farm *was* sold.

Because this rule sometimes creates some strained sentences, it is sometimes best to avoid the construction altogether and to write:

Both the husband and the wife *need* advice.

The senator and his assistants *were* praised.

The president *is* just as responsible as the secretary.

The store and the farm *were* sold.

f. A singular subject followed by a phrase containing a plural noun requires a singular verb.

The *attitude* of these men *is* definitely hostile.

The *leader* of the rebel forces *has* been captured.

One of the women in the back row *looks* sick.

A *list* of the names of all survivors *is* on file.

In conversation, a plural modifier immediately before a verb often leads to a plural verb. This is most likely to happen in sentences like the last example, in which the subject is followed by a long modifier containing two plural nouns. This colloquial usage has less justification in writing, since the more deliberate nature of writing and revision makes it easier to identify *list* as a singular subject requiring a singular verb.

g. Indefinite pronouns such as *anybody, anyone, each, either, everybody, neither, nobody, no one,* and *somebody* generally require a singular verb.

Anybody who does that *is* just reckless.

Anyone who wants to *has* the right to split this with me.

Each of them *makes* fifty dollars a week.

Somebody has been using my bicycle.

Nobody in town *admits* having seen him.

Everybody has the same chance.

h. The pronouns *any* and *none* take either singular or plural verbs.

Are any of you *going* to the show?

Any of these times *is* satisfactory.

None works so faithfully as he.

None are expected from the district.

i. When the subject is a relative pronoun, the verb agrees with the antecedent of that pronoun.

He is one of the *men who act* as advisers.

This is one of those *problems that have* two solutions.

j. When the expletive *there* or the adverb *here* comes at or near the beginning of a sentence, the verb agrees with the subject that follows the verb.

Here *is* your *money.*

Here *are* the *receipts.*

There *are* no second *chances.*

There *are* a *man* and a *boy* in that boat.

Is there a *chance* of his winning?

Were there many *people* present?

This usage is not strictly observed in speech, because most people at times begin a sentence with an expletive followed by a single subject and then add more subjects before finishing the sentence. For example:

Did I see anyone you know at the party? Well, there was Juana Salazar, and Rae Carroll, and Dan Snyder.

In speech, you cannot conveniently revise the verb to take care of these additional subjects. But you do have such an opportunity in writing, and hence a plural verb is expected in such sentences.

k. When a sentence begins with the expletive *it*, the verb is always singular, regardless of the number of the subject.

It *is* the *Johnsons.*

It *is we* whom they want.

l. The complement of the verb *to be* does not affect the number of the verb.

Books are her chief source of enjoyment.

Her chief *source* of enjoyment *is* books.

One *thing* you must be ready for *is* their attempts to break up the meeting.

Their *attempts* to break up the meeting *are* one thing you must be ready for.

If this rule produces an awkward sentence, the wisest thing to do is to revise the sentence.

Awkward	Revised
The amusing *thing* about campaign speeches *is* the attempts that both sides make to represent themselves as the only friends of the people	In campaign speeches, it is amusing to see how both sides attempt to represent themselves as the only friends of the people.

m. A collective noun takes a singular verb when the class it names is thought of as a unit, a plural verb when the members of the class are thought of as individuals.

Singular	Plural
The jury *is* finally complete.	The jury *were* divided in their opinions.
The family *holds* an annual reunion.	My family *have* never been able to agree.
The clergy *is* wretchedly underpaid.	The clergy *are* supporting this proposal from their pulpits.

This rule also applies to such nouns as *number, part,* and *rest.*

Singular	Plural
A large number *is* expected.	A number of errors *have* been found.
Only part of the order *was* delivered.	A great part of the people *have* no opinion on the question.
The rest of the page *is* illegible.	The rest of the votes *are* about equally divided among the three candidates.

n. Titles of books, magazines, movies, newspapers, plays, and the like take a singular verb.

Brideshead Revisited is a fine novel.

The Outcasts was not a success at the box office.

The *New York Times* is his bible.

o. Plural numbers take a singular verb when they are used in a phrase to indicate a sum or a unit.

A million dollars *is* a great deal of money.

Ten years *is* too long to wait.

Nine percent *is* good interest.

Forty hours *is* the regular work week.

p. Certain nouns that are plural in form generally take a singular verb. Some of these are *civics, economics, electronics, linguistics, mathematics, measles, mumps, news, physics, semantics.*

Economics *has* been called the dismal science.

No news *is* good news.

Semantics *is* the study of meanings.

Exercise   Which of the forms in parentheses is the right one?

1. Neither he nor his sons (was, were) present at the reading of the will.

2. Neither my sister nor my mother (plans, plan) to attend the physical fitness sessions for women.

3. The instructor as well as the students (was, were) at fault.

4. Each of the candidates for the position (has, have) exceptionally high qualifications.

5. He is one of the students who (plans, plan) to attend the extra class session tomorrow.

6. There (is, are) both food and firewood in the snowbound cabin.

7. The jury (is, are) expected to reach its decision very quickly.

8. Fifty hours (is, are) the amount of work time I contracted for.

9. It (is, are) the Joneses who are particularly concerned about the new zoning regulations.

10. The jury (is, are) to be isolated in individual hotel rooms each night during the trial.

GF5   Pronoun-Antecedent Agreement

1. Pronouns agree with their antecedents in gender, number, and person.

The **antecedent** of a pronoun is the noun or pronoun to which it refers. In "The children missed their parents," the antecedent of *their* is *children,* and in "She packed her suitcase," the antecedent of *her* is *She.* The rule requires that if the antecedent is plural, the pronoun must be plural *(their)*; if the antecedent is feminine, the pronoun must take the feminine form *(she, her)*; if the antecedent is declined for person, the pronoun should be in the same person. But a pronoun need not agree with its antecedent in case, since it takes its case from its function in its own clause.

Example

The *men* got *their* wages.

Explanation

Their *is third person plural to agree with* men. *The plural form of the pronoun is the same for all genders.*

Example	**Explanation**
The *girl* found *her* watch.	*Her is third person feminine singular to agree with* girl.
The *boy* misses *his* dog.	*His is third person masculine singular to agree with* boy.
The *plane* changed *its* course.	*Its is third person neuter singular to agree with* plane.
Mario and *Carlos* are looking for *their* parents.	*Two or more antecedents connected by* and *take a plural pronoun.*

Troublesome Constructions

Most troubles with agreement of pronouns occur in only a few constructions, and arise because of conflict between formal and colloquial usage. Generally, in formal usage the *form* of the antecedent, not its *meaning*, determines the number of the pronoun; whereas in colloquial usage number tends to be governed by *meaning*. For example, *everybody* is singular in form but plural in meaning, because it refers to more than one person. Formally, *everybody* requires the singular *his* or *her*; colloquially, *everybody* is often followed by the plural *their*.

a. *Each, either,* or *neither,* **followed by a phrase containing a plural noun, takes a singular pronoun.**

Each of the girls is sure *she* is going to win.

Neither of the men would admit *his* mistake.

Either of these women may lose *her* position.

b. *Everybody, each, either, everyone, neither, nobody,* **or** *a person* **takes a singular pronoun.**

Each has *his or her* own group of supporters.

Everybody had *his or her* work in good shape.

Nobody had *his or her* speech ready today.

Everyone was keeping *his or her* fingers crossed.

A *person* who begins to cut classes may find *himself or herself* in trouble.

As these examples show, English does not have a singular personal pronoun that refers to both male and female in such sentences as "Each student should do ____ own work." Formerly, the masculine form of the pronoun was used when the sex of the antecedent was unknown or when the antecedent referred to both sexes. But most people now urge that the linguistic discrimination implied in this traditional use should be avoided whenever possible. If the use of both masculine and feminine forms results in an awkward construction (as in some of the examples above), a sentence may be recast in the plural or reworded to eliminate the gender form. For example: "Students should do their own work"; "Nobody had a speech ready today"; "Cutting classes may lead to trouble."

c. The impersonal *one* takes the third person pronoun unless the style is very formal.

One must watch *his or her* step with that group.

One can't really blame *himself or herself* for that.

If *one* had a second chance, how much wiser *he or she* might be.

In a very formal style the impersonal pronoun is sometimes used throughout.

Under such conditions *one* laments *one's* utter incapacity to be of any genuine service.

One finds *oneself* wishing that the evidence were more convincing.

d. A collective noun takes either a singular or a plural pronoun, depending on whether the group is considered as a unit or as a number of individuals.

Singular	Plural
The *family* keeps pretty much to *itself*.	The *family* may have *their* private quarrels, but *they* always agree in public.
The judge reprimanded the *jury* for *its* disregard of the evidence.	At the request of the defense attorney, the *jury* were polled and *their* individual verdicts recorded.
The *team* had *its* back to the wall.	The *team* are electing *their* captain.

e. The relative pronoun *who* is used when the antecedent is a person; *which* is used when the antecedent is a thing; *that* is used to refer to persons, animals, or things.

This is the *man who* drove the car.

The *girl who* found it is here.

The *woman that* I mean had brown hair.

Here is the *parcel which* (or *that*) she left.

This is the *cow that* jumped over the moon.

The possessive form *whose* is theoretically limited to persons, but it is often used when the more formal *of which* seems awkward.

The *nation whose* conscience is clear on that score is exceptional.

The *newspaper whose* reporters are most alert gets the most scoops.

Exercise   **Indicate which of the forms in parentheses is the preferred form.**

1. Each boy must take (his, their) turn.

2. Nobody will commit (himself or herself, themselves) to a definite plan.

3. One shouldn't be too confident until (one has, you have) tried it.

4. The team lost (its, their) opening game at home and won the first game (it, they) played away from home.

5. The horse (who, that) won the Kentucky Derby went on to win the Preakness and the Belmont.

6. My high school graduating class will hold (its, their) first reunion this Christmas.

7. Neither of the bicycles (is, are) worth (its, their) price.

8. Everybody has (his or her, their) own opinion about what we should do.

9. The janitor (who, which) found the money was given a reward.

10. The faculty are quite divided about whom (it, they) (wants, want) to be the next president.

GF6   Vague Pronoun Reference

A pronoun should refer clearly to a specific antecedent. If it refers to a whole clause, or to one of two possible antecedents, or to a unidentified antecedent, the reference may be vague.

Vague reference	Explanation	Revision
I lost a front tooth, *which* embarrassed me.	Which *refers to the whole main clause. In the revision the sentence is recast in order to avoid the vague reference.*	Losing a front tooth embarrassed me.

Vague reference	Explanation	Revision
Because Kyle is more interested in literature than in biology, he sometimes slights *it*.	*The pronoun* it *has no clear antecedent and might refer to either literature or biology. The revision avoids the ambiguity.*	Kyle's interest in literature sometimes makes him slight biology.
The crash is being investigated. At present *they* think the planes must have collided.	*The antecedent of* they *is not identified. The statements would be improved by substituting the noun* investigators *for the nonspecific pronoun.*	The crash is being investigated. At present the investigators think the planes must have collided.

Exercise

Revise the following sentences to make all pronoun references clear:

1. The defendant was visibly upset. At that very moment they were in the next room deciding his fate.

2. We have already overspent our budget for the play, but we need money for props and for set construction, which is a major problem.

3. In revival meetings it is customary for them to offer testimonies.

4. Hunters should be careful about how they carry guns when they are loaded.

5. Mark Twain did not like his early work on *Huckleberry Finn,* which caused him to consider destroying the partially completed manuscript.

6. The figure skaters anxiously awaited the decision as they tabulated their score cards.

7. Fred and Sue agreed to have a church wedding, which pleases their parents.

8. My job in New York was only three blocks from my apartment and the working hours were during the daytime, which pleased my mother.

9. Kemper would draw sketches of birds and trees which showed where his interests lay.

10. Students living in an apartment must do their own cooking and cleaning, which will take some of their time.

GF7 Faulty Complement

1. **Avoid using an illogical or awkward construction as a complement of the verb *to be*.**

The verb *to be* is usually either an auxiliary verb ("I *am* learning") or a linking verb ("Honesty *is* the best policy"). As a linking verb, it joins its complement to its subject and thus acts as a kind of equal sign: honesty = best policy. Readers expect two things of this linking verb: (1) that it will be followed by a complement, and (2) that the complement can be logically equated with the subject. They will be bothered if either of these expectations is not met.

Thus if they read the sentence, "Honesty is in the little details of everyday life," they will miss the promised linking relationship and will want to make the sentence read, "Honesty is best expressed in the little details of everyday life," thus changing *is* from a linking to an auxiliary verb ("*is* expressed").

Similarly, readers who meet the sentence, "Honesty is what you do in such a situation," will feel that the complement throws the equation out of balance, since it equates the abstract noun *honesty* with a statement of action. They will want to revise the sentence to read, "The honest thing to do in such a situation is to tell the truth," so that each side of the equation refers to an action (*to do* and *to tell*).

To avoid such annoying constructions, make sure that the complement of *to be* can be logically equated with the subject. If it cannot, or if the equation results in a wordy or awkward sentence, either revise the form of the complement or rewrite the sentence to get rid of the linking verb.

Illogical or awkward complement	Explanation	Revised sentence
Before I built the house, all I had learned about carpentry was from watching my father.	*The equation requires some statement of what I knew, not how my knowledge was obtained. Of the various possible revisions, perhaps the best is to substitute a more active verb that does not promise an equation.*	Before I built the house, all that I knew about carpentry *I had learned from* watching my father.
The chief disadvantage of weeping willows is the branches are brittle and break easily.	*The omission of* that *between* is *and the branches invites the misreading that* branches *is the complement. When* that *is inserted, however, the complement is seen to be the entire clause, of which* branches *is the subject.*	The chief disadvantage of weeping willows is *that* the branches are brittle and break easily.

2. Avoid the use of *is when, is where,* and *is if* when the complement of *to be* is intended to describe or define the subject.

This advice is a special application of the more general statement given in rule 1. The use of an adverbial clause instead of a noun phrase or clause is one kind of illogical complement that occurs frequently in student definitions. This error and its revision are illustrated by the following examples:

Faulty complement	Explanation	Revision
Plagiarism is *when you represent another person's writing as your own.*	*The reader expects to find out what* plagiarism *is, not when* it is. *The construction calls for a noun phrase similar to the italicized phrase at the right.*	Plagiarism is *the representation of another's writing as one's own.*
Manslaughter is *where a person is killed deliberately but without premeditation.*	*Again, the construction requires a statement of what* manslaughter *is, not where* it is.	Manslaughter is *the deliberate but unpremeditated killing of a person.*
A comma splice is if a comma is used to separate two independent sentences that are not connected by a coordinating conjunction.	*The complement should tell what a comma splice is, not how a comma splice is made. Use a noun such as* use *at the right.*	A comma splice is *the use of a comma to separate two independent sentences that are not connected by a coordinating conjunction.*

3. Use the adjective form as the complement of a sensory verb.

A **sensory verb** is one that identifies some action of the senses — seeing, hearing, feeling, tasting, smelling. Because the complement of a sensory verb usually describes the subject rather than the action of the verb, it should be an adjective, not an adverb. Turning the construction around and expressing the complement as an adjective, as in the parenthetical phrases below, helps illustrate the adjectival function of the complement:

The table feels smooth. (smooth-feeling table)

The barrel looks clean. (clean-looking barrel)

That note sounded flat. (flat-sounding note)

The syrup tasted sweet. (sweet-tasting syrup)

To use an adverb after these verbs would suggest that the writer was describing the manner in which the feeling, looking, sounding, and tasting were performed. Unless the modifier completing a sensory verb is clearly intended to describe the action suggested by the verb, an adjective is the correct form. The adverb is appropriate in the following sentences:

The blind man touched the paper lightly.

The doctor tasted the liquid cautiously.

Exercise

Revise the following sentences to correct faulty complements:

1. My only preparation for college chemistry was from a junior high school course in general science.

2. I feel badly about having caused you so much trouble.

3. Forgery is when one signs another person's name to a document.

4. I heard on last night's news where flooding has reached disaster proportions in some areas of the country.

5. Goal tending is if a defensive basketball player touches the ball after it has begun its downward path toward the goal.

6. The result of our conference was in reaching complete accord.

7. The most unusual food I have ever had was when I ate a serving of boiled snails.

8. In tennis a double fault is where the server fails twice successively to hit the ball into the appropriate part of the opponent's court.

9. The boxer's chief disadvantage is his opponents have learned that he has a "glass chin."

10. The judge explained that perjury is if a witness lies under oath.

GF8   Confusion of Adjective and Adverb

Modifiers that are faulty because of word order are discussed in **WO2**. This section is limited to errors in the forms of modifiers.

1. Do not use an adjective to modify a verb.

Adjective for adverb	Correct
The old car still runs *good*.	The old car still runs *well*.

Adjective for adverb

Do it as *careful* as you can.

Listen *close* to what I tell you.

Correct

Do it as *carefully* as you can.

Listen *closely* to what I tell you.

2. Do not use an adjective to modify an adverb or another adjective.

Adjective for adverb

He is *considerable* better today.

It is *sure* difficult to decide.

Correct

He is *considerably* better today.

It is *surely* difficult to decide.

3. Do not use an adverb as the complement of a sensory verb unless you clearly intend to modify the verb, not the subject.

See **GF7.**

4. When a modifier could modify either a noun or a verb, indicate by the form which one you intend.

Adverb

Tie the knot *tightly* and *securely.*

Her husband held her *firmly.*

John spoke out *forthrightly.*

Adjective

Tie the boat *tight* to the dock.

He kept his resolutions *firm.*

His answers seemed *forthright.*

Exercise

Rewrite the following sentences to revise or delete faulty modifiers:

1. Speak gentle though you feel angry.

2. We are sure pleased that you could work with us today.

3. The polluted pond smelled horribly.

4. Fasten the hatches secure, for we expect strong wind and high waves tonight.

5. React as calm as you possibly can.

6. We have just come from a real exciting movie.

7. When Laura saw the grade on her history exam, she looked happily.

8. Keep him safely until the danger is past.

9. Now listen careful while I tell you once again.

10. I am considerable poorer for having bought a used car.

P   PUNCTUATION

The common marks of punctuation are the following:

period	.	quotation marks	" "
comma	,		or ' '
semicolon	;	apostrophe	'
colon	:	dash	—
question mark	?	parentheses	( )
exclamation mark	!	square brackets	[ ]

Most of these marks have highly specialized functions, and once these functions are understood, it is easy enough to use the specialized punctuation marks correctly. The chief exception, perhaps, is the comma, which is at once the most common mark of punctuation and the one with the most complex uses.

P1   Uses of the Comma

The comma is used to make the internal structure of a sentence clear. It does so in three general ways: (1) by separating elements that might otherwise be confused, (2) by setting off interrupting constructions, and (3) by marking words out of normal order.

1. Use commas to separate elements that might otherwise seem to run together. Use them as separators in the following ways:

a. To prevent a confused, ambiguous, or awkward reading.

The most important use of the comma is to prevent a confused, ambiguous, or awkward reading. All other uses are subordinate to this one. Notice how the confused sentences at the left are made clear at the right by the use of commas.

Ambiguous	**Explanation**	**Clear**
Mr. Smith our milkman has been hurt.	*Is this a statement to or about Mr. Smith?*	Mr. Smith, our milkman has been hurt.
		or
		Mr. Smith, our milkman, has been hurt.

Ambiguous	Explanation	Clear
I do not care for money isn't everything.	*In order that* money *will not seem to complete* care for, *a comma should be inserted after* care.	I do not care, for money isn't everything.
A hundred yards below the bridge was flooded.	*Comma necessary to avoid misreading of* bridge *as the object of* below.	A hundred yards below, the bridge was flooded.

b. To separate two main clauses joined by a coordinating conjunction *(and, or, nor, but, for)*.

The comma prevents possible misinterpretation on first reading; specifically, it keeps the subject of the second main clause from being misread as a second object in the first clause.

He sold his tractor and his fields went unplowed.

The club owner traded the catcher and the shortstop, his roommate, was angry.

In both these sentences the noun following the conjunction appears at first glance to be part of a compound object of the first verb. A comma before the conjunction shows clearly that the two nouns are in different clauses:

He sold his tractor, and his fields went unplowed.

The club owner traded the catcher, and the shortstop, his roommate, was angry.

When there is no danger of a confused reading, the comma becomes less necessary and may be omitted.

c. To separate elements in a series.

Churchill promised the English only *blood, sweat, toil,* and *tears.*

Reading, swimming, and *dancing* are my favorite recreations.

It was said of Washington that he was *first in war, first in peace,* and *first in the hearts of his countrymen.*

North passed, East bid two spades, South bid three hearts, and *West doubled.*

We were tired, hungry and *disconsolate.*

As these illustrations show, a series may consist of clauses, phrases, or single words, and all items in a series should have the same grammatical form. The comma before the conjunction joining the last two items in a series is optional and may be omitted, as it is in the last example.

Commas are not used to separate adjectives in series under the following conditions:

1. When the adjectives do not individually modify the same headword. For example, in "a new silk dress," *silk* modifies *dress,* but *new* modifies *silk dress.* This kind of sequence is different from the kind of sequence in "a dark, drizzly, cold day," in which each adjective individually modifies *day.*

2. When the series is so commonly used that there is no need to separate the adjectives: "a nice little old lady" or "a red white and blue flag."

d. To separate contrasted elements in a "this, not that" construction.

He is sick, not drunk.

We are disgusted, not angry.

This is a problem that must be handled with sympathy, not harshness.

e. To separate directly quoted material from such speech tags as "he said," "she answered," and "we replied."

She said, "You are only half right."

"This," I declared, "is the last straw."

"Nobody asked you, sir," she said.

"But," he asked, "what if they do decide to come?"

Since the quotation marks themselves set off the quoted material, no confusion would result if the comma were omitted; but convention requires the comma. Whether the punctuation should come *inside* or *outside* the quotation marks is discussed in **P9**.

f. To separate elements in dates, addresses, and place names.

August 4, 1983; February 19, 1984 — (comma between day and year)

She dated the check January 23, 1983, before remembering that the year was now 1984. — (comma between day and year and after year)

875 Main Street, Galesburg, Illinois — (comma between street and city and between city and state)

Chicago, Illinois, is the third-largest city in this country.	(comma before and after the state)
He was born in London, England.	(comma between city and country)

g. In the following miscellaneous constructions: in figures —

22,745; 1,000,000; 150,743,290

in names followed by titles —

R. W. Leeds, M.D.

at the end of the salutation in informal letters —

Dear Joe,

after an introductory *yes* or *no* —

Yes, I'll do it.

Exercise

In the following sentences insert commas if they are needed for ease of reading or are conventionally required:

1. The largest city in the world is Jacksonville Florida if you judge by area not population.

2. I'll have orange juice waffles with maple syrup and black coffee.

3. When we finished sanding and staining the desk looked beautiful.

4. "But the name is Manson not Mason" said Aunt Lois.

5. After all it was not such a difficult shot for a professional.

6. The yard was strewn with empty cartons newspapers scraps of lumber and discarded tires.

7. Throughout his speech was a masterful exhibition of how to talk around a question without answering it.

8. Father went to the airport to meet his sister and Mother came with me to the reception.

9. Lyndon Baines Johnson, thirty-sixth President of the United States, was born near Stonewall Texas on August 27 1908 and died on January 22 1973.

10. No I cannot wait any longer for the train leaves in ten minutes.

2. Use commas to set off an interrupting construction.

Any element that comes between a subject and its verb, a verb and its object or complement, or any two elements not normally separated may be called an *interrupting construction.* If the interruption is awkward, it should be avoided; but many interrupters are necessary. These should be set off by commas, so that a reader can recognize the basic pattern of the sentence.

But you must distinguish between constructions that actually interrupt and those that come between related elements without interrupting them. For example, in

The girl, *you say,* has gone.

the italicized clause comes between subject *(girl)* and verb *(has gone).* The interrupter need not occupy this position. The sentence could have been written

You say that the waiter has gone.

The waiter has gone, you say.

But in the sentence

The waiter *you want* has gone.

the italicized clause identifies the particular girl and cannot be moved without weakening the sentence. The clause modifies the subject so closely that we may consider "The girl you want" as the "whole subject" of *has gone.* A modifying phrase or clause which is so closely related to another element that it is felt to be a part of that element should not be set off with commas, since the commas would distort the relationship, not clarify it. The italicized modifiers in the following sentences are so necessary that they are not considered interrupting constructions:

The man *with him* is his brother.

The woman *at the piano* is his wife.

The leader *of the revolt* has been captured.

As you study the following uses of commas to set off interrupting constructions, notice this about them: *an interrupting construction between subject and verb, or verb and object, or verb and complement requires two commas to enclose it.* These commas act like mild parentheses and *are always used in pairs.*

a. To set off an appositive.

An **appositive** is a noun or pronoun, a noun phrase, or a noun clause that is considered grammatically equivalent to the noun or pronoun it refers to:

His father, *the president of the company,* will be responsible.

They want us, *you and me,* to go.

I felt that her main point, *that everybody must be on time,* was directed chiefly at me.

I want to see Dr. Roberts, *the guidance counselor.*

The first three examples show that the appositive is often a particular kind of interrupter. The fourth appositive does not interrupt the main clause, but is conventionally separated from the rest of the sentence by a comma.

But when an appositive is necessary to identify the subject, it is not considered an interrupting construction and is not set off with commas:

Your son *John* called.

John is necessary to identify the son who called.

b. To set off nouns of address.

A **noun of address** is a common or proper noun used to name a listener to whom we are speaking directly: "I wish, *Dad,* that you would reconsider your decision." "I understand, *Mrs. Ellison,* that you are now a grandmother." Such nouns may come at the beginning, middle, or end of a sentence, so that strictly speaking they are not always interrupters. But they are always set off from the rest of the sentence by commas.

I would like to ask you, *Mr. Johnson,* for your opinion.

Sir, I'd like to ask a question.

Listen, *chum,* I've had enough of you!

I wish I were going with you, *Brenda.*

c. To set off conjunctive adverbs and other transitional markers.

Conjunctive adverbs (*however, moreover, therefore,* and the like), sometimes called **transitional connectives,** are adverbs that serve to connect main clauses or sentences. Usually they provide a transition between two such statements, and they come *near,* or *at,* the beginning of the second one.

We planned our demonstration for noon sharp. We thought, moreover, that we could bring it off.

Most students seemed excited enough. Some, however, were already expressing doubts.

Commas around *therefore* are sometimes omitted.

I am therefore canceling the order.

d. To set off a nonrestrictive modifier.

A modifier of a noun is said to be **restrictive** when it specifies a particular member or members of a group. In "The President *who said that* was Lincoln," the italicized modifier restricts the whole class of Presidents to a particular one. When a modifier does not limit a class to a particular group or individual but modifies the whole class, it is said to be **nonrestrictive.** Thus in "The President, *who is both the chief of state and the leader of his party,* holds one of the most powerful offices in the world," the italicized modifier refers to all Presidents of the United States and does not restrict the statement to any particular one. It is nonrestrictive.

A modifier of a verb or predicate is restrictive when it limits the action of the verb. Thus in "I'll go *if I must,*" the italicized conditional clause states under what conditions the going will occur. Similarly, in "I did it *because I was forced to,*" the italicized clause states why the speaker had to do a particular thing. In both examples the information provided by the modifier is so closely related to the action indicated by the verb that the meaning of the whole sentence would be considerably changed if the modifier were omitted.

The following sentences illustrate the punctuation of restrictive and nonrestrictive modifiers:

Restrictive	Nonrestrictive
All students *who were absent* will be required to do an additional assignment.	College graduates, *who represent a superior intellectual group,* must accept the responsibility of leadership.
Soldiers *who have flat feet* are not assigned to the infantry.	Soldiers, *who are selected by physical fitness tests,* should show a sickness rate lower than that of the total population.
He comes and goes *as he pleases.*	Just one more picture, *if you please.*
Speak *when you are spoken to.*	He asked me, *when she had gone,* who she was.

The best practical test of whether a modifier is restrictive in its context is to see if leaving it out would seriously distort the meaning of the sentence. Restrictive modifiers are so closely related to their headwords that they cannot be left out without distortion of the original meaning. Nonrestrictive modifiers, by contrast, can be omitted without significant change in the meaning. Compare the following omissions with the original versions above:

All students . . . will be required to do an additional assignment.	(This is not what the original statement meant.)
College graduates . . . must accept the responsibility of leadership.	(This is substantially what the original statement meant.)
Soldiers . . . are not assigned to the infantry.	(Not the original meaning.)
Soldiers . . . should show a sickness rate lower than that of the total population.	(The original meaning has not been substantially changed.)
He comes and goes.	(This was not the idea of the original sentence.)
Just one more picture.	(The omission does not change the meaning.)
Speak.	(The omission distorts the original meaning.)
He asked me . . . who she was.	(No significant change of meaning.)

Exercise

In the following sentences, provide commas to set off appositives, nouns of address, conjunctive adverbs, and nonrestrictive modifiers. Some sentences may require no additional punctuation.

1. Dad did you know that Dr. Jones our chemistry professor once played professional hockey?

2. Mary asked, "Joe why don't you talk to the man in charge the managing editor?"

3. Yes her mother is a doctor — not however of medicine but of philosophy.

4. The man who said that must have been joking.

5. The man whoever he is must be found.

6. Don't shoot till you see the whites of their eyes.

7. Dean asked me when he called last night if we were still going to have the picnic.

8. The children looking very disappointed thanked us anyway.

9. The instructor said in addition that some of the test answers were illegible.

10. I left a call with the switchboard operator to be sure of getting up in time to catch my plane.

11. Dad you said we could go if we had finished our work. You promised moreover that we could use the car even though the direction signal is not working.

12. A radio report which may or may not be true states that John Whalen our line coach has an offer from a professional team that he will probably accept.

13. The challenger who was clearly the underdog before the match made his defeat of the champion look so easy that the sportswriters began to hail him as one of the truly great champions.

14. However the wig that she bought in the bargain basement was the best of the three.

15. The bus driver Mr. Peterson who is usually an easygoing person was in a bad mood today scolding the children at the slightest provocation.

3. Use commas to mark an inversion.

a. To emphasize an inverted element.

Any word, phrase, or clause written out of its normal position is said to be *inverted.* To emphasize an inverted element, a writer sets it off with commas.

Myself, I will vote in favor of it.

Except for physics, my courses are not difficult.

But if the inversion is so common as to seem normal, the comma is usually omitted. No commas would be used in the following inversions:

Yesterday I had a bad time of it.

In 1913 the concept of total war was unknown.

In the following sentences the verbs are underlined.

b. To set off a long introductory phrase or an adverbial clause preceding the main clause.

When a sentence opens with a long phrase or adverbial clause, use a comma between this element and the main clause:

1. *Pulling over to the curb at the first opportunity,* I waited for the fire engines to pass.

2. *If there is going to be any difficulty about this request,* I would rather withdraw it.

3. *Being ignorant of the facts of the situation,* I could say nothing.

4. *When you say that,* smile.

This usage is often considered optional, but the comma is generally used under the following conditions:

1. when the opening phrase contains a verbal, as in examples 1 and 3

2. when it is a subordinate clause, as in example 2

3. when it is an obvious inversion, as in example 4

The comma should always be used if it makes the meaning clearer and the reading easier.

Exercise   In the following sentences insert commas to set off inversions and introductory constructions where desirable.

1. Whatever he says take it with a grain of salt.

2. Whatever he says will be worth listening to.

3. If he is going to fly off the handle like that at the slightest provocation I think you should stop dating him.

4. As far as I know they plan to stay here this summer.

5. Whatever the merits of the proposal it comes too late to be considered.

6. Whether you like it or not this is the final decision.

7. After the show we walked home together.

8. Since he has not answered any of our letters even those we sent by registered mail we must assume that he is not interested.

9. Knowing that his only chance to win might depend on stealing second base the manager sent in a runner for Milney.

10. Confused and hurt by her parents' attitude the girl ran sobbing to her room.

P2   Misuse of the Comma

Too many commas can be more annoying than too few. Observe the following "don'ts":

1. Do not use a comma instead of a period between sentences.

Using a comma instead of a period between sentences may cause serious misinterpretation. (See "Comma Splice," **S5**.)

Common splice	Clear
He spoke very quietly, as I listened, I had the impression that he was speaking to himself.	He spoke very quietly. As I listened, I had the impression that he was speaking to himself.
There was nothing more to be said, when they took that attitude, further negotiation became impossible.	There was nothing more to be said. When they took that attitude, further negotiation became impossible.

2. Do not use a comma between closely related elements except to mark an interrupting construction.

The comma should reveal the structure of a sentence, not disguise it. Closely related elements (subject and verb, verb and object, verb or noun and modifier) should not normally be separated. If these elements must be interrupted, using a pair of commas to enclose the interrupting construction helps to bridge the interruption.

Faulty comma	Correct
My car, is at the service station.	My car, which is at the service station, needs a thorough overhauling right away.
He said, that he would try.	He said, when I asked him, that he would try.
The student who lost his money, may need it badly.	The student, who had lost money on other occasions, was reprimanded for his carelessness.

The last pair of illustrations contrasts a restrictive and a nonrestrictive clause (see page 662). There should be no comma in the sentence at the left because the subordinate *who*-clause is a restrictive modifier.

3. Do not use commas excessively.

It is not necessary to use commas in a particular construction simply because convention recommends them. Convention describes general practice and should usually be followed, but there are times when slavishly following the rules will chop a sentence to pieces. In such cases omit any punctuation that is not necessary to control the reading of the sentence. Exception: You may not omit commas that set off nonrestrictive modifiers or appositives.

The following examples illustrate excessive and adequate punctuation:

Excessive

However, it is not, in my opinion, desirable.

Yesterday, a little, old lady, in a dilapidated, old Ford, picked me up and brought me home.

Sometimes, she would appear in an elaborate beach outfit, sometimes, she wore a simple, white suit, and, occasionally, she put on a red, white, and blue bathing suit, with a detachable skirt.

Adequate

However, it is not in my opinion desirable.

Yesterday a little old lady in a dilapidated old Ford picked me up and brought me home.

Sometimes she would appear in an elaborate beach outfit, sometimes she wore a simple white suit, and occasionally she put on a red white and blue bathing suit with a detachable skirt.

P3   Uses of the Semicolon

1. Use a semicolon to separate closely related independent clauses not connected by a conjunction.

Try this one; it looks like your color.

His mother won't let him; she is afraid he might get hurt.

Your car is new; mine is eight years old.

In each of these sentences a period could be used instead of the semicolon. But the clauses, even though grammatically independent, are felt to be so closely related that a period makes too sharp a separation.

The semicolon provides a more emphatic separation than the comma; it affords a closer tie than the period. It is therefore the most suitable mark to balance two contrasted ideas parallel in form:

Take care of the children; the adults can take care of themselves.

It was not the hours or the pay that discouraged me; it was the constant monotony of the work.

2. Use a semicolon between independent clauses joined by a transitional connective (conjunctive adverb).

Transitional connectives are words like *also, besides, consequently, furthermore, hence, however, in addition, likewise, moreover, nevertheless, still, then, therefore.* Since these connectives are not subordinating conjunctions, they require a stronger mark of punctuation than a comma.

His argument has some merit; *however,* he goes too far.

His eyes went bad; *consequently,* he had to resign his job as a proofreader.

She argued brilliantly; *still,* her opponent had the stronger case.

3. Use a semicolon to separate elements in a series that themselves contain commas.

Among those present were Dr. Holmes, pastor of the First Methodist Church; A. C. Levitt, superintendent of schools; B. L. Rainey, manager of the Benson Hotel; and M. T. Cord, vice president of Miller and Sons.

Commas between the elements in this series would be confused with the commas that set off the appositives.

P4 Misuse of the Semicolon

1. Do not use a semicolon as the equivalent of a colon.

Although the names suggest a close relationship, the semicolon and the colon have quite different uses and are not interchangeable. The colon (see **P7**) is used chiefly to indicate that something is to follow, usually a series of items; the semicolon separates parallel elements and is never used to introduce a series. In the following examples the faulty semicolon is followed by the correct colon in parentheses:

My records show that the following students have not handed in the assignment; (:) Mr. Andrews, Mr. Richardson, Mr. Smith, and Ms. Wallace.

Dear Sir; (:) May I call your attention to an error. . . .

2. Do not use a semicolon as the equivalent of a comma.

A semicolon cannot be substituted for a comma between a main clause and a subordinate construction. In the following examples the faulty semicolon is followed by the correct comma in parentheses:

Although I seldom have trouble with grammar or spelling; (,) I never seem to use the right punctuation.

We stayed up until two o'clock in the morning; (,) hoping that they would arrive.

P5   ## The Period

1. A period is used to mark the end of a declarative sentence.

Unless a sentence is intended as a question, a command, or an exclamation, it is declarative and is closed by a period.

Today is Tuesday.

We have three days to go.

2. A period is used to mark an accepted abbreviation such as the abbreviation of a title —

Col., Dr., Hon., Mrs., Rev.

degree —

B.A., B.S., M.D., Ph.D.

name —

John A. Jones, Chas. W. Brown

month —

Jan., Feb., Aug., Nov.

state —

Ala., Ga., Me., Ill., Wash. (*but also:* AL, GA, ME, IL, WA — no period is used in the capital-style, two-letter state abbreviations)

miscellaneous —

Ave., St., vol., p., U.S.A., B.C., A.D.

Notice, however, that periods are not used in such shortened forms as *exam, gym, prom, per cent, 1st, 2nd, 3rd.* Periods are usually omitted also in abbreviations of government agencies — *USNR, TVA, AEC, FBI, CIA.*

3. A period is used before a decimal and between dollars and cents.

The error is less than .01 inch.

The correct answer is 57.39.

The price tag read $11.98.

P6   Question and Exclamation Marks

1. The main use of the question mark is to indicate that a sentence is to be understood as a question.

Whose is this?

You mean he's ill?

But if the question is a courteous way of stating a request, the end punctuation is a period, not a question mark:

Will you please hand in your papers now.

The question mark is sometimes used in parentheses to query the accuracy of the preceding word:

These amateurs (?) make a comfortable living out of sports.

As a device for irony, however, it is generally weak. Avoid:

Those funny (?) remarks are uncalled for.

Notice that a question reported in indirect discourse does not take a question mark:

They asked where we were going.

2. The exclamation mark is used to show that a statement is imperative or that it is spoken with strong emotion.

Be quiet!

Don't just stand there! Do something!

Oh, what a mess!

P7   The Colon

Use a colon:
1. To indicate that something is to follow, especially a formal statement or series.

Here are the facts: The money was there five minutes before he entered the room; it was missing immediately after he left; the next day he bought a new record player, though he had already spent all this month's allowance.

2. In place of a comma before long direct quotations.

In his most famous speech Bryan said: "You shall not press down upon the brow of labor a crown of thorns; you shall not crucify mankind upon a cross of gold."

This is her statement as reported in the papers: "I have never advocated such ideas; I do not advocate them now; I do not approve of them; I have no reason to believe that I ever will approve of them."

3. Before a clause that restates in different words the idea of the preceding clause.

Romeo and Juliet is one of the great experiences in film. It is not, to be sure, the greatest: the creation of new dramatic poetry is more important than the re-creation of old.

Except for differences of subject matter, the rules of grammar are in essence like the laws of physics and chemistry: they are scientific generalizations about the facts.

In such uses the clause after the colon says, in another way, what the clause before the colon has already said. But the restatement is not needless repetition: it illustrates or amplifies the content of the preceding clause.

4. Between clauses when the second clause provides an example of something stated in the first.

Very few tennis players can be called superstars: Martina Navratilova is one of those few.

5. In certain specialized uses: after the salutation in formal letters —

Dear Sir:

between hours and minutes —

The train is due at 8:36.

between chapter and verse in Biblical citations —

Isaiah 12:2–4

between volume and page in a magazine citation —

College English 29:253–285

between place and publisher in a bibliography —

Boston: Houghton Mifflin

P8   Quotation Marks

This section is limited to the use of quotation marks. The position of other punctuation in relation to quotation marks is treated separately in the next section.

Quotation marks may be double (" ") or single (' ').

Double Quotation Marks

1. Double quotation marks have the following uses:

a. To enclose the actual words of a speaker (direct discourse).

I said, "That's your worry."

"Jean," he said, "you can't do that!"

"What is the matter?" she asked.

Because all the words of a speaker are enclosed in quotation marks, an interrupting "he said," "she replied," or the like requires two sets of quotation marks in the sentence. Notice also that when direct discourse is reported as indirect discourse, quotation marks are not used.

She asked what was the matter.

b. To identify words that are being discussed as words.

The word "garage" comes from French; the word "piano" comes from Italian.

"Buxom" originally came from the Old English verb meaning "to bend."

This use of quotation marks to call attention to a word is sometimes extended to include technical terms (*A "field" in mathematics is not what it is in agriculture*) and slang terms (*Her brother "socked" her in the eye and "beaned" her with a ruler*). Though occasionally acceptable, this usage is often overdone. Quotation marks do not make a term appropriate. If a word is appropriate in context, it can usually stand without quotation marks; if it is not appropriate, it should not be used.

Another method, preferred by some writers, is to underline or italicize the word being cited (see page 698).

To be is the trickiest verb in the language.

c. To enclose the titles of essays, short stories, articles, poems, paintings, songs, television programs, and the like (but not books).

(For an alternative form for paintings and musical compositions, see page 698.)

I think Hemingway's best short story is "The Snows of Kilimanjaro."

It was Linda Ronstadt who sang "Desperado."

Two of my otherwise highbrow mother's favorite television programs were "Dallas" and "Three's Company."

He says that Da Vinci's "Mona Lisa" is a portrait of an Italian noblewoman.

d. In bibliographies, to distinguish the title of a selection from that of the book from which it is taken.

Faulkner, William. "Two Soldiers." In *Collected Stories of William Faulkner*. New York: Random House, 1950.

For additional examples of this use, see pages 508–513. Notice that titles of books are either underlined or set in italics, not enclosed in quotation marks.

Single Quotation Marks

2. Single quotation marks are used to mark quotations within quotations.

When it is necessary to include one set of quotation marks within another, the internal quotation is placed within single marks, the longer quotation within double marks:

When the director said, "Let's try that passage again, beginning with 'Once more into the breach,' and remember that this is a battle, not a declamation contest," there was an audible Bronx cheer from one of the veterans.

P9   Punctuation with Quotation Marks

The question often comes up whether punctuation should be placed *inside* or *outside* quotation marks. The procedure recommended by the *MLA Handbook* is to place commas and periods *inside* the quotation marks, and all other marks *outside* them. But if a question mark or exclamation mark is part of the quotation, it is placed *inside* the quotation marks. This recommendation may be detailed as follows:

1. When the quoted words are followed by a comma, put the comma inside the quotation marks.

"If you insist," I said, "I'll do it."

The word "bread," for example, has both standard and slang meanings.

A comma after "he said," "she replied," and similar tags should be placed immediately after these phrases, as in the first example above.

2. A period, like a comma, always goes inside the quotation marks.

That is not the way to spell "eclectic."

He said, "You can always count on Tom to muddy the issue."

3. If a quotation ends with both single and double quotation marks, the final period comes inside both sets of marks.

Here is an excerpt from my brother's letter: "Today in class Mr. Blair quoted Wordsworth's line 'A six years' darling of a pigmy size,' and said it appeared in one edition as 'A six years' darling of a pig my size.' "

4. If the quotation is a question, the question mark goes inside the quotation marks; if the whole sentence in which a quotation appears is a question but the quotation is not, the question mark goes outside.

Somebody yelled, "Why don't you go home?"	(What was yelled was a question.)
Did he actually say, "Let Williams do it"?	(The quotation is not a question, but the whole sentence is. The question mark goes outside the quotation marks, and no other end punctuation is used.)
Well, how *do* you spell "eclectic"?	(The whole sentence is a question, not just the word "eclectic.")

5. The exclamation mark, like the question mark, goes inside if the quotation itself is an exclamation; otherwise it goes outside.

"Get out of my sight!" he yelled.	(The quoted portion is an exclamation.)
But I *did* say "Friday"!	(The whole sentence is an exclamation; "Friday" is not.)
His only answer was "Nonsense!"	(Only the quoted word is an exclamation.)

6. If a semicolon is used to separate a quotation from the rest of the sentence, it always goes outside the quotation marks.

He said, "You can be confident that I'll do it"; but I was not the least bit confident.

7. When a dash is used to indicate that a remark was left unfinished, it is included within the quotation marks.

Occasionally speakers are interrupted or for some reason fail to finish what they have begun to say. Whenever this happens, a dash is used to show that the quotation is not finished.

"But Mary said — " she began, then stopped suddenly.

Nicholson said loudly, "In my opinion, our instructor is — " Just then the instructor walked into the room.

Notice that a concluding period is not used after the dash.

P10   The Apostrophe

The apostrophe (') has three general uses:
1. To indicate the possessive case of nouns and some pronouns.

To indicate the possessive, an apostrophe followed by *s* is added to the regular form of the following types of nouns and pronouns:

1. both singular and plural nouns that do not end in *s:*

boy's, girl's, ox's, mouse's, tooth's, antenna's

men's, women's, oxen's, mice's, teeth's, antennae's

2. singular nouns ending in *s:*

James's, Charles's, Keats's, Burns's, Dickens's

Usage for this group varies. Some writers omit the final *s: James', Charles'.* When a noun already contains two or more *s* sounds, these writers are especially reluctant to add the final *s.* They would strongly prefer, for example, *Massachusetts', mistress', Jesus'.* But since most written communications are not read aloud, the repetition of *s* sounds is not so objectionable as it might seem to be. With singular nouns ending in *s,* then, follow your own preference.

3. indefinite pronouns:

anybody's, anyone's, everybody's, one's, nobody's, someone's

An apostrophe without an *s* is added to form the possessive of plural nouns that end in *s.* Most plural nouns, of course, fit into this category.

babies' clothing, lions' manes, birds' nests, teachers' personalities

2. To indicate the omission of letters or figures.

I've, can't, hasn't, isn't, '48 (1948), the class of '71

3. To indicate the plural of letters or figures.

Let's begin with the *A*'s.

Mr. Cardoza's application was misfiled among the *K*'s.

Her *S*'s look like *8*'s.

P11   Ellipsis

1. The basic use of an ellipsis (...) is to mark the omission of one or more words from a quotation.

If the omitted words were preceded in the original quotation by a comma or other punctuation mark necessary to the meaning of the shortened quotation, the punctuation mark is given and then the three dots of the ellipsis (, . . .). If the ellipsis comes at the end of a sentence, it is followed by a fourth dot to mark the concluding period (. . . .). The following ellipses (note the plural form) illustrate the conventions:

Original quotation

In a famous speech after the British defeat at Dunkirk, Churchill said: "Even though large tracts of Europe and many old and famous States have fallen or may fall into the grip of the Gestapo and all the odious apparatus of Nazi rule, we shall not flag or fail. We shall go on to the end. We shall fight in France, we shall fight on the seas and oceans, we shall fight with growing confidence and growing strength in the air, we shall defend our island, whatever the cost may be. We shall fight on the beaches, we shall fight on the landing grounds, we shall fight in the fields and in the streets, we shall fight in the hills; we shall never surrender, and even if, which I do not for a moment believe, this island or a large part of it were subjugated and starving, then our Empire beyond the seas, armed and guarded by the British Fleet, would carry on the struggle, until, in God's good time, the new world, with all its power and might, steps forth to the rescue and the liberation of the old."

Elliptical quotation

In a famous speech after the British defeat at Dunkirk, Churchill said: ". . . we shall not flag or fail. We shall go on to the end. . . . We shall fight on the beaches, . . . we shall fight in the fields and in the streets . . . ; we shall never surrender. . . ."

2. A second use of ellipsis is to indicate that a progression of numbers continues beyond the last figure given.

1, 4, 7, 10, 13, . . .

P12   Dash

The dash should not be used as a general utility mark in place of a comma, period, semicolon, or colon. It is a specialized punctuation mark that serves the following purposes:

Use the dash:
1. To stress a word or phrase at the end of a sentence.

In the whole world there is only one person he really admires — himself.

And now it is my pleasure to present a man whom we all know and admire and to whom we are all deeply indebted — the Reverend Dr. Mason.

Absence makes the heart grow fonder — of somebody else.

2. To set off a summary of, or conclusion to, an involved sentence.

To live as free people in a free country; to enjoy, even to abuse, the right to think and speak as we like; to feel that the state is the servant of its people; to be, even in a literal sense, a trustee and a partner in the conduct of a nation — all this is what democracy means to us.

3. To mark an interrupted or unfinished construction.

"I'd like to," he said, "but I'm — "
"You're what?" I asked.
"Well, I'm — I — you see, I've never done anything like that before, and I won't — I mean, I see no reason to start now."

4. In pairs, to set off a pronounced interruption.

There will never again be — you may be sure of this — so glorious an opportunity.

This answer — if we can call it an answer — is completely meaningless.

P13   Parentheses and Brackets

Parentheses

1. The three most common uses of parentheses are:

a. To enclose an explanation, qualification, or example.

His wife (he married about a year ago) is a member of a fine New England family.

Nice (in the old sense of "discriminating") has almost fallen out of use.

Foreign words (*data,* for example) slowly become naturalized and lose their foreign characteristics.

b. To enclose cross-references.

(See Appendix A.)

(See page 271.)

(Consult *Webster's Biographical Dictionary.*)

George Bellows described the world of sports in vivid oil paintings like *Dempsey and Firpo* (see Plate VI).

c. In formal business transactions, to repeat a sum previously stated in words.

I enclose three hundred dollars ($300.00) to cover my share of the costs.

Brackets

Square brackets are used chiefly to enclose an editorial or a clarifying explanation or comment within a passage being edited, reported, or quoted. The words within the brackets are supplied by the editor or reporter. The Latin word *sic,* meaning "thus," is included in brackets after an error to indicate that the error is in the original statement.

The entry reads, "The father died of numonia [sic]."

Smith is unjustified in claiming, "What he [Faulkner] meant to write is 'back door,' not 'black door.' "

Review Exercises

Where necessary, rewrite the following sentences, inserting appropriate punctuation. If sentences are correct as they stand, simply mark them OK.

1. **Mr. Reynolds the insurance agent had not arrived by nine o'clock.**

2. I wonder whats keeping him Dad grumbled. Are you sure that he said he would call at eight o'clock.

3. Yes quite sure I replied. He said to me Tell your father I will call at eight o'clock.

4. I have not seen Mrs. Manlin for some time since her husband was killed she spends a lot of time at her mother's place.

5. Gutenberg the inventor of movable type was motivated by a desire to make the Bible more widely available.

6. I hear that the man who was responsible for the accident has been arrested.

7. The speaker who was obviously embarrassed said that he did not answer questions of such a personal nature.

8. No wonder her hair looks different she's wearing a wig.

9. Some of the shutters had fallen to the ground others were hanging from one corner and a few were firmly locked in place across the windows.

10. Seated at the speakers' table were Fred Hanley, superintendent of schools, Dr Mason, dean of the College of Education, Mrs Helen Loftus, president of the Parent Teachers Association, and the chairman, Professor Robbins.

11. The girl who received first prize a silver cup was our neighbors' daughter.

12. A dog that's frightened by the sound of gunshots is no good for hunting.

13. However important these facts may have been eight years ago they have no significance today.

14. Trevino despite the pressure he was under continued to joke with the gallery.

15. He said when I asked him that he expected to take a brief vacation.

16. She said When I asked his opinion he answered if you want legal advice I'll be glad to talk with you in my office.

17. Donald said if I remember correctly that he would be out of town for the next three or four days.

18. Where the old ice house used to be there is now a little stone cottage with a white picket fence around it.

19. Giggling almost hysterically the children either could not or would not explain what had happened.

20. Mules though less speedy than horses in open country are both faster and surer on those narrow mountain tracks.

The following selection is now punctuated only at the ends of the sentences. Add whatever internal punctuation you think necessary and be able to explain why.

The plight of a normal person who finds himself committed to a mental institution and unable to convince anyone he is not insane is a standard plot for horror fiction. But in a remarkable study last week Dr David L Rosenhan professor of psychology and law at Stanford University and seven associates reported just such a nightmare in real life. To find out how well psychiatric professionals can distinguish the normal from the sick they had themselves committed to mental institutions. Their experiment reported in the journal *Science* clearly showed that once inside the hospital walls everyone is judged insane.

The pseudopatients five men and three women included three psychologists a pediatrician a psychiatrist a painter and a housewife all of whom were certifiably sane. In the course of the three-year study the volunteers spent an average of nineteen days in a dozen institutions private and public in New York California Pennsylvania Oregon and Delaware. Each pseudopatient told admitting doctors that he kept hearing voices that said words like empty hollow and void suggesting that the patient found his life meaningless and futile. But beyond falsifying their names and occupations all the volunteers described their life histories as they actually were. In so doing they gave the doctors every chance to discern the truth. I couldn't believe we wouldnt be found out Rosenhan told *Newsweek*'s Gerald Lubenow. But they werent. At eleven hospitals the pseudopatients were promptly diagnosed as schizophrenic and at the twelfth as manic-depressive.

As soon as they had gained admission the volunteers studiously resumed normal behavior. They denied hearing voices and worked hard to convince the staff members that they ought to be released. But such efforts were to no avail doctors and nurses interpreted everything the pseudopatients did in terms of the original diagnosis. When some of the volunteers went about taking notes the hospital staff made such entries in their records as patient engages in writing behavior. The only people who realized that the experimenters were normal were some of the patients. Youre not crazy said one patient. Youre a journalist or a professor. Youre checking up on the hospital. (Copyright Newsweek, Inc. 1973, reprinted by permission.)

MECHANICS

Sp   ## Spelling

If you have trouble with spelling, the first step toward improvement is to take an inventory of your errors. In a notebook keep a written record of the words *that you actually misspell in your writing.* This is your basic list. Review it periodically and keep it up to date by crossing out the words you have mastered and by adding new words that you have recently misspelled.

When you study your list, concentrate on the *part* of the word that you have misspelled. Generally people misspell not words, but syllables. For example, most students who misspell *secretary* interchange the second and third vowels; most misspellings of *tragedy* come from placing an extra *d* before the *g;* and misspellings of such words as *receive, belief,* and *friend* come from reversing the *i* and *e.* Identifying your specific errors allows you to concentrate on the syllable in which the error occurs.

For words that prove unusually troublesome it often helps to learn or invent some memorizing device: a rule, a slogan, a jingle — anything, no matter how absurd, that will remind you of the correct spelling of a particular syllable. The rule of "*i* before *e* except after *c,*" which is stated as a jingle on page 685, and the rules for prefixes and suffixes are generally useful memorizing devices. It may help, too, to remember statements like "A good secretary keeps a secret," "Remember the gum in argument," and "Every cemetery has a meter in the middle." Or you may capitalize the danger spots in practice — *tRAGedy, mainTENance, desPERate.* If these devices help you, use them; if not, invent your own.

Finally, so far as possible, don't worry about spelling while writing the first drafts of your papers. Wait until revision. If you break off writing a paragraph to use the dictionary, you may lose a thought you cannot recapture. Put a check in the margin and go on. Then, when the first draft is finished, you can look up the spellings of all the words you have checked. Indeed, a writer with severe spelling troubles should proofread every draft of each paper at least once for spelling alone.

In short, then: (1) keep a spelling record, (2) study it at regular intervals, (3) identify the trouble spot in each word, (4) figure out a way to remember the correct spelling, and (5) check your spelling when you proofread.

The Most Common Traps in Spelling

Although any word that is not spelled the way it sounds may give trouble, six types of words are especially likely to cause errors. Let us look briefly at these error-causing word types.

Words containing a "colorless" vowel A vowel in an unstressed position (*ago*, *agent*, *awkward*, *maintenance*, *incredible*, *bachelor*) is likely to be pronounced as a very weak "uh." This sound is called the *colorless*, or *neutral*, *vowel*. Because its sound gives no clue to its spelling, the colorless vowel is responsible for many spelling errors. There is nothing to guide you in spelling this sound. The only solution is to memorize the vowel in any word that repeatedly causes trouble. The best help is a memorizing device, such as magnifying the syllable in question — *balANCE*, *independENT*, *eliGIble*, *sponSOR*, *forEIGN*, *chaufFEUR*.

Words with ie *or* ei Words like *niece*, *receive*, and *friend* are frequently misspelled through the interchanging of the *e* and the *i*. Most of these errors may be easily removed by following rule 4 on page 685 and memorizing the eleven exceptions.

Words with similar sounds but different meanings Such words as *altar, alter; peace, piece; weak, week; weather, whether* are easily confused, as are the contrasted pairs given on page 686.

Words with irregular plural forms Most English nouns are made plural by the addition of *-s* to the singular form. All plurals formed in any other way may be considered irregular. The most troublesome plurals to spell are those of nouns ending in *o* or *y*. Such nouns have regular *s* plurals when the *o* or *y* immediately follows a vowel *(cameo, cameos; key, keys; studio, studios)*, but are generally irregular when the *o* or *y* follows a consonant *(cargo, cargoes; veto, vetoes; lady, ladies; torpedo, torpedoes)*. See rules 6 and 7 on page 685.

Words in which the final consonant is doubled before a suffix beginning with a vowel Some words double a final consonant before adding a suffix beginning with a vowel *(refer, referred)*, while others do not *(benefit, benefited)*. This inconsistency causes many spelling errors, and the "rule" is so cumbersome and has so many exceptions that students often prefer to study the individual words that cause them trouble. The more useful part of the rule concerning doubled consonants is given as rule 9 on page 686.

Common exceptions to general rules Any exceptional spelling is likely to be difficult because of the tendency to make it conform to the regular pattern. For example, a student who is not sure how to spell *seize* is likely to interchange the *e* and *i* because of the *i*-before-*e* rule. Similarly, the rule that a silent *e* at the end of a word is retained in adding a suffix beginning with a consonant leads many students to misspell *argument*. Words like these are exceptions to general rules and cause many spelling errors. The only safe procedure is to *memorize the exceptions along with the rule*. Whenever a rule is given in the following pages, the common exceptions are noted as well. Study these as carefully as you study the rule itself.

Rules of Spelling

Only the most useful rules are given here.

1. The prefixes *un-, dis-, mis-* do not affect the spelling of the root.

Thus, *unafraid* but *unnecessary; disappoint* but *dissatisfy; misrepresent* but *misspell.* And

unable, unknown, unopened; *but* unnatural, unnerved, unnoticed

disable, disorder, disregard; *but* disservice, dissimilar, dissolve

misbehave, misconduct, misguided; *but* misshapen, misspent, misstatement

2. When a suffix beginning with a consonant is added to a word ending in silent *e,* the *e* is retained.

absolutely, achievement, extremely, indefinitely, sincerely

Exceptions to this rule include *argument, awful, duly, ninth, probably, truly, wholly.*
    Three common words have alternative spellings: *abridgment, abridgement; acknowledgment, acknowledgement; judgment, judgement.*

3. When a suffix beginning with a vowel is added to a word ending in silent *e,* the *e* is dropped unless it is required to indicate pronunciation or to avoid confusion with a similar word.

accumulating, achieving, boring, coming, grievance, icy

Following are examples of the kinds of exceptions mentioned in the rule:

a. *e* retained to keep *c* or *g* soft

advantageous, changeable, courageous, manageable, noticeable, outrageous, peaceable, serviceable, singeing, tingeing, vengeance

b. *e* to prevent mispronunciation

canoeist, eyeing, hoeing, mileage, shoeing

c. *e* kept to prevent confusion with other words

dyeing, singeing

4. The order of the vowels in the *ie* combination *(ceiling, niece)* is explained in the jingle:

> **Write *i* before *e***
> **Except after *c***
> **Or when sounded like *ay***
> **As in *neighbor* and *weigh*.**

Exceptions to the rule include *counterfeit, either, foreign, forfeit, height, leisure, neither, seize, seizure, sovereign, weird.*

5. Words ending with the sound "seed" are usually spelled *-cede*.

accede, concede, intercede, precede, recede, secede

There are only four exceptions to this rule. Three of them end in *ceed (exceed, proceed, succeed);* the fourth is the only English word that ends in *sede (supersede).*

6. Singular nouns ending in a consonant plus *y* form their plurals by changing the *y* to *i* before adding *-es*.

This rule also applies to the third person singular of verbs.

ally, allies; baby, babies; city, cities; cry, cries; try, tries

The plurals of proper names often add *-s* immediately after the *y* and are an exception: *the Kellys, the Marys, the Sallys.*

Notice that singular nouns ending in a vowel plus *y* are regular and simply take on an *-s* on becoming plural: *attorneys, donkeys, valleys.*

7. Singular nouns ending in a consonant plus *o* generally form their plurals by adding *-es*.

buffaloes, cargoes, echoes, heroes, potatoes, torpedoes, vetoes

There are many exceptions. The chief exceptions are musical terms: *altos, bassos, pianos, solos, soporanos.* Others are *autos, cantos, dynamos, Eskimos, quartos.*

Notice that singular nouns ending in a vowel plus *o* are regular and simply add *-s* to form the plural: *cameos, folios, radios, studios.*

8. Most singular nouns ending in *s, ss, sh, ch, x,* or *z* form their plurals by adding *-es*.

Jameses, Joneses, ashes, bushes, matches, pitches, foxes, taxes, buzzes

Exceptions include *fish* and *Swiss* (both of which are plural as well as singular forms) and borrowed Greek nouns ending in *is* (*ellipsis, ellipses; thesis, theses*).

9. Words of one syllable double the final consonant before adding a suffix beginning with a vowel if (1) they end in a single consonant, and (2) they contain a single vowel.

begging, fitting, spinning

This rule holds only if *both* conditions are satisfied. Thus a word of one syllable ending in *two* consonants does not double the final consonant before a suffix beginning with a vowel (a*ct*ing, a*sk*ed, pa*rt*ing, si*ft*ed). And a one-syllable word containing *two* vowels does not double the final consonant (bea*r*ing, cree*p*ing, dea*l*ing, ree*l*ing, soa*r*ing).

Review Exercises

1. Errors in the following words may be classified as errors in spelling or errors in diction, since both meaning and spelling are involved in their correct use. Check those words that you are unsure of and look them up in the Checklist of Troublesome Usages, which begins on page 720.

access–excess	formally–formerly
adapt–adopt	ingenious–ingenuous
advice–advise	irrelevant–irreverent
affective–effective	judicial–judicious
all together–altogether	loath–loathe
allusion–illusion	loose–lose
capital–capitol	luxuriant–luxurious
censor–censure	moral–morale
cite–sight–site	personal–personnel
complement–compliment	principal–principle
continual–continuous	prophecy–prophesy
council–counsel	respectfully–respectively
decent–descent	right–rite
desert–dessert	sensual–sensuous
economic–economical	stationary–stationery
elicit–illicit	suit–suite
emigrant–immigrant	troop–troupe
eminent–imminent	

2. Following is a list of words frequently misspelled by college students. Underline those words that you know you have trouble with and review them from time to time. The list may also serve as a handy reference when you proofread your papers.

abbreviate
absence
absurd
accelerate
accidentally
accommodate
accomplish
according
accumulate
accustom
achievement
acoustics
acquaintance
acquitted
across
address
aggravate
aggression
airplane
alleviate
alley
allotted
allowed
ally
although
always
amateur
ambiguous
ammunition
among
amount
analogous
analysis
analyze
annual
antecedent
anxiety
apartment
apparatus
apparent
appearance
appropriate
arctic
argument
arising

arithmetic
arouse
arranging
article
artillery
ascend
association
athlete
athletics
attempt
attractive
audible
audience
authorities
automobile
auxiliary
awkward
bachelor
balance
balloon
barbarous
barring
battalion
bearing
becoming
beggar
beginning
believe
beneficial
benefited
biscuit
boundaries
breathe
brilliant
Britain
Britannica
bulletin
buoyant
bureau
buried
burying
business
busy
cafeteria
calendar

candidate
carburetor
carrying
casualties
causal
ceiling
celebrity
cemetery
certain
changeable
changing
characteristic
chauffeur
chief
choosing
chosen
clause
climbed
clothes
colloquial
colonel
column
coming
commission
commitment
committed
committee
companies
comparatively
compel
compelled
competent
competition
complaint
completely
compulsory
concede
conceivable
conceive
condemn
condescend
connoisseur
conqueror
conscience
conscientious

considered
consistent
contemptible
control
controlled
convenient
copies
corner
coroner
corps
corpse
costume
countries
courteous
courtesy
cries
criticism
criticize
cruelty
cruise
curiosity
curriculum
custom
cylinder
dealt
debater
deceitful
deceive
decide
decision
defendant
deferred
deficient
definite
definition
democracy
dependent
descendant
description
desirable
despair
desperate
destruction
developed

development
diaphragm
diary
dictionary
dietitian
difference
digging
diphtheria
disappearance
disappoint
disastrous
discipline
discussion
disease
dissatisfied
dissipate
distribute
doesn't
dominant
don't
dormitories
dropped
drunkenness
echoes
ecstasy
efficiency
eighth
eligible
eliminate
embarrass
emphasize
employee
encouraging
encyclopedia
enthusiastic
environment
equipment
equipped
equivalent
erroneous
especially
eventually
exaggerate
exceed

excel
excellent
exceptional
excitement
exercise
exhaust
exhilaration
existence
experience
explanation
extensive
extracurricular
extremely
exuberance
fallacious
fallacy
familiar
fascinate
February
fiery
financial
financier
forehead
foreign
foremost
forfeit
forty
frantically
fraternities
friend
fulfill, fulfil
gaiety
generally
genius
genuine
glorious
government
grammar
grandeur
grievous
guarantee
guardian
guidance
handicapped

handkerchief
harass
hearse
height
heinous
heroes
hesitancy
hindrance
hoarse
hoping
horde
humorous
hurries
hygiene
hypocrisy
hysterical
illiterate
illogical
imaginary
imagination
imitative
immediately
implement
impromptu
inadequate
incidentally
incredible
indefinitely
independent
indicted
indispensable
inevitable
influential
innocent
inoculate
intellectual
intelligence
intentionally
intercede
interested
interpret
interrupt
irreligious
irresistible

irresponsible
itself
judicial
khaki
knowledge
laboratory
legitimate
leisure
library
lightning
literature
loneliness
losing
magazine
magnificent
maintain
maintenance
maneuver
manual
manufacture
mathematics
mattress
meant
medicine
medieval
messenger
millionaire
miniature
minute
mischievous
misspelled
modifies
modifying
momentous
mosquitoes
mottoes
mountainous
murmur
muscle
mysterious
necessary
necessity
neither
nervous

nevertheless
nickel
niece
ninety
ninth
noticeable
notorious
nowadays
obedience
obliged
obstacle
occasionally
occur
occurred
occurrence
official
omission
omit
omitted
opinion
opportunity
optimistic
organization
original
orthodox
outrageous
overrun
pamphlet
parallel
parliament
participle
particularly
pastime
peaceable
perceive
perform
permissible
perseverance
persuade
phrase
physical
physician
picnicked
piece

playwright	remembrance	specifically
pleasant	reminiscence	specimen
possess	rendezvous	spontaneous
possessive	repetition	statement
possible	replies	statue
potatoes	representative	stomach
practice	reservoir	stopped
prairie	resistance	strength
preceding	restaurant	strenuously
predominant	rhetoric	stretched
preference	rheumatism	struggle
preferred	rhythmical	studying
prejudice	ridiculous	subordinate
preparation	sacrifice	subtle
prevalent	sacrilegious	succeed
primitive	safety	success
privilege	salary	successful
probably	sanctuary	suffrage
professor	sandwich	superintendent
prominent	scarcely	supersede
pronounce	scene	suppress
pronunciation	scenic	surprise
propeller	schedule	swimming
protein	secretarial	syllable
psychology	secretary	synonym
pursue	seized	synonymous
pursuing	sensible	tangible
putting	sentence	tariff
quantity	sentinel	tasting
quarantine	separate	technical
questionnaire	sergeant	technique
quizzes	severely	temperament
realize	shining	tenant
recede	shriek	tendency
receipt	siege	thorough
receive	sieve	thought
receiving	similar	tournament
recognize	sincerely	traffic
recommend	sincerity	tragedy
reference	skeptical	transferred
referred	slight	tremendous
relevant	soliloquy	tries
religion	sophomore	truly
religious	source	twelfth

typical	vengeance	wiry
tyranny	victorious	woman
unanimous	view	women
undoubtedly	vigilant	won't
unnecessary	vigorous	worried
until	village	worrying
usage	villain	writing
useful	warrant	written
using	warring	yacht
usually	weird	your
vacancy	welfare	you're (you are)
vacuum	whole	zoology
valuable	wholly	

Abr   Abbreviations

In general, abbreviations should satisfy two conditions: they must be standard forms recognized by dictionaries, and they must be appropriate to the context. The first condition rules out such slang abbreviations as *b.f.* (boyfriend) and *n.g.* (no good). The second implies that many standard abbreviations *(advt., Ave., Feb., Xmas)* are inappropriate in most student essays and that abbreviations of certain titles *(Col., Dr., Mrs., Ms., Rev.)* are used only when followed by the name of the person to whom the title applies.

The following is a summary of the most common standard abbreviations. For the correct form of abbreviations not included in this list, you should consult your dictionary.

Abbreviations may be used for: bibliographical terms —

cf., vol., pp.

names of days (in dates only) —

Sun., Mon., Tues., Wed., Thurs., Fri., Sat.

names of months (in dates only) —

Jan., Feb., Aug., Sept., Oct., Nov., Dec.

names of organizations —

AFL, U.S. Steel, IBM, YMCA, UNESCO

names of government agencies (abbreviations of government agencies generally do not require periods) —

CIA, FBI, HUD, SEC, TVA

names of states (in addresses only), and signs.

When the context permits, the following signs are used as abbreviations: & (ampersand; see Glossary), $ (dollar), £ (British pound sterling), % (per cent), and " " (ditto marks, used in tabulations to repeat the item immediately above the marks).

Caps   Use of Capital Letters

1. Capitalize the first word of every sentence and of every line of regular poetry.

Ask for Mr. Lane. He is in charge of services.

Too bad! Better luck next time.

Earth has not anything to show more fair;
Dull would he be of soul who could pass by
A sight so touching in its majesty. . . .
    — Wordsworth, "Composed upon Westminster Bridge"

2. Capitalize the first word of a direct quotation.

Who said, "We have met the enemy, and they are ours"?

She looked puzzled and asked, "For example?"

3. Capitalize proper nouns.

She works for the National Broadcasting Company.

I find French easier than German.

The Amazon is longer than the Mississippi.

Note: Words that were originally proper nouns but have taken on more general meanings are regarded as common nouns and are not capitalized: *boycott, calico, china* (dishes), *port* (wine), *tweed*.

4. Capitalize adjectives formed from proper nouns.

They seem to be ignorant of the *American* point of view.

There is a *Miltonic* quality in this verse.

The inductive method has been called the *Baconian* method.

Note: Words originally derived from proper nouns cease to be capitalized when they are used as allusions rather than as direct references to the original noun. For example, *colossus, draconian, herculean, meandering,* and *panic* do not take capitals. *Philippic* is capitalized when it refers directly to the orations made by Demosthenes but not when it is used to describe some other denunciatory speech.

5. Capitalize nouns or pronouns referring to the deity. Also capitalize *Bible* and *Biblical* when they refer to Scripture.

God, Lord, our Father, Savior, Messiah, Trinity, Holy Ghost, He, His, Him

Although she does not seem to be a particularly religious person, she reads a passage from the Bible every day.

Note: When *bible* and *biblical* do not refer to Scripture, they are not capitalized: "*Das Kapital* is the bible of the Communist party." Some dictionaries also accept *biblical* as an alternative spelling of *Biblical*.

6. Capitalize names of offices only when they are used as titles.

Capitalized	Not capitalized
District Attorney Johnson	Tell it to the district attorney.
Prime Minister Thatcher	Heath is a former prime minister.
The death of Chairman Mao resulted in major changes in official Chinese policies.	Stella Iantosca was made chairperson of the committee.
Professor Swanson	She is a college professor.

Note: *President, Presidential, Presidency,* and *Executive* are capitalized when they refer to the office of President of the United States: "One of these men will be our next President"; "the Presidency is at stake"; "Executive privilege." The same style is followed for *Vice President* and its derivatives.

7. Capitalize *north, south, east,* and *west* and their derivatives only when they refer to geographical areas.

Capitalized	Not capitalized
We found the South charming.	Next year we are going south.
Her parents live in the East.	New York is east of Chicago.
They live on the West Side.	The west side of the field is wet.
The Southern armies fought gallantly.	The house has a fine southern exposure.

8. Capitalize titles of books, names of magazines, titles of plays, and the headings of chapters or sections of a work.

The general practice is to capitalize all significant words in a title, including the first word.

A Child's History of the United States

The Return of the Native

Mourning Becomes Electra

Some publishers, however, capitalize every word in the title.

A Child's History Of The United States

Either form is acceptable, but be consistent.

9. Capitalize the names of days of the week, months, and holidays.

New Year's Day will fall on Tuesday.

The favorite vacation months are July and August.

10. Avoid unnecessary capitalization

In general, do not use capitals unless they are required by one of the conventions stated above. The modern tendency is to use capitals sparingly. Especially avoid unnecessary capitalization of the names of the seasons, of family relationships *(father, mother, sister, uncle)*, and of such words as *army, college, freshman, navy, sophomore, university,* unless they are being considered as proper nouns.

Capitalized	Not capitalized
He is a captain in the Army of the United States.	In foreign affairs an army is a political instrument.
Whom do you pick in the Army-Navy game, General?	The general said we must have an army and a navy second to none.
Uncle Bill and Aunt Martha are here.	All the uncles and aunts were present.
Where is Sanford Community College?	He wants a college education.
Boston University will have a strong team next year.	He is a university professor.
Are you going to the Freshman Mixer?	Are you a freshman or a sophomore?
The Summer Festival starts next week.	I like summer best and winter least.
Oh, Mother, I can't do that!	Is your mother at home?

Hyph   Hyphenation

Hyphens are used for two purposes: to divide a word at the end of a line, and to join two or more words of a compound that is not written solid.

1. Use a hyphen to break a word at the end of a line.

This use of the hyphen is less frequently necessary in typed or handwritten copy than it is in print. In your writing, words should be broken at the ends of lines only when failure to hyphenate would result in obviously long or short lines. If hyphenation seems necessary, the following conditions should be observed:

a. Do not break words of one syllable.

If there is not room at the end of a line for a word such as *burst, change, drink, through,* carry the whole word over to the next line.

b. Break words only between syllables.

When in doubt about syllabication, consult your dictionary.

c. Do not separate a suffix of fewer than three letters from the rest of the word or break on a one-letter prefix.

An *-ing* may be carried over to the next line, but single letters or *-al, -le, -ly,* and *-ed* endings should not be. Words like *about, against,* and *open* should not be broken.

d. Break compound words between the elements of the compound.

Compound word	End-of-line hyphenation
armchair	arm- chair
blackbird	black- bird
sailboat	sail- boat
self-denial	self- denial (not: self-de- nial)

e. Subject to the limitations stated in rules b and c, hyphenate between prefix and root or between root and suffix.

Between prefix and root	Between root and suffix
ante- cedent	adapt- able
be- loved	back- ward
com- mit	depend- able
con- tagious	ego- ism
dis- appear	kitchen- ette
inter- rupt	lemon- ade
intro- duce	mile- age
per- suade	racket- eer
trans- late	trouble- some

2. Use a hyphen between elements of a compound when usage calls for it.

Hyphenation of compounds varies so much that (1) for any particular word, the only safe authority is a reliable, up-to-date dictionary, and (2) whenever usage is uncertain, a writer is allowed a choice between competing usages.

Some compounds *(applesauce, blackboard, steamship)* are written solid; others *(dirt cheap, place kick, wedding ring)* are nearly always written as separate words; still others *(father-in-law, ready-made, up-to-date)* are hyphenated.

A hyphen is required in the following types of compounds:

a. Hyphenate a compound modifier preceding a noun.

> a self-made man, a well-dressed woman, a pay-as-you-go tax, a round-by-round report, an off-the-cuff judgment, a tear-jerking film, a Sunday-morning golf game, a heart-to-heart talk

Compound numerical modifiers follow this rule: "twenty-seven dollars," "one hundred and twenty-five pounds," "a two-thirds majority." When a compound numeral is used as a noun, it is hyphenated: "All the men in Ward Room II should be commended, for all twenty-five of them volunteered for special duty." But whole numbers below twenty-one are single words and are not hyphenated: "their nineteenth anniversary," "the sixteenth of May."

Notice that a compound modifier *following* a noun is usually not hyphenated: "The woman was well dressed"; "The machine is worn out."

b. Hyphenate a compound consisting of a prefix and a proper noun.

pro-Russian, un-American, anti-Castro

c. Hyphenate compounds of *ex* ("former") and a noun.

ex-wife, ex-sweetheart, ex-President

d. Hyphenate to avoid confusion with another word.

re-cover (to prevent confusion with *recover*)

re-creation (to prevent confusion with *recreation*)

e. Hyphenate most compounds beginning with *self*.

self-satisfied, self-government, self-conceit

But *selfless* and *selfsame* are written solid.

Ital   Use of Italics and Underlining

Words in print are made to stand out by using a special kind of slanting type called *italic;* they are similarly set off in manuscript or typewritten material by underlining.

1. Italics or underlining is used for the following purposes:

a. To indicate that a word is still considered a foreign element in the language.

In printed material	In manuscript
were *en rapport*	were en rapport
voted *in absentia*	voted in absentia

b. To mark titles of books, magazines, newspapers, movie and stage productions, musical compositions, and paintings, and the names of airplanes, ships, and trains.

In printed material	In manuscript
Mencken's *The American Language*	Mencken's The American Language
last month's *Esquire*	last month's Esquire
Beethoven's *Eroica*	Beethoven's Eroica
Da Vinci's *Last Supper*	Da Vinci's Last Supper
Lindbergh's *Spirit of Saint Louis*	Lindbergh's Spirit of Saint Louis
the French liner, the *France*	the French liner, the France

But notice that (1) Bible is not italicized and (2) titles of musical compositions, paintings, and other works of art may be either italicized or enclosed in quotation marks (see page 673).

c. To call attention to a word being named.

In printed material	In manuscript
The word *judgment* has two spellings.	The word judgment has two spellings.
What does *discriminate* mean?	What does discriminate mean?

Quotation marks are also used for this purpose (see page 673), but when in a printed work it is necessary to place quotation marks around a great many single words, an editor will sometimes attempt to improve the appearance of the page by substituting italics for quotation marks. The need for this substitution almost never exists in student writing.

d. To emphasize a word, letter, or number.

In printed material	In manuscript
Not *moral,* but *morale.*	Not <u>moral</u>, but <u>morale</u>.
Is this letter an *a* or an *o?*	Is this letter an <u>a</u> or an <u>o</u>?

No

Forms of Numbers

Whether numbers should be written in words *(twenty-five)* or figures *(25)* depends partly on the nature of the writing. In scientific, statistical, and technical writing, figures are used whenever possible. In essays and literary publications, numbers are more frequently written in words, and the more formal the style is, the less often are figures used.

1. Figures are used in writing days, hours, and street numbers.

January 22, 1980   5:00 A.M.   17 Main Street

January 1   6:15 P.M.   417 Fifth Avenue

Notice that figures are used for street numbers but that street names, even when they are numbers, are usually written out and capitalized to avoid confusion with other numbers.

2. Figures are used in recording sums of money other than round sums.

$2.75; 98 cents (*but:* a hundred dollars; thirty cents)

If the style is informal, even round sums may be expressed as figures.

$40 million; 100 dollars; 30 cents; 40,000 spectators

3. Use figures for large numbers that would be awkward to write out.

365 days; 1,760 yards; 14,320 students

4. Use figures in citing volume, chapter, and page references.

This whole question is discussed in Volume 2 of Brand's work.

Soil erosion is discussed in Chapter 5, beginning on page 84.

5. Do not use figures at the beginning of a sentence.

Sixty percent is a passing grade. (*not:* 60% is a passing grade.)

6. Generally avoid figures when a number can be conveniently expressed in one word.

one, five, third, quarter, twelve

But in an informal style and in scientific writing, numbers over ten are frequently expressed in figures.

7. Do not use figures in a formal invitation or reply.

on Saturday the twenty-third of June

at seven o'clock in the evening

This most formal usage is an exception to the practice recommended in rule 1 above.

8. Roman numerals are used chiefly as volume and chapter numbers in some books and as page numbers in the front matter of books.

Because Roman numerals are so little used, many people have trouble reading them. If you are one of these people, you will find that most of the difficulty is eliminated once you recognize the key numerals and understand the principle by which they are combined.

The key numerals are i (1), v (5), x (10), l (50), c (100), d (500), m (1,000). Occasionally these are written in capitals: I, V, X, L, C, D, M. The basic principle is that a higher number is created either by adding a numeral to a lower number — xi, for example is x (10) plus i (1), or 11 — or by subtracting a numeral from a higher number — xc is c (100) minus x (10), or 90.

Units	Tens	Hundreds
i(1)	x(10)	c(100)
ii(2)	xx(20)	cc(200)
iii(3)	xxx(30)	ccc(300)
iv(4)	xl(40)	cd(400)
v(5)	l(50)	d(500)
vi(6)	lx(60)	dc(600)
vii(7)	lxx(70)	dcc(700)
viii(8)	lxxx(80)	dccc(800)
ix(9)	xc(90)	cm(900)

*Review
Exercise*

In the following sentences make any corrections that you think would be necessary in a college composition.

1. Doctor Lindon is a chemistry prof at the U of Toronto.

2. Columbus discovered America in anno Domini fourteen hundred and ninety-two.

3. 4 days after medication the sore was completely healed.

4. Her father is a Lt. Col. in the army of the U.S.

5. That is a Senior course. Freshman and Sophomores are not eligible for it, but Juniors may take it with the Instructor's permission.

6. My father's birthday falls on father's day this year.

7. When he got out of the Navy he studied for the ministry.

8. It has rained heavily on each of the last 5 days.

9. Faulkner incorporated altered versions of several of his short stories, including Spotted Horses, in his novel The Hamlet.

10. What day of the week was new year's day in 1973?

11. Rev. David Smith lives at seventy-one Grand Ave.

12. Bill says that his Mother-in-law is one of the finest women he knows.

13. The birth certificate shows that he was born on January thirty-one at five minutes after eleven, post meridiem.

14. The bill came to $6.15. That was fifteen cents more than I had.

15. The King James bible is called the Authorized Version. It was translated by a committee of biblical scholars.

16. 78 was the median score on this test; the highest score was 98, and the lowest, 39.

17. I suppose pas de deux and tour jeté are French terms, but what do they mean?

18. The word is concave, not convex.

19. As a star in many american and european movies of the twenties and thirties, including Emperor Jones, Othello, King Solomon's Mines, and The Proud Valley, Paul Robeson is one of the great figures in black film history.

20. The careers of Harry S. Truman and Lyndon B. Johnson, although different in many respects, show interesting similarities. Both were democratic senators who were elected vice presidents and succeeded to the presidency on the death of a president. After serving the unexpired term they were elected chief executive, served four years, and refused to run again. They died within a month of each other, and for the first time in our history the American flag flew at half-mast to honor simultaneously the memory of two presidents.

Glossary of Grammatical and Literary Terms

This glossary is a reference section that explains grammatical and literary terms. Page references following an explanation refer you to a fuller treatment in the text. Words not listed in this glossary may be checked in the index at the end of the book.

absolute   An element that has no specific grammatical relationship to any other term in a sentence, yet clearly belongs in the sentence.

> *Nonsense,* it is all a hoax.
>
> *Good heavens,* is it that late?
>
> *No,* I won't do it.
>
> He said — *believe it or not* — that he had played in the Rose Bowl.

accent marks   When French words are written in English, their accent marks *(café, mère, fête)* are treated as part of their spelling, but when such words are no longer considered foreign, the accent mark generally is dropped. When in doubt whether the accent mark is needed, consult your dictionary.

In English, accent marks are used chiefly to indicate primary and secondary stress: *ak′ sent′*.

accusative case   In modern English, the objective case, as in *him, her, me, us, them.*

acronym   An abbreviation pronounced as a word and made up of the first letters of the title being abbreviated: *CORE* (Congress of Racial Equality), *NASA* (National Aeronautics and Space Administration).

active voice   One of two "voices" of a verb, the other being *passive.* See **voice.**

A.D.   Abbreviation for Latin *anno Domini,* "in the year of the Lord." Opposite of B.C., "before Christ." Used to distinguish dates before and after the beginning of the Christian era: "He lived from 31 B.C. to A.D. 12"; "From 100 B.C. to 100 A.D. is two hundred years." Note that B.C. always follows the figure; A.D. may follow or precede the figure.

adjectives and adverbs   Adjectives and adverbs can often but not always be distinguished by their forms. Most adverbs end in *-ly,* but so do a few adjectives: *silly, lively, manly.* A few adverbs (among them *clean, fast, straight*) do not have *-ly* endings, and some have two forms: *late, lately; loud, loudly; slow, slowly.* Adjectives and adverbs are best recognized by their function in a sentence: adjectives modify nouns or pronouns; adverbs modify verbs, adjectives, or other adverbs. See also **comparison.**

agreement   The convention that verbs agree in number with their subjects and that pronouns agree in gender, number, and person with their antecedents.

alliteration Repetition of the same consonant, especially an initial consonant, in several nearby words in prose or poetry: "*T*ippecanoe and *T*yler *t*oo"; "The *m*oan of doves in i*mm*emorial el*m*s, / And *m*urmuring of innumerable bees." Alliteration is a common device in poetry, but it should be used with restraint in ordinary prose since its overuse or inappropriate use may seem affected.

A.M., P.M., a.m., p.m. Abbreviations for the Latin phrases *ante meridiem* ("before noon"), *post meridiem* ("after noon"). The abbreviation A.M. is used to indicate the period from midnight to noon; P.M. from noon to midnight: "He works from 8 P.M. to 4 A.M." These abbreviations can be used only after a figure. Either capital or small letters may be used in manuscript, and in printed books small capitals frequently are used.

analogy in argument See pages 361–365.

analogy in language The process by which words change their forms to fit a dominant pattern. Because the dominant way of forming the past tense in English is to add *-ed* or *-d* to the present tense, small children are likely to say "buyed" for *bought* and "catched" for *caught* by analogy with *cried, sighed, tried,* and the like. Similarly, the regular pattern of forming English plurals is to add *-s* to the singular form, so foreign words imported into English tend to adjust to this pattern. Thus the Latin plural *gymnasia* becomes *gymnasiums* and the Hebrew plural *cherubim* becomes *cherubs.*

antagonist See **protagonist.**

antecedent The noun or pronoun to which a following pronoun refers.

anticlimax The putting of a minor fact or detail at the end of a sentence or passage where a reader expects a climactic point: "I recommend Miss Smith for her high intelligence, moral integrity, and attractive smile." Putting the least important information at the end can destroy the effectiveness of a sentence. However, skillful writers deliberately employ anticlimax for humorous effect. In *Pudd'nhead Wilson* Mark Twain says, "Adam and Eve had many advantages, but the principal one was that they escaped teething."

antonym A word opposite in meaning to a given word. Thus, *love* is the antonym for *hate.*

apposition In grammar, two constructions are in apposition when the second follows and identifies the first, as in "Mr. Botts, *the chemistry teacher,* has resigned."

Arabic numerals The numbers 1, 2, 3, etc., as contrasted with Roman numerals I, II, III, etc.

assonance The similarity of vowel sounds in words that do not rhyme (w*e*, w*ee*p; f*i*ne, wh*i*te).

asterisk The sign "*." A single asterisk is sometimes used as a footnote marker. A row of asterisks is sometimes used to indicate that the action of the story has been broken off or to suggest that time has passed.

auxiliary verb   A "helping" verb that combines with another verb to form a verb phrase: "I *am* going"; "He *has been* talking." The most common auxiliaries are *be, can, do, have, may, must, ought, shall, will.*

basic sentence   A sentence in its simplest form, usually just a subject and predicate without any modifiers: "The rain came." "She laughed." See page 232.

B.C.   See **A.D.**

big words   The stylistic fault of using longer and more learned words than the context requires.

blank verse   Unrhymed verse with the dominant metrical pattern of five feet to a line, each foot containing one unstressed and one stressed syllable. The following line from Marc Antony's funeral oration illustrates the pattern:

If you have tears, prepare to shed them now.

caret   The symbol " ∧," used to identify the place in a printed, typed, or written line at which something is to be inserted.

case   A system of inflection that shows the relation of nouns and pronouns to other words in the sentence. See pages 637–640.

circumlocution   Literally, "roundabout speech." An attempt to avoid a direct statement by a circuitous reference, as in "She is expecting an addition to the family" for "She is pregnant."

clause   A group of words containing its own subject and predicate. When a clause can stand alone as a sentence, it is a *main clause;* when it acts as the subject, object, complement, or modifier within a sentence, it is a *subordinate clause.*

cliché   A synonym for "trite expression." See pages 295–298.

clipped words   Any word formed by clipping off part of a longer word, as *cab* or *taxi* from *taxicab,* or *phone* from *telephone.* Clipped words are not considered abbreviations and are not followed by periods. They are generally acceptable in all but the most formal of styles. Common examples are *ad, auto, bike, bus* (from *omnibus*), *exam, flu* (from *influenza*), *gas* (from *gasoline*), *gym, lab, mike* (from *microphone*), *photo, tarp* (from *tarpaulin*), *vet* (from *veteran* or *veterinarian*), *wig* (from *periwig*), *zoo* (from *zoological garden*).

coherence   The quality of being logically integrated. In composition, chiefly used to refer to the integration of sentences within a paragraph. See pages 209–216.

collective noun   A noun that refers to a group or class of individuals: *army, audience, committee, team.* For the agreement of a collective noun and its verb, see pages 645–646.

colorless vowels   When vowels are in an unstressed position, they are sometimes pronounced as a weak "uh," as in *ago*, sof*a*, bal*a*nce, ag*e*nt, el*e*phant, incred*i*ble, bach*e*lor, cor*o*ner, nerv*ou*s. Such colorless vowels frequently cause spelling errors. See page 683.

comma splice   The use of a comma instead of a period or semicolon between two independent clauses that are not connected by a conjunction. See pages 607–609.

comparison   A change in the form of an adjective or adverb to show degree of comparison. There are three degrees: positive, comparative, superlative. There are three methods of indicating comparison in English: (1) adding *-er* for the comparative and *-est* for the superlative; (2) prefixing *more* for comparative and *most* for superlative; (3) using different words for each degree. Methods 1 and 2 are regular; 3 is irregular.

	Positive	**Comparative**	**Superlative**
Method 1:	strong	stronger	strongest
Method 2:	beautiful	more beautiful	most beautiful
Method 3:	good, well	better	best
	bad, ill	worse	worst
	far	farther, further	farthest, furthest
	little	less, lesser	least
	much, many	more	most

complement   Literally, a completing construction. Used in grammar chiefly to refer to the construction that completes a linking verb. See page 600.

compound verbs   Two or more finite verbs in the same clause: "He *called* and *apologized* for his error."

compound words   Combinations of two or more words, the parts of which may be written solid *(blindfold)*, hyphenated *(father-in-law)*, or separately *(blood bank)*. When in doubt about the spelling, consult your dictionary.

conjugation   The inflection of a verb to show its different forms, chiefly those indicating number, person, and tense.

conjunction   Also called *connective*. See below.

connective   Also called *conjunction*. See pages 601–602.

connotation   See pages 270–271.

context   The situation or environment in which a word or statement occurs. It may be verbal, physical, or psychological. A *verbal context* is the surrounding words in a sentence or paragraph. Thus in "That strike *looked like a ball to me*," the italicized words form a verbal context that tells a listener which of several meanings of *strike* to choose. A *physical context* is the physical environment in which an utterance is made, as when miserable weather conditions provide an ironic meaning for "Nice day, isn't it?" A *psychological context* is the state of mind in which a statement is made, as when a frustrated child screams at its mother, "I hate you!" These contexts must be considered in interpreting the statement. Any interpretation that ignores the context may seriously distort what was meant.

coordination   The combining of grammatical structures into pairs or series having the same grammatical function and form. See pages 236–238.

copula   See **linking verb.**

couplet   Two successive lines of poetry that rhyme, as in Coleridge's

The one red leaf, the last of its clan,
That dances as often as dance it can, . . .

dangling modifier   Any modifier that has nothing to modify in a sentence. See pages 611–613.

dative case   In Old English and in some other languages, generally the case of the indirect object; in Modern English expressed by word order ("He gave *me* the book") or by a prepositional phrase ("Send it to *her*").

deadwood   The use of unnecessary words that should be pruned from a sentence. See pages 260–263.

declension   The inflection of a noun to show its different forms for number and case.

definite article   *The* as contrasted with the indefinite article *a* or *an.*

demonstrative   *This, that, these, those* are called demonstratives when they are used as pointing words: "This is the man"; "That coat is mine."

denotation   See pages 270–271.

dialects   Variant forms of a common language which show differences in pronunciation, vocabulary, and grammar characteristic of a particular regional or social group. See "Standards of Usage," pages 596–598.

diphthong   A combination of two vowel sounds run together to sound like a single vowel. Examples are the "ah-oo" sounds combining into a single sound in *shroud* and *cloud* and the "aw-ee" sounds combining in *boy* and *toy.*

direct discourse   A quotation of the exact words of a speaker or writer as contrasted with *indirect discourse,* in which the content of the message is reported but not quoted. Contrasted in

He said, "Send me a copy of the letter." (direct discourse)
He told me to send him a copy of the letter. (indirect discourse)

direct object   See **object.**

distance   A term used in a discussion of style to indicate a writer's attitude toward the reader. See pages 307–309.

documentation   The citing of the source of information either in a footnote or an endnote. See pages 500–507.

e.g.   An abbreviation for the Latin phrase *exempli gratia* ("for the sake of example"; "for example"). Used to introduce an example in publications, such as dictionaries, in which space must be conserved.

ellipsis   A punctuation mark consisting of three dots (. . .) used to indicate the omission of words within a statement. See pages 477, 498, 677–678.

elliptical construction   A construction which is literally incomplete but in which the missing terms are understood.

> I am taller than he (is tall).
> Who told him? (It was) Not I (who told him).

endnotes   Notes placed at the end of a paper or article to identify the sources from which the information was obtained. For the form of such notes, see pages 504–507.

epigram   A short, pithy statement, usually witty or cynical, in either prose or verse.

> Yes, the meek shall inherit the earth — six feet of it.

> Here lies our sovereign lord, the King,
> Whose word no man relies on,
> Who never said a foolish thing,
> And never did a wise one.

etymology   The study of the derivation of words.

euphemism   A word or phrase used as a substitute for a term with unfavorable connotations. A common example is the use of "lady dog" or "girl dog" for *bitch*. When used to refer to a female dog, *bitch* is no more objectionable a word than *doe* or *mare;* but as a slang word it has acquired such unfavorable connotations that some people avoid it altogether and use the euphemisms given above.

expletive   In such sentences as "There are two answers to the question" and "It seems to me that you are mistaken," the words *There* and *It* are called *expletives.* In these sentences the order is expletive–verb–subject, the expletive occupying the normal position of the subject.

fallacy   An error in reasoning. For common fallacies, see pages 365–372.

figure of speech   A literary device that involves an imaginary comparison between two things that are normally quite unlike. The most common figures of speech are discussed on pages 282–287.

fine writing   Often used as an uncomplimentary term for writing that, because of its attempts to be "literary," is artificial or pretentious.

finite verb   A verb form that can be conjugated to show number, person, and tense and can serve as a predicate in a sentence, as contrasted with infinitives, participles, and auxiliary verbs, which cannot be so conjugated or used.

footnotes   Notes used at the foot of a page to identify a source of information. See also **endnotes.**

free verse   Poetry that does not conform to conventional meter and rhyme patterns but has cadence, lines of irregular length, and imagery — for example, these lines from Amy Lowell's "A Decade":

> When you came, you were like red wine and honey,
> And the taste of you burnt my mouth with its sweetness.
> Now you are like morning bread,
> Smooth and pleasant.
> I hardly taste you at all for I know your savour,
> But I am completely nourished.

function words   Words used chiefly to show grammatical relationships between sentence elements: "worked *at* the store," "students *in* class," "ran *and* played," "laughed *because* he won."

gender   A grammatical division of words into masculine, feminine, and neuter categories. Grammatical gender is important in highly inflected languages such as Latin and German. It is only partly related to differences in sex. For example, *nauta* ("sailor") in Latin is a feminine noun, *das Kind* ("child") in German is neuter. Except for personal pronouns *(he, she, it)* and a few feminine forms of nouns *(actress, niece)*, English makes little use of grammatical gender.

genitive case   The possessive case.

gerund   The *-ing* form of a verb when used as a noun: "*Sewing* bored her."

headword   The chief word in a phrase: a noun modified by one or more adjectives ("an old tall *tale*"), or a verb modified by one or more adverbs ("they *danced* mechanically"), or a noun in a prepositional phrase ("at the *beginning*").

historical present   Also called *dramatic present.* The use of the present tense in narrative style to record action in the past: "His friends *try* to persuade him to escape, but Socrates *reasons* with them and *shows* them he must die."

homonyms   Words that are pronounced alike: *air, heir; blew, blue.*

hyperbole   An obvious exaggeration as in "When she said she would tell my father, I was scared to death."

idiom   A usage characteristic of the language or dialect in which it is used. We say "How do you do?"; the French say "How do you carry yourself?" Neither of these expressions is more logical than the other. One is an English idiom, the other a French idiom.

Because idioms are traditional rather than logical, they can be learned only by experience, not by rule. There is, for example, no rule that will tell you in advance what preposition to use with what verb. You say "aim *at*," "abide *by*," "account *for*," "meet *with*," and "move *on*." A foreigner who knows what *get* means will find that that knowledge is of little use in interpreting the meaning of "get ahead," "get along," "get away," "get by," "get on," "get over," "get through," "get with it."

i.e. An abbreviation of the Latin phrase *id est* ("that is"), used to introduce a restatement or an explanation of a preceding word or phrase. Its use is generally confined to publications in which space must be conserved.

imperative mood See **mood.**

indefinite article *A* or *an* as contrasted with the definite article *the*.

indicative mood See **mood.**

indirect object See **object.**

infinitive A verbal form, usually prefixed by *to* (*"to have* and *to hold"*) that can serve as a subject, object, complement, or modifier in a sentence but cannot serve as a verb. See pages 602–603, 635–636.

inflection Changes in the basic form of a word to indicate such grammatical concepts as case, number, tense, person, and degree. The system of a verb's inflection is called its *conjugation*, that of nouns and pronouns is their *declension*, and that of adjectives and adverbs is their *comparison*.

intensives Such modifiers as *much, so, too, very* are called intensives when they merely add emphasis to the words they modify: "much obliged," "so tired," "too bad," "very good." The pronouns that combine with *-self* may also be used as intensives: "You *yourself* are the best judge"; "He built the cabin *himself*"; "She *herself* is to blame"; "I will do it *myself*"; "We *ourselves* were surprised at the news"; "They *themselves* must accept responsibility."

interjection A word, phrase, or clause used as an exclamation, usually to suggest some degree of emotion. Examples are

Oh no, don't do that!

For heaven's sake, take it easy!

You better believe I'll do it.

Wow! What a blunder!

The name comes from a Latin phrase meaning "to throw in." Interjections have no grammatical relation to other parts of the sentence: they do not act as subjects, verbs, modifiers, objects, complements, or connectives, and can sometimes stand alone as sentences or sentence fragments. See **absolute.**

intransitive See **verb.**

irony A mode of statement in which the writer implies almost the opposite of what is explicitly stated. The writing proceeds on two levels at the same time: one stating a literal meaning and the other suggesting to the reader a quite different implied meaning. The most famous example in English is Jonathan Swift's *A Modest Proposal,* which, under the guise of proposing a workable plan for improving the economy of Ireland, makes a scathing criticism of England's exploitation of the Irish. See the passage from *The Adventures of Huckleberry Finn* on page 310 of this book.

jargon   See pages 292–295.

linking verb   (copula) A verb that is neither transitive (that is, requires an object) nor intransitive, but is completed by a noun, pronoun, or adjective acting as a complement. The most common linking verb is some form of the verb *to be,* but *become, feel, look, seem, smell, taste,* and some other verbs may link the subject to a complement: "His uncle *is* a minister"; "Tom *was* late"; "That dress *becomes* her"; "We *felt* disappointed"; "It *smells* bad"; "They *look* tired." In each of these sentences the construction following the italicized linking verb completes the verb but is not an object.

localism   Any usage that is confined to a particular region.

loose sentence   A technical term used to describe a sentence in which the main clause is completed before the end. The opposite of a periodic sentence. Loose sentences are standard sentences and should not be thought faulty.

lower case   A printer's term for small letters, in contrast with *caps* (capital letters). Printers and editors abbreviate *lower case* to *l.c.*

main clause   See **clause**

malapropism   A humorous, though unintentional, confusion of words similar in form and sound: "Henry VIII died of an *abbess* on his knee". The error is named for Mrs. Malaprop, a character in Sheridan's play *The Rivals,* whose speech often illustrates this kind of confusion.

mechanics   In composition, a general term for matters of spelling, capitalization, hyphenation, abbreviation, and the like. See pages 682–702. The term is sometimes extended to details of grammar, punctuation, and usage generally.

meter   From Latin and Greek words meaning "measure." In poetry, lines are measured by feet, and feet are measured by stressed and unstressed syllables.

Measurement of feet	Measurement of lines
˘ ′ = iambic *(ăgó)*	monometer = 1 foot
′ ˘ = trochaic *(bóuntў)*	dimeter = 2 feet
˘ ˘ ′ = anapestic *(ŭnăwáre)*	trimeter = 3 feet
′ ˘ ˘ = dactylic *(beáutĭfŭl)*	tetrameter = 4 feet

Measurement of feet	Measurement of lines
´ ´ = spondaic *(báckstáge)*	pentameter = 5 feet
˘ ˘ = pyrrhic *(mŭrmŭr)*	hexameter = 6 feet
	heptameter = 7 feet

In the scansion of poetry these two kinds of measurement join. For example: iambic tetrameter ("Whŏse wóods/ thĕse áre/ Ĭ thínk/ Ĭ knów"); anapestic trimeter ("Thŏugh Ĭ sáng/ ĭn mў cháins/ lĭke thĕ séa"); trochaic trimeter followed by iambic trimeter ("Áy, thĕ/ báll ĭs/ flўĭng,/ Thĕ láds/ plăy heárt/ ănd soúl").

Middle English   English language and literature from 1100 to 1500.

mixed metaphor   A metaphor that confuses two or more images. See page 298.

Modern English   English language and literature since 1500.

mood   Of the three moods of English verbs — indicative, imperative, and subjunctive — the indicative is by far the most common. A verb is in the indicative mood unless

1. it expresses a command or entreaty ("*Sit* down!" "Please *listen* to me"), in which case it is in the imperative mood.
2. it is used in one of the following ways, in which case it is in the subjunctive mood:
   a. to express a condition contrary to fact: "If I *were* you, I would go."
   b. to grant a concession: "*Be* it as you say."
   c. to state an improbability: "If this *were* the end of the matter, I'd be happy."
   d. to conduct certain parliamentary proceedings: "I move that the committee *go* on record"; "It is moved and seconded that this measure *be* adopted."

The form used for the imperative mood is always the same as the first principal part. The subjunctive, once fully inflected, is so little used in Modern English that you need consider only the forms for the simple present and past tenses of the verb *to be*. These are *be* for all persons in the singular and plural of the simple present, and *were* for all persons in the singular and plural of the simple past.

MS., ms.   Abbreviations for *manuscript*. The plural is *MSS.* or *mss.*

Ms.   An abbreviation (pronounced "Miz") used to address a woman without indicating whether she is married *(Mrs.)* or unmarried *(Miss).*

nominative case   The case of a noun or pronoun when it is used as a subject; sometimes called the *subjective* case.

nonrestrictive modifier   See the discussion of restrictive and nonrestrictive modifiers on pages 662–663.

nonstandard usage   Any usage not accepted as standard English: "they was"; "he ain't"; "them's my books."

noun   A part of speech usually inflected for number and case and used as subject, object, or complement in a sentence: *man, action, house, flower.* It may be used in the possessive case as a modifier: "the *man's* garden."

noun clause   A subordinate clause serving usually as the subject, object, or complement in a sentence — that is, used in the positions in which a noun is normally used.

object   A noun, pronoun, or noun clause that completes the action of a transitive verb: "We bought the *car*"; "I asked *her*"; "She said *that she would think about it.*" In these examples the italicized words are *direct objects.* An *indirect object* identifies the recipient of the action indicated by a verb-object combination: "We bought *Dad* a car"; "The children gave *her* a party"; "He gave the *beggar* a dollar."

Old English   English language and literature from 700 to 1100. There is no surviving Old English literature from before 700.

onomatopoeia   The use of words that sound like the things they represent: *buzz, crack, cuckoo, hiss, meow, purr.*

parallelism   See pages 238–242.

paraphrase   The restatement of someone else's writing in one's own language.

parenthetical construction   A parenthetical element interrupts the flow of the discourse in order to give an explanation, qualification, or example. For the punctuation of parenthetical or interrupting constructions, see pages 657–658.

parts of speech   In traditional grammar the eight parts of speech are nouns, pronouns, verbs, adverbs, adjectives, prepositions, conjunctions, and interjections.

passive voice   See **voice.**

period fault   An error caused by using a period between parts of a sentence. See pages 604–605.

periodic sentence   See pages 249–252.

persona   The personality a writer reveals in his or her writing. The term originally meant "mask" and referred to the practice in ancient Greek drama of wearing different masks for different roles. See also **voice** (in writing).

personification   See page 286.

phonetics   The science dealing with the sounds of language. The sounds are represented by phonetic symbols that ignore the appearance of a word and record only its pronunciation. When words are spelled as they are pronounced, the spelling is said to be phonetic; thus *tho* is a phonetic spelling, but *though* and *colonel* are not.

phonology   The study of the sounds in speech. Phonology includes *phonemics* (the study of small units of sound) and *phonetics* (see above).

plagiarism   A literary fraud in which one writer represents as his or her own the work of another. In its most blatant form the plagiarized material is copied from its source without quotation marks and without acknowledgment. To avoid unintentional plagiarism in a paper, follow the practices recommended on pages 499–500.

P.M., p.m.   See **A.M.**

précis   A summary that preserves the organization and principal content of an original longer work.

predicate   That part of a sentence that makes a statement about the subject. The predicate may consist of an intransitive verb, with or without modifiers; or of a transitive verb and its object, with or without modifiers; or of a linking verb and its complement, with or without modifiers.

predicate adjective   An adjective that completes a linking verb: "His mother is *sick*"; "Oh, it is *beautiful!*"; "I am *afraid.*"

predicate noun   Same function as *predicate adjective* above: "Her mother is a *writer*"; "Her brother became a successful *lawyer.*"

prefix   A word or syllable placed before the root of another word to form a new word: *anti*bodies, *pre*writing, *mis*used, *un*able.

premise   That part of an argument from which the conclusion is drawn. See pages 343–348.

preposition   A connective word that links a following noun or pronoun to another word in the sentence, usually a noun or verb: "He sat *on* the desk"; "There is room *at* the top"; "We looked *into* it."

prepositional phrase   A phrase consisting of a preposition, its object, and the modifiers of the object. Prepositional phrases act as adjectives ("His house *in the country* has been sold") or adverbs ("You will find her *in the kitchen*").

principal parts   See **verb.**

pronoun   Pronouns are usually divided into five classes: personal, relative, reflexive, demonstrative, and indefinite.

Personal pronouns refer to nouns and may serve as subjects, objects, complements, and modifiers in sentences. The following chart shows their inflection for person, gender, number, and case:

Number	Case	1st person	2nd person	3rd person		
				mas.	fem.	neut.
Singular	Subjective	I	you	he	she	it
	Possessive	my (mine)	your(s)	his	her(s)	its
	Objective	me	you	him	her	it

Plural				
Subjective	we	you	they	
Possessive	our(s)	your(s)	their(s)	all genders
Objective	us	you	them	

Relative pronouns *(that, who, which, what, and their compounds with -ever)* are called relative because they "relate" a subordinate clause to an antecedent in a main clause. They thus act as subordinating connectives. Of these pronouns only *who* and its compounds are inflected for case: *who* (subjective), *whose,* (possessive), *whom* (objective).

When a pronoun object refers to the same antecedent as the subject in such a way that the subject performs the action of the verb on itself, the pronoun is called *reflexive.* Examples are "She hurt *herself,*" "He blamed *himself,*" "They corrected *themselves.*"

Demonstrative pronouns *(this, that)* are inflected only for number *(these, those)* and agree in number with the nouns they modify: "*this* kind," "*these* kinds."

Indefinite pronouns *(all, any, both, each, either, none, one, somebody, and the like)* often refer to antecedents that are less definite than those of other pronouns. Except for the possessive form in *one's, everybody's, nobody's, somebody's,* they are not inflected.

protagonist   The principal character in a story. He or she may be opposed by an *antagonist.* These words come from the Greek *agonistes,* meaning "competitors in games," and the prefixes *pro-* ("for") and *anti-* ("against"). In Shakespeare's *Othello,* Othello is the protagonist and Iago the antagonist.

quatrain   In poetry, a stanza of four lines, either rhymed or unrhymed.

referent   A term used in a discussion of meaning to indicate the thing to which a word refers. *Referent* is pronounced with the stress on the first syllable.

restrictive modifiers   See the discussion of restrictive and nonrestrictive modifiers on pages 662–663.

Roman numerals   See pages 700–701.

run-on sentence   See pages 606–607.

semantics   That part of the study of language that is concernd with meaning as contrasted with phonetics (pronunciation), morphology (form), and syntax (grammatical relations within a sentence).

sentence   A unit of discourse consisting of a subject and predicate and their modifiers, if any. Sentences may be classified either rhetorically or grammatically. In Chapter 7 of this book they are classified rhetorically as basic, balanced, and periodic. Grammatically they are classified as simple, compound, complex, and compound-complex, each of which categories is illustrated below.

1. *Simple.* One clause, a main clause: "Charlie shot a squirrel."
2. *Compound.* Two or more main clauses: "Charlie shot a squirrel, and Beth scolded him."

3. *Complex.* One main clause and one or more subordinate clauses: "Charlie shot a squirrel while he and Beth were walking in the woods."

4. *Compound-complex.* Two or more main clauses and one or more subordinate clauses: "Charlie shot a squirrel and Beth gathered wildflowers while they were walking in the woods."

sentence fragment   See pages 604–605.

series   Parallel constructions arranged in succession: "She was *tall, tanned,* and *lean.*" The elements of a series may be single words, phrases, or subordinate or main clauses, but all elements must have the same grammatical form. See page 657.

sic   A term inserted into a quotation, usually in square brackets, to notify the reader that the word preceding *sic* was written in the form given: "The sign said firmly: 'No person will be allowed on the premises unless duely [sic] authorized.' "

silent letters   Letters that are not pronounced — the *k* in *knot*, the *b* in *climb*, the *p* in *psychology.*

slanting   Selecting material so that it suggests a judgment that could not be made if all the material available were presented. See pages 335–337.

split infinitive   An infinitive is "split" when one or more words come between the marker *to* and the rest of the infinitive: *"to* wholly *comprehend."* When the split results in an awkward construction ("He wanted *to* at the same time *protect* his family"), it should be avoided; but if it provides a desired emphasis ("The prosecution failed *to* completely *demolish* the alibi") there can be no reasonable objection to it.

spoonerism   An unintentional shift in the sounds of a word — "She slyly shipped aboard" for "She shyly slipped aboard." The error is named for the Rev. William A. Spooner, who often made such mistakes.

strong verb   One of a class of irregular verbs that form the past tense and past participle by changing the vowel of the present tense: *break, broke, broken; ride, rode, ridden.*

stylebooks   Books that offer advice about details of usage. Three of the best stylebooks are the *MLA Handbook* (Modern Language Association), *A Manual of Style* (University of Chicago Press), and the *United States Government Printing Office Style Manual.*

subjunctive   One of three moods of English verbs, the other two being imperative and indicative. See **mood.**

subordinate clause   See **clause.**

subordination   The reduction of a main clause to a subordinate clause or phrase. See pages 242–244.

suffix   A syllable added at the end of a word to make a derived word, as in *like + ly = likely; child + hood = childhood.*

syllogism   A form of deductive argument that can be presented as a conclusion drawn from a major and minor premise.

> *major premise:*   Mammals bear their young alive.
> *minor premise:*   Whales are mammals.
> *conclusion:*   Whales bear their young alive.

symbol   (in literature)   See pages 416–417.

synonyms   Two or more words with the same meaning. Contrasted with antonyms, which have opposite meanings. *Brave* and *valiant* are synonyms; *brave* and *cowardly* are antonyms.

syntax   That part of the study of language that is concerned with the relations of words within a sentence.

tense   The system of changes in the form of verbs to indicate the time at which an action took place.

theme   Used in two ways in a composition course: (1) the dominant idea of an essay or book as in "The theme of the essay is that self-deception is the commonest of vices"; (2) a general name for a composition assignment as in "Write a 500-word theme for Monday." The first meaning is synonymous with *thesis* as it is used in this book.

tone   The attitudes of a writer toward the subject and the reader as these attitudes are revealed in the written material. See pages 301–302.

tragic flaw   In Greek tragedy, a decisive flaw or weakness in the hero's character that brings about his or her downfall. For example, it is the rashness of Oedipus at critical moments in his life that contributes to his unintentional violation of the moral laws and to the punishment he imposes upon himself. The term has been extended to English tragedy: Macbeth's tragic flaw is excessive ambition, and Othello's is irrational jealousy.

transition   From a Latin root meaning "to go across." Transitions link one part of a paper to another. The transitional devices may be individual words, phrases, clauses, sentences, or short paragraphs. See pages 212–215, 220–221.

transitive   See **verb.**

verb   Such words as *be, caught, do, eat, pray, run, said, thought, walked* belong to a large class of words that name actions or states of being and are inflected for number, person, tense, and mood. Each verb has four *principal parts,* from which its various forms are derived. The accompanying table shows the principal parts of regular and irregular verbs.

	Present tense	Present participle	Past tense	Past participle
Regular	walk	walking	walked	walked
	deal	dealing	dealt	dealt
	have	having	had	had
Irregular	buy	buying	bought	bought
	speak	speaking	spoke	spoken
	bet	betting	bet	bet
	am, are	being	was, were	been

As this table shows, the present participle is formed by adding *-ing* to the present-tense form. In regular verbs both the past tense and the past participle are formed by adding the suffix *-ed, -d,* or *-t* to the present-tense form. Most irregular verbs form the past tense by changing the vowel of the present tense: *buy, bought; speak, spoke.* Some, like *buy,* retain the past-tense form for the past participle; others, like *speak,* retain the vowel change but add *-en* for the past participle. Some irregular verbs, like *bet,* retain the same form in all principal parts: *cast, cost, hit, hurt, let, put, set, shed, shut, split, spread, thrust.* The verb *to be* is so irregular that we will treat it separately after we have discussed the inflection of the other verbs.

Inflection for person and number. The only inflection for person and number occurs in the form for the third person singular, which is marked by the addition of *-s* to the present form. Thus: "I (we, you, they) *walk,*" but "he (she, it) *walks.*" Slight variations of this rule are *have* and *do,* which in the third person singular become *has* and *does,* respectively. Otherwise, the same form is used for all persons in both singular and plural, whether the verb is regular or irregular.

Inflection for tense. Although many tenses can be identified in English, we will deal here with only the six basic tenses.

1. *Simple present:* They walk.   They speak.
2. *Present perfect:* They have walked.   They have spoken.
3. *Simple past:* They walked.   They spoke.
4. *Past perfect:* They had walked.   They had spoken.
5. *Simple future:* They will walk.   They will speak.
6. *Future perfect:* They will have walked.   They will have spoken.

An inspection of these tenses shows that the simple present and the simple future come from the first principal part, although the simple future also uses the auxiliary verb *will;* the simple past comes from the past-tense form; and all the perfect tenses combine the past participle with the auxiliary verb *have* or *had.*

The inflection of the verb *to be* in these six tenses is as follows:

1. *Simple present: am* in first singular, *is* in third singular, *are* in the rest

2. *Present perfect: have been* in all persons and numbers except *has been* in third singular.

3. *Simple past: was* in first and third singular, *were* in all others

4. *Past perfect: had been* in all persons and numbers

5. *Simple future: will be* throughout, except that *shall* may be used for *will* in first person singular and plural

6. *Future perfect: will have been* throughout, except that *shall* may be used for *will* in first person singular and plural

Inflection for mood. See **mood.**

Verbs are also identified as *transitive* or *intransitive.* A verb is transitive when it requires an object to complete the predicate ("We *left* him alone"); when it does not require an object, it is intransitive ("All the girls *have left*").

verbal   See pages 602–603.

voice   (of verb)   English verbs have two voices: *active* ("A man opened the door") and *passive* ("The door was opened by a man"). When a verb is changed from active to passive, the object of the active verb becomes the subject of the passive verb. The passive voice is formed by adding the past participle to the appropriate tense form of the verb *to be:* "The door *is opened (was opened, will be opened)."*

voice   (in writing)   A term used in a discussion of style to identify the person or personality speaking in a literary work. See page 418.

vulgate   Synonymous with *nonstandard;* any usage characteristic of uneducated speech.

A Checklist of Troublesome Usages

This checklist identifies certain words and constructions that sometimes require attention in composition classes. Some of the entries are pairs of words that are quite different in meaning yet similar enough in spelling to be confused (see **principal–principle**); some, such as the use of *without* as a synonym for *unless,* are nonstandard usages that are not acceptable in college writing (see **without = unless**); some are informal constructions that may be appropriate in some situations but not in others (see **guess**).

The judgments recorded here about usage are based on the Usage Notes contained in *The American Heritage Dictionary,* supplemented by the following sources: *Webster's Third New International Dictionary, Webster's New World Dictionary,* Theodore M. Bernstein's *The Careful Writer,* Margaret M. Bryant's *Current American Usage,* Bergen and Cornelia Evans's *A Dictionary of Contemporary Usage,* and Robert C. Pooley's *The Teaching of English Usage.* Because these authorities do not always agree, it has sometimes been necessary for the authors of this textbook to decide which judgments to accept. In coming to decisions, we have attempted to represent a consensus, but readers should be aware that on disputed items the judgments recorded in this checklist are finally those of the authors.

Because dictionaries do not always distinguish between formal, informal, and colloquial usage, it has seemed useful in the checklist to indicate whether particular usages would be appropriate in college writing. The usefulness of this advice, however, depends on an understanding of its limitations. In any choice of usage, the decision depends less on what dictionaries or textbooks say than on what is consistent with the purpose and style of the writing. The student and instructor, who alone have the context of the paper before them, are in the best position to answer that question. All that the checklist can do is to provide a background from which particular decisions can be made. The general assumption in the checklist is that the predominant style in college writing is informal rather than formal or colloquial. This assumption implies that calling a usage informal in no way suggests that it is less desirable than a formal usage.

access–excess   *Access* means "approach" or "admission": "an access road"; "having access to the records." *Excess* means "beyond what is normal or desirable": "He worries to excess"; "a tax on excess profits."

ad   *Ad* is the clipped form of *advertisement.* The full form is preferable in a formal style, especially in letters of application. The appropriateness of *ad* in college writing depends on the style of the paper.

adapt–adopt   *Adapt* means "to adjust to meet requirements": "The human body can adapt itself to all sorts of environments"; "It will take a skillful writer to adapt this novel for the movies." *Adopt* means "to take as one's own" ("He immediately adopted the idea") or — in parliamentary procedure — "to accept as law" ("The motion was adopted").

advice–advise   The first form is a noun, the second a verb: "I was advised to ignore his advice."

affect–effect   Both words may be used as nouns, but *effect*, meaning "result," is usually the word wanted: "His speech had an unfortunate effect"; "The treatments had no effect on me." The noun *affect* is a technical term in psychology. Though both words may be used as verbs, *affect* is the more common. As a verb, *affect* means "impress" or "influence": "His advice affected my decision"; "Does music affect you that way?" As a verb, *effect* is rarely required in college writing but may be used to mean "carry out" or "accomplish": "The pilot effected his mission"; "The lawyer effected a settlement."

affective–effective   See **affect–effect.** The common adjective is *effective* ("an effective argument"), meaning "having an effect." The use of *affective* is largely confined to technical discussions of psychology and semantics, in which it is roughly equivalent to "emotional." In this textbook *affective* is used to describe a tone that is chiefly concerned with creating attitudes in the reader. See pages 302–307.

aggravate   *Aggravate* may mean either "to make worse" ("His remarks aggravated the dispute") or "to annoy or exasperate" ("Her manners aggravate me"). Both are standard English, but there is still some objection to the second usage. If you mean *annoy, exasperate,* or *provoke,* it would be safer to use whichever of these words best expresses your meaning in preference to *aggravate.*

ain't   Except to record nonstandard speech, the use of *ain't* is not acceptable in college writing.

alibi   The use of *alibi* as a verb ("He alibied for me") is not acceptable. Its use as a noun in the legal sense of being elsewhere when a crime was committed ("The police could not disprove the suspect's alibi") is thoroughly acceptable. Its use to mean "excuse" ("She had a good alibi for being late") is a colloquial usage to which there is some objection in college writing. *Excuse* is the preferred word.

all (not all that)   The use of "not all that interested" to mean "not much interested" is generally not acceptable in college writing.

all the farther, further   Colloquial in some areas but generally unacceptable in college writing. Use "as far as."

all together–altogether   Distinguish between the phrase ("They were all together at last") and the adverb ("He is altogether to blame"). *All together* means "all in one place"; *altogether* means "entirely" or "wholly."

allow   When used to mean "permit" ("No smoking is allowed on the premises"), *allow* is acceptable. Its use to mean "think" ("He allowed it could be done") is nonstandard and is not acceptable in college writing.

allusion–illusion   An *allusion* is a reference: "The poem contains several allusions to Greek mythology." An *illusion* is an erroneous mental image: "Rouge on pallid skin gives an illusion of health."

alright A common variant spelling of *all right,* but there is still considerable objection to it. *All right* is the preferred spelling.

among, between See **between, among.**

amount, number *Amount* suggests bulk or weight: "We collected a considerable amount of scrap iron." *Number* is used for items that can be counted: "He has a large number of friends"; "There are a number of letters to be answered."

an Variant of indefinite article *a.* Used instead of *a* when the word that follows begins with a vowel sound: "an apple," "an easy victory," "an honest opinion," "an hour," "an unknown person." When the word that follows begins with a consonant, or with a *y* sound or a pronounced *h,* the article should be *a:* "a yell," "a unit," "a history," "a house." Such constructions as "a apple," "a hour" are nonstandard. The use of *an* before *historical* is an older usage that is now dying out.

and/or Many people object to *and/or* in college writing because the expression is associated with legal and commercial writing. Generally avoid it.

angle The use of *angle* to mean "point of view" ("Let's look at it from a new angle") is acceptable. In the sense of personal interest ("What's your angle?"), it is slang.

anxious = eager *Anxious* should not be used in college writing to mean "eager," as in "Gretel is anxious to see her gift." *Eager* is the preferred word in this context.

any = all The use of *any* to mean "all," as in "He is the best qualified of any applicant," is not acceptable. Say "He is the best qualified of all the applicants," or simply "He is the best-qualified applicant."

any = any other The use of *any* to mean "any other" ("The knife he bought cost more than any in the store") should be avoided in college writing. In this context, use "any other."

anyone = all The singular *anyone* should not be used in writing to mean "all." In "She is the most talented musician of anyone I have met here," drop "of anyone."

anywheres A nonstandard variant of *anywhere.* It is not acceptable in college writing.

apt = likely *Apt* is always appropriate when it means "quick to learn" ("He is an apt student") or "suited to its purpose" ("an apt comment"). It is also appropriate when a predictable characteristic is being spoken of ("When he becomes excited he is apt to tremble"). In other situations the use of *apt* to mean "likely" ("She is apt to leave you"; "He is apt to resent it") may be too colloquial for college writing.

as = because *As* is less effective than *because* in showing causal relation between main and subordinate clauses. Since *as* has other meanings, it may in certain contexts be confusing. For example, in "As I was going home, I decided to telephone," *as* may mean *while* or *because.* If there is any possibility of confusion, use either *because* or *while* — whichever is appropriate.

as = that   The use of *as* to introduce a noun clause ("I don't know as I would agree to that") is colloquial. In college writing, use *that* or *whether.*

as to, with respect to = about   Although "as to" and "with respect to" are standard usage, many writers avoid these phrases because they sound stilted: "I am not concerned as to your cousin's reaction." Here "about" would be more appropriate than either "as to" or "with respect to"; "I am not concerned about your cousin's reaction."

at   Avoid the redundant *at* in such sentences as "Where were you at?" and "Where do you live at?"

author (verb)   *Author* is not fully accepted as a verb. "To write a play" is preferable to "to author a play."

awful, awfully   The real objection to *awful* is that it is worked to death. Instead of being reserved for situations in which it means "awe inspiring," it is used excessively as a utility word. (See pages 289–290.) Use both *awful* and *awfully* sparingly.

bad = badly   The ordinary uses of *bad* as an adjective cause no difficulty. As a predicate adjective ("An hour after dinner I began to feel bad"), it is sometimes confused with the adverb *badly.* After the verbs *look, feel,* and *seem,* the adjective is preferred. Say "It looks bad for our side," "I feel bad about the quarrel," "Our predicament seemed bad this morning." But do not use *bad* when an adverb is required, as in "He played badly," "a badly torn suit."

bank on = rely on   In college writing "rely on" is generally preferred.

being as = because   The use of *being as* for "because" or "since" in such sentences as "Being as I am an American, I believe in democracy" is nonstandard. Say "Because I am an American, I believe in democracy."

between, among   In general, use *between* in constructions involving two people or objects and *among* in constructions involving more than two: "We had less than a dollar between the two of us"; "We had only a dollar among the three of us." The general distinction, however, should be modified when insistence on it would be unidiomatic. For example, *between* is the accepted form in the following examples:

> He is in the enviable position of having to choose between three equally attractive young women.
>
> A settlement was arranged between the four partners.
>
> Just between us girls . . . (when any number of 'girls' is involved)

between you and I   Both pronouns are objects of the preposition *between* and so should be in the objective case: "between you and me."

bi-, semi- *Bi-* means "two": "The budget for the biennium was adopted." *Semi-* means "half of": *semicircle. Bi-* is sometimes used to mean "twice in." A bimonthly paper, for example, may be published twice a month, not once every two months, but this usage is ambiguous; *semimonthly* is preferred.

but that, but what In such a statement as "I don't doubt but that you are correct," *but* is unnecessary. Omit it. "I don't doubt but what . . ." is also unacceptable. Delete "but what" and write *that*.

can = may The distinction that *can* is used to indicate ability and *may* to indicate permission ("If I can do the work, may I have the job?") is not generally observed in informal usage. Either form is acceptable in college writing.

cannot help but In college writing, the form without *but* is preferred: "I cannot help being angry." (Not: "I cannot help but be angry.")

can't hardly A confusion between *cannot* and *can hardly*. The construction is unacceptable in college writing. Use *cannot, can't,* or *can hardly*.

capital–capitol Unless you are referring to a government building, use *capital.* The building in which the U.S. Congress meets is always capitalized ("the Capitol"). For the various meanings of *capital,* consult your dictionary.

censor–censure Both words come from a Latin verb meaning "to set a value on" or "tax." *Censor* is used to mean "appraise" in the sense of appraising a book or a letter to see if it may be released ("All outgoing mail had to be censored") and is often used as a synonym for "delete" or "cut out" ("That part of the message was censored").

Censure means "to evaluate adversely" or "to find fault with" or, as a noun, "rebuke": "The editorial writers censured the speech"; "Such an attitude will invoke public censure."

center around Some people object to the contradiction between *center,* which means "focus," and *around:* "The question of his eligibility centers around the accuracy of the registrar's report." Since *around* adds nothing of value in the sentence, "centers on" is the preferred form.

cite–sight–site *Cite* means "to refer to": "He cited chapter and verse." *Sight* means "spectacle" or "view": "The garden was a beautiful sight." *Site* means "location": "This is the site of the new plant."

commentate *Commentate* is not generally accepted either as a transitive verb ("Howard Cosell commentated the game between the Bears and the Vikings") or as an intransitive verb ("He has commentated for CBS ever since I can remember"). Use *announced* or *reported,* or rephrase the sentence to use an appropriate noun: *commentator, announcer, reporter.*

compare, contrast *Compare* can imply either differences or similarities; *contrast* always implies differences. *Compare* can be followed by either *to* or *with.* The verb *contrast* is usually followed by *with.*

Compared to her mother, she's a beauty.

I hope my accomplishments can be compared with those of my predecessor. His grades this term contrast conspicuously with the ones he received last term.

complected Nonstandard form of *complexioned*. Not acceptable in college writing.

complement–compliment Both words can be used as both nouns and verbs. *Complement* speaks of completion: "the complement of a verb"; "a full complement of soldiers to serve as an honor guard"; "Susan's hat complements the rest of her outfit tastefully." *Compliment* is associated with praise: "The instructor complimented us for writing good papers."

complement of *to be* The choice between "It is I" and "It's me" is a choice not between standard and nonstandard usage but between formal and colloquial styles. This choice seldom has to be made in college writing, since the expression, in whatever form it is used, is essentially a spoken rather than a written sentence. Its use in writing occurs chiefly in dialogue, and then the form chosen should be appropriate to the speaker.

The use of the objective case in the third person ("That was her") is less common and should probably be avoided in college writing except when dialogue requires it.

consensus of opinion Because *consensus* means "collective opinion," the addition of *of opinion* is redundant. In the following sentence *of opinion* should be deleted: "The leader asked for an informal show of hands so she could discover whether there was a consensus of opinion."

considerable The use of *considerable* as a noun ("I have spent considerable on this project") is not appropriate in college writing. Write "considerable money" or "a considerable amount of money." The adjective form ("I was considerable surprised") is not acceptable when the adverbial form *considerably* is needed.

continual–continuous Both words refer to a continued action, but *continual* implies repeated action ("continual interruptions," "continual disagreements"), whereas *continuous* implies that the action never ceases ("continuous pain," "a continuous buzzing in the ears").

cope The verb *cope*, meaning "to contend with," is usually followed by the preposition *with* and its object: "We found it difficult to cope with inflated prices."

could of = could have Although "could of" and "could have" often sound alike in speech, *of* is not acceptable for *have* in college writing. In writing, "could of," "should of," "would of," "might of," and "must of" are nonstandard.

council–counsel *Council* is a noun meaning "a deliberative body": "a town council," "a student council." *Counsel* can be either a noun meaning "advice" or a verb meaning "to advise": "to seek a lawyer's counsel," "to counsel a person in trouble." One who offers counsel is a *counselor:* "Because of his low grades Quint made an appointment with his academic counselor."

credible–creditable–credulous All three words come from a Latin verb meaning "to believe," but they are not synonyms. *Credible* means "believable" ("His story is credible"); *creditable* means "commendable" ("John did a creditable job on the committee") or "acceptable for credit" ("The project is creditable toward the course requirements"); *credulous* means "gullible" ("Only a most credulous person could believe such an incredible story").

cute A word used colloquially to indicate the general notion of "attractive" or "pleasing." Its overuse shows lack of discrimination. A more specific term is often preferable.

His daughter is cute.   (lovely? petite? pleasant? charming?)

That is a cute trick.   (clever? surprising?)

He has a cute accent.   (pleasant? refreshingly unusual?)

She is a little too cute for me.   (affected? juvenile? clever?)

data is Because *data* is the Latin plural of *datum*, it logically requires a plural verb, and always does in scientific writing: "These data have been double checked." In popular usage *datum* is almost never used and *data* is treated as a singular noun and given a singular subject: "The data has been double checked." Either "data are" or "data is" may be used in popular writing, but only "data are" is acceptable in scientific writing.

debut *Debut* is a noun meaning "first public appearance." It is not acceptable as a transitive verb ("The Little Theater will debut its new play tonight") or as an intransitive verb ("Cory Martin will debut in the new play").

decent–descent A decent person is one who behaves well, without crudeness and perhaps with kindness and generosity. *Decent* can mean "satisfactory" ("a decent grade," "a decent living standard"). *Descent* means "a passage downward"; a descent may be either literal ("their descent into the canyon") or figurative ("hereditary descent of children from their parents," "descent of English from a hypothetical language called Indo-European").

desert–dessert The noun *desert* means "an uncultivated and uninhabited area"; it may be dry and sandy. *Desert* can be an adjective: "a desert island." The verb *desert* means "to abandon." A *dessert* is a sweet food served as the last course at the noon or evening meal.

different than Although both "different from" and "different than" are common American usages, the preferred idiom is "different from."

disinterested–uninterested The distinction between these words is that *disinterested* means "unbiased" and *uninterested* means "apathetic" or "not interested." A disinterested critic is one who comes to a book with no prejudices or prior judgments of its worth; an uninterested critic is one who cannot get interested in the book. Dictionaries disagree about whether this distinction is still valid in contemporary usage and sometimes treat the words as synonyms. But in college writing the distinction is generally observed.

don't *Don't* is a contraction of "do not," as *doesn't* is a contraction of "does not." It can be used in any college writing in which contractions are appropriate. But it cannot be used with a singular subject. "He don't" and "it don't" are nonstandard usages.

double negative The use of two negative words within the same construction. In certain forms ("I am not unwilling to go") the double negative is educated usage for an affirmative statement; in other forms ("He hasn't got no money") the double negative is nonstandard usage. The observation that "two negatives make an affirmative" in English usage is a half-truth based on a false analogy with mathematics. "He hasn't got no money" is unacceptable in college writing, not because two negatives make an affirmative, but because it is nonstandard usage.

economic–economical *Economic* refers to the science of economics or to business in general: "This is an economic law"; "Economic conditions are improving." *Economical* means "inexpensive" or "thrifty": "That is an economical purchase"; "He is economical to the point of miserliness."

effect–affect See **affect–effect.**

effective–affective See **affective–effective.**

either Used to designate one of two things: "Both hats are becoming; I would be perfectly satisfied with either." The use of *either* when more than two things are involved ("There are three ways of working the problem; either way will give the right answer") is a disputed usage. When more than two things are involved, it is better to use *any* or *any one* instead of *either:* "There are three ways of working the problem; any one of them will give the right answer."

elicit–illicit The first word means "to draw out" ("We could elicit no response from them"); the second means "not permitted" or "unlawful" ("an illicit sale of drugs").

emigrant–immigrant An emigrant is a person who moves *out of* a country; an immigrant is one who moves *into* a country. Thus, refugees from Europe and elsewhere who settled in the United States were emigrants from their native countries and immigrants here. A similar distinction holds for the verbs *emigrate* and *immigrate.*

eminent–imminent *Eminent* means "prominent, outstanding": "an eminent scientist." *Imminent* means "ready to happen" or "near in time": "War seems imminent."

enormity, enormous, enormousness *Enormous* refers to unusual size or measure — synonyms are *huge, vast, immense:* "an enormous fish," "an enormous effort." *Enormousness* is a noun with the same connotations of size and can be applied to either good or bad effects: "The enormousness of their contribution is only beginning to be recognized"; "The enormousness of the lie almost made it believable." But *enormity* is used only for evil acts of great dimension: "The enormity of Hitler's crimes against the Jews shows what can happen when power, passion, and prejudice are all united in one human being."

enthused   *Enthused* is colloquial for *enthusiastic:* "The probability of winning has caused them to be very enthused about the campaign." In college writing use *enthusiastic.*

equally as   In such sentences as "He was equally as good as his brother," the *equally* is unnecessary. Simply write "He was as good as his brother."

etc.   An abbreviation for the Latin *et cetera,* which means "and so forth." It should be used only when the style justifies abbreviations and then only after several items in a commonly used kind of series have been identified: "The data sheet required the usual personal information: age, height, weight, marital status, etc." An announcement of a painting contest that stated, "Entries will be judged on the basis of use of color, etc.," would not tell contestants very much about the standards by which their work is to be judged. Avoid the redundant *and* before *etc.*

excess–access   See **access–excess.**

expect = suppose or suspect   The use of *expect* for *suppose* or *suspect* is colloquial. In college writing use *suppose* or *suspect:* "I suppose you have written to him"; "I suspect that we have made a mistake."

fact   Distinguish between facts and statements of fact. A fact is something that exists or existed. It is neither true nor false; it just *is.* A statement of fact, or factual statement, may be true or false, depending on whether it does or does not report the facts accurately. But there are no true or false facts.

   Avoid padding a sentence with unnecessary use of "a fact that," as in "It is a fact that all the public opinion polls predicted Truman's defeat in the 1948 election." The first five words of that sentence add no meaning. Similarly, "His guilt is admitted" says all, in fewer words, that is said by "The fact of his guilt is admitted."

famous, notorious   *Famous* is a complimentary and *notorious* an uncomplimentary adjective. Well-known people of good repute are famous; those of bad repute are notorious, or infamous.

farther–further   The distinction that *farther* indicates distance and *further* degree is not unanimously supported by usage studies. But to mean "in addition," only *further* is used: "Further assistance will be required."

feature = imagine   The use of *feature* to mean "give prominence to," as in "This issue of the magazine features an article on juvenile delinquency," is established standard usage and is appropriate in college writing. But this acceptance does not justify the slang use of *feature,* meaning "imagine," in such expressions as "Can you feature that?" "Feature me in a dress suit," "I can't feature him as a nurse."

fewer = less   *Fewer* refers to quantities that can be counted individually: "fewer male than female employees." *Less* is used for collective quantities that are not counted individually ("less corn this year than last") and for abstract characteristics ("less determination than enthusiasm").

field *Field,* in the sense of "an area of study or endeavor," is an overused word that often creates redundance: "He is majoring in the field of physics"; "Her new job is in the field of public relations." Delete "the field of" in each of these sentences.

finalize One of many *-ize* words that people associate with business and government jargon. Avoid *finalize* in college writing.

fine = very well The colloquial use of *fine* to mean "very well" ("He is doing fine in his new position") is probably too informal for most college writing.

flaunt = flout Using *flaunt* as a synonym for *flout* confuses two different words. *Flaunt* means "to show off": "She has a habit of flaunting her knowledge to intimidate her friends." *Flout* means "to scorn or show contempt for": "He is better at flouting opposing arguments than at understanding them." In the right context either word can be effective, but the two words are not synonyms and cannot be used interchangeably.

formally–formerly *Formally* means "in a formal manner": "They dressed formally." *Formerly* means "previously": "He was formerly with A. C. Smith and Company."

fortuitous–fortunate *Fortuitous* means "by chance," "not planned": "Our meeting was fortuitous; we had never heard of each other before." Do not confuse *fortuitous* with *fortunate,* as the writer of this sentence has done: "My introduction to Professor Kraus was fortuitous for me; today she hired me as her student assistant." *Fortunate* would be the appropriate word here.

funny Often used in conversation as a utility word that has no precise meaning but may be clear enough in its context. It is generally too vague for college writing. Decide in what sense the subject is "funny" and use a more precise term to convey that sense. See the treatment of vagueness on pages 289–292.

get A utility word. *The American Heritage Dictionary* lists thirty-six meanings for the individual word and more than sixty uses in idiomatic expressions. Most of these uses are acceptable in college writing. But unless the style is deliberately colloquial, avoid slang uses of *get* meaning "to cause harm to" ("She'll get me for that"), "to cause a negative reaction to" ("His bad manners really get me"), "to gain the favor of" ("He tried to get in with his boss"), and "to become up-to-date" ("Get in the swing of things").

good The use of *good* as an adverb ("He talks good"; "She played pretty good") is not acceptable. The accepted adverbial form is *well.*

This discussion does not apply to the use of *good* as an adjective after verbs of hearing, feeling, seeing, smelling, tasting, and the like. See **bad.**

good and Used colloquially as an intensive in such expressions as "good and late," "good and ready," "good and tired." The more formal the style, the less appropriate these intensives are. In college writing use them sparingly, if at all.

guess The use of *guess* to mean "believe," "suppose," or "think" ("I guess I can be there on time") is accepted by all studies on which this list is based. There is still objection to its use in formal college writing, but it should be acceptable in an informal style.

had (hadn't) ought Nonstandard for *ought* and *ought not.* Not acceptable in college writing.

hanged, hung Alternative past participles of *hang.* For referring to an execution, *hanged* is preferred; in other senses, *hung* is preferred.

hopefully Opinion is divided about the acceptability of attaching this adverb loosely to a sentence and using it to mean "I hope": "Hopefully, the plane will arrive on schedule." This usage is gaining acceptance, but there is still strong objection to it. In college writing the safer procedure is to avoid it.

idea In addition to its formal meaning of "conception," *idea* has acquired so many supplementary meanings that it must be recognized as a utility word. Some of its meanings are illustrated in the following sentences:

The idea (thesis) of the book is simple.

The idea (proposal) she suggested is a radical one.

I got the idea (impression) that he is unhappy.

It is my idea (belief, opinion) that they are both wrong.

My idea (intention) is to leave early.

The overuse of *idea,* like the overuse of any utility word, makes for vagueness. Whenever possible, use a more precise synonym.

illicit–elicit See **elicit–illicit.**

illusion–allusion See **allusion–illusion.**

immigrant–emigrant See **emigrant–immigrant.**

imminent–eminent See **eminent–imminent.**

imply–infer The traditional difference between these two words is that *imply* refers to what a statement means, usually to a meaning not specifically stated but suggested in the original statement, whereas *infer* is used for a listener's or reader's judgment or inference based on the statement. For example: "I thought that the weather report implied that the day would be quite pretty and sunny, but Marlene inferred that it meant we'd better take umbrellas." The dictionaries are not unanimous in supporting this distinction, but in your writing it will be better not to use *imply* as a synonym for *infer.*

individual Although the use of *individual* to mean "person" ("He is an energetic individual") is accepted by the dictionaries, college instructors frequently disapprove of this use, probably because it is overdone in college writing. There is no objection to the adjective *individual,* meaning "single," "separate" ("The instructor tries to give us individual attention").

inferior than Possibly a confusion between "inferior to" and "worse than." Say "inferior to": "Today's workmanship is inferior to that of a few years ago."

ingenious–ingenuous *Ingenious* means "clever" in the sense of "original": "an ingenious solution." *Ingenuous* means "showing frank simplicity": "Her ingenuous confession disarmed those who had been suspicious of her motives."

in regards to The only acceptable form in writing is "in regard to."

inside of, outside of *Inside of* and *outside of* generally should not be used as compound prepositions. In place of the compound prepositions in "The display is inside of the auditorium" and "The pickets were waiting outside of the gate," write "inside the auditorium" and "outside the gate."

Inside of is acceptable in most college writing when it means "in less than": "I'll be there inside of an hour." The more formal term is *within*.

Both *inside of* and *outside of* are appropriate when *inside* or *outside* is a noun followed by an *of* phrase: "The inside of the house is quite attractive"; "He painted the outside of his boat dark green."

in terms of An imprecise and greatly overused expression. Instead of "In terms of philosophy, we are opposed to his position" and "In terms of our previous experience with the company, we refuse to purchase its products," write "Philosophically, we are opposed to his position" and "Because of our previous experience with the company, we refuse to purchase its products."

invite (noun) Sometimes used for *invitation*, as in "an invite to the picnic." In college writing *invitation* is preferred.

irregardless A nonstandard variant of *regardless*. Do not use it.

irrelevant–irreverent *Irrelevant* means "having no relation to" or "lacking pertinence": "That may be true, but it is quite irrelevant." *Irreverent* means "without reverence": "Such conduct in church is irreverent."

it's me This construction is essentially a spoken one. Except in dialogue, it rarely occurs in writing. Its use in educated speech is thoroughly established. The formal expression is "It is I."

judicial–judicious Judicial decisions are related to the administering of justice, often by judges or juries. A judicious person is one who demonstrates good judgment: "A judicious person would not have allowed the young boys to shoot the rapids alone."

kind of, sort of Use a singular noun and a singular verb with these phrases: "That kind of person is always troublesome"; "This sort of attitude is deplorable." If the sense of the sentence calls for the plural *kinds* or *sorts*, use a plural noun and a plural verb: "These kinds of services are essential." In questions introduced by *what* or *which*, the singular *kind* or *sort* can be followed by a plural noun and verb: "What kind of shells are these?"

The use of *a* or *an* after *kind of* ("That kind of a person is always troublesome") is usually not appropriate in college writing.

kind (sort) of = somewhat   This usage ("I feel kind of tired"; "He looked sort of foolish") is colloquial. The style of the writing will determine its appropriateness in a paper.

latter   *Latter* refers to the second of two. It should not be used to refer to the last of three or more nouns. Instead of *latter* in "Michigan, Alabama, and Notre Dame have had strong football teams for years, and yet the latter has only recently begun to accept invitations to play in bowl games," write *last* or *last-named,* or simply repeat *Notre Dame.*

learn = teach   The use of *learn* to mean "teach" ("He learned us arithmetic") is nonstandard and is not acceptable in college writing.

leave = let   The use of *leave* for the imperative verb *let* ("Leave us face it") is not acceptable in college writing. Write "Let us face it." But *let* and *leave* are interchangeable when a noun or pronoun and then *alone* follow: "Let me alone"; "Leave me alone."

lend   See **loan, lend.**

less   See **fewer.**

liable = likely   Instructors sometimes object to the use of *liable* to mean "likely," as in "It is liable to rain," "He is liable to hit you." *Liable* is used more precisely to mean "subject to" or "exposed to" or "answerable for": "He is liable to arrest"; "You will be liable for damages."

like = as, as though   The use of *like* as a conjunction ("He talks like you do"; "It looks like it will be my turn next") is colloquial. It is not appropriate in a formal style, and many people object to it in an informal style. The safest procedure is to avoid using *like* as a conjunction in college writing.

loan, lend   Both forms of the verb are accepted in educated American usage. *Lend* is the preferred form.

loath–loathe   The form without *e* is an adjective meaning "reluctant," "unwilling" ("I am loath to do that"; "He is loath to risk so great an investment"), and is pronounced to rhyme with *both.* The form with *e* is a verb meaning "dislike strongly" ("I loathe teas"; "She loathes an unkempt man") and is pronounced to rhyme with *clothe.*

loose–lose   The confusion of these words causes frequent misspellings. *Loose* is most common as an adjective: "a loose button," "The dog is loose." *Lose* is always used as a verb: "You are going to lose your money."

luxuriant–luxurious   These words come from the same root but have quite different meanings. *Luxuriant* means "abundant" and is used principally to describe growing things: "luxuriant vegetation," "a luxuriant head of hair." *Luxurious* means "luxury-loving" or "characterized by luxury": "He finds it difficult to maintain so luxurious a lifestyle on so modest an income"; "The furnishings of the clubhouse were luxurious."

mad = angry or annoyed   Using *mad* to mean "angry" is colloquial: "My girl is mad at me"; "His insinuations make me mad." More precise terms — *angry, annoyed, irritated, provoked, vexed* — are generally more appropriate in college writing. *Mad* is, of course, appropriately used to mean "insane."

majority, plurality   Candidates are elected by a *majority* when they get more than half the votes cast. A *plurality* is the margin of victory that the winning candidate has over the leading opponent, whether the winner has a majority or not.

mean = unkind, disagreeable, vicious   Using *mean* to convey the sense "unkind," "disagreeable," "vicious" ("It was mean of me to do that"; "He was in a mean mood"; "That dog looks mean") is a colloquial use. It is appropriate in most college writing, but since using *mean* loosely sometimes results in vagueness, consider using one of the suggested alternatives to provide a sharper statement.

medium, media, medias   *Medium*, not *media*, is the singular form: "The daily newspaper is still an important medium of communication." *Media* is plural: "Figuratively, the electronic media have created a smaller world." *Medias* is not an acceptable form for the plural of *medium*.

might of   See **could of.**

mighty = very   *Mighty* is not appropriate in most college writing as a substitute for *very*. Avoid such constructions as "He gave a mighty good speech."

moral–morale   Roughly, *moral* refers to conduct and *morale* refers to state of mind. A moral man is one who conducts himself according to standards for goodness. People are said to have good morale when they are cheerful, cooperative, and not too much concerned with their own worries.

most = almost   The use of *most* as a synonym for *almost* ("I am most always hungry an hour before mealtime") is colloquial. In college writing *almost* would be preferred in such a sentence.

must (adjective and noun)   The use of *must* as an adjective ("This book is must reading for anyone who wants to understand Russia") and as a noun ("It is reported that the President will classify this proposal as a must") is accepted as established usage by the dictionaries.

must of   See **could of.**

myself = I, me   *Myself* should not be used for *I* or *me*. Avoid such constructions as "John and myself will go." *Myself* is acceptably used as an intensifier ("I saw it myself"; "I myself will go with you") and as a reflexive object ("I hate myself"; "I can't convince myself that he is right.")

nauseous = nauseated   *Nauseous* does not mean "experiencing nausea"; *nauseated* has that meaning: "The thought of making a speech caused her to feel nauseated." *Nauseous* means "causing nausea" or "repulsive": "nauseous odor," "nauseous television program."

nice   A utility word much overused in college writing. Avoid excessive use of *nice* and, whenever possible, choose a more precise synonym.

That's a nice dress.   (attractive? becoming? fashionable? well-made?)

She's a nice person.   (agreeable? charming? friendly? well-mannered?)

nice and   Intensives like "nice and easy" and "nice and comfortable" are colloquial. The more formal the style, the less appropriate such expressions are.

notorious   See **famous.**

nowheres   Nonstandard variant of *nowhere.* Do not use it in college writing.

off, off of = from   Neither *off* nor *off of* should be used to mean "from." Write "Jack bought the old car from a stranger," not "off a stranger" or "off of a stranger."

OK, O.K.   Its use in business to mean "endorse" is generally accepted: "The manager OK'd the request." In college writing *OK* is a utility word and is subject to the general precaution concerning all such words: do not overuse it, especially in contexts in which a more specific term would give more efficient communication. For example, contrast the vagueness of *OK* at the left with the discriminated meanings at the right.

The mechanic said the tires were OK.   The mechanic said the tread on the tires was still good.

The mechanic said the pressure in the tires was satisfactory.

one   See **you = one.**

only   The position of *only* in such sentences as "I only need three dollars" and "If only Mother would write!" is sometimes condemned on the grounds of possible ambiguity. In practice, the context usually rules out any but the intended interpretation, but a change in the word order would often result in more appropriate emphasis: "I need only three dollars"; "If mother would only write!"

on the part of   The phrase "on the part of" ("There will be some objection on the part of the students"; "On the part of businesspeople, there will be some concern about taxes") often makes for a wordy style. Simply say "The students will object," "Businesspeople will be concerned about taxes."

outside of   See **inside of.**

party = person   The use of *party* to mean "person" is appropriate in legal documents and the responses of telephone operators, but these are special uses. Generally avoid this use in college writing.

per = a   "You will be remunerated at the rate of forty dollars per diem" and "The troops advanced three miles per day through the heavy snow" show established use of *per* for *a.* But usually "forty dollars a day" and "three miles a day" would be more natural expressions in college writing.

percent, percentage *Percent* (alternative form, *per cent*) is used when a specific portion is named: "five percent of the expenses." *Percentage* is used when no number is given: "a small percentage of the expenses." When *percent* or *percentage* is part of a subject, the noun or pronoun of the *of* phrase that follows determines the number of the verb: "Forty percent of the wheat is his"; "A large percentage of her customers pay promptly."

personal–personnel *Personal* means "of a person": "a personal opinion," "a personal matter." *Personnel* refers to the people in an organization, especially employees: "Administrative personnel will not be affected."

plenty The use of *plenty* as a noun ("There is plenty of room") is always acceptable. Its use as an adverb ("It was plenty good") is not appropriate in college writing.

plurality See **majority.**

première *Première* is acceptable as a noun ("The première for the play was held in a small off-Broadway theater"), but do not use it as a verb ("The play premièred in a small off-Broadway theater"). Write "The play opened . . ."

preposition (ending sentence with) A preposition should not appear at the end of a sentence if its presence there draws undue attention to itself or creates an awkward construction: "They are the people whom we made the inquiries yesterday about." But there is nothing wrong with writing a preposition at the end of a sentence to achieve an idiomatic construction: "Isn't that the man you are looking for?"

principal–principle The basic meaning of *principal* is "chief" or "most important." It is used in this sense both as a noun and as an adjective: "the principal of a school," "the principal point." It is also used to refer to a capital sum of money, as contrasted with interest on the money: "He can live on the interest without touching the principal." *Principle* is used only as a noun and means "rule," "law," or "controlling idea": "the principle of 'one man, one vote' "; "It is against my principles."

prophecy–prophesy *Prophecy* is always used as a noun ("The prophecy came true"); *prophesy* is always a verb ("He prophesied another war").

proved, proven When used as past participles, both forms are standard English, but the preferred form is *proved:* "Having proved the first point, we moved to the second." *Proven* is preferred when the word is used primarily as an adjective: "He is a proven contender for the championship."

quote The clipped form for *quotation* ("a quote from *Walden*") is not acceptable in most college writing. The verb *quote* ("to quote Thoreau") is acceptable in all styles.

rarely ever, seldom ever The *ever* is redundant. Instead of saying "He is rarely ever late" and "She is seldom ever angry," write "He is rarely late" and "She is seldom angry."

real = really (very) The use of *real* to mean "really" or "very" ("It is a real difficult assignment") is a colloquial usage. It is acceptable only in a paper whose style is deliberately colloquial.

refer back A confusion between *look back* and *refer*. This usage is objected to in college writing on the ground that since the *re-* of *refer* means "back," *refer back* is redundant. *Refer back* is acceptable when it means "refer again" ("The bill was referred back to the committee"); otherwise, say *refer* ("Let me refer you to page 17").

respectfully–respectively *Respectfully* means "with respect": "respectfully submitted." *Respectively* means roughly "each in turn": "These three papers were graded respectively A, C, and B."

right (adv.) The use of *right* as an adverb is established in such sentences as "He went right home" and "It served her right." Its use to mean *very* ("I was right glad to meet him") is colloquial and should be used in college writing only when the style is colloquial.

right–rite A *rite* is a ceremony or ritual. This word should not be confused with the various uses of *right*.

said (adj.) The use of *said* as an adjective ("said documents," "said offense") is restricted to legal phraseology. Do not use it in college writing.

same as = just as The preferred idiom is "just as": "He acted just as I thought he would."

same, such Avoid using *same* or *such* as a substitute for *it, this, that, them*. Instead of "I am returning the book because I do not care for same" and "Most people are fond of athletics of all sorts, but I have no use for such," say "I am returning the book because I do not care for it" and "Unlike most people, I am not fond of athletics."

scarcely In such sentences as "There wasn't scarcely enough" and "We haven't scarcely time," the use of *scarcely* plus a negative creates an unacceptable double negative. Say "There was scarcely enough" and "We scarcely have time."

scarcely than The use of "scarcely than" ("I had scarcely met her than she began to denounce her husband") is a confusion between "no sooner . . . than" and "scarcely . . . when." Say "I had no sooner met her than she began to denounce her husband" or "I had scarcely met her when she began to denounce her husband."

seasonable–seasonal *Seasonable* and its adverb form *seasonably* mean "appropriate(ly) to the season": "She was seasonably dressed for a late-fall football game"; "A seasonable frost convinced us that the persimmons were just right for eating." *Seasonal* means "caused by a season": "increased absenteeism because of seasonal influenza," "flooding caused by seasonal thaws."

seldom ever See **rarely ever.**

-selfs   The plural of *self* is *selves*. Such a usage as "They hurt themselfs" is nonstandard and is not acceptable in college writing.

semi-   See **bi-, semi-.**

sensual–sensuous   *Sensual* has unfavorable connotations and means "catering to the gratification of physical desires": "Always concerned with satisfying his sexual lust and his craving for drink and rich food, the old baron led a totally sensual existence." *Sensuous* has generally favorable connotations and refers to pleasures experienced through the senses: "the sensuous comfort of a warm bath," "the sensuous imagery of the poem."

shall, will   In American, as contrasted with British, usage the dominant practice is to use *will* in the second and third persons to express either futurity or determination, and to use either *will* or *shall* in the first person.

In addition, *shall* is used in statements of law ("Congress shall have the power to . . ."), in military commands ("The regiment shall proceed as directed"), and in formal directives ("All branch offices shall report weekly to the home office").

should, would   These words are used as the past forms of *shall* and *will* respectively and follow the same pattern (see **shall, will**): "I would [should] be glad to see him tomorrow"; "He would welcome your ideas on the subject"; "We would [should] never consent to such an arrangement." They are also used to convert a *shall* or *will* in direct discourse into indirect discourse.

Direct discourse	**Indirect discourse**
"Shall I try to arrange it?" he asked.	He asked if he should try to arrange it.
I said, "They will need money."	I said that they would need money.

should of   See **could of.**

sight–site–cite   See **cite–sight–site.**

so (conj.)   The use of *so* as a connective ("The salesperson refused to exchange the merchandise; so we went to the manager") is thoroughly respectable, but its overuse in college writing is objectionable. There are other good transitional connectives — *accordingly, for that reason, on that account, therefore* — that could be used to relieve the monotony of a series of *so*'s. Occasional use of subordination ("When the salesperson refused to exchange the merchandise, we went to the manager") would also lend variety to the style.

some   The use of *some* as an adjective of indeterminate number ("Some friends of yours were here") is acceptable in all levels of writing. Its use as an intensive ("That was some meal!") or as an adverb ("She cried some after you left"; "This draft is some better than the first one") should be avoided in college writing.

somewheres   Nonstandard variant of *somewhere.* Not acceptable in college writing.

sort of   See **kind of.**

stationary-stationery *Stationary* means "fixed" or "unchanging": "The battle front is now stationary." *Stationery* means "writing paper": "a box of stationery." Associate the *e* in *stationery* with the *e*'s in *letter*.

suit-suite The common word is *suit*: "a suit of clothes"; "Follow suit, play a diamond"; "Suit yourself." *Suite,* pronounced "sweet," means "retinue" ("The President and his suite have arrived") or "set" or "collection" ("a suite of rooms," "a suite of furniture"). When it refers to furniture, an alternative pronunciation is "suit."

sure = certainly Using *sure* in the sense of "certainly" ("I sure am annoyed"; "Sure, I will go with you") is colloquial. Unless the style justifies colloquial usage, use *certainly* or *surely*.

swell = good, fine Using *swell* as a synonym for *good* or *fine* ("It was a swell show"; "We had a swell time") is slang. It is generally inappropriate in college writing.

take and This usage ("In a fit of anger he took and smashed the bowl") is not acceptable in college writing. Simply use *smashed:* "In a fit of anger he smashed the bowl."

terrific Used at a formal level to mean "terrifying" ("a terrific epidemic") and at a colloquial level as an intensive ("a terrific party," "a terrific pain"). Overuse of the word at the colloquial level has made it almost meaningless.

thusly Not an acceptable variant of *thus*.

tough The use of *tough* to mean "difficult" ("a tough assignment," "a tough decision") and "hard fought" ("a tough game") is accepted without qualification by reputable dictionaries. But its use to mean "unfortunate," "bad" ("The fifteen-yard penalty was a tough break for the team"; "That's tough") is colloquial and should be used only in a paper written in a colloquial style.

troop-troupe Both words come from the same root and share the original meaning, "herd." In modern usage *troop* can refer to soldiers and *troupe* to actors: "a troop of cavalry," "a troop of scouts," "a troupe of circus performers," "a troupe of entertainers."

try and "Try to" is the preferred idiom. Write "I will try to do it" in preference to "I will try and do it."

type = type of *Type* is not acceptable as a variant form of *type of*. In "That type engine isn't being manufactured anymore," add *of* after *type*.

uninterested-disinterested See **disinterested-uninterested.**

unique The formal meaning of *unique* is "sole" or "only" or "being the only one of its kind": "Adam was unique in being the only man who never had a mother." The use of *unique* to mean "rare" or "unusual" ("Americans watched their television sets anxiously as astronauts in the early moon landings had the unique experience of walking on the moon") has long been popular, but some people still object to this usage. The use of *unique* to mean merely "uncommon" ("a unique sweater") is generally frowned upon. *Unique* should not be modified by adverbs that express degree: *very, more, most, rather.*

up The adverb *up* is idiomatically used in many verb-adverb combinations that act as verbs — "break up," "clean up," "fill up," "get up," "tear up." Avoid unnecessary or awkward separation of *up* from the verb with which it is combined, since such a separation makes *up* look at first like an adverb modifying the verb rather than an adverb combining with the verb in an idiomatic expression. For example, "They held the cashier up" and "She made her face up" are awkward. Say "They held up the cashier," "She made up her face."

use to The *d* in "used to" is often not pronounced; it is elided before the *t* in *to*. The resulting pronunciation leads to the written expression "use to." But the acceptable written phrase is "used to": "I am used to the noise"; "He used to do all the grocery shopping."

used to could Nonstandard for "used to be able to." Not acceptable in college writing.

very A common intensive, but avoid its overuse.

wait on *Wait on* means "serve": "A clerk will be here in a moment to wait on you." The use of *wait on* to mean "wait for" ("I'll wait on you if you won't be long") is a colloquialism to which there is some objection. Use *wait for:* "I'll wait for you if you won't be long."

want in, out, off The use of *want* followed by *in, out,* or *off* ("The dog wants in"; "I want out of here"; "I want off now") is colloquial. In college writing supply an infinitive after the verb: "The dog wants to come in."

want to = ought to, should Using *want to* as a synonym for *should* ("They want to be careful or they will be in trouble") is colloquial. *Ought to* or *should* is preferred in college writing.

ways Colloquial for *way* in such sentences as "You must have come a long ways." Use *way* instead of *ways.*

where ... at, to The use of *at* or *to* after *where* ("Where was he at?" "Where are you going to?") is redundant. Simply write "Where was he?" and "Where are you going?"

will, shall See **shall, will.**

-wise Avoid adding the suffix *-wise,* meaning "concerning," to nouns to form such combinations as *budgetwise, jobwise, tastewise.* Some combined forms with *-wise* are thoroughly established *(clockwise, otherwise, sidewise, weatherwise),* but the fad of coining new compounds with this suffix is generally best avoided.

without = unless *Without* is not accepted as a conjunction meaning "unless." In "There will be no homecoming festivities without student government sponsors them," substitute *unless* for *without.*

with respect to   See **as to.**

worst way   When "in the worst way" means "very much" ("They wanted to go in the worst way"), it is too informal for college writing.

would, should   See **should, would.**

would of   See **could of.**

would have = had   *Would* is the past-tense form of *will,* but its overuse in student writing often results in awkwardness, especially, but not only, when it is used as a substitute for *had.* Contrast the following sentences:

Awkward	**Revised**
If they *would have done* that earlier, there *would have been* no trouble.	If they *had done* that earlier, there *would have been* no trouble. *or:* *Had* they *done* that earlier, there *would have been* no trouble.
We *would want* some assurance that they *would accept* before we *would make* such a proposal.	We *would want* some assurance of their acceptance before we *made* such a proposal.

In general, avoid the repetition of "would have . . ." in the same sentence.

Xmas   An abbreviation for *Christmas* much used in business and advertising. The full word is preferred in college writing.

you = one   The use of *you* as an indefinite pronoun instead of the formal *one* is characteristic of an informal style. If you adopt *you* in an informal paper, be sure that this impersonal use will be recognized by your readers; otherwise, they are likely to interpret a general statement as a personal remark addressed specifically to them.

Generally avoid shifting from *one* to *you* within a sentence. See pages 613–616.

yourself   *Yourself* is appropriately used as an intensifier ("You yourself told me that") and as a reflexive object ("You are blaming yourself too much"). But usages such as the following are not acceptable: "Marian and yourself must shoulder the responsibility" and "The instructions were intended for Kate and yourself." In these two sentences, replace *yourself* with *you.*

The plural form is *yourselves,* not *yourselfs.*

Index of Authors and Titles

This index contains the names of all authors whose work is quoted in the text and the titles of all full-length selections and longer excerpts. Names of student writers and titles of student writing are indicated by an asterisk (*); they are also indexed in greater detail in the main index, which begins on page 743.

Index

Authors and titles of all writers and works quoted in the text — both professional and student — will be found in the Index of Authors and Titles, which begins on page 741. Because student writers and writing play a critical role in many chapters in the text, they are also indexed in further detail in this index.